The United Nations and Changing World Politics

The revised and updated Introduction to this classic text situates the UN in substantially changing world politics, including:

- The election of the ninth Secretary-General, António Guterres;
- The burgeoning of "new nationalisms" worldwide, including most importantly in the Trump administration's Washington, DC, and Brexit;
- The continuing proliferation of such non-state actors as ISIS and those in the "third UN," including developmental and humanitarian NGOs.

Essential to all classes on the UN, International Organizations, and Global Studies, this interim edition of *The United Nations and Changing World Politics* is refreshed for students and scholars alike.

Thomas G. Weiss is Presidential Professor at the City University of New York's Graduate Center and Director-Emeritus of the Ralph Bunche Institute for International Studies.

David P. Forsythe is the Charles J. Mach Distinguished Professor Emeritus of Political Science at the University of Nebraska-Lincoln.

Roger A. Coate is Paul D. Coverdell Professor of Public Policy at Georgia College & State University and Distinguished Professor Emeritus of Political Science at the University of South Carolina.

Kelly-Kate Pease is Professor of International Relations at Webster University in St. Louis and the Director of the International Relations Program Worldwide. She also serves as a Fellow in the Institute for Human Rights and Humanitarian Studies.

THE UNITED NATIONS AND CHANGING WORLD POLITICS

REVISED and UPDATED with a NEW INTRODUCTION

EIGHTH EDITION

THOMAS G. WEISS,
DAVID P. FORSYTHE,
ROGER A. COATE AND
KELLY-KATE PEASE

Routledge
Taylor & Francis Group

NEW YORK AND LONDON

Eighth edition published 2020

by Routledge
52 Vanderbilt Avenue, New York, NY 10017

and by Routledge
2 Park Square, Milton Park, Abingdon, Oxon, OX14 4RN

Routledge is an imprint of the Taylor & Francis Group, an informa business

© 2020 Taylor & Francis

First published by Westview Press 2017

Library of Congress Cataloging-in-Publication Data
A catalog record has been requested for this book

ISBN: 978-0-367-35391-9 (pbk)
ISBN: 978-0-8133-5047-9 (ebk)

Typeset in Minion Pro
by codeMantra

Visit the eResources: www.routledge.com/9780367353919

Contents

Tables and Illustrations

Acknowledgments

This text builds on seven previous editions, which would not have been as insightful without the contributions of many individuals over the years. Four outside reviewers read the original manuscript of the first edition in 1993. Craig Murphy of Wellesley College and Lawrence Finkelstein, then at Northern Illinois University, are both recognized scholars of international organization and world politics; they provided comments through the cooperation of the International Organization Section of the International Studies Association (ISA). Two other readers, unknown to us, were provided by Westview Press. A discussion group focused on this manuscript at the annual meeting of the Academic Council on the United Nations System (ACUNS) in Montreal in June 1993. Other ISA panels focused on the book at the 2002 conference in New Orleans and the one in 2013 in Toronto. Thus this book is in many ways a product of the ISA and ACUNS.

We would like to express our special gratitude to those staff members of our respective academic institutions who—with good humor and professionalism—assisted in the preparation of the various versions of the manuscript over time. We thank Danielle Zach, Janet Reilly, and Elisa Athonvarangkul at the Ralph Bunche Institute for International Studies of the Graduate Center of the City University of New York for their essential contributions. Without the help of Susan Costa, Mary Lhowe, Melissa Phillips, Fred Fullerton, and Laura Sadovnikoff at Brown University's Watson Institute, the earliest editions would have been considerably slower in appearing and certainly less well presented. Another word of appreciation goes to those younger researchers who have helped at one stage or another in framing arguments, checking facts and endnotes, and prodding their mentors: Peter Breil, Christopher Brodhead, Cindy Collins, Paula L'Ecuyer, Jean Garrison, Mutuma Ruteere, Barbara Ann Rieffer, Lekesha Harris, Peter Söderholm, Corinne Jiminez, and Caitlin Creech.

We are delighted that David Malone agreed to grace these pages with an original foreword to this eighth edition. From his current position as rector at the UN University in Tokyo, he brings to bear not only his own insights as a researcher but also a distinguished career as a Canadian diplomat and manager of the International Research Development Centre and the International Peace Institute.

Finally, we also are honored to acknowledge those colleagues and friends who contributed their insights in forewords to previous editions. Inis L. Claude, in his foreword to the second edition, captured the prominence the UN enjoyed in the immediate post–Cold War era and foreshadowed the challenges faced by the UN in the wake of disintegrating states. In the third edition, Leon Gordenker cautioned that no single theory can capture the complexities of the UN policies and processes and prodded us to consider what encourages the UN to influence global life and what holds it back. In the fourth, James O. C. Jonah noted that the role of the secretariat and the secretary-general is too often downplayed and needs further elucidation if we are to understand how and why the UN behaves as it does. Richard Jolly set the pessimistic tone of the 2005 World Summit in the fifth edition's foreword, noting that the decade-long effort to reform the UN was systematically undermined by the neoconservative administration of George W. Bush; coupled with the U.S. invasion of Iraq in 2003 without Security Council authorization, the UN suffered a critical leadership deficit. The foreword of the sixth edition, by Ramesh Thakur, highlighted the political changes in important states, including the United States, and stressed that, on balance, the world is a better and safer place because of the UN. The foreword to the previous edition was crafted by Michael Doyle, who emphasized the ongoing experiments with the responsibility to protect. Because of space constraints, we are no longer able to present the full texts of these previous forewords; however, they are available on the publisher's website at www.westviewpress.com.

Although only the authors are responsible for the final version, we acknowledge with gratitude the time and effort that others have put into improving our work.

Thomas G. Weiss
David P. Forsythe
Roger A. Coate
Kelly-Kate Pease
May 2016

Foreword to the Eighth Edition

It is rare for a comprehensive textbook of this nature to evolve into an eighth edition. Why has demand for the approach of these authors withstood the test of time so well?

The volume is structured with great clarity and its tone is one of skeptical inquiry rather than either uncritical admiration for, or instinctive bashing of, the United Nations (UN). It situates the UN in the circumstances that determine its role in international politics: global distribution of power and world order, in a dispensation of sovereign states vying with each other for advantage, while a growing number of other actors in international relations, including those of the third UN so impressively documented in these pages, seek to advance their own interests and views within the UN's chambers (or to telegraph their messages against the backdrop of the UN's headquarters).

The United Nations is an organization of member states, which came together under a Charter that was agreed to after contentious debates in San Francisco in 1945. Originally cast as an alliance of countries fighting the Axis powers of World War II, it sought, as the end of that conflagration approached, to channel international relations through a permanent multilateral conference (as occurred in the nineteenth century with the Vienna Conference followed by the Concert of Nations and, in a more a structured form, after World War I with the League of Nations). This permanent grouping of states came to equip itself over time with a large, sophisticated secretariat; a number of specialized agencies, programs, and funds; and a range of affiliations to other international organizations active in fields the UN (at least initially) left to them.

Delegations at San Francisco had lofty ambitions for the UN and granted its Security Council unique powers under international law to coerce compliance with its wishes. But the scope for action enjoyed by the UN was long qualified in various fields by the intensity of the Cold War. Today the UN is hamstrung by the financial pressures experienced within the industrialized world after years of stagnation or very slow growth following the financial crisis of 2008. The UN has never been good at editing itself. Its activities have tended to be additive and overlapping rather than disciplined and self-denying. And the need for financial restraint nowadays is proving stressful for this and other self-indulgent international organizations.

The UN is sometimes derided as a talking shop. It does host a great deal of speechifying and grandstanding, much of it vacuous. But it was meant to bring the world together, even if in disagreement. It has done this very well since its inception, but with increasing sprawl as more and more issues are addressed by an ever-expanding list of interlocutors, from UN bodies, governments, civil society, and other actors. Results have often been disappointing. But sometimes apparently slow, even failing negotiating processes have, in the long run, produced important results. The human rights field, an argumentative and much-fought-over one that the UN's treaties, decisions, institutions, debates, and activities have vastly expanded, is an obvious example of how over time the UN has provided sharper meaning to vague notions evoked in the Charter, and encouraged action all over the world to achieve specific objectives to enhance a range of freedoms and entitlements.

Until recently, the UN's seventy years have unfolded in clearly demarcated periods: that of the Cold War, during which some of its bodies faced circumscribed potential, notably the Security Council, while others thrived; and the post–Cold War era, during which the council's potential was unlocked, but with mixed results. Meanwhile, the rest of the UN system started to suffer from bloat, characterized by repetitive debates; outdated North-South confrontations bearing little relation to the growing diversity of the Global South, marked by the emergence of meaningful global powers in its midst, such as India, South Africa, and Brazil; and negotiating habits that increasingly failed to deliver positive outcomes, for example, at the Copenhagen climate change negotiations in 2009. Further, an air of artificiality overtook some UN negotiation outcomes in 2016, as donor countries double or triple-counted purported financial commitments to international objectives. They had by then also fiddled with their own key definition of what constitutes Official Development Assistance (ODA) to include domestic resettlement costs for refugees, seriously eroding some European ODA programs.

But we may now be entering into a third period of UN endeavor, marked by global economic distress and a return of great power rivalry. This has seen the Russian Federation and the United States not only backing different actors in the Syrian crisis since 2011 but undertaking military operations above Syrian soil that create real risks of an unintended clash between them. While the Security Council's work on conflicts in Africa, which takes up about 85 percent of its time and accounts for a similar range of its decisions and reports, remains largely consensual, sharp disagreements over Libya, the Ukraine, and Syria could contaminate the rest of the Security Council's agenda unless handled more successfully in the future than in the past.

While human rights have emerged as the third pillar of the UN—as often described by Secretaries-General Kofi Annan and Ban Ki-moon—the relevance of the UN's work on development has seemed increasingly questionable. Beyond the setting of global goals, which had some mobilizing effect, it has become clear that the UN has had little to do with the success of development efforts since the turn of the millennium. These have been domestically driven, albeit supported in many cases by the improved mix of policies often advocated at the international level. The impressive gains in many developing countries over the past fifteen years, notably marked by accelerating growth in Asia and Africa (while Latin America focused more on social development and protection), stand in contrast to the dismal performance of the industrialized world since 2008. They underpinned the overall attainment of many of the Millennium Development Goals (MDGs) and targets.

Starting in 2012 with discussions at the Rio+20 Conference on Sustainable Development, and with input from a variety of sources, UN member states developed a new set of Sustainable Development Goals (SDGs), more than doubling their number (from eight to seventeen) and agreeing on 169 targets flowing from them—without yet having developed indicators by which their attainment could be measured. UN delegations seemed unfazed by widespread criticism beyond their own rarefied circles that no government could cope with a prescription of this scope and detail, ultimately leaving it to governments to pick and choose which targets to adopt as priorities, and to cherry-pick in reporting on themselves.

Exhaustion and ill humor also marked negotiations toward a new agreement on climate change after implementation of the legally binding Kyoto Protocol largely disintegrated in slow motion following its first commitment period (2008–2012), having proved hopeful but unbalanced. Member states, negotiating seemingly nonstop throughout 2014 and 2015, produced ever more bracketed text over which disagreement was often fierce. They were only rescued from this unproductive track by China and the United States, neither of which had committed to implementation of the Kyoto Protocol's emission reduction provisions. Washington and Beijing agreed on a voluntary-commitment approach backed by specific pledges from each, an approach that came to be adopted by other countries throughout 2015. In part because of the relentless pressure and diplomacy applied to all countries by the French hosts of the summit on this issue, on December 12, 2015, agreement was reached in Paris on a new global course. The agreement picked up on that of China and the United States, marked by indicative voluntary commitments by virtually all countries to limit and reverse their carbon footprint over coming decades, with these commitments to be reviewed every five years with the aim of improving on them. While disappointing to many, the outcome involved commitments from all the major players, even if not in binding terms, a major improvement on the Kyoto Protocol. It is likely that pressure will only grow on capitals the world over, for domestic as well as international reasons, to curb carbon and other noxious emissions, thus validating the modest first steps taken in Paris.

Of note is that on both climate change and the SDGs, when UN processes fail to provide a convincing prescriptive approach, governments are left to offer and adopt à la carte approaches to a vast menu of policy options and outcome objectives (as much to their own people as at the international level). To some of us, this seems a sensible outcome, as economic, social, and development policies need to be internally driven, while seeking, however selectively, to attain a number of international standards and emerging norms.

Meanwhile, humanitarian action, on which the UN had for many years played second fiddle to the International Red Cross system, became a growth center both for UN organizations and for the Security Council in the immediate post–Cold War period, absorbing large amounts of funding nominally targeted by the Organisation for Economic Co-operation and Development's country donors, with UN agencies, funds, and programs competing for humanitarian roles of various sorts. This remarkable increase in humanitarian assistance since the end of the Cold War has helped significantly drive down mortality rates in war-torn countries in the course of the past two decades, reflected, for instance, in significant reduction in child mortality rates even in war-torn countries. And yet, humanitarian assistance is rarely turned into sustainable development gains, and with a resurgence of civil wars over the past decade, humanitarian distress around the world is again on the rise, highlighted by the fact that the number of forcibly displaced and other distressed migrant persons in 2015 was the highest since the end of World War II.

Within the UN itself, attention focused on a growing imbalance of power within the UN Security Council, whose five permanent members (P5) had come to dominate not only its decision making but all aspects of its work. This domination includes the selection of the next secretary-general, who will succeed Ban Ki-moon on January 1, 2017, with attention for the first time focusing primarily on women candidates. The risk to the permanent members that now comprehensively control the action and decision-making in the council is that others may simply abandon the game or selectively withhold consent for the preferences of the P5, for which they need only seven votes to block action. Key decision making may migrate to other forums with outcomes merely brought to the Security Council for its formal imprimatur and for access to its binding legal powers.

Pressure has grown for a more transparent and open selection of the next secretary-general. Ideas include the demand for candidates to introduce themselves and their ideas to the wider membership and the possibility of several candidates being recommended by the Security Council to the UN General Assembly rather than the single candidate that has been customary since 1945. There is increasing focus on the role of the General Assembly in electing the secretary-general, currently a pro forma one but potentially a more dynamic process, rather than solely on the role of the Security Council in recommending a candidate (or perhaps one day, several candidates). Unless the council proves more consultative in response to widespread unhappiness in the General Assembly and civil society over its limited agency in this key election, it is not inconceivable in decades ahead that the General Assembly could fail to provide the necessary votes to confirm the candidate recommended by the Council and elect instead another of its own preference, thus triggering UN constitutional tensions.

In sum, this splendid volume, so ably structured and rooted in deep knowledge of the institution, makes clear that the UN is an aging institution. At seventy, it is experiencing trouble both in its working methods and in its ability to adapt to new global geopolitical and economic dispensations that no longer conform to the familiar Cold War, post–Cold War, and North-South divides, much as national representatives sometimes seem to want to cling to these. Each chapter of the book is rooted in authoritative scholarly literature and features sharp, lucid analysis. It elegantly spans the academic disciplines of law, public policy, political science, development studies, and international relations. It will helpfully support teaching at the undergraduate and graduate levels in any of these fields and across them.

I am honored, through these brief lines, to be associated with this remarkable, enduring venture.

David M. Malone
Rector of the UN University
Undersecretary-General
of the United Nations
Tokyo, Japan
December 2015

Acronyms

AFISMA	African-led International Support Mission in Mali
AIIB	Asian Infrastructure and Investment Bank
AMIS	African Union Mission in Sudan
ASEAN	Association of Southeast Asian Nations
AU	African Union
BINUCA	Integrated Peacebuilding Office in the Central African Republic
BRICS	Brazil, Russia, India, China, and South Africa
CAR	Central African Republic
CAT	Committee against Torture
CDC	Centers for Disease Control and Prevention
CEDAW	Committee on the Elimination of Discrimination Against Women
CERD	Committee on the Elimination of Racial Discrimination
CESCR	Committee on Economic, Social, and Cultural Rights
CHR	Commission on Human Rights
CIA	Central Intelligence Agency
CIS	Commonwealth of Independent States
COP	Conference of the Parties
CRC	Committee on the Rights of the Child
CSCE	Conference on Security and Cooperation in Europe
CSD	Commission on Sustainable Development
CSR	corporate social responsibility
CTC	Counter-Terrorism Committee
CTTF	Counter-Terrorism Task Force
DAC	Development Assistance Committee
DESA	United Nations Department for Economic and Social Affairs
DHA	Department of Humanitarian Affairs
DPKO	Department of Peacekeeping Operations
DPRK	Democratic People's Republic of Korea
DSB	Dispute Settlement Body
DSP	Dispute Settlement Panel
EC	European Community
ECA	Economic Commission for Africa

ECAFE	Economic Commission for Asia and the Far East
ECE	Economic Commission for Europe
EC-ESA	Economic and Social Affairs Executive Committee
ECHA	Executive Committee for Humanitarian Affairs
ECLA	Economic Commission for Latin America
ECLAC	Economic Commission for Latin America and the Caribbean
ECOMOG	Military Observer Group of the Economic Community of West African States
ECOSOC	Economic and Social Council
ECOWAS	Economic Community of West African States
EPTA	Expanded Programme of Technical Assistance
ERC	emergency relief coordinator
ESCAP	Economic and Social Commission for Asia and the Pacific
ESCWA	Economic and Social Commission for Western Asia
EU	European Union
FAO	Food and Agriculture Organization
FMLN	Frente Farabundo Martí para la Liberación Nacional (Farabundo Martí National Liberation Front)
FUNDS	Future United Nations Development System
G7	Group of Seven
G8	Group of Eight
G20	Group of Twenty
G77	Group of 77
GATT	General Agreement on Tariffs and Trade
GCC	Gulf Cooperation Council
GDP	gross domestic product
GEF	Global Environment Facility
HIPC	Heavily Indebted Poor Countries Initiative
HIV/AIDS	human immunodeficiency virus/acquired immunodeficiency syndrome
HLP	High-level Panel on Threats, Challenges and Change
HLPF	High-level Political Forum on Sustainable Development
HRC	Human Rights Council
IAEA	International Atomic Energy Agency
IASC	Inter-Agency Standing Committee
IBRD	International Bank for Reconstruction and Development
ICC	International Criminal Court
ICCPR	International Covenant on Civil and Political Rights
ICISS	International Commission on Intervention and State Sovereignty
ICJ	International Court of Justice
ICRC	International Committee of the Red Cross
ICSID	International Centre for Settlement of Investment Disputes
ICSU	International Council of Scientific Unions
ICT	information and communications technology

ICTR	International Tribunal for Rwanda
ICTY	International Tribunal for the former Yugoslavia
IDA	International Development Association
IDF	Israel Defense Forces
IDP	internally displaced person
IFC	International Finance Corporation
IFI	international financial institution
IFOR	Implementation Force (in the former Yugoslavia)
IGBP	International Geosphere-Biosphere Programme
IGO	intergovernmental organization
IHL	international humanitarian law
ILO	International Labour Organization
IMF	International Monetary Fund
IMO	International Maritime Organization
INTERFET	International Force in East Timor
IOC	International Oceanographic Commission
IPCC	Intergovernmental Panel on Climate Change
ISG	International Securities Group
ISIS	Islamic State in Iraq and Syria
ITU	International Telecommunications Union
IUCN	International Union for the Conservation of Nature and National Resources
KFOR	Kosovo Force
KLA	Kosovo Liberation Army
LGBT	lesbian, gay, bisexual, and transgender
MCA	Millennium Challenge Account
MDA	Magen David Adom (Israeli aid society)
MDG	Millennium Development Goal
MDGR	Millennium Development Goal Report
MIGA	Multilateral Investment Guarantee Agency
MINUCI	United Nations Mission in Côte d'Ivoire
MINURCAT	United Nations Mission in the Central African Republic and Chad
MINUSCA	United Nations Multidimensional Integrated Stabilization Mission in the Central African Republic
MINUSMA	United Nations Multidimensional Integrated Stabilization Mission in Mali
MINUSTAH	United Nations Stabilization Mission in Haiti
MISCA	International Support Mission to the Central African Republic
MNF	Multinational Force
MONUC	United Nations Observer Mission in the Democratic Republic of the Congo
MSC	Military Staff Committee
NAM	Non-Aligned Movement

NATO	North Atlantic Treaty Organization
NDB	New Development Bank
NGLS	Non-Governmental Liaison Service
NGO	nongovernmental organization
NIEO	New International Economic Order
NPT	Nuclear Non-Proliferation Treaty
NSA	nonstate actor
NTB	nontariff barrier
OAS	Organization of American States
OAU	Organization of African Unity
OCHA	Office for the Coordination of Humanitarian Affairs
ODA	overseas development assistance
ODC	Overseas Development Council
OECD	Organisation for Economic Co-operation and Development
OHCHR	Office of the High Commissioner for Human Rights
OIC	Organization of Islamic Cooperation
ONUB	United Nations Operation in Burundi
ONUC	United Nations Operation in the Congo
ONUCA	United Nations Observer Group in Central America
ONUSAL	United Nations Observer Mission in El Salvador
ONUVEH	United Nations Observer Mission to Verify the Electoral Process in Haiti
ONUVEN	United Nations Observer Mission to Verify the Electoral Process in Nicaragua
OPCW	Organization for the Prohibition of Chemical Weapons
OPEC	Organization of Petroleum Exporting Countries
OSCE	Organization on Security and Cooperation in Europe
OSG	Office of the Secretary-General
P5	permanent five members of the Security Council
PBC	Peacebuilding Commission
PBF	Peacebuilding Fund
PBSO	Peacebuilding Support Office
PEPFAR	President's Emergency Plan for AIDS Relief
PLO	Palestine Liberation Organization
R2P	responsibility to protect
Rio+20	UN Conference on Sustainable Development
RUF	Revolutionary United Front
SAARC	South Asian Association for Regional Cooperation
SAP	structural adjustment program
SARS	severe acute respiratory syndrome
SCOPE	Scientific Committee on Problems of the Environment
SCSL	Special Court for Sierra Leone
SDG	Sustainable Development Goal
SMG	Senior Management Group

SUNFED	Special United Nations Fund for Economic Development
SWAPO	South-West Africa People's Organization
TDB	Trade and Development Board
TNC	transnational corporation
TPP	Trans-Pacific Partnership
TRIMS	trade-related investment measures
TRIPS	Trade-Related Aspects of Intellectual Property Rights
UDHR	Universal Declaration of Human Rights
UDI	unilateral declaration of independence
UNAMET	United Nations Mission in East Timor
UNAMID	United Nations/African Union Hybrid Mission in Darfur
UNAMIR	United Nations Assistance Mission in Rwanda
UNAMSIL	United Nations Mission for Sierra Leone
UNAVEM	United Nations Angola Verification Mission
UNCDF	United Nations Capital Development Fund
UNCED	United Nations Conference on Environment and Development
UNCHE	United Nations Conference on the Human Environment
UNCSD	UN Conference on Sustainable Development
UNCTAD	United Nations Conference on Trade and Development
UNDG	United Nations Development Group
UNDOF	United Nations Disengagement Observer Force
UNDP	United Nations Development Programme
UNDRO	United Nations Disaster Relief Office
UNEF	United Nations Emergency Force
UNEP	United Nations Environment Programme
UNESCO	United Nations Educational, Scientific and Cultural Organization
UNFICYP	United Nations Peacekeeping Force in Cyprus
UNFPA	United Nations Population Fund
UNGOMAP	United Nations Good Offices Mission in Afghanistan and Pakistan
UNHCR	United Nations High Commissioner for Refugees
UNICEF	United Nations Children's Fund
UNIFEM	United Nations Development Fund for Women
UNIFIL	United Nations Interim Force in Lebanon
UNIIMOG	United Nations Iran-Iraq Military Observer Group
UNITA	National Union for the Total Independence of Angola
UNITAF	Unified Task Force (in Somalia)
UNMEE	United Nations Mission in Ethiopia and Eritrea
UNMEER	United Nations Mission for Ebola Emergency Response
UNMIH	United Nations Mission in Haiti
UNMIK	United Nations Interim Administration Mission in Kosovo
UNMIL	United Nations Mission in Liberia
UNMIS	United Nations Mission in the Sudan
UNMISET	United Nations Mission of Support in East Timor

UNMISS	UN Mission in South Sudan
UNMIT	United Nations Integrated Mission in Timor-Leste
UNMOGIP	United Nations Military Observer Group in India and Pakistan
UNMOVIC	United Nations Monitoring, Verification, and Inspection Commission
UNOCI	United Nations Operation in Côte d'Ivoire
UNOMSIL	United Nations Observer Mission in Sierra Leone
UNOSOM	United Nations Operation in Somalia
UNPROFOR	United Nations Protection Force (in the former Yugoslavia)
UNRWA	UN Relief and Works Agency
UNSAN	Union of South American Nations
UNSMIH	United Nations Support Mission in Haiti
UNSMIL	United Nations Support Mission in Libya
UNTAC	United Nations Transitional Authority in Cambodia
UNTAET	United Nations Transitional Administration in East Timor
UNTAG	United Nations Transition Assistance Group in Namibia
UNTSO	United Nations Truce Supervision Organization
UPR	Universal Periodic Review
UPU	Universal Postal Union
USSR	Union of Soviet Socialist Republics
WACAP	World Alliance of Cities Against Poverty
WCRP	World Climate Research Programme
WFF	Worldwide Fistula Fund
WFP	World Food Programme
WHO	World Health Organization
WMD	weapon of mass destruction
WMO	World Meteorological Organization
WTO	World Trade Organization

New Nationalisms, the UN, and Turbulence: An Introduction

O UR LATE COLLEAGUE Jim Rosenau wrote eloquently about the conundrums of the international system:

> To anticipate the prospects for global governance in the decades ahead is to discern powerful tensions, profound contradictions, and perplexing paradoxes. It is to search for order in disorder, for coherence in contradiction, and for continuity in change. ... It is to look for authorities that are obscure, boundaries that are in flux, and systems of rule that are emergent. And it is to experience hope embedded in despair.[1]

Previous editions of this textbook acknowledged that, as quoted above, the evolution of the United Nations (UN) system was primarily affected by the complexities of world politics, and that the future was notoriously difficult to predict. When we finalized our previous edition, few anticipated the strength of the broad attacks on multilateral arrangements, the latter often called globalism, which manifested themselves in 2016 and thereafter. It is no exaggeration to posit that they have called into question many aspects of the UN in particular and of international cooperation in general. These events include the election of Donald Trump as the 45th President of the United States (U.S.), the referendum in the United Kingdom (U.K.) favoring British withdrawal (usually dubbed "Brexit") from the European Union (EU), and various other electoral campaigns often summarized under the rubric of the rise of right-wing populism. The year 2016 also witnessed the selection of António Guterres as the ninth UN Secretary-General.

We put the eighth edition into press in fall 2016 before the widespread nature of nativist discontent became so visible—there is no index entry for Trump or Brexit. Because most of the data and analyses in that text remain valid and do not merit a thorough revision, and because it will take time to sort out the more enduring aspects of current trends, we have left the bulk of the book intact except for this revised and expanded introduction. Its fundamental purpose is to try and understand the basics of recent developments with a central focus on implications for the United Nations. To do that, we first back up in time before returning to the other central components in this kick-off chapter; there follows a discussion of the "three" United Nations (member states, secretariats, and non-state actors); an overview of basics; UN principles; and central themes.

MOVING BACK IN TIME

"The war to end all wars" was the label given prematurely by H.G. Wells and Woodrow Wilson to World War I, which ended over a century ago. At the time, multilateral relations and international organizations were in their infancy. Experiments with public international unions, conference diplomacy, and the expansion of multilateral relations beyond Europe remained fledgling. The first experiment with universal multilateralism in 1919, the League of Nations, sought to manage the challenges posed by the increasing lethality of warfare and institutionalize the evolving norm of the illegality of aggressive war. This new world organization built upon the U.S. war aims, laid out in President Wilson's Fourteen Points speech before Congress, that were proposed to serve as the foundation for post-war peace. The highly touted fourteenth point called for the creation of "[A] general association of nations ... formed under specific covenants for the purpose of affording mutual guarantees of political independence and territorial integrity to great and small states alike." Also included among the fourteen war aims were liberal ideological tenants, such as: absolute freedom of navigation [point II]; removable of all economic barriers to free trade [point III]; and "adjustment of all colonial claims, based upon a strict observance of the principle that in determining all such questions of sovereignty the interests of the populations concerned must have equal weight with the equitable government whose title is to be determined"—e.g., self-determination [point V].

These three points were, of course, not so subtle jabs at the norms and practices of the imperial states still prominent at the time—the U.K., France, and Italy. The leaders of these three empires—Lloyd George, Georges Clemenceau, and Vitorio Orlando—did not warmly embrace Wilson's points. Portugal was not a major player in 1919, only a waning colonial power, and did not close out its last colonies until the mid-1970s, the last formal empire to do so. In addition, the United States never joined the League of Nations, which embodied these liberal ideals. For these and many other reasons, this first great experiment aimed at creating a rules-based international order failed.

Yet, the League of Nations laid the foundation for its successor, the United Nations Organization (UNO). Behind U.S. and U.K. leadership, the original twenty-six (later forty-four) countries allied to fight fascism during World War II signed the Declaration by United Nations on January 1, 1942, thus beginning the second great experiment in universal international organization, an experiment that continues today.[2] In 1945, when the fifty-one original member states signed the formal UN Charter in San Francisco, the war against fascism and Japanese imperialism still was being fought and won. The price of a third world war was too great as the nuclear era had begun with the U.S. atomic bombing of Hiroshima, barely six weeks after the ink had dried on the UN Charter. If the League of Nations and the United Nations manifested one cornerstone thought, it was this: an unregulated or pure state system of world affairs was too dangerous. A crying need existed for a rules-based order, monitored by a universal international organization.

Three quarters of a century has elapsed since the member states of the United Nations Alliance began laying the institutional foundations of the post-war liberal world order—the UN system. It was a product of pragmatism and a pressing need to change the way states conducted their international affairs. The founders saw the UN as a way of harnessing state power for the management of important global problems: in the words of one analyst, "Its wartime architects bequeathed us this system as a realist necessity vital in times of trial, not as a liberal accessory to be discarded when the going gets rough."[3] In reality, the UN was the result of both realist and liberal thinking. The authoritative Security Council with its five permanent members recognized the importance of linking norms to power. The rest of the UN system reflected many liberal ideas such as equal voting in the General Assembly, endorsement of human rights, attention to underdevelopment, and more.

The UN system was fashioned plural and decentralized; it was never intended to approximate a formal world government. The primary purpose of the UN is to maintain international peace and security, and addressing socioeconomic issues (such as human rights and development) are ways to indirectly prevent war by promoting economic prosperity and human dignity at home and abroad. Franklin Delano Roosevelt (FDR), among others, believed strongly that the origins of World War II lay in the economic and social misery of the 1920s. Those conditions gave rise to aggressive fascism in Europe. So even as the world conflagration continued, the U.S.-led United Nations Alliance began putting in place a broad UN cooperation system. Beginning with the United Nations Conference on Food and Agriculture in early summer 1943—laying the foundation for establishing the Food and Agricultural Organization (FAO)—and the founding of the United Nations Relief and Rehabilitation Administration (UNRRA) on November 9, 1943, members of the United Nations, under vigorous American leadership, incrementally designed and created a new world order. Within a matter of six months, the United Nations Monetary and Financial Conference established the core rules of the Bretton Woods system—prefacing the founding of the International Bank for Reconstruction and Development (IBRD or World Bank) and the International Monetary Fund (IMF). This decentralized system of multilateral agencies represented a grand design of sorts for building, maintaining, and promoting international peace and prosperity. At the same time, FDR understood that the future of the world would be greatly affected by U.S. relations with the Soviet Premier Josef Stalin. One had to do two things at the same time: seek security arrangements among the Great Powers, and attack the socio-economic ills that gave rise to various discontents, frustrations, and anger.

The construction of what Margaret Karns and Karen Mingst have called the "centerpiece of global governance" in this new order,[4] the UNO, took place incrementally via major power negotiations during the war. These initial negotiations, unlike the others, were carried out almost exclusively at the level of heads of government and their immediate representatives. The Big Three's negotiations—Winston Churchill joined Roosevelt and Stalin—set in play the construction of a collective security organization mandated to promote and maintain global peace and security as well as post-war prosperity. However, even before World War II was over, FDR was dealing more and more with Stalin, with Churchill pushed to a second tier. As always, diplomacy reflected power. Later lesser powers affected the wording of the UN Charter in various ways, but these changes did not alter the core conceptions established by the most powerful states of the 1940s.

Consistently, there were two prongs to the quest for a peaceful and progressive world order—the management of violence and attention to the socio-economic context that might give rise to violence. As for the second of these, the UNO was supposed to resemble, at least in part, a "town meeting of the world where public opinion is focused as an effective force."[5] It was to serve as a facilitator for the spread of liberal norms and practices, as a center for the harmonization of national policies, and, in Roosevelt's words, as a catalyst "to assist the creation, through international cooperation, of conditions of stability and well-being necessary for peaceful and friendly relations among nations."[6] At the same time, the UNO's role in the economic and social areas was greatly limited. The associated, yet autonomous, UN specialized agencies, and the Bretton Woods institutions in particular— the World Bank and the IMF—in the economic area, would presumably serve to transform the world's social and economic realm.

U.S. Secretary of State Cordell Hull put it this way in a 1943 radio address to the American people:

> We know that political controversies and economic strife among nations are fruitful causes of hostility and conflict. But we also know that economic stagnation and distress, cultural backwardness, and social unrest within nations, wherever they exist, may undermine all efforts for stable peace. *The primary responsibility for dealing with these conditions rests on each and every nation concerned.* But each nation will be greatly helped in this task by the establishment of sound trade and other economic relations with other nations, based on a comprehensive system of mutually beneficial international cooperation, not alone in this respect, but also in furthering educational advancement and in promoting observance of basic human rights [emphasis added].[7]

Thus, the UNO was clearly the centerpiece, but by itself—namely, its core organs— was never envisioned to be sufficient for creating the conditions necessary for promoting and maintaining peace and security. This would be the responsibility of the specialized agencies and the Bretton Woods institutions, with the world organization playing a supplemental role of standard setter, town meeting, and, when necessary and consensually agreed upon by the major powers, peace enforcer of the world.

As for the other prong or path to peace and security, the victors of World War II knew a lot about the importance of coercive power. FDR's September 1943 "four policemen" conceptualization clearly acknowledged that reality:

[I]t is my thought that time is an essential in disseminating the ideals of peace among the very diverse nationalities and national egos of a vast number of separate peoples who, for one reason or another over a thousand years, have divided themselves into a hundred different forms of hate. ... Therefore, I have been visualizing a superimposed—or if you like it, a superassumed—obligation by Russia, China, Britain and ourselves that we will act as sheriffs for the maintenance of order during the transition period.[8]

A new world order, yes, but still one dominated by the major powers, which acknowledged straightforwardly a long history of violence by the more powerful in world affairs. The rules for the Security Council clearly manifested this projected dominance: five permanent members, the veto provision, and the broad authority of the council even to take action that overrode other treaty provisions. The Security Council could do pretty much whatever it desired, if its members agreed. The UNO reflected power politics wrapped in a legally binding multilateral agreement, plus progressive politics designed to cure the contextual evils of the world. There was a preferred position for states with power—above all, the United States and the Union of Soviet Socialist Republics (U.S.S.R.), which would soon become known as "the superpowers—which less powerful states agreed to by ratifying the UN Charter. In return, they got attention to their concerns mostly in parts of the UN beyond the Security Council.

The history of the UN has been filled with the trials and tribulations of collective security and the attempt to construct and maintain a new liberal global political-economic order since World War II.[9] In this context, Part 1 of this book details the evolving efforts of the United Nations to directly combat threats to international peace and security. Chapter 1 introduces the theory of collective security and explains how international cooperation is fostered through key Charter provisions involving the pacific settlement of disputes, enforcement, and respect for regional arrangements. Chapter 2 examines UN security efforts during the early part of the Cold War and shows how the UN innovated with the creation of peacekeeping. It also examines the early use of economic sanctions as a public policy tool. Chapter 3, "UN Security Operations after the Cold War, 1988–1998," and Chapter 4, "Security Operations since 1999," explain the renaissance in UN security activities, including the expansion of peacekeeping and peace enforcement operations, and the evolution of the international norm, the responsibility to protect (R2P). Chapter 5 discusses the contemporary political dynamics at the UN and reviews reform proposals that would make it better able to address the challenges of failed states, terrorism, and proliferation of weapons of mass destruction.

Part 2 of the book introduces UN efforts to promote and protect international human rights and humanitarian principles, not only as a strategy for maintaining international peace and security, but as something intrinsically valuable to individuals and worthy of pursuit in world politics. Chapter 6 traces the origins of UN actions on behalf of human rights and humanitarian principles. Chapter 7 focuses on how the UN has helped create and implement these rights and principles through various multilateral and intergovernmental bodies. Chapter 8 centers on UN developments in the field of human rights, exploring the role of such non-state actors as independent experts and nongovernmental organizations (NGOs).

The book's Part 3 describes the efforts by the UN to build consensus around the idea of sustainable human development. Chapter 9 examines the evolution of development thought and explores international attempts to build a humane capitalist world order. Chapter 10 focuses on how the UN formulates public policy related to human security and explains the complexities of international environmental protection. The role of the United Nations in promoting development and human security in the context of the Millennium Development Goals and the Sustainable Development Goals is the focus of Chapter 11.

The United Nations and Changing World Politics is still about the competition to shape and determine values, as well as the distribution of resources within the international community of states. Thus, its focus is the nature and dynamics of a central part of world order and global governance. This begs the question of how the United Nations actually functions. Who are the actors that constitute the "United Nations" and what values and principles do they prefer? What determines which values and preferences will prevail and why? What are the central principles, rules and norms that frame and shape this competition? What main forces, tensions, contradictions, and paradoxes have been at play and what challenges do they continue to present? After all, no world government exists to authoritatively set the rules of the world or to serve as the final arbiter of disputes. The remainder of this introduction is devoted to answering these questions about the "real" United Nations. It is not a moral magic bullet that independently can solve global problems. It is a political and legal institution mostly controlled by states but with a role for various non-state actors as well.

WHAT IS THE UNITED NATIONS?

Many journalists and other observers often use phrases like "the UN failed" (to stop ethnic cleansing in the Balkans) or "the UN was successful" (in checking Iraqi aggression against Kuwait). This phraseology obscures a complex reality. The UN is many different things. The term "United Nations" is often used as a short cut for the UNO. At other times, it is used to refer to the complex and interdependent system of intergovernmental organizations, termed the "UN system." As discussed below, meaning makes a difference as regards understanding and comprehending the UN's role in global governance and the challenges thereto.

The UN is a broad and complex system of policymaking and administration in which some decisions are made by member states and others by professional civil servants who are not instructed by states. Moreover, NGOs, corporations and private individuals pressure state and UN officials and seek to influence decision- and policy-making processes. Analytically, the UN is really three different, yet interactive, entities that often cooperate but also can work at cross purposes. Each of these entities represents complex interests, some of which strive to maintain the status quo and others of which seek substantive change. This is why the story of the UN is one of simultaneous continuity and change.[10]

The First UN. The first UN is an institutional framework through which member states conduct their multilateral diplomacy and play out their foreign policies. For centuries, much of international relations has centered on the relations and interests of states. Governments of states have found it in their self-interest, as well as their collective interest, to act multilaterally to confront shared problems. States have organized and agreed to certain norms, rules, and procedures that govern their relations. The first UN is a multilateral framework comprised of member states that bring their different aspirations, values, ideologies, and capabilities to the table. States with more capabilities, including the capability to structure the rules to reflect their values and preferences, tend to have a greater say in the first UN. As such, political will and capability often determine which values and preferences will prevail and why. The first UN, then, is primarily an intergovernmental organization (IGO), an arena in which member states may pursue or channel their foreign policies, multilaterally.

At the same time, UN structures and processes also frame and even constrain the exercise of state power. The UN Charter is the closest thing there is to a global constitution. When state actors comply with the Charter and use UN procedures, their policies acquire the legitimacy that stems from adherence to international law. They also acquire the legitimacy that stems from collective political approval. This is especially true when it comes to using military force in international relations. Normally, policies that are seen as legal and collectively approved are more likely than not to be successful. The weight of collective political approval also may induce recalcitrant state authorities to accept a UN policy, decision, or program. It is better to have UN approval than otherwise.

The first UN is in essence an institutional arena in which politics among member states is carried out. At the first UN, the organizations' governing bodies are populated and controlled by representatives of member states. This means government officials are responsible to and represent specific countries. In the UNO, for example, these organs include the Security Council, the General Assembly, the Economic and Social Council (ECOSOC), the Human Rights Council, and the list goes on. Other UN agencies are, more or less, structured similarly. Since member states provide direction to their representatives, it is not surprising that these various entities are inherently politicized. State representatives decide; and when UN decisions involve force, economic resources, or considerable diplomatic pressure, those necessities essentially borrowed from member states. The clash of values and interstate rivalries that are present in world politics are also manifest in the first UN. Moreover, in the context of the Security Council, the concert of the five permanent (and veto-wielding) members—the P5—is required. This check was intended by the institution's founders, and it is embodied in the Charter. The General Assembly and other official UN delegate bodies that adopt most of the important "UN" resolutions are made up of states.

Without political agreement in the first UN, "the UN" is severely restricted in what it can accomplish. This was the case in 1945, and since then it has not been altered in any fundamental way. At times the United Nations is placed on the back burner, as it was for much of the Cold War. Major states bypassed the world organization on important international security issues, instead favoring action outside it. At other times the first UNO was front and center as it was during the 1990s, with a major collective security action (Iraq in 1991) and a surge in peacekeeping and peace-enforcement operations. The post-September 11, 2001 era has seen the efficacy of the first UN in security matters wax and wane depending on the extent to which important states—especially the United States, China, and Russia—can agree on policy decisions. State decisions about power and policy constitute the primary force driving events at the UN. In this regard, the Middle East has served as the first UN's "Achilles heel," accounting for the overwhelming number of vetoes in the Security Council since 1975. When important states show a convergence in policy, then the UN can be allowed to act.

From the initiation of the first peacekeeping mission in 1948 through the end of 2018, the UN had deployed seventy-one of them in the field.[11] Of these, fourteen were still active at that time with a combined personnel of about 90,000[12] and a total budget for July 1, 2018 to June 30, 2019 of $6.7 billion.[13] The largest contemporary field missions were the UN Mission in South Sudan (UNMISS), the United Nations Organization Stabilization Mission in the Democratic Republic of the Congo (MONUSCO), the United Nations Multidimensional Integrated Stabilization Mission in Mali (MINUSMA), and the United Nations Multidimensional Integrated Stabilization Mission in the Central African Republic (MINUSCA); collectively they accounted for about 63 percent of the total peace operations budget. In addition, there were twenty-two active political missions and good offices engagements.[14] While these activities required consensus in the Security Council and funding and troop contributions from states, the second UN of staff members was responsible for their implementation.

The Second UN. By design, the secretariats of UN organizations are administrative. The secretaries-general (or head of other bodies) and the international civil service constitute the second UN, which is the system of decision and policy making by UN officials who are legally independent and not completely instructed by states. Neither the UN Secretary-General nor the heads of the WHO, ILO, and UNESCO, to give a few examples, are supposed to take instructions from his/her home state but rather is instructed by state members through resolutions adopted. While states set the agendas and pay the bills (sometimes), UN staff at all levels have margins for maneuver and initiative. It would be a strange civil service, national or international, that consisted only of slavish bureaucrats.

UN staff have expertise, knowledge, and independent diplomatic skills, which Michael Barnett and Robert Duvall have indicated is a source of "power."[15] The position of agency head helps member states reduce the transaction and information costs associated with multilateral action and can help clarify preferences and alternatives. It offers the possibility of neutrality and adds to a sense of legitimacy in numerous situations. While the second UN cannot function well if its actions and decisions stray too far from the preferences of powerful member states, it can exercise some agency and engages in mediation and education. It may suggest new ideas. It also performs an important monitoring function that provides state representatives with the quality data necessary to make good decisions. The second UN can also push and prod member states, reminding them of their obligations under the Charter and other areas of international law.

The second UN is unusually positioned as the guardian of UN principles and values. It certainly does not have the sole voice on how to interpret their meaning and application of the Charter, but it does have some legal and moral authority. The Charter confers some independent authority on the secretary-general, who may address the Security Council and makes an annual report on the UN's work to the General Assembly, focusing attention on certain problems and possible solutions. Numerous UN organizations, funds, programs, and specialized agencies are staffed by independent personnel paid by regular UN budgets, and others are financed through voluntary contributions. Some are on permanent, long-duration contracts but others on short-term ones. As indicated above, authority—and the influence and power flowing from it—also may be transferred by intergovernmental bodies to independent UN personnel. The UN Security Council may decide to create a peacekeeping force but then turns over many specifics and mechanics to the secretary-general, who in turn relies upon force commanders and special representatives. Within the broad confines of this system, UN personnel exercise considerable influence as relatively autonomous actors not fully controlled by states. Their authority is not supranational but can be significant, especially if exercised out of the limelight. They cannot instruct states how to act, but they may be able to induce states to behave in certain ways. Moreover, they can improve the lives of millions of people by cooperating and coordinating with states and NGOs.

The Third UN. Another dimension of the UN is the network of NGOs, experts, corporate executives, media representatives, and academics who work closely with the first and second UN.[16] Their presence is often ignored when thinking about the theory and practice of the world organization.[17] With the backing or the blessing of important member states, the second UN often will bring in independent experts to serve on *ad hoc* commissions or as advisors or envoys. Technically, these individuals are not formal employees of the second UN, but they may become influential because they usually have extensive prior work experience with member states and/or UN agencies. These quasi-representatives of the UN, and the services that they render, reflect how the second UN can extend the influence of UN symbols and prestige.

Nearly four thousand NGOs have some form of officially recognized consultative or observer status within the UN, which means that member states have formally acknowledged their competency and compatibility with the Charter; they are permitted to participate in international conferences. NGOs perform two basic kinds of roles within UN politics. First, NGOs represent an important lobbying force for policies or changes in existing policy developed by the first UN and the second UN. They do this by providing collecting and disseminating data and through advocacy. They facilitate relationships with state and IGO officials and also provide ordinary citizens with a vehicle for meaningful participation in UN affairs.

Second, NGOs play a significant subcontracting role in delivering humanitarian and development aid. The first and the second UN often turns to NGOs to provide assistance, expertise, and educational services during routine field operations to foster development and in complex emergencies. NGOs also perform a crucial monitoring role, for example related to detention facilities in conflict situations. NGOs monitor and assess the status of human rights and humanitarian principles as well as progress on development indicators or environmental conditions. They also help set, and measure progress toward, socioeconomic benchmarks. Increasingly, private NGOs are active and sometimes influential in their interactions with the intergovernmental system.

The Three Together. The first, the second, and the third United Nations cohere—often without much seeming coherence—into what most observers lump together, "the United Nations." This tripartite conceptualization holds both in regard to the core UNO and the larger UN system of otherwise autonomous organizations. Throughout this text, the distinction between these three UNs is noted, as appropriate. When UN forums controlled by states reach decisions, the first UN is in play. Similarly, when the secretary-general or a high commissioner (or their subordinates) decide and act, the second UN is engaged. When independent experts and NGOs influence, pressure, or educate state and IGO officials or provide services, the third UN is at work.

The relationships among the various UNs are interactive and dynamic. Reports from the secretary-general or his staff may influence the first UN. NGOs may influence important member states in taking a particular stance. The second and third UN rely on states for funding, visas, and protection. Relationships are not always constructive or free of conflict. The second UN, although in theory independent from state control and responsible only to the Charter, is often stymied and even marginalized by member states. Also, fealty to the Charter does not make officials from the second UN immune from making poor choices or performing sub-optimally. NGOs can complicate UN politics. For example, faith-based NGOs have been extremely influential in shaping UN policy related to women's sexual and reproductive health rights, international development, and human rights and the defamation of religion.[18] This brings them into conflict with the more secular and progressive elements of the United Nations.

United Nations Secretary-General António Guterres. (UN PHOTO 709941/MARK GARTEN)

The second UN cannot function without funds appropriated by the first UN governing bodies and actually paid by member states. And, since the early 1980s, the UN has continuously staggered through budget crisis after crisis. Not only was 2018 no less so, but even more so. For UN fiscal year (FY) 2018, only forty-eight member states had paid their dues in full to the regular budget by the due date (February 9, 2018). As of end July, only one hundred and twelve of them had paid their dues in full, and Secretary-General António Guterres warned member states in a letter of an impending budget crisis if this situation continued.[19] As of September 30, 2018, a total of U.S. $1.1 billion remained unpaid, and as of end October, forty-seven member states still were in arrears. Leading the list of deadbeats was the United States—the UN's largest contributor. Despite claimed FY budget-cycle issues, Washington could have paid on October 1; but, as has become the norm of slow or non-payment, had not. In regard to the peace-keeping budget—a separate budget in UN accounting—a total of $2.5 billion was in arrears.[20]

The General Assembly's appointment of the ninth UN Secretary-General provides an example of the dynamic forces and tensions in the relationships among the three United Nations. Whereas all prior selections of Secretaries-General had been the exclusive and private purview of closed negotiations among the "electoral college" of the Permanent Five (P5) members of the Security Council, the 2016 recommendation of a single candidate reflected pressures for a more participatory process. On September 22, 2015, the General Assembly adopted resolution 69/321, which called for a more open format for the selection process would proceed. It began with a call for nominations set out in a joint letter by the presidents of the Security Council and General Assembly. An overarching set of criteria was included, including a person

> who embodies the highest standards of efficiency, competence and integrity and demonstrates a firm commitment to the purposes and principles of the United Nations, and invites Member States to present candidates with proven leadership and managerial abilities, extensive experience in international relations and strong diplomatic, communication and multilingual skills.

For only the second time—the first was in 1996—the campaigns for the U.S. president and the UN secretary-general ran in parallel.[21] Both were protracted. The UN version produced a slate of thirteen nominees—seven of whom were women, whereas over the previous seven decades only three were actively considered for the top post. All candidates pursued their campaigns in person and through lobbyists, while the "1-for-7-billion" civil society campaign pestered member states. The process certainly was more open and transparent than previous ones, although only an inveterate Pollyanna would have hoped to eliminate completely backroom horse-trading in the Security Council.

In a break from previous practice, the General Assembly gathered for two-hour hearings with each candidate from April to September 2016; it also organized an open public event for all of them; and civil society debates in New York and London augmented the intergovernmental gatherings. Curricula vitae were available for public and private scrutiny. Candidates circulated "vision statements," which contained thoughts about how to reshape the unwieldy, so-called UN family.

The front-runner for several months and winner of five straw polls in the usually divided Security Council, Guterres secured its recommendation. The General Assembly endorsed his candidacy by acclamation in early in October 2016. Having previously served for two successful terms first as prime minister of Portugal and as head of the Office of the UN High Commissioner for Refugees (UNHCR), his distinguished government and UN management experience, together with his evident energy and diplomatic finesse, made him the best of the declared candidates.

In short, the selection process no longer resembled a papal conclave. Arguably, Guterres would not have emerged under the old rules—he obviously is not a Central European woman, when geographical rotation dictated an Eastern European and many insisted on a female. Moreover, his predecessor undoubtedly would not have been selected in 2006 had the new procedures been in effect. Perhaps these welcome, albeit modest, steps are harbingers of a more merit-based and transparent process that will have knock-on effects for other senior positions in the second UN. This result appeared to have been the case in the May 2017 election of WHO Director-General Tedros Adhanom Ghebreyesus and the November 2017 election of UNESCO Director-General Audrey Azoulay. It could have an impact at the World Bank and International Monetary Fund, whose top jobs have always been reserved for U.S. and European nationals, respectively.

We have gone on at length about the selection not only because of its importance for a textbook on the United Nations, but also because of how it demonstrates the reality of the three United Nations. The reform of the selection process for the UN's top job—part of the first UN affecting the second UN—resulted from a combination of General Assembly resolutions from the first UN with external pressure from civil society organizations from the third UN. Internally, two caucusing groups also helped to move the issue forward. These were the Accountability, Coherence, and Transparency (ACT) group, made up of twenty-five small member states from various regions, and the Non-Aligned Movement (NAM). These sub-groups from the first UN felt substantial pressure from the concerted campaign by the broad-based coalition of some seven hundred and fifty NGOs in the "1 for 7 Billion: Find the Best UN Leader."[22] In summary, the head of the second UN reflected hybrid efforts by the first UN and the third UN.

UNO BASICS: AN OVERVIEW

UN agencies are political institutions, and UN politics involves the exercise of power—either hard power (coercive) or soft power (influence). Since power is needed to make and implement policy, member states of the first UN naturally seek allies. Academic and diplomatic observers have put forward varied generalizations about the political alliances, coalitions, or blocs within the United Nations. During the Cold War era the countries of the West—that is, the Western industrialized democracies that are members of the Organization for Economic Co-operation and Development (OECD), sometimes joined by Israel—constituted the so-called First World. "Developing countries," basically all of Asia, Africa, and Latin America, have been examined under the rubrics of the "Third World," the "Global South," the "Non-Aligned Movement" (NAM), and the "Group of 77" (or G77, for the original constellation of seventy-seven states, which has now grown to some one hundred and thirty-five members). The "socialist countries," when the Soviet Union and its bloc existed, were also called the "East" and the "Second World." The West and the East, in a curious bit of mathematical geography, were added together to constitute the North, or the developed countries, in juxtaposition to the Global South, or the developing countries. The North-South conflict represents the difference in values and preferred outcomes between wealthier and developing states.

Although these distinctions roughly correspond to the bulk of voting patterns during the Cold War, they have become considerably less useful over time. Not only did the bloc of European socialist states and the Soviet Union cease to exist, but also some of this terminology was never accurate: Cuba was hardly nonaligned, and the socialist countries of Eastern Europe were not nearly as economically developed as the West, with some at levels comparable to the Third World. In the past, it was conventional to speak of the Third World as if it were homogeneous, with little hesitation in grouping Singapore's and Chad's economies or Costa Rica's and North Korea's ideologies. Now, it is common to point out that developing countries consist of a series of crosscutting alignments reflecting the heterogeneous character of their economies and ideologies.[23] On a few issues, however, developing countries do show truly common interests. In such instances the North-South divide continued to be salient. For example, during the 2006 negotiations to create the Human Rights Council, a classic North-South divide was observed on many questions. Frequently, however, developing countries subdivide along different lines according to the issue before the UN: between radicals and moderates, between Islamic and non-Islamic, between those in the region and outside, between maritime and landlocked, between those achieving significant economic growth and otherwise. Also, the emergence of the BRICS (Brazil, Russia, India, China, and South Africa) association signifies a potentially formidable political alliance that might challenge the dominance of traditional Western values and preferences at the UN.[24] The organization of the powerful countries of North and South into the Group of 20 (G20) defies categorization but their decisions weigh heavily on international deliberations in light of their group's geopolitical weight.[25] Within the Western group there have always been numerous differences, which regularly come to the fore. Divisions among and within all groups over the pursuit of war against Iraq in 2003 were one example.

The previous paragraph was historically accurate when the previous edition of this textbook went to press. It now needs to be interpreted in the light of ongoing, contemporary developments whose impacts are far from certain. The Western coalition at the UN has badly fractured, with the Trump Administration publicly castigating most of its traditional allies on various issues, even engaging in ad hominem attacks on several Western leaders. Meanwhile, Brazil's November 2018 elections resulted in the presidency of Jair Bolsonaro—called by some the "Trump of the Tropics—whose negative impact on Brazil's leadership in such multilateral efforts as climate change and in the BRICS is likely. Accompanying leadership scandals in Brazil and South Africa have been their sluggish economies along with Russia's. Caucusing power among the members of the first UN is not what it was merely two years ago.

Structurally, the UN recognizes five regional groupings of states: Africa, Asia-Pacific, Eastern Europe, Latin America-Caribbean, and Western Europe and Others (including the United States, Australia, New Zealand, Japan, Canada, and Israel). Membership on such important bodies as the Security Council, the ECOSOC, and the Human Rights Council is comprised on a geographical-distribution basis. These regional groupings are responsible for selecting which of their member states will stand for election, so intra-regional politics as well as intra-council politics are at play. Moreover, powerful member states, such as the United States, Japan, and Germany, are known to wield their financial influence to induce the political support of developing countries for council policies.[26] The same is true for other states like China and Saudi Arabia.

The second UN, while comprised of purportedly independent officials, is not immune to politics. UN officials have their own preferences and interpretations of UN values and principles and use UN symbols and procedures to achieve them. Organizational heads may align with certain states or groups of states. For example, at one point during the 1980s UNESCO's director-general was accused of being too aligned with developing countries, which precipitated the withdrawal of the United States and the United Kingdom.[27] After rejoining UNESCO following an absence of almost two decades, the United States withdrew again officially at the end of 2018 after not paying its assessed contribution since 2010. The precipitating event was the 2010 decision by the "first UNESCO"—the General Conference—in admitting Palestine as a member state. In both cases, however, UNESCO's Second UN was forced to bear the brunt of U.S. ire and was confronted with overnight losses of over 20 percent of its core budget. A similar link to domestic politics over Israel-Palestine took place in late 2017 when Washington predictably vetoed (score 14-1) a Security Council resolution criticizing the wisdom of moving Israel's capital to Jerusalem. When the General Assembly voted likewise, the administration froze the remaining U.S. contribution to the UN Relief and Works Agency (UNRWA) and then eliminated completely its contribution (close to half of its budget) in 2018 with an obvious negative impact on the second UN's delivery of assistance to Palestinian refugees.

The politics of the third UN are also dynamic as civil society actors compete for influence and resources. NGO interactions with the first UN and second UN have greatly expanded since the mid-1990s and the role of NGOs in UN politics is now institutionalized.[28] NGOs are diverse in terms of their orientation and tactics and are partners with the UN in field operations. The commissioning of NGOs in the peacebuilding work of the UN has real policy consequences on the ground in places like Bosnia, Haiti, Iraq, Afghanistan, and Sierra Leone.[29] NGOs can complicate traditional forms of diplomacy and also be a catalyst for policy and change. In sum, the United Nations is a world organization comprised of member states and UN personnel along with independent experts, the media, business, and NGOs. These three parts of the UN are wrestling with the twenty-first century's most pressing problems of insecurity, abuses of human rights, and lack of sustainable human development. These latter three substantive issues encompass the central challenges to improving the human condition. They are also the central focus of this book.

THE PRINCIPLES OF THE UNITED NATIONS

The institutional framework of the UNO, as specified in the UN Charter, rests on a number of organizing principles, most importantly for example: the sovereign equality of its member states; the peaceful settlement of disputes; the nonuse of force in international relations; and nonintervention in the domestic jurisdiction of member states. These principles influence the political dynamics at the UNO. When states join the UNO, they agree to respect these principles and to take separate and joint action to assist in the world organization's main purposes: maintaining international peace and security and promoting economic and social cooperation. This includes promoting and protecting human rights and humanitarian principles. The UN Charter is a bridge between the older Westphalian norms of sovereignty and nonintervention with relatively newer norms such as the pacific settlement of disputes and the prohibition of the threat and use of force in international relations.

One needs to recognize that because of political calculations, at least some of the various UN principles are either contradictory or oxymoronic—requiring shrewd diplomacy to manage or finesse. The Preamble to the UN Charter sets out many laudatory purposes, then declares that the UN cannot "intervene in matters essentially within the domestic jurisdiction of any state." This phrase was written by John Foster Dulles, an advisor to the U.S. delegation at the San Francisco Conference that approved the language in the UN Charter. He was trying to placate especially Southern Senators concerned about UN action regarding treatment of African-Americans. Dulles and his superiors were trying to ensure U.S. membership in the UN and avoid a repeat of the Senate's rejection of the League of Nations. In pursuit of that goal, U.S. policy and resulting legal language was to weaken many UN efforts to improve things, especially appalling human rights conditions in many places. In fairness to Dulles, Roosevelt often talked about the projected UN as a great problem solver, but he also argued that national independence and sovereignty remained intact. In this sense, many officials associated with the founding of the UN were not that dissimilar from Woodrow Wilson and those who founded the League of Nations. They wanted a general international organization to help solve problems, but did not want to give up national prerogatives to get it.[30]

State Sovereignty. The legal foundations of sovereignty are centuries deep. When the Peace of Westphalia essentially ended European religious wars in 1648, powerful political circles accepted that the world should be divided into territorial states. Before that time, dynastic empires, city-states, feudalistic orders, clans and tribes, churches, and a variety of other arrangements organized persons into groupings for personal identity and problem solving. From about the middle of the fifteenth century to the middle of the seventeenth, the territorial state emerged, first in Europe and then elsewhere, as the basic unit of social and political organization that supposedly commanded primary loyalty and was responsible for order, and eventually for justice and prosperity, within a state's territorial boundaries. European rulers found the institution of the state useful and perpetuated its image; then politically aware persons outside the West adopted the notion of the state to resist domination by European states.

Other groupings also persisted. In nineteenth-century Europe, Napoleon sought to substitute a French empire for several states, European imperialism thrived, and much colonialism persisted in Africa until the 1960s—some would argue it continues informally today. Despite these exceptions and the endurance of clan, ethnic, and religious identities, most of those exercising power increasingly promoted the perception that the basic political-legal unit of world affairs was the state: an administrative apparatus with a supposed monopoly on the legitimate use of force over a specific geographical area, with a stable (non-nomadic) population. Frequently, the territorial state is referred to as the "nation-state." This label is not totally false, but it can be misleading because nations and states are not the same. A nation is a people (a group of persons professing solidarity on the basis of language, religion, history, or some other bonding element) linked to a state. Legally speaking, where there is a state, there is a nation, but there may be several peoples within a state. For example, the citizens of Switzerland (officially the Helvetian Confederation) are, by legal definition members of the Swiss nation, but in social reality the Swiss state includes four peoples: the Swiss-Germans, the Swiss-French, the Swiss-Italians, and the Swiss-Romanisch. The confusing notion of a multinational state also has arisen alongside divided nations (East and West Germany between 1945 and 1989, and North and South Korea today) and states with irredentist claims (Serbia and Russia). The members of the United Nations are territorial states (with the exception of the Vatican), but this only begs the question of who is a national people entitled to a state. Many persons in existing states, from Belgium to Sri Lanka, from the United Kingdom to Canada, have not fully and finally settled this issue.

• The emergence of the territorial state was accompanied by the notion that the state was sovereign. Accordingly, the sovereignty of all other social groupings was legally subordinated to the state's sovereignty. Political and legal theorists argued that sovereignty resided in territorial states' rulers, who had ultimate authority to make policy within a state's borders. Those who negotiated the two treaties making up the Peace of Westphalia in 1648 wanted to stop the religious wars that had brought so much destruction to Europe. They specified that whoever ruled a certain territory could determine the religion of that territory. State sovereignty was an idea that arose in a particular place at a particular time and then became widely accepted as European political influence spread around the world. The argument was about legal rights, but it was intended to affect power. All states were said to be sovereign equals, regardless of their actual "power"—meaning capability to influence outcomes. They had the right to control policy within their jurisdictions even if they did not have the power to do it. Framed in the language of the abstract state, sovereignty enhanced the power of those persons making up the government that represented the state.

Sovereignty was designed to produce order, legitimize existing power arrangements, and stop violence between and within states over religious questions. However, did state sovereignty become, on balance, an idea that guaranteed international instability? Was it necessary to think of relations between and among states as anarchical—not in the sense of chaos but in the sense of interactions among equal sovereigns recognizing no higher rules and organizations? Of course, the more powerful states, while agreeing that all states were equally sovereign, repeatedly violated the domestic jurisdiction of the weaker states—what Stephen Krasner has dubbed "organized hypocrisy."[31] State sovereignty, originally designed to produce order and to buttress central authority within the state, led to negative external consequences, the main one being that central authority over global society and interstate relations was undermined. All territorial states came to be seen as equal in the sense of having ultimate authority to prescribe what "should be" in their jurisdictions. No outside rules and organizations were held to be superior to the state. Only those rules consented to, and only those organizations voluntarily accepted, could exist in interstate relations based on the logic of the Westphalian system of world politics.[32] Thus, states were legally free to make war, violate human rights, neglect the welfare of citizens, and damage the environment.

State sovereignty is not a physical fact, like energy or a doorknob. It is a social fact; it is widely accepted and becomes part of the dominant psychology. The process of "socially constructing" the notion of sovereignty means that it has evolved to mean different things in different eras. At one time, sovereignty meant a state had the ultimate and absolute right to govern, even if that meant practicing slavery or systematically persecuting women or minorities. Today, such state behavior invites at least international opprobrium and at times even intervention. In political reality in the modern Westphalian interstate legal order, the attribute of sovereignty is primarily determined by established states recognizing the sovereign status of new or existing governments. Thus, to a majority of the member states in the UN, Palestine has been de facto granted sovereignty, despite U.S. remonstrations to the contrary.

Who should govern and by what means are the kinds of questions raised at the UN? For example, by 1992 the state had disintegrated in the geographical area known as Somalia, which is to say that the governing system for the territory did not function. With no effective government to represent the state, should the UN be the organization ultimately responsible for ending disorder and starvation and helping to reestablish the state? If disputes within a recognized state, such as the former Yugoslavia in the early 1990s, lead to mass murder, mass migration, and mass misery, should the UN be ultimately responsible? Or, as was the controversial case in Kosovo in 1999, should another multilateral organization—to wit, the North Atlantic Treaty Organization (NATO)—override claims to sovereignty by Serbia (the successor state to Yugoslavia) if the Security Council is paralyzed? If the UN is responsible and decides to act, should the UN delegate its authority to specific states to determine the means of protecting civilians, even if it involves supporting opposition forces intent on overthrowing a brutal dictator, as in Libya in 2011? If states fail to take action in relation to major violations of international criminal law (individual responsibility for genocide, war crimes, crimes against humanity, and ethnic cleansing), should the International Criminal Court (ICC) have the right to prosecute and convict the individuals responsible?

Governments act in the name of states to determine how to manage certain transnational problems. On occasion, they have agreed to let an international organization have the ultimate say as to what should be done. For example, more than forty states in the Council of Europe have consented to the European Convention on Human Rights. Under this treaty, the European Court of Human Rights has the ultimate say as to the correct interpretation of the convention, and the court regularly issues judgments to states concerning the legality of their policies. If one starts, as do European governments, with the notion that states are sovereign, then these states have used their sovereignty to create international bodies that restrict their own authority. Among these states, the protection of human rights on a transnational basis is valued more highly than complete state independence. States have used their freedom to make policies that reduce their freedom. Initial sovereignty, linked to territory, has been used to restrict that sovereignty by an international body acting primarily on transnational considerations. This European situation is atypical of interstate relations and the nature of interstate relations is not likely to change in the foreseeable future. Indeed, the Brexit vote in part represented a pushback against the authority of European multilateralism. In other states on the continent as well, there was much criticism of the authority and power of EU policy making.

There are a few other examples of supranational authority in world politics. Although much noise arises in the United States about the right of the dispute panels of the World Trade Organization (WTO) to dictate policy to states, this international grant of authority is modest. States ultimately decide whether to apply sanctions for violations of WTO rules. Power, especially economic power, influences the efficacy of sanctions authorized under such rules. So when WTO's Dispute Settlement Panel (DSP) rules that a U.S. policy violates WTO strictures, sometimes the United States changes its policy, sometimes it does not, and sometimes Washington engages in protracted negotiations with other states that make it difficult to decide whether the United States is complying with the DSP ruling. In any case, the purportedly most powerful state has agreed to abide by rules and decisions of an international organization in pursuit of mutually beneficial, regulated free trade.

Most states, and none more than those that have achieved formal independence after the UN's founding, sometimes value state sovereignty more than supranational cooperation to improve security, protect human rights, or pursue sustainable development. For many, it is a matter of national identity and pride, and also protection against large bully or "rogue" states. Older states also highly value state sovereignty, demonstrated by Trump's use of the term some twenty-one times in his first address in September 2017 to the General Assembly.[33] Edward Luck has pointed out the example of American exceptionalism and traditional skepticism about inroads on its authority within the UN.[34] As Richard Haass puts it in an understatement, "Americans have traditionally guarded their sovereignty with more than a little ferocity."[35] Jack Goldsmith, an official in George W. Bush's Justice Department, and afterward a member of the Harvard Law School faculty, regards most international law and organization, including the concept of war crimes, with great skepticism, seeing them as limits on what a president thinks is needed to protect American homeland security.[36] China, too, argues that only the state, not outside parties, can determine what is best for the Chinese people, whether in the realm of security, human rights, or sustainable human development. As noted above, by 2015, the United Kingdom was showing irritation with the intrusive decisions of both the European Union and the Council of Europe, accompanied by a more traditional and less cooperative nationalism could be found in public opinion polls and electoral outcomes. In short, international cooperation exists at various levels but usually falls short of being anything like permanently and irrevocably supranational. International organizations normally lack the formal capacity to override independent state decisions on an ongoing, broad, and settled basis. This rule is certainly true of the United Nations.

The bigger picture is worth emphasizing. From about 2016, especially across the Western developed democracies, there was a backlash against many multilateral organizations and regimes. A dominant lesson of history was implicitly reconsidered. Heretofore, a basic principle was widely accepted: after 1914 and then 1939, a pure state system was seen as too dangerous and ineffective. From 2016 a new (or perhaps better, "recycled") principle competed: many international arrangements restricted state sovereignty too much. More than one national leader talked about returning to the days of greater national freedom, which meant reducing the role of international rules and regulations, not to mention reducing the number of foreign born in their societies. To overstate the matter for emphasis, it was as if one should return to 1913 and the days of an absolute sovereignty with few international restrictions on its exercise. In this context, Britain voted to leave the European Union; the recently-elected Trump Administration pulled out of the Trans Pacific Partnership on Trade (TPP) as well as the Paris Agreement on Climate Change, including reneging on its commitment to the Green Climate Fund; the Orban government in Hungary touted the virtues of a traditional illiberal Christian democracy with less limitation by European regional law or UN refugee law; and the list of backpedaling actions goes on. The most pronounced anti-UN actions were by the Trump Administration, which also ripped up the P5+1 Iran nuclear deal; stopped financing the UN Population Fund (UNFPA); pulled out of the Human Rights Council (HRC) and the Global Compact for Safe, Orderly and Regular Migration; and announced the intention to withdraw from even the most technical of international organizations, the Universal Postal Union (UPU).

Ironically, at the very same time of widespread disenchantment with international arrangements, as the peoples and states of the world become more interconnected and interdependent, materially and morally, demands increased in some circles of opinion for more effective international management even at the expense of state sovereignty. Indeed, the "responsibility to protect" (R2P) civilians has emerged as a mainstream concern—at least on paper.[37] Demand is growing in some circles for better transnational management of pressing problems, especially in cases of humanitarian disasters, climate change, and pandemics.[38] More effective global governance is necessary, even if there remains strong resistance to a global government. This dynamic plays out daily at the United Nations. In 2016, a distinguished historian published the following:

> as we have come increasingly to live in an age of globalization, as the barriers created by the Cold War have crumbled, international institutions, worldwide means of communication, multinational companies, and many other influences have eroded national boundaries and begun to bind us all together as a global human community.[39]

Yet it was precisely at this time that many leaders and followers in the West longed for "the good old days" embodying less foreign influence in their countries, and fewer foreign born therein. Nativism, xenophobic nationalism, and right-wing populism were back with a vengeance. Cosmopolitanism, in which identity with the nation was blended with international standards benefitting all, was out—or certainly much weakened.[40]

In addition, in many parts of the world existing states are under pressure from within because a variety of groups—usually loosely called "ethnic," although they often are based on religious, linguistic, or other cultural characteristics—demand some form of sovereignty and self-determination. Many demands cause problems, but conflict is particularly pronounced when self-determination takes the form of a demand for a people's right to construct a new state. In these cases, the idea of accepting the territorial state as the basic unit of world politics is not at issue, at least in principle. What is at issue, and often fought over, is which groupings of people should be recognized as a state, and in what territorial boundaries. Kosovo and Palestine are cases in point. So was the Tamil area of Sri Lanka or the Biafra area of Nigeria. The question of Kurdistan remains unresolved with regard to Turkey, Iraq, Iran, and Syria. Less toxic cases arise with regard to Scotland, Catalonia, and Québec. There has never been agreement in the abstract concerning who is a national people entitled to the right of national self-determination.

State sovereignty persists in the perceptions of most political elites. Each annual session of the UN General Assembly reaffirms it in principle. But state sovereignty, linked to the power and independence of those who govern in the name of the state, is not the only value in world politics. Other values can challenge state sovereignty, including enhanced security, respect for human rights and humanitarian principles, and sustainable human development. The precise boundaries of state sovereignty are elusive and the leaders of the second UN are often tasked with testing those boundaries. Boutros Boutros-Ghali, then secretary-general, argued in 1992 that the time of absolute sovereignty had passed. In *Foreign Affairs* he wrote,

> The centuries-old doctrine of absolute and exclusive sovereignty no longer stands, and was in fact never so absolute as it was conceived to be in theory. A major intellectual requirement of our time is to rethink the question of sovereignty.[41]

His successor, Kofi Annan, was even more outspoken on the subject:

> State sovereignty, in its most basic sense, is being redefined—not least by the forces of globalization and international cooperation. States are now widely understood to be instruments at the service of their peoples, and not vice versa. At the same time individual sovereignty—by which I mean the fundamental freedom of each individual, enshrined in the charter of the UN and subsequent international treaties—has been enhanced by a renewed and spreading consciousness of individual rights. … This developing international norm in favour of intervention to protect civilians from wholesale slaughter will no doubt continue to pose profound challenges to the international community. In some quarters it will arouse distrust, skepticism, even hostility. But I believe on balance we should welcome it.[42]

Indeed, Annan was instrumental in leading international efforts to re-conceptualize sovereignty as R2P. Subsequent chapters discuss the development of this norm as a guiding international principle, but for our purposes here, R2P means responsible sovereignty. According to Ban Ki-moon, Annan's successor

> [p]roperly understood, R2P is an ally of sovereignty, not an adversary. Strong States protect their people, while weak ones are either unwilling or unable to do so. Protection was one of the core purposes of the formation of States and the Westphalian system. By helping States meet one of their core responsibilities, R2P seeks to strengthen sovereignty, not weaken it.[43]

Yet the Trump Administration, with its strong unilateralists like the third national security advisor, John Bolton, definitely did not agree with the internationalist views noted above by secretaries-general despite Bolton's earlier posting as the U.S. permanent representative to the United Nations. The foreign policy of the organization's most important state and funder had changed. It no longer clearly and consistently sought to play the role of hegemon striving to construct a rules-based world order cemented on liberal values as institutionalized in the UN and other international organizations. It sought national advantage through bullying tactics with scant regard for human rights and humanitarian values. In this orientation, it effectively mimicked the foreign policies of China and Russia. At home and abroad in many states, it was tough times for most liberal values[44]—even liberal economics featuring the laws of supply and demand, as compared to diktats from the White House.

World politics consists, in large part, of managing the contradictions between conceptions of state sovereignty, on the one hand, and the desirability of advancing other values, on the other hand. These contradictions are not the only ones in world politics, and managing them is not the only pressing need, but they constitute the fault lines that permeate the United Nations.

The Peaceful Settlement of Disputes. Upon joining the UN, member states are obligated to settle disputes nonviolently using agreed upon mechanisms of conflict resolution. Disputes may be territorial or involve differences regarding who controls the government or represents the state. Conflicts also may arise over resources or property. Member states use a variety of methods to resolve their conflict. Traditional diplomacy is usually the preferred means but states also may adjudicate disputes using international law and courts. When formal legal remedies are not available or desirable, member states turn to mediation and arbitration. Mediation is a non-binding form of conflict resolution in which a skilled mediator attempts to find a solution that is acceptable to the parties, rather than deciding questions of legality or who is right or wrong. Arbitration is quite similar but more formal in that the parties agree ahead of time to be bound by the arbiter's decision.

Independent commissions of inquiry and international claims and compensation bodies are also useful tools.[45] Independent commissions may be appointed by the UN Security Council or the Human Rights Council to investigate a conflict and to reduce the risk of conflict escalation. International claims and compensation bodies assist in the reconciliation process by helping parties recover from damages and loss. One of the central roles of the second UN is to assist member states in peacefully settling their disputes. UN personnel are routinely called upon to use their "good offices" to negotiate conflict among member states. By employing their relative neutrality, expertise, and the prestige of their office, UN personnel can help mediate conflicts and use UN symbols to help de-escalate conflict situations.

The Nonuse of Force. For about a century leading up to 1919 and the League of Nations, traditional international law considered resorting to war to be within the sovereign competence of states.[46] If state officials perceived that their interests justified force, it was used. But increasingly state authorities, not just ivory-tower academics or pacifists, have agreed that changing patterns of warfare require international attempts to avoid or constrain force. The history of efforts to eliminate war through development of international norms has been recently reviewed,[47] although it remains probable that the absence of great power war since 1945 owes much to destructive weaponry. Interest in peace and security has been combined with an interest in state authority, power, and independence. The result is international norms and organizations that continue to depend on state authority and power even as those norms and organizations try to restrain the threat and use of military force.

State actors originally thought that their best interests were served by absolute sovereignty and complete freedom in the choice of policy. Many then also learned that this was a dangerous and frequently destructive situation. From the viewpoint of their own interests, limiting the recourse to and the process of force was highly desirable. That led to the part of international law called *jus ad bellum* (law regulating recourse to war) and *jus in bello* (law regulating the conduct of war). International laws and organizations were developed to contribute to state welfare even as they limited state freedom.[48]

Article 2 (4) of the UN Charter effectively bans the threat or use of force in international relations. The only exceptions are in cases of individual self-defense/collective self-defense (Article 51) or when authorized by the UN Security Council using the enforcement provisions under Chapter VII. The general prohibition against the threat and use of force is revolutionary because aggressive war is outlawed and using military force is limited. Even in cases of self-defense or collective defense, the use of force must be necessary and proportional to the threat or attack. The idea was that states could avoid the dangerous consequences of violent conflict by limiting when force could legitimately be used and then even if violence does break out, limiting war's harmful effects.

Since the formal creation of the UN in 1945, nonetheless, member states have threatened and used force repeatedly. As subsequent chapters show, the Security Council has had limited success in confronting uses of military force, especially by veto-wielding powers protecting themselves or their allies. Change does not occur overnight nor is it necessarily progressive. But the UN Charter, following the experiment of the League of Nations Covenant, has changed the narrative. The politics involving the use of the force in the UN era have centered on interesting legal claims of self-defense rather than the sovereign right of states to act to their perceived national interests. States have gone to great lengths to be invited by some national or regional authority to intervene militarily. Some member states have invoked the notion of anticipatory self-defense claiming they do not have to wait until attacked before responding with force. Other states have made claims to a form of extended self-defense claiming the right to use force to protect their nationals abroad. Many developing states, especially during the colonial era, argued they had a right to delayed self-defense in that they are entitled to use military force to rid themselves of colonial rule or foreign occupation. The use of force, long after the initial attack had occurred, was justified in the name of national liberation or self-determination. Some states and non-state actors have attempted to carve out yet another exception to the general prohibition against the threat and use of force. When confronted with genocide, crimes against humanity, and gross violations of human rights and humanitarian principles, the use of military force may be legitimate in order to preserve human dignity. Much of UN politics centers on how and when military force should be authorized, and how to respond to unauthorized or questionable uses of military force.

Nonintervention. The principle of nonintervention, already discussed as to its origins, is a companion to both sovereignty and the nonuse of force. Prior to the UN, nonintervention was seen as an essential complement to sovereignty. Respect for sovereignty meant states had a duty to respect the domestic jurisdiction of their counterparts. Under the Westphalian system, what fell within the domestic jurisdiction of states was quite broadly defined.[49] If states systematically, as a matter of policy, discriminated against racial minorities, women, or indigenous populations, it was an internal matter. If a state conducted a brutal counter-insurgency campaign within its territory, even in a colony, that fell under a state's domestic jurisdiction.

However, whether a matter is solely within the domestic jurisdiction of a state is largely dependent on world politics. At one time, states practiced slavery and formal colonialism. These practices are no longer permitted. The Permanent Court of International Justice in the "Nationalities Decrees in Tunis and Morocco" (1923) viewed matters not regulated by international law as the "exclusive" jurisdiction of states. The extent of this jurisdiction varies with the development of international relations and, thus, is relative.[50]

UN Charter Article 2 (7)—undoubtedly its most quoted provision—indicates that

> Nothing contained in the present Charter shall authorize the United Nations to intervene in matters which are essentially within the domestic jurisdiction of any state or shall require the Members to submit such matter to settlement under the present Charter; but this principle shall not prejudice the application of measures under Chapter VII.

Unfortunately, the Charter does little to clarify what matters fall within the domestic jurisdiction of states. The principle of nonintervention is complicated by disagreements as to what behavior constitutes "intervention." For some states, the mere discussion of a state's human rights record constitutes intervention, while others see such discussion as a legitimate part of world politics. Most see the use of military force as intervention but many disagree about whether providing weapons or financial and political support to groups in another state constitutes intervention. Does the use of sanctions and incentives to induce states to change their domestic policies amount to intervention?

Contemporary world politics determine what matters are deemed internal, and what behaviors constitute intervention. Thus, nonintervention has no set definition. Legal scholars have attempted to define it as "dictatorial interference."[51] They generally hold that the threat and use of force constitute intervention, as do non-forcible means of coercion such as sanctions and international judicial pursuit. The discussion, scrutiny, and the usual horse-trading involved in world politics do not. Political definitions of course can differ from legal ones. In 1965 during the height of the decolonization process, the General Assembly sought to prohibit armed intervention, as well as "all other forms of interference" in both the internal and external affairs of states in resolution 2131 (XX). The resolution also attempted to limit what outside states could do to influence internal struggles for self-determination and national liberation. The resolution says that no state should "interfere in the civil strife of another state" and all states shall

> respect the right of self-determination and independence of peoples and nations, to be freely exercised without any foreign pressure and with absolute respect for human rights and fundamental freedoms. Consequently, all States shall contribute to the complete elimination of racial discrimination and colonialism in all is forms and manifestations.

Understood in the context of the decolonization process, the member states of the General Assembly were expressing their preferences and concerns about how states compete with each other to shape political outcomes.

Many developing countries, having fought hard for their sovereignty and the right to determine their internal affairs, understandably are especially reluctant to weaken the principle of nonintervention, however ill-defined. The principle is subordinate to the Chapter VII enforcement provisions. When the Security Council identifies events occurring within the jurisdiction of a member state as a threat to international peace and security, then nonintervention gives way to the authority of the UN. According to Article 2(5), member states are obligated to support the UN and not assist states against which the UN is taking enforcement action. With the advent of the UN system, sovereignty and nonintervention are no longer sacrosanct principles of world order. They are conditioned by other principles: the nonuse of force, the pacific settlement of disputes, and respect for international law and obligations contained in the UN Charter.

This commentary makes clear that the core UN principles not only are important for building a world order and global governance worthy of support but also are themselves subject to debate. Their application is an essential element of international politics. The contested nature of these principles is not unusual. If we take the United States and its constitutional principles for comparison, we find ongoing debates over: federalism and states' rights, the meaning of "equal protection of the laws," the scope of congressional war powers, whether free speech in the First Amendment regulates campaign contributions, the proper understanding of religious freedom, and so forth.

So far in this section, we have discussed logical and legal interpretations of UN Charter principles. A closing word is in order consistent with the macro theme of this book, namely that world politics determines the ultimate meaning of UN principles—and ultimately UN action in their shadow. International norms do not implement themselves. Actors take the norms and push or ignore them in daily affairs. The most powerful actors remain states. Thus, whether the elastic, and sometimes competing, principles of the UN are brought to bear on a situation, and in what form, depend on malleable state policies.

Using the example of human rights and politics since 2016 is particularly illustrative. The United States up to that time, and in an elevated way since about 1976, was content to have human rights on the international agenda. It did not consider all forms of international attention to human rights as protected by the domestic jurisdiction and non-interference principles. Since the start of the Trump Administration, it is no longer clear how much this powerful democracy would be interested in human rights as pursued through the UN. The details cannot be covered in this introduction, but at a minimum we note a general tendency for Washington to downplay systematic attention to human rights issues worldwide.

Where human rights inform Trump foreign policy, that situation tends to be politicized and inconsistent. Human rights criticism is trotted out against enemies, such as Iran, but not for Saudi Arabia or Israel. The Saudi killing of a journalist, a U.S. legal resident, in Turkey in 2018, was clearly secondary to U.S. commercial and other self-interests. Attention to the atrocities against the Rohingya in Myanmar was episodic and insignificant especially after Rex Tillerson left as secretary of state. If U.S. foreign policy were to continue to evolve as a series of self-serving transactions without great strategic coherence, and without consistent moral underpinnings, principled attention to human rights at the UN will suffer. It is definitely not the case that preceding governments in Washington manifested consistent interest in effective human rights protections abroad. However, the Trump Administration's disdain was especially pronounced as demonstrated by the withdrawal from the Human Rights Council—"a cesspool of bias" in U.S. ambassador Nikki Haley's description. Primarily driven by the treatment of Israel, the withdrawal overlooked the considerable good done by that HRC, as shown by its investigation of Myanmar and calls for action on the Rohingya atrocities. When the world's leading democracy dismisses democracy promotion and human rights protections, UN Charter principles are marginalized. They do not implement themselves.

ENDURING TENSIONS AND CENTRAL THEMES

Sovereignty and the fundamental challenges that it poses, as well as the complexities inherent in its practice, represent the most fundamental obstacles confronting the UN. As argued, understandings of sovereignty change according to the ever-evolving world political climate—the political version of "climate change" in international relations. As this book's title implies, *The United Nations and Changing World Politics*, we emphasize the impacts and implications of change and continuity in the world political climate on the UN system.[52] In addition to its foundation in the principle of sovereignty and the associated Westphalian interstate order, one of us has identified three other major ailments: "North-South Theater"; the feudal nature of the UN system and the resulting dysfunction; and the UN system's overwhelming bureaucracy and the paucity of leadership.[53]

In summer 2018 shortly before we wrote this introduction, a series of articles in *Foreign Affairs* probed these issues. These weaknesses have caused some, including Graham Allison, to question whether the UN system, and indeed the much talked about quest for a rules-based, liberal world order, is anything more than a propaganda campaign designed to divert from the realities of a harsh power politics in world affairs.[54] On the other hand, Daniel Deudney and John Ikenberry continued to stress the reality of an incomplete liberal world order, with the UN at its center.[55] We are in the latter camp; we have noted the reality, for example, of numerous security field missions authorized by the UN Security Council. Subsequent chapters show that UN approved criminal courts have led to the conviction and incarceration of various miscreants from the Balkans, Africa, and elsewhere. UN organizations have delivered humanitarian relief and development projects. UN action is real, substantive, and has had an impact.

One can perhaps best understand this divergence of opinion about the importance of the UN by thinking of international relations as a game played primarily on two chessboards. The first involves a struggle for dominant power and is mostly rules-free. Here one finds the United States helping to overthrow elected governments (e.g., Iran in 1953, Guatemala in 1954, and Chile in 1973), manipulating foreign elections (e.g., Italy during the early days of the Cold War), and engaging in other covert interventions via the Central Intelligence Agency (CIA) and other parts of the "deep state." The Soviet Union acted in similar fashion, as did many other governments. The view in Washington was that there could be no rules-based world order if the bad guys won the power struggle, so one had to violate the desired rules to avoid that outcome. One could not have a liberal world order if the communists or radical Jihadists won the struggle for dominant power. At the same time, one tried to establish liberal multilateral arrangements with cooperating partners. In brief, Washington played on both chessboards.

Melvyn Leffler captured this Janus-faced reality by summarizing U.S. diplomatic history:

> the strategic logic that made the United States great in the 20th century is simple and still applies today; preserve an open international order and thwart adversaries ... from gaining control ... Deter and contain. Then seek to coopt and integrate adversaries into the multilateral institutions ... designed to promote the rule of law, nurture non-discriminatory trade, encourage open market places, protect human rights, and strengthen civil society.[56]

That is, deter and contain, then coopt into liberal multilateral regimes.

What is striking since 2016 is the extent to which Trump's foreign policy has largely abandoned—or significantly undermined and damaged—the second objective, namely to incorporate as many states as possible into multilateral arrangements that advance traditional goals such as mutual security, human rights and humanitarian values, and sustainable development (in particular, coping with climate change). While Trump foreign policy continues tough action on the first chessboard such as fighting radical Jihadists in the Middle East and Africa, they have severely damaged but not completely abandoned the second chessboard. While especially Republicans have long been prone to criticize the UN, it is not clear if the Trump Administration has a grand strategy for its foreign policy, and where the UN might fit in that strategy—if one exists.

If we scrutinize current U.S. foreign policy as reflected in impulsive presidential tweets or comments to journalists, the White House clearly disparages the world body as mostly a waste of money accompanied by an aversion to collaborative decision-making in any context. Given its power and as the largest source of financing, Washington has an unusual ability to wreak political and financial havoc, but we should not forget that the current administration's assault on multilateralism is not the first low point in U.S.–UN relations. For example, the 1975 General Assembly "Zionism is racism" resolution 3379 alienated Washington for forty years until its repeal. The 1985 Kassebaum amendment (named after the former Republican Senator from Kansas) demanding more large funders' control over UN spending created financial headaches with U.S. arrears until Ted Turner eased the pain with a private donation a decade and a half later. Washington pulled out of the ILO in 1977 when the American trade-union leader George Meany insisted that the appointment of a senior Soviet official endangered American and other workers; but the U.S. rejoined three years later.

It also is important to note that in many developed liberal democracies, there has been strong discontent on the political right, feeling that the status quo, featuring much multilateralism, has been injurious to their interests and values. This generalization is true in Germany, France, Italy, the Czech Republic, Hungary, and elsewhere. Moreover, this introduction has highlighted the current administration's actions toward the UN and the multilateral menaces in the "Age of Trump";[57] but he is hardly alone. Nativist-populist "ages" are everywhere: of Putin, Erdogan, Xi, Modi, Bolsonaro, Duterte, Netanyahu, al-Sisi, Orban, Maduro, Obrador, and rising right-wing parties across Europe and elsewhere. Together, they pose a death-threat to global cooperation. An opinion piece in Bloomberg described the challenge of relevance for the UN in stark terms:

> If the United Nations were a stock or an index fund, you might want to short it. Founded in 1945 to "maintain international peace and security," the UN in recent years has been mostly powerless to stop slaughter in Syria, Yemen and Myanmar. Civil conflicts are nearing post-Cold War highs. The number of displaced people has hit a new record. After decades of improvement, more of the world's poor are going hungry. The gap between what the UN seeks and receives for humanitarian relief is greater than ever. Gridlock at the Security Council is worsening. The organization's biggest shareholder, the U.S., is withdrawing its support, creating an opening for a takeover by powers with decidedly illiberal interests.[58]

With these grim political facts in mind, readers should keep in mind several central themes as they peruse the following pages. First, we reiterate that the story of the UN is one of continuity and change. A fundamental continuity is that the political will of the first UN, especially of the great powers, is a prerequisite for UN decisions and effectiveness. Power matters and the way that member states apply their power has an impact on the efficacy of the UN in managing global problems. Another continuity is that world politics are dynamic, leading to ups-and-downs in UN responses to major issues. These fluctuations mostly depend on the policies of member states and the skill of their leaders. At the same time with regard to change, most alterations at the UN are undramatic and certainly not transformational. Rather they are incremental and non-linear. Setbacks happen, and once-effective strategies need to evolve to adjust to new realities. It is impossible to assess what might have happened had the UN acted or not. What is possible is to trace how and why the UN was created, and how it has adapted to a constantly changing political, economic, and social environment.

Second, history is important. The present and the future have a history. When seemingly new issues arise, they always have a background that affects their management or disposition. When former colonies are asked to support a proposed UN action to protect human rights inside abusive states, they are often reluctant to do so—recalling their domination by powerful western imperial powers in the past. When U.S. secretary of state Colin Powell spoke at the UN Security Council in early 2003 about whether Iraq had complied with previous council resolutions demanding disarmament, many commentators referred back to the council of 1962. Then, U.S. permanent representative Adlai Stevenson dramatically confronted the Soviet Union over the issue of Soviet nuclear missiles in Cuba. In 2003 the United States did not have the same kind of compelling evidence—the same kind of "smoking gun" presented some forty years earlier. Indeed, the "evidence" was later exposed as false. Nonetheless, UN history was part of the drama for Powell's presentation. The 2003 events, in turn, will shape future UN efforts at disarmament and nonproliferation. History does not necessarily determine the future, but history provides insights and frequently circumscribes policy options and prescriptions. The history of the UN in authorizing military force, deploying peacekeeping forces, coordinating humanitarian assistance, and promoting sustainable development affects new policy decisions and directions. Knowing this history is essential for understanding what is politically correct or incorrect, political viable or infeasible in the contemporary world organization.

Third, public international law as an institution exerts real influence on real political struggles. Like all public law, international law is not simply a technical subject independent of politics, but is itself part of world politics. International law is formulated through a political process, frequently revolving around a variety of actors in a variety of UN forums. Consequently, public international law interacts with world politics, sometimes shaping it greatly and sometimes only slightly or not at all.

Much of world politics centers on the networks of actors of the first, second, and third United Nations who are focusing on and tackling the same problems. The proliferation and diversity of actors complicates analysis and creates additional challenges, forcing us to rethink how we imagine global governance.[59] The creation of the United Nations in 1945 ushered in hopes that a new and effective world order could be created based on security, freedom, and welfare; however, today, it is clear that the one hundred and ninety-three governments of the first UN do not always agree on those values, much less how to pursue them. If we add in the various armed groups outside of the UN system (many supported by member states)—for instance, the Islamic state in eastern Syria and western Iraq, Boko Haram in northern Nigeria, Al Qaeda, and religious and nationalist militias—pessimists might conclude that the contents of the UN Charter, Universal Declaration of Human Rights, and 1949 Geneva Conventions appear meaningless historical footnotes. Moreover, armed non-state radicals reject not only international human rights and the laws of war, but also plurality and religious and cultural diversity. Nevertheless, the UN framework represents a relevant vehicle for trying to manage these thorny challenges.

For as Secretary General Dag Hammarskjöld famously once said, "the purpose of the UN is not to get us to heaven but to save us from hell." One reason that we are not in his netherworld already is the existence of the United Nations.[60] Indeed, it is an embedded part of today's world order and often taken for granted, which represents a different danger. "We are barely conscious of the continuing stabilizing role it plays in setting the broad parameters for the conduct of international relations," is how Australia's former prime minister Kevin Rudd framed the issue during his unsuccessful campaign for Secretary-General. "If the UN one day disappears, or more likely just slides into neglect, it is only then that we would become fully away of the gaping hole this would leave in what remained of the post-war order."[61] In that case, historian David Mayer reminds us, "the liberal order conceived just after World War II will appear to future generations as a thing of relative wholesomeness."[62]

Multilateralism of all stripes is under siege. In this context, the United Nations, warts and all, remains essential. "We are calling for a great reawakening of nations," is how Donald Trump concluded his 2017 remarks to the General Assembly. He ignored the fact that the United States created the world organization to curb the demonstrated horrors of nations and of nationalism. Instead, we are hoping that the readers of this introduction and this book will call for a great reawakening of the United Nations.

NOTES

1. James N. Rosenau, "Governance in the Twenty-first Century," *Global Governance* 1, no. 1 (1995): 13.

2. Dan Plesch and Thomas G. Weiss, eds., *Wartime Origins and the Future United Nations* (London: Routledge, 2015).

3. Dan Plesch, "How the United Nations Beat Hitler and Prepared the Peace," *Global Society* 22, no. 1 (2008): 137–158; and Dan Plesch, *America, Hitler and the UN: How the Allies Won World War II and Forged a Peace* (London: Tauris, 2011).

4. Margaret Karns, Karen Mingst, and Kendal Stills, *International Organizations: The Politics and Processes of Global Governance*, 3rd ed. (Boulder, Colo.: Lynne Rienner, 2015), 109–160.

5. John Foster Dulles, "The General Assembly," *Foreign Affairs* (October 1945): 165.

6. Cited in Cordell Hull, *The Memoirs of Cordell Hull*, 2 vols. (New York: The MacMillan Company, 1948), 1646–1647.

7. Cited by Clive Archer, *International Organizations*, 3rd ed. (London and New York: Routledge, 2001), 5.

8. Franklin D. Roosevelt, "Letter to George W. Norris, September 21, 1943," in *The Roosevelt Letters*, ed. Elliott Roosevelt, vol. 3 (London: George G. Harrup & Co., Ltd., 1952), 473–474.

9. Donald Puchala, Roger Coate, and Katie Laatikainen, *United Nations Politics: International Organization in a Divided World* (New York: Prentice-Hall, 2007); and Vaughan Lowe, Adam Roberts, Jennifer Welsh, and Dominik Zaum, eds., *The United Nations Security Council and War: The Evolution of Thought and Practice Since 1946* (Oxford: Oxford University Press, 2008).

10. See Thomas G. Weiss and Sam Daws, "The United Nations: Continuity and Change" in *The Oxford Handbook on the United Nations*, ed. Weiss and Daws (Oxford: Oxford University Press, 2018), 3–40.

11. UN, "List of Peacekeeping Operations 1948–2018," available at https://peacekeeping.un.org/sites/default/files/180413_unpeacekeeping-operationlist_2.pdf

12. UN, "Summary of Contributions to UN Peacekeeping by Country, Mission and Post: Police, UN Military Experts on Mission, Staff Officers and Troops, 31 September 2018," available at https://peacekeeping.un.org/sites/default/files/3_country_and_mission_7.pdf

13. UN, "Approved Resources for Peacekeeping Operations for the Period from 1 July 2018 to 30 June 2019," UN document A/C.5/72/25, July 5, 2018, available at http://undocs.org/A/c.5/72/25

14. UN, "United Nations Peace Operations," available at www.unmissions.org/#block-views-missions-political-missions

15. Michael Barnett and Raymond Duvall, eds., *Power in Global Governance* (Cambridge: Cambridge University Press, 2005).

16. Thomas G. Weiss, Tatiana Carayannis, and Richard Jolly, "The 'Third' United Nations," *Global Governance* 15, no. 1 (2009): 123–142. This is a major theme in the capstone volume from the United Nations Intellectual History Project by Richard Jolly, Louis Emmerij, and Thomas G. Weiss, *UN Ideas That Changed the World* (Bloomington: Indiana University Press, 2009); and the topic for Tatiana Carayannis and Thomas G. Weiss, *The "Third" United Nations: How Non-State Actors Help the UN Think* (Cambridge: Polity, forthcoming).

17. Thomas Davies, ed., *Routledge Handbook NGOs and International Relations* (London: Routledge, 2020) and *NGOs: A New History of Transnational Civil Society* (Oxford: Oxford University Press, 2014); William DeMars and Dennis Dijkeul, eds., *The NGO Challenge for International Relations Theory* (London: Routledge, 2015); Joel Oestereich, ed., *International Organizations as Self-Directed Actors: A Framework for Analysis* (London: Routledge, 2012); Molly Ruhlman, *Who Participates in Global Governance: States, Bureaucracies, and NGOs in the United Nations* (London: Routledge, 2014); Peter Willetts, *Non-Governmental Organizations in World Politics* (London: Routledge, 2011); and Nora McKeon, *The United Nations and Civil Society* (London: Zed, 2009).

18. Jeffery Haynes, *Faith-Based Organization at the United Nations* (New York: Palgrave MacMillan, 2014).

19. *The Guardian*, "UN 'Running Out of Cash' and Facing Urgent Cuts, Warns Chief," www.theguardian.com/global-development/2018/jul/27/un-running-out-of-cash-and-facing-urgent-cuts-warns-chief-antonio-guterres

20. UN Committee on Contributions, "Contributions Received for 2018 for the United Nations Regular Budget, available at www.un.org/en/ga/contributions/honourroll.shtml

21. See Thomas G. Weiss and Tatiana Carayannis, "Windows of Opportunity for UN Reform: Historical Lessons for the Next Secretary-General," *International Affairs* 92, no. 2 (2017): 309–326.

22. Yvonne Terlingen, "A Better Process, a Stronger UN Secretary-General: How Historic Change Was Forged and What Comes Next," *Ethics & International Affairs* 31, no. 2 (2017): 115–127.

23. Soo Yeon Kim and Bruce Russett, "The New Politics of Voting Alignments in the United Nations General Assembly," *International Organization* 50, no. 4 (1996): 629–652; and Evan Luard, *A History of the United Nations: The Years of Western Domination* (London: Macmillan, 1982).

24. Cedric de Coning, Thomas Mandrup, and Liselotte Odgaard, eds., *The BRICS and Coexistence: An Alternative Vision of World Order* (New York: Routledge, 2015); Peter Ferdinand, "Rising Powers at the UN: An Analysis of the BRICS in the General Assembly,"

Third World Quarterly 35 (2014): 376–391; and David Petrasek, "New Powers, New Approaches? Human Rights Diplomacy in the 21st Century," *International Journal of Human Rights* 10 (2013): 6–15.

25. Andrew Cooper and Ramesh Thakur, *The Group of 20 (G20)* (London: Routledge: 2013).

26. James Raymond Vreeland, *The Political Economy of the United Nations Security Council: Money and Influence* (New York: Cambridge University Press, 2014).

27. Roger A. Coate, *Unilateralism, Ideology, & U.S. Foreign Policy: The United States In and Out of UNESCO* (Boulder, Colo.: Lynne Rienner, 1988).

28. Kerstin Martens, *NGOs and the United Nations: Institutionalization, Professionalization and Adaptation* (Basingstoke, U.K.: Palgrave Macmillan, 2005), 2.

29. Henry F. Carey, *Privatizing the Democratic Peace: Policy Dilemmas of NGO Peacebuilding* (Basingstoke, U.K.: Palgrave Macmillan, 2011).

30. In general, see Stewart Patrick, *The Sovereignty Wars: Reconciling America with the World* (Washington, DC: Brookings, 2018).

31. Stephen D. Krasner, *Sovereignty: Organized Hypocrisy* (Princeton, N.J.: Princeton University Press, 1999).

32. Despite the notion of the sovereign equality of states, all sorts of unequal relations have been formally approved. See Jack Donnelly, "Sovereign Inequality and Hierarchy in Anarchy: American Power and International Society," in *American Foreign Policy in a Globalized World*, ed. David P. Forsythe, Patrice C. McMahon, and Andy Wedeman (New York: Routledge, 2006), 81–104.

33. Donald J. Trump, "Remarks by President Trump to the 72nd Session of the United Nations General Assembly." United Nations General Assembly. United Nations Headquarters, New York. September 19, 2017.

34. Edward Luck, *Mixed Messages: American Politics and International Organization, 1919–1999* (Washington, D.C.: Brookings Institution, 1999).

35. Richard N. Haass, *The Opportunity: America's Moment to Alter History's Course* (New York: Public Affairs, 2005), 41.

36. Jack Goldsmith, *The Terror Presidency* (New York: Norton, 2008).

37. International Commission on Intervention and State Sovereignty, *The Responsibility to Protect* (Ottawa: ICISS, 2001). See also Gareth Evans, *The Responsibility to Protect* (Washington, D.C.: Brookings Institution, 2008); Alex Bellamy, *Responsibility to Protect: The Global Effort to End Mass Atrocities* (Cambridge: Polity, 2009); Thomas G. Weiss, *Humanitarian Intervention: Ideas in Action*, 3rd ed. (Cambridge: Polity, 2016); and Ramesh Thakur, *The United Nations, Peace and Security: From Collective Security to the Responsibility to Protect*, 2nd ed. (Cambridge: Cambridge University Press, 2017).

38. Thomas G. Weiss and Ramesh Thakur, *Global Governance and the UN: An Unfinished Journey* (Bloomington: Indiana University Press, 2010).

39. Richard J. Evans, *The Pursuit of Power: Europe 1815–1914* (London: Penguin, 2017), xvii.

40. On the concept of cosmopolitan nationalism, see Patrice C. McMahon and David P. Forsythe, *American Exceptionalism Reconsidered: The United States, Human Rights, and World Order* (New York and London: Routledge, 2017).

41. Boutros Boutros-Ghali, "Empowering the United Nations," *Foreign Affairs* 72, no. 5 (1992–1993): 98–99.

42. Kofi Annan, "Two Concepts of Sovereignty," *The Economist*, September 18, 1999.

43. Secretary General SG/SM/11701, July 15, 2008, Department of Public Information.

44. David P. Forsythe, "Hard Times for Universal Human Rights, But …," *Australian Journal of Human Rights* 23, no. 4 (Fall, 2018): 281–291.

45. Ian Brownlie, "The Peaceful Settlement of International Disputes," *The Chinese Journal of International Law* 8, no. 2 (2009): 267–283; and John R. Crooks, "The U.S. and International Claims and Compensation Bodies," in *The Sword and the Scales: the United States and International Courts and Tribunals*, ed. Cesare P.R. Romano, (New York: Cambridge University Press, 2009), 297–319.

46. Stephen C. Neff, *War and the Law of Nations: A General History* (Cambridge: Cambridge University Press, 2005).

47. Oona A. Hathaway and Scott J. Shapiro, *The Internationalists: How a Radical Plan to Outlaw War Remade the World* (New York: Simon & Schuster, 2017).

48. Adam Roberts and Richard Guelff, eds., *Documents on the Laws of War*, 3rd ed. (Oxford: Oxford University Press, 2000).

49. R.J. Vincent, *Nonintervention and International Order* (Princeton, N.J.: Princeton University Press, 1974).

50. *Summaries of Judgements, Advisory Opinions, and Orders of the Permanent Court of International Justice* (United Nations, 2013), 7, available at http://legal.un.org/PCIJsummaries/documents/english/PCIJ_FinalText.pdf

51. Lassa Oppenheim, *International Law: A Treatise*, vol. 1 (London: Longmans, 1920), 221; R.J. Vincent, *Nonintervention and International Order* (Princeton, N.J.: Princeton University Press, 1974), 13.

52. Thomas G. Weiss and Rorden Wilkinson, "Continuity and Change in Global Governance," in *Rising Powers, Global Governance, and Global Ethics*, ed. Jamie Gaskarth (London: Routledge, 2015), 41–56; and "Change and Continuity in Global Governance," *Ethics & International Affairs* 29, no. 4 (2015): 397–406.

53. Thomas G. Weiss, *What's Wrong with the United Nations and How to Fix It*, 3rd ed. (Cambridge: Polity Press, 2016).

54. Graham Allison, "The Truth about the Liberal Order," *Foreign Affairs* (June 2018), available at www.foreignaffairs.com/authors/graham-allison

55. Daniel Deudney and G. John Ikenberry, "Liberal World: The Resilient Order," *Foreign Affairs*, www.foreignaffairs.com/articles/world/2018-06-14/liberal-world; Rebeccad Friedman Lissner and Mira Rapp-Hooper, "The Liberal World Order is More than a Myth," *Foreign Affairs* (June 2018), available at www.foreignaffairs.com/articles/world/2018-07-31/liberal-order-more-myth?cid=int-now&pgtype=hpg&region=brl

56. Melvyn Leffler, "The Strategic Thinking that made America Great," *Foreign Affairs* (July–August 2018), available at www.foreignaffairs.com/articles/2018-08-10/strategic-thinking-made-america-great

57. Thomas G. Weiss, "The UN and Multilateralism in the Age of Trump," *Global Summitry* 5, no. 1 (2019 forthcoming).

58. James Gibney, "The UN's Darkest Hour," Bloomberg online, September 23, 2018; www.bloombergquint.com/opinion/the-united-nations-and-u-s-disengagement-under-trump

59. See Thomas G. Weiss and Rorden Wilkinson, *Rethinking Global Governance* (Cambridge: Polity, 2019); and Michael Zürn, *A Theory of Global Governance: Authority, Legitimacy, and Contestation* (Oxford: Oxford University Press, 2018).

60. Thomas G. Weiss, *Would the World Be Better without the UN?* (Cambridge: Polity, 2018).

61. Kevin Rudd, "My 10 Principles to Reform the United Nations, before It's Too Late," *The Guardian*, August 7, 2016.

62. David Allan Mayer, *America and the Postwar World: Remaking International Society, 1945–1956* (New York: Routledge, 2018), 8.

PART ONE

INTERNATIONAL PEACE
AND SECURITY

CHAPTER 1

The Theory and Practice of UN Collective Security

THE PRIMARY PURPOSE OF the UN is to maintain international peace and security through what is broadly referred to as collective security. Collective security is premised on the idea that security is in the interest of all states, and threats to security often require a coordinated international response. States agree to confront security threats and to share in the costs of maintaining or enforcing the peace. The primary mechanisms for collective security in the UN Charter are the commitment to the peaceful settlement of disputes (Chapter VI), peace enforcement (Chapter VII), and the respect for regional arrangements (Chapter VIII).[1] This chapter explores the theory and practice of collective security at the UN by examining the requisites for successful collective security, and the roles of the UN Security Council, General Assembly, and secretary-general in supporting the arrangements. It concludes with an examination of the role of regional intergovernmental organizations (IGOs) in maintaining international peace and security.

COLLECTIVE SECURITY

Initially, collective security was conceived as being guaranteed by the Chapter VII enforcement provisions of the UN Charter. This conception of collective security can be traced through a long history of proposals that deal with war and peace.[2] The central thread is the same: all states would join forces to prevent one of their number from using coercion to gain advantage. Under such a system, no government could conquer another or otherwise disturb the peace for fear of retribution from all other governments. An attack on one would be treated as an attack on all. The notion of self-defense, universally agreed on as a right of sovereign states, was expanded to include the international community's right to prevent war.[3]

The apparent simplicity of the logic of collective security contrasts with the difficulties in its application. In theory, successful collective security depends on three factors: consensus, commitment, and organization.[4] Consensus refers to the recognition by members that a threat to international peace and security exists. Members of a collective security arrangement, especially the most powerful members, must agree that a threat to the peace or a breach of the peace has occurred, or they must at least stand aside (i.e., abstain) when others wish to act. When the UN was founded in 1945, the central concern was states invading other states and grabbing territory. After World War II, the land grab was rare and the violent conflicts that did arise instead centered on who controlled governments, decolonization, and related civil strife. States provided arms and aid to governments they liked and provided assistance to opposition groups in states they did not like. Some states funded nongovernmental organizations (NGOs) in other states that promoted democracy, human rights, and the rule of law, though this was seen by others as fomenting rebellion and subverting the recognized governments. Did such actions disturb the peace or threaten stability? Deciding which behaviors constitute a threat to international peace and security is one of the central challenges for the UN. Since 1945, states have not been consistently willing to characterize all uses of force, outside of self-defense, as a threat to or breach of the peace.

If and when member states agree that some use of force is unacceptable, they must then agree on what to do about it. Should states impose economic sanctions, use military force, or a combination of both? This is where commitment factors in: Once a course of action has been decided, then states must be committed to that course of action and have contingency plans if it falters. They must be willing to bear the costs and sacrifice their national interests for the collective good—or define their national interest as coterminous with general peace and stability.

Finally, if the first two conditions can be met, then there must be organization. That is, agreed-on mechanisms, rules, and procedures must exist for carrying out a course of action. If sanctions are imposed, how will member states enforce them, detect cheating, or evaluate their political and social impact? If military force is approved, which states will conduct the operations, and how will they be monitored? These kinds of policy choices are complicated and represent the kind of questions member states wrestle with at the UN. The record of the world organization in collective security is determined in large part by its ability to meet the conditions of consensus, commitment, and organization in practice.

The Security Council and Collective Security

Chapter V of the UN Charter designates the Security Council as the organ primarily responsible for maintaining international peace and security. Unlike in the League of Nations, all UN member states are legally required to abide by Security Council resolutions that constitute decisions that relate to enforcement actions.[5] The Charter originally specified that the Security Council would have eleven members, but in 1965 the council's membership was increased to fifteen to better reflect the expanded UN after decolonization. In this "first UN", intergovernmental body, the most powerful states are accorded special responsibilities and privileges. The five permanent members (the P5) are the United States, the Soviet Union (now Russia), the United Kingdom, France, and China. Each state of the P5 has veto power. They pay more of the bills, and no decision can be made on nonprocedural questions unless they concur or at least agree to abstain. The veto power ensures that no enforcement action can take place against one of the great powers. Such an action could start a major war—the very thing that the United Nations was established to forestall. By preventing action against a permanent member, the veto saves the organization from wrecking itself in operations against its most powerful members. Enforcement actions can be undertaken only with great power consensus, the first key element for collective security.

The remaining ten members are elected to two-year terms by the General Assembly. When electing the nonpermanent members, the assembly tries to maintain a geographical balance by including representatives of the four major regions of the world: usually three from Africa, two from Asia, three from Europe, and two from Latin America. After expanding in 1965, the Security Council altered its decision-making process, reducing the mathematical weight that the permanent members hold in the voting. Nine affirmative votes are now needed to pass a resolution.

The presidency of the council revolves monthly among council member states and plays a critical role in setting the agenda and smoothing the way to a vote. Some disagreement during the formal voting process has been reduced by efforts to gain consensus before any vote, though this process may lead to soft or unclear resolutions or statements. The president meets with the secretary-general to identify the parties to a dispute, negotiates with the permanent members to try to ensure that the veto will not be used, and consults with the elected members of the Security Council and other relevant groups or actors. Accordingly, unified decision making is facilitated, and disunity in the council can be reduced.[6] Sometimes a president decides to push a particular theme for a month—for example, protection of civilians or peacebuilding.

The General Assembly and Security

The Security Council is not the only organ of the first UN with a role in maintaining international peace and security. The General Assembly, where every member state is represented, serves as a more open forum for discussion of security matters. Under the UN Charter (Articles 10 and 11), it may consider and make recommendations regarding the maintenance of international peace and security. The General Assembly's role in international peace and security increased for a time with the passage of the Uniting for Peace Resolution in 1950. This resolution, which can be initiated by either the General Assembly or the Security Council, was first enacted to allow the assembly to address North Korean aggression in South Korea. This was a reaction to the Security Council's inaction after its initial condemnation of aggression and approval of assistance to South Korea. The absence by the boycotting Soviet Union (protesting Taiwan's occupation of the "Chinese seat" on the council in spite of the 1949 military victory by the Chinese communists under Mao Zedong) had permitted the initial call for assistance and linked the UN to the subsequent military action against North Korea and its allies. But once Moscow ended its boycott and entered the fray, the Security Council was paralyzed by the Soviet veto. The Uniting for Peace Resolution was not used again until 1956, when permanent members were involved in two crises. The General Assembly approved UN actions in the Suez crisis because effective action in the Security Council had been blocked by France and Britain; earlier that year, the assembly had censured Moscow's use of armed force in Hungary. Another use was in 1960, after the Security Council became deadlocked over the Congo operation primarily because the Soviet Union and the United States supported different sides in the conflict.

The Uniting for Peace Resolution has been invoked ten times, the last being against Israel in 1997 for its policies in the occupied territories. Although several NGOs from the third UN called on the General Assembly to invoke the resolution in response to the U.S. invasion of Iraq in 2003, no state on the Security Council or in the General Assembly has formally called for its consideration in recent years. Given its sporadic use, the efficacy of the Uniting for Peace Resolution for enhancing the General Assembly's role in international security is subject to considerable skepticism.

When the Security Council is paralyzed, the General Assembly can at least be a sounding board for international views. It has overwhelmingly condemned Syria's war on its own people in five different resolutions since 2011 and even called upon Syrian president Assad to step down. In 2014 the General Assembly passed a resolution condemning Russia's annexation of Crimea with only twelve member states voting against it. However, the assembly can only make nonbinding recommendations, including statements of condemnation, relating to international peace and security. Only the Security Council can make decisions that are binding on member states.

The Secretary-General and Security

The second UN also has an important role in the maintenance of international peace and security.[7] The Charter spells out some of these actors: the executive head of the organization (the secretary-general) and the professional staff (the secretariat). Selected by the General Assembly upon the recommendation of the Security Council, the secretary-general is effectively the chief executive officer (although the Charter specifies "chief administrative officer"). Today's professional and support staff number approximately fifty-five thousand in the UN proper and an additional twenty-five thousand in the specialized agencies. These figures represent substantial growth from the five hundred employees in the UN's first year at Lake Success and the peak total of seven hundred staff employed by the League of Nations.[8] In matters of peace and security, several departments are involved, including the undersecretaries-general for political affairs, humanitarian affairs, and peacekeeping operations. Depending on the number of peace operations under way at any moment, somewhere between ten thousand and one hundred thousand UN soldiers, police, and other special personnel have served under the secretary-general.

Beyond organizing and directing staff, the secretary-general plays an instrumental role in the mediation of disputes, negotiations between or among warring parties, and deployment of UN-sponsored forces. This role reaches beyond that assigned to any other international official—although many ask whether the role is more "secretary" or "general."[9] An important mechanism in this regard is the appointment of special and personal representatives or envoys of the secretary-general, who undertake missions in conflict areas.[10] This step is approved by the Security Council and is often taken when the council is divided and unable to act.

Additionally, Article 99 of the UN Charter makes it possible for the secretary-general to "bring to the attention of the Security Council any matter which in his opinion may threaten the maintenance of international peace and security," although it has been invoked only three times. If the council is unwilling to act, as one UN staff member said, there is no point in diving into an empty swimming pool. Even without formally invoking Article 99, the secretary-general can still press his views behind the scenes with various states. His personal judgment and readiness to run risks and take initiatives are crucial to fulfilling the job description.

The secretary-general's actions are closely scrutinized by governments. Depending on the political climate, criticism can be scathing, and it certainly affects the UN Secretariat. Secretary-General U Thant was stridently criticized by the West for pulling UN troops from the Sinai in 1967, just as Trygve Lie, the first secretary-general, and Dag Hammarskjöld had been criticized by the Soviet bloc for their respective actions in Korea and the Congo. U Thant was also criticized by Washington for his clear opposition to the U.S. presence in Vietnam. More recently, Secretaries-General Javier Pérez de Cuéllar, Boutros Boutros-Ghali, and Kofi Annan have been criticized for their actions in the Persian Gulf, Bosnia, Somalia, and Iraq. The eighth occupant of the job, Ban Ki-moon, assumed office in January 2007 and has been criticized for his lack of leadership in the area of international peace and security.[11] The ninth secretary-general will assume office in January 2017 and should expect, as with many visible policy positions, criticism to go with the territory. However, since the time of Trygve Lie and the Korean War, the secretary-general has rarely issued a harsh public judgment concerning armed conflict involving P5 states, since he is not effective if he loses the confidence of any state with the veto. The secretary-general walks a tightrope, needing to appear independent and not simply a pawn of any or all of the P5 states, even while maintaining their confidence and support. If from time to time he must speak out in a critical way, it cannot be to the point that he becomes persona non grata to any of the Big Five.

Legal Basics

Most Security Council and General Assembly resolutions constitute recommendations, legally speaking. When dealing with peace and security issues, the council usually acts under Chapter VI, not Chapter VII. Chapter VI deals with the pacific settlement of disputes. Under this part of the Charter the council suggests to parties how they might resolve their disputes. Traditional peacekeeping, even though UN personnel may be lightly armed, takes place under Chapter VI. UN peacekeepers do not shoot their way into situations; they proceed with the consent of the parties, usually to supervise some cease-fire or other agreement. But the theory of the Charter's operation always entailed the notion that persuasion under Chapter VI should be seen against the more coercive possibilities under Chapter VII. If the parties cannot agree, upon pacific urging of the Security Council under the purview of Chapter VI, they might face sanctions under Chapter VII.

One of the great complexities facing the UN in the twenty-first century is that although the Charter was written for states, much political instability and violence arise today either from violence within states or from violence across state boundaries by nonstate actors (NSAs). This is further complicated by state actors funding and supporting NSAs. The problems in Somalia and Liberia, to name just two, arose from the absence of a functioning state and a government capable of speaking in the name of the state. In Sri Lanka, armed Tamils sought to violently carve out a new state in the north of that island. In Libya and Syria today, armed factions vie with the existing regime for control of the government. Particularly after September 11, 2001, the importance of transnational NSAs, including the Islamic State in Iraq and Syria (ISIS), Boko Haram, Al Qaeda, and other militant groups has become obvious.

This reality has implications for contemporary meanings of Article 2 (7) of the UN Charter, which prohibits the UN from intervening in the domestic jurisdiction of a state. In the context of failed states or humanitarian crises generated by state and nonstate actors, can the UN and its member states intervene in matters previously considered to be part of domestic jurisdiction? It is fairly well settled (both in the Charter and in practice) that if the UN Security Council decides (under Chapter VII) that an internal situation constitutes a threat to international peace and security, then the UN can intervene. The fault line in the politics of the first UN today is who can act and how when the Security Council will not.

Enforcement

Collective security, whether to confront traditional forms of interstate aggression or to address instability occurring materially within the territory of a state, requires organization. However, although Article 43 obligates states to conclude an agreement with the Military Staff Committee (MSC), a subsidiary of the Security Council, whereby military forces are made available to the UN, no state has ever concluded such an agreement. Most states do not agree on that kind of delegation of power resources. The Cold War pushed the MSC to the back burner and eventually Article 43 became a dead letter. In 2004 the High-level Panel on Threats, Challenges and Change (HLP), and in 2005 then secretary-general Annan in his publication *In Larger Freedom: Towards Development, Security and Human Rights for All*, recommended that the MSC be formally abolished.[12] At the 2005 World Summit, the General Assembly recommended that the Security Council review the composition and mandate of the MSC. Hence, the body exists in theory, but in practice the council and secretary-general are left with the task of constructing military forces mostly anew for each crisis in which a UN military presence is contemplated. It is hard to believe that large-scale UN peace operations, which, after all, started in 1956, still remain on such shaky and ad hoc organizational ground.[13]

The UN, thus, has been forced to resort to a "sheriff's posse"[14] approach to responding to crises—as in Korea, Iraq, Somalia, Haiti, East Timor, and Libya. In effect, the UN delegates its Chapter VII authority to others. The legal foundation for such a delegation is strong, especially since the Chapter VII authority is broad and over fifty years of state practice demonstrates a clear pattern of tasking member states, the secretary-general, regional organizations, and international criminal courts to carry out Security Council decisions. While the authority and the competency of the council to delegate are broad, it is not allowed to delegate two kinds of powers.[15] First, the council cannot delegate the authority to determine whether a threat to the peace or a breach of the peace has occurred. Second, it cannot delegate unrestricted command and control of enforcement to others. That is, the council should maintain oversight.

As we will see in later discussions of Iraq and Libya, Security Council control of delegated collective security enforcement operations has proven more problematic in practice than in theory. Nevertheless, the UN has entered into a "contract" with the United States or other major powers or regional organizations to enforce UN policy in countering either aggression or threats to peace and security. In the former Yugoslavia following the Dayton accords, the North Atlantic Treaty Organization (NATO) became the UN's agent. This is not so different from the Rhodesian situation in the 1960s and 1970s, when the Security Council authorized the British navy to enforce the mandatory economic embargo in Mozambican territorial waters. This approach has the advantage of efficiency, which is no small matter when lives are on the line. But it has the drawback of the loss of UN control over its own decisions, diminishing the organization's capacity for oversight of what is done in its name.

Gaps Between Theory and Practice

Experience with UN collective security indicates considerable gaps between theory and practice. First, some states have refused to join a collective-sanctioning effort because they have already defined their friends and enemies. During the Cold War, the United States would not have joined in a UN effort at collective security against one of its NATO allies, nor would the Soviet Union have done so against its Warsaw Pact allies. In an exceptional move, the United States did oppose the British, French, and Israeli invasion of Egypt in 1956 and eventually helped to roll it back by diplomacy. But the United States never seriously considered UN sanctions against its allies in 1956, precisely because it wanted to maintain their cooperation in the Cold War. Friends and allies might have shifted a bit after the Cold War, but the desire to protect friends has not. Under true collective security, all aggressors have to be treated the same. All threats to and breaches of the peace have to be firmly and automatically opposed.

Second, there is the fundamental problem of power. Since 1945 the international community of states has had major and insurmountable problems in applying collective security against a nuclear state, especially the P5.[16] The Security Council is constrained procedurally by the veto. By design, the Security Council is supposed to act only when there is concurrence among the P5. How could one justify the massive destruction that could result from trying to apply forcible collective security against such a state, even if clear-cut aggression had occurred? The nuclear problem also extends to other states that possess nuclear weapons, such as India, Israel, Pakistan, and North Korea.

The problem of regulating powerful potential aggressors goes beyond the nuclear question. Many states control sufficient conventional forces, biological and chemical weapons of mass destruction, or economic resources so that collective security against them would be highly disruptive and costly to international society. For this reason, the vast majority of states have been content with diplomatic and symbolic opposition to such acts as the U.S. invasions of Grenada and Panama in the 1980s or Iraq in 2003 or the Soviet/Russian invasions of Hungary and Czechoslovakia in the 1950s and 1960s and Georgia and Ukraine in 2010s, knowing full well that any attempt at military or economic sanctions would be disruptive and ineffectual. The great powers are not the only ones difficult to manage. Lesser powers with considerably less economic and military strength can still be important actors, depending on issues and timing.

Third, collective security can be costly to those supporting it. Sanctions cut both ways, affecting not only the aggressor but the defenders. Communist Bulgaria voted in the UN for sanctions against white-minority rule in South Africa in the 1980s but also sold arms to South Africa under the table. Bulgaria did not want to miss out on profits from the arms trade despite its formal support for economic collective security against the white-minority government in Pretoria. It was one thing for states to accept that apartheid constituted a threat to the peace. It was another for them to engage collectively against apartheid at a cost to their own narrow national interests. Similarly, UN sanctions against Iraq in the 1990s and Sudan in 2005 were undermined by major trading partners.

Fourth, the concept of collective security is based on the assumption that all victims are equally important: that the international community of states will respond in the same way to an attack on Bosnia or Armenia as to an attack on Kuwait or Germany.[17] Historical evidence shows that most states have differentiated between countries worth defending and otherwise. In 1991 the United States was

A wide view of the Security Council meeting on the situation in Syria. September 16, 2015, United Nations, New York. (UN PHOTO 642775/LOEY FILIPE)

willing to disrupt its home front by putting almost half a million military personnel into the liberation of oil-rich Kuwait. But the United States did not respond so decisively at about the same time in the early 1990s when Serbia tried to enlarge itself at the expense mainly of neighboring Bosnia. U.S. officials stated openly that since U.S. national interests were not involved, the government was prepared to let Europeans handle a European problem. It was only later, when continued atrocities led to increased demands for international action, that Washington and the rest of the UN Security Council were roused to a more determined response.

Collective security could make the state system more humane by making it more secure. Forms of collective security have worked at times. Iraqi aggression against Kuwait was rolled back in 1991 through collective force authorized by the UN, as was a military coup in Haiti after UN-sponsored economic sanctions fell short. At the time of this writing, UN and other sanctions had brought Iran to the negotiating table, with the UN Security Council seeing the possibility of an Iranian nuclear weapons program as a definite threat to the peace. But these tend to be the exceptional examples proving the general rule that collective security, either military or economic, is exceedingly difficult to organize and enforce. States have numerous narrow national interests that they are reluctant to see overridden in the name of generalized peace or justice. Member states of the Security Council also may genuinely disagree as to when coercive economic and military enforcement measures are justified. Such was the case in 2002 and 2003, when the council was divided over how to enforce disarmament measures in Iraq. Similarly, the P5 has been unable to agree on what to do about the violence and humanitarian situation in Syria beginning in 2011, as armed conflict has dragged on and claimed more than 250,000 lives while uprooting over half of Syria's population. If agreement on international enforcement issues were easier, one might aspire to world government, not just collective security.[18]

As the following chapters illustrate, the difficulties with enforcement have led the member states of the first UN to innovate with alternatives to collective security. States push and prod other states to use less coercive mechanisms, such as legal remedies, mediation, and arbitration. They also created "peacekeeping" in 1948 (discussed in Chapter 2) as a halfway measure between the peaceful settlement of disputes and enforcement. The peacekeeping innovation has evolved considerably to include extensive peacebuilding in postconflict societies.

REGIONAL ARRANGEMENTS

Is it more appropriate to deal with local conflict through multilateral organizations whose scope is regional (for instance, the European Union, NATO, or the Arab League) or universal (for instance, the United Nations)?[19] Chapter VIII of the UN Charter indicates a preference for regional management of regional conflict. Regional organizations, when and where they exist, are often an appropriate locus for action because instability often poses a greater threat to regional actors than those farther away. At the outset of the present Charter regime, the preference for peaceful settlement was clearly articulated. Even Article 21 of the Covenant of the League of Nations noted the validity of regional understandings as a basis for maintaining peace. Nevertheless, one of the most controversial aspects at the San Francisco conference was the relative balance between regionalism and universalism.[20] While the creation of the Security Council, with its enforcement power, gave globalism a significant edge over regionalism, Chapter VIII, "Regional Arrangements," was also considered essential. The basic idea, called subsidiarity, is that the organization closest to the conflict should take action, if possible, before asking the universal UN to get involved. That way, the Security Council remains an option if regional efforts fall short. Chapter VIII was designed to limit Security Council deliberations to the most severe and intractable disputes.

Article 52 of Chapter VIII declares, "Nothing in the present Charter precludes the existence of regional arrangements or agencies dealing with matters relating to the maintenance of international peace and security" under the condition that "their activities are consistent with the Purposes and Principles of the United Nations." This article encourages states to use regional organizations before directing their conflicts to the Security Council and also recommends that the council make use of regional arrangements. Articles 53 and 54 define relations between the UN and regional organizations by prohibiting the latter from taking peace and security measures without Security Council authorization and by insisting that regional organizations inform the council of their activities.

The active use of the veto throughout the Cold War not only prevented the use of the Security Council but also meant that regional organizations sometimes provided the United States and the Soviet Union with convenient pretexts for containing disputes within organizations that were themselves under superpower control. Crises in Guatemala, Cuba, Panama, and the Dominican Republic were relegated to the Organization of American States, dominated by the United States. Hungary and Czechoslovakia were in the jurisdiction of the "socialist community" of the Warsaw Pact, dominated by the Soviet Union.

The supposed deficiencies of universal international organizations and the resulting apparent strengths of regional ones should be examined in light of the ambiguity of "region" as a concept, the overstretched capacities of the UN in international peace and security, and the purported better familiarity with local crises by the member states of regional organizations. The framers deliberately avoided precision in the language in Chapter VIII, thereby allowing governments the flexibility to fashion instruments to foster international peace and security. Although the commonsensical notion of region is related to geography, the ambiguity of the Charter means that a region can also be conceived of geopolitically, culturally, ideologically, and economically. Such groups could include treaty-based organizations that predate or postdate the United Nations or ad hoc mechanisms created to deal with a specific concern. In addition to including such geographic entities as the African Union or the Organization of American States (OAS), the Charter's definition of a regional organization might also include NATO, the Organization of Islamic Cooperation, and the Organisation for Economic Co-operation and Development (OECD). The emergence of such "subregional" units as the Gulf Cooperation Council (GCC) and the Southern African Development Coordination Conference are potentially significant.[21] The concept of regionalism remains ambiguous and therefore contested. The upside might be a more flexible response to crises.

A second issue concerns institutional resources. The United Nations continues to experience grave financial difficulties and lacks sufficient and qualified staff. The great powers appear reluctant to pay for substantial administrative expansion of UN conflict management. The end of East-West tensions diminished Western interests in many regional conflicts. Moreover, the "war on terrorism" introduced other priorities, not just in the United States but worldwide. Governing elites and publics sought to divert expenditure from foreign policy to postponed domestic economic and social needs. Smaller powers traditionally active in peacekeeping are unlikely to continue to pick up more of the tab. They share the economic problems of the larger states. The 2005 World Summit failed to approve any significant additional resources for the UN, and it even stumbled over giving the secretary-general more authority for budget and management decisions. Such a change would have implied reducing the control by the General Assembly, where developing countries are the majority, in favor of the UN's central administration, where the perception is that Western donors (and especially Washington) are in control.

In this context, regional approaches to crisis management and conflict resolution might seem attractive. States near a country in conflict suffer most from the destabilizing consequences of war in their area. They receive most of the refugees and bear the political, social, and economic consequences, willingly or unwillingly, of combatants from neighboring countries seeking sanctuary. They face the choice of pacifying and repatriating combatant and noncombatant aliens on their territory or of resisting hot pursuit by those from whom these refugees have fled. Local conflict and the consequent perceptions of regional instability dampen investment flows and retard growth. They divert public resources into defense expenditures.

States from a region at war appear to be well suited to mediating local conflicts. They understand the dynamics of the strife and of the cultures involved more intimately than outsiders do. Leaders are far more likely to have personal connections to the involved parties, and these connections may be used as a basis for mediation. Involvement by other regional powers or organizations is less likely to be perceived by the international community as illegitimate interference than would involvement by extraregional organizations. Finally, issues of local conflict are far more likely to be given full and urgent consideration in regional gatherings than in global ones, as the latter have more extensive agendas.

The apparent advantages of regional institutions may exist more in theory than in practice, however. In reality, most of these organizations are far less capable than the United Nations. The comparative advantage of organizations in the actual region in conflict is more than offset by such practical disadvantages as partisanship, resource shortages, and rivalries. Apart from very unusual cases (such as NATO), regional organizations lack military capacity, diplomatic leverage, and economic resources. Furthermore, regional organizations are also plagued by the same problems often facing the world organization—achieving consensus, commitment, and organization.

Many of the factors favoring regional organizations are questionable. Regional actors do tend to suffer most from the destructive consequences of conflict among their neighbors. At the same time, they frequently have stakes in these conflicts, are committed to one side or another, and stand to benefit by influencing outcomes. Sometimes they are even active participants. In this sense, their interests are more complex than many proponents of regional organizations suggest. Their shared interest in the public good of regional stability is often accompanied by unilateral interest in obtaining specific favorable outcomes. A favorable result for one regional power is likely to enhance its regional position at the expense of other countries, which are likely to oppose such initiatives. In the terminology of international relations theory, we have simultaneous considerations of "absolute gain" (stability) and "relative gain" (power). There is no certainty that stability will predominate. Situating crises in their regional historical and political contexts enhances this overall argument considerably.

Africa

In Africa, the paralysis and bankruptcy of the Organization of African Unity (OAU)—now renamed the African Union (AU)—in curbing intervention and in managing the civil war in Angola (1975–2002) reflected deep disagreement among its own members about the desirable outcome of the process of liberation. Even though its headquarters was in Addis Ababa, the OAU also was inept in helping to end the Ethiopian civil war (1974–1991). The lack of any substantial OAU initiative also arose because other African states were deeply implicated in the conflict in pursuit of diverging national interests. Similar difficulties were evident in OAU efforts to cope with crises in Chad, Somalia, Liberia, and Sierra Leone during the Cold War. The new AU proved largely irrelevant to the bloodletting in the Congo and was slow to respond to the crisis in Darfur. More recently, the AU has become more visible and active in conflicts ranging from South Sudan and Somalia to the Congo and Burundi. The Economic Community of West African States (ECOWAS) has compiled a mixed record in trying to pacify Liberia, Sierra Leone, and recently Côte d'Ivoire. ECOWAS was one of the first voices to condemn the 2012 military coup d'état in Mali and the first to act to begin the process of brokering a deal that would bring about elections. Still, ECOWAS was forced to appeal to the UN and wealthier states for diplomatic and financial support, and could do little to confront the Islamist insurgency in northern Mali, which required a UN-sanctioned French intervention in 2013. Similarly, it was British troops who stopped the bloodletting in Sierra Leone, rather than any African organization troops in the country. ECOWAS field missions usually depend heavily on the Nigerian military, which has been both corrupt and ineffective in facing Boko Haram in northeast Nigeria.

Asia

In South Asia, it is hard to see how any regionally based initiative could have settled the Afghan civil war (1978–1996), not only because of the presence of Soviet forces earlier, but also because India had no interest in seeing a pro-Pakistani or Islamic fundamentalist regime in Kabul. To take a more extreme case, the capacity of the South Asian Association for Regional Cooperation (SAARC) to act as a neutral mediator of the conflict between India and Pakistan over Kashmir is extremely problematic; the two principal members of the organization are the very states involved. SAARC has shown some promise in coordinating responses to poverty and environmental degradation but remains deficient with security issues such as terrorism.[22] SAARC had little or no role in Sri Lanka's prolonged and bloody civil war between the government and the Tamil Tigers. This conflict was brought to an end through a brutal governmental victory, with no effective involvement by any outsiders.

Elsewhere on the continent, efforts by the Association of Southeast Asian Nations (ASEAN) to resolve the Cambodian conflict were handicapped by differing conceptions of Chinese and Vietnamese threats to the region. Member states have more informal security arrangements rather than regional collective security.[23] The secessionist conflict in Indonesia involving East Timor was resolved only when the UN Security Council authorized the Australian-led International Force in East Timor (INTERFET) to restore peace and security on the island, an action taken with the acquiescence of the Indonesian government.

The Americas

In Central America, the OAS could not deal effectively with civil wars in Nicaragua and El Salvador during the 1980s because of the U.S. failure to abide by the essential norm of nonintervention in its pursuit of a unilateral agenda to prevent Marxist revolutions. For similar reasons, the OAS could not resolve instability in Honduras after a military coup ousted an elected president in 2009. The United States refused to defer to OAS diplomacy and pursued its own agenda. Dissatisfaction with the OAS and U.S. policies led South American states to create the Union of South American Nations (UNSAN), but its defense arm is still in the conceptualization stage.

Europe

Regional security in Europe is complex, consisting of overlapping, yet divergent, security organizations that include NATO, the European Union (EU), and the Organization for Cooperation and Security in Europe (OSCE). The capacity of the EU (and its predecessor EC, the European Community) to come up with an effective response to the violence and instability resulting from the disintegration of Yugoslavia beginning in 1991 was constrained by deep differences of opinion between France and Germany. Furthermore, disagreements among NATO members long hampered military humanitarianism in Bosnia and Herzegovina. The crisis in the Ukraine (2014–present) is testing the capacity of all European organizations to confront Russia's military assertiveness in Russian-speaking areas of Europe. Despite U.S. president Barack Obama's commitment to add seventeen thousand American soldiers to the fifty thousand NATO troops in Afghanistan in 2009, the alliance has found it difficult to sustain long-term engagements because of political pressures on domestic fronts. NATO and the United States ended their combat mission in 2014, with decidedly mixed results. Continuing disputes surrounding burden sharing within the alliance led the well-regarded former U.S. secretary of defense Robert Gates to scold NATO allies for their lack of military spending and political will in the UN-delegated collective security operation in Libya. He warned that NATO had "a dim if not dismal future."[24]

In short, regional organizations replicate regional power imbalances. They may be used by the more powerful to expand their influence at the expense of the weak. This problem has appeared, or is likely to appear, in regions where power imbalances are so substantial that it is not possible for weaker states in coalition to balance against the strong. Cases in point include Russia in Europe, South Africa in southern Africa, Nigeria in West Africa, India in South Asia, Indonesia in Southeast Asia, and the United States in the Americas.

Regional organizations have traditionally demonstrated their greatest structural weaknesses in dealing with civil war, the main growth industry for international conflict managers. This shortcoming follows in part from the international legal impediments associated with the doctrine of nonintervention in internal affairs. These impediments have proven even more acute for many countries in the Global South, preoccupied as they are with exerting control over their own tenuous bases of power.[25] The reluctance to become involved in civil armed conflict reflects the sensitivity of regional powers to creating precedents that might later be used to justify intervention in their own countries. In Africa, for example, many governments are themselves threatened by the possibility of internal war, which leads to caution about fostering norms and precedents that would legitimize regional involvement in such conflicts. Developing states, which have experienced the yoke of colonialism and struggled to gain their independence, tend to jealously guard their sovereign prerogatives. Ironically, the challenge to the sovereignty of colonial powers facilitated the decolonization process, and now the states that benefited from that challenge are among the staunchest defenders of state sovereignty. Respect for conventional definitions of sovereignty has verged on slavishness—allowing repression and the license to murder. This weakness is likely to play out more strongly at the regional level. For all of these reasons, the general case for reliance on regional organizations is weak, as was very much in evidence in Zimbabwe, where the African Union stood on the sidelines in the face of Robert Mugabe's destructive repression.

Actions in the wake of the Arab Spring may result in a rethinking of these long-standing generalizations. The visible support by the Arab League and the GCC for establishing a no-fly zone in Libya was essential to mobilizing support for Security Council resolution 1973. And later in Syria, this striking change continued as the Arab League in particular was clear in condemning Bashar al-Assad. Despite the vetoes, threatened and real, from Russia and China, it also put forward a peace plan within the UN and established the joint Arab League–UN mission led by a succession of special envoys—Kofi Annan, Lakhdar Brahimi, and Staffan de Mistura. The GCC approved a Saudi-led military intervention in Yemen in 2015 and the UN Security Council has followed up with an arms embargo against rebels in Yemen. But regional organizations dealing with the Middle East have lacked the military power to put a decisive end to the violence and instability there.

The United Nations and regional organizations have resorted to creative measures to address violence and conflict. The Gulf War in 1991 and the creation of safe havens for Iraqi Kurds are clear and successful illustrations of military "delegating" to the Allied Coalition, as was NATO's presence in Bosnia from 1995 until December 2004. A more controversial and less successful example was Somalia, where a U.S.-led effort was mounted to break the back of warlord-induced famine. Moreover, three Security Council decisions in July 1994 indicated the relevance of military intervention by major powers in regions of their traditional spheres of influence: a Russian plan to deploy its troops in Georgia to end the three-year-old civil war; the French intervention in Rwanda to cope with genocidal conflict; and the U.S. plan to spearhead a military invasion to reverse the military coup in Haiti. More recently the UN delegated security operations to the United Kingdom in Sierra Leone (2000); to Australia in East Timor (2000); and to France in Côte d'Ivoire (2011), Mali (2013), and the Central African Republic (2014). Regional organizations have also turned to delegation. In 1994 the then Conference (now Organization) on Security and Cooperation in Europe (CSCE or OSCE) authorized troops from the Commonwealth of Independent States and other OSCE member states following a cease-fire between the Republic of Azerbaijan and the self-proclaimed Nagorno-Karabakh. Similarly, ECOWAS authorized a contingent of largely Nigerian troops to stabilize Liberia and Sierra Leone.

The record of regional arrangements has not been consistently superior to the UN's record. Yet the evident gap between the UN's capacities and persistent demands for help could be filled by regional powers, or even hegemons, operating under the scrutiny of a wider community of states.[26] The argument has become stronger in light of the experience in Kosovo and the smooth handover in Timor-Leste from the Australian-led force to the UN one in February 2000, followed by the return of the Australians when violence renewed in 2006.

Events in Côte d'Ivoire demonstrated the ad hoc and changing efforts to manage conflict and security. While the Security Council may pass resolutions in New York, implementing them may result in shifting ad hoc arrangements, given the lack of dependable resources on which the UN can rely. Here the AU's diplomacy was ultimately unsuccessful but helpful in making the final UN decisions, as was pressure by ECOWAS to act militarily.[27] The absence of a meaningful threat to actually deploy military force in 2010–2011 to oust Laurent Gbagbo and install Alassane Ouattara in Côte d'Ivoire illustrated what happens when a viable military option is not in the international toolkit. The eventual ouster of incumbent Ggagbo followed action by the 1,650-strong French Licorne force as the avant-garde of the UN peace operation and a half year of dawdling. The unavailability or unwillingness to apply armed force abetted Gbagbo's intransigence as Côte d'Ivoire's disaster unfolded. Nevertheless, the role of the UN Security Council in authorizing and reviewing the use of force was central throughout.

The capacity of regional organizations to outperform the UN in the management of conflict is in doubt, with the possible exception of Europe, and the potential of regional organizations needs to be tempered with the reality of recent efforts. Since 1945, untold numbers of wars have broken out, and tens of millions of people have perished as a result.[28] According to the logic of the Charter, the leadership for the UN's peace and security duties rests on the shoulders of a small segment of the international community of states, notably the great powers on the Security Council. Conflict between the United States and the Soviet Union poisoned the atmosphere and prevented their working together on most security issues during the Cold War. After the Cold War, world politics often made it impossible to act collectively and states often chose to disobey or ignore the prohibitions and restrictions on the use of force. In place of the ideal collective security system, the UN developed an alternative to mitigate certain kinds of conflicts: peacekeeping. We now turn to this story.

NOTES

1. Bruno Simma, ed., *The Charter of the United Nations: A Commentary,* 2nd ed. (Oxford: Oxford University Press, 2002).

2. F. H. Hinsley, *Power and the Pursuit of Peace* (Cambridge: Cambridge University Press, 1963); S. J. Hambleben, *Plans for World Peace Through Six Centuries* (Chicago: University of Chicago Press, 1943); and F. P. Walters, *A History of the League of Nations,* 2 vols. (London: Oxford University Press, 1952).

3. Thomas G. Weiss and Ramesh Thakur, *Global Governance and the UN: An Unfinished Journey* (Bloomington: Indiana University Press, 2010), 55–90.

4. Robert Riggs and Jack Plano, *The United Nations: International Organization and World Politics,* 2nd ed. (Belmont, Calif.: Wadsworth, 1994), 100.

5. See Loraine Sievers and Sam Daws, *The Procedure of the UN Security Council,* 4th ed. (Oxford: Oxford University Press, 2014); and Vaughan Lowe, Adam Roberts, Jennifer Welsh, and Dominik Zaum, eds., *The United Nations Security Council and War: The Evolution of Thought and Practice Since 1945* (Oxford: Oxford University Press, 2008). See also Edward C. Luck, *The UN Security Council: Practice and Promise* (London: Routledge, 2006); Ian Hurd, *After Anarchy: Legitimacy and Power in the United Nations Security Council* (Princeton, N.J.: Princeton University Press, 2007); and David L. Bosco, *Five to Rule Them All: The Security Council and the Making of the Modern World* (Oxford: Oxford University Press, 2009).

6. Johan Kaufmann, *United Nations Decision-Making* (Rockville, Md.: Sijthoff and Noordhoff, 1980), 43–52; and James P. Muldoon et al., *Multilateral Diplomacy and the United Nations Today* (Boulder, Colo.: Westview, 1999).

7. Leon Gordenker, *The UN Secretary-General and Secretariat,* 2nd ed. (London: Routledge, 2010).

8. Thant Myint-U and Amy Scott, *The UN Secretariat: A Brief History (1945–2006)* (New York: International Peace Academy, 2007), 126–128.

9. Simon Chesterman, ed., *Secretary or General? The UN Secretary-General in World Politics* (Cambridge: Cambridge University Press, 2007).

10. Cyrus R. Vance and David A. Hamburg, *Pathfinders for Peace: A Report to the UN Secretary-General on the Role of Special Representatives and Personal Envoys* (New York: Carnegie Commission on Preventing Deadly Conflict, 1997).

11. James O. C. Jonah, "Ki-moon as Key Player: The Secretary-General's Role in Peace and Security," *Harvard International Review* (Spring 2011): 59–63.

12. *In Larger Freedom: Towards Development, Security and Human Rights for All,* UN document A/59/2005, March 21, 2005.

13. Michael W. Doyle and Nicholas Sambanis, *Making War and Building Peace: United Nations Peace Operations* (Princeton, N.J.: Princeton University Press, 2006).

14. Brian Urquhart, "Beyond the 'Sheriff's Posse,'" *Survival* 32, no. 3 (1990): 196–205.

15. Danesh Sarooshi, *The United Nations and the Development of Collective Security: The Delegation by the UN Security Council of Chapter VII Powers* (Oxford: Oxford University Press, 1999), 32–33.

16. Jane Boulden, Ramesh Thakur, and Thomas G. Weiss, eds., *The United Nations and Nuclear Orders* (Tokyo: UN University Press, 2009).

17. Justin Gruenberg, "An Analysis of the United Nations Security Council Resolutions: Are All Countries Treated Equally?" *Case Western Reserve Journal of International Law* 41 (2009): 469–511.

18. Chapter 12 of Inis L. Claude Jr., *Swords into Plowshares: The Problems and Progress of International Organization*, 4th ed. (New York: Random House, 1971), remains the best single treatment of collective security. See also his *Power and International Relations* (New York: Random House, 1962); Ernst B. Haas, "Types of Collective Security: An Examination of Operational Concepts," *American Political Science Review* 49, no. 1 (1955): 40–62; Thomas G. Weiss, ed., *Collective Security in a Changing World* (Boulder, Colo.: Lynne Rienner, 1993); and George W. Downs, ed., *Collective Security Beyond the Cold War* (Ann Arbor: University of Michigan Press, 1994).

19. S. Neil MacFarlane and Thomas G. Weiss, "Regional Organizations and Regional Security," *Security Studies* 2, no. 1 (1992): 6–37; and Alexander Orakhelashvili, *Collective Security* (Oxford: Oxford University Press, 2011).

20. Francis O. Wilcox, "Regionalism and the United Nations," *International Organization* 19, no. 3 (1965): 789–811; and Tom J. Farer, "The Role of Regional Collective Security Arrangements," in *Collective Security in a Changing World*, ed. Thomas G. Weiss (Boulder, Colo.: Lynne Rienner, 1993), 153–189.

21. William T. Tow, *Subregional Security Cooperation in the Third World* (Boulder, Colo.: Lynne Rienner, 1990).

22. Zahid Shahab Ahmed, *Regionalism and Regional Security in South Asia: The Role of SAARC* (Surrey, U.K.: Ashgate, 2013).

23. Hiro Katsumata, "East Asian Regional Security Governance: Bilateral Hard Balancing and ASEAN's Informal Cooperative Security," in *Comparative Regional Security Governance*, ed. Shaun Breslin and Stuart Croft (New York: Routledge, 2012), 72–93.

24. Thom Shanker and Steven Erlanger, "Blunt U.S. Warning Reveals Deep Strains in NATO," *New York Times*, June 10, 2011, www.nytimes.com.

25. Mohammed Ayoob, *The Third World Security Predicament: State Making, Regional Conflict, and the International System* (Boulder, Colo.: Lynne Rienner, 1995); and Brian Job, ed., *The Insecurity Dilemma: National Security of Third World States* (Boulder, Colo.: Lynne Rienner, 1992).

26. Jarat Chopra and Thomas G. Weiss, "Prospects for Containing Conflict in the Former Second World," *Security Studies* 4, no. 3 (1995): 552–583; Lena Jonson and Clive Archer, eds., *Peacekeeping and the Role of Russia in Eurasia* (Boulder, Colo.: Westview, 1996); and Alan K. Henrikson, "The Growth of Regional Organizations and the Role of the United Nations," in *Regionalism in World Politics: Regional Organizations and World Order*, ed. Louise Fawcett and Andrew Hurrell (Oxford: Oxford University Press, 1995), 122–168.

27. Thomas J. Bassett and Scott Straus, "Defending Democracy in Côte d'Ivoire," *Foreign Affairs* 90, no. 4 (2011): 130–140.

28. The annual publication of the International Institute for Strategic Studies, *Strategic Survey*, updates these numbers and is published by Oxford University Press.

CHAPTER 2

UN Security Efforts
During the Cold War

T HE UN CHARTER'S REQUIREMENT for unanimity among the permanent members of the Security Council reflected the realities of the power politics of the day and historical norms of European interstate relations. The council was created less out of naive idealism and more out of a hardheaded effort to mesh state power with international law, a traditional approach to effective enforcement. However, the underlying requirement that members would agree was not borne out with any frequency during the Cold War. The veto held by the UN's five permanent members (P5)—the United States, the Soviet Union (now Russia), the United Kingdom, France, and China—was not the real problem; disagreement among those with power was. Still, with the help of the second UN, specifically the secretary-general, member states tried to craft multilateral responses to threats to international peace and security. They innovated with peacekeeping and experimented with multilateral sanctions as mechanisms to restore order.

THE EARLY YEARS: PALESTINE, KOREA, SUEZ, THE CONGO

The onset of the Cold War ended the great-power cooperation on which the postwar order had been predicated. Nonetheless, the UN became involved in four major security crises: Palestine (1948), Korea (1950), Suez (1956), and the Congo (1962). After Israel declared its independence in 1948, war broke out between it and its four neighbors: Egypt, Jordan, Lebanon, and Syria. Soon thereafter, the Security Council ordered a cease-fire under Chapter VII and ultimately created an observer team, the United Nations Truce Supervision Organization (UNTSO), under Chapter VI to supervise it. UNTSO observer groups were deployed, unarmed, along the borders of Israel and its neighbors and operated with the consent of the parties involved. Close to six hundred observers were eventually deployed, including army units from Belgium, France, the United States, and Sweden. Troops had no enforcement mandate or capability, but their presence deterred truce violations. To exercise their mandates without relying on military might, they relied on the moral authority of the United Nations. Also, warring parties knew that their truce violations would be objectively reported to UN headquarters in New York for possible further action. Although observers wore the uniforms of their respective national armies, their first allegiance theoretically was to the world organization, symbolized by UN armbands. Later, blue helmets and berets became the trademark of UN peacekeepers. The observers were paid by their national armies and granted a stipend by the world organization. UNTSO's activities continue to be financed from the UN's regular operating budget.

UNTSO has performed a variety of important tasks. UNTSO observers set up demilitarized zones along the Israeli-Egyptian and Israeli-Syrian borders, established Mixed Armistice Commissions along each border to investigate complaints and allegations of truce violations, and verified compliance with the General Armistice Agreements. UNTSO unfortunately also contributed to a freezing of the conflict. From 1949 to 1956 and then to 1967, the main parties to the conflict were unwilling to use major force to break apart the stalemate. UNTSO was there to police the status quo. Being freed from major military violence, the parties lacked the necessary motivation to make concessions for a more genuine peace. This problem of UN peacekeeping contributing to freezing but not resolving a conflict was to reappear in Cyprus and elsewhere.

The first coercive action taken in the name of the United Nations concerned the Korean Peninsula and was arguably a type of collective security.[1] World War II left Korea divided, with Soviet forces occupying the North and U.S. forces the South. The UN call for withdrawal of foreign troops and elections throughout a unified Korea was opposed by communist governments, leading to elections only in the South and the withdrawal of most U.S. troops. In 1950 forces from North Korea (the Democratic People's Republic of Korea), which was informally allied with the Soviet Union and China, attacked South Korea (the Republic of Korea). The United States moved to resist this attack.

At the first UN, the Soviet Union was boycotting the Security Council to protest the seating of the Chinese government in Taiwan as the permanent member instead of the Chinese communist government on the mainland. Knowing the Security Council would not be stymied by a Soviet veto and could move to adopt some type of resolution on Korea, the United States referred the Korean situation to the council. The council passed a resolution under Chapter VII declaring that North Korea had committed a breach of the peace and recommended that UN members furnish all appropriate assistance (including military assistance) to South Korea. The Truman administration ordered U.S. military forces to Korea, albeit before the Security Council approved that particular course of action. The Soviet Union abandoned its boycott and returned to its council seat, thereby thwarting any additional measures. Under U.S. leadership, the General Assembly improvised, passing the Uniting for Peace Resolution to continue support for the South in the name of the United Nations.

Security Council resolutions on Korea provided broad international legitimacy to U.S. decisions among noncommunist countries. The Truman administration was determined to stop communist expansion in East Asia. It proceeded without a congressional declaration of war or any other specific authorizing measure, and it was prepared to proceed without UN authorization—although once this was obtained, the Truman administration emphasized UN approval in its search for support both at home and abroad. The General Assembly action deputized the United States to lead the defense of South Korea in the name of the United Nations. When the early tide of the contest turned in favor of South Korea, Truman decided to carry the war all the way to the Chinese border. This was a fateful decision: by bringing Chinese forces into the fight in major proportions, it prolonged the war until 1953, when a stalemate restored the status quo. All important strategic and tactical decisions pertaining to Korea that carried the UN's name were made by the United States. Other states, such as Australia and Turkey, fought for the defense of South Korea, but that military effort was essentially a U.S. operation behind the UN flag.

The defense of South Korea was not exactly a classic example of collective security if the UN Charter is the guide. A truncated Security Council clearly labeled the situation a breach of the peace and authorized the use of military force, something that would not occur again during the Cold War. Neither the council nor its Military Staff Committee really controlled the use of UN symbols. No Article 43 agreements transferring national military units to the UN were concluded. At the second UN, Secretary-General Trygve Lie (of Norway) played almost no role once he declared himself against the North Korean invasion. The Soviet Union stopped treating him as the UN's head, and he was eventually forced to resign (the only such resignation to date) because of his perceived ineffectiveness. Legally correct in his public stand against aggression, he was left without the necessary political support of a major power, Moscow. Subsequent secretaries-general learned from his mistake, representing Charter values but without completely antagonizing the permanent members whose support was necessary for successful UN action.

The 1956 Suez Canal crisis resulted in the first large-scale use of what became known as peacekeepers, to separate warring parties. France, Britain, and Israel had attacked Soviet-backed Egypt against the wishes of the United States, claiming a right to use force to keep the Suez Canal open after Egyptian president Gamal Abdel Nasser had closed it. Britain and France used their vetoes, blocking action by the Security Council. The General Assembly resorted to the Uniting for Peace Resolution—this time for peacekeeping, not enforcement—and directed Secretary-General Dag Hammarskjöld (of Sweden) to create a force to supervise the cease-fire between Israel and Egypt once it had been arranged. The first UN Emergency Force (UNEF I) oversaw the disengagement of forces and served as a buffer between Israel and Egypt. In this instance, the United States and the Soviet Union were not so far apart. U.S. president Dwight D. Eisenhower acted in the spirit of collective security by preventing traditional U.S. allies from proceeding with what he regarded as aggression. UN peacekeeping in 1956 and for a decade thereafter was hailed as a success.

The efforts by the world organization to deal with one of the most traumatic exercises in decolonization—in the former Belgian Congo (then Zaire and more recently the Democratic Republic of Congo)—illustrated the limits of peacekeeping. The ONUC (the French acronym for the United Nations Operation in the Congo)[2] almost bankrupted the world organization and also threatened its political life. Secretary-General Hammarskjöld would lose his own life in a suspicious plane crash in the region but had already developed the precedents for the preventive diplomacy that has characterized the behavior of secretaries-general since.[3]

This armed conflict was both international (caused by Belgium's intervention in its former colony) and domestic (caused by a province's secession within the new state). The nearly total absence of a government infrastructure led to a massive involvement of UN civilian administrators in addition to twenty thousand UN soldiers. After using his Article 99 powers to get the world organization involved, Secretary-General Hammarskjöld became embroiled in a situation in which the Soviet Union, its allies, and many nonaligned countries supported the national prime minister, who was subsequently murdered while detained; the Western powers and the UN organization supported the president. At one point the president fired the prime minister, and the prime minister fired the president, leaving no clear central authority in place. The political vacuum created enormous problems for the United Nations as well as opportunities for action.

Instead of neutral peacekeepers, UN forces became an enforcement army for the central government, which the UN Secretariat created with Western support. This role was not mandated by the General Assembly or Security Council, and in this process the world organization could not count on cooperation from the warring parties within the Congo. Some troop contributors resisted UN command and control; others removed their soldiers to register their objections. The Soviet Union, and later France, refused to pay assessments for the field operation. This phase of the dispute almost destroyed the UN, and the General Assembly had to suspend voting for a time to dodge the question of who was in arrears on payments and thus who could vote. Moscow went further in trying to destroy Hammarskjöld's independence by suggesting the replacement of the secretary-general with a troika (a three-person administrative structure at the top of the organization). Four years later, the UN departed from a unified Congo, an accomplishment. Nevertheless, it had acquired an operational black eye in Africa because of its perceived partisan stance. No UN troops were sent again to Africa until the end of the Cold War (to Namibia). The UN also incurred a large budgetary deficit and developed a hesitancy to become involved in internal wars. Questions about funding lay unresolved, to arise again in later controversies.

The 1973 Arab-Israeli War ended with the creation of the second United Nations Emergency Force (UNEF II). The UNEF model of a lightly armed interpositional force became the blueprint for other traditional peacekeeping operations. UNEF II comprised troops from Austria, Finland, Ireland, Sweden, Canada, Ghana, Indonesia, Nepal, Panama, Peru, Poland, and Senegal—countries representing each of the world's four major regions. The operation consisted of over seven thousand persons at its peak. UNEF II's original mandate was for six months, but the Security Council renewed it continually until 1979, when the U.S.-brokered Israeli-Egyptian peace accord was signed. UNEF II functioned as an impartial force designed to establish a demilitarized zone, supervise it, and safeguard other provisions of the truce. Small-scale force was used to stop those who tried to breach international lines. The presence of UNEF II had a calming influence on the region by ensuring that Israel and Egypt were kept apart. The success of both UNEF I and II, and the problems with the operation in the Congo, catalyzed traditional peacekeeping, the subject to which we now turn.

UNDERSTANDING PEACEKEEPING

The effective projection of military power under international control to enforce international decisions against aggressors was supposed to distinguish the United Nations from the League of Nations. The onset of the Cold War made this impossible on a systematic basis—in fact, the first fifty vetoes in the first decade were Moscow's. A new means of peace maintenance was necessary, one that would permit the world organization to act within carefully defined limits when the major powers agreed or at least acquiesced.

UN peacekeeping proved capable of navigating the turbulent waters of the Cold War through its neutral claims and limited range of activities. Again, global politics circumscribed UN activities. Although peacekeeping is not specifically mentioned in the Charter, it became the organization's primary function in the domain of peace and security. The use of sizable troop contingents for this purpose is widely recognized as having begun during the 1956 crisis in Suez. Contemporary accounts credit Lester B. Pearson, then Canada's secretary of state for external affairs and later prime minister, with proposing to the General Assembly that Secretary-General Hammarskjöld organize an "international police force that would step in until a political settlement could be reached."[4]

Close to five hundred thousand military, police, and civilian personnel—distinguished from national soldiers by their trademark powder blue helmets and berets—served in UN peacekeeping forces during the Cold War, and some seven hundred lost their lives in UN service during this period. Alfred Nobel hardly intended to honor soldiers when he created the peace prize that bears his name, and no military organization had received the prize throughout its eighty-seven-year history. This changed in December 1988, when UN peacekeepers received the prestigious award. This date serves as the turning point in the following discussion to distinguish UN security activities during and after the Cold War.

The Cold War and the Birth of Peacekeeping, 1948–1988

The lack of any specific reference to peacekeeping in the Charter led Hammar-skjöld to coin the poetic and apt expression "Chapter six and a half," which referred to stretching the original meaning of Chapter VI. And certainly peacekeeping "can rightly be called the invention of the United Nations," as Secretary-General Boutros Boutros-Ghali later claimed in *An Agenda for Peace*.[5] The lack of a clear international constitutional basis makes a consensus definition of peacekeeping difficult, particularly because peacekeeping operations have been improvised in response to the specific requirements of individual conflicts. Despite the lack of consensus and the multiplicity of sources,[6] former UN undersecretary-general Marrack Goulding provided a sensible definition of peacekeeping: "United Nations field operations in which international personnel, civilian and/or military, are deployed with the consent of the parties and under United Nations command to help control and resolve actual or potential international conflicts or internal conflicts which have a clear international dimension."[7]

The first thirteen UN peacekeeping and military observer operations deployed during the Cold War are listed in Table 2.1.[8] Five were still in the field in mid-2016. From 1948 to 1988, peacekeepers typically served two functions: observing the peace (that is, monitoring and reporting on the maintenance of cease-fires) and keeping the peace (that is, providing an interpositional buffer between belligerents and establishing zones of disengagement). The forces were normally composed of troops from small or nonaligned states, with permanent members of the Security Council and other major powers making troop contributions only under exceptional circumstances. Lightly armed, these neutral troops were symbolically deployed between belligerents who had agreed to stop fighting; they rarely used force and then only in self-defense and as a last resort. Rather than being based on any military prowess, the influence of UN peacekeepers in this period resulted from the cooperation of belligerents mixed with the moral weight and diplomatic pressure of the international community of states.[9]

Peacekeeping operations essentially defend the status quo. They help suspend a conflict and create political space so that belligerents can be brought closer to the negotiating table. However, these operations do not by themselves guarantee the successful pursuit of negotiations. They are often easier to institute than to dismantle, as the case of over five decades of this activity in Cyprus demonstrates. The termination of peacekeeping operations creates a vacuum and may have serious consequences for the stability of a region, as happened in 1967 at the outbreak of the Arab-Israeli War following the withdrawal of UNEF I at Egypt's request.

The UN Disengagement Observer Force (UNDOF) represents a classic example of international compromise during the Cold War. This operation was designed as a microcosm of geopolitics, with a NATO member and a neutral on the pro-Western Israeli side of the line of separation, and a member of the Warsaw Pact and a neutral on the pro-Soviet Syrian side. UNDOF was established on May 31, 1974, upon the conclusion of disengagement agreements between Israel and

Members of the Polish contingent of the United Nations Disengagement Observer Force (UNDOF) on patrol. June 26, 2008, Golan Heights, Syria. (UN PHOTO 184767/GEMOT PAYER)

Syria that called for an Israeli withdrawal from all areas it occupied within Syria, the establishment of a buffer zone to separate the Syrian and Israeli armies, and the creation of areas of restricted armaments on either side of the buffer zone. UNDOF was charged with verifying Israel's withdrawal, establishing the buffer zones, and monitoring levels of militarization in the restricted zones.

UNDOF employed as many as 1,250 armed soldiers, including 90 military observers. Troop deployment emphasized equal contributions by countries that were either politically neutral or sympathetic to the West or East. Originally, Peru, Canada, Poland, and Austria provided troops for the operation. Canadian and Peruvian forces operated along the Israeli side; Polish and Austrian forces operated on the Syrian side.

Despite the declared hostility between Israel and Syria, UNDOF has proven instrumental in maintaining peace on the Golan Heights. The size and weapons of the force clearly are inadequate to halt any serious incursions, but the two longtime foes want the force there. Thus, since 1977 no major incidents between the two states have occurred in areas under UNDOF's jurisdiction. Success is attributable to several factors: the details of the operation were thoroughly defined before its implementation, leaving little room for disagreement; Israel and Syria cooperated with UNDOF; and the Security Council supported the operation fully. The ongoing civil war in Syria (discussed in Chapter 4) has destabilized the Golan Heights somewhat. Syrian rebels kidnapped twenty-one peacekeepers for

TABLE 2.1 UN PEACEKEEPING OPERATIONS
DURING THE COLD WAR AND DURING THE INITIAL THAW

Years Active	Operation
1948–Present	United Nations Truce Supervision Organization (UNTSO, based in Jerusalem)
1949–Present	United Nations Military Observer Group in India and Pakistan (UNMOGIP)
1956–1967	United Nations Emergency Force (UNEF I, Suez Canal)
1958	United Nations Observation Group in Lebanon (UNOGIL)
1960–1964	United Nations Operation in the Congo (ONUC)
1962–1963	United Nations Force in New West Guinea (UNSF, in West Irian)
1963–1964	United Nations Yemen Observation Mission (UNYOM)
1964–Present	United Nations Peacekeeping Force in Cyprus (UNFICYP)
1965–1966	United Nations India-Pakistan Observation Mission (UNIPOM)
1965–1966	Mission of the Representative of the Secretary-General in the Dominican Republic (DOMREP)
1973–1979	Second United Nations Emergency Force (UNEF II, Suez Canal and later the Sinai Peninsula)
1974–Present	United Nations Disengagement Observer Force (UNDOF, Golan Heights)
1978–Present	United Nations Interim Force in Lebanon (UNIFIL)
1988–1990	United Nations Good Offices Mission in Afghanistan and Pakistan (UNGOMAP)
1988–1991	United Nations Iran-Iraq Military Observer Group (UNIIMOG)
1989–1990	United Nations Transition Assistance Group (UNTAG, in Namibia)
1989–1991	United Nations Angola Verification Mission (UNAVEM I)
1989–1992	United Nations Observer Group in Central America (ONUCA)

three days and the UN was forced to withdraw from vulnerable positions as a result.[10] Increased rebel activity in the region poses a significant threat to the lightly armed observer force.

Principles of Traditional Peacekeeping

The man who helped give operational meaning to "peacekeeping," Brian Urquhart, summarized the following characteristics of UN operations during the Cold War: consent of the parties, continuing strong support of the Security Council, a clear and practicable mandate, nonuse of force except as a last resort and in self-defense, the willingness of troop contributors to furnish military forces, and the willingness of member states to make available requisite financing.[11] Developing each of the characteristics serves as a bridge to our discussion of subsequent UN efforts that extend beyond traditional limitations because many of these traditional standard operating procedures would need to be set aside or seriously modified to confront the challenges of many post–Cold War peace operations.

Principle #1: Consent Is Imperative Before Operations Begin. In many ways, consent is the keystone of traditional peacekeeping, for two reasons. First, it helps to insulate the UN decision-making process against great-power dissent. For example, in Cyprus and Lebanon the Soviet Union's desire to obstruct was overcome because the parties themselves had asked for UN help.

Second, consent greatly reduces the likelihood that peacekeepers will encounter resistance while carrying out their duties. Peacekeepers are physically in no position to challenge the authority of belligerents (either states or opposition groups), and so they assume a nonconfrontational stance toward local authorities. Traditional peacekeepers do not impinge on sovereignty. In fact, it is imperative to achieve consent before operations begin.

The emphasis that traditional missions place on consent does have drawbacks, as two observers summarized: "Peacekeeping forces cannot often create conditions for their own success."[12] For example, belligerents will normally consent to a peacekeeping mission once wartime goals have been achieved or losses have made belligerents war weary. In instances where neither of these conditions has been met, it becomes necessary to find alternate ways to induce warring parties to achieve and maintain consent. Moreover, major powers need to pressure their clients not only to consent but also to negotiate. When political will is lacking, either wars continue unaddressed by the organization or UN peacekeepers become inextricably tied down in conflict, neither able to bring peace to the area nor able to withdraw from it. For example, the United Nations Peacekeeping Force in Cyprus (UNFICYP), originally deployed in 1964 to separate warring Turkish and Greek Cypriot communities and then given a new mandate in 1974, remains in the field because consent for deployment has not been matched by a willingness to negotiate the peace. Likewise, the United Nations Military Observer Group in India and Pakistan (UNMOGIP), established in 1949; UNDOF, created in 1974; and the United Nations Interim Force in Lebanon (UNIFIL), deployed in 1978, all continue to operate because of the absence of political conditions allowing for their removal.

Principle #2: Peacekeeping Operations Need Full Support from the Security Council. Such support is necessary not only in the beginning stages of the mission, when decisions regarding budgets, troop allotments, and other strategic priorities are made, but also in its later stages, when mandates come up for renewal. The host of problems in the Congo illustrates the dangers of proceeding without the support of the major powers in the Security Council. Backing by both the United States and the Soviet Union of UNEF I in the General Assembly was the only case in which the United States and the Soviet Union abandoned the Security Council and then resorted to the General Assembly to get around a veto. A practice has developed for the Security Council to renew the mandate of missions several times—frequently semiannually for years on end—so as to keep pressure on parties who may be threatened with the possible withdrawal of peacekeepers. Full Security Council support also enhances the symbolic power of an operation.

Principle #3: Participating Countries Need to Provide Troops and to Accept Risks. Successful peacekeeping missions require the self-sustained presence of individual

Canadian and Swedish soldiers serving with the United Nations Peacekeeping Force in Cyprus (UNFICYP) read *The Blue Beret*, a UNFICYP newspaper. April 18, 1964, Nicosia, Cyprus. (UN PHOTO 52051/BZ)

peacekeeping battalions, each of which is independent but also functions under UN command. Frequently they deploy in areas of heavy militarization. Mortal danger exists for peacekeepers. Governments that provide troops must be willing to accept the risks inherent in a given mission, and they also must be able to defend such expenditures and losses before their parliaments.

Principle #4: Permanent Members Do Not Normally Contribute Troops Except for Logistical Support. Providing logistical support has become a specialty of the United States, which during the Cold War essentially airlifted most start-up troops and provisions for UN operations. Keeping major powers from an active role in peacekeeping was imperative for the perceived neutrality that successful peacekeeping strives to attain. Washington and Moscow were thought to be especially tainted by the causes they supported worldwide.

The experience with exceptions to this rule has been mixed. Because of the special circumstances involved in Britain's possession of extraterritorial bases on the island of Cyprus, the United Kingdom has been involved in UN operations there from the outset; that effort has been worthwhile. The experience of French peacekeepers deployed in UNIFIL in Lebanon was a source of problems because of France's perceived involvement as an ex-colonial power on the Christian side of the conflict. Consequently, French troops came under attack by local factions and were forced to withdraw from the zone of operations and to remain in the UN compound.

Principle #5: A Clear and Precise Mandate Is Desirable. The goals of the mission should be clear, obtainable, and known to all parties involved. Enunciation of the mission's objectives reduces local suspicion. Yet a certain degree of flexibility is desirable so that the peacekeepers may adapt their operating strategies to better fit changing circumstances. The goals of the operation may be expanded or reduced as the situation warrants. In fact, diplomatic vagueness may at times be necessary in Security Council voting to secure support or to keep future options open.

Principle #6: Force Is Used Only in Self-Defense and as a Last Resort. Peacekeepers derive their influence from the diplomatic support of the international community, and therefore they use force only as a last resort and in self-defense. *The Peacekeeper's Handbook* states this wisdom: "The degree of force [used] must only be sufficient to achieve the mission on hand and to prevent, as far as possible, loss of human life and/or serious injury. Force should not be initiated, except possibly after continuous harassment when it becomes necessary to restore a situation so that the United Nations can fulfill its responsibilities."[13]

Peacekeeping techniques differ greatly from those taught to most soldiers and officers by their national training authorities. In the past only the Scandinavian states and Canada have trained large numbers of their recruits and officers specifically for peacekeeping. Soldiers from other countries have often found themselves unprepared because the prohibition against the use of force contradicts their standard military training. Thus, the administrative, technological, and strategic structures that sustain peacekeeping have reflected the need for professional diplomatic and political expertise more than the need for professional soldiers.

"Chapter Six and a Half" on Hold, 1978–1988

From 1948 to 1978 thirteen UN peacekeeping operations took place. In the ten years after 1978, however, no new operations materialized, even as a rash of regional conflicts involving the superpowers or their proxies sprang up around the globe.[14] The last operation approved before the decade-long hiatus highlights the difficulties the UN encountered during this period. UNIFIL in Lebanon was beset with problems similar to those experienced in the Congo during the 1960s, where domestic conflict and an absence of government structures had given the world organization an operational black eye.[15] UNIFIL's difficulties illustrate the dangers inherent in operations that lack both clear mandates and the effective cooperation of belligerents, and that exist amidst political chaos and great-power disagreement.

UNIFIL was established at the Security Council's request on March 19, 1978, following Israel's military incursion into southern Lebanon. Israel claimed that military raids and shelling by members of the Palestine Liberation Organization (PLO) who were based in southern Lebanon threatened Israeli peace and security. Israel's harsh military response embarrassed its primary ally, the United States. Washington used its influence in the Security Council to create UNIFIL as a face-saving means for Israel to withdraw when criticism of its tactics became widespread. The UNIFIL duties included confirming the Israeli withdrawal; establishing and maintaining an area of operations; preventing renewed fighting among the PLO, Israel, and the Israeli-backed Southern Lebanese Army; and restoring Lebanese sovereignty over southern Lebanon.

At UNIFIL's maximum strength, over seven thousand soldiers were deployed, including contingents from Canada, Fiji, France, Ghana, Iran, Ireland, Nepal, the Netherlands, Nigeria, Norway, and Senegal. UNIFIL encountered significant problems as a result of the conflicting interests of the major parties involved in southern Lebanon. Israel refused to cede control of the South to UNIFIL, choosing instead to rely on the Southern Lebanese Army, which resisted UNIFIL's efforts to gain control in the area. The PLO demanded that it be allowed to operate freely in the South to continue its resistance against Israel. The Lebanese government insisted that UNIFIL assume control of the entire region. Consequently, UNIFIL found itself sandwiched between the PLO and the Southern Lebanese Army and routinely came under fire. In 1982, as Israel reinvaded Lebanon and marched to Beirut, UNIFIL stood by, powerless, in the face of Israel's superior firepower and the unwillingness of troop contributors or the UN membership to resist. UNIFIL's refusal to stand its ground echoed Egypt's 1967 request to withdraw UNEF I; once UN troops were pulled out, war ensued. UNIFIL's mandate was rejuvenated and renewed in 2006, after the cessation of another round of hostilities, and it remains in operation today.

Much of the impetus for the increased tension between East and West and for the end of new UN deployments came from the United States after the Reagan administration took office in 1981. Elected on a platform of anticommunism, the rebuilding of the national defense system, and fiscal conservatism, the administration was determined to roll back Soviet gains in the Third World. Neoconservatives in Washington scorned the world organization and cast it aside as a bastion of Third World nationalism and support for communism. The UN's peacekeeping operations were tarred with the same brush. The Reagan administration also refused to pay its assessed dues (including a portion of the assessment for UNIFIL, which Washington had originally insisted on).[16] The organization was in near bankruptcy at the same time that U.S. respect for international law seemed to evaporate and unilateral action gained favor.[17] Intervening in Grenada, bombing Libya, and supporting insurgencies in Nicaragua, Angola, Afghanistan, and Cambodia attested to U.S. preferences in the 1980s. The Soviet Union countered these initiatives. Central America, the Horn of Africa, much of southern Africa, and parts of Asia became battlegrounds and flash points for the superpowers or their proxies.

ECONOMIC SANCTIONS

Short of sending international forces, a group of states may attempt to isolate an aggressor or forestall a breach of the peace by cutting off diplomatic or economic relations with a view toward altering offensive behavior. These are coercive, albeit nonforcible, actions—the first step in Chapter VII's enforcement progression. Diplomatic and economic sanctions are significantly more emphatic than the usual political influence that makes up the everyday stuff of foreign policy, even if less emphatic than the dispatch of troops.

On a spectrum ranging from political influence to outside military intervention, economic sanctions are enforcement measures that fall far short of military force. For the same reasons that real collective security was not possible during the Cold War, these milder forms of enforcement were also largely underused. The exceptions were against two pariahs, Rhodesia and South Africa, whose domestic racist policies were widely condemned. As a reaction to Rhodesia's unilateral declaration of independence (UDI) from the United Kingdom in 1965, the Security Council in 1966 ordered limited economic sanctions under Chapter VII of the Charter for the first time in UN history.[18] Whether the trigger was due more to the UDI or to the human rights situation for Africans is debatable, but the result was that the council characterized the domestic situation as a "threat to the peace." The council toughened the stance against the white-minority government by banning all exports and imports (except for some foodstuffs, educational materials, and medicines). These sanctions became "comprehensive" in 1968.

The sanctions initially were costly for the government of Rhodesian prime minister Ian Smith. But, ironically, they eventually helped immunize the country against outside pressure because they prompted a successful program of import substitution and the diversification of its economy. Although most members of the UN complied, some of those who counted did not. The United States, for example, openly violated sanctions after the Byrd amendment by Congress allowed trade with Rhodesia, even though the United States had voted for sanctions in the Security Council. According to U.S. judicial doctrine, if Congress uses its statutory authority to violate international law intentionally, domestic courts will defer to congressional action in U.S. jurisdiction. Many private firms as well as some other African countries also traded with Rhodesia, including the neighboring countries of Mozambique (a Portuguese colony) and the Republic of South Africa, then under white minority rule.

Although the Security Council authorized a forceful blockade to interrupt supplies of oil and the British navy halted a few tankers, there was insufficient political will at the first UN to effectively blockade the ports and coastlines of Mozambique and South Africa. Hence, the Security Council helped but can hardly be credited with the establishment of an independent Zimbabwe in 1979. The UN's use of economic sanctions in this case was more important as legal and diplomatic precedent than as effective power on the ground.

UN-imposed sanctions against South Africa reflected the judgment that racial separation (apartheid) within the country was a threat to international peace and security. Limited economic sanctions, an embargo on arms sales, boycotts against athletic teams, and selective divestment were all part of a visible campaign to isolate South Africa. These acts exerted pressure, but it is difficult to quantify their impact. Initially, South Africa's high-cost industry thrived by trying to replace missing imports (as had Rhodesia's), and it even managed to produce a variety of sophisticated arms that eventually became a major export. The transition to democracy (and the end of white rule) probably resulted more from the dynamics of the internal struggle by the black majority and the end of the Cold War than from sanctions. No doubt sanctions contributed to altering the domestic balance by demonstrating the risks and the costs of being isolated, but measuring their precise impact requires greater empirical work.[19]

The Rhodesian and South African experiences show how the UN, through the Security Council, can link the domestic policies of states to threats to international peace and security and thereby justify Chapter VII action. The council expanded the definition of a threat by the use of sanctions as enforcement tools for a domestic issue, and thereby set an important precedent. UN sanctions are analytically distinct from bilateral economic sanctions or those imposed by treaty (for example, the Montreal Protocol to protect the ozone layer). The UN Charter never uses the word *sanctions* in Chapter VII, but Article 41 speaks of "measures not involving the use of armed force," which "are to be employed to give effect to its decisions." The continued use of partial or comprehensive sanctions has come under increased criticism because of their impact on vulnerable populations within targeted countries, a subject to which we return at the end of Chapter 3.

NOTES

1. Leon Gordenker, *The UN Secretary-General and the Maintenance of Peace* (New York: Columbia University Press, 1967); and Leland M. Goodrich, *Korea: A Study of U.S. Policy* (New York: Council on Foreign Relations, 1956).

2. The tradition of acronyms in English was set aside as operations in Spanish-speaking and French-speaking countries became more widespread.

3. Bertrand G. Ramcharan, *Preventive Diplomacy at the UN* (Bloomington: Indiana University Press, 2008).

4. Max Harrelson, *Fires All Around the Horizon: The UN's Uphill Battle to Preserve the Peace* (New York: Praeger, 1989), 89.

5. Boutros Boutros-Ghali, *An Agenda for Peace: Preventive Diplomacy, Peacemaking, and Peace-Keeping: Report of the Secretary-General Pursuant to the Statement Adopted by the Summit Meeting of the Security Council on 31 January 1992* (New York: United Nations, 1992), para. 46.

6. United Nations, *The Blue Helmets: A Review of United Nations Peace-Keeping*, 2nd ed. (New York: UNDPI, 1990), 4; Alan James, *Peacekeeping in International Politics* (London: Macmillan, 1990), 1; and Boutros-Ghali, *Agenda*, para. 20.

7. Marrack Goulding, "The Changing Role of the United Nations in Conflict Resolution and Peace-Keeping," speech given at the Singapore Institute of Policy Studies, March 13, 1991, 9. See also his "The Evolution of Peacekeeping," *International Affairs* 69, no. 3 (1993): 451–464, and *Peacemonger* (London: John Murray, 2002).

8. Thomas G. Weiss and Jarat Chopra, *Peacekeeping: An ACUNS Teaching Text* (Hanover, N.H.: Academic Council on the United Nations System, 1992), 1–20. The United

Nations published its own volume, *The Blue Helmets*, in 1985, which was revised in 1990 and 1996. Updates are now on the United Nations website at www.un.org. See also Rosalyn Higgins, *United Nations Peacekeeping: Documents and Commentary*, vols. 1–4 (Oxford: Oxford University Press, 1969–1981).

9. John Mackinlay, *The Peacekeepers: An Assessment of Peacekeeping Operations at the Arab-Israel Interface* (London: Unwin Hyman, 1989); Augustus Richard Norton and Thomas G. Weiss, *UN Peacekeepers: Soldiers with a Difference* (New York: Foreign Policy Association, 1990); William J. Durch, ed., *The Evolution of UN Peacekeeping* (New York: St. Martin's Press, 1993); Paul F. Diehl, *International Peacekeeping* (Baltimore: Johns Hopkins University Press, 1993); and Adekeye Adebajo, *UN Peacekeeping in Africa: From the Suez Crisis to the Sudan Conflicts* (Boulder, Colo.: Lynne Rienner, 2011).

10. Richard Gowan, "For U.N. and Europe, a Peacekeeping Crisis in Lebanon," *World Politics Review* (March 25, 2013): 1.

11. Brian Urquhart, "Beyond the 'Sheriff's Posse,'" *Survival* 32, no. 3 (1990): 198, and *A Life in Peace and War* (New York: Harper and Row, 1987).

12. John Mackinlay and Jarat Chopra, "Second Generation Multinational Operations," *Washington Quarterly* 15, no. 3 (1992): 114.

13. International Peace Academy, *Peacekeeper's Handbook* (New York: Pergamon, 1984), 56.

14. S. Neil MacFarlane, *Superpower Rivalry and Third World Radicalism: The Idea of National Liberation* (Baltimore: Johns Hopkins University Press, 1985); Elizabeth Kridl Valkenier, *The Soviet Union and the Third World: An Economic Bind* (New York: Praeger, 1983); and Jerry F. Hough, *The Struggle for the Third World: Soviet Debates and American Options* (Washington, D.C.: Brookings Institution, 1986).

15. Bjorn Skogmo, *UNIFIL: International Peacekeeping in Lebanon* (Boulder, Colo.: Lynne Rienner, 1989); and Emmanuel A. Erskine, *Mission with UNIFIL: An African Soldier's Reflections* (New York: St. Martin's Press, 1989).

16. Jeffrey Harrod and Nico Shrijver, eds., *The UN Under Attack* (Aldershot, U.K.: Gower, 1988).

17. David P. Forsythe, *The Politics of International Law: U.S. Foreign Policy Reconsidered* (Boulder, Colo.: Lynne Rienner, 1990).

18. Henry Wiseman and Alistair M. Taylor, *From Rhodesia to Zimbabwe: The Politics of Transition* (New York: Pergamon, 1981); and Stephen John Stedman, *Peacemaking in Civil War: International Mediation in Zimbabwe, 1974–1980* (Boulder, Colo.: Lynne Rienner, 1991).

19. Taehee Whang and Hannah June Kim, "International Signaling and Economic Sanctions," *International Interactions* 41, no. 3 (2015): 427–452.

CHAPTER 3

UN Security Operations After the Cold War, 1988–1998

A s the cold war was winding down, the United Nations underwent an important transition. The new Soviet leader Mikhail Gorbachev sought to reduce East-West tensions by reinvigorating multilateralism generally and UN peacekeeping more particularly.[1] The Soviet Union made payments on its UN debt of over $200 million in 1987, generating renewed international interest in the United Nations and collective security. Among other things, the first and second UNs were helpful to Gorbachev, as UN peacekeeping provided a face-saving means to withdraw from what he called the "bleeding wound of Afghanistan."[2]

Changes in the Soviet Union's attitude toward the UN influenced the international climate and more particularly the U.S. approach to the world organization. In 1988 on the eve of leaving office, President Ronald Reagan abruptly altered his public stance and praised the work of the organization, the secretary-general, and UN peacekeepers. After helping to spearhead attacks that had led to almost a decade of UN bashing, he declared at the General Assembly that "the United Nations has the opportunity to live and breathe and work as never before" and vowed to repay U.S. debts to the organization. This orientation was continued by President George H. W. Bush, a former U.S. permanent representative to the world body. Great-power cooperation grew, allowing the Security Council to resume part of its role as a guarantor of international peace and security. The UN provided a convenient way for Paris, London, and Moscow to maintain international preeminence despite their declining economic, political, and military significance. The UN also enabled the United States to proceed as a hegemonic rather than dominant power, allowing it to act through the UN on the basis of cooperation rather than having to coerce other states into compliance. Beginning in 1988, collegiality and regular collaboration among great powers in the Security Council were politically possible.

UN MILITARY OPERATIONS, 1988–1993

After a ten-year gap in deploying new UN security operations, five post–Cold War operations (listed at the top of Table 3.1) were launched in rapid succession: in Afghanistan and Pakistan, astride the Iran-Iraq border, and in Angola, Namibia, and Central America (for Nicaragua). These were largely traditional peacekeeping operations, but they also incorporated some improvisations characteristic of the evolution of UN peacekeeping. They mainly were extensions of the time-tested recipe. In particular, all enjoyed the consent of belligerents and relied on defensive concepts of force employed by modestly equipped UN soldiers, very few of whom came from armies of the major powers. Of the peace operations begun between 1988 and 1998 (Table 3.1), two also fall into the traditional peacekeeping category: the follow-up operation in Angola and the one in the Western Sahara.[3] However, in Namibia and Central America, large numbers of civilians and civil society actors worked in tandem with soldiers. The third UN was beginning to take shape and influence outcomes in the field. The first supervision of domestic elections as well as the collection of weapons from insurgents took place in Nicaragua. These set precedents and illustrated the UN's capacity for growth and innovation in a new era, just as improvisation and task expansion had been present earlier.

Three operations begun during this period are so different in scope and mandate that to characterize them as "peacekeeping" stretches analytical categories to the breaking point. UN operations in Cambodia, the former Yugoslavia, and Somalia are examples of the new challenges facing the UN. The evolution of these and two subsequent operations (Rwanda and Haiti) also illustrates the limits of UN military operations. Another UN operation in the Iraq-Kuwait war merits a separate discussion because its deployment followed the first UN collective security action of the post–Cold War era.

THE REBIRTH OF PEACEKEEPING

The UN Good Offices Mission in Afghanistan and Pakistan (UNGOMAP), the UN Iran-Iraq Military Observer Group (UNIIMOG), the first UN Angola Verification Mission (UNAVEM I), and the UN Transition Assistance Group in Namibia (UNTAG) were missions that renewed peacekeeping's visibility and perceived workability in the international arena of conflict resolution. UNGOMAP, UNIIMOG, and UNTAG are also significant because they afforded the UN the opportunity to demonstrate its usefulness in war zones, a capacity frozen from 1978 to 1988. Successes built confidence and allowed the UN to move back toward center stage, and the operations provided the space to experiment with innovations beyond the scope of previous deployments.

These operations are examples of "observation," a diverse set of tasks that occupies the least controversial part of the peacekeeping spectrum. Traditionally, observation has meant investigation, armistice supervision, maintenance of a

TABLE 3.1 UN PEACE AND SECURITY OPERATIONS, 1988-1998

Years Active	Operation
1988–1990	United Nations Good Offices Mission in Afghanistan and Pakistan (UNGOMAP)
1988–1991	United Nations Iran-Iraq Military Observer Group (UNIIMOG)
1989–1990	United Nations Transition Assistance Group (UNTAG, in Namibia)
1989–1991	United Nations Angola Verification Mission (UNAVEM I)
1989–1992	United Nations Observer Group in Central America (ONUCA)
1991–1992	United Nations Advance Mission in Cambodia (UNAMIC)
1991–1995	United Nations Observer Mission in El Salvador (ONUSAL)
1991–1995	United Nations Angola Verification Mission II (UNAVEM II)
1991–2003	United Nations Iraq-Kuwait Observer Mission (UNIKOM)
1991–Present	United Nations Mission for the Referendum in Western Sahara (MINURSO)
1992–1993	United Nations Transitional Authority in Cambodia (UNTAC)
1992–1993	United Nations Operation in Somalia I (UNOSOM I)
1992–1994	United Nations Operation in Mozambique (ONUMOZ)
1992–1995	United Nations Protection Force, former Yugoslavia (UNPROFOR)
1993–1994	United Nations Mission Uganda-Rwanda (UNOMUR)
1993–1995	United Nations Mission in Somalia II (UNOSOM II)
1993–1996	United Nations Mission in Haiti (UNMIH)
1993–1996	United Nations Assistance Mission in Rwanda (UNAMIR)
1993–1997	United Nations Observer Mission in Liberia (UNOMIL)
1993–Present	United Nations Observer Mission in Georgia (UNOMIG)
1994–1994	United Nations Aouzou Strip Observer Group (UNASOG, Chad/Libya)
1994–2000	United Nations Mission of Observers in Tajikistan (UNMOT)
1995–1996	United Nations Confidence Restoration Operation, Croatia (UNCRO)
1995–1997	United Nations Angola Verification Mission III (UNAVEM III)
1995–1999	United Nations Preventive Deployment Force, former Yugoslav Republic of Macedonia (UNPREDEP)
1995–2002	United Nations Mission in Bosnia and Herzegovina (UNMIBH)
1996–1997	United Nations Support Mission in Haiti (UNSMIH)
1996–1998	United Nations Transitional Administration for Eastern Slavonia, Baranja and Western Sirmium (UNTAES)
1996–2002	United Nations Mission of Observers in Prevlaka (UNMOP)
1997–1997	United Nations Verification Mission in Guatemala (MINUGUA)
1997–1997	United Nations Transition Mission in Haiti (UNTMIH)
1997–1999	United Nations Observer Mission in Angola (MONUA)
1997–2000	United Nations Civilian Police Mission in Haiti (MIPONUH)
1998–1998	United Nations Civilian Police Support Group (UNCPSG)
1998–1999	United Nations Observer Mission in Sierra Leone (UNOMSIL)
1998–2000	United Nations Mission in the Central African Republic (MINURCA)

cease-fire, supervision of plebiscites, oversight of the cessation of fighting, and reports to headquarters. It has been expanded to include the verification of troop withdrawal, the organization and observation of elections, the voluntary surrender of weapons, and human rights verification. These operations are distinct from the other traditional task: interposition, or placing peacekeepers between belligerents along a cease-fire line.

UNGOMAP verified the withdrawal of Soviet troops from Afghanistan after 1988. The Soviet Union had entered the country in 1979 to ensure a friendly Afghan government in Kabul. By the early 1980s Afghanistan had become Moscow's Vietnam. The Soviets had become inextricably tied down in an unwinnable conflict against the mujahideen, armed local groups backed by Pakistan, the United States, and a few others, such as Saudi Arabia. The Gorbachev administration sought a face-saving device to extricate itself. The 1988 Geneva Accords provided the means to achieve Soviet withdrawal, mutual noninterference and nonintervention pledges between Pakistan and Afghanistan, the return of refugees, and noninterference pledges from the United States and the Soviet Union. These accords had been brokered by the United Nations and the indefatigable efforts of Undersecretary-General Diego Cordovez.

The deployment of UNGOMAP was not accompanied by enough political will from the first UN to implement the international agreements concerning peace, elections, and disarmament. The symbolic size of the operation—only fifty officers divided between Islamabad and Kabul—attested to its inability to independently perform tasks other than reporting on the Soviet withdrawal after the fact. The operation paved the way to a potential peace by reducing the direct East-West character of the conflict; however, the power vacuum left by the Soviet withdrawal also set the stage for the rise of the Taliban, which provided sanctuary to Al Qaeda.

In 1988 the Iran-Iraq War drew to a close with over 1 million lives lost. The Security Council ordered a cease-fire in 1987, with the compulsory intent provided for under Chapter VII to set up UNIIMOG the following year to maintain the cease-fire astride the international border. UNIIMOG established cease-fire lines between Iranian and Iraqi troops, observed the maintenance of the cease-fire, and investigated complaints to defuse minor truce violations before they escalated into peace-threatening situations. Composed of only three hundred fifty unarmed observers from some twenty-five states, UNIIMOG played a useful role in preserving the cease-fire between Iran and Iraq, two countries whose mutual antagonism continued after hostilities ceased. In its first five months alone, UNIIMOG investigated some two thousand complaints of truce infractions.

In 1988 Angola, Cuba, and South Africa signed a trilateral agreement that provided for the simultaneous withdrawal of Cuban troops from Angola and of South African troops and administrators from Namibia. This diplomatic breakthrough was monitored successfully by the first United Nations Angola Verification Mission, which led the way for the UN-sponsored peace process that brought Namibian independence on March 21, 1990, from South Africa's illegal colonial rule. The second UNAVEM was problematic because civil war returned despite

Secretary-General Javier Pérez de Cuéllar inspects the Kenyan battalion honor guard at the UN Transition Assistance Group (UNTAG) Military Headquarters in Suiderhof Base, Windhoek, Namibia. He is accompanied by Lt. General Prem Chand, Force Commander of UNTAG. July 1, 1989. (UN PHOTO 75912/MILTON GRANT)

UN-supervised elections at the end of 1992; the difficulties faced by this group are discussed with other problematic operations later in this chapter.

UNTAG was established to facilitate and monitor South Africa's withdrawal from Namibia, to set up free and fair elections, and to determine the future government and constitution of Namibia. This was one of the last major decolonization efforts under UN auspices. UNTAG was tasked with monitoring and facilitating the departure of South Africa's army and the withdrawal and confinement of fighters of the South-West Africa People's Organization (SWAPO) to base camps in Angola. It also monitored the southwest African police force controlled by South Africa to prevent meddling in the election, oversaw the repeal of discriminatory laws that threatened the fairness of the election, helped ensure the respect for amnesty for political prisoners, and provided for the return of all Namibian refugees. UNTAG also registered voters and facilitated information about the election process.

At its maximum deployment, nearly 8,000 persons were involved in UNTAG: about 4,500 military personnel, 2,000 civilian personnel, and 1,000 police officers. It was the first sizable operation in Africa since the contested one in the Congo almost three decades earlier that gave the UN a black eye. In spite of initial difficulties, the belligerents, in particular South Africa, were committed to making the operation work. UNTAG is generally considered a success, and Secretary-General Javier Pérez de Cuéllar viewed it as one of his singular accomplishments. Virtually the entire population was registered to vote. SWAPO won forty-one of seventy-two seats in the Constitutional Constituents Assembly and was duly empowered to lead the formation of the Namibian government. On March 21, 1990—ahead of schedule and under budget—Pérez de Cuéllar swore in Sam Nujoma as president of Namibia.

UNTAG provides a helpful analytical hinge between the old and new types of UN peace operations. It went smoothly because traditional rules were followed, especially consent and minimal use of force. At the same time, it undertook several new tasks related to civil administration, elections, human rights monitoring, and police activities. They foreshadowed new UN tasks that would more routinely intrude into the affairs of sovereign states.

MOVING TOWARD THE NEXT GENERATION

The work of the second UN in Central America during the late 1980s and early 1990s signaled the progressive movement toward a new generation of peacekeeping and peace-enforcement operations.[4] World politics was changing, and so were the possibilities for UN action. The United Nations Observer Group in Central America (ONUCA), the United Nations Observer Mission to Verify the Electoral Process in Nicaragua (ONUVEN), and the United Nations Observer Mission in El Salvador (ONUSAL) illustrate the complex transition that UN peace and security functions began to undergo. These also set the stage for the UN-sponsored Chapter VII enforcement action against Iraq. ONUSAL in particular shows the independent nature of the second UN when states give the world organization some political room to maneuver.

In the late 1980s, the conclusion of the so-called Esquipulas II agreements between the countries of Central America—Nicaragua, Costa Rica, El Salvador, Guatemala, and Honduras—began the peace process that ended a decade of civil war and instability in the region. The cornerstone of the agreements involved setting up free and fair elections in Nicaragua. In addition to calling for elections, they prohibited aid to rebel groups and the use of a state's territory for guerrilla operations in another. ONUCA (1989–1992) was established to ensure that these provisions were respected. Although ONUCA was officially an "observer" mission, its duties were far-reaching. They included verifying that all forms of military assistance to insurgent forces had ceased and preventing states from sponsoring such activity for infiltration into neighboring countries. ONUCA observers made spot checks and random investigations of areas prone to guerrilla activity along the borders of Nicaragua, El Salvador, Guatemala, Honduras, and Costa Rica. Although the signatories to Esquipulas II were expected to cooperate with ONUCA, the participation of the Nicaraguan resistance movement, the Contras, was not ensured until after the electoral defeat of the Sandinista government in February

1990. ONUCA military observers operated in a tense, potentially dangerous situation in which armed attacks were possible.

ONUCA's mandate expanded after the Nicaraguan election to include demobilizing the Contras. Bases were set up inside the borders of Nicaragua, where many rebel soldiers came and handed over some of their weapons and military equipment to ONUCA soldiers, who destroyed them and helped to advance demilitarization. In spite of the continued existence of arms among disgruntled partisans of both the Contra and the Sandinista causes, this was the first instance of UN involvement in demilitarization through the physical collection and destruction of armaments. This task is important for conflict resolution in areas where heavily armed regular as well as irregular forces need to be drastically reduced before any meaningful consultative process can occur. The collection of arms has been integrated into numerous subsequent UN peacekeeping operations and has been made even more rigorous.[5]

ONUVEN was created to ensure the fairness of elections in Nicaragua and is the first example of UN observation of elections inside a recognized state, an extraordinary intrusion according to conventional notions of domestic jurisdiction. It operated in tandem with ONUCA's soldiers, but ONUVEN consisted of some 120 civilian observers who monitored elections from start to finish to ensure that they were free and fair. These members of the second UN verified that political parties were equitably represented in the Supreme Electoral Council; that there was political, organizational, and operational freedom for all political parties; that all political parties had equal access to state television and radio broadcasts; and that the electoral rolls were drawn up fairly. It also reported any perceived unfairness to the Supreme Electoral Council, made recommendations about possible remedial action, and reported to the secretary-general.

Another unusual development was the extent to which the UN operations were linked with supporting efforts from regional and nongovernmental organizations.[6] The UN and the Organization of American States (OAS)—in particular, the secretaries-general of the UN and the OAS—cooperated closely in diplomacy and in civilian observation. During the Nicaraguan elections, a host of nongovernmental groups, such as former U.S. president Jimmy Carter's Council of Freely Elected Heads of Government, provided additional outside observers as part of a large international network. Nongovernmental organizations (NGOs) on the ground shaped the political dynamics and helped implement UN policies in many Central American peace operations.[7]

The operation began in August 1989 and ended in February 1990 with the surprising electoral defeat of the Sandinista government. ONUVEN's success—which was fortified by its links to the OAS and private groups—enhanced the prospects of UN election-monitoring teams working within the boundaries of states. This practice has gained wider international acceptance even when no armed conflict has taken place. For instance, from June 1990 to January 1991, the United Nations Observer Mission to Verify the Electoral Process in Haiti (ONUVEH) performed tasks similar to ONUVEN's missions in Nicaragua, which set the stage for subsequent UN action when the duly elected government of Jean-Bertrand Aristide was overthrown. ONUVEN's civilian composition changed the content of peacekeeping's definition by blurring the distinction between civilian and military operations and between security and human rights.

In El Salvador, ONUSAL was an essential element in helping to move beyond a decade of brutal civil war in which over seventy-five thousand people had been killed and serious human rights abuses had taken place. The government and rebel sides, and their foreign backers, came to a stalemate. This created the conditions for successful and creative UN mediation. Negotiations under the good offices of the UN secretary-general led to a detailed agreement on January 1, 1992, which was actually initialed a few hours after Javier Pérez de Cuéllar had completed his second five-year term.

An essential component of moving beyond the war was the use of UN civilian and military personnel in what, by historical standards, would have been seen as unacceptable outside interference in purely domestic affairs. Ongoing human rights abuses were to be prevented through an elaborate observation and monitoring system that began before an official cease-fire. Previous violations by both the army and the government as well as by the armed opposition, the Farabundo Marti National Liberation Front (FMLN), were to be investigated by a truth commission. The highly controversial findings—including the documentation of a former president's approval of a dissident archbishop's assassination and the incrimination of a sitting defense minister in other murders—served to clear the air. A second commission was also established to identify those military personnel who had committed major human rights violations.

In addition, ONUSAL personnel collected and destroyed weapons and helped oversee the creation of a new national army staff college, where students included former members of the armed opposition in addition to new recruits and members of the national army. Some of the early UN involvement on the ground in El Salvador took place even before the cease-fire was signed, thus putting UN observers at some risk.

MOVING TOWARD ENFORCEMENT

The creative adaptations by the UN's member states and civil servants are as important as the grand visions and long-term plans for international organizations. Political changes and crises occur, and then the United Nations reacts and adapts. Precedents are created that circumscribe what is possible later. UN actions in the Persian Gulf beginning in 1990 set important precedents relating to collective security, humanitarian actions, and sanctions.

On August 2, 1990, Iraqi armed forces swept past the border of neighboring Kuwait and quickly gained control of the tiny, oil-rich country. The invasion met with uniform condemnation in the United Nations, including the Security Council's first unequivocal statement about a breach of the peace since 1950 and the

Korean War. From early August until the end of the year, the Security Council passed twelve resolutions directed at securing Iraq's withdrawal from Kuwait. The council invoked Chapter VII, Articles 39–41, to lay the guidelines for the first post–Cold War enforcement action. Resolutions 661 of August 6 and 665 of August 25 called on member states to establish economic sanctions against Iraq and to militarily enforce them if necessary. Resolution 678 of November 29 authorized member states to use "all necessary means" to expel Iraq from Kuwait and thus represented a major shift in strategy. The organization's experience during the Persian Gulf War contains valuable lessons about the needs of a workable collective-security system for the future.

At Washington's insistence, the date of January 15, 1991, was negotiated as the deadline for Iraq to withdraw from Kuwait or else face the use of military force. Iraq remained in Kuwait past this date, and the U.S.-led coalition of twenty-eight states began military operations two days later.[8] A bombing campaign commenced, followed by a ground war one month later with about half a million U.S. military personnel. The coalition's victory reversed the Iraqi invasion and occupation at minimal cost in blood and treasure. It also placed the United Nations at the center of the international security stage.

Members of the Allied Coalition lost relatively few lives, but tens of thousands of Iraqi civilians and soldiers were killed, raising questions about the proportionality of UN-sponsored actions.[9] The Security Council's process of decision making and the conduct of the war have led some critics to be skeptical about the precise value of the Gulf War as a precedent for subsequent Chapter VII enforcement action.[10] Dominance by the United States, the decision to replace nonforcible sanctions with military force as the dominant means of ensuring Iraq's compliance with the organization's wishes, the extensive use of military means that ensued, and the UN's inability to command and control the operation are also concerns. Each of these criticisms raises serious questions about the ability of the UN's collective-security apparatus to function in a variety of contexts.

Criticisms of UN Involvement in the 1991 Gulf War

The first criticism of the Persian Gulf War—that the United States too easily employed the United Nations to rubber-stamp its own agenda—was a general criticism of geopolitics after the disappearance of the Soviet Union as a superpower. Washington used its influence to foster perceived national interests, creating and maintaining a diverse coalition against Iraq. The process by which the coalition was created illustrated the extent to which the political first UN had become a reflection of U.S. influence. The UN had never been a completely neutral arena: Western dominance in the early years had been partially replaced beginning in the 1960s by the Third World's "automatic majority" in the General Assembly, but not in the Security Council. Yet the United States was able to use its considerable political and economic clout in the Security Council to ensure that its Persian Gulf agenda was approved. Political concessions were provided to the Soviet Union to gain its approval for enforcement and to China for its abstentions (instead of vetoes). The United States promised financial aid and debt relief to a number of developing countries for their votes and withdrew aid commitments to Yemen in retribution for its opposing the use of force. This is the way a hegemonic power is supposed to operate, making the "side payments" necessary to get many other states to consent to what the hegemon desires.[11] Moreover, Kuwait, a member state of the UN, had been attacked by traditional means; the question of aggression or breach of the peace was clear.

A second criticism centers on how the nonforcible economic sanctions mandated by the Security Council were replaced by forcible military ones after only three months. According to Article 42, the Security Council may authorize force after all other means of settlement, and economic sanctions in particular, have proven inadequate. Yet the Security Council chose to use military force before the sanctions had had a chance to take full effect. Critics pointed out that in South Africa, by contrast, partial sanctions had not been discarded in favor of military force even though that country's racist policy had been condemned for decades. They also noted that Israel's expansion and continued occupation of territories from 1967 had not been met with either economic or military sanctions.

Sanctions can take a long time to work, and some doubt their efficacy as violence often continues and can even increase under a sanctions regime. Their use became widespread enough that David Cortright and George Lopez called the 1990s the "sanctions decade."[12] When economic sanctions were applied later to Haiti, some observers said military force should have been used earlier and would have caused less suffering. The record regarding the use of sanctions and military force suggests that the politics of the day determines a course of action and, ultimately, the sequence in which action occurs. For instance, the UN continued to use economic sanctions against Iraq after the end of formal military operations, and they were removed with UN approval after the U.S. invasion in 2003.

The third criticism of the handling of the 1991 Persian Gulf War is that no limits on the use of force were enacted, and that the world organization exerted no oversight of the U.S.-led military operation. According to the Charter, military enforcement operations are to be directed and controlled by the Military Staff Committee so that the UN can exercise control and military forces can be held accountable to the international community for their actions. As in Korea forty years earlier, command and control of the Gulf War was in the hands of the U.S.-led coalition forces. Only this time, in the Persian Gulf, there was no blue flag and no decision specifically authorizing the preponderant U.S. role. The Security Council was essentially a spectator, but U.S. leadership appeared necessary for reasons of efficiency as well as political support.

Resolution 678 authorized "all necessary means" and made no restrictions on what kind of, how much, and how long force could be used. According to critics, the United States had left with a blank check to pursue the expulsion of Iraq. Authorizations of this kind may run contrary to the Charter, especially as it relates to the delegation of its Chapter VII authority. Still, the Persian Gulf War provides the first example of the existing security apparatus in an enforcement action in

Members of the Security Council vote to use "all necessary means" to uphold its resolutions if Iraq does not withdraw from Kuwait by January 15, 1991. November 29, 1990, United Nations, New York. (UN PHOTO 31700/MILTON GRANT)

the post–Cold War era. Although the organization proved successful in achieving its stated objective—expelling Iraq from Kuwait—the way that this goal was achieved continues to be debated by diplomats, lawyers, and scholars. There was simply no alternative but to "delegate" to the twenty-eight members of the U.S.-led coalition. In view of the UN's limited capacities, such a procedure for enforcement seems inevitable for the foreseeable future.

Forceful Action in Northern Iraq on Behalf of Humanitarian Values

On April 5, 1991, the Security Council passed resolution 688. It declared that Saddam Hussein's repression of Kurdish and Shiite populations constituted a threat to international peace and security. It insisted that Iraq allow access to international relief organizations so that they could care for the beleaguered groups. Elite troops from the United States, the United Kingdom, France, and the Netherlands moved into Iraq—without explicit approval from the Security Council—and carved out a safe haven above the thirty-sixth parallel, which they guarded to ensure the security of UN relief operations. The council had already taken a broad view of its duty to protect human rights in Rhodesia and South Africa, but this resolution was a dramatic and straightforward linkage between human rights and international peace and security. The notion of human security inside states was much discussed in the corridors of the UN. In Iraq, the Hussein government eventually agreed to the presence of UN guards providing security to agencies working with Iraqi Kurds, but obviously under Western military pressure.

Many in the West applauded resolution 688 as a vigorous step toward enforcing human rights protection,[13] but others feared the precedent. "Who decides?" became a rallying cry for those, particularly in the Global South, who opposed granting the Security Council, dominated by Western foreign policy interests, the authority of Chapter VII to intervene for arguably humanitarian reasons. Later military responses with a humanitarian justification—in Somalia, Bosnia and Herzegovina, Rwanda, Haiti, Kosovo, and East Timor—served to keep the debate alive about the weight accorded state sovereignty relative to the international protection of human rights. The theme of humanitarian intervention reappears in later humanitarian crises, as does its reformulation as the "responsibility to protect" (R2P).[14]

SANCTIONS IN THE POST-COLD WAR ERA: HUMANITARIAN DILEMMAS

Economic sanctions have long been seen as a policy option to give teeth to international decisions. While UN-approved sanctions against Rhodesia and South Africa were exceptional, during the 1990s the Security Council resorted to them more than a dozen times. Partial or comprehensive sanctions were levied against Iraq, the states of the former Yugoslavia, Libya, Liberia, Somalia, Haiti, and Rwanda. Moreover, the council also imposed them on several nonstate actors, including the Khmer Rouge in Cambodia (when it was called Kampuchea), the National Union for the Total Independence of Angola (UNITA), and the Taliban in Afghanistan.

Sanctions pose three pertinent challenges. The first results from the nature of modern warfare as exemplified by the 1991 Persian Gulf War.[15] The Gulf crisis dramatizes the extent to which the international responses in modern armed conflicts can themselves do serious harm to innocent and powerless civilians. The political strategies adopted, the economic sanctions imposed, and the military force authorized by the Security Council not only created additional hardships but also complicated the ability of the UN's own humanitarian agencies to help civilians caught in the throes of conflict.

Before the Security Council decides on sanctions with potentially major humanitarian consequences, organizations with humanitarian competence and responsibilities should be consulted. Whether the impact is on citizens in the pariah country or elsewhere, the staff of the major entities of the second UN—the United Nations Children's Fund (UNICEF), the United Nations High Commissioner for Refugees (UNHCR), the World Health Organization (WHO), and the World Food Programme (WFP)—are well situated to warn against, anticipate, and monitor the consequences. Private humanitarian NGOs consult regularly with UN bodies and can provide detailed and specialized information on the humane impact of sanctions. Among these, the International Committee of the Red Cross (ICRC) usually has personnel on the ground as well as a reputation for accurate reporting.

In Iraq, the decision to use economic sanctions to force compliance with weapons inspections had damaging effects on women and children. The ICRC and a few other agencies reported on the looming crisis in the first half of the 1990s. UNICEF in 1999 found that 90,000 deaths occurred yearly in Iraq as a result of sanctions, and 5,000 children a month were dying.[16] The gender dimensions of sanctions are often overlooked, as women and girls tend to bear the brunt as they sacrifice their food rations for the male members of their families. If the Security Council decides to proceed, governments could provide resources to the UN system so that it could respond fully to the immediate and longer-term human consequences of sanctions.[17] These options clearly were not explored during the 1991 Persian Gulf crisis.

The second challenge is an eminently practical one. How long should a sanctions regime be maintained when it is clear that civilians are suffering? Resolution 688 insisted that Iraq provide the United Nations with humanitarian access to its people, a watershed for the UN.[18] Yet Iraq reacted negatively against assertive humanitarianism, creating havoc for UN and NGO efforts. International assistance flowed more easily to minority populations in revolt against Baghdad than to civilians in equal need in parts of the country under the central government's control. Eventually, the Security Council approved a program of allowing Iraq to sell oil to pay for food and other civilian needs, which in turn led to numerous abuses.

The third challenge relates to timing the deployment of UN military forces in conjunction with economic sanctions. The UN Charter assumes that nonforcible sanctions should be tried first; only when they fail should collective military action ensue. The suffering civilian populations of the former Yugoslavia and Haiti provided compelling reasons to rethink the conventional wisdom about sequencing. In the former Yugoslavia, vigorous and earlier preventive deployment of UN soldiers to Bosnia and Herzegovina (rather than just to Croatia, with a symbolic administrative presence in Sarajevo) might have obviated the later need for sanctions to pressure Belgrade and Serbian irregulars and might have prevented that grisly war. This reasoning justified in part the preventive positioning of UN observers as part of the United Nations Protection Force (UNPROFOR) in Macedonia in December 1992. In Haiti, some observers, with considerable reason, queried whether an earlier military enforcement action to restore an elected government would have entailed far less civilian suffering than extended economic sanctions did, particularly because the willingness to use such overwhelming force was visible in September 1994. In short, the reluctance to use force may not always be a good thing, if delay means that civilians suffer and aid agencies are projected into conflict as a substitute for military intervention.

OPERATIONAL QUANDARIES: CAMBODIA, THE FORMER YUGOSLAVIA, SOMALIA, RWANDA, AND HAITI

Several UN operations during the 1990s highlight the inadequacy of traditional peacekeeping to meet the challenges of the new world disorder. The UN Transitional Authority in Cambodia (UNTAC), the UN Protection Force in the former

Yugoslavia (UNPROFOR), the first and second UN Operations in Somalia (UN-OSOM I and II), the UN Assistance Mission in Rwanda (UNAMIR), and the UN Mission in Haiti (UNMIH) represent experiments by the world body to respond in new ways to different kinds of armed conflicts. These operations were qualitatively and quantitatively different from UN operations during the Cold War. The formal consent of the parties simply did not mean very much on the ground. The military effectiveness required from, and the dangers faced by, UN military forces went far beyond the parameters of traditional lightly armed peacekeepers. Moreover, these operations suggest the magnitude of the new demands on the UN for services that threatened to overwhelm troop contributors and to break the bank. If classic peacekeeping was said to be based on Chapter "VI.5," these new field operations could be considered part of Chapter "VI.9"—that is, very close to the war-fighting orientation of Chapter VII. Indeed, a criticism waged later by David Rieff was that the gentle vocabulary—especially the word *humanitarian*—sugarcoated the reality that these efforts were ugly and constituted war.[19]

After stable levels of about ten thousand troops and a budget of a few hundred million dollars in the early post–Cold War period, the numbers jumped rapidly. In the mid-1990s, seventy to eighty thousand blue-helmeted soldiers were authorized by the UN's annualized peacekeeping budget, which approached $4 billion in 1995. Accumulated total arrears in these years hovered around $3.5 billion—almost equal to this budget and approaching three times the regular UN budget. The roller-coaster ride continued between 1996 and 1998, when both the number of soldiers and the budget dropped precipitously by two thirds, at least partially reflecting the world organization's overextension and administrative indigestion. It changed again in the new millennium as police efforts in Kosovo and military ones in East Timor and the Congo began. Throughout, arrears remained at a critical level, and the world organization's cash reserves often covered barely one month's expenditures.

What exactly were the operational quandaries? The Cambodian operation amounted to the UN's taking over all of the important civilian administration of the country while simultaneously disarming guerrillas and governmental armed forces. The UN registered most of the nation's citizens for the first democratic election in the country's history. The UNTAC deployment was based—as are most UN undertakings—on national budgetary projections out of touch with real military requirements. These estimates were based on best-case scenarios; the situation on the ground was closer to worst-case ones.

Japan's desire—sustained in part by U.S. and other pressures—to make a large contribution to this operation in its own region, despite its postwar pacifist constitution, was important. Despite many problems and sometimes fatal attacks on its personnel, Japan stayed the course in Cambodia—in part because it was urged to do so by Yasushi Akashi, a Japanese national who was head of the UN operation in that country. Also, Japan wanted to prove that it deserved a seat on an expanded Security Council, which provided another reason for its larger role in UN security policy.

United Nations Transitional Authority in Cambodia (UNTAC) military observers distributing radios donated by Japanese nongovernmental organizations. UNTAC used radio to convey information about an upcoming election, scheduled for May 1993. August 1, 1992, Kompong Speu, Cambodia. (UN PHOTO 121634/PERNACA SUDHAKARAN)

Years of internal conflict had left Cambodia's infrastructure devastated and its population displaced. In response, the United Nations invested over $1.6 billion and over twenty-two thousand military and civilian personnel. Yet UNTAC's success was hardly a foregone conclusion, particularly in light of the Khmer Rouge's unwillingness to respect key elements of agreements and Prince Norodom Sihanouk's stated position that the peace process and elections should continue with or without the Khmer Rouge. Failure here could have seriously undermined the confidence of member states attempting an undertaking of this scale or complexity elsewhere.

The May 1993 elections were a turning point. A Khmer Rouge attack on a UN fuel and ammunition dump three weeks before the elections exposed how inadequately prepared UN soldiers were to resist even symbolic military maneuvers, let alone a return to full-scale civil war. However, the elections were held and returned Prince Sihanouk to power as the head of a coalition that included the former government and part of the opposition—but excluded the Khmer Rouge. The UN's achievement was that the Cambodian people struggled for power for the first time by means of a secret ballot.

The former Yugoslavia was the UN's first military operation on European soil after many years in which armed conflicts seemed to be an exclusive monopoly of the Global South. The violent dissolution of the former Yugoslavia caused a human displacement of a magnitude not seen in Europe since World War II. The region was plagued by warring factions, ethnic cleansing, detention camps, refugees, killing, systematic rape, and other atrocities committed by all sides. The UN's initial security involvement in Croatia, with close to fourteen thousand peacekeepers, achieved some objectives, such as implementing the cease-fire between Croatia and the Yugoslav Federation. The UNPROFOR mandate was expanded to neighboring Bosnia and Herzegovina in part to alleviate the human suffering and ensure the delivery of humanitarian assistance to Muslims and Croats under siege from Serbia and Serbian militias.

The 1,500 UN soldiers initially assigned to the Sarajevo area quickly proved inadequate. The Security Council later authorized adding 8,000 soldiers to protect humanitarian convoys and to escort detainees in Bosnia and Herzegovina. The United Nations also asked NATO to enforce a no-fly zone for Serbian aircraft. The secretary-general insisted that these additional humanitarian soldiers be provided at no cost to the world organization, and NATO countries responded affirmatively. U.S. airdrops of food to isolated and ravaged Muslim communities, while largely symbolic, helped saved lives. Yet these efforts were insufficient to halt the bloodshed or inhibit the carving up of Bosnia and Herzegovina by the Serbs and Croats.

After months of efforts by the UN special envoy, former U.S. secretary of state Cyrus Vance, and the European Community's mediator, former British foreign minister David Owen, a tenuous plan to create a "Swiss-like" set of ten semi-autonomous ethnic enclaves within Bosnia and Herzegovina was finally agreed by the belligerents. The Vance-Owen plan was undermined almost immediately by renewed Serbian and Croatian military offensives; by 1993 Serbia controlled 70 percent of the territory, and Croatia held 20 percent. The Bosnian Muslims were left with what were ironically called UN safe areas, which were anything but safe, as these areas were systematically attacked.

The situation in the Balkans deteriorated and demonstrated that the first and second UN can provide the means for governments to pretend to be doing something without really doing very much at all. There was a shift from Chapter VI to Chapter VII operations, but without the necessary political will or military wherewithal to make the shift work. Given their traditional operating procedures and constraints, UN soldiers were not strong enough to deter the Serbs. But they did deter the first UN from more assertive political and military intervention under Chapter VII because UN troops, along with humanitarian workers, were vulnerable targets. Assistance to refugees saved lives but also helped foster ethnic cleansing by cooperating in the forced movement of unwanted populations.

The initial UN response was followed by a steadily growing number of additional UN troops that, although mainly from NATO countries, were also feeble. No-fly zones were imposed but not fully enforced; other forms of saber rattling, including low-altitude sorties over Serbian positions and warnings about possible retaliatory air strikes, were tried; and the Security Council passed what the *Economist* called "the confetti of paper resolutions."[20] As Lawrence Freedman observed at the time, the Security Council "experimented with almost every available form of coercion short of war."[21] UN token measures did little to halt Serbian irredentism and consolidation of territory in either Croatia or Bosnia, nor did these measures prevent the initial expansion of Croatian claims in Bosnia. The UN mandatory arms embargo instituted in September 1991 had benefited primarily the Serbs, who controlled the bulk of the military hardware of the former Yugoslav army. UN soldiers were powerless to deter the Serbs, and the vulnerability of UN "protectors" was regularly invoked by Europeans as a rationale *against* more forceful military measures.

The idea of "safe areas" brought derision because, with only slight hyperbole, the least safe places in the Balkans were under UN control. In summer 1995, two of these safe areas in eastern Bosnia were overrun by Bosnian Serbs. Srebrenica, a Muslim enclave, was the scene of the largest massacre in Europe since 1945, where some eight thousand men and boys were systematically executed. Srebrenica had been designated a UN safe haven after the UN brokered an agreement between Muslims and Serbs to disarm the enclave in return for UN protection against Serb forces. The agreement provided a modicum of safety for a time, but as the political and military situation in Bosnia deteriorated, the Serbs moved against the "safe haven." Bosnian Muslim fighters also used Srebrenica as a base for staging attacks on Serb forces outside. The outgunned UN peacekeeping unit withdrew from Srebrenica (after the death of one Dutch soldier), leaving its inhabitants vulnerable to the advancing Serb forces, whose known tactics included mass execution, systematic rape, and forced expulsion. Shortly before this horrific incident, Serbs had chained UN blue helmets to strategic targets to prevent NATO air raids.[22] Srebrenica became a conversation stopper in UN circles. UN peacekeepers in Croatia were unable to implement their mandate because they received no cooperation from the Croats or Krajina Serbs. In Bosnia, UN forces were under Chapter VII but lacked the capability to apply coercive force across a wide front. Shortly before resigning in January 1994 from a soldier's nightmare as UN commander in Bosnia, Lt. Gen. Francis Briquemont lamented the disparity between rhetoric and reality: "There is a fantastic gap between the resolutions of the Security Council, the will to execute those resolutions, and the means available to commanders in the field."[23]

The first UN was unwilling to authorize or supply sufficient military might in the former Yugoslavia until August 1995. The inaction left many of the inhabitants of the region mistrustful of the United Nations and lent a new and disgraceful connotation to the word *peacekeeping*. Bound by the traditional rules of engagement (fire only in self-defense and only after being fired upon), UN troops never fought a single battle with any of the factions in Bosnia that routinely disrupted relief convoys. The rules of engagement led to the appeasement of local forces rather than to the enforcement of UN mandates.

A much heavier dose of NATO's bombing and U.S. arm-twisting proved necessary to compel the belligerents, sequestered at Ohio's Wright-Patterson Air Force Base in November 1995, to reach a political settlement. The Dayton peace agreements laid the groundwork for military deployment by almost sixty thousand NATO soldiers, one third from the United States, in the International Force (IFOR). The deployment of NATO-led peacekeepers and the creation of a police force served to stabilize Bosnia-Herzegovina. However, such a large military deployment was accompanied by additional problems. Bosnia-Herzegovina became a center of human trafficking into Western Europe and the locus of an active sex industry. UN officials were accused of corruption, facilitating the trafficking, and looking the other way regarding the behavior of many peacekeepers, despite a trio of former staff members' exposure of stunning details of several operations that tarnished the image of UN personnel in the Balkans.[24] In fact, the sexual behavior of peacekeepers has become one of the more serious issues facing current UN peace operations.[25]

Somalia provided another complicated challenge for UN involvement in internal wars with the breakdown in local governance, or "complex emergencies." Like Bosnia, Somalia was an example of violent fragmentation, yet, unlike Bosnia, one without an ethnic logic. In Somalia, a single ethnic group sharing the same religion, history, and language split into heavily armed clans. Somalia had no government in any meaningful sense, and one third of the population risked death from starvation because the violence prevented humanitarian aid workers from reaching the needy.

In August 1992, the Security Council authorized three to four thousand UN soldiers (UNOSOM I) to protect the delivery of humanitarian assistance to Somalia under Chapter VII. While the council made formal reference to Chapter VII, quiet diplomacy obtained the consent of the leading clans for deployment of UN force. That force was directed initially not against clan leaders but against bandits interfering with relief. The most important delivery point for relief was not a UN agency but rather the private International Committee of the Red Cross. UNHCR in particular had retired to the sidelines in neighboring Kenya while awaiting the end of hostilities.

In December 1992, the lame-duck president George H. W. Bush moved vigorously to propose a U.S.-led humanitarian intervention. Within days of the passage of Security Council resolution 794, the first of what would become over twenty-seven thousand U.S. troops arrived to provide a modicum of security to help sustain civilians. They were augmented by ten thousand soldiers from twenty-two other countries. This effort was labeled Operation Restore Hope from the American side, or the Unified Task Force (UNITAF), an acronym that reflected the Security Council's authorization to use force to ensure the delivery of humanitarian relief. UNITAF was always under U.S. operational command. With virtually no casualties, humanitarian space was created, and modest disarming of local bandits began.

UNITAF ceased operations in April 1993, when the second phase of the UN Operation in Somalia began as authorized by Security Council resolution 814. The secretary-general, for the second time, directly commanded a military force deployed under Chapter VII. The Security Council authorized UNOSOM II under

Chapter VII to use whatever force was necessary to disarm Somali warlords who refused to surrender their arms and to ensure access to suffering civilians. At its maximum strength, some twenty thousand soldiers and eight thousand logistical troops from thirty-three countries were deployed.

Almost three thousand civilian officials were expected to take over the administration of the country. Significantly, the United States initially remained on the ground with logistics troops for the first time under the command of a UN general—who was an officer from a NATO country, Turkey. Another thirteen hundred soldiers, including four hundred Army Rangers, were held in reserve as a "rapid-reaction force" in boats offshore. These units were strictly under U.S. command.

In retaliation against attacks on UN peacekeepers and aid personnel, U.S. Cobra helicopter gunships were called in by the UN command in June and July 1993 against the armed supporters of one of the main belligerents, General Mohammed Aideed. These attacks were followed by the arrival of U.S. Army Rangers later in the summer. These violent flare-ups put the UN in the awkward position of retaliation, which elicited more violence. The assassination of foreign journalists and aid workers and further attacks on U.S. troops—including the ugly scene in October 1993, when the body of a dead Ranger was dragged by crowds through the streets of Mogadishu in front of television cameras—further inflamed the situation. Washington blamed the UN for the deaths of U.S. soldiers. This questionable blame game led to a "Somalia syndrome" whereby the Pentagon would balk at any further association with a UN multilateral operation.

The U.S. military involvement in the Horn of Africa is criticized on numerous grounds. First, the military was obsessed with the capture of Aideed, which resembled a Wild West hunt, complete with a wanted poster. Hunting a single individual in a foreign and unforgiving land can be demoralizing for troops. Second, the United States was slow to engage in disarmament and nation building. A striking disequilibrium between the military and humanitarian components existed as the costs of Operation Restore Hope alone, at $1 billion, amounted to three times the U.S. total aid contribution to Somalia since independence. Seven months of UNOSOM II in 1993 were estimated to cost $1.5 billion, of which the lowest estimate for humanitarian aid was 0.7 percent of the total and the highest, 10 percent.[26] Also, as UN objectives expanded, resources were actually reduced.

When the last UN soldiers pulled out of Somalia in March 1995, the impact of military and humanitarian help was unclear. Three years and some $4 billion had left the warring parties better armed, rested, and poised to resume civil war. But the worst starvation had been brought under control. Today Somalia remains without a viable national government, although concerted diplomatic efforts continue. It is a haven for extremists and now also known for its pirates, who hijack commercial ships and luxury yachts in the Indian Ocean.

An even worse horror story developed simultaneously in East Africa, where long-standing social tensions within Rwanda led to the genocide of some eight hundred thousand people, mainly of Rwanda's Tutsi minority. The genocide was instigated by extremists who rallied the Hutu majority to turn on their Tutsi neighbors. UN peacekeeping forces (UNAMIR) had been present in Kigali for about eight months prior to the genocide. The mandate was to facilitate the Arusha Peace Accord, which was designed to end the Rwandan civil war between the Hutu-dominated government and the Tutsi rebels, the Rwandan Patriotic Front (RPF), who were based in neighboring Uganda and had unsuccessfully tried to capture power a few years earlier. Following the downing of the president's plane under suspicious circumstances, the genocide commenced on April 6, 1994, and within a week over fifty thousand Tutsis were murdered. On April 16, the Hutu extremists mutilated and killed ten Belgian UN peacekeepers. The Belgian government ordered its troops home, and the UN Security Council dramatically cut the UN peacekeeping force, leaving only a token mission. This reduction came in spite of the previous request of the Canadian commander of the blue helmets, Roméo Dallaire, for an augmented force and a warning that genocide was planned by Hutu extremists. As the UN withdrew, the Hutu extremists committed slaughter unimpeded, killing even the Tutsis and moderate Hutus who were under UN protection. As the scale of the killings became more widely known, the Security Council wrestled with whether the killings constituted genocide.[27] Members refrained from calling it genocide because such a designation might have a corresponding legal obligation to act. Ironically, Rwanda was seated on the Security Council as one of the nonpermanent members, and sadly, no other members asked Rwanda to explain the killings. The genocide ended as the rebel Tutsi army (the RPF) invaded from neighboring Burundi and overthrew the Hutu government.

The Security Council now found itself "gravely concerned," as two million persons were displaced within Rwanda, while another 2 million refugees, mostly Hutus, fled into neighboring states. The council authorized two stand-alone initiatives. First, following an announcement by Paris that it was planning on intervening, the council passed resolution 929 under Chapter VII authorizing the French-led Opération Turquoise to stabilize the southwestern part of the country. One effect was that the French used their presence to protect their Hutu allies and their families (who were now refugees in dire need of international assistance after having been favored by French assistance for a number of years) from the invading Tutsi army, despite Hutu participation in the genocide. Second, the UN authorized a massive two-month logistics effort through the U.S. operation Support Hope in July and August to provide relief to the Hutu refugees in the Goma region of Zaire. Numerous national contingents also deployed to this region in support of the assistance efforts by the UNHCR. Arguably, Opération Turquoise prevented another refugee crisis of the record-setting magnitude of the one in May in Goma, where almost a million Rwandan refugees appeared virtually overnight, but it also protected many members of the former regime who had participated in the killings. The crisis was accompanied by a cholera epidemic that is estimated to have killed between fifty and eighty thousand people.[28]

Massive amounts of food, clothing, medicine, shelter, and water were delivered. Outside armed forces thus made essential contributions by using their unexcelled logistical and organizational resources, but only after the genocide had occurred. Rapid military action in April proved totally unfeasible, but the costs of the genocide, massive displacement, and a ruined economy (including decades of wasted development assistance and outside investment) were borne almost immediately afterward by the same governments that had refused to respond militarily a few weeks earlier. The refugee camps established by the UNHCR in Goma and elsewhere after the genocide were militarized: they were taken over by the Hutu extremists, who had established themselves there and used them as military bases to launch attacks against Tutsis in Rwanda. The inability of the second UN to control the refugee camps and the repeated attacks by Hutu extremists from the Congo prompted Rwanda to invade the Congo, sparking an African "world war" involving nine nations and what may be 5 million deaths,[29] although that figure has been disputed and may be closer to 1 million.[30]

The UN's response to the Rwandan genocide stands as one of its greatest acknowledged failures. Several years later, Secretary-General Kofi Annan, who had been in charge of the UN's peacekeeping department in New York during the crisis, felt compelled during a visit to Kigali to confess, "We must and we do acknowledge that the world failed Rwanda at that time of evil. The international community and the United Nations could not muster the political will to confront it."[31] A later statement continued, "There was a United Nations force in the country at the time, but it was neither mandated nor equipped for the kind of forceful action which would have been needed to prevent or halt the genocide. On behalf of the United Nations, I acknowledge this failure and express my deep remorse."[32] It was Annan who had "buried" the cable from General Dallaire asking for a proactive role to head off the mass murder.[33] In his mind at the time, Annan was acting to save the second UN from controversy, but Rwandans paid the price.

Meanwhile in the Caribbean, nine months after the United Nations had overseen the first democratic elections in Haiti, the populist priest Jean-Bertrand Aristide was overthrown by a military junta led by General Raoul Cédras. This is interesting for a number of reasons. Although Haiti had not really endured a civil war, it had all the attributes of a failed state—in particular, political instability, widespread poverty, massive emigration, and human rights abuses. It also became the target of international coercive actions—that is, both nonforcible and forcible sanctions under Chapter VII of the UN Charter similar to those in the other war-torn countries analyzed earlier. However, the basis for outside intervention was the restoration of a democratically elected government. This precedent has widespread potential implications because of its relevance for other countries in political crises.

Multilateral military forces were essential to the solution that ultimately resulted in late 1994. First, however, came the embarrassing performance of the initial UN Mission in Haiti (UNMIH I), including the retreat by the USS *Harlan County*, which carried unarmed American and Canadian military observers, in September 1993 following a rowdy demonstration on the docks in Port-au-Prince. In September 1994, the first soldiers of the UN-authorized and U.S.-led

Members of the Jordanian battalion of the United Nations Stabilization Mission in Haiti rescue children from an orphanage destroyed by Hurricane Ike.
(UN PHOTO 192376/MARCO DORMINO)

Multinational Force (MNF) landed in Haiti on the basis of Security Council resolution 940. What Pentagon wordsmiths labeled Operation Uphold Democracy grew quickly to twenty-one thousand troops—almost all American except for one thousand police and soldiers from twenty-nine countries, mostly from the eastern Caribbean. This operation ensured the rapid departure into comfortable exile of the illegal military regime and the restoration of the elected government.

The MNF was prepared to use overwhelming military force—although it did not have to: only a single military person was killed in action, and the local population was almost universally supportive—to accomplish two important tasks with clear humanitarian impacts. First and most immediately, the MNF brought an end to the punishing economic sanctions that had crippled the local economy and penalized Haiti's most vulnerable groups. Second, the MNF established a secure and stable environment that stemmed the tide of asylum seekers, facilitated the rather expeditious repatriation of about 370,000 of them, and immediately stopped the worst human rights abuses. Once the MNF achieved its goals at the end of March 1995, the next UN Mission in Haiti (UNMIH II) took over, which was replaced by the even smaller UN Support Mission in Haiti (UNSMIH) in July 1996. A small UN presence was continued for the remainder of the decade.

Yet a decade after the initial intervention and in spite of subsequent stabilization missions, Haiti was still characterized by political instability, violence, kidnapping, and widespread poverty. The United Nations returned to the island nation in 2004, in response to armed conflict between Aristide and his opponents, who after taking control of the northern part of the country threatened to march on the capital, Port-au-Prince. With Aristide's flight into exile in Africa in February 2004, and following the interim president's request, the Security Council authorized an MNF led by the United States, which was followed up by the 7,500-strong UN Stabilization Mission in Haiti (MINUSTAH). Armed gangs, probably working in tandem with certain political factions, actually killed some blue helmets. Under the stress of the action, their Brazilian commander apparently took his own life.

The stabilization mission did little to improve the police and judiciary or alter the fundamental economic situation. The disparity in the distribution of wealth and power between a tiny elite and the vast majority of the population made Haiti one of the world's most polarized societies; this inequality had led to the rise and fall of Aristide. In 2010 the misery and impoverishment of the Haitian people were further exacerbated by the 7.0-magnitude earthquake that leveled much of the island nation, killing over three hundred thousand people and leaving over 1 million homeless.

As in other military interventions for humanitarian or other purposes, the initial perception that the interests of key states were threatened spurred leadership and risk taking. The location of this crisis brought into prominence not just the United States but also Canada and several Caribbean countries. Washington was and is particularly anxious to end the perceived "flood" of boat people upsetting the demographics and politics of such places as south Florida and Louisiana. The success of the military deployment was dramatic, notwithstanding that it was authorized to restore democracy rather than respond to a complex emergency. Both the U.S. Congress and the Pentagon were initially lukewarm about what turned out to be a successful operation in the short term.

The most significant feature of the international responses just discussed has been the willingness to address, rather than ignore, fundamental problems within the borders of war-torn states—at least at times. As the UN Development Programme (UNDP) calculated, eighty-two armed conflicts broke out in the first half decade following the collapse of the Berlin Wall, and seventy-nine were intrastate wars; in fact, two of the three remaining ones (Nagorno-Karabakh and Bosnia) also could legitimately have been categorized as civil wars.[34] But trying to put a lid on civil wars is not the same as a persistent effort to deal with their root causes. Having gone from famine to feast in the mid-1990s, the second United Nations had a bad case of institutional indigestion.

LESSONS LEARNED

What lessons emerged for the United Nations from security operations after the Cold War, from 1988 to 1998? These operations represent a qualitatively different kind of peace mission from the world organization's previous experiments. UN efforts in Cambodia and El Salvador were ambitious, complex, and multidisciplinary. They represent the first UN attempts at creating or re-creating civil order and respecting the rule of law where governance and stability had either broken down or been nonexistent. They entail reconstructing the social and economic infrastructure, building democratic political institutions, providing humanitarian assistance, and much more. This task expansion changed the character of the humanitarian agencies and led to much soul searching.[35]

"Learning by doing" seems the order of the day. Not to act seems unthinkable to many, especially in light of Srebrenica and Rwanda. But how to act remains uncertain in an ever-evolving international environment. In the twenty-first century we can conceive of traditional peacekeeping and complex peacekeeping, both operating under Chapter VI of the Charter, as well as additional tasks that come close to war fighting and Chapter VII. Traditional peacekeeping is primarily neutral interposition to supervise cease-fire lines and other military demarcations. Complex peacekeeping involves a range of tasks mostly intended to move post-conflict or failed states toward a liberal democratic order.[36] In such places as the Balkans, the UN has attempted no less than to change an illiberal region into a liberal one—on a stable, permanent basis.

The two dominant norms of world politics during the Cold War—namely, that borders were sacrosanct and that secession was unthinkable—no longer generate the enthusiasm that they once did, even among states. At the same time, an almost visceral respect for nonintervention in the internal affairs of states has made way for a more subtle interpretation, according to which on occasion the rights of individuals take precedence over the rights of repressive governments and the sovereign states they represent.

Until early in 1993, the dominant perception of outside intervention under UN auspices was largely positive. The United Nations seemed on a roll, first by reversing Iraq's aggression against Kuwait, followed closely by the dramatic life-saving activities by the U.S.-led coalitions in northern Iraq and initially in Somalia. The UN was successful in Central America, especially El Salvador. In spite of the lack of resolve, Bosnia showed that world politics had evolved to the point where governments and insurgents would no longer be allowed to commit abuses with impunity. The emphasis on protecting persons inside states led the UN, particularly the second and third UN, to a focus on human security. This focus coexists alongside the older notion of traditional interstate military security.[37]

NOTES

1. Thomas G. Weiss and Meryl A. Kessler, "Moscow's U.N. Policy," *Foreign Policy* no. 79 (Summer 1990): 94–112; Thomas G. Weiss and Meryl A. Kessler, eds., *Third World Security in the Post–Cold War Era* (Boulder, Colo.: Lynne Rienner, 1991); Thomas G. Weiss and James G. Blight, eds., *The Suffering Grass: Superpowers and Regional Conflict in Southern Africa and the Caribbean* (Boulder, Colo.: Lynne Rienner, 1992); and G. R. Berridge, *Return to the UN* (London: Macmillan, 1991).

2. Gorbachev's 1988 comments about the war can be found in "The Soviet Occupation of Afghanistan," *Afghanistan and the War on Terror, PBS NewsHour*, October 10, 2006, http://www.pbs.org/newshour/indepth_coverage/asia/afghanistan/soviet.html.

3. An indication of the growing importance of this phenomenon is a publication from the Center on International Cooperation, *Annual Review of Global Peace Operations*, which was first published in 2006.

4. Tom J. Farer, ed., *Beyond Sovereignty: Collectively Defending Democracy in the Americas* (Baltimore: Johns Hopkins University Press, 1996); David P. Forsythe, "Human Rights and International Security: United Nations Field Operations Redux," in *The Role of the Nation-State in the 21st Century: Human Rights, International Organisations, and Foreign Policy: Essays in Honor of Peter Baehr*, ed. Monique Castermans-Holleman, Fried van Hoof, and Jacqueline Smith (The Hague: Kluwer Law International, 1998), 265–276.

5. Mats R. Berdal, *Disarmament and Demobilisation After Civil Wars* (Oxford: Oxford University Press, 1996).

6. Rodrigo Tavares, *Regional Security: The Capacity of International Organizations* (London: Routledge, 2010); and Monica Herz, *The Organization of American States: Global Governance Away from the Media* (London: Routledge, 2011).

7. S. Neil MacFarlane and Thomas G. Weiss, "The United Nations, Regional Organizations, and Human Security: Building Theory in Central America," *Third World Quarterly* 15, no. 2 (1994): 277–295; Laura MacDonald, "Globalising Civil Society: Interpreting International NGOs in Central America," *Millennium* 23, no. 2 (1994): 267–285.

8. Washington's shift to forcible liberation occurred just after U.S. congressional elections. The Senate approved of the new strategy by only five votes, which almost led to a constitutional crisis in the United States over war powers.

9. Oscar Schachter, "United Nations Law in the Gulf Conflict," and Burns H. Weston, "Security Council Resolution 678 and Persian Gulf Decision Making: Precarious Legitimacy," *American Journal of International Law* 85, no. 3 (1991): 452–473, 516.

10. Stephen Lewis, Clovis Maksoud, and Robert C. Johansen, "The United Nations After the Gulf War," *World Policy Journal* 8, no. 3 (1991): 539–574.

11. Robert J. Lieber, ed., *Eagle Rules: Foreign Policy and American Primacy in the Twenty-First Century* (Upper Saddle River, N.J.: Prentice-Hall, 2002), chap. 1.

12. David Cortright and George A. Lopez, *The Sanctions Decade: Assessing UN Strategies in the 1990s* (Boulder, Colo.: Lynne Rienner, 2000); and David Cortright and George A. Lopez, *Sanctions and the Search for Security: Challenges to UN Action* (Boulder, Colo.: Lynne Rienner, 2002).

13. Mario Bettati and Bernard Kouchner, *Le Devoir d'ingérence* (Paris: De Noël, 1987).

14. International Commission on Intervention and State Sovereignty, *The Responsibility to Protect* (Ottawa: ICISS, 2001). For a view about the dangers, see Robert Jackson, *The Global Covenant: Human Conduct in a World of States* (Oxford: Oxford University Press, 1998).

15. Larry Minear and Thomas G. Weiss, "Groping and Coping in the Gulf Crisis: Discerning the Shape of a New Humanitarian Order," *World Policy Journal* 9, no. 4 (1992): 755–777.

16. UNICEF, "Results of the 1999 Iraq Child and Maternal Mortality Survey," July 23, 1999, http://www.unicef.org/newsline/99pr29.htm.

17. Richard Jolly and Ralph van der Hoeven, eds., "Adjustment with a Human Face—Record and Relevance," special issue, *World Development* 19, no. 12 (1991). For general

discussions, see Lori Fisler Damrosch, "The Civilian Impact of Economic Sanctions," in *Enforcing Restraint: Collective Intervention in Internal Conflicts*, ed. Lori Fisler Damrosch (New York: Council on Foreign Relations, 1993), 274–315; and Patrick Clawson, "Sanctions as Punishment, Enforcement, and Prelude to Further Action," *Ethics & International Affairs* 7 (1993): 17–37.

18. Jarat Chopra and Thomas G. Weiss, "Sovereignty Is No Longer Sacrosanct: Codifying Humanitarian Intervention," *Ethics & International Affairs* 6 (1992): 95–117; and David J. Scheffer, "Toward a Modern Doctrine of Humanitarian Intervention," *University of Toledo Law Review* 23, no. 2 (1992): 253–293.

19. David Rieff, *At the Point of a Gun: Democratic Dreams and Armed Intervention* (New York: Simon & Schuster, 2006).

20. "In Bosnia's Fog," *Economist*, April 23, 1994, 16.

21. Lawrence Freedman, "Why the West Failed," *Foreign Policy* 97 (Winter 1994–1995): 59.

22. Netherlands Institute for War Documentation, *Srebrenica, a "Safe" Area: Reconstruction, Background, Consequences, and Analyses of the Fall of a Safe Area* (Amsterdam: Boom Publishers, 2002); Jan Willem Honig and Norbert Both, *Srebrenica: Record of a War Crime* (London: Penguin, 1996); and David Rohde, *Endgame: The Betrayal and Fall of Srebrenica* (Boulder, Colo.: Westview, 1998).

23. "U.N. Bosnia Commander Wants More Troops, Fewer Resolutions," *New York Times*, December 31, 1993.

24. Kenneth Cain, Heidi Postlewait, and Andrew Thomson, *Emergency Sex and Other Desperate Measures: A True Story from Hell on Earth* (New York: Hyperion, 2004).

25. UN General Assembly, *A Comprehensive Strategy to Eliminate Future Sexual Exploitation and Abuse in United Nations Peacekeeping Operations*, UN document A/59/710, March 24, 2005.

26. Debarati G. Sapir and Hedwig Deconinck, "The Paradox of Humanitarian Assistance and Military Intervention in Somalia," in *The United Nations and Civil Wars*, ed. Thomas G. Weiss (Boulder, Colo.: Lynne Rienner, 1995), 168.

27. See "The Triumph of Evil," *PBS Frontline*, January 26, 1999, http://www.pbs.org/wgbh/pages/frontline/shows/evil.

28. Larry Minear and Philippe Guillot, *Soldiers to the Rescue: Humanitarian Lessons from Rwanda* (Paris: OECD, 1996); Gérard Prunier, *The Rwanda Crisis: History of a Genocide* (New York: Columbia University Press, 1995); Joint Evaluation of Emergency Assistance to Rwanda, *The International Response to Conflict and Genocide: Lessons from the Rwandan Experience*, 5 vols. (Copenhagen: Joint Evaluation of Emergency Assistance to Rwanda, 1995).

29. Sadako Ogata asked the Security Council to control the Hutu militia in the refugee camps, but the members lacked the necessary fortitude for a proper response. Ogata then contracted with Zaire, as it then was, to provide security in the camps—less than an ideal solution. See Sadako Ogata, *The Turbulent Decade: Confronting the Refugee Crisis of the 1990s* (New York: W. W. Norton, 2005), chap. 3.

30. The Human Security Report Project, *Miniatlas of Human Security* (Brighton: UK Myriad Editions, 2008), 13.

31. Kofi Annan, Address to the Parliament of Rwanda, Kigali, May 7, 1998, document SG/SM/6552.

32. Kofi Annan, "Statement on Receiving the Report of the Independent Inquiry into the Actions of the United Nations During the 1994 Genocide in Rwanda," United Nations, New York, December 16, 1999.

33. Roméo Dallaire, *Shake Hands with the Devil: The Failure of Humanity in Rwanda* (Toronto: Brent Beardsley, 2004). See further Michael N. Barnett, *Eyewitness to a Genocide: The United Nations and Rwanda* (Ithaca, N.Y.: Cornell University Press, 2002); and the UN's own hard-hitting report from an independent inquiry, available at http://www.un.org/Docs/journal/asp/ws.asp?m=S/1999/1257.

34. United Nations Development Programme, *Human Development Report 1994* (New York: Oxford University Press, 1994), 47.

35. Michael Barnett, "Humanitarianism Transformed," *Perspectives on Politics* 3, no. 4 (2005): 723–740; and Janice Stein, "Humanitarianism as Political Fusion," *Perspectives on Politics* 3, no. 4 (2005): 740–744.

36. Forsythe, "Human Rights and International Security."

37. Rob McRae and Don Hubert, eds., *Human Security and the New Diplomacy: Protecting People, Promoting Peace* (Montreal: McGill-Queen's University Press, 2001). See also S. Neil MacFarlane and Yuen Foong Khong, *Human Security and the UN: A Critical History* (Bloomington: Indiana University Press, 2006).

CHAPTER 4

Security Operations Since 1999

THE RESPONSIBILITY TO PROTECT

An interesting lens through which to examine normative and operational change emerging from ongoing UN security operations is the development of the responsibility to protect (R2P). In 2001 the International Commission on Intervention and State Sovereignty (ICISS) issued *The Responsibility to Protect*, which provides a snapshot of issues surrounding nonconsensual international military action to foster humanitarian values.[1] The ICISS was responding to two sets of events. The first were several moral pleas in 1999 from the future Nobel laureate, UN secretary-general Kofi Annan, who argued that human rights concerns transcended claims of sovereignty, a theme that he put forward more delicately a year later at the Millennium Summit.[2] The reaction was loud, bitter, and predictable, especially from China, Russia, and throughout the Global South. "Intervention"—for whatever reasons, including humanitarian—remained taboo.[3] The second set of events concerned the weak, untimely, and inadequate reactions by the Security Council in Rwanda and the Balkans. In both cases, the Security Council was unable to act expeditiously and authorize the use of military force to protect vulnerable populations. The role of humanitarian concerns as a possible exception to the general prohibition on the threat and use of military force is one of the most salient dimensions of contemporary UN security operations.

The ICISS report encapsulated three conceptual developments. First, and most critically, R2P infused state sovereignty with a human rights dimension—that is, sovereignty was not a license to do as state authorities wished but was contingent on respecting minimal human rights standards. The standards were not particularly high—not committing mass atrocity crimes or allowing others to do so—but sovereignty was no longer accepted as absolute, and this clearly represents a substantial normative change in international relations. Second, R2P reformulated the conceptual basis for humanitarian intervention. It called for moving away

The United Nations and its secretary-general, Kofi Annan, received the Nobel Peace Prize in Oslo, Norway, on the 100th anniversary of the prestigious award. December 10, 2001. (UN PHOTO 100552/SERGEY BERMENIEV)

from the rights of interveners (outsiders) toward the rights of victims (insiders) and the responsibility if not the obligation of outsiders to act. R2P included action not only to intervene when large-scale loss of life occurs but also to prevent armed conflicts and to help mend war-torn societies. Third, the ICISS proposed a new international default setting: a modified just-war doctrine for future interventions to sustain humanitarian values or human rights. As such, just cause, proportionality, likelihood of success, and right authority (ideally, the Security Council) were seen as essential elements of a responsible decision to act.

The ICISS report was influential in laying the intellectual foundation for changing the way the UN conducts security operations, especially enforcement. In 2003 Secretary-General Annan appointed the High-level Panel on Threats, Challenges and Change (HLP), which consisted of sixteen former government officials, including Brent Scowcroft, the former national security adviser for President George H. W. Bush. The HLP was tasked with identifying the principal threats facing the international community and developing proposals to reform the UN to meet its new challenges. The panel issued its final report, *A More Secure World: Our Shared Responsibility*, in December 2004, and embraced the emerging concept of R2P as a legitimate reason for authorizing military force.

The HLP report laid the political foundation for the secretary-general's recommendations, published as *In Larger Freedom: Towards Development, Security, and Human Rights for All* (2005). Both documents, in turn, were used to set the stage for the 2005 World Summit, dubbed "San Francisco II" for its ambitious task of remaking the UN after six decades. The distance between these documents and the decisions taken at the 2005 World Summit reflects the difference between what knowledgeable government and UN officials deem necessary and what is politically possible among member states. A great deal of consensus existed on the threats facing the international community of states; however, important political differences remained on definition, priorities, strategies, and implementation. The interplay between the first and second United Nations illustrates the complexities of governance on international security issues.

The debate at the 2005 World Summit centered on the conditions under which the UN should authorize military force. This invariably involves determining what constitutes an imminent threat to international peace and security, and how to respond to situations in which governments are unable or unwilling to protect their citizens against mass atrocity crimes (genocide, crimes against humanity, war crimes, and ethnic cleansing). These issues are contentious and divisive in the best of times and even more so in the not so best of times. And these were the not so best of times for the UN, as the United States, under President George W. Bush, was particularly hostile to the world organization and systematically sought to undermine its legitimacy. An odd alliance emerged between the United States and the many developing countries: they would support the status quo by avoiding formal criteria for authorizing force and language that would formally allow for humanitarian intervention in cases of genocide. The former served the interests of the United States, whose use of force in Iraq in 2003 is still widely criticized, and the latter served the interests of many developing countries concerned that any right to humanitarian intervention would threaten their hard-won but shaky sovereignty. The summit outcome reiterated the prohibition against the use of force in international relations except in self-defense, with no reference as to what constitutes an imminent threat as it relates to self-defense. It also reiterated that the primary responsibility to protect lies with states and that the first duty of the international community of states is to use appropriate nonviolent means to protect populations. The UN may "take collective action, in a timely and decisive manner, through the Security Council, in accordance with the Charter, including Chapter VII, on a case-by-case basis and in cooperation with relevant regional organizations as appropriate, should peaceful means be inadequate and national authorities are manifestly failing to protect their populations from genocide, war crimes, ethnic cleansing, and crimes against humanity."[4] In diplomatic-speak, the international community of states avoided declaring a formal right to humanitarian intervention, yet left open the possibility that military intervention could be authorized if the Security Council had the political will to determine that such situations constituted a threat to international peace and security.

Why was this such a sea change? During the Cold War, the Security Council was largely missing in action regarding humanitarian matters. No resolutions mentioned the humanitarian aspects of any armed conflict from 1945 until the Six-Day War of 1967.[5] The first mention of the International Committee of the Red Cross (ICRC) was not until 1978. And in the 1970s and 1980s, "the Security Council gave humanitarian aspects of armed conflict limited priority."[6] During the first half of the 1990s, it passed twice as many resolutions as during the first forty-five years of UN history. They contained repeated references, in the context of Chapter VII, to humanitarian crises amounting to threats to international peace and security and repeatedly requested belligerents to respect the principles of international humanitarian law.[7]

The humanitarian imperative that gave rise to R2P is evidenced by the growing demand of UN security activities. In recent years, the Security Council held sessions on the situations in Kosovo, Sierra Leone, Western Sahara, Ethiopia/ Eritrea, Somalia, Guinea-Bissau, Congo, Burundi, Macedonia, Croatia, Bosnia and Herzegovina, Central African Republic, Georgia, Tajikistan, Afghanistan, Iraq and Kuwait, Haiti, Cyprus, Lebanon, Syria, Israel, Iran, Libya, Sudan, Syria, Mali, and Ukraine. When peacekeeping operations are authorized, many now include a mandate to use force to protect civilians. In the face of these crises, the critical question confronting the UN is how to respond effectively when demand so clearly outstrips supply—in short, how to "muddle through." The answer to this question emerges on a case-by-case basis, yet with each new response seemingly informed by and building on the last. Table 4.1 illustrates the UN's peace and security operations since 1999. The following discussion illustrates the evolution in UN security operations, many with a humanitarian dimension and robust military requirements. While not all the ongoing peacekeeping operations are detailed, those discussed expose the strengths and weaknesses of contemporary UN security operations. The examples also illustrate a shift from traditional peacekeeping activities, such as observing cease-fires and providing a buffer between warring parties, to peacebuilding responsibilities that involve creating stable, democratic institutions. An important dimension of R2P is the responsibility of the international community to help societies rebuild after atrocities.

STABILIZED SECURITY OPERATIONS

The evolution of R2P as a guiding principle of UN peace and security operations has been fueled by the shortcomings of past interventions as well as contemporary challenges. From Kosovo to Syria, the UN has sought to protect civilians from atrocities and gross violations of human rights. When governments have been unable or unwilling to protect civilians, the UN as stepped in with peacekeeping, peacebuilding, and on occasion by authorizing the use of military force.

TABLE 4.1 UN PEACE AND SECURITY OPERATIONS, 1999–PRESENT

Years Active	Operation
1999–2002	United Nations Transitional Administration in East Timor (UNTAET)
1999–2005	United Nations Mission in Sierra Leone (UNAMSIL)
1999–Present	United Nations Organization Mission in the Democratic Republic of the Congo (MONUC)
1999–Present	United Nations Interim Administration Mission in Kosovo (UNMIK)
2000–2008	United Nations Mission in Ethiopia and Eritrea (UNMEE)
2002–2005	United Nations Mission of Support in East Timor (UNMISET)
2003–Present	United Nations Mission in Liberia (UNMIL)
2004–Present	United Nations Operation in Côte d'Ivoire (UNOCI)
2004–Present	United Nations Stabilization Mission in Haiti (MINUSTAH)
2004–2006	United Nations Operation in Burundi (ONUB)
2005–Present	United Nations Mission in the Sudan (UNMIS)
2006–2012	United Nations Integrated Mission in Timor-Leste (UNMIT)
2006–Present	United Nations Interim Force in Lebanon (UNIFIL)[a]
2007–2010	United Nations Mission in the Central African Republic and Chad (MINURCAT)
2007–Present	African Union/United Nations Hybrid Mission in Darfur (UNAMID)
2008–Present	United Nations Integrated Peacebuilding Office in Sierra Leone (UNIPSIL)
2010–Present	United Nations Organization Stabilization Mission in the Democratic Republic of the Congo (MONUSCO)
2011–Present	United Nations Interim Security Force for Abyei (UNISFA)
2011–Present	United Nations Mission in the Republic of South Sudan (UNMISS)
2013-Present	United Nations Multidimensional Integrated Stabilization Mission in Mali (MINUSMA)
2014-Present	United Nations Multidimensional Integrated Stabilization Mission in the Central African Republic (MINUSCA)

[a] UNIFIL was created in 1978 to monitor an Israeli withdrawal from Lebanon; however, the mission was significantly enhanced following the outbreak of violence between Israel and Lebanon in July 2006.

Kosovo

In 1999 NATO militarily intervened in Kosovo arguably to stop the gross violations of human rights and ethnic cleansing being perpetrated by the Serbian military. Depending on how one reads the script of diplomatic code embedded in Security Council resolutions, NATO's action could be argued to represent a breach of international law or to have been launched with the council's implicit approval. The secretary-general of NATO, Javier Solana, chose the latter interpretation of Security Council resolution 1199. The Independent Commission on Kosovo, composed largely of human rights proponents, called the intervention "illegal but legitimate"—that is, without the Security Council's blessing but justified in human terms.[8] On the other hand, both Russia and China condemned the action as illegal. Russia weakened its own position and made a tactical blunder by introducing a council resolution criticizing the NATO bombing and asking that it be halted. The resolution's defeat by a wide margin (12–3) enhanced the status of NATO's action even if it did not make the illegal (that is, against the Charter's rules) legal. Secretary-General Annan drew considerable fire for his speech at the opening of the General Assembly in September 1999, when he wished the Security Council had been able to give explicit approval to the bombing yet nonetheless could not condone idleness in the face of Serb atrocities.[9]

Diplomacy had failed to change Serbian policy. Time and again Yugoslav president Slobodan Milošević demonstrated his blatant disregard for negotiated agreements. In late January 1999, U.S. officials shifted away from a diplomatic approach and threatened military action. Secretary-General Annan had apparently arrived at a similar conclusion. In a statement before NATO leaders in Brussels, he indicated that indeed force might be necessary. In doing so, he praised past UN-NATO collaboration in Bosnia and suggested that a NATO-led mission under UN auspices might well be what was needed. He concluded:

> The bloody wars of the last decade have left us with no illusions about the difficulty of halting internal conflicts by reason or by force particularly against the wishes of the government of a sovereign state. Nor have they left us with any illusions about the need to use force, when all other means have failed.[10]

But neither NATO nor the UN was willing to give up totally on diplomacy. In February 1999 in Rambouillet, France, the so-called contact group—the United States, France, Germany, Italy, Russia, and the United Kingdom—hosted a peace conference that sought to broker a solution between Yugoslavia and an Albanian Kosovar delegation. Talks foundered, and the situation in Kosovo continued to deteriorate. On March 24, NATO began a seventy-seven-day aerial bombardment of Serbian targets. Soon after the bombing started, Serbian security forces launched an all-out campaign to exorcise Kosovo of its predominant ethnic-Albanian population. Initially, the intervention accelerated flight and humanitarian suffering, as 1.8 million Kosovar Albanians were forcibly displaced. As NATO's intervention progressed, air strikes intensified until finally, in the context of a Russian-mediated settlement, Milošević agreed on June 3 to an immediate and verifiable end to the violence and repression and to the withdrawal of all Serbian security forces. Almost immediately the refugees began returning home.

Other aspects of the agreement included the deployment under UN auspices of an effective international civilian and security presence with substantial NATO participation, the establishment of an interim administration, safe return of all refugees and displaced persons, demilitarization of the Kosovo Liberation Army (KLA), and a substantially self-governing Kosovo.

On June 10, 1999, the Security Council, in a 14–0–1 vote (China abstained), adopted resolution 1244 authorizing an international civil and security presence in Kosovo under UN auspices. NATO's preceding "humanitarian war" had been unusual to say the least, and many aid agencies had trouble pronouncing those two words together and choked trying to say "humanitarian bombing."[11] But the new UN peace mission, the UN Interim Administration Mission in Kosovo (UNMIK), was unprecedented in its nature and scope. NATO authorized forty-nine thousand Kosovo Force (KFOR) troops to maintain order and security, and meanwhile UNMIK was to assume authority over all the territory and people of Kosovo, including judicial, legislative, and executive powers. It was to move the region toward self-governance; perform all normal civilian administrative functions; provide humanitarian relief, including the safe return of refugees and displaced persons; maintain law and order and establish the rule of law; promote human rights; assist in reconstructing basic social and economic infrastructure; and facilitate a democratic political order.

The mission was pathbreaking in integrating several non-UN international organizations under a unified UN leadership around four substantive pillars: civil administration (UN-led); humanitarian affairs (UNHCR-led); reconstruction (European Union–led); and democratic institution building (OSCE-led). The scope could hardly have been more ambitious. Civil administration, for example, was comprehensive and included health, education, energy and public utilities, post and telecommunications, judicial, legal, public finance, trade, science, agriculture, environment, and democratization. Over eight hundred thousand people had to be repatriated. Over 120,000 houses had been damaged or destroyed. Schools needed to be reestablished; food, medical aid, and other humanitarian assistance provided; electrical power, sanitation, and clean water restored; land mines cleared and security ensured; and so on.

Although the initial UNMIK mandate was twelve months, it remains in Kosovo today. UNMIK's day-to-day functions are modest. Military forces have been reduced, elections held, and the rebuilding of a society begun. Serious problems persist regarding continued ethnic violence, the status of the Serb minority, widespread unemployment, and the thriving sex trade. In 2004 ethnic Albanians rioted and attacked ethnic Serbs in the volatile and ethnically mixed city of Mitrovica, killing nineteen people. Both NATO and UNMIK were criticized for not protecting Serbian enclaves or confronting the rioters.[12] This outbreak of ethnic violence, and UNMIK and NATO's inability to prevent it, plagued the negotiations on the most serious and intractable of Kosovo problems: the final status of the mostly Albanian province.

Deadlines for negotiating the final status of Kosovo came and went. Initial negotiations launched in 2005 by Special Envoy Marti Ahtisaari, the former Finnish president and UN undersecretary-general, began with a plan that called for Kosovo's formal independence from Serbia. This was immediately rejected by Serbia with the backing of Russia and China. These states said such a plan would inspire other separatist movements and set a dangerous precedent. Negotiations were then turned over to the so-called troika of the European Union, the United States, and Russia, and another deadline was set for December 10, 2007.

Backed by Russia, Serbia offered Kosovo the autonomous status it enjoyed under the former Yugoslavia prior to the rise of Milošević; however, Serbia would retain sovereignty over the province. Kosovo, backed by the United States and the European Union, wanted formal independence—indeed, the substantial (90 percent) Albanian majority had overwhelmingly voted for independence—with special political protections for the Serb minority in Kosovo. The UN and the European Union (EU) were in an awkward position because Security Council resolution 1244 reaffirms the sovereignty and territorial integrity of the Federal Republic of Yugoslavia, of which Kosovo was a part. With Serbia as the internationally recognized successor state, Kosovo falls under Serbia's sovereignty.

The situation came to a head with Kosovo's unilateral declaration of independence in February 2008. The secession of a former part of a sovereign state (Serbia) with international assistance (as Kosovo was a UN protectorate since 1999) was particularly problematic for Moscow because it faced similar tensions in Chechnya. While Albanians celebrated in the streets in the new capital, Pristina, Serbs in their enclave to the north confronted NATO troops and threatened to secede as well. Serbs in Belgrade burned the U.S. embassy, as Washington and several Western states recognized a sovereign Kosovo. The EU's common foreign policy was anything but: Greece, Italy, Cyprus, Romania, and Spain still oppose formal recognition.

In 2008 the General Assembly approved Serbia's bid to ask the International Court of Justice (ICJ) for an advisory opinion on the legality of Kosovo's unilateral declaration of independence. In this much anticipated opinion, the ICJ deftly and narrowly concluded in 2010 that the declaration had not violated international law.[13] The ICJ chose neither to address the legal consequences of such declarations nor to say whether Kosovo was a state. It avoided giving primacy to either the principle of sovereignty or that of self-determination. Rather, the analysis was confined to the narrow question of Kosovo and found nothing in international law preventing a unilateral declaration of independence.

By mid-2015 over one hundred states had formally recognized Kosovo. The UN and its member states, as well as the EU, are still striving for a mediated solution between Kosovo and Serbia, with predictably mixed results. A compromise between the parties was reached, allowing Kosovo to represent itself at international meetings. The deal said that the word *republic* would not appear next to the name "Kosovo" and instead a footnote would be added referencing Security Council resolution 1244 and the ICJ advisory opinion.[14] This compromise represented an important step toward EU membership for Serbia and recognition of Kosovo by Serbia. However, Serbia continues to claim that it will never formally recognize Kosovo. Meanwhile, violence breaks out occasionally in Serbian enclaves in northern Kosovo, and in April 2012 Serbia's plans for local elections in Kosovo forced NATO to send reinforcements to its peacekeeping mission. However, the instability and sporadic violence did not derail the 2013 Brussels Agreement, which put Serbia and Kosovo on the path to normalizing relations. The EU enticed Serbia to agree to the Brussels framework by offering the possibility of acceding to EU membership. While specifics are still being negotiated, the conflict in Kosovo has stabilized and appears close to being resolved.

Timor-Leste (East Timor)

After seventeen years of UN-mediated efforts to resolve the status of East Timor, an agreement was reached on May 5, 1999, between Indonesia and Portugal (the only remaining Western colonial power). The two states agreed that the UN secretary-general would be responsible for organizing and conducting a popular consultation to determine whether the people of East Timor would accept or reject a special autonomous status within the unitary Republic of Indonesia. A rejection of such special status meant that the UN would administer the territory during its transition to independence. Security Council resolution 1246 established the UN Mission in East Timor (UNAMET) with the mandate of conducting such a consultation; after several postponements, the popular vote was held, and the special autonomy status option was overwhelmingly rejected in favor of independence.

News of the outcome stirred pro-integration forces backed by armed militias to violence. Within a matter of weeks nearly a half million East Timorese were displaced from their homes and villages. Indonesian military troops and police were either unwilling or unable to restore order, and the security situation deteriorated. In September, the Security Council, in resolution 1264, authorized the creation of a multilateral force to restore order and protect and support UNAMET. Member states were welcomed to lead, organize, and contribute troops to such a force. Sitting in the wings ready to act, an Australian-led force began arriving in East Timor less than a week later. Numerous arms had been twisted in Jakarta so that Indonesia "requested" the coalition force. In less than a month general order was restored, and the Indonesian People's Consultative Assembly voted on October 19 to formally recognize the results of the popular consultation. The following week the Security Council unanimously approved resolution 1272, establishing the UN Transitional Administration in East Timor (UNTAET).

The nature and scope of the UNTAET mission were ambitious and wide-ranging.[15] As in the case of Cambodia, a country with substantial interests and motivation (in this case, Australia) took the military lead. It was empowered to exercise all legislative and executive powers and judicial authority; establish an effective civil administration; assist in developing civil and social services; provide security and maintain law and order; ensure the coordination and delivery of humanitarian assistance, rehabilitation, and development assistance; promote sustainable development; and build the foundation for a stable liberal democracy. To carry out this mandate, authorization was given for a military component of 8,950 troops, 200 observers, and a civilian police component of up to 1,640 personnel. By 2000 the processes of reconstruction and state building were well under way, and in 2002 East Timor became the 191st member of the United Nations with its new name: Timor-Leste.

In mid-2006 skeptics' fears were confirmed with the explosion of violence in Dili and the hurried return of Australian soldiers to restore order and security. The violence was sparked by former soldiers who rebelled against the newly

Ana Vaz (second from right), a Formed Police Unit officer of the United Nations Mission in Timor-Leste from Portugal, speaks to a Rapid Intervention Unit officer of the Timor-Leste police about protecting the trucks distributing food to internally displaced persons with the help of the International Organization for Migration and the World Food Programme. (UN PHOTO 186422/MARTINE PERRET)

elected civilian government. In August 2006, the Security Council created the United Nations Integrated Mission in Timor-Leste (UNMIT) through resolution 1704, with a mandate to help the current government consolidate stability and keep the peace. Continued violence (and the emergency return of Australian troops in 2007) has forced the Security Council to extend the mandate of UNMIT annually since. The UN also established the Independent Special Commission of Inquiry for Timor-Leste[16] to investigate the violence and make recommendations regarding how to hold those responsible accountable through the domestic legal system. Most of the recommendations were not implemented, but the report does create an official narrative of the events.

In 2012 largely peaceful first-round elections were held and hailed as a success by Timor-Leste president José Ramos-Horta.[17] The Nobel Peace Prize winner who served as prime minister and president said that the elections demonstrated the willingness of the Timorese to take their battles to the polls instead of the street. Ironically, Ramos-Horta was on the ballot but lost to former rebel leader, José Maria Vasconcelos, whom the Independent Special Commission had recommended be prosecuted for supplying illegal arms during the 2006 violence. Depending on circumstances, national reconciliation sometimes can trump accountability. Successful parliamentary elections followed in July 2012 and the mission closed in December 2012, having successfully assisted in stabilizing the situation and promoting reconciliation.

Sierra Leone

The year 1999 brought both sorrow and hope to the people of Sierra Leone, who were reeling from over eight years of civil war. The bloody civil war that had intensified during 1998 turned even bloodier in January 1999, when rebel forces once again captured the capital, Freetown, and launched a four-day spree of killing and destruction. Judges, journalists, human rights workers, government officials, civil servants, churches, hospitals, prisons, UN offices, and others were targets of the rebel alliance, comprising forces of the former junta and the Revolutionary United Front (RUF). Complicating and fueling the conflict was the material support of the RUF by neighboring Liberia. Liberian president Charles Taylor provided sanctuary to RUF rebels and used the RUF to gain control of Sierra Leone's diamond mines. Over six thousand were killed, and about 20 percent of the total stock of dwellings was destroyed. The UN Observer Mission in Sierra Leone (UNOMSIL), which had been established in June 1998, was evacuated.[18]

Fighting continued throughout the spring and early summer, uprooting more than a million people, about 450,000 of whom fled to neighboring Guinea. The issue remained on the Security Council agenda, and the council kept extending UNOMSIL's mandate several months at a time. Finally, on July 7, 1999, the Lomé Peace Agreement was negotiated between the government and the RUF. The Security Council responded positively to this move and on August 20 unanimously adopted resolution 1260, extending and expanding the UNOMSIL mandate. The UN presence was further expanded in October, when the council adopted resolution 1270, creating a new mission, the UN Mission for Sierra Leone (UNAMSIL), which mandated the tasks of establishing a presence at key locations throughout the country to assist the government of Sierra Leone in implementing the disarmament, demobilization, and reintegration of rebel troops; ensuring the security and freedom of movement of UN personnel; monitoring adherence to the ceasefire agreement of May 18; encouraging the parties to create confidence-building mechanisms and support their functioning; facilitating the delivery of humanitarian assistance; supporting the operations of UN civilian officials, including the special representative of the secretary-general and his staff, human rights officers, and civil affairs officers; and providing support, as requested, for the elections, which are to be held in accordance with the present constitution of Sierra Leone.

Initially, the UN mission did not go well, in part because member states predictably failed to follow through on the UNAMSIL mandate with the necessary resources. The force of six thousand soldiers (from Nigeria, Kenya, and Guinea) was authorized under Chapter VII to use force if necessary to protect UN personnel and civilians threatened with imminent physical violence. However, the security situation was unstable, as forty-five thousand combatants remained armed and in control of the diamond mines. In May 2000, nearly five hundred

UNAMSIL peacekeepers were kidnapped and held hostage by rebels. At the same time, the United Kingdom sent heavily armed forces to protect and extricate its nationals from the deteriorating security situation in Freetown.[19] Although unplanned, events on the ground played out such that UNAMSIL and U.K. forces worked together to stabilize Freetown and restore order to outlying regions. As the British began to draw down troops in 2001, Security Council resolution 1346 expanded the peacekeeping force to 17,500 soldiers.

UNAMSIL and U.K. military forces successfully locked down Sierra Leone militarily and deterred rebel groups from pursuing violence as a political strategy.[20] However, militaries and soldiers are often ill-suited for the other necessary elements of peacekeeping, such as humanitarian activities and postconflict reconciliation.[21] Part of the problem centers on how to square the militarized masculinity associated with being a soldier in war-fighting situations with the requirements of maintaining peace.[22] Soldiers are trained for fighting, not reconstruction. At the same time, properly trained civilian corps can make important progress in deepening political integration, reaching compromises among multiple and competing parties, and building the institutions of civil society. Sierra Leone, as well as other cases discussed thus far, represents the informal and often ill-defined relationship between state military power and UN peacekeeping and peacebuilding capacities.

In 2005 UNAMSIL completed its mission. The newly created Peacebuilding Commission (PBC, discussed in more detail in the next chapter) decided in 2006 to undertake missions in Sierra Leone and Burundi as pilots for the new and more concentrated UN efforts in postconflict countries. By selecting two of the more troubled African countries, the PBC took on exceptional challenges. The commission's mandate is to "marshal resources at the disposal of the international community to advise and propose integrated strategies for post-conflict recovery, focusing attention on reconstruction, institution-building and sustainable development, in countries emerging from conflict." Its report on Sierra Leone notes that while important political progress has been made, "the majority of the population remains extremely insecure because of poverty, lack of access to justice, lack of employment opportunities, high crime rates and corruption. The situation is even more difficult for young people and women, who face additional marginalization and discrimination. Many of the root causes of conflict, such as lack of employment for the large youth population, the proliferation of small arms, inadequate State capacity to deliver basic services, corruption and instability in the region, persist today."[23] In 2007 the UN Peacebuilding Fund (PBF), which supports PBC missions, allocated $35 million for youth employment, good governance, justice and security, and capacity building for public administrations. Sierra Leone remains an important test for the nascent Peacebuilding Commission and the Peacebuilding Fund. Subsequently, the PBC focused its work on building multiparty dialogue and democratic governance, combating corruption, and preparing for elections.[24] Successful elections mean Sierra Leone can make the transition from late-stage peacebuilding toward longer-term development.[25]

Creating a positive peace increasingly involves the use of international and hybrid courts to address war crimes and crimes against humanity. Beginning with the former Yugoslavia and Rwanda in the 1990s, UN security efforts have often entailed a legal dimension to end or mitigate the culture of impunity for violence and to help societies turn the page on armed conflict. Discussed in more detail in Chapter 7, it is worth mentioning here that these courts are important tools to help restore international peace and security and provide a form of restorative justice. In 2000, at the request of Sierra Leone, the Security Council authorized the secretary-general to work with Sierra Leone to create what is now known as the Special Court for Sierra Leone (SCSL) to prosecute those who bear the greatest responsibility for violations of international and Sierra Leonean law. The SCSL successfully prosecuted and convicted thirteen people, including former Liberian president Charles Taylor in 2012, for aiding and abetting war crimes. It was closed in 2013 and replaced by the Residual Special Court for Sierra Leone to oversee remaining court obligations such as witness protection, supervision of sentences, and maintenance of the court archives.

The hard-fought progress of stabilizing Sierra Leone and building a sustainable peace was threatened in 2014 with the outbreak of Ebola, a virus that causes hemorrhagic fever, internal bleeding, organ failure, and death. The outbreak affected large areas of West Africa, and Sierra Leone had considerable difficulty in containing it. The UN responded to the unprecedented health crisis in the region by creating the United Nations Mission for Ebola Emergency Response (UNMEER) to coordinate multilateral and local efforts to stop the outbreak, treat the sick, and preserve stability. UNMEER is the UN's first emergency health mission and its pathbreaking work adds yet another dimension to contemporary security challenges.

Côte d'Ivoire

UN peace operations in Côte d'Ivoire date back to 2003, when the Security Council created the United Nations Mission in Côte d'Ivoire (MINUCI) to facilitate the implementation of the Linas-Marcoussis Agreement (which ended the Ivoirian civil war) and to complement the Economic Community of West African States (ECOWAS) and French peacekeeping forces that had been deployed since 2002. After the agreement was concluded, violent demonstrations erupted in Côte d'Ivoire as the parties backtracked on their negotiated agreements. At the behest of France, the Security Council adopted resolution 1528, under Chapter VII, which established a peace operation of about seven thousand troops—the United Nations Operation in Côte d'Ivoire (UNOCI). It became operational in 2004 and was authorized to use force to protect civilians. The council also authorized France to use all necessary means to support UNOCI.

Similar to the other UN missions discussed earlier in this chapter, the UNOCI mandate was extensive, including monitoring the cease-fire, disarming militias, establishing law and order, and preparing for national elections. While UNOCI helped to stabilize parts of the country, forces loyal to President Laurent Gbagbo routinely clashed with French forces. After an eruption of intense hostilities, the UN helped broker the Ouagadougou Agreement in 2007 that called for a transitional government, free and fair elections, and a phased withdrawal of UNOCI and French forces after elections. In 2010 those elections were held and led to a presidential runoff between Gbagbo and the former prime minister, Alassane Ouattara. Preelection violence erupted as Gbagbo and Ouattara supporters clashed. As election results clearly indicated a victory for Ouattara, pro-Gbagbo forces took to the streets and killed civilians. Gbagbo refused to cede power and used military force to confine Ouattara in a hotel surrounded by his UNOCI bodyguards. The military used heavy artillery in the capital, causing mass casualties. In December 2010, Ouattara requested the ICC to investigate the postelection violence, and the ICC opened an official investigation.

Most of the international community of states recognized Ouattara as the duly elected president, and in 2011 the Security Council passed resolution 1975 calling on Gbagbo to step down. Even though UN secretary-general Ban Ki-moon has been widely criticized for his ambivalence toward UN military deployments and his doubts regarding the UN's ability to manage and direct such operations, he urged UNOCI and French forces to halt the military assault on the capital with backing of the Security Council.[26] By April 2011, with the independent French forces playing a leading role, Gbagbo surrendered and was taken into custody. The ICC unsealed a secret arrest warrant for Gbagbo, and the Security Council cooperated with the ICC by lifting the travel ban against Gbagbo, which facilitated his transfer to The Hague.[27] Today, Ouattara is the recognized president of the country, and Laurent Gbagbo sits in an ICC cell facing criminal charges. The UNOCI mandate is reviewed annually, and troops remain on the ground supporting the Ivoirian government.

The eventual ouster of incumbent Gbagbo followed robust military action by the 1,650-strong French Licorne force as the avant-garde of the UN peace operation, but only after a half year of dawdling. The contrast with what happened in Libya, described later, suggests why military humanitarianism is a necessary, if insufficient, component of the responsibility to protect. The unwillingness to apply armed force abetted Gbagbo's intransigence as the disaster in Côte d'Ivoire unfolded. Was it really necessary to sustain war crimes, crimes against humanity, a million refugees, and a ravaged economy? International military action could have taken place earlier.

EVOLVING SECURITY OPERATIONS

Lebanon—Again

On July 12, 2006, Hezbollah, an Iranian-backed militia based in Lebanon, conducted a raid into Israel, kidnapping and later executing two Israel Defense Forces (IDF) soldiers. In the past, such raids have been used against Israel as a negotiating tactic to secure the release of Islamic militants held in Israeli prisons. Israel responded by launching a large-scale war against Hezbollah, beginning with air strikes on Hezbollah strongholds in southern Lebanon. Hezbollah responded by launching rockets into the Israeli cities of Kiryat Shmona and Haifa, leading to further escalation by Israel. IDF forces in massive attacks, including the use of cluster bombs, destroyed a substantial part of the economic infrastructure of Lebanon and eventually entered southern Lebanon to create a buffer zone between Hezbollah rockets and Israeli territory. After nearly a month of intense fighting, in which more than twelve hundred civilians were killed and more than four thousand wounded, the Security Council approved resolution 1701, which called for a cease-fire and the deployment of the United Nations Interim Force in Lebanon (UNIFIL) into southern Lebanon. UNIFIL was created in 1978 to deal with earlier crises in Lebanon. Before the 2006 deployment, UNIFIL forces needed to be increased from some two thousand to a more robust fifteen thousand soldiers. Its mandate also had to be expanded.

According to resolution 1701, UNIFIL's mandate is to monitor the cease-fire, assist the Lebanese government in deploying its troops into southern Lebanon, and aid in the delivery of humanitarian assistance or the safe return of displaced persons. Most important, 1701 calls for UNIFIL to create a zone along the Israeli-Lebanon border where the only armed personnel are members of the Lebanese military or UNIFIL. Finally, the Security Council authorized UNIFIL to use appropriate military force as necessary to carry out its mandate.

Empowering UNIFIL to fulfill its mandate was not without problems. Two issues generated considerable media attention and debate at the UN. The first issue centered on rules of engagement for UNIFIL. Although it was authorized to use military force, questions remained about whether it should attempt to disarm or engage Hezbollah directly. The answers to these questions would directly affect the second issue of the composition of UNIFIL forces. France, which helped broker the cease-fire, was widely expected to contribute the bulk of the military forces and lead UNIFIL, but announced in mid-August that it would contribute only two hundred soldiers and provide some logistical support.[28] After a few days of widespread criticism, it offered to contribute four hundred soldiers, generating even more criticism. Only after Italy offered to contribute two thousand troops and lead UNIFIL did France agree to send two thousand soldiers.

By the end of 2015, UNIFIL had 11,430 military troops from thirty-eight countries and an annual operating budget of $509 million.[29] By most accounts, the mission has been successful. It has deterred violence in the border region, observed the Israeli withdrawal, and assisted with the deployment of Lebanese troops. The mixture of local armed forces with UN military forces was yet another departure for peace operations. The problems of command and control seemingly have been overcome, largely because the combined forces have not yet encountered a serious challenge. The deterrent capacity of UNIFIL is due in large part to its military strength, which includes significant naval as well as land forces.[30] Although UNIFIL is a more traditional peacekeeping operation in that it

United Nations Interim Force in Lebanon troops observe Section 83 near the Blue Line on the border between Lebanon and Israel. (UN PHOTO 123914/MARK GARTEN)

is deployed with the consent of the parties, it is robust and allowed to use military force beyond self-defense. Nevertheless, UNIFIL lacks the capacity as well as the mandate to undertake postconflict peacebuilding, which is desperately needed in the war-ravaged country.

UNIFIL faces several challenges. The first concerns the sustainability of the mission. Fielding such a large and well-equipped military force indefinitely tests the resolve of the first and second UN, especially in the absence of a stable political solution regarding the leadership of the Lebanese government. A series of political murders decimated the leadership of pro-Western forces in Lebanon, while Hezbollah, backed by Iran and Syria, has increased its political influence. A second challenge centers on balancing the security of UNIFIL forces with the security of civilians in the border region. UNIFIL has been criticized for spending more time protecting itself than preventing Hezbollah rocket attacks in Israel, raising questions of whether it has become a victim of "soldier safety first," or the so-called UN peacekeeping syndrome.[31] At the same time, UNIFIL has done useful work in clearing land mines and other weapons, including cluster bombs, making civilian lives considerably safer. To date, neither Hezbollah nor Israel has really challenged UNIFIL. Hezbollah sporadically fires rockets at Israel, and Israel occasionally violates Lebanese airspace by conducting air patrols; however, these incidents have not posed a significant impediment to UNIFIL's operations. Given that Hezbollah is not averse to terrorist attacks against UN personnel, and in the past Israel has ignored UNIFIL and in the 1980s invaded Lebanon, questions remain about what will happen if or when UNIFIL comes into violent conflict with the well-armed Hezbollah or Israel or both.

For the time being, the southern border of Lebanon is secure. Now the eastern border is at risk with the civil war raging in neighboring Syria and the influx of over 1 million refugees. The Security Council extends the mission of UNIFIL annually; however, efforts in 2014 to change the UNIFIL mandate to include deployments to the east have been rejected by the Hezbollah-dominated government. The political instability emanating from Tunisia, Egypt, Yemen, Libya, Syria, and other Middle Eastern states has not yet been transmitted to Lebanon, but UNIFIL's maritime operations have intercepted ships containing weapons destined for armed gangs in Syria. Concerns also remain that Hezbollah, backed by Syria and Iran, could be drawn in more directly to the conflict with militants from the Islamic State in Iraq and Syria (ISIS) and other militant Sunni rebel groups allied against the Assad regime.

Darfur, Sudan

The Darfur crisis is the culmination of a series of unresolved conflicts resulting from Sudan's decolonization in 1956. After Sudan gained independence from the United Kingdom, it descended into an almost continual civil war, which pitted the central government in Khartoum in the north against rebel groups in the south, east, and west. Darfur, in the western part of Sudan, is home to two insurgencies, the Sudan Liberation Army and the Justice Equality Movement. Intense fighting erupted in 2003 between Sudanese government forces and the Sudan Liberation Army, creating a humanitarian crisis for civilians in the area. After sustaining attacks in the north, Sudanese government forces, along with Arab militias known as the *janjaweed*, attacked towns and villages in Darfur with little regard for civilians. Claiming that the civilian population was harboring the insurgents, government and *janjaweed* forces razed entire communities and pursued a scorched-earth policy. Although estimates vary, it is commonly thought that since 2003 upward of three hundred thousand people have lost their lives and over 2.5 million people been displaced.

In the case of Darfur, the relative effectiveness of regional versus universal organizations comes back into focus as a theme.[32] Both the African Union (AU) and the UN have been involved in efforts to resolve this complex armed conflict and to protect the civilian population. The AU took the lead in mediating peace talks and successfully brokering an important cease-fire in 2004. It also deployed its first peacekeeping mission, the African Union Mission in Sudan (AMIS), to monitor the cease-fire in 2004 and to help build a secure environment for delivering humanitarian assistance. Originally consisting of 150 troops, AMIS expanded over the next few years to comprise 7,000 troops. AMIS was plagued by poor funding, poor equipment, and poor training—in short, nothing like the force that would be necessary to improve conditions in an area the size of France. Moreover, its mandate did not include disarmament or the use of force to protect civilians. The cease-fire brokered in 2004 did not hold, and neither did a series of cease-fires in 2006 and 2007. Attacks on civilians continued. To complicate matters further, AMIS peacekeepers and humanitarian aid workers also became targets of government, *janjaweed*, and insurgent forces.

The United Nations initially played a supporting role to the African Union by highlighting human rights abuses and keeping pressure on Khartoum. UN agencies and personnel, such as the UN coordinator for Sudan and the UN high commissioner for human rights, reported that gross violations and ethnic cleansing were commonplace in Sudan as early as 2004. In September 2004, U.S. secretary of state Colin Powell used the term *genocide* to describe the actions of the Sudanese government, sparking an international debate among practitioners and scholars about whether events on the ground actually constituted genocide, and the U.S. House of Representatives voted unanimously that this was the case.[33] The Security Council, with resolution 1564, invited the secretary-general to create the Independent Commission of Inquiry on Darfur to investigate whether genocide was occurring in Sudan, and while the commission stopped short of calling the violence genocide, it did find that serious crimes were being committed. This report eventually led the council to refer the matter to the International Criminal Court (ICC), a remarkable occurrence given the U.S. antagonism to the ICC (U.S. and Chinese abstentions allowed the resolution to pass).[34]

The ICC has since issued indictments against two Sudanese officials for their role in the conflict. In 2008 the ICC prosecutor sought an indictment against Sudanese sitting president Omar Hassan al-Bashir and in March 2009 the court issued an arrest warrant for him (see Chapter 9). Some critics question the wisdom of such an indictment when UN and AU officials are seeking more cooperation and consent from Khartoum about security operations in the field. Ever since the International Military Tribunal in Nuremberg that tried German officials for war crimes, such indictments have been a common bone of contention between those who seek to turn a page on armed conflict and those who view impunity as a longer-run threat to society. Security Council resolution 1590 created the United Nations Mission in Sudan (UNMIS) in 2005 to monitor the Comprehensive Peace Agreement signed between rebel groups and the Sudanese government. The main thrust of the agreement was to end hostilities in southern Sudan, but it was also seen as a framework for ending hostilities throughout Sudan, including Darfur. UNMIS was additionally tasked with providing political and logistical support to the floundering AMIS with the hope of stabilizing peacekeeping operations. The mandate of UNMIS included protecting civilians; however, its primary operations were in southern Sudan, where until recently a relative peace prevailed and the civilian population was not at risk.

The Security Council was, and remains, deeply divided between members who want to authorize a more forceful UN response and those members, such as Russia and China, who are wary of infringing on Sudanese sovereignty, which is augmented by their desire to protect their commercial (oil and arms) trade. As such, most of the Darfur resolutions passed by the Security Council have been watered down so that a consensus could be reached. Still, the Security Council was able to place limited, but targeted, sanctions on certain individuals and authorize an arms embargo and no-fly zone.[35] Sudan resisted accepting UN peacekeepers, claiming that the deployment of a peacekeeping force would amount to a Western recolonization of Sudan, an argument that still resonates with many developing countries. As a compromise, Sudan accepted a small, underfunded, and poorly equipped AU mission. UNMIS was accepted later only because its principal task is to monitor the cease-fire created by the Comprehensive Peace Agreement and to "support" AMIS. In 2006 the Security Council, in resolution 1706, in theory expanded the scope, military troop levels, and mandate of UNMIS. The intent was to deploy UN peacekeepers to Darfur; however, in a Security Council compromise, the resolution also called for Sudan's consent. Needless to say, the government in Khartoum never gave its consent, and limited progress has been made to protect civilians in Darfur.

The UN's supporting role did pave the way for an unprecedented hybrid peacekeeping force between the UN and the African Union. With its July 2007 resolution 1769, the Security Council finally authorized the creation of a more robust peacekeeping force, armed with a mandate to protect civilians. This new peacekeeping operation, called United Nations/African Union Mission in Darfur (UNAMID), involved folding in AMIS forces and beefing up the entire mission to include twenty-six thousand soldiers, most of whom were uniformed military, and a few thousand police personnel. The resolution authorized the UN to assume peacekeeping duties in Darfur on December 31, 2007. The existence of UNAMID

Chinese engineers working for the United Nations/African Union Mission in Darfur unload their equipment kits upon arrival in Nyala, Sudan. (UN PHOTO 190255/STUART PRICE)

was seen by some as an early success for Secretary-General Ban Ki-moon, who is largely credited with gaining China's acquiescence to the mission.[36]

Unfortunately, UNAMID did not get off to a good start. Khartoum appointed ICC-indicted Ahmad Harun to coordinate and oversee the deployment of UNAMID. By late 2008, the force was less than half strength (with seven thousand soldiers coming from the beleaguered AU mission already in Darfur) and without the necessary logistical and communications support.[37] In addition, Sudan objected to non-Muslim and non-African contingents and kept changing the terms of the mission's mandate. UNAMID also came under fire from Sudanese government forces and by various rebel factions. Seven UNAMID peacekeepers were killed in a rebel ambush in July 2008. As a result, and after the ICC prosecutor sought the indictment against al-Bashir in August 2008, UNAMID convoys were attacked by government forces. In what many saw as a textbook case for the "responsibility to protect," the new norm seemed very much in question, since moral rhetoric and political reality were so distinct.

Violence in Darfur has ebbed and flowed, and the worst of the mass killings have eased. However, a 2015 report by Human Rights Watch evoked the atrocities committed earlier and detailed campaigns involving war crimes and crimes against humanity in 2014 by the so-called Rapid Support Forces.[38] The al-Bashir government severely constrains the movements of UNAMID peacekeepers, who have been held hostage and of whom 145 have lost their lives. In 2014, just as UNAMID was approaching full strength, UN Security Council resolution 2173 reduced the number of peacekeepers to just under sixteen thousand. In 2015 the UN secretary-general opened talks with Sudan to withdraw the entire force. Under increased pressure from Sudan and shifting international priorities, the ongoing drawdown reflects a political stalemate in the Security Council regarding the best strategies for promoting stability and protecting civilians in the region.

Moreover, international attention has also shifted back to the south, as the Khartoum government recognized the results of a referendum that paved the way for the UN's newest member state (its 193rd) in July 2011: South Sudan. Virtually from the end of independence celebrations, however, Sudan and South Sudan have resorted to force to try to resolve their border and economic issues. The two states exchanged military blows over contested oil fields, prompting the African Union to call on the states to withdraw troops from the disputed area and for the Security Council to issue a Chapter VII decision. The civil war within South Sudan complicates an already difficult political landscape. The UN Mission in South Sudan (UNMISS)—some 11,000 soldiers and 1,200 police—has a Chapter VII mandate to protect civilians but is not only inadequate for that purpose but also has no mandate to protect the territory of South Sudan.

Libya

The contagion of the Arab Spring, a movement against autocratic governments that originated in December 2010 in Tunisia, spread to Libya in January 2011 when civilians and opposition groups took to the streets to protest the authoritarian dictatorship of Muammar Gaddafi, who had ruled Libya since his 1969 coup d'état. The Gaddafi regime, already notorious for its repressiveness, responded with tanks, heavy artillery, and snipers. Suspected dissenters were rounded up and tortured.[39] Opposition forces organized the National Transitional Council (NTC) and claimed to be the legitimate representative of the Libyan people.[40] The opposition soon took control of the strategic city of Benghazi, prompting Gaddafi to threaten an all-out assault and promising no mercy for rebels. His usual rhetoric was surpassed by a vile menace against those "cockroaches" and "rats" who opposed him (the same dehumanizing terms used in 1994 by Rwanda's genocidal government).

The international community of states responded on national, regional, and global levels. European and North American governments condemned the assaults on civilians, as did the African Union, the European Union, the Arab League, and the Organization of the Islamic Conference. Secretary-General Ban Ki-moon and UN high commissioner for human rights Navi Pillay condemned the excessive use of force, and by the end of February, Libya was squarely on the Security Council's agenda.

The mere consideration of military force for Libya undoubtedly made the initial decisions on other Chapter VII measures easier. Security Council resolution 1970 contained a package of actions: an arms embargo, assets freeze, travel bans, and an inquiry by the International Criminal Court. These relatively robust stances, for the UN at least, were agreed unanimously in late February 2011, instead of being the most that might have been expected after months or years of protracted deliberations. Predictably, Gaddafi responded with even greater violence, and regional organizations (the African Union and the Islamic Conference) condemned that response and called for all necessary means to protect civilians.

In March 2011, after considerable behind-the-scenes negotiation securing the abstentions of veto-holding Russia and China, the UN Security Council passed resolution 1973, which authorized the creation of a no-fly zone and all necessary measures to ensure compliance with the order to cease attacks on civilians. After forces loyal to Gaddafi violated the terms of resolution 1973, and only thirty-six hours after approval of the resolution, French, British, and U.S. fighter jets and cruise missiles began to hammer Libyan military positions.

Resolution 1973 noted that both NATO and the Arab League were ready to act in support of the resolution. NATO took the lead in enforcing the no-fly zone (fourteen NATO states and four Arab states participated in military operations) and eventually providing air cover for advancing opposition forces. NATO airstrikes continued for seven months, much to the dismay of those who initially supported international action, apparently thinking that Gaddafi would back off. But he was eventually captured and brutally killed by opposition forces in October 2011. During the seven months of NATO operations against Libyan forces, the NTC gained wider recognition as the voice of the Libyan people, and in September the UN General Assembly allowed the NTC to represent Libya in that body.[41]

The Security Council, through resolution 2009, created the United Nations Support Mission in Libya (UNSMIL) to help with the transition. Unlike traditional peacekeeping, UNSMIL is a peacebuilding mission, run by the UN Department of Political Affairs, whose emphasis is on diplomatic and political support, creating a light UN footprint.

The Security Council set precedents for applying R2P in justifying both resolutions 1970 (which had unanimous support) and 1973 (which no country voted against, although there were five abstentions). In addition, the Human Rights Council referred to R2P for the first time in resolution S-15/1, which led to the General Assembly's resolution 65/60 to suspend Libya—the first time that an elected member state had been suspended from such a position. Critically, some ten council decisions involved the R2P norm, and six of those took place in 2011 alone and a seventh in 2012.

While ultimately successful in removing Gaddafi from power, the use of force by NATO, with UN blessing, generated three broad criticisms.[42] The first, and perhaps most important, was that NATO interpreted resolution 1973 to mean whatever it wanted and went well beyond what was apparently authorized. Russia, China, India, Brazil, and Germany abstained from resolution 1973; however, their representatives later expressed concerns that NATO had done more than enforce the no-fly zone or use deadly force to protect civilians.[43] It had effectively become the air force of the opposition. NATO provided technical assistance and intelligence, and credible evidence suggests that Libyan opposition forces were supported by foreign special forces on the ground.[44] The criticism from China and Russia was particularly pointed, raising concerns that the contortion of resolution 1973 from the responsibility to protect civilians to regime change would mean no future support for R2P initiatives.[45] That fear was at least initially borne out by the Security Council's inability to take action in Syria.

The theatrical huffing and puffing was reminiscent of earlier high-voltage and high-decibel criticism that confronted the emergence of R2P ten years earlier.[46] For many critics, those seeking to make "never again" more than a slogan were not necessarily on the side of the angels. The feigned surprise among the harshest critics is hard to take seriously. It makes sense to expect that international action will result in altered behavior away from abhorrent practices by a pariah government like Tripoli's—that is, causing the Gaddafi regime to halt abuse and negotiate an end to repression and violence. If no such change in behavior occurs, and in Libya it did not, a change in regime should not come as a surprise but as the logical outcome of deploying R2P military force.

The concern that R2P is a ruse for Western imperialism or a pretext for regime change seems quaint or disingenuous but remains resonant. While Libya may have helped reorient policy and decision makers toward realizing the centrality of R2P for both normative and operational issues, it has also provoked doubts and stimulated anew thoughts of buyer's remorse. Such ruminations were clear in the proposal from Brazil at the sixty-sixth session of the General Assembly in fall 2011. It argued that "the international community, as it exercises its responsibility to protect, must demonstrate a high level of responsibility while protecting."[47] Brazil's support for human rights and unwillingness to be seen as unenthusiastic about R2P were clear, along with its unease about the use of military force for regime change. The idea of "responsibility while protecting" has been embraced by R2P skeptics as a necessary evolution in defining when to use military force to protect civilian populations from repressive governments. In any case, the ethics surviving any decisions about life-and-death matters in this field are thorny.[48]

Second, as has always been the case for delegated operations, the Security Council exercised no effective oversight of the use of force it approved. Reports of civilian casualties and the unwillingness of NATO officials to investigate have drawn criticism.[49] The Human Rights Council appointed the International Commission of Inquiry on Libya, which issued a report in March 2012 that highlighted crimes by both the regime and the opposition forces; it indicated NATO's "demonstrable determination to avoid civilian casualties" but also "confirmed civilian casualties and found targets that showed no military utility."[50] The UN Security Council seems reluctant to pressure the current Libyan government given the fluidity of events on the ground. Gaddafi's son, Saif el Islam, for instance, is in Libyan custody although under ICC indictment. Libyan officials want to try him in Libya; in the view of the ICC, however, Libya lacks the domestic legal structures to ensure a fair trial in accordance with international standards. Still, the Security Council is reluctant to press for his extradition. The United Nations lacks the capacity to carry out enforcement missions on its own and must take more responsibility for actions done in its name.

Third, the violent instability and increased militancy in the aftermath of the UN-authorized intervention raises questions as to whether the civilian population has actually benefited from the implementation of R2P without the necessary follow-on peacebuilding and peacekeeping efforts. The media, including the *Economist* and the *Guardian*, have reported on the deteriorating security situation in Libya and the dramatic increase in human rights violations. One study suggests that the intervention actually prolonged the violence, exacerbated human rights abuses, prolonged humanitarian suffering, and increased Islamic radicalism.[51] Libya, for all intents and purposes, has descended into a civil war and the first and second UN have no clear strategy to deal with the unintended consequences of their actions. Libya's weak and fragmented government is as grave a threat to human dignity as a brutal dictator bent on crushing the opposition.

Syria

The popular uprisings of the Arab Spring found their way to Syria in March 2011, as mass protests against forty years of al-Assad family rule broke out across the country. The government of Bashar al-Assad, responding to what it said were "terrorist acts," arrested hundreds, and security forces fired on protesters. This initially slow-motion crisis took place simultaneously with the Libyan conflict. The controversies surrounding the Libyan operation spilled over into UN deliberations regarding Syria, with Russia and China unwilling to consider UN-authorized co-ercion. While the exact number of civilian casualties is impossible to calculate, estimates in 2016 hovered around two hundred and fifty thousand.

The situation in Syria is considerably more complicated, chancy, and confused than in Libya.[52] Whereas the latter's relatively cohesive opposition movement was run from inside and spoke with one voice, Syria's was initially based outside as well as inside the country, dispersed geographically, and divided politically. The more visible but fractious central opposition group in exile, the Syrian National Council, was divided among the Muslim Brotherhood (itself split into more and less tolerant factions) and two other Islamist organizations, the National Action Group and the Syria National Movement. Inside the country, eclectic and ragtag groups of fighters and unarmed protesters agreed on little except that al-Assad must go. They were unable to coalesce into a unified force, they had no common ideology, and they lacked a clear chain of command to coordinate operations, protests, or arms supplies.

Moreover, instead of virtually an entire country (other than those on his pay-roll) being mobilized against Gaddafi, a substantial number of Syrians supported the regime in Damascus and cities like Aleppo, or at least stood on the sidelines waiting to see who ended up on top. Unlike Libya, which has virtually a single ethnic group (Arabized Berbers, mostly all Sunni Muslims), Syria is strikingly diverse: while Arabs constitute 90 percent of the population, there are substantial numbers of Kurds, Armenians, and others. Sunni Muslims constitute some three quarters of the Muslim population, but over 15 percent are Alawites, Druze, and other sects. In addition to the possible intra-Muslim divide, there is also the likely cleavage with the 10 percent of the population who are Christian. In comparison to the largely desert-like Libya with a few isolated cities, Syria's numerous urban and suburban areas meant that surgical airstrikes were implausible and that sig-nificant civilian deaths from military action were guaranteed. Unlike Libya's small mercenary army (mostly Berbers from Northern Mali), which quickly de-fected or departed, the Syrian armed forces remained well equipped, disciplined, and loyal.

Buoyed by its effective activism in Libya, the Arab League called upon Syria to cease attacks against civilians. In November 2011, the Arab League suspended Syria, called for an Arab League observer mission, and imposed economic sanc-tions. These steps did little to curb the violence, and in January 2012 the Arab League proposed a plan that called for al-Assad to transfer power and begin talks to form a transitional government. The Arab League also presented the plan to the UN Security Council and asked for its support.

The draft Security Council resolution supporting the plan was vetoed by Russia and China in February 2012.[53] Those states thought the resolution sent an unbal-anced message by emboldening opposition forces and supporting regime change. After the resounding double veto, Syrian violence escalated, this time involving not only government attack on civilians but insurgent attacks on government forces and personnel. After more than a year of al-Assad's murderous repression, the Arab League and the UN appointed a joint envoy, former UN secretary-general Kofi Annan, to negotiate a political solution. Annan's plan consisted of a cease-fire, humanitarian access, and the deployment of three hundred unarmed monitors to replace the handful of Arab League observers. The Security Council created the United Nations Supervision Mission in Syria (UNSMIS) in 2012.

The litany of ineffective international actions in Syria demonstrates that a robust R2P response is never automatic. Public lamentations were audible as Syrian security forces deployed tanks, warships, and heavy weapons against civilians who were increasingly mixed with fighters. Despite strong condemnatory statements of al-Assad's crimes against humanity, no decision with teeth was possible because China and Russia routinely threatened to veto or vetoed even the most watered-down proposals. In August 2012, Annan resigned, citing the intransigence of the al-Assad regime and conflict on the Security Council. In the face of increasing violence, the UN decided to end UNSMIS when its mandate expired; however, it did appoint Lakhdar Brahimi to replace Annan to continue the negotiations to end the violence.

Brahimi encountered even more grave difficulties in negotiating a resolution to the Syrian conflict. In September 2013, a sarin gas attack in a Damascus suburb, followed by chemical weapons use in Aleppo and elsewhere, shocked the international community. Western powers contemplated military action against Syrian government forces without Security Council authorization. Russian president Vladimir Putin took the extraordinary step of writing an opinion piece in the *New York Times* to caution against such a move. Putin claimed it was not clear who used the weapons and argued that:

> The potential strike by the United States against Syria, despite strong opposition from many countries and major political and religious leaders, including the pope, will result in more innocent victims and escalation, potentially spreading the conflict far beyond Syria's borders. A strike would increase violence and unleash a new wave of terrorism. It could undermine multilateral efforts to resolve the Iranian nuclear problem and the Israeli-Palestinian conflict and further destabilize the Middle East and North Africa. It could throw the entire system of international law and order out of balance .[54]

Putin's public diplomacy about the unintended consequences of intervention, coupled with a corresponding plan to disarm Syria of chemical weapons put forth by Russia and China dissuaded the United States from following through on its threat. The framework agreement worked out between Russia and the United States was approved by the Security Council in resolution 2118. The resolution declared that the use of chemical weapons was a threat to international peace and security and endorsed the destruction of Syrian chemical weapons under the auspices of the Organization for the Prohibition of Chemical Weapons (OPCW). The resolution also stated that noncompliance would result in Chapter VII enforcement, although another council resolution would be required to authorize military force. After initial wrangling and false starts, the chemical weapons in Syria were rather quickly removed and destroyed by the OPCW. A year later, the OPCW reported that 96 percent of Syrian chemical weapons stockpiles had been destroyed.[55] In May 2014, Brahimi resigned and was replaced by another special envoy, Staffan de Mistura.

The expeditious disarmament process shows that when the important members of the first UN can agree, then even the most complicated problems can be addressed. Unfortunately, people do not die by chemical weapons alone. They die from small arms fire, improvised explosive devices, and war-induced starvation and disease. The violence and killing continues in Syria, with upward of 250,000 dead and half of the prewar population displaced. The human catastrophe is exacerbated by government helicopters' dropping barrel bombs containing chlorine as well as the massacres and beheadings by some rebel factions (including ISIS and ISIS-related terrorist groups).

The brutality and lethality of nonstate actors (NSAs) has emerged as a cross-regional problem in the Middle East and North Africa. These NSAs use violence to overthrow repressive governments, but replacing one group of tyrants with another does little to improve human dignity. Moreover, humanitarian intervention can unleash serious unintended consequences. The crisis in Syria is symptomatic of a wider problem that requires a wider regional solution. While this is cause for pessimism, it important to recall that R2P is a principle and not a tactic, and the principle has influenced the international response in Syria even if international action was considerably slower and less robust than in Libya and Côte d'Ivoire. The transformation of international attitudes is remarkable compared to the deafening silence that greeted the 1982 massacre by Hafez al-Assad (the father of Bashar) of some forty thousand people in an artillery barrage of Hama. Today, there is a steady stream of hostile condemnations of his son's machinations from a host of actors: the UN's Joint Office on the Prevention of Genocide and R2P called for a halt to crimes against humanity; the Human Rights Council condemned the crimes by a crushing vote and published a report detailing extensive crimes; the United States, the European Union, and other states imposed sanctions; the Arab League condemned the actions, formulated a peace plan, and sent human rights monitors; and the UN General Assembly initially condemned the violence and supported the peace plan with a two-thirds majority, and later even more overwhelmingly condemned Bashar al-Assad's unbridled crackdown on his population and specifically called for his resignation. Only twelve states voted against it.

The Syrian crisis is far from abating. The flow of refugees and migrants from the region has had a dramatic impact in Europe, and members of the EU struggle to formulate a common policy and cost-sharing plan. At the 2015 General Assembly summit, Russian president Putin argued it was a mistake for the UN not to work constructively with al-Assad. Russia has also intervened militarily in Syria to help prop up the regime, striking at Western-backed rebels and occasionally ISIS militants. The first UN is divided, with important member states disagreeing as to the cause of the crisis and how to resolve it.

Mali

In January 2012, the Tuareg (a seminomadic Berber group), loosely allied with several Islamic militant groups, including Al Qaeda in the Islamic Maghreb, attacked government offices in remote areas of northern Mali. The Tuareg have long had a difficult, complicated, and often violent relationship with the Malian central government. Many of the Tuareg fighters in this particular rebellion had served as mercenaries in the Libyan army and returned to the area after the fall of the Gaddafi regime. The military setbacks in the north destabilized the already weak central government in Bamako far to the southwest. In March 2012, the government was overthrown by military officers and Mali descended into chaos. ECOWAS condemned the coup d'état and began the process of negotiating a deal that would have the military step down and hold elections.

In the absence of a functioning government, the loose Tuareg-Islamic alliance seized control of several northern regions; in April 2012, the alliance declared the area an independent Islamic state. In the south, ECOWAS and the AU were trying to restore the constitution diplomatically, and also working to reestablish the territorial integrity of Mali. ECOWAS and Mali appealed to the UN Security Council for a stabilization force throughout the summer, but council members were reluctant to authorize such a force absent a functioning government and with the situation on the ground so opaque and fluid. By August 2012, a fragile national unity government had formed in the south, but in the north the Tuareg-Islamic alliance fractured. The Tuareg were routed by their former allies, and the in-fighting killed thousands. Several hundred thousand were forced to flee to neighboring countries or become internally displaced. Islamic militias also destroyed mosques and cultural sites. The Security Council and ICC prosecutor publicly warned militant groups that the destruction of shrines and cultural sites was a war crime.

The humanitarian situation continued to deteriorate; and in the fall of October 2012, the Security Council responded with resolution 2071. This resolution demanded an end to attacks on civilians and authorized the UN secretary-general to work with ECOWAS and AU officials in planning for an international military force.[56] Resolution 2085 (December 2012) authorized the deployment of the African-led International Support Mission in Mali (AFISMA) with a mandate to help strengthen Mali's military and to assist the fledgling government's primary responsibility to protect the population from gross violations of human rights and crimes against humanity. AFISMA took several months to get off the ground.

The declared Islamic state in north Mali continues to be seen as a clear threat to international peace and security especially by Western members of the UN Security Council, who see it as a direct threat to European security.[57] When the Islamic forces in the north successfully pushed south in late December 2012– early January 2013, several council members decided more forceful action was necessary. At the invitation of the Malian government, France launched military strikes against the Islamists (who were advancing toward Bamako) on January 10, 2013. The action, called Operation Serval, was perceived as legal because it was done at the invitation of the Malian government and the UN Charter allows for collective self-defense. France also claimed Operation Serval was consistent with Security Council resolution 2085. While the council did not explicitly authorize this particular use of military force, it gave its "blessing" to the French use of force.[58]

In April 2013, Security Council resolution 2100 cited Chapter VII to create the United Nations Multidimensional Integrated Stabilization Mission in Mali (MINUSMA), which contained a robust mandate to use force to protect civilians. It also welcomed the response of France and identified several of the belligerents as terrorist organizations.[59] The complex mission involves assisting transitional authorities, implementing a transitional roadmap, human rights monitoring, and creating humanitarian space. France also was authorized to use force in support of MINUSMA. This peace enforcement operation in Mali got off to a slow start because of the usual logistical problems of getting member states to provide troops, materiel, and funding. The initial deployment of MINUSMA was really a "rehatting" of approximately six thousand AFMISA troops already in Mali. The French military and MINUSMA did create a stable, yet fragile, environment that allowed for presidential elections and provisional peace talks. However, violence in the north escalated and the UN has been unable to project sufficient force to tamp down the unrest. By the end of 2013, MINUSMA was only at half of its mandated strength of 11,200 and was forced to withdraw from key areas in the north. It has subsequently returned to full authorized strength.

An interesting dimension of this peacekeeping/peace enforcement mission is that Security Council member states, including China, have committed combat troops.[60] The UN has also taken sides in the conflict, identifying specific groups as terrorist organizations. This reality has contributed to the attractiveness of MINUSMA as a target of rebel and Islamist groups. To date, forty-nine peacekeepers have lost their lives, including twenty in October 2014. Despite its robust mandate, MINUSMA has had a difficult time protecting civilians. Reports suggest some peacekeepers have used excessive force against civilians during demonstrations, which highlights some of the difficulties of dealing with the local populations during domestic conflicts. The complex mission suffered numerous military setbacks, and military skirmishes with rebel and insurgent groups are becoming more frequent.[61] Gains made by the French intervention in the north have been rolled back and the fragile Malian government, with its rampant corruption, struggles to govern.

The Central African Republic

For decades, the Central African Republic (CAR) has been plagued with civil violence that pitted the minority Muslim population against the Christian majority and Christian-dominated government. The UN Integrated Peacebuilding Office in the Central African Republic (BINUCA) began operations in 2010 to strengthen peace and democratic institutions. In December 2012, an alliance of

Muslim groups, called the Seleka, launched a series of attacks that prompted a brutal government response. The UN-AU brokered a peace accord in January 2013, but Muslim rebels attacked the capital, Bangui, and forced the CAR president to flee in March 2013. The leader of the rebellion, Michel Djotodia, suspended the constitution and dissolved the government. Despite strong international and domestic opposition, Djotodia became president of the CAR as part of a transition government in August 2013. The CAR quickly descended into rival ethnic and religious violence that killed thousands and displaced tens of thousands more. In December 2013, the Security Council authorized an AU-led peacekeeping mission, the International Support Mission to the Central African Republic (MISCA) supported by French military forces (Operation Sangaris). Under Chapter VII, UN Security resolution 2127 authorized military force to protect civilians, allowing MISCA to support the stabilization of the country and the transition to a democratic government based on previous agreements. It also authorized the creation of an Independent Commission of Inquiry to investigate violations of human rights and humanitarian principles that bordered on genocide and ethnic cleansing as Christian militias, known as the anti-Balaka, systematically targeted Muslim civilians as well as suspected rebels. The Security Council also authorized the UN secretary-general to plan for the transition of MISCA from an AU to a UN peacekeeping force.

The violence continued and the arrival of foreign fighters from around the region led to an escalation in atrocities. In January 2014, Djotodia resigned, and in April 2014, the Security Council authorized the creation of the United Nations Multidimensional Integrated Stabilization Mission in the Central African Republic (MINUSCA). MINUSCA officially took over from MISCA in September 2014 with its principal mandate to protect civilians. It is also charged with facilitating the delivery of humanitarian assistance and human rights monitoring. Its other responsibilities, such as assisting with the disarmament and demobilization of warring parties, have been pushed to the back burner as few have been willing to lay down their arms. France continues to have troops on the ground to provide protection to the airport and other strategic areas. However, it plans to withdraw all troops by the end of 2015. Their mission has been rocked by scandal with allegations of child sexual abuse by French soldiers. The government of France was criticized by UN High Commissioner for Human Rights Zeid Ra'ad Al-Hussein for being slow to investigate the allegations.[62] Ironically, a decade earlier Al-Hussein wrote a report for Secretary-General Annan calling for "zero tolerance" for such abuse.[63] Even more ironically, a senior UN whistle-blower working for Al-Hussein who leaked an internal report was fired—but then reinstated by an administrative tribunal—after exposing alleged child abuse by French forces in a Security Council–approved but French-led mission in the Central African Republic. Echoing previously reported abuse in Haiti, Liberia, and the Democratic Republic of the Congo, the report finds that children displaced by war were molested and raped in exchange for food, and the UN has done nothing as yet to hold peacekeepers accountable. Amid the public outcry, Ban Ki-moon fired Babacar

Gaye, the head of the United Nations mission in the Central African Republic, the first such firing of a mission head in recent memory.

The UN itself reported almost five hundred similar allegations between 2008 and 2013, which suggests the extent to which Zeid's original efforts have failed to end the culture of impunity.[64] This issue in fact has dogged the UN's various peace operations since the 1990s because the world organization has no authority to investigate or punish misconduct, a right jealously guarded by the nearly 120 states that have contributed soldiers to peace operations over the last half century.

The uproar over these allegations, while justified, distracts from the scale of the atrocities that occurred in the CAR. According to the Independent Commission of Inquiry on the Central African Republic, there is ample evidence of war crimes and crimes against humanity. [65] The Muslim population was systematically targeted, causing many to flee to neighboring countries or to be internally displaced. The international community of states interceded in the conflict and helped slow the escalating violence. Some areas of the CAR are still inaccessible and much remains to be done in terms of reintegration and repatriation.

WHITHER THE RESPONSIBILITY TO PROTECT?

Dilemmas remain as Libya—a country with no history of democratic rule and plenty of evidence of ethnic feuds and bitterness—hurtles headlong into a new era.[66] Côte d'Ivoire appears to be turning a page: it is returning displaced persons, soothing memories of massacres, and alleviating human suffering. Syria continues to hemorrhage, Mali smolders, and the CAR remains on the brink of disintegrating. Let us be clear: R2P is not a panacea. But it is a step in the right normative direction away from genocide and crimes against humanity. Gary Bass's *Freedom's Battle: The Origins of Humanitarian Intervention* concludes, "We are all atrocitarians now—but so far only in words, and not yet in deeds."[67]

In the abstract, R2P suggests that state sovereignty is not absolute but contingent on responsible governmental behavior. If a government egregiously violates international law, and in particular if it allows atrocities or is the perpetrator of such abuse, its claims to sovereignty will be reviewed and maybe restricted or even overturned by the Security Council. A standard of consistent implementation is a fool's errand. In terms of applying the emerging norm, Syria is not Libya, and Sri Lanka is not Côte d'Ivoire. Political interests and will vary from case to case. Coming to the rescue may not be popular when blood and treasure are involved. Military intervention even for human protection purposes is not a favored option when a quagmire looms. Particularly difficult to sustain for democratic states is a foreign venture costing the lives of their military personnel, but when no traditional self-interests seem at stake. That has not changed since Somalia in the early 1990s.

The UN's track record in the twenty-first century is disputed.[68] On the one hand, the organization has fielded significant security operations in some of the world's most troubled hot spots and saved and improved lives.[69] Often this has been done with the "coerced consent" of the parties involved—for instance, Serbia in Kosovo and Indonesia in East Timor. At the end of 2015, the United Nations was engaged in sixteen peacekeeping operations and when those missions are fully deployed, well over 106,000 uniformed personnel will be in the field from some 120 troop-contributing member states.[70]

On the other hand, important states, such as China and Russia, along with some countries in the Global South, have created a backlash against the responsibility to protect. Despite the norm's approval of paragraphs 138 and 139 of the *World Summit Outcome Document*, evidence of buyer's remorse continues to surface in New York, as some of the usual suspects who are uneasy with any incursions into human rights are up in arms and trying to argue that the emerging norm is no longer emerging and should not be described as having emerged.[71] At the same time, there is ample cultural evidence across the Global South to sustain robust and justifiable humanitarian action.[72] Support by countries in the region for outside intervention in Libya was also noteworthy as was fulsome rhetorical support by regional organizations for action in Côte d'Ivoire and Syria.

Civil society's norm entrepreneurs, those who establish or set standards, can make a difference. R2P supporters continue to advocate for an alternative vision that is intellectually and doctrinally coherent and clearly expressed. The long-term goal is protecting the essence of the norm such that it triggers effective action to save lives from mass atrocities. The R2P notion is complex and multifaceted. In discussing the need for conceptual clarity, some observers hope the responsibility to protect can be a springboard for all international responses to prevent and resolve armed conflicts, while others see it as a framework for international efforts to protect civilians, and still others as a framework for military intervention. Whatever else, R2P is fundamentally about overriding sovereignty when mass atrocities occur, and so the concept will always be contested.

It is important to place these developments within a historical context. With the possible exception of the prevention of genocide after World War II, no idea has moved faster or farther in the international normative arena than the responsibility to protect. It was not so long ago—in 1995—that the Commission on Global Governance proposed amending the UN Charter to explicitly permit Chapter VII military action with a humanitarian justification.[73] The recommendation was moot: the interventions of the 1990s show that the Security Council has recognized that massive human suffering constitutes a sufficient threat to international peace and security to justify forceful action. José Alvarez observes the acceleration in the usual pace for normative development: "Traditional descriptions of the requisites of custom—the need for the passage of a considerable period of time and the accumulation of evidence of the diplomatic practices between sets of states reacting to one another's acts—appear increasingly passé."[74]

What is perhaps most important is the reconceptualization of state sovereignty—from being an absolute barrier to outside action, to having the duty to protect human rights and respect human security.[75] After centuries of more or less passive and mindless acceptance of the proposition that state sovereignty was a license to kill and repress, it is now clear that sovereigns must govern responsibly.

As in other arenas, actions speak louder than words. And in this latter regard, the international response to Burmese policy in the wake of a devastating cyclone in May 2008, for example, can only give pause. That military government was clearly insensitive to the humanitarian needs of many of its coastal citizens, who were further impoverished and sometimes displaced by natural disaster, after tens of thousands had been killed. Yet important outsiders, such as China, were not much interested in compelling the government to act on behalf of those in need, and so the government's sluggish response continued for some time. This insensitivity involved the refusal to give permission to U.S. Navy vessels and others waiting offshore for permission to provide assistance. The ships eventually sailed away for lack of sovereign consent, although the predicted mass starvation and disease did not transpire.

In short, we can say that the R2P norm has moved quickly but that the concept is young. Edward Luck provides a note of caution: "Like most infants, R2P will need to walk before it can run."[76] We see that R2P is an idea, and we should remind ourselves that ideas matter, for good and for ill. Political theorist Daniel Philpott's study of revolutions in sovereignty demonstrates that they are driven primarily by the power of ideas,[77] and we are in the midst of a revolution in which state sovereignty is becoming more contingent on upholding basic human rights values. Gareth Evans encourages us: "And for all the difficulties of acceptance and application that lie ahead, there are—I have come optimistically, but firmly, to believe—not many ideas that have the potential to matter more for good, not only in theory but in practice, than that of the responsibility to protect."[78]

NOTES

1. International Commission on Intervention and State Sovereignty, *The Responsibility to Protect: Report* (Ottawa: ICISS, 2001). See also Thomas G. Weiss and Don Hubert, *The Responsibility to Protect: Research, Bibliography, and Background* (Ottawa: ICISS, 2001). For interpretations by some of the major participants, see Gareth Evans, *The Responsibility to Protect: Ending Mass Atrocity Crimes Once and for All* (Washington, D.C.: Brookings Institution, 2008); Thomas G. Weiss, *Humanitarian Intervention: Ideas in Action*, 3rd ed. (Cambridge: Polity, 2016); and Ramesh Thakur, *The United Nations, Peace and Security: From Collective Security to the Responsibility to Protect* (Cambridge: Cambridge University Press, 2006). See also Anne Orford, *International Authority and the Responsibility to Protect* (Cambridge: Cambridge University Press, 2011); Alex Bellamy, *The Responsibility to Protect* (Cambridge: Polity, 2009); James Pattison, *Humanitarian and the Responsibility to Protect: Who Should Intervene?* (Oxford: Oxford University Press, 2010); and Aidan Hehir, *The Responsibility to Protect: Rhetoric, Reality and the Future of Humanitarian Intervention* (Basingstoke, U.K.: PalgraveMacmillan, 2012).

2. Thomas G. Weiss, "The Politics of Humanitarian Ideas," *Security Dialogue* 31, no. 1 (2000): 11–23.

3. Mohammed Ayoob, "Humanitarian Intervention and International Society," *Global Governance* 7, no. 3 (2001): 225–230; and Robert Jackson, *The Global Covenant: Human Conduct in a World of States* (Oxford: Oxford University Press, 1998).

4. General Assembly, *2005 World Summit Outcome*, para. 139.

5. Christine Bourloyannis, "The Security Council of the United Nations and the Implementation of International Humanitarian Law," *Denver Journal of International Law and Policy* 20, no. 3 (1993): 43.

6. T. A. van Baarda, "The Involvement of the Security Council in Maintaining International Law," *Netherlands Quarterly of Human Rights* 12, no. 1 (1994): 140.

7. Martha Finnemore, *The Purpose of Intervention: Changing Beliefs About the Use of Force* (Ithaca, N.Y.: Cornell University Press, 2003).

8. Independent Commission on Kosovo, *Kosovo Report: Conflict, International Response, Lessons Learned* (Oxford: Oxford University Press, 2000).

9. Kofi A. Annan, "Secretary-General's Speech to the 54th Session of the General Assembly," September 20, 1999.

10. UN Press Release SG/SM/6878, January 28, 1999.

11. Adam Roberts, "NATO's 'Humanitarian War' in Kosovo," *Survival* 41, no. 3 (1999): 102–123.

12. See Human Rights Watch, "Kosovo: Failure of NATO, U.N. to Protect Minorities," July 27, 2004, www.hrw.org/english/docs/2004/07/27/serbia9136.htm.

13. *Accordance with International Law of Unilateral Declaration of Independence in Respect of Kosovo, Advisory Opinion*, http//www.icj-cij.org/docket/files/141/15987.pdf. For discussions of this opinion, see "Recent International Advisory Opinion," *Harvard Law Review* 124 (2011): 1098–1105; Ralph Wilde, "Accordance with International Law of Unilateral Declaration of Independence in Respect of Kosovo, Advisory Opinion," *American Journal of International Law* 105, no. 2 (2011): 301–307; Marc Weller, "Modesty Can Be a Virtue: Judicial Economy in the ICJ Kosovo Opinion?" *Leiden Journal of International Law* 24, no. 1 (2011): 127–147.

14. Matthew Brunwasser, "Kosovo and Serbia Reach Key Deal," *New York Times*, February 24, 2012.

15. Michael G. Smith with Moreen Dee, *Peacekeeping in East Timor: The Path to Independence* (Boulder, Colo.: Lynne Rienner, 2003).

16. The Report of United Nations Independent Special Commission of Inquiry for Timor-Leste, document S/2006/628, October 2, 2006, www.ohchr.org/Documents/Countries/COITimorLeste.pdf.

17. José Ramos-Horta, "Elections to Be Proud Of," *New York Times*, April 18, 2012.

18. Funmi Olonisakin, *Peacekeeping in Sierra Leone: The Story of UNAMSIL* (Boulder, Colo.: Lynne Rienner, 2008).

19. See "Sierra Leone Profile," BBC News, http://news.bbc.co.uk/2/hi/africa/country_profiles/1065898.stm.

20. David Curran and Tom Woodhouse, "Cosmopolitan Peacekeeping and Peacebuilding in Sierra Leone: What Can Africa Contribute?" *International Affairs* 83, no. 6 (2007): 1055–1070.

21. Thierry Tardy, "The UN and the Use of Force: A Marriage Against Nature," *Security Dialogue* 38 (March 2007): 49–70.

22. Sandra Whitworth, *Men, Militarism, and UN Peacekeeping: A Gendered Analysis* (Boulder: Colo.: Lynne Rienner, 2004).

23. General Assembly document A/61/901 and Security Council document S/2007/269, www.mofa.go.jp/mofaj/gaiko/peace_b/pdfs/sil_070514_missionrep.pdf.

24. Peacebuilding Commission, *Review of the Outcome of the High-Level Special Session of the Peacebuilding Commission on Sierra Leone*, PBC/4/SLE/3, October 1, 2010.

25. Statement by Ambassador Guillermo E. Rishchynski, Permanent Representative of Canada to the United Nations to the Security Council on the Situation in Sierra Leone, March 22, 2012.

26. Richard Gowan, "Floating Down the River of History: Ban Ki-moon and Peacekeeping, 2007–2011," *Global Governance* 17 (2011): 400.

27. Hemi Mistry and Deborah Ruiz Verduzco, "The UN Security Council and the International Criminal Court: International Law Meeting Summary, with Parliamentarians for Global Action," Chatham House, March 12, 2012, http://www.chathamhouse.org/sites/default/files/public/Research/International%20Law/160312summary.pdf.

28. Colum Lynch, "France Declines to Contribute Major Force for UN Mission," *Washington Post*, August 16, 2006.

29. UNIFIL Facts and Figures, http://www.un.org/en/peacekeeping/missions/unifil/facts.shtml.

30. David Axe, "UN Adds Bulk to Peacekeeping Forces in Lebanon," *Aviation Week*, February 7, 2007.

31. Andrzej Sitkowski, *UN Peacekeeping: Myth and Reality* (Westport, Conn.: Praeger Security International, 2006).

32. Dave Benjamin, "Sudan and the Resort to Regional Arrangements: Putting Effect to the Responsibility to Protect?" *International Journal of Human Rights* 14 (April 2010): 233–245.

33. Scott Strauss, "Darfur and the Genocide Debate," *Foreign Affairs* 84 (2005): 123–133; Noelle Quenivet, "The Report of the International Commission of Inquiry on Darfur: The Question of Genocide," *Human Rights Review* 7 (July 2006): 38–68; and Gérard Prunier, *Darfur: The Ambiguous Genocide* (Ithaca, N.Y.: Cornell University Press, 2007).

34. Corrina Heyder, "The U.N. Security Council's Referral of the Crimes in Darfur to the International Criminal Court in Light of U.S. Opposition to the Court," *Berkeley Journal of International Law* 24 (2006): 650–671.

35. Alex J. Bellamy and Paul D. Williams, "The UN Security Council and the Question of Humanitarian Intervention in Darfur," *Journal of Military Ethics* 5 (June 2006): 144–160.

36. "The Rewards of Beavering Away," *Economist*, January 3, 2008.

37. For a discussion, see Thomas G. Weiss and Martin Welz, "Military Twists and Turns in World Politics: Downsides or Dividends for UN Peace Operations?" *Third World Quarterly* 36, no. 8 (2015): 1493–1509.

38. Human Rights Watch, *Men with No Mercy*, September 2015, https://www.hrw.org/report/2015/09/09/men-no-mercy/rapid-support-forces-attacks-against-civilians-darfur-sudan.

39. For a timeline of events, see "Libya Profile," BBC News, http://www.bbc.co.uk/news/world-africa-13755445.

40. Mehrdad Payandeh, "The United Nations, Military Intervention and Regime Change in Libya," *Virginia Journal of International Law* 52 (2012): 372.

41. UN Press Release, GA/11137, September 16, 2011.

42. See Dag Hennriksen and Ann Karin Larsen, eds., *The Political Rationale and International Consequences of the War in Libya* (Oxford: Oxford University Press, 2016); and Mónica Serrano and Thomas G. Weiss, eds., *The International Politics of Human Rights: Rallying to the R2P Cause?* (London: Routledge, 2014).

43. Alex Bellamy and Paul D. Williams, "The New Politics of Protection: Côte d'Ivoire, Libya and the Responsibility to Protect," *International Affairs* 4 (2011): 845.

44. The use of special forces in Libya has been reported by the *Mirror, Guardian, Al Jazeera,* CNN, and Fox News.

45. Richard Norton Taylor, "Libya Mission 'Has Made UN Missions to Protect Civilians Unlikely,'" *Guardian* (London), March 18, 2012, http://www.guardian.co.uk/world/2012 /mar/19/libya-un-missions-civilians.

46. Thomas G. Weiss, "RtoP Alive and Well After Libya," *Ethics & International Affairs* 25, no. 3 (2011): 287–292.

47. "Letter Dated 9 November 2011 from the Permanent Representative of Brazil to the United Nations Addressed to the Secretary-General," UN document A/66/551-S/2011/701, 1.

48. Hugo Slim, *Humanitarian Ethics: A Guide to the Morality of Aid in War and Disaster* (Oxford: Oxford University Press, 2015); Michael Barnett and Thomas G. Weiss, *Humanitarianism Contested: Where Angels Fear to Tread* (London: Routledge, 2011); and Michael Barnett and Thomas G. Weiss, eds., *Humanitarianism in Question: Politics, Power, Ethics* (Ithaca, N.Y.: Cornell University Press, 2008).

49. Amnesty International Report, March 19, 2012; C. J. Chivers and Eric Schmitt, "In Strikes on Libya by NATO, an Unspoken Civilian Toll," *New York Times*, December 17, 2011.

50. *Report of the International Commission of Inquiry on Libya*, Human Rights Council document A/HRC/19/68, March 2, 2012, 1.

51. Alan J. Kuperman, "A Model Humanitarian Intervention?" *International Security* 38, no. 1 (Summer 2013): 105–136.

52. This account draws on Thomas G. Weiss, "Military Humanitarianism: Syria Hasn't Killed It," *Washington Quarterly* 37, no. 1 (2014): 7-20.

53. "Security Council Fails to Adopt Draft Resolution on Syria as Russian Federation, China Veto Text Supporting Arab League's Proposed Peace Plan," UN Security Council, SC/10536, February 4, 2012, http://www.un.org/News/Press/docs/2012/sc10536.doc.htm.

54. Vladimir Putin, "A Plea for Caution from Russia: What Putin Has to Say to Americans About Syria," *New York Times*, September 11, 2013, http://www.nytimes.com /2013/09/12/opinion/putin-plea-for-caution-from-russia-on-syria.html.

55. UN News Centre, "Ninety-six Percent of Syria's Declared Chemical Weapons Destroyed—UN-OPCW Mission Chief," (September 4, 2014), http://www.un.org/apps/news /story.asp?NewsID=48642#.VUf7q4l0xjo.

56. UN News Centre, "Adopting Resolution 2071 (2012) Security Council Demands that Armed Groups Cease Human Rights Abuses, Humanitarian Violations in Northern Mali (October 12, 2012), http://www.un.org/press/en/2012/sc10789.doc.htm

57. Gorm Rye Olsen, "Fighting Terrorism in Africa by Proxy: The USA and the European Union in Somalia and Mali," *European Security* 23, no. 3 (September 2014): 290-306.

58. Karine Bannelier and Theodore Christakis, "Under the UN Security Council's Watchful Eyes: Military Intervention by Invitation in the Malian Conflict," *Leiden Journal of International Law* 25, no. 4 (December 2013): 855–874.

59. Thomas G. Weiss and Martin Welz, "The UN and the African Union in Mali and Beyond: A Shotgun Wedding?" with Martin Welz, *International Affairs* 90, no. 4 (2014): 889–905.

60. *Economist,* "Over There," June 15, 2013, 44.

61. Adam Nossiter, "Attacks on U.N. Force Add to Unrest in Mali," *New York Times,* May 1, 2015, A6.

62. Somini Sengupta, "U.N. Official Accuses France of Delays in Child Sex Abuse Case," *New York Times,* May 9, 2015, A9.

63. Zeid Ra'ad Al-Hussein, "A Comprehensive Strategy to Eliminate Future Sexual Exploitation and Abuse in United Nations Peacekeeping Operations," UN document A/59/710, March 24, 2005.

64. There was widespread media coverage of the leaked report. For example, see http://www.aljazeera.com/news/2015/06/peacekeepers-accused-swapping-goods-sex -150611110949806.html.

65. *Final Report of the International Commission of Inquiry on the Central African Republic, received from the Chair of the Commission in Accordance with Security Council Resolution 2127 (2013)*, UN document S/2014/928, December 22, 2014.

66. The argument and conclusion draw on Thomas G. Weiss, "Humanitarian Intervention and US Policy," in *Great Decisions*, ed. Karen Rohan (New York: Foreign Policy Association, 2012).

67. Gary J. Bass, *Freedom's Battle: The Origins of Humanitarian Intervention* (New York: Knopf, 2008), 382.

68. See Michael Doyle and Nicholas Sambanis, *Making War and Building Peace: United Nations Peace Operations* (Princeton, N.J.: Princeton University Press, 2006); and Sebastian von Einsedel, David Malone, and Bruno Stagno, eds., *The United Nations Security Council: From Cold War to the 21st Century* (Boulder, Colo.: Lynne Rienner, 2016)

69. John Kabia, *Humanitarian Intervention and Conflict Resolution in West Africa: From ECOMOG to ECOMIL* (Burlington, Vt.: Ashgate, 2009).

70. Paul D. Williams, *Enhancing U.S. Support for Peace Operations in Africa*, Council Special Report No. 73 (New York: Council on Foreign Relations, 2015).

71. Thomas G. Weiss, "Reinserting 'Never' into 'Never Again': Political Innovations and the Responsibility to Protect," in *Driven from Home: Protecting the Rights of Forced Migrants*, ed. David Hollenbach (Washington, D.C.: Georgetown University Press, 2010), 207–228.

72. Rama Mani and Thomas G. Weiss, eds., *The Responsibility to Protect: Cultural Perspectives from the Global South* (London: Routledge, 2011).

73. Commission on Global Governance, *Our Global Neighborhood: The Report of the Commission on Global Governance* (Oxford: Oxford University Press, 1995), 90.

74. José E. Alvarez, *International Organizations as Law-Makers* (Oxford: Oxford University Press, 2005), 591.

75. Daniel Philpott, *Revolutions in Sovereignty: How Ideas Shaped Modern International Relations* (Princeton, N.J.: Princeton University Press, 2001).

76. Edward C. Luck, "The United Nations and the Responsibility to Protect," *Policy Analysis Brief* (Muscatine, Ia.: Stanley Foundation, 2008), 8.

77. Daniel Philpott, *Revolutions in Sovereignty: How Ideas Shaped Modern International Relations* (Princeton, N.J.: Princeton University Press, 2001).

78. Evans, *The Responsibility to Protect*, 7.

CHAPTER 5

Confronting Contemporary Challenges

Many challenges and opportunities face the United Nations as it confronts evolving security threats in an uncertain political and financial environment. Combating terrorism and the proliferation of weapons of mass destruction (WMD) requires sustained and concerted effort among the member states of the first UN. It also requires leadership and a general consensus on goals and strategies. Unfortunately, the politics of the first UN remain polarized, and few states have the capability and will to lead. At the second UN, the election of a ninth secretary-general (to assume responsibilities in January 2017), the safety of UN personnel, the proliferation of nonstate actors (NSAs), and the scarcity of financial and military resources preoccupy UN officials. Efforts to reform the institution to make it more effective operationally repeatedly encounter roadblocks even though reform of the Security Council, peacekeeping operations, and the secretariat are critical for strengthening the UN as a whole.[1] This chapter is devoted to exploring how the UN, broadly defined, confronts these contemporary challenges.

SECURITY CHALLENGES

The events of September 11, 2001, brought into sharper focus the post–Cold War world's problems of disarmament and the nonproliferation and regulation of WMDs. The possibility that terrorist groups could get their hands on WMDs and use them in civilian and urban centers emerged as a critical security concern on the UN agenda. Moreover, the concern that rogue regimes would ally with terrorist groups—exemplified by Washington's tenuous and ultimately erroneous linkage of Saddam Hussein and Al Qaeda—rendered the issue of WMDs even more urgent for UN member states. UN efforts to build consensus around a coherent security strategy have met with varying degrees of success depending on the issue, circumstances, and states involved.

Terrorism

Until the 1990s, terrorism was dealt with almost entirely by the General Assembly, which approached the issue as a general problem of international law. [2] The twelve existing UN conventions related to terrorism identify particular forms of outlawed action but contain no definition of terrorism per se.[3] The lack of consensus among member states about the definition exposes a rift in the world organization. Defining terrorism reflects many concerns of states, such as their wanting to protect the option of small-scale and supposedly nonstate violent resistance to foreign occupation, such as the French resistance against Germany in the 1940s, the Afghan resistance against the Soviet Union in the 1980s, or Iraqi resistance against the United States in the 2000s. Other states want to protect the option of using small-scale and supposedly nonstate force to harass what they see as unjust domination, as the American colonists did early on against their British masters. Today, many developing countries and nonstate actors justify armed violence in the name of fighting for national liberation or resisting foreign occupation— hence the oft-used phrase "one person's terrorist is another's freedom fighter." Complicating matters further is the extent to which the term *terrorism* can be applied to state behavior, through a state's direct uses of violence or its direct or indirect support of NSAs that employ or enable violence. Some uses of force by Israel and the United States resulting in civilian casualties are mentioned in the same breath as suicide bombers. State military and financial aid for opposition groups in other states (e.g., Libya and Syria) who then set off car bombs in urban areas could constitute state-supported terrorism.

The UN's High-level Panel on Threats, Challenges and Change (HLP) confronted these traditional stumbling blocks head-on by offering a synthesis of what they viewed as an area of consensus: "Attacks that specifically target innocent civilians and non-combatants must be condemned clearly and unequivocally by all."[4] The secretary-general added that their "proposal has clear moral force."[5] While a clear definition of terrorism continues to elude member states, for the first time in UN history the heads of state and government at the 2005 World Summit issued an unqualified condemnation. They agreed to "strongly condemn terrorism in all forms and manifestations, committed by whomever, wherever and for whatever purposes."[6] However, earlier and clearer language stating that targeting civilians could not be justified—even for movements resisting occupation—had been removed. On balance, the summit added momentum to the secretary-general's evolving counterterrorism strategy. The summit's clear condemnation of terrorism was a step forward, fully consistent with the laws of war. It has ethical content, contains the basis for a future treaty that would reinforce existing humanitarian law, and places the UN near the center of the fight against terrorism—at least in terms of important norms, if not operational decisions.

Several points have become clear over the years. Attacks on civilians who take no active part in hostilities are prohibited by international humanitarian law, specifically the 1949 Geneva Conventions and Additional Protocols of 1977. Various other treaties prohibit attacks on diplomats and interference with civilian aircraft. Thus, the international community of states can reach and has reached agreement on prohibited targets of violence, thereby bypassing disagreement on an all-encompassing definition of terrorism.

The Security Council became more focused on terrorism primarily at the instigation of the United States and in response to key events: several aerial incidents in the late 1980s, including the downing of a Pan American flight over Lockerbie, Scotland; the attempted assassination of Egyptian president Hosni Mubarak in 1995; and the bombings of U.S. embassies in East Africa in 1998. In each case, the Security Council responded by imposing sanctions against Libya, Sudan, and Afghanistan for refusing to extradite suspects. Sanctions contributed to curbing state terrorism by Libya and Sudan but were ineffective in altering the behavior of the Taliban and Al Qaeda. Such groups tend to "situate themselves outside of the international system and reject its institutions and norms."[7] This is especially true of the Islamic State of Iraq and Syria (ISIS), which rules through violence and without regard for human rights or international humanitarian law.

The Security Council's approach changed in the aftermath of September 11. It acted immediately and endorsed measures ranging from approval of the use of force in self-defense to requiring member states to undertake wide-ranging and comprehensive measures against terrorism. Previously an issue drawing inconsistent attention from the General Assembly and the Security Council, terrorism quickly became a persistent and systematic focus at the UN.

The council's responses are noteworthy. Resolution 1368, passed the day after the attacks on U.S. territory, recognized "the inherent right of individual or collective self-defense." This was the first time that the right to self-defense was formally recognized as a legitimate response to nonstate violence. A few weeks later, the Security Council passed a comprehensive resolution outlining a series of wide-ranging measures to be undertaken by states to "prevent and suppress" terrorist acts. Resolution 1373 detailed the requirements for member states, including changes to national legislation. The resolution established the Counter-Terrorism Committee (CTC) to monitor member-state implementation of these measures. Once again the council had shrunk the domain of purely domestic affairs, in that national legislation involving tax laws for contributions to charities was subjected to international monitoring and mandates. And the Security Council went further in resolution 1540, unsettling some states as well as international lawyers, by using Chapter VII to call on states to enact national legislation intended to prohibit nonstate actors from acquiring WMDs. Resolution 1540 also mandated that states detail to the Security Council, through a committee, their legislative and administrative efforts to curb the proliferation of WMDs.

The General Assembly's work in developing international conventions on terrorism, while subsequently overshadowed by the Security Council, remains important.

The most significant advantage of the assembly is that it is an inclusive forum involving all member states. It is also the place where decisions about allocating organizational resources are made, thus giving it a direct impact on determining the administrative capability of the world organization to deal with terrorism. Still, this organizational capacity is greatly affected by the political will of member states. Thus, codification of emerging norms can perhaps better take place in a forum that can take a comprehensive, politically informed, and longer-term view.

The second UN also has a role to play in curbing terrorism. The secretary-general and the secretariat have the ability to take a less reactive, more comprehensive approach.[8] After September 11, Kofi Annan established a Policy Working Group on terrorism to examine how the UN should deal with the phenomenon.[9] In 2006 the General Assembly agreed to the UN Global Counter-Terrorism Strategy, which enables the UN to take a more coordinated approach to combating terrorism by building state capacity. Most of the heavy lifting in implementing the strategy is done by the Counter-Terrorism Task Force (CTTF), which is chaired by the Office of the Secretary-General (OSG). Ban Ki-moon has made combating terrorism a priority and, in his first year of office in 2007, launched an online handbook on counterterrorism to help states, agencies, and regional organizations coordinate operations.[10] Eight working groups have been established to comprehensively deal with the multiple dimensions of counterterrorism: Preventing and Resolving Conflict, Supporting and Highlighting Victims of Terrorism, Countering the Use of the Internet for Terrorism, Preventing and Responding to WMD Terrorism, Tackling Financing of Terrorism, Strengthening the Protection of Vulnerable Targets, Protecting Human Rights While Countering Terrorism, and Border Management. These groups were highlighted by Secretary-General Ban in his remarks to the Symposium on International Counter-Terrorism Cooperation.[11] The CTTF has a comprehensive strategy to combat the appeal of terrorist acts and to undermine the perceived legitimacy of such acts among different constituencies.

The disturbing fact remains that such groups as ISIS continue to recruit adherents from around the world despite its record of beheading detainees, torture, selling women and girls into sexual slavery, and other atrocities, including the destruction of cultural monuments. ISIS has also been able to inspire and even instruct homegrown terrorists to carry out attacks in such places as Paris, Brussels, and San Bernardino. The fact remains that states (e.g., Iran) continue to publicly support armed nonstate actors (e.g., Hezbollah), which carry out violations of human rights and humanitarian law. The fact remains that Russia continues to support armed nonstate actors in eastern Ukraine, which led to the shooting down of a Malaysian civilian airliner with much loss of life. Over a decade since 9/11, the UN remains the only global forum where the international community of states can develop strategies to reduce attacks on civilians.

WMDs and Nonproliferation

The UN's efforts to grapple with the threats to world peace posed by weapons of mass destruction extend back to the founding of the world body. Although absent from the Charter, eliminating atomic weapons arsenals and other weapons adaptable to mass destruction was the centerpiece of the General Assembly's first resolution in 1946.[12] The long-standing efforts of the first and second UNs to regulate WMDs—nudged along by nongovernmental organization (NGO) members of the third UN that are far more adamant about their elimination—have met varying degrees of success in at least three ways.

First, the UN is a forum for negotiations among states, for example, through the General Assembly and its First Committee, and the Conference on Disarmament—which is not formally part of the UN but reports to the assembly and is staffed by UN officials.[13] Among the major treaties concluded under UN auspices is the 1968 Nuclear Non-Proliferation Treaty (NPT). The only countries that have not joined the regime are India, Pakistan, and Israel; and in 2003 North Korea withdrew. The NPT rests on an asymmetric agreement between nuclear and nonnuclear states, committing the latter to forgo the acquisition of nuclear weapons in exchange for the use of nuclear technology for peaceful purposes (energy, medical, etc.). This technology is provided largely by the former, and the use of the nuclear technology is monitored by the International Atomic Energy Agency (IAEA). Another dimension of this asymmetric bargain is that the nuclear-armed states are to reduce their stockpiles with the eventual goal of total disarmament. September 11 generated increased emphasis, especially by the United States, on nonproliferation. In particular, it shined a spotlight on the possibility of "rogue regimes" acquiring nuclear and other WMD capabilities, an issue that only became more acute with North Korea's acquisition of nuclear weapons and extended negotiations about Iran's looming capacity to do so. In addition to the NPT, other major treaties include the 1972 Biological Toxins and Weapons Convention, the 1993 Chemical Weapons Convention, and the Comprehensive Test Ban Treaty, which the General Assembly adopted in 1996 but which has not yet entered into force. Second, the UN also has a limited role in directly implementing arms control agreements. It collaborates with the IAEA, which conducts inspections to verify that nuclear materials and activities are not used for military purposes. The UN also works with the Organization for the Prohibition of Chemical Weapons and the Preparatory Commission for the Comprehensive Nuclear-Test-Ban Treaty Organization. Third, the UN has also engaged in coercive disarmament, either through implementing sanctions or the threat of military force. These roles of the UN in international nonproliferation efforts are perhaps better illustrated in the negotiations surrounding the WMD programs of Iraq, North Korea, and Iran.

Iraq. After the Gulf War of 1990–1991, the Security Council passed resolution 687, which required Iraq to declare its WMD programs and facilities; imposed sanctions; and established intrusive weapons inspections bodies, such as the UN Special Commission (UNSCOM). UNSCOM uncovered nuclear, chemical, and biological weapons programs and oversaw the destruction of Iraq's chemical weapons and facilities as well as the country's biological weapons industry. UNSCOM's activities, however, were compromised by not only Iraqi deception but also its association with the U.S. Central Intelligence Agency (CIA), which led the Hussein regime to expel the commission and ban IAEA inspections in 1998. This brought to the forefront the issue of the autonomy of multilateral monitoring organizations that lack their own intelligence-gathering capacity. Subsequently the UN Monitoring, Verification, and Inspection Commission (UNMOVIC) was established and began a round of renewed weapons inspections in 2002.

By the end of 2002, the George W. Bush administration was determined to overthrow Saddam Hussein on the pretense that his regime had violated previous council resolutions and was engaging in the development of WMDs, which could potentially fall into the hands of terrorist groups, particularly Al Qaeda. The United Kingdom sided with the United States, but the other members of the P5—France, Russia, and China—along with other council members—staunchly opposed the use of force to disarm Iraq without the passage of more time and an additional resolution authorizing force from the Security Council. A fact that apparently had escaped notice was Saddam Hussein's reluctance to declare that he had few WMDs for fear of exposing his weakness, particularly vis-à-vis Iran.

The debate among the members of the first UN about how to deal appropriately with Iraq reflects the nature of power and how it manifests in the world organization—and world politics more generally. In a world in which a nonstate terrorist actor attacked the sole superpower, the struggle over resolutions in the Security Council and the publication of a new doctrine of a very broad anticipatory self-defense, or preventive, war (incorrectly, in international legal terms, dubbed "preemption" by U.S. officials),[14] are relevant to assessing the role of international law and the UN. Also relevant is the United States' and Great Britain's taking forceful action without UN authorization and the U.S. declaration of a goal of "regime change" in Iraq. The interplay of law and politics is part and parcel of understanding the UN's role in world affairs.

The U.S. invocation of self-defense against terrorism in response to September 11, and its military campaign in Afghanistan to dislodge a government that was intertwined with a terrorist network, was approved by the Security Council. The U.S. focus on WMDs in Iraq that might be put at the disposal of terrorists was placed within the framework of previous UN resolutions, thus indicating that traditional concerns about state security are by no means incompatible with international law and organization. Up to this point, basic U.S. foreign policy was largely consistent with and supportive of international law and the UN. Moreover, then president George W. Bush was persuaded by British prime minister Tony Blair and U.S. secretary of state Colin Powell to return to the council in the fall of 2002, even after the United States had started its military buildup in the Persian Gulf during the preceding summer. These actions indicate that the United Nations still matters and that obtaining international legitimacy through UN endorsement still counts for something, even to the United States, whose government under the George W. Bush administration believed in doctrinaire unilateralism.[15]

The rest of the story about Iraq and the UN in 2003 demonstrates that a fundamental point had not changed since 1945 and the ratification of the UN Charter, namely that the members of the Security Council need to be in agreement for it to be effective, diplomatically and militarily.[16] The council was in agreement up to a point, demanding Iraqi compliance with previous disarmament resolutions and stating in resolution 1441 that serious consequences would follow upon further noncompliance. The United States tried to get the council to state that the time for diplomacy had ended and that military responses were in order. But Washington was unable to muster the evidence needed to get nine votes for its draft resolution (cosponsored by the United Kingdom and Spain), much less counter an expected veto of its proposal by France, Russia, and China. Except for those of its three sponsors and perhaps Bulgaria, votes for war were hard to come by. This was a remarkable turn of events. In the fall of 2001 when the council had endorsed U.S. military strikes on the Taliban government in Afghanistan, which had supported the Al Qaeda network, and in fall 2002, the council had unanimously called for Iraq's rapid disarmament or it would face "serious consequences." This time such states as France and Russia did not believe, for good reasons, that the United States had demonstrated a substantial link between Iraq and the terrorist attacks on New York and the Pentagon. The Bush administration's argument that in the future Saddam Hussein might cooperate with terrorists in some type of attack on the United States seemed too amorphous for many states to justify an invasion of Iraq. Even council members basically friendly toward the United States, such as Chile and Mexico, were reluctant to endorse this new Bush doctrine, a broad interpretation of preventive war.

The U.S. stance was controversial and departed from the notion in international law of a limited preemption doctrine that might be appropriate when threats were immediate and overwhelming, leaving no time for further diplomacy. This approach, articulated in the nineteenth century by U.S. secretary of state Daniel Webster in the *Caroline* affair—when Canadian loyalists to the British crown destroyed a U.S. ship that was being used to supply arms and other provisions to Canadian rebels—was replaced by the Bush administration with the much broader standard of a possible and distant threat. This latter standard was not in line with customary international legal norms and not a doctrine that many states wanted the council to endorse in the Iraqi case.[17] The Bush doctrine of preemption would open a large Pandora's box. Would, for example, Russia have the unilateral right to use force in a neighboring state, absent any approval to do so by other states individually or the UN collectively?

There were other complications. Based on the earlier efforts at monitoring in Iraq,[18] the council had created a new weapons inspection regime centered on UNMOVIC for chemical and biological weapons and relied on the IAEA for nuclear weapons. These two UN agencies, one ad hoc and one permanent, had elicited some cooperation from Saddam Hussein—in the context of a U.S. military buildup in the Persian Gulf that eventually reached about three hundred thousand soldiers. Many states wanted to avoid war by giving these UN inspection teams more time to work, whereas the United States and its allies, especially Britain, felt that Iraq could always evade the more important inspection efforts. Moreover, Washington was concerned that protracted diplomacy would undercut its military pressure.

Some states also thought that the United States had always been more interested in removing the Saddam Hussein regime than in making serious arguments about homeland security. Indeed, both Clinton and Bush administration officials had talked of removing the Hussein regime long before the 9/11 attacks.

Many subplots were at work to fracture the Security Council over what to do about Iraq. Some observers thought that France was again deliberately taking anti-American positions and demonstrating a persistent effort to play the role of global power despite its limited economic and military capacities. Some thought that Russia was only too happy to cause trouble for a United States that had seemed disdainful of a major Russian role after the Cold War. Moreover, Moscow had substantial economic interests both in Iraq and in a continued high price for oil, one of Russia's chief exports. Both France and Russia had businesses that benefited extensively from the $64 billion Oil-for-Food Programme. Germany, a nonpermanent member at the time, opposed U.S. policy so as to appeal to domestic public opinion and win elections—at least in the view of many commentators. Some thought that the Bush administration was never interested in the type of multilateral diplomacy that constrained decision making in Washington, and that the Bush team simply wanted to use its power superiority to take out what it perceived as a "rogue state" and part of "the axis of evil"—even absent any substantial connection to Al Qaeda or any other group interested in attacks on the United States.

As in 1999 on the question of Kosovo, in 2003 the Security Council was unable to present a united front regarding Iraq. Unlike Kosovo, the United States could not fall back on the collective approval of the liberal democratic states making up NATO, because NATO itself was divided over Iraq, as were the members of the European Union. The United States could only seek legitimization through a "coalition of the willing," albeit a less impressive one than had been mobilized in 1991 (to push Iraq from Kuwait). The question of the collective authorization of force is a perennial one in international relations, especially when an armed attack against a state has not occurred. The Iraq case casts a pall over how the first UN deals with similar threats. The dangers posed by the spread of WMDs remain, and the UN and its most powerful member states have had to confront the international instability associated with the nuclear ambitions of North Korea and Iran.

North Korea. North Korea has been especially problematic as it tries to renegotiate its six decades of antagonistic relations with the United States. It has acquired crude nuclear weapons, and there is considerable evidence of its deliberate proliferation of such devices. In 2006 North Korea tested a series of long-range missiles in violation of past agreements. The Western powers immediately sought a strong Chapter VII decision ordering North Korea to cease developing and testing missiles and to prevent other member states from assisting them. China and Russia insisted on a watered-down version that excluded any reference to Chapter VII, which meant excluding any possibility of coercive measures to give teeth to the resolution.[19] The first Security Council decision about North Korea since 1993,[20] the July 2006 resolution 1695 condemned the missile tests and demanded that North Korea return to the Six-Party Talks (a negotiating forum consisting of China, the United States, Russia, Japan, South Korea, and North Korea).

Three months later, North Korea detonated a nuclear weapon. Western reaction was fast and furious, but again China was reluctant to punish its ally and insisted that it would veto any council resolution that allowed the possibility of the use of force.[21] When resolution 1718 was eventually passed, it invoked Chapter VII, but only Article 41 permitting sanctions, not Article 42 allowing military force. Resolution 1718 represents incremental progress in dealing with the development of WMDs and the ability to deliver such weapons. It also created a panel of experts to assist states in enforcing sanctions. But sanctions did little to deter North Korea's rogue behavior.

In September 2007 an Israeli raid destroyed a Syrian nuclear reactor that had been supplied by North Korea. The international reaction was surprisingly tight-lipped, and even Syria did not ask for a Security Council meeting. The IAEA launched an investigation into the site and after being stymied by Syria for several years, in 2011 referred Syria to the Security Council for noncompliance with its international obligations under the NPT. While some members of the council wanted sanctions, Russia and China were reluctant to impose them over a site and situation that no longer existed.[22]

In 2009, in what many observers saw as clear violation of 1718, North Korea launched a ballistic missile. The Security Council was unable to reach consensus about a response, but the test of yet another nuclear weapon resulted in Security Council resolution 1874, which enhanced sanctions and also placed an arms embargo against North Korea. The travel ban and financial restrictions of resolution 1718 also were strengthened. With the seizures of ships and cargo, along with targeted sanctions against key North Korean officials and companies, the international community of states stepped up the pressure.

The next major crisis centered on a series of events that started with the sinking of a South Korean warship, the *Cheonan*, in March 2010 in disputed waters on the maritime border between the two Koreas. Several days later, North Korea announced that it was starting construction on a nuclear reactor, thereby once again derailing the Six-Party Talks. The illness of Kim Jong Il simultaneously raised concerns about leadership succession and control of the North's nuclear arsenal. In 2010 Kim Jong Un, the youngest son of Kim Jong Il, was elevated to key positions within the North Korean hierarchy, fueling speculation that his father was terminally ill. Kim Jong Un assumed leadership in 2011 after the death of his father and in 2012 decided to launch a satellite. The launch failed, but the Security Council condemned it and expanded and tightened sanctions under previous resolutions.[23] Concerns about future developments in the North Korean nuclear arsenal continue as North Korea continues its militaristic provocations, but China and Russia remain obstacles to tougher measures, as their muted response to yet another test in early 2016 suggests. This time North Korea claimed to have tested a hydrogen bomb, although intelligence reports are skeptical of the veracity of that claim. It is unclear whether tougher measures or even Beijing's and Moscow's intransigence really matter because once nuclear weapons are acquired by a state, the risk of the Security Council's sanctioning an armed attack declines significantly.[24] In short, North Korea remains a security, WMD, and proliferation challenge.

Iran. While similar in many respects, Iran is qualitatively different. Iran is not as isolated and autarkic a pariah as North Korea. It is a large, diverse, and complicated state and a major player in the region, with an essential role in Iraq, Afghanistan, Syria, Lebanon, and the Persian Gulf. Nevertheless, Iran (along with Iraq and North Korea) had been identified as a part of the "axis of evil" in the famous 2002 State of the Union address by President George W. Bush. At the time of the speech, the Iranian president was a moderate, but he was quickly undermined domestically after Bush's declaration, and hard-line elements soon assumed power.

Unlike its nondeclared but nuclear neighbor Israel, Iran has been a member of the NPT since 1968 and embarked on a comprehensive nuclear energy program with the blessing and cooperation of the United States and under the auspices of the IAEA. After the 1979 Islamic Revolution, however, Washington suspended its cooperation and forced Iran to abandon its nuclear energy program. In 1989 Iran restarted the program, this time working with France, China, and Russia and under the supervision of the IAEA. Sometime in 2002, Iran quietly began construction of a nuclear reactor, a uranium enrichment program, and a heavy-water facility (which produces deuterium, used in atomic bombs). Iran did not initially notify the IAEA, although it did agree to IAEA inspections in 2003.[25] After those inspections, the IAEA reported that Iran was noncompliant with its obligations under the NPT, especially as it related to its enrichment activities. Iran responded by agreeing to talks with France, Germany, and the United Kingdom.

After negotiations stalled, the IAEA referred Iran to the Security Council in 2006. The central problem is that the NPT allows for states to pursue and use nuclear technology for peaceful purposes under IAEA supervision. States that have complex and developed nuclear energy programs also have the technical know-how and material capability to create nuclear weapons. That is, these states are nuclear weapon–capable or "nuclear latent states."[26] Germany, Japan, the Netherlands, South Africa, Turkey, and Brazil are nuclear latent states. Iran claims that it is only seeking to peacefully develop nuclear energy, as all countries have a right to do under the NPT. Moreover, three permanent members of the Security Council have lucrative contracts with Iran to develop that energy. Enriching uranium is necessary for nuclear energy, but enriching uranium to weapons grade is a relatively modest additional step involving more centrifuges and longer processing. The IAEA found evidence of weapons-grade uranium, prompting the referral to the Security Council. The council issued a Presidential Statement calling on Iran to suspend its enrichment activities and to ratify and implement the Additional Protocol of the NPT that governs enriching technologies.[27] Iran refused, and the council passed resolution 1696 under Chapter VII, which made the Presidential Statement binding on Iran. Iran continued to defy the council, which relied on resolutions 1737 and 1803 to impose targeted sanctions again in 2007. Russia also suspended its cooperation in building a nuclear power plant.

In 2008 Iran successfully launched a ballistic missile as part of its space program; however, the dual use alarmed many, especially in Israel and the West. In March 2008 the Security Council tightened sanctions with resolution 1835, this time banning trade in items that have both military and civilian uses. Iran responded by testing intermediate and long-range missiles. U.S. president Barack Obama, elected later that year, promised Iran more dialogue on its nuclear program; however, optimism waned when Iran's president Mahmoud Ahmadinejad declared victory over the "green movement" in a disputed election in June. Iran also acknowledged a secret nuclear facility near Qom and test-fired additional missiles. In 2010, after several IAEA plans were developed and rejected, the three Western powers of the P5 began negotiations for tougher sanctions. Resolution 1929 expanded the arms embargo and tightened financial and shipping restrictions.[28] The resolution also targeted the financial interests of the Iranian Revolutionary Guard.

The Arab Spring's turmoil was a momentary distraction, but Russia and China would not support stronger Security Council actions. As such, by 2012 the European Union (EU) and the United States implemented stronger sanctions on their own, clamping down on the Iranian Central Bank and embargoing Iranian oil. Other countries to varying degrees reduced Iranian oil imports. Covert operations of dubious legality have also hampered Iranian nuclear ambitions. A computer worm debilitated several key systems, and illegal centrifuges were sabotaged prior to purchase. Several Iranian nuclear scientists were assassinated in Iran, and one defected to the United States (although Iran claims he was kidnapped). The crisis remained in a dangerous phase and seemed nowhere near resolution.

The election of Hassan Rouhani in 2013 (and the reelection of Barack Obama the previous fall) renewed hope that diplomacy might resolve the conflict surrounding Iran's nuclear program centered on 6+1 talks (the P5, Germany, and Iran). By summer 2015, Iran and its interlocutors had agreed on a deal in which various sanctions would be progressively relaxed as international inspections confirmed that Iranian nuclear developments remained below the level needed for a breakout toward a nuclear weapon. In essence, Iran agreed not to seek to "weaponize" its nuclear energy program for fifteen years, in return for a progressive relaxation of broad and crippling UN sanctions. The Security Council endorsed the complicated agreement in July 2015 in resolution 2231.

The Iranian nuclear "deal" became the subject of much debate around the world, especially in United States and Israel as well as in Iranian political circles. Critics contended that the deal's terms did not really solve the problem of Iran and nuclear weapons but merely kicked the can down the road. Israel and other detractors also alleged that Iran would not act in good faith under its terms, and that the relaxation of sanctions would lead to more money for Iran to pursue the development of nuclear weapons either through its own policies, those of Hezbollah, or the deep reach of the Revolutionary Guards.

The Obama administration argued that it was worth taking a risk for peace that continued sanctions and threats of force would not be as good as this negotiated arrangement, and that in the coming years Iran might be brought into the community of respected nations rather than remaining a dangerous revolutionary actor. The Obama team feared that absent this agreement, Israel would be inclined to strike Iran militarily, the United States would be drawn into that conflict, and all parties would be worse off—with Iran in that event definitely moving to "weaponize" its nuclear program. In addition, Iran might well serve as an important partner in dealing with ISIS in Iraq and Syria.

Israel along with its supporters, particularly in conservative circles within the United States, strongly opposed the deal. Many Sunni Arab states, caught up in a regional competition with Shia Iran, also had strong misgivings. Although these critics had no persuasive alternative to what the negotiating group and the UN Security Council had endorsed, nevertheless vigorous debate continues with many uncertainties about the evolution of events.

POLITICAL CHALLENGES

The UN faces several challenges that are political in nature. Disagreements over leadership and resources impact the operational effectiveness of the UN and affect its ability to protect its personnel in conflict zones.

Leadership of the First UN

A void of leadership persists at the first UN. Without the support of the remaining superpower—and a question as to how "super" the United States is—the world body continues to face marginalization on many issues relating to international peace and security. Inspired, capable leadership is necessary to build a relative consensus among diverse actors regarding the strategies for handling today's security problems. Washington's decisions to invade Iraq in 2003 (without Security Council authorization) and systematically undermine the UN from 2001 to 2008 compromised its ability to lead the institution.[29] The 2008 election of Barack Obama renewed hope that Washington would assume a constructive leadership role at the United Nations. President Obama initially appointed his confidante Susan Rice as the U.S. permanent representative to the world organization and elevated that position to cabinet level. Compared to his predecessor, Obama demonstrated greater interest in multilateral approaches to many problems. The Obama team showed awareness of the limits of American power and resources and, consequently, the need to adjust to a more multilateral world. At the same time, the administration, like its predecessors, also has demonstrated a willingness to act unilaterally or bypass multilateral forums.

The administration sought to reengage with the UN on many levels, and Rice was a strong and measured voice on the Security Council. On such issues as Libya and Sudan, the Obama team has stressed the need for council approval for any outside intervention.[30] At the same time, it was under no illusion as to what the world organization could accomplish, and its approach has been pragmatic yet inconsistent.[31] It has not hesitated to resort to controversial unilateralism, as in drone attacks in Pakistan and Yemen, where it believes its security interests are threatened. However, the Obama administration has not joined the International Criminal Court (ICC), which requires an uphill battle for advice and consent in the Senate; has taken a hands-off approach to Sudan and boycotted a meeting on racism in solidarity with Israel; and has failed to follow up the Goldstone report for the Human Rights Council, which criticized Israeli and Palestinian actions in Gaza.[32] President Obama's reelection in 2012 signaled that the United States would remain engaged with the UN on selected issues when multilateralism has a reasonable chance of success both domestically and internationally. Susan Rice assumed a new role as the national security advisor, and Samantha Power was appointed to replace her at the U.S. Permanent Mission in New York. Power's journalistic and academic writings speak strongly of the need for the international community of states, including the United States, to protect civilians when their governments are unwilling or unable to do so. She is also keenly aware that humanitarian action creates additional and sometimes intractable complications.[33] These concerns played out particularly in the Syrian conflict, as the Obama team abjured decisive intervention despite the mounting numbers of deaths and uprooted citizens.

Even if Washington wished to lead in the Security Council, China and Russia often have very different perspectives. On the one hand, they may genuinely feel that sanctions, military force, and muscular peace operations have little utility in resolving largely civil conflicts, and may contribute to instability and human suffering by "freezing" armed conflict. They may genuinely feel that traditional notions of sovereignty and the inviolability of a state's territory are more conducive to world order.[34] On the other hand, China and Russia are autocratic states that give other authoritarian regimes the diplomatic cover to pursue WMDs or policies that result in gross violations of human rights.[35] The distance between liberal democracies and autocracies is slowly rising to the level of another cold war and presents serious impediments for managing the world's problems. In particular, Russia's provocative and aggressive policies in neighboring Georgia and Ukraine have complicated limited cooperation in other areas, such as the civil war in Syria and Iran's nuclear program. China also is pressing its claims to sovereignty over contested islands in the South China Sea and has openly disdained universal human rights. The Security Council is divided and cannot act in these kinds of situations, which encourages some member states to move unilaterally if and when they think they have the power to go it alone successfully.

Another related cleavage centers on what action is permissible by states and the UN in the territory of another state. Western and UN-supported NGOs in

Ukraine and Georgia have drawn the ire of Russia. China contests human rights organizations in Tibet and Uyghur regions and is among the many states that censor the Internet. For many states, the instability and turmoil in Ukraine and in states associated with the Arab Spring are being fostered by foreign-sponsored NGOs. Some scholars and observers see the current crisis in Ukraine as a result of the West's decision to expand NATO and export democracy.[36]

Leadership of the Second UN

When the P5 are able to reach a consensus, it must have the organizational support of the second UN to carry out policy decisions. Hence, the leadership provided by the secretary-general is also a central political concern.[37] Both Kofi Annan and Boutros Boutros-Ghali came under fire, especially in the United States and international media, for mismanagement of the Oil-for-Food Programme and the alleged corruption of staff and family members.[38] Although the scale of corruption was not extreme, the United States cited the kickbacks and inept oversight as reasons to end the standoff between Iraq and the UN in the lead-up to the 2003 war. A strong and independent Office of the Secretary-General is crucial for UN legitimacy and for conflict resolution. Efforts to undermine the integrity and independence of the OSG, coupled with scandal and mismanagement, have done little to strengthen the UN's major representative to the rest of the world. The five-volume report issued in 2005 by the commission headed by former Federal Reserve chairman Paul A. Volcker cast a shadow over Kofi Annan.[39]

Annan's successor was a South Korean career diplomat with little prior experience within the UN itself. The first years of Ban Ki-moon's tenure yielded a few diplomatic victories, such as obtaining Chinese consent to a UN peacekeeping mission in Darfur and the successful resolution of the crisis in Côte d'Ivoire. However, concrete successes have been few and far between for a secretary-general who has far less charisma and presence than his two immediate predecessors and who prides himself on his invisibility.[40] Ban has singled out climate change and R2P as his signature issues, and in June 2012 he was elected to a second term, the earliest such reelection in UN history. It should be kept in mind that the P5 states usually prefer low-key secretaries-general, as they do not wish to contend with dynamic personalities whom they do not control. It is for that reason that the United States vetoed the reelection efforts of Boutros Boutros-Ghali.

As Ramesh Thakur points out, "The single most important challenge for the secretary-general is to provide leadership: the elusive ability to make others connect emotionally and intellectually to a larger cause that transcends their immediate self-interest. Leadership consists of articulating a bold and noble vision for the international community, establishing standards of achievement and conduct for states and individuals, explaining why they matter, and inspiring or coaxing everyone to adopt the agreed benchmarks as their own goals."[41] Ban's quiet approach is preferred by states who appreciate his deference, but his successor will have to be reform-minded and attempt to build bridges between competing

Secretary-General Ban Ki-moon addresses the staff members of the Office of the UN High Commissioner for Refugees. (UN PHOTO 201380/JEAN-MARC FERRÉ)

worldviews. As world politics is no longer solely the domain of states, the head of the second UN can make an essential contribution.

Civil society and other members of the third UN are seeking a stronger voice in UN affairs, including the selection of the secretary-general. A more transparent process for selecting the secretary-general has been on the reform agenda for years. Many are dissatisfied with a process by which the P5 effectively choose the candidate behind the scenes (based, in part on informal criteria, such as geography), who then stands for election by the General Assembly with the outcome all but predetermined. In some circles there is a strong push for a female secretary-general.[42] For only the second time—the first was in 1996—the electoral campaigns for the U.S. president and the UN secretary-general have run in parallel.

The Safety of UN Personnel

Since the 1990s UN staff have been killed, kidnapped, and physically and sexually assaulted in record numbers. Personnel were targets in places as varied as Bosnia, Lebanon, Congo, Sudan, Rwanda, Iraq, Afghanistan, Kosovo, Algeria, Cambodia, and Mali. This challenge has become particularly acute since the bombings of the UN headquarters in Iraq in August and September 2003 in which 22 were killed and 162 injured. Not only were tensions exacerbated between the United States and the UN because U.S. occupying forces were unable to provide a secure environment for UN personnel, but as the *Report of the Independent Panel on the Safety and Security of UN Personnel in Iraq* stated, the attacks were "signals of the emergence of a new and more difficult era for the UN system."[43] Since 2012, 480

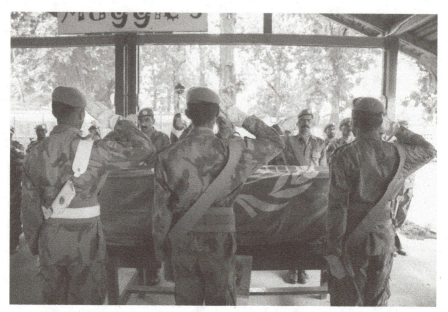

The UN Multidimensional Integrated Stabilization Mission in the Central African Republic (MINUSCA) holds a memorial ceremony at its headquarters in honor of two of its peacekeepers. Sepoy Fahad Iftikhar of the mission's Pakistani contingent was killed in an ambush, and Chief Caporal Nizi Giyi Mana Jean Paul of the Burundian contingent died from malaria in the Bangui. October 13, 2014, Bangui, Central African Republic. (UN PHOTO 609887/ NEKTARIOS MARKOGIANNIS)

peacekeepers have lost their lives. The UN must be able to defend itself if it is to continue humanitarian and development operations in conflict zones. This new security environment involving failed and failing states and terrorism requires that the UN move beyond merely guarding against criminal and opportunistic attacks and develop a comprehensive strategy for protecting personnel in conflict areas.

The same security problems confront private relief and development organizations that work in tandem with UN programs. In 2007 UN and private aid agencies were targeted by terrorists in Algeria. The attack on UN facilities killed 41 people, including 17 UN personnel. Secretary-General Ban responded by unveiling plans to create another independent panel to investigate the attacks in Algeria and other security threats UN personnel face around the world. Algeria responded negatively, claiming it was not consulted and therefore would not consent to the investigation. NGO aid workers are routinely kidnapped and killed in active war zones, such as Sudan, Afghanistan, Yemen, Mali, Iraq, and Syria. The protection of second and third UN personnel is further complicated when the first UN formally decides to take sides in a conflict as it has in Mali and the Central African Republic (CAR). Humanitarian principles of neutrality, impartiality, and nondiscrimination are compromised and members of a peacekeeping mission or humanitarian aid workers can be seen as the enemy. When the Security Council empowers peacekeepers with enforcement mandates that target specific groups, the UN's role as an arbiter can be called into question.[44]

The Proliferation of Actors

Another related political challenge centers on the proliferation of actors, particularly nonstate actors.[45] The nature and dynamics of peaceful relationships require that the UN pay more attention to NSAs and differentiate among them based on their importance to the issue at hand, especially in the humanitarian arena. The origins of armed conflicts, as well as their mitigation and management, must be conceived broadly enough to include diverse group of nongovernmental actors, such as clans, "terrorist groups," social movements, as well as mainstream NGOs, such as Oxfam or Human Rights Watch and the International Committee of the Red Cross. People make war, and people respond to it. Experience in Sudan, for example, suggests that the second UN is frequently at a disadvantage in dealing with insurgents.[46] Private relief agencies, however, may be better placed than intergovernmental ones for delivering aid in certain war zones.

Resources

The UN simply does not have enough money to properly conduct peace operations. It also does not have adequate resources to properly fight poverty, promote economic and social development, or protect and promote human rights. Many member states, including the United States, are in arrears of their regular and peacekeeping dues (which are assessed separately). In 2014 member states owed more than $3.4 billion. Compared to the annual global defense expenditures of over $1 trillion, the amount contributed to peacekeeping seems trivial. If every country devoted 1 percent of its defense budget to UN efforts, $10 billion would be readily available. Other measures, such as surcharges on the sale of weaponry and on the use of UN-provided services—for example, ensuring the right of passage for ships—could help provide additional income. The solution supported long ago by an independent group of bankers and politicians is that governments must respect their international treaty obligations to pay the bills for UN security operations.[47] This recommendation seems straightforward enough, but the UN's long-standing resource problems only have been exacerbated by the global financial crisis, economic recession, and slow recovery, as states are either reducing their budgets or devoting scarce resources to domestic initiatives so as to stabilize their economies and their debts.

THE CHALLENGES OF REFORM

The world organization has been continually discussing the need for substantive reform for at least a quarter century.

Reforming the First UN

Reform of the first UN is difficult because member states are reluctant to give up their privileges or influence. Some fear a first UN with more authority, while others are quite comfortable with that UN in a supporting role or as a foreign policy tool. Reform of the Security Council's permanent membership is seemingly a permanent agenda item in New York, with little likelihood of being resolved anytime soon.[48] Possibilities for long-range reform involve changes in the Security Council's permanent membership; shorter-range reform, longer and more frequent terms on the council for influential countries. However, each major structural reform would give rise to new matters requiring consideration: Which developing countries should be added? Should they be the most powerful or populous? What about the voice of the small and powerless, or of traditional supporters of multilateralism from the Nordic countries? After a civil war, should a splintered state retain its seat? Why should economic powers whose constitutions impede overseas military involvement (i.e., Germany and Japan) be given a seat at all? Should there be three permanent European members, and what about the European Union? Which countries should wield vetoes? Should not all regions have at least one permanent member?

The HLP attempted to answer some of these questions in 2004 by proposing two models for Security Council reform.[49] Both are based on regional representation in that they create new council seats (expanding the council from fifteen to twenty-four members) and distribute them among four major regional areas: Africa, Asia-Pacific, Europe, and the Americas. The models do not expand the veto or change the veto among the existing five permanent members. The models also address several principles designed to avoid many of the issues here discussed. The first principle is that all members of the council have enhanced financial, military, and diplomatic responsibilities to the UN. Second, the models bring more countries, especially countries from the Global South, into the decision-making process. Third, the models may not impair the council's effectiveness. Finally, both models increase democracy and accountability. As might be expected, these proposals as well as newer ones remain on the drawing boards.

Unfortunately, the best member states could muster at the 2005 World Summit, given the tense political environment, was to reaffirm their desire to make the council more representative and recommend "that the Security Council continue to adapt its working methods so as to increase the involvement of States not members of the Council in its work, as appropriate, enhance its accountability to the membership and increase the transparency of its work."[50] At least the verbal jousting and rhetoric over the years have created a permissive environment that helped facilitate pragmatic modifications in working methods. These have injected more openness, accountability, and diverse inputs into council deliberations and should be expanded.[51]

In 2008 the General Assembly decided to take a stab at council reform with the commencement of the "intergovernmental negotiations on Security Council reform in informal plenary of the General Assembly." This basically meant that they would establish a working group within the assembly to keep the dialogue going. Not surprisingly, little progress has been made as the same disagreements on size, representation, and the veto persist. In 2014 the president of the General Assembly, John Ashe, attempted to jump-start the process by presenting a "nonpaper" of similar ideas; however, Ashe was arrested and accused of bribery in October 2015 and little has come of it. The present situation is analogous to a group of doctors who all agree on the patient's illness but cannot agree on the remedy; and then for those who agree, the prescription is not available. All agree that council membership is out of date relative to realities in world affairs, but none can come up with a workable formula for new membership that satisfies the leading stakeholders.

Reform of Peace Operations

Reforming the second UN to make it more effective in carrying out peace operations means changing the way peacekeeping is conducted, placing greater emphasis on peacebuilding in postconflict societies, and strengthening the secretariat. The evolution of peace operations illustrates a general failure to distinguish between the military operations that the second UN can manage (traditional and even slightly muscular peacekeeping) and those that it cannot and should not (enforcement). As Michael Mandelbaum asserts, "the U.N. itself can no more conduct military operations on a large scale on its own than a trade association of hospitals can conduct heart surgery."[52] Enforcement seems best left to the militaries of states that have council authorization. Modest reform in this area includes creating mechanisms for greater council oversight over state uses of force in the UN's name.

Reforming and strengthening traditional and slightly muscular peacekeeping began in earnest in 2000 when Secretary-General Annan appointed a high-level international panel to examine critically the UN's handling of peace operations. Led by Lakhdar Brahimi, the panel found a great deal to criticize, especially after full assessments of operations in Rwanda and Bosnia. The Brahimi Report's blunt language focused on getting states to take their responsibilities seriously, on creating clear mandates and reasonable goals, and on providing well-trained and well-equipped troops. Not surprisingly, consensus among member states was not achieved, and most of the report's recommendations were not implemented. The secretary-general must go begging and start from scratch for new peacekeeping forces. The difficulty in fielding missions and getting them up to full strength is repeated in new operations, such as Mali and the Central African Republic. UN peacekeeping, even of the traditional type, remains unsystematic and essentially ad hoc in composition and deployment.

In 2008 the Department of Peacekeeping Operations (DPKO) produced the "Capstone Document" that outlined the guidelines for effective peacekeeping. It reiterated the basic principles of peacekeeping: the consent of the parties involved, impartiality, and nonuse of force except in cases of self-defense (and defense of the mandate). It also reiterated that there must be a peace to keep, and that missions must have clear mandates and obtainable goals. The full support of the Security Council along with the resources necessary were cited as prerequisites for success. The DPKO also turned the spotlight on itself, stressing the need for better planning and execution of missions. This includes understanding missions in terms of their start-up, mandate implementation, and exit phases.

The central contradiction for most peacekeeping operations is that the maintenance of international peace and security involves tackling problems that states cannot or do not want to handle themselves. In addition, the nature of contemporary operations is often "neither fish nor fowl" (or neither peacekeeping nor peace enforcement), which one analyst has labeled with the oxymoron "enforcement peacekeeping."[53] In addition, contemporary peace operations also require the integration of a number of activities conducted by other parts of the UN system.[54] Member states often want to "do something" (or convey the impression that they do) but not badly enough to invest a lot of their blood and treasure. They also disagree as to what is causing problems and therefore the solutions. As such, a solution or "success" is not really possible and the task at hand is to manage a situation to prevent it from getting worse or spiraling out of control. The UN thus lurches from one crisis to another, with lessons either disregarded or not applicable to the crise de jour.

At the same time, the Security Council continues to authorize complex, multidimensional missions with robust mandates to use force to protect civilians. Member states are still slow to provide the human and financial resources, and questions remain whether peacekeepers can actually protect civilians. A 2014 UN internal oversight report found that peacekeepers rarely used force to protect civilians in conflict zones and that attacks frequently occurred against civilians in areas under the responsibility of UN peacekeepers.[55] The report also found that the peacekeepers did use force in their own immediate self-defense. The backlash against the report by member states revealed a deep division between the poorer states that provide the troops and the richer states that provide the funding.[56] Poorer states resent criticism and point out that the peacekeepers have not received a raise in over ten years. Recent peacekeeping gatherings have been mixed with acrimony as the first and second UN wrangle over how to improve effectiveness.

In October 2014, Secretary-General Ban established the High-Level Independent Panel on Peace Operations, led by José Ramos-Horta, the 1996 Nobel laureate from Timor-Leste. Ban hoped that the panel's recommendations would lead the way forward.[57] Predictably the panel reiterated past recommendations (regarding the necessary political support and the provision of recourses) and also urged that UN peace operations not engage in military counterterrorism activities. Despite widespread criticism, empirical evidence suggests that UN peace operations can be effective in protecting civilians when sufficient military force is deployed.[58] While peacekeepers seem reluctant to use force to protect civilians, their presence and activities do deter attacks.

Members of the Nepalese contingent serving with the United Nations Multi-dimensional Integrated Stabilization Mission in Mali (MINUSMA) listen to Major General Michael Lollesgaard, force commander of MINUSMA, as he addresses the troops during his visit to the airstrip in Kidal, northern Mali. September 15, 2015. (UN PHOTO 642473/ MARCO DOMINO)

A very specific, recurring, and embarrassing problem is sexual exploitation and abuse by peacekeepers. Member states included strong language in the 2005 World Summit Outcome Document and urged that UN policies of zero tolerance and zero impunity be implemented without delay. The formal procedures to curb sexual abuse represent an important first step in restoring the credibility of UN peacekeepers. They include education programs and policies dealing with complaints. Part of the problem is that peacekeeping operations include national military contingents, civilian police and military observers, UN civilian staff, volunteers, and subcontractors.[59] Each subgroup of a peacekeeping force has different procedures for handling allegations and complaints. For military forces, it is up to national authorities of troop-contributing states to investigate and punish their soldiers. The most that the UN can do is to insist that troop contributors repatriate soldiers to their home countries. The formal change in procedures in terms of reporting incidents does not necessarily translate into a formal change in attitudes. A decade ago a report issued by Refugees International suggested that the procedures are not being fully implemented because the "boys will be boys" attitude in peacekeeping missions breeds tolerance for exploitation and abuse.[60] Rapes continue to be dismissed as simple acts of prostitution. Anna Shotton, author of that report, nonetheless argues that progress has been made. In the past, the UN had only occasionally repatriated uniformed personnel, but in the twenty months preceding her report the UN had completed 221 investigations, which resulted in the firing of ten civilian employees and the repatriation of eighty-eight military personnel, including six commanders. Still, much work remains to be done in prosecuting sex crimes by troop-contributing states and on changing the attitudes among the armed forces involved in peace missions. The 2015 controversy over allegations of sex abuse and child rape by French troops in the Central African Republic as well as by UN troops in the same area of operations demonstrates that the issue has not disappeared.

Perhaps the most significant accomplishment of the 2005 World Summit relating to peace operations was the decision to create the Peacebuilding Commission (PBC). The PBC actually represents "follow-through," or learning based on previous UN peacekeeping and peacemaking activities in such places as Somalia, Sierra Leone, Haiti, Liberia, Democratic Republic of Congo (DRC), and Rwanda. It is necessary to rebuild state capacity, not as nostalgia for the national security state of the past but as a clear recognition that a modicum of state capacity is a prerequisite for peace or development. Trying to restore broken states along this path was clearly a challenge emerging from the UN's main growth industry, and, just as clearly, the incoherence of UN efforts in picking up the pieces from conflict was no longer desirable.

The decision to establish the PBC in spring 2006 was a positive step toward improving UN efforts to prevent conflict relapse in war-torn countries that have turned a page on armed conflict, and a response to a growing arena of demand for the UN's operations.[61] Its mandate is to propose integrated strategies for postconflict stability, ensure predictable financing for recovery, draw international attention to the tasks, provide recommendations and information to improve coordination, and develop best practices requiring the collaboration of a variety of actors.

The PBC's Organization Committee comprises thirty-one members: seven from the Security Council, seven from the UN Economic and Social Council (ECOSOC), five of the main financial contributors to the United Nations, five of the top military contributors to the world organization's peace operations, and seven elected by the General Assembly to redress geographical imbalances that may result from the other selection criteria. The PBC also includes country-specific committees, which tailor programs to include country representatives and relevant contributors in each case.

The Organizational Committee oversees an expanding "second UN" related to peacebuilding. Member states at the World Summit requested that the secretary-general establish a Peacebuilding Support Office (PBSO) within the secretariat, whose staff could assist and support the PBC as well as advise the secretary-general. The PBSO also oversees the Peacebuilding Fund (PBF), established in 2006 with a target of $250 million. In 2015 deposits reached about $630 million, with a total portfolio of approximately $651 million.[62] The aim of the fund is to provide initial support for peacebuilding and kick-start donor investment in long-term recovery. If managed effectively, the fund has the potential to reduce waste and the duplication of efforts and to enhance coordination among financial sources.

During its first year, the Peacebuilding Commission allocated some \$35 million to Burundi and Sierra Leone. The PBSO has also approved emergency funding for more urgent peacebuilding activities in the Central African Republic, Guinea, Côte d'Ivoire, Haiti, Liberia, and Kenya. In 2014 the PBC was one of the first to sound the alarm about the Ebola outbreak in West Africa, in part because several of the affected countries were on its agenda, and yet another source of instability was hardly a welcome development for those seeking to build the foundations for peace.

Like all international organizations, the PBC is not without shortcomings.[63] It is a subsidiary body of both the General Assembly and the Security Council, which exacerbates reporting problems. Moreover, it is an advisory rather than a decision-making body; it has no enforcement mechanisms. As one analyst notes, "The advisory nature of the PBC—coupled with the stipulation that it 'shall act in all matters on the basis of consensus of its members'—seems at odds with the very concept of the body assuming the final responsibility for peacebuilding."[64]

Moreover, there is some overlap between the PBSO and the activities entrusted to the Department of Political Affairs and the Department of Peacekeeping Operations, which exposes the potential for turf battles. Nevertheless, the creation of the PBC, PBSO, and PBF is an important step toward enhancing the coordination, efficiency, and effectiveness of postconflict stability and reconciliation efforts financed and supervised by the United Nations. Indeed, in operational terms, many donor countries are channeling more of their assistance to conflict-prone countries—already 38 percent in 2011[65]—and see this arena as a comparative advantage for the United Nations.[66]

Reform of the Second UN

Reforming and strengthening the secretariat is essential for the UN to continue in its mission. However, reforming a bureaucracy is no easy task. As Franklin D. Roosevelt once famously said when he tried to alter the U.S. Navy, it is like "punching a feather bed. You punch it with your right and your left until you are finally exhausted, and then you find the damn bed just as it was before you started punching."[67] Bureaucracies carry out large, complex tasks and to be able to do so, they must be hierarchically structured, specialized, and governed by rules (or standard operating procedures). Specialization is important because it allows each agency and office to develop an expertise; however, as a bureaucracy grows to address new challenges, new offices are created and relations with existing offices can become competitive and lead to a duplication of services.

Such a hierarchical structure is often frustrating and daunting, but it is necessary to carry out complicated policy and provide continuity when personnel change. Hence, most reform often starts at the top. When then secretary-general Kofi Annan unveiled his strategy for a "quiet revolution" to reform the world organization in 1997, he initiated measures to make the UN a more effective mechanism for administering and managing peace operations.[68] The creation and effective implementation of a rationalized cabinet system, consisting of the Senior Management Group (SMG) with division heads and an executive committee system, introduced a greater degree of horizontal cooperation than had been the case before. Senior officials throughout the organization (including those based in Geneva and Vienna through teleconferencing) were to meet weekly with the secretary-general. In addition, the Executive Committee on Peace and Security, which brings together those senior officials whose units deal with peacekeeping, holds biweekly discussions. This process is supplemented with a number of issue-specific task forces, including ones for each multidisciplinary peace operation, as well as special meetings involving a much wider set of actors who serve as operational partners in the field, including development and humanitarian agencies and international financial institutions.

How full or empty the reform glass happens to be depends on the observer. In 2008, shortly after leaving his post as deputy secretary-general and prior to becoming the U.K.'s minister for Africa, Asia, and the United Nations, Mark Malloch Brown commented that no topic, not even sex, was more popular than reform around water coolers or over coffee. Neither governments nor Secretary-General Ban Ki-moon understood "the scale of change required." Member states "would have to rise above their own current sense of entrenched rights and privileges and find a grand bargain to allow a new more realistic governance model for the UN." But, he continued, "that may take a crisis."[69]

The ability of the secretariat and thereby of the Security Council to monitor enforcement operations has long been a subject of heated discussions.[70] The 1991 Persian Gulf War represented the first military enforcement action of the post–Cold War era, but the UN secretary-general and the secretariat were on the sidelines when decisions were made about how to wage the ground war. Although Security Council authorizations were politically useful, coalition forces were not accountable to the world organization. This pattern has been repeated in enforcement and peacekeeping operations in Mali, Libya, Kosovo, and Afghanistan. Increasing the secretary-general's influence over Security Council decision making and subsequent UN military operations is problematic. Article 99 of the Charter supposedly empowers the secretary-general to bring the council's attention to matters that he believes could threaten international peace and security. Greater use of this article could allow the secretary-general to place issues on the council's agenda that otherwise might be avoided because of their sensitivity, but he thereby risks alienating states and cannot be effective if he offends one of the P5. Hence, this option is rarely used.

The Office of the Secretary-General has also asked for a mandate to request advisory opinions from the International Court of Justice (ICJ) under Article 96 of the Charter. Such a course of action could allow the organization's head to help refine the legitimate definitions of those situations that present threats to the peace as well as to provide more concrete policy options that are both politically and legally acceptable. One key to advisory opinions is asking a question and getting a specific-enough response. Like all courts, the ICJ oftentimes avoids the substance of an issue and relies on procedural interpretations to set aside a case. Time is also a problem because the ICJ never acts quickly—an understatement of some magnitude because, until recently, the court decided only a case or two a year. Moreover, given that the United States has made clear that it does not want the International Criminal Court second-guessing its decisions about choice of weapons and targets in armed conflict, it is highly doubtful that the United States—or Russia or China—would welcome the secretary-general's raising similar questions of the ICJ.

Agreement on standards may be increasingly necessary, however. Resolutions are often kept vague to secure intergovernmental assent ("all necessary means" in the war against Iraq created a host of questions about proportionality, and "all measures necessary" was quintessential UN doublespeak that did not permit sufficient action to help Bosnia's Muslims). The language of international decisions is sometimes too elliptical to allow a determination of which concrete actions and procedures would constitute legitimate follow-up. The secretary-general—and not just the General Assembly and the Security Council—should be authorized to request advisory opinions from the ICJ to help reduce the criticism of selective application by the Security Council of the principles guiding its decision making. Although seeking the court's opinion would be harmful in the midst of a crisis, judgments eventually could be useful in anticipating future contingencies and establishing precedents.

As part of reform, steps have been taken to enhance the secretariat's means of fact-finding so that the secretary-general can improve his access to timely, unbiased, and impartial accounts of dangerous situations. Special units have proliferated that focus exclusively on early warning and prevention. The mandate of these units is to provide greater access to information about potential threats to the peace, thus enhancing the secretariat's ability to launch preventive diplomacy and possibly to recommend preventive deployment. Of course, much more could be done, and the Office of the Secretary-General could and should be equipped and staffed to act as an effective crisis-monitoring center for events that threaten the peace.

The end of the Cold War permitted the world organization to move toward reviving old-fashioned ideals of an objective and competent international civil service, on which the organization was supposedly founded.[71] The success of the organization's activities begins and ends with the people in its employ. A long-ignored reality is the need to overhaul the international civil service, for which qualifications have long been secondary to geographic and political considerations, and within which women have hardly played a role commensurate with their potential.[72]

This reality became more obvious with the Oil-for-Food Programme debacle. Along with the sexual scandals involving peacekeepers highlighted earlier, the Volcker report demonstrated serious flaws in management and judgment by the central administration, which is almost universally agreed to be inefficient, politicized, and in desperate need of repair. The preface to the fourth Volcker report

contained language that could have been written by an American neoconservative but nonetheless is apt: "The inescapable conclusion from the Committee's
work is that the United Nations Organization needs thoroughgoing reform—and
it needs it urgently."[73]

Not much has substantively changed since 2005, although the first and second
UN have taken concrete steps to strengthen the role of women. In 2000 the Security
Council passed resolution 1325 to ensure that peace operations and postconflict
reconstruction would be sensitive to gender and gendered inequalities. Violence,
sanctions, and poverty have disparate impacts on women and these are often overlooked by states and organizations. The council lent considerable legitimacy to
reform efforts involving gender equity.[74] Resolution 1325 and the overall reform
effort have led to substantive reforms dealing with sexual abuse by peacekeepers
and within UN agencies themselves. To take stock after fifteen years and six additional resolutions on women, peace, and security, the Security Council approved a
high-level review to assess progress at the national, regional, and global levels of the
original 1325 resolution. Radhika Coomaraswamy, previously special representative of the secretary-general on children and armed conflict and special rapporteur
on violence against women, led the advisory group for the global study. The group
found that while important strides have been made, the mainstreaming of gender
in peace operations still has not become standard practice and the funding for programs supporting women in peace and security efforts remains "abysmally low."[75]

The primary vehicle for empowering women within the UN system is UN
Women. Created in July 2010 by the General Assembly, it merged four smaller
bodies devoted to advancing women. The mission of UN Women is to support
governments and intergovernmental organizations in implementing standards
and meeting their obligations under national and international law.[76] Michelle
Bachelet, the former president of Chile, was appointed the first undersecretary-general and executive director of UN Women and served until 2013. She was
replaced by Phumzile Mlambo-Ngcuka who has made monitoring the progress
of gender equality within the UN system a priority. While early in its life, UN
Women has emerged as pivotal in relation to international peace and security.[77]
It is now at the decision-making table regarding peacebuilding activities, security and justice, gender- and sex-based violence, and postconflict humanitarian
planning. The role of UN Women in development is a necessary institutional reform for improving the lives of women and meeting the Sustainable Development
Goals (SDGs; see Chapter 12 for more about these).

INCREMENTAL CHANGE

The glacier-like pace of reform is due in large part to fundamental political disagreements between North and South and between the liberal democracies and
autocratic states.[78] It also reflects the nature of bureaucracies in general, which
are designed to provide stability regardless of changes in personnel. Structural

alterations in one area require changes in another and soon a full renovation is required. Hence, inertia remains a dominant force, especially in areas of substantive disagreement. In a globalizing world, the UN is the only institution with global values but remains controlled by states; and nonstate actors have very limited leverage. The third UN represents a global cosmopolitanism in which NGOs, corporations, the media, and private citizens are demanding a greater voice in the formulation of UN policy and greater transparency in the selection of key personnel.[79] Their voices, concerns, and preferences need to be heard everywhere, but nowhere more than in the security arena, where not only are decisions on current crises made but also legal precedents.[80] While high-level panels and commissions of inquiry are important vehicles for modest civil society participation, more needs to be done to incorporate the third UN in the day-to-day maintenance of international peace and security. Leveraging and improving relations with the third UN is essential for managing the complex problems of violent conflict, gross violations of internationally recognized human rights, and promoting sustainable human development.

NOTES

1. Two important UN reports on this topic are *Report of the Panel on United Nations Peace Operations*, UN document A/55/305-S/2000/809, August 21, 2000; and *Report of the High-Level Independent Panel on United Nations Peace Operations*, UN document A/70/95-S/2015/446, June 17, 2015.

2. This discussion draws on Jane Boulden and Thomas G. Weiss, "Whither Terrorism and the United Nations?" in *Terrorism and the United Nations: Before and After September 11*, ed. Jane Boulden and Thomas G. Weiss (Bloomington: Indiana University Press, 2004), 3–26. See also Thomas G. Weiss, Margaret E. Crahan, and John Goering, eds., *War on Terrorism and Iraq: Human Rights, Unilateralism, and U.S. Foreign Policy* (London: Routledge, 2004).

3. Adam Roberts, "Terrorism and International Order," in *Terrorism and International Order*, ed. Lawrence Freedman, Christopher Hill, Adam Roberts, R. J. Vincent, Paul Wilkinson, and Philip Windsor (London: Routledge, 1986), 9–10; and M. J. Peterson, "Using the General Assembly," in Boulden and Weiss, *Terrorism and the United Nations*, 173–197.

4. *A More Secure World: Our Shared Responsibility—Report of the High-Level Panel on Threats, Challenges, and Change* (New York: United Nations, 2004), para. 161. See "The Report of the High-Level Panel on Threats, Challenges and Change," *Security Dialogue* 36, no. 3 (2005): 361–394; and Paul Heinbecker and Patricia Goff, eds., *Irrelevant or Indispensable? The United Nations in the 21st Century* (Waterloo, Ontario: Wilfred Laurier University Press, 2005).

5. Kofi Annan, *In Larger Freedom: Towards Development, Security and Human Rights for All*, UN document A/59/2005, March 21, 2005, para. 91.

6. *2005 World Summit Outcome*, UN resolution A/60/1, October 24, 2005, para. 81.

7. Chantal de Jonge Oudraat, "The Role of the Security Council," in Boulden and Weiss, *Terrorism and the UN*, 151–172.

8. Peter Romaniuk, *Multilateral Counter-Terrorism: The Global Politics of Cooperation and Contestation* (London: Routledge, 2010).

9. *Report of the Policy Working Group on the United Nations and Terrorism*, UN document A/57/273/S/2002/875.

10. See statements by Secretary-General Ban at www.un.org/terrorism/sg.shtml.

11. Secretary-General Ban Ki-moon, "Remarks at Symposium on International Counter-Terrorism Cooperation," New York, September 19, 2011.

12. This discussion relies on the work of Nina Tannenwald, "The UN and Debates Over Weapons of Mass Destruction," in *The United Nations and Global Security*, ed. Richard M. Price and Mark W. Zacher (New York: Palgrave, 2004), 3–20.

13. Jane Boulden, Ramesh Thakur, and Thomas G. Weiss, eds., *The United Nations and the Nuclear Challenges* (Tokyo: UN University Press, 2009).

14. George W. Bush, in an address to cadets at the U.S. Military Academy (West Point) on June 1, 2002, described the role of preventive war in U.S. foreign policy and national defense, saying that Americans needed "to be ready for preemptive action when necessary to defend our liberty and to defend our lives."

15. John Ruggie, "Doctrinal Unilateralism and Its Limits: America and Global Governance in the New Century," in *American Foreign Policy in a Globalized World*, ed. David P. Forsythe, Patrice C. MacMahon, and Andrew Wedeman (New York: Routledge, 2006), 31–50.

16. Rosemary Foot, S. Neil MacFarlane, and Michael Mastanduno, eds., *U.S. Hegemony and International Organizations: The United States and Multilateral Institutions* (Oxford: Oxford University Press, 2003).

17. Anthony Clark Arend and Robert J. Beck, *International Law and the Use of Force: Beyond the UN Charter Paradigm* (London: Routledge, 1993). On the Bush doctrine as a violation of the UN Charter, see Tom J. Farer, "Beyond the Charter Frame: Unilateralism or Condominium," *American Journal of International Law* 96, no. 2 (2002): 359–364. Yoram Dienstein, in *War, Aggression, and Self-Defense*, 2nd ed. (Cambridge: Cambridge University Press, 1994), endorses the notion of anticipatory self-defense as found in Israel's first use of force in 1967.

18. Jean E. Krasno and James R. Sutterlin, *The United Nations and Iraq: Defanging the Viper* (Westport, Conn.: Praeger, 2003).

19. Alexander Bernard and Paul J. Leaf, "Modern Threats and the United National Security Council," *Stanford Law Review* 62 (2010): 1395–1443.

20. Security Council Press Release, SC/8778, July 15, 2006, http://www.un.org/News/Press/docs/2006/sc8778.doc.html.

21. Bernard and Leaf, "Modern Threats," 1420.

22. "UN Nuclear Watchdog Refers Syria to Security Council," BBC News, June 9, 2011, http://www.bbc.co.uk/news/world-middle-east-13717874.

23. "Security Council Strongly Condemns DPR Korea's Satellite Launch Attempt," UN News Centre, April 2012, http://www.un.org/apps/news/story.asp?NewsID=41784&Cr=Democratic&Cr1=Korea.

24. David Sobek, Dennis M. Foster, and Samuel B. Robinson, "Conventional Wisdom? The Effect of Nuclear Proliferation on Armed Conflict, 1945–2001," *International Studies Quarterly* 56, no. 1 (2012): 149–162.

25. Kelly-Kate Pease, *International Organizations: Perspective on Governance in the Twenty-First Century*, 5th ed. (New York: Longman, 2012), 144–146.

26. Maria Rost-Rublee, "Taking Stock of the Nuclear Proliferation Regime: Using Social Psychology to Understand Regime Change," *International Studies Review* 10, no. 3 (2008): 421.

27. Presidential Statements are often used by the Security Council when it lacks the necessary consensus to pass a resolution. This statement (S/PRST/200/15) was issued on March 29, 2006. See N. Jansen Calamita, "Sanctions, Countermeasures and the Iranian Nuclear Issue," *Vanderbilt Journal of Transnational Law* 42 (November 2009): 1393–1442.

28. "Security Council Imposes Additional Sanctions on Iran," Security Council SC/9948, June 9, 2010, http://www.un.org/News/Press/docs/2010/sc9948.doc.htm.

29. President Bush's controversial recess appointment of outspoken UN critic John Bolton in 2005 as the U.S. representative to the UN raised serious questions about Washington's ability to provide constructive leadership. Bolton was forced to leave his position after his recess appointment expired in 2007, and Bush appointed Zalmay Khalilzad to the post. The former U.S. ambassador to Afghanistan and Iraq was far more polished and diplomatic than Bolton, but he hailed from the same neoconservative school that generally distrusts multilateralism.

30. "US Hits Out at Russia and China After UN Security Council Veto," *Guardian* (London), October 5, 2011, http://www.guardian.co.uk/world/video/2011/oct/05/us-russia -china-un-syria-video.

31. Lise Morje Howard, "Sources of Change in United States–United Nations Relations," *Global Governance* 16, no. 4 (2010): 485–503.

32. Stephen Schlesinger, "Bosom Buddies? Ban and Obama's Curious Relations," *World Policy Journal* 27, no. 1 (2010): 87–95.

33. Samantha Power, *The Problem from Hell: America and the Age of Genocide* (New York: Basic Books, 2013).

34. Bernard and Leaf, "Modern Threats," 1414.

35. Robert Kagan, *The Return of History and the End of Dreams* (New York: Knopf, 2008).

36. John J. Mearsheimer, "Why the Ukraine Crisis Is the West's Fault," *Foreign Affairs* 93, no. 5 (2014): 1–12.

37. Bertrand G. Ramcharan, *The UN and Preventive Diplomacy* (Bloomington: Indiana University Press, 2008).

38. Jeffrey A. Meyer and Mark G. Califano, *Good Intentions Corrupted: The Oil-for-Food Scandal and the Threat to the U.N.* (New York: PublicAffairs, 2006).

39. The complete reports by Paul A. Volcker, Richard J. Goldstone, and Mark Pieth are available at www.iic-offp.org.

40. "The Rewards of Beavering Away," *Economist*, January 3, 2008.

41. Ramesh Thakur, "The Next U.N. Secretary-General," *Japan Times*, February 10, 2015, http://www.japantimes.co.jp/opinion/2015/02/09/commentary/world-commentary /next-u-n-secretary-general.

42. Natalie Samarasinghe, "Electing the Ninth Secretary-General," *FUNDS Briefing* #34, October 2015. See also the 1 for 7 Billion website at http://www.1for7billion.org as well as www.womansg.org and www.equalitynow.org.

43. *Report of the Independent Panel on the Safety and Security of UN Personnel in Iraq*, October 20, 2003, http://www.un.org/News/dh/iraq/safety-security-un-personnel-iraq.pdf.

44. John Karlsrud, "The UN at War: Examining the Consequences of Peace-Enforcement Mandates for the UN Peacekeeping Operations in the CAR, the DRC, and Mali." *Third World Quarterly* 36, no. 1 (January 2015): 40–54.

45. Thomas G. Weiss and Peter J. Hoffman, "Making Humanitarianism Work," in *Making States Work: State Failure and the Crisis of Governance*, ed. Simon Chesterman, Michael Ignatieff, and Ramesh Thakur (Tokyo: UN University Press, 2005), 296–317. See also Michael Barnett and Thomas G. Weiss, eds., *Humanitarianism in Question: Politics, Power, Ethics* (Ithaca, N.Y.: Cornell University Press, 2008).

46. Larry Minear et al., *Humanitarianism Under Siege: A Critical Review of Operation Lifeline Sudan* (Trenton, N.J.: Red Sea, 1991); and Francis M. Deng and Larry Minear, *The Challenges of Famine Relief: Emergency Operations in the Sudan* (Washington, D.C.: Brookings Institution, 1992).

47. Paul Volcker and Shijuro Ogata, *Financing an Effective United Nations: A Report of the Independent Advisory Group on U.N. Financing* (New York: Ford Foundation, 1993).

48. For an up-to-date survey, see Peter Nardin, *UN Security Council Reform* (London: Routledge, 2016). For earlier discussions, see Edward C. Luck, *Reforming the United Nations: Lessons from a History in Progress*, United Nations Occasional Paper no. 1 (New Haven, Conn.: ACUNS, 2003), 7–16; Brian Urquhart and Erskine Childers, *A World in Need of Leadership: Tomorrow's United Nations—A Fresh Appraisal* (Uppsala, Sweden: Dag Hammarskjöld Foundation, 1996); Commission on Global Governance, *Our Global Neighborhood: The Report of the Commission on Global Governance* (Oxford: Oxford University Press, 1995); South Centre, *For a Strong and Democratic United Nations: A South Perspective on UN Reform* (Geneva: South Centre, 1995); and Erskine Childers and Brian Urquhart, *Renewing the United Nations System* (Upland, Penn.: Diane Publishing, 1999).

49. *A More Secure World*, paras. 247–260.

50. General Assembly, *2005 World Summit Outcome*, para. 154.

51. Thomas G. Weiss, *Overcoming the Security Council Impasse: Envisioning Reform*, United Nations Occasional Paper no. 14 (Berlin: Friedrich Ebert Stiftung, 2005).

52. Michael Mandelbaum, "The Reluctance to Intervene," *Foreign Policy* 95 (Summer 1994): 11.

53. Mateja Peter, "Between Doctrine and Practice: The UN Peacekeeping Dilemma," *Global Governance* 21, no. 3 (2015): 351–370.

54. Anna Powles, Negar Partow, and Nick Nelson, eds., *United Nations Peacekeeping Challenge: The Importance of the Integrated Approach* (Surrey, U.K.: Ashgate, 2015).

55. See A/68/787 (March 7, 2014). Summary found at the Office of Internal Oversight Services, https://oios.un.org/page?slug=evaluation accessed May 30, 2015.

56. Somini Sengupta, "Beleaguered Blue Helmets: What Is the Role of UN Peacekeepers," *New York Times*, July 12, 2014.

57. United Nations, *Uniting Our Strengths for Peace—Politics, Partnership and People*, Report of the High-Level Independent Panel on Peace Operations, June 16, 2015, http://www.un.org/sg/pdf/HIPPO_Report_1_June_2015.pdf.

58. Lisa Hultman, Jacob Kathman, and Megan Shannon, "United Nations and Civilian Protection in Civil War," *American Journal of Political Science* 57, no. 4 (October 2013): 875–891.

59. Muna Ndulo, "The United Nations Responses to Sexual Abuse and Exploitation of Women and Girls by Peacekeepers During Peacekeeping Missions," *Berkeley Journal of International Law* 27, 1 (2009): 147.

60. Warren Hoge, "Report Finds U.N. Peacekeeping Isn't Moving to End Sex Abuse by Peacekeepers," *New York Times*, October 19, 2005.

61. Roland Paris, *After War's End: Building Peace After Civil Conflict* (Cambridge: Cambridge University Press, 2004).

62. See Peacebuilding Fund, "Trust Fund Fact Sheet," http://mptf.undp.org/factsheet /fund/PB000.

63. Advisory Group of Experts for the 2015 Review of United Nations Peacebuilding Architecture, *The Challenge of Sustaining Peace*, UN document A/69/968; S/2015/490, June 29, 2015.

64. Alberto Cutillo, *International Assistance to Countries Emerging from Conflict: A Review of Fifteen Years of Interventions and the Future of Peacebuilding*, International Peace Academy, Security-Development Nexus Program, February 2006, 60. For a general discussion, see Rob Jenkins, *Peacebuilding: From Concept to Commission* (London: Routledge, 2013).

65. OECD, *Fragile States 2014: Domestic Resource Mobilisation in Fragile States* (Paris: OECD, 2014), 24.

66. See Stephen Browne and Thomas G. Weiss, eds., *Peacebuilding Challenges for the UN Development System* (New York: Future UN Development System Project, 2015).

67. Quoted in Graham Allison, "Conceptual Models and the Cuban Missile Crisis," *American Political Science Review* 63 (September 1969): 701–702.

68. Kofi Annan, "The Quiet Revolution," *Global Governance* 4, no. 2 (1998): 123–138.

69. Mark Malloch Brown, "Can the UN Be Reformed?" *Global Governance* 14, no. 1 (2008): 7–8.

70. See an earlier discussion by John Mackinlay, "The Requirement for a Multinational Enforcement Capability," in *Collective Security in a Changing World*, ed. Thomas G. Weiss (Boulder, Colo.: Lynne Rienner, 1993), 139–152.

71. The classic treatment is by Dag Hammarskjöld, *The International Civil Servant in Law and in Fact: A Lecture Delivered to Congregation on 30 May 1961* (Oxford: Clarendon, 1961). See also Thomas G. Weiss, *What's Wrong with the United Nations and How to Fix It*, 3rd ed. (Cambridge: Polity, 2016).

72. Christine Chinkin and Hilary Charlesworth, *The Boundaries of International Law: A Feminist Analysis* (New York: Juris Publications, 2000).

73. Paul A. Volcker, Richard J. Goldstone, and Mark Pieth, *The Management of the United Nations Oil-for-Food Programme*, vol. 1: *The Report of the Committee*, September 7, 2005, 4, http://www.iic-offp.org/Mgmt_Report.htm.

74. Laura Shepherd, "Power and Authority in the Production of the United Nations Security Council Resolution 1325," *International Studies Quarterly* 52, no. 2 (June 2008): 383–404.

75. *Preventing Conflict, Transforming Justice, Securing the Peace: A Global Study on the Implementation of Security Council Resolution 1325*, 14, accessed December 12, 2015, http://www.unwomen.org/~/media/files/un%20women/wps/highlights/unw-global-study -1325-2015.pdf.

76. UN Women's website has details; see http://www.unwomen.org/about-us/about -un-women.

77. Fleur Roberts, "Understanding the Need for UN Women: Notes for New Zealand Civil Society," *Women's Studies Journal* 25 (2011): 31–46.

78. Spencer Zifcak, *United Nations Reform: Heading North or South* (New York: Routledge, 2009); Peter G. Danchin and Horst Fischer, eds. *United Nations Reform and the New Collective Security* (Cambridge: Cambridge University Press, 2010).

79. Giovanni Finizio and Ernesto Gallo, eds. *Democracy at the UN: UN Reform in the Age of Globalization* (Brussels: Peter Lang, 2013), especially Part II; Molly Ruhlman, *Who Participates in Global Governance? States, Bureaucracies, and NGOs in the United Nations* (London: Routledge, 2014); and Rodney Bruce Hall, ed., *Reducing Armed Violence with NGO Governance* (London: Routledge, 2014).

80. Vesselin Popovski and Trudy Fraser, eds., *The Security Council as Global Legislator* (London: Routledge, 2014).

PART TWO

HUMAN RIGHTS AND HUMANITARIAN AFFAIRS

CHAPTER 6

The United Nations, Human
Rights, and Humanitarian Affairs

O NE OF THE CENTRAL roles of the UN is to advance human dignity, which can be done through attention to human rights law, to international humanitarian law, and to humanitarian principles. This chapter describes and analyzes the explosion of UN human rights efforts since the 1940s. It also covers the basics of international humanitarian law, which is negotiated outside the UN but increasingly involves the world organization in its implementation and seeks to relieve human suffering. Humanitarian efforts may bypass discussion of human rights. For example, in the diplomacy of the Conference on Security and Cooperation in Europe during the Cold War, some families divided by the Iron Curtain were reunited purely with the objective of achieving a humane outcome, sidestepping debates about rights to emigrate or to pursue family unification. Likewise, foreign assistance is provided for victims of earthquakes and other natural disasters at least in part because of humane considerations, regardless of whether persons have a legal right to that international assistance.

The distinctions between human rights, international humanitarian law, and humanitarian action are often blurred, but all are part of a general rubric of "humanitarianism."[1] At the first UN, a great many international actions are undertaken for mixed motives with various justifications. In 1992 the Security Council authorized the use of force, in effect, to curtail starvation in Somalia. To some, this was a response to the codified human rights to life, adequate nutrition, and health care. To others, this was acting humanely to alleviate suffering. The council later stipulated that to interfere with humanitarian relief was a war crime, which brought humanitarian law into play. The concept of international security was expanded to include human security so that the Security Council could respond with a binding decision. Whether outside troops went into Somalia for reasons of human rights or humanitarian affairs was a theoretical distinction without operational significance.

The second UN may be involved in a situation because it is oriented toward humane outcomes, regardless of whether the language of international human rights is employed. Increasingly, UN civil servants try to organize and coordinate humanitarian relief in peace and war. They also try to alleviate the plight of refugees and internally displaced persons (IDPs) who have been uprooted by various events.

The nongovernmental organizations (NGOs) of the third UN are almost always involved in matters of human dignity: providing information to UN human rights monitoring agencies, doing the dangerous work of relief on the ground in war zones to identify just two of the many activities. NGOs respond to natural disasters in such numbers that after the earthquake of 2010, Haiti was often called the "Haitian Republic of NGOs." Increasingly, human rights groups, such as Amnesty International and Human Rights Watch, concern themselves with the part of the laws of war pertaining to civilians and detained fighters in war, not just with human rights standards in peace. Given the extent of violence in the world, those concerned about individuals in dire straits need to be aware of international humanitarian law for armed conflict and the long effort to create humanitarian space in the midst of what belligerents call "military necessity." Other members of the third UN also come into the picture—for instance, the media in reporting on abuses or disasters, and those businesses pursuing policies of corporate social responsibility (CSR).

Human rights and humanitarian standards are always under some kind of challenge. Two examples illustrate this point. The human rights of women across the world remain at risk because women lack the same legal status as men and in some societies are even treated as property. For some, the oppression of women is the twenty-first century's most pervasive human rights problem.[2] Violence against women remains a basic issue, and while some governments may not directly target women, private actors, such as family members, social groups, and employers, do. Direct physical threats are complicated by a pervasive mindset that works against women, whereby women are systematically denied equal protection and access to food, health, education, and the right to participate in public life. If the human rights of half the population are in question, then the very idea of universal human rights is also in question. Even where women have the same legal status as men, cultural practices and norms often dictate a subordinate position of women in society.

The so-called era of terrorism is a second example of a challenge to human rights. Alan Dershowitz, a lawyer at Harvard University, openly advocated torture as a legitimate security measure under certain conditions.[3] Another prominent public intellectual, Michael Ignatieff—who had directed a human rights center at Harvard before being elected to the Canadian parliament and has now returned to the university—argued that even liberal democracies could understandably violate even the most basic human rights when faced with major threats to national security.[4] In January 2003 the *Economist* ran a cover story under the title "Is Torture Ever Justified?" This focus was a follow-up to a *Washington Post* story reporting that in its war on terrorism, the United States was using "stress and duress" interrogation techniques on prisoners detained in Afghanistan and at its detention facility in Guantánamo Bay, Cuba, where more than thirty prisoners had attempted suicide. At the infamous prison in Iraq, Abu Ghraib, U.S. personnel subjected prisoners in 2003 to torture and cruel treatment. The United States also transferred certain prisoners to such states as Egypt, Morocco, Jordan, and Syria, where interrogation procedures were, euphemistically speaking, harsh. All of this was coupled with secret CIA detention facilities, acknowledged by President George W. Bush, in Eastern Europe and elsewhere.

In 2009 President Obama signed executive order 13491 prohibiting torture and ensuring lawful interrogation. While this put an end to most Bush-era tactics, some defenders of prisoner abuse continue to argue that "enhanced interrogation techniques" are lawful and give rise to important actionable intelligence.[5] In that same year the president ordered the closing of the Guantánamo Bay detention facility but was blocked by Congress. In March 2011, hemmed in by congressional legislation, he reluctantly signed another executive order that allowed for unlimited administrative detention at Guantánamo Bay, as well as having to accept controversial military commissions rather than trials in federal courts. Obama has also made extensive use of drones to target and kill terror suspects, raising concerns about the human rights dimensions of these kinds of extrajudicial killings.[6] It is not clear that all of those so attacked were active combatants.

If the first example, of the rights of women, indicates many challenges to human rights norms particularly in the non-Western world, the second example about torture raises serious questions about the commitment by Western democracies to human rights and humanitarian principles and policies as they pertain to suspected terrorists.

UNDERSTANDING HUMAN RIGHTS

Since 1945, states have used their plenary or constitutive sovereignty to create international human rights obligations that in turn have restricted their operational sovereignty. The international law of human rights, developed on a global scale mostly at the United Nations, clearly regulates what legal policies states can adopt even within their own territorial jurisdictions. International agreements on human rights norms have been followed at least occasionally by concrete, noteworthy developments showing that international organizations have begun to reach deeply into matters that were once considered the core of national domestic affairs.

The process by which a territorial state's assumed sovereignty has given way to shared authority and power between the state and international organizations is not a recent phenomenon. These changes accelerated with the start of the United Nations in 1945, became remarkable from about 1970, and became spasmodically dramatic from about 1991. The UN's role in human rights remains one of the more provocative subjects of the twenty-first century, what Roger Normand and Sarah Zaidi have aptly called "the unfinished revolution."[7] Acknowledging these historical changes concerning the United Nations and human rights is not the same as being overly optimistic about these developments. Indeed, some UN proceedings on human rights would "depress Dr. Pangloss," the character in Voltaire's *Candide* who believes that all is for the best in this best of all possible worlds.[8] Although noteworthy in historical perspective, UN activity concerning human rights often displays an enormous gap between the law on the books and the law in action. At any given time or on any given issue, state expediency may supersede the application of UN human rights standards. Revolutionary change in a given context may not be institutionalized in UN machinery;[9] similar situations can give rise to different UN roles and different outcomes for human rights. A number of states, some of them with democratic governments, have opposed progressive action for human rights at the United Nations. If the international movement for human rights means separating the individual from full state control, then this movement has not always been well received by those who rule in the name of the state. They may be primarily interested in stability, order, national power, wealth, and/or independence.

The territorial state remains the most important legal-political entity in the modern world despite the obvious importance of ethnic, religious, and cultural identifications and an increasing number of actors in civil society everywhere. Thus, many ethnic and religious groups try to capture control of the government so that they can speak officially for the state. Some groups may attempt to secede from an existing state and create a new state that has international recognition and possesses sovereignty. The state constitutes the basic building block of the United Nations. State actors primarily shape the world organization's agenda and action on human rights, although states are pushed and pulled by other actors, such as private human rights groups and UN secretariat officials. Developments at the UN concerning human rights have sometimes been remarkable. However, in general, state authorities still control the most important final decisions, and traditional national interests still trump individual human rights much of the time in international relations. States have primary responsibility for the protection of human rights, yet they are often the primary violators of international human rights.

Positive and negative developments concerning the United Nations and human rights were evident at the 1993 World Conference on Human Rights in Vienna.[10] The Vienna conference was the last major global conference relating to human rights, and many states reaffirmed their commitment to universal human rights. A small minority of delegations, especially from Asia and the Middle East, argued for cultural relativism in a strong form: namely, that there were few or no universal human rights, mostly only rights specific to various countries, regions, or cultures.[11] Some of the delegates making arguments in favor of strong cultural relativism were representing states that were party to numerous human rights treaties, without reservations.

A large number of NGOs attended the conference and tried to focus on concrete rights violations in specific countries, but most governments wanted to deal with abstract principles, not specific violations. At the same time that the U.S. delegation took a strong stand in favor of internationally recognized human rights in general, the Bill Clinton administration refused to provide military specialists and protective troops to conduct an investigation into war crimes in Serbian-controlled territory in the Balkans. These examples show that a certain diplomatic progress concerning international human rights was accompanied by much controversy and reluctance to act decisively on specifics.

Human rights are fundamental entitlements of persons, constituting means to the end of minimal human dignity or social justice. If persons have human rights, they are entitled to a fundamental claim that others must do, or refrain from doing, something. Under the Westphalian system of international relations, which the UN modifies but does not fundamentally contradict, states are primarily responsible for order and social justice in their jurisdictions. Their governments are the primary targets of these personal and fundamental claims. If an individual has a right to freedom from torture, governments are obligated to ensure that torture does not occur in their jurisdiction. Likewise, if an individual has a right to adequate health care, governments are obligated to ensure that such care is provided to every person in their jurisdiction.

The legal system codifies what are recognized as human rights at any point in time. The legal system, of course, recognizes many legal rights. The ones seen as most fundamental to human dignity—that is, a life worthy of being lived—are called human rights. There is a difference between fundamental human rights and other legal rights that are perhaps important but not, relatively speaking, fundamental. This theoretical distinction between fundamental and important rights can and does give rise to debate.[12] Is access to minimal health care fundamental, and thus a human right, as the Canadian legal system guarantees? Or is that access only something that people should have if they can afford it, as the U.S. system implies? Why does the U.S. legal system recognize a patient's legal right to sue a doctor for negligence but not allow that same person access to adequate health care as a human right?

The origin of human rights outside of codification in the legal system is also debated. Legal positivists are content to accept the identification of human rights as found in the legal system. But others, especially philosophers, wish to know what "true" or "moral" human rights exist independent from any legal codification. Natural law theorists, for example, believe that human rights exist in natural law as provided by a supreme being. Analytical theorists believe there are moral rights associated inherently with persons; the legal system only indicates a changing view of what these moral rights are.[13] Michael Ignatieff argues that we now have human rights at home and abroad not because of philosophy but because of history. If one reads history and notes the chronic abuse of individuals by public authorities, and if one notes that the societies that accept human rights do a better job of providing for the welfare of their citizens, that is sufficient justification for human rights.[14] Despite the long-standing debate about the ultimate origin of human rights, many societies have come to some agreement about fundamental personal rights, writing them into national constitutions and other legal instruments. In international society some formal agreement exists on what constitutes universal human rights.[15]

International Origins

When important territorial states arose and became consolidated in the middle of the seventeenth century, human rights were treated, if at all, as national rather than international issues. Indeed, the core of the 1648 Peace of Westphalia, designed to end the religious wars of Europe, indicated that the territorial ruler would henceforth determine the territory's religion. In the modern language of rights, freedom of religion, or its absence, was left to the territorial ruler. The dominant international rule was what today we call state sovereignty. Any question of human rights was subsumed under that ordering principle. International order was based on the principle of noninterference in domestic affairs.

Later, the Americans in 1776–1787 decided to recognize human rights, and the French in 1789 attempted to do so, both revolutions referring to such rights as universal.[16] These revolutions had no immediate legal effect, and sometimes no immediate political effect, on other countries. In fact, many non-Western peoples and their rulers were not immediately affected by these two revolutions, oriented as they were to definitions of what were then called "the rights of man." Many non-Western societies, such as China, relied primarily on enlightened leaders for human dignity and social justice. Such leaders might be seen as limited by social or religious principles, but they were not widely seen as limited by the personal rights of their "subjects." A pervasive view, but by no means totally shared, is that the idea of universal human rights was a Western invention in both theory and practice, but ethical considerations from many cultures affected European and North American thought.[17]

During the middle of the nineteenth century, the West was swept by a wave of international sentiment.[18] Growing international concern for the plight of persons without regard to nationality laid the moral foundations for a later resurrection and expansion of the notion of personal rights. Moral concern led eventually to an explosion in human rights developments, even if the notion of human rights was not particularly resurrected then.[19] In some ways Marxism was part of this European-based transnational concern for the individual, since Karl Marx focused on the plight of the industrialized worker everywhere under early and crude capitalism. But he was not a persistent or consistent champion of all individual rights, being especially critical of unbridled property rights.

Early Marxism had its moral dimensions about individual suffering. Two other moral or social movements occurred about the same time and are usually cited as the earliest manifestations of internationally recognized human rights. In the 1860s, about the time Marx wrote *Das Kapital*, a Swiss businessman named Henry Dunant started what is now called the International Red Cross and Red Crescent Movement. Dunant was appalled that in the 1859 Battle of Solferino in what is now Italy, which was entangled in the war for the Austrian succession, wounded soldiers were simply left on the battlefield.[20] Armies had no adequate medical corps. European armies had more veterinarians to care for horses than doctors to care for soldiers.[21] Dunant envisioned what became national Red Cross (or, in Muslim states, Red Crescent) societies, and these putatively private agencies not only geared up for practical action in war but also lobbied governments for new treaties to protect sick and wounded soldiers. In 1864 the first Geneva Convention for Victims of War was concluded, providing legal protection to fighters disabled in international war and the medical personnel who cared for them. According to a third protocol added to the 1949 Geneva Conventions in December 2005, politically neutral emblems recognized for certain aid societies in armed conflict are the Red Cross, the Red Crescent, and the Red Crystal. Other neutral emblems are also recognized.[22] Today the International Red Cross and Red Crescent Movement encompasses over 186 national Red Cross or Red Crescent societies, the associated but autonomous International Federation of Red Cross and Red Crescent Societies, and the independent International Committee of the Red Cross (ICRC).

The antislavery movement was another nineteenth-century effort to identify and correct a problem of human dignity on an international basis. By 1890 in Brussels, all the major Western states finally signed a multilateral treaty prohibiting the African slave trade. This capped a movement that had started about the turn of the nineteenth century in Britain. Just as private Red Cross organizations had pushed for protection and assistance for victims of war, so the London-based Anti-Slavery Society (today, Anti-Slavery International) and other private groups pushed the British government in particular to stop the slave trade. Britain outlawed the trade in the first decade of the nineteenth century; obtained a broader, similar international agreement at the Congress of Vienna in 1815; and thereafter used the British navy, among other means, to try to enforce its ban on the slave trade.

The early resistance by the United States and other major slave-trading states was overcome by the end of the century. Yet an international agreement on principles and applications, reaching deeply into the European colonies in Africa, was necessary to significantly reduce this long-accepted and lucrative practice. In the twentieth century freedom from slavery, the slave trade, and slavery-like practices came to be accepted as an internationally recognized human right. Its roots lay in the transnational morality of the nineteenth century.

During the nineteenth century from time to time domestic pressure on such leading Western powers as Britain and France resulted in use of force abroad to "save strangers" or protect certain individuals from massacres—what today we call atrocities.[23] These "interventions" mostly occurred in "the sick man of Europe"—namely the Ottoman Empire. So it was that the Greek, Bulgarian, and Syrian peoples under Ottoman rule benefited from British and French (even sometimes Russian) military action. These early "humanitarian interventions" often displayed a religious link, with "Christian nations" acting on behalf of "Christian peoples" menaced by Islamic (that is, Turkish or Ottoman) authorities. While episodic and unsystematic, such action also contributed to a growing concern for the fate of persons regardless of national borders. Of course, not all menaced groups were so fortunate in attracting outside protectors, as the fate of Armenians in the Ottoman Empire demonstrated.[24]

This trend of focusing on human need across national borders increased during the League of Nations era, although the League's Covenant contained no human rights provisions and most efforts to focus on human dignity met with less than full success in an era of fascism, militarism, nationalism, racism, and isolationism. The Versailles conference in 1919 represented efforts to write into the Covenant rights to religious freedom and racial equality. The British even proposed a right of outside intervention into states to protect religious freedom. These proposals failed largely because of Woodrow Wilson. Despite a Japanese push for the endorsement of racial equality, the U.S. president was so adamantly against any mention of race that U.S. and British proposals on religious freedom were withdrawn.[25] During the 1930s the League's assembly debated the merits of an international agreement on human rights in general, but French and Polish proposals to this effect failed. Some states were opposed in principle, and some did not want to antagonize Nazi Germany, given the prevailing policy of accommodation or appeasement. Nevertheless, the language of universal human rights was appearing more and more in diplomacy.

International efforts to codify and institutionalize labor rights were more successful. The International Labour Organization (ILO) was created and based in Geneva alongside the League. Its tripartite membership consisted of government, labor, and management delegations from each member state. This structure was conducive to the approval of a series of treaties and other agreements recognizing labor rights, as well as to the development of mechanisms to monitor state practice under the treaties. The ILO thus preceded the United Nations but continued after 1945 as a UN specialized agency. It was one of the first international organizations to monitor internationally recognized rights—in this case labor rights—within states.[26]

Although the Covenant failed to deal with human rights in general, its Article 23 indicated that the League should be concerned with social justice. In addition to calling for international coordination of labor policy, the article called on member states to take action on such matters as "native inhabitants," "traffic in women and children," "opium and other dangerous drugs," "freedom of communications," and "the prevention and control of disease." Precise standards, however, were decidedly lacking in these issue areas.

The League of Nations was connected to the minority treaties designed for about a dozen states after World War I in an effort to curtail the ethnic passions that had contributed to the outbreak of the Great War in the Balkans. Only a few states were legally obligated to give special rights to minorities. The system of minority treaties did not function very well under the acute nationalist pressures of the 1930s. So dismal was the League record on minority rights that global efforts at minority protection per se were not renewed by the United Nations until the 1980s—a gap of about fifty years.

The League's mandate system sought to protect the welfare of dependent peoples. The Permanent Mandates Commission supervised the European states that controlled certain territories taken from the losing side in World War I. Those

European states were theoretically obligated to rule for the welfare of dependent peoples. Peoples in "A" mandates were supposed to be allowed to exercise their collective right to self-determination in the relatively near future. The Permanent Mandates Commission was made up of experts named by the League Council, and it established a reputation for integrity—so much so that the controlling states regarded it as a nuisance. The League of Nations tried to promote "humane values"—a synonym for "social justice." It was concerned with human dignity, in some cases seeking to improve the situation of persons without actually codifying their rights. In so doing it laid the foundation for later rights developments.

These and other developments in the late nineteenth and early twentieth centuries expressed "an epochal shift in moral sentiment."[27] The growing "moral interdependence" was to undergird the creation of human rights "regimes" in the UN era.[28] This moral solidarity was not cohesive enough to eradicate many of the ills addressed. How could it be, when in the 1930s some major states (Germany, Italy, and Japan) were glorifying brutal power at the service of particular races or nationalities? The Soviet Union had an extensive record of brutal repression and exploitation within its borders, using mass murder and starvation as a policy tool to obtain compliance.[29] The United States enforced legally sanctioned racial segregation and discrimination as well as blatantly racist immigration and miscegenation laws. Thus, while a shift occurred toward a cosmopolitan morality that tended to disregard national boundaries and citizenship, a "thick morality" still centered on national communities and was subject to the disease of chauvinistic nationalism. "Thin morality" was left for international society. Prevailing wisdom was that governments existed to pursue the national interest, whereas attention to the plight of others abroad was a distinctly secondary consideration.

When the United Nations was created in 1945, a growing corpus of legal and organizational experience existed that the international community could draw on in trying to improve international order and justice. By 1948, conventional wisdom held that internationally recognized human rights would have to be reaffirmed and expanded, not erased. For example, the League of Nations Refugee Office (under different names with different mandates) had earlier sought to help refugees, which in 1951 led the UN to sponsor a treaty on refugee rights and establish the Office of the United Nations High Commissioner for Refugees. However, the UN would have to devise further, better ways of improving human dignity, through both law and organization.

BASIC NORMS IN THE UN ERA

In the post–World War II era, the international community sought to embed a particular set of values and standards regulating the behavior of states. These values and standards were thought to contribute to international peace and stability and were incubated both within and outside the UN.

Charter Norms

The UN Charter became the first general treaty to obligate states to promote human rights, despite the fact that early drafts of the Charter did not refer to human rights. The addition of human rights language preceded widespread knowledge about the extent of the Holocaust and other World War II atrocities.[30] Intellectual opinion in the United States and United Kingdom pushed for an endorsement of human rights as a statement about the rationale for World War II. This development built on the Atlantic Charter issued by the United States and Britain early in 1941. Franklin D. Roosevelt stressed the importance of four freedoms, including freedom from "want." A handful of Latin American states joined in this push to emphasize human rights as a statement about civilized nations. Eleanor Roosevelt became an outspoken champion of human rights in general and women's rights in particular. In the UN Human Rights Commission, however, which Eleanor Roosevelt chaired in the 1940s, the most outspoken advocate for women's rights was the Indian representative, Hansa Mehta.

Unlike the Wilson administration in 1919, the Truman administration agreed to a series of statements on human rights in the Charter and successfully lobbied the other victorious great powers. This decision was not easy, particularly given the continuation of legally sanctioned and widely supported racial discrimination within the United States. Whether this administration was genuinely and deeply committed to getting human rights into the Charter[31] or whether it was pushed in that direction by others[32] remains a point of historical debate. Harry Truman made no mention of the 1948 Universal Declaration of Human Rights in his memoirs. U.S. support for UN human rights language remained general and judicially unenforceable.[33]

Why Joseph Stalin accepted early UN human rights statements is unclear, especially given the widespread political murder and persecution within the Soviet Union in the 1930s and 1940s. Perhaps the USSR saw this human rights language as useful in deflecting criticism of Soviet policies, particularly since the Charter language was vague and not immediately followed by specifics on application. Perhaps Stalin saw the language of rights as useful in his attempt to focus on socialism—that is, he accepted the general wording on rights as it was intended to concentrate only on social and economic rights.[34] This would not be the last time the Soviet Union underestimated the influence of language written into international agreements. The 1975 Helsinki Accord, and especially its provisions on human rights and humanitarian affairs, generated pressures that helped weaken European communism. The Soviet Union initially resisted human rights language in the accord, but it eventually accepted that language in the mistaken notion that the codification and dissemination of human rights would not upset totalitarian control.[35]

The United Kingdom accepted the Charter language on human rights with the understanding that it would not be applied in British colonies. For Winston Churchill, who had helped author ringing pronouncements about human rights during World War II to highlight enemy atrocities, the British Empire should continue, with all that it implied about an unequal status for nonwhite peoples. In this view he was not dissimilar from the American founding fathers, albeit two centuries earlier, whose proclamations about rights were not intended for women, slaves, or Native Americans.

The 1945 Charter statements on human rights, although more progressive than some had originally wanted, were vague. Nevertheless, they provided the legal cornerstone or foundation for a later legal and diplomatic revolution. The Charter's preamble states that a principal purpose of the UN is "to affirm faith in fundamental human rights." In Article 1, the Charter says that one of the purposes of the organization is to promote and encourage "respect for human rights and for fundamental freedoms for all without distinction as to race, sex, language, or religion." In Article 55, the Charter imposes on states these legal obligations:

> With a view to the creation of conditions of stability and well-being which are necessary for peaceful and friendly relations among nations based on respect for the principle of equal rights and self-determination of peoples, the United Nations shall promote:
>
> A. higher standards of living, full employment, and conditions of economic and social progress and development;
> B. solutions of international economic, social, health, and related problems; and international cultural and educational cooperation; and
> C. universal respect for, and observance of, human rights and fundamental freedoms for all without distinction as to race, sex, language, or religion.

Article 56 states that "all Members pledge themselves to take joint and separate action in cooperation with the Organization for the achievement of the purposes set forth in Article 55."

The language of Article 55 endorses the notion of human rights because they were linked to international peace and security. Western democracies believed that states respecting human rights in the form of civil and political rights would not make war on others. In this view, brutal authoritarian states, those that denied civil and political rights, were inherently aggressive, whereas democracies were inherently peaceful. At the same time, many accepted the notion of human rights by seeing them as a means to human dignity, not necessarily or primarily as a means to ensure international peace.

Both motivations drove the diplomatic process regarding human rights in 1945. Some policymakers genuinely saw human rights as linked to peace, and others may have accepted that rationale as a useful justification for promoting human dignity. Motivation and justification are not the same,[36] but separating the two is difficult. The relationship between human rights and peace has intrinsic importance to world politics. A clear correlation between at least some human rights and peace has importance not only for a direct and "micro" contribution to human dignity but for a contribution to human dignity in a "macro" sense by enhancing international—and perhaps national—security and stability through eliminating major violence.

The connection between various human rights and international and national peace—with *peace* defined as "the absence of widespread violence between or within countries"—has been widely researched. The following five statements summarize some of that voluminous research. First, consolidated liberal democratic governments (those that emerge from, and thereafter respect, widespread civil and political rights) tend not to engage in international war with one another.[37] Documenting international war between or among democracies is difficult, and some scholars believe that the absence of war is not because of democracy. The United Kingdom and the United States fought in 1812, but one scholar holds that because of the severely limited franchise, the United States did not become a democracy until the 1820s and Britain not until the 1830s.[38]

The debate about threshold conditions for democracy continues. One view is that the United States did not become a democracy until women, or half of the population, gained the franchise. In the American Civil War, the Union and the Confederacy both had elected presidents, but the Confederacy was not recognized as a separate state by many outsiders, and it also severely restricted the voting franchise. At the start of World War I, Germany manifested a very broad franchise, but its parliament lacked authority and the kaiser went unchecked in making much policy. Even though some scholars think the historical absence of war between democracies is either a statistical accident or explicable by security factors, other scholars continue to insist that consolidated liberal democracies (as compared to transitional democracies and illiberal democracies) do not often make war on each other.[39] But one must remain cautious about the accuracy and durability of this apparent pattern.

Second, liberal democratic governments have used covert force against other elected governments that are not perceived to be truly in the liberal democratic community. During the Cold War the United States used force to overthrow some elected governments in developing countries—for example, Iran in 1953 (Mohammed Mossadeq was elected by Iran's parliament), Guatemala in 1954 (Jacobo Arbenz Guzmán was genuinely if imperfectly elected in a popular vote), Chile in 1973 (Salvador Allende won a plurality), and Nicaragua after 1984 (some international observers regarded Daniel Ortega as genuinely if imperfectly elected).[40] Several democracies used force to remove the Patrice Lumumba government in the Congo in the 1960s; those elections, too, were imperfect but reflected popular sentiment.[41]

Third, some industrialized liberal democratic governments seem to be war-prone and clearly have initiated force against authoritarian governments. Britain, France, and the United States are among the most war-prone states, owing perhaps to their power or geography. Liberal democratic governments initiated hostilities in the Spanish-American War of 1898 and the Suez crisis of 1956, not to mention U.S. use of force in Grenada and Panama in the 1980s and in Iraq in 2003.

Fourth, human rights of various types do not correlate clearly and easily with major national violence, such as civil wars and rebellions.[42] In some of these situations a particular human rights issue may be important—for example, slavery in the American Civil War, ethnic and religious persecution in the Romanian violence of 1989, and perceived ethnic discrimination in contemporary Sri Lanka. But in other civil wars and similar domestic violence, human rights factors seemed not to be a leading cause—for example, the Russian civil war of 1917 and the Chinese civil war in the 1930s. The Universal Declaration of Human Rights presents itself, in part, as a barrier to national revolution against repression. This follows the Jeffersonian philosophy that if human rights are not respected, revolution may be justified. But the link between human rights violations and national revolutionary violence is difficult to verify as a prominent and recurring pattern. A number of repressive and exploitative governing arrangements have lasted for a relatively long time while various rights-protective governments have yielded under violent pressure to more authoritarian elites.

Fifth, armed conflict seems clearly to lead to an increase in human rights violations.[43] If some uncertainty remains about whether liberal democracy at home leads to a certain peace abroad, a reverse pattern does not seem open to debate. When states participate in international and internal armed conflict, there is almost always a rise in violations of rights of personal integrity and an increase in forced disappearance, torture, arbitrary arrest, and other violations of important civil rights. Human rights may or may not lead to peace, but peace is conducive to enhanced human rights.

Core Norms Beyond the UN Charter

The UN Charter presented the interesting situation of codifying a general commitment to human rights before an international definition or list of human rights was developed. To answer the question of what internationally recognized human rights states are obligated to apply, the United Nations developed the Universal Declaration of Human Rights (UDHR) in an effort to specify Charter principles. On December 10, 1948—December 10 is now recognized as International Human Rights Day—the General Assembly adopted the UDHR without a negative vote (but with eight abstentions: the Soviet Union and its allies, Saudi Arabia, and South Africa). This resolution, not legally binding at the time of adoption, listed thirty human rights principles covering perhaps sixty rights. They fell into three broad clusters.[44]

First-generation negative rights are the individual civil and political rights that are well known in the West. They are called "first-generation" because they were the ones first endorsed in national constitutions and called "negative" because civil rights in particular blocked public authority from interfering with the private person in civil society. These were the rights to freedom of thought, speech, religion, privacy, and assembly, plus the right to participate in the making of public policy. In the view of some observers, these are the only true human rights. In the view of others, these are the most important human rights, because if one has civil and political rights, one can use them to obtain and apply the others. In the

Mrs. Eleanor Roosevelt of the United States holding a Declaration of Human Rights poster in French. November 1, 1949, United Nations, Lake Success, New York. (UN PHOTO 83980)

view of still others, these rights are not so important because if one lacks the material basics of life, such as food, shelter, health care, and education, then civil and political rights become relatively meaningless.

Second-generation positive rights are socioeconomic rights.[45] They are called "second-generation" because they were associated with various twentieth-century revolutions emphasizing a redistribution of the material benefits of economic growth, and "positive" because they obligate public authority to take positive steps to ensure minimal food, shelter, and health care. European states, Japan, and Canada have enshrined these rights in their welfare states, and these rights have been rhetorically emphasized in many developing countries. How important these rights are is still a matter of debate. In the United States, the Democratic Carter and Clinton administrations accepted them in theory and gave them some rhetorical attention but never fully embraced them. Republican administrations from Ronald Reagan to George W. Bush rejected them as dangerous to individual responsibility and leading to big government.

Third-generation solidarity rights are the rights emphasized by some contemporary actors. They are called "third-generation" because they followed the other two clusters and also are called "solidarity" because they pertain to collections of persons—for instance, indigenous peoples—rather than to individuals. Later formulations have included claims to a right to peace, development, and a healthy environment as the common heritage of humankind. Under some national laws, groups receive formal recognition. Some minorities are guaranteed a certain number of seats in parliament. Other peoples are recognized as holding collective title to land. Whether some of these group arrangements should be called collective human rights of universal validity remains controversial.

One collective right, a people's right to self-determination, has been much discussed, especially since the end of World War I. The principle of national self-determination is recognized as the first article in both the International Covenant on Civil and Political Rights and the International Covenant on Economic, Social and Cultural Rights. Thus, the collective right to self-determination is cast in modern times as a human right. This general principle, however, has not translated into specific rules indicating which group is a national people with this right and which is not. Also lacking is a clear indication of what "self-determination" means, and the options range from various forms of internal autonomy to full independence. Unfortunately, most claims to self-determination are resolved by politics, including violent politics, rather than peaceful change under judicial supervision.

Parsing rights into several categories or "generations" is perhaps useful to summarize developments, but analytical care is necessary. To apply negative rights, positive action must be taken. States must develop legislation to protect civil and political rights and spend billions each year to see that they are respected. Second-generation socioeconomic rights are sometimes seen as emanating from non-Western and socialistic actors, but they were emphasized by the Catholic Church as well as by the state of Ireland and various Latin American states relatively early on. Collective rights can also pertain to individuals. Moreover, they are not so new. The right to national self-determination is actually a right of peoples or nations that has been (a vague) part of international law for decades.

A prevalent view, articulated nicely by Mary Robinson—the former president of Ireland who stepped down in September 2002 as the UN high commissioner for human rights and since has headed an NGO, Realizing Rights-Ethical Globalization Initiative—is that all of the generations should be viewed as a "package."[46] All internationally recognized rights were important and interdependent. At the same time, however, the Security Council created international criminal tribunals for the former Yugoslavia and Rwanda with legal jurisdiction for genocide, war crimes, and crimes against humanity. This suggested that the right to be free from these violations was more important or more basic. UN member states created the International Criminal Court with the same focus. The structure of the International Covenant on Civil and Political Rights suggests that even within that category of rights some rights are core, permitting no violation even in national emergencies, while other rights can be suspended in exceptional times. Debate abounds about whether there should be some prioritizing of human rights action. Also, in international law there is the concept of *jus cogens*: fundamental legal rights that can never be abridged, even by other rights developments. No definitive list of *jus cogens* has ever been approved by states, but a virtually universal view is that some human rights, such as freedom from genocide and summary execution and torture, are part of *jus cogens*. This consideration again leads to the conclusion that some human rights are more basic than others. The notion of "responsibility to protect" indicates that mass atrocities, such as genocide, crimes against humanity, war crimes, and ethnic cleansing, should receive special attention. Much practice in International Relations suggests that "atrocity crimes" constitute the priority for human rights action.

The United States is an outlier among states that traditionally support human rights. It has not ratified three of seven core treaties—the ones protecting economic, cultural, and social rights; protecting children's rights; and eliminating discrimination against women. Within the Group of 8 (G8)—the seven most powerful Western democracies (including Japan) and the Russian Federation (when not excluded from that grouping)—the United States is the only country that has not ratified any of these. And in the expanded G20, the United States finds itself in the company of China, South Korea, Saudi Arabia, and South Africa in not ratifying one or more of these treaties. Moreover, even when ratifying such human rights treaties as the Convention on the Prevention and Punishment of the Crime of Genocide and the Covenant on Civil and Political Rights, the United States adds reservations and other statements that prevent the treaties from having domestic effect, which, as a former State Department lawyer noted, makes it very difficult to get international law introduced into courts within the United States.[47]

No state voting for the Universal Declaration of Human Rights has succeeded in meeting all its terms through national legislation and practice. This vote was the homage that vice paid to virtue. This would not be the last time that state diplomacy presented a large measure of hypocrisy. Yet most contemporary states want to be associated with the notion of human rights. Of the UN's 193 member states, 168 had formally accepted the civil-political covenant by mid-2015, and 164 the economic-social-cultural covenant.

The practical impact of the UDHR is considerable. Its principles have been endorsed in numerous national constitutions and other legal and quasi-legal documents. All the new or newly independent European states that once had communist governments accepted its principles in theory in the 1990s. Of the eight states abstaining in 1948, seven had renounced their abstention by 1993. Only Saudi Arabia continued to object openly to the declaration. In reality, however, among the five permanent members of the UN (P5), China saw civil and political rights as a dangerous development coming from the West that threatened Chinese stability and cohesion, and likewise in Russia Vladimir Putin has tolerated little effective dissent from his autocratic rule.

Having adopted the declaration in 1948, UN member states turned to an even more specific elaboration of internationally recognized human rights. The

The "Allée des drapeaux" ("Flags Way") at the Palais des Nations, seat of the UN Office at Geneva (UNOG). April 9, 2015. (UN PHOTO 628375/JEAN-MARC FERRÉ)

decision was made to negotiate two separate core human rights treaties, one on civil and political rights and one on social, economic, and cultural rights. This was not done only, or even primarily, because of theoretical or ideological differences among states. The different types of rights also were seen as requiring different types of follow-up. A widely held view was that civil-political rights could be implemented immediately, given sufficient political will, and were enforceable by judicial proceedings. By comparison, socioeconomic rights were seen as requiring certain policies over time, as greatly affected by economic and social factors, and hence as not subject to immediate enforcement by court order. The more recent approach within the United Nations, in the General Assembly and elsewhere, is to blur distinctions and consider rights comprehensively.

By 1956 the two UN covenants, or multilateral treaties, were essentially complete on the two clusters of rights. By 1966 they were formally approved by states voting in the General Assembly, the time lag indicating that many states were unenthusiastic about the emergence of human rights treaties limiting state sovereignty. By 1976 a sufficient number of state adherences had been obtained to bring the treaties into legal force by parties giving their formal consent. Few followed the example of the United States of accepting one but rejecting the other (the United States became a party to the civil-political covenant in 1992, with reservations, but not to the socioeconomic covenant). Most states have accepted both covenants.

These three documents—the 1948 Universal Declaration of Human Rights and the two 1966 UN covenants—make up what was not included in the UN's Charter: an International Bill of Rights, or a core list of internationally recognized human rights that would have similar status to the Bill of Rights in the U.S. Constitution. Most of the treaty provisions are clarifications of, and elaborations on, the thirty norms found in the declaration. There are a few discrepancies. The declaration notes a right to private property, but this right was not codified in the two covenants. After the fall of communism, the General Assembly on several occasions returned to a recognition of property rights. As already noted, there was a broad and formal acceptance of this International Bill of Rights, even though there is no such official label or document. But from either 1966 or 1976, depending on which date is emphasized, there was a core definition of universal human rights in legally binding form.

The contours of the third UN took shape around the monitoring process designed to specify what the treaties meant. Both covenants are overseen by committees of independent experts, not governmental representatives. More than fifty states (not including the United States) have agreed to allow their citizens to petition the UN Human Rights Committee (after exhausting national efforts) alleging a violation of the civil-political covenant by a government. The Human Rights Committee is not a court but a "monitoring mechanism" that can direct negative publicity toward an offending and recalcitrant government. It works to prod governments toward fulfilling their international commitments. All states that have accepted the socioeconomic covenant are automatically supervised by a UN Committee of Experts. After a slow start, that committee, too, began a systematic effort to persuade states to honor their commitments. Part of the process involves state parties submitting reports that detail their implementation of the treaties. Unfortunately, a number of governments are tardy in filing reports with both the Human Rights Committee under the civil-political covenant and the Committee of Experts under the socioeconomic covenant—and many of the reports that are submitted are incomplete or poorly done. Nevertheless, the promotion and protection of human rights has expanded beyond states and their representatives.

Supplementing (and Challenging) the Core

During most of the UN era, states were willing to endorse abstract human rights. But until the 1990s, they were not willing to create specialized human rights courts or even to make the global treaties enforceable through national courts. Traditionally, in the absence of dependable adjudication, states tried to reinforce the International Bill of Rights, while protecting their legal independence, by negotiating more human rights treaties. This is a way to bring diplomatic emphasis to a problem, to raise awareness of a problem, or to further specify state obligation in the hope that specificity will improve behavior.

About one hundred international human rights instruments exist. These include conventions, protocols, declarations, codes of conduct, and formal statements of standards and basic principles. Table 6.1 summarizes part of the situation. Despite overlap and duplication, the United Nations has overseen the emergence of treaties on racial discrimination, apartheid, political rights of women, discrimination against women, slavery, the slave trade and slavery-like practices, genocide, hostages, torture, the nationality of married women, stateless persons, refugees, marriage, prostitution, children, and discrimination in education. The ILO has sponsored treaties on forced labor, the right to organize, and rights to collective bargaining, among others. A number of supplemental human rights treaties are in varying stages of negotiation at the United Nations, including those on indigenous peoples, forced disappearances, persons with disabilities, and minorities. A collective right to development has been declared by various UN bodies, including the General Assembly, and may become the subject matter of a treaty.

Regional human rights developments are noteworthy because depending on the area, developments either supplement or challenge the UN core. The regional human rights regime created in Western Europe serves as an excellent model for the international protection of human rights. The European Convention on Human Rights and Fundamental Freedoms defined a set of civil and political rights. For a time the European Commission on Human Rights served as a collective conciliator, responding to state or private complaints to seek out-of-court settlements. The European Court of Human Rights existed to give binding judgments about the legality of state policies under the European Convention on Human Rights. Today, the European Court of Justice (part of the European Union) is empowered to hear human rights cases alongside the European Court of Human Rights (part of the Council of Europe).

All states in the Council of Europe bound themselves to abide by the convention. All governments allowed their citizens to have the right of individual petition to the commission, a body that could then—failing a negotiated agreement—take the petition to the European Court of Human Rights. All states eventually accepted the court's supranational authority. Member states voluntarily complied with its judgments (or at least with parts of judgments) holding state policies illegal. Such was the political consensus in support of human rights within the Council of Europe. This regional international regime for human rights functioned through international agencies made up of uninstructed individuals rather than state officials, although there was also a Committee of Ministers made up of state representatives.

In the mid-1990s, the Council of Europe's members progressively moved toward giving individuals standing to sue in the European Court of Human Rights without having the commission represent them. Thus an individual would have almost the same legal "personality" or status in the court as a state. Persons came to acquire both substantive and procedural rights of note, a distinctive feature, since formerly it was possible to present a case—or have full "personality," in the language of international lawyers—only as a state.

The European system for the international protection of civil and political rights under the European Human Rights Convention generated such a large number of cases that, to streamline procedure, the commission was done away with. Individuals were allowed to proceed directly to a lower chamber of the

TABLE 6.1 UN HUMAN RIGHTS CONVENTIONS

Convention (grouped by subject)	Year Opened for Ratification	Year Entered into Force	Number of Parties
General Human Rights			
International Covenant on Civil and Political Rights	1966	1976	167
Optional Protocol to the International Covenant on Civil and Political Rights (private petition)	1966	1976	114
Second Optional Protocol to the International Covenant on Civil and Political Rights (abolition of death penalty)	1989	1991	75
International Covenant on Economic, Social, and Cultural Rights	1966	1976	160
Racial Discrimination			
International Convention on the Elimination of All Forms of Racial Discrimination	1966	1969	175
International Convention on the Suppression and Punishment of the Crime of Apartheid	1973	1976	108
International Convention Against Apartheid in Sports	1985	1988	60
Rights of Women			
Convention on the Political Rights of Women	1953	1954	122
Convention on the Nationality of Married Women	1957	1958	74
Convention on Consent to Marriage, Minimum Age for Marriage, and Registration of Marriages	1962	1964	55
Convention on the Elimination of All Forms of Discrimination Against Women	1979	1981	187
Optional Protocol to the Convention on the Elimination of All Forms of Discrimination Against Women (communication procedures)	1999	2000	104
Slavery and Related Matters			
Slavery Convention of 1926, as amended in 1953	1953	1955	99
Protocol Amending the 1926 Slavery Convention	1953	1953	61
Supplementary Convention on the Abolition of Slavery, the Slave Trade, and Institutions and Practices Similar to Slavery	1956	1957	123
Convention for the Suppression of the Traffic in Persons and the Exploitation of the Prostitution of Others	1950	1951	82

continues

TABLE 6.1 *(continued)*

Convention (grouped by subject)	Year Opened for Ratification	Year Entered into Force	Number of Parties
Refugees and Stateless Persons			
Convention Relating to the Status of Refugees	1951	1954	145
Protocol Relating to the Status of Refugees (extends time of original convention)	1967	1967	146
Convention Relating to the Status of Stateless Persons	1954	1960	76
Convention on the Reduction of Statelessness	1961	1975	48
Other			
Convention on the Prevention and Punishment of the Crime of Genocide	1948	1951	142
Convention on the International Right of Correction	1952	1962	17
Convention on the Non-Applicability of Statutory Limitations of War Crimes and Crimes Against Humanity	1968	1970	54
Convention Against Torture and Other Cruel, Inhuman, or Degrading Treatment or Punishment	1984	1987	153
Convention on the Rights of the Child	1989	1989	193
Optional Protocol to the Convention on the Rights of the Child (on the Involvement of Children in Armed Conflict)	2000	2002	150
Optional Protocol to the Convention on the Rights of the Child (on the Sale of Children, Child Prostitution, and Child Pornography)	2000	2002	160
Optional Protocol to the Convention Against Torture, and other Cruel, Inhuman or Degrading Treatment or Punishment	2002	2006	73
Optional Protocol to the Convention of Persons with Disabilities	2006	2008	148

European Court of Human Rights for an initial review of the admissibility of their complaint. If the complaint met procedural requirements, the individual could then move on to the substantive phase, basically on an equal footing with state representatives. The European situation shows that supranational, effective protection of human rights is possible in international relations when there is sufficient political will. Unfortunately, the European situation also shows how far the UN system and other regional organizations have to go before they can provide the same sort of human rights protection.

However, as of 2015, this regional human rights system was under stress. Russia and, to a lesser extent, Turkey were increasingly authoritarian and unsympathetic to many of the values of the European Convention on Human Rights. Even the United Kingdom was increasingly critical of regional international organizations that intruded too deeply into traditional British life, with much criticism of the European Union and Council of Europe.

A troubling development for the convergence of human rights norms is the proliferation of regional human rights regimes that are weaker than or inconsistent with UN standards. In the Americas, the human rights architecture is as long-lived as Europe's and has the same constitutive elements: an intergovernmental organization (the Organization of American States); a founding legal framework (the 1948 Declaration on the Rights and Duties of Man and the 1968 Inter-American Convention on Human Rights); an "independent" commission of experts (the Inter-American Commission on Human Rights); and a judicial body (the Inter-American Court on Human Rights). While the commission and court may hear complaints and petitions, they will only do so with the consent of state parties. The United States has not consistently led on human rights in the Americas, and no English-speaking government in the hemisphere has ratified the human rights treaty or accepted the court. The United States has signed but has never ratified the convention, and it has eschewed the jurisdiction of the court. Venezuela renounced the convention in 2012.

Regional organizations such as the League of Arab States, the Organization of Islamic Cooperation (OIC), and the Association of Southeast Asian Nations (ASEAN) have embraced different human rights norms in their respective human rights regimes. [48] The Arab League and OIC articulate different rights for women and hold that Islam is the source of human rights. Some of the punishments contained in sharia law are harsh and incongruent with international human rights law. The Arab Charter on Human Rights equates Zionism with racism and has several anti-Zionist references. The ASEAN regime excludes important civil rights and the commission is an intergovernmental body made up of state representatives, rather than independent experts.

The human rights regime in Africa is loosely organized, complicated by overlapping organizations that reflect the continent's diversity. North Africa and the Middle East states culturally have more in common with the Arab League and the OIC than with states in southern Africa. The African Union (AU) succeeded the Organization of African Unity in 2001 and adopted the latter's human rights framework. This framework includes the African Charter on Human and Peoples' Rights, also known as the Banjul Charter, as well as a commission and later, a court. The African regime is not well developed largely because it is underresourced and has very little state political will supporting it.[49] It is unique in that it contains the collective rights to the self-determination of peoples and the right of peoples to natural resources, but the actualization of those rights has been problematic. Also, when the African Court of Justice and the African Court on Human and Peoples' Rights were merged to streamline human rights protection, AU member states decided to give heads of state immunity from war crimes and crimes against humanity prosecutions.[50] The African Union backed Kenya's leaders in resisting efforts by the International Criminal Court to hold them legally accountable for inciting ethnic violence in relation to electoral campaigns.

INTERNATIONAL HUMANITARIAN LAW (HUMAN RIGHTS DURING WAR)

Technically outside the domain of the UN, treaties on international humanitarian law, often viewed as human rights in armed conflict, are sponsored by the International Committee of the Red Cross and Switzerland, which is the official depository for international humanitarian law (IHL). In this regard, diplomatic events that technically fall outside the UN, especially related to IHL, contributed to further specifying international standards on human rights and humanitarian affairs. IHL sought to protect human dignity in armed conflicts, just as human rights law sought to protect human dignity more generally.

In 1949 the international community of states adopted four conventions for victims of war. Initially drafted by the ICRC in consultation with governments, the Geneva Conventions of August 1949 sought to codify and improve on the humanitarian practices undertaken during World War II. For the first time in history, a treaty was directed to the rights of civilians in international armed conflict and in occupied territory resulting from armed conflict. Each of the four Geneva Conventions of 1949 contained an article (hence Common Article 3) that extended written humanitarian law into internal armed conflict. The ICRC, although technically a private Swiss NGO, was given the right in public international law to see detainees resulting from international armed conflict.[51] And for the first time in history, civilians in occupied territory were recognized as having a right to humanitarian assistance.

This body of humanitarian law—from one point of view the international law for human rights in armed conflict and from another the laws of war—was further developed in 1977 through two protocols (or additional treaties): Protocol I for international armed conflict and Protocol II for internal (or noninternational) armed conflict. Normative standards continued to evolve. For the first time in the history of warfare, Protocol I prohibited the starvation of civilians as a legal means of warfare. Protocol II represented the first separate treaty on victims in internal war. In 2005 Additional Protocol III was added, regulating neutral emblems for aid societies. Among its practical effects was allowing the official Israeli aid society, Magen David Adom (MDA), to be recognized into the International Red Cross and Red Crescent Movement. Before, since MDA used the Red Shield of David as its emblem, it could not be officially recognized by the ICRC or admitted into the Federation of Red Cross and Red Crescent Societies. For many states, what was at issue was indirect recognition of the legitimacy of the state of Israel through accommodation of its official aid society. For that reason, Protocol III was approved not by consensus but by contested vote. The protocol allowed use of a Red Crystal, in addition to the Red Cross and Red Crescent, as approved neutral emblems, to which national emblems could be added. Thus MDA could now use the Red Crystal in international operations devoid of religious or historical significance, along with its red six-sided star within Israeli territory only. Such were the complications when humanitarian considerations collided with state strategic calculation.

Diplomatic activity on setting human rights and humanitarian standards shows that human rights and humanitarianism have been formally accepted as a legitimate part of international relations. Most states do not oppose these normative developments in the abstract—that is, they do not dispute that international law should regulate the rights of persons even when persons are within states in "normal" times. This generalization also pertains to international or internal armed conflict and to public emergency—although some rights protections can be modified in these exceptional situations. All states are now parties to the 1949 Geneva Conventions and Additional Protocols. However, considerable disagreements continue to exist on some definitions and implementations of certain rights and principles. The diplomatic record confirms that while most states no longer view many human rights matters as essentially within their domestic jurisdiction, they are not necessarily happy with all the existing norms, which many deem overly Western. The next chapter details how the United Nations, broadly defined, applies human rights standards in a challenging political environment.

NOTES

1. Michael J. Barnett, *Empire of Humanity: A History of Humanitarianism* (Ithaca, N.Y.: Cornell University Press, 2011). See also Gary J. Bass, *Freedom's Battle: The Origins of Humanitarian Intervention* (New York: Knopf, 2008).

2. Nicholas Kristof and Sheryl WuDunn, *Half the Sky: Turning Oppression into Opportunity for Women Worldwide* (New York: Random House, 2010).

3. Dana Priest and Barton Gellman, "For CIA Suspects Abroad, Brass-Knuckle Treatment," *Washington Post*, December 27, 2002. This article generated virtually no immediate reaction in official Washington. Compare "Is Torture Ever Justified?" *Economist*, January 11–17, 2003. Harvard University law professor Alan Dershowitz defended some use of torture in a debate with Kenneth Roth of Human Rights Watch on NBC's *Today Show*, March 4, 2003.

4. Michael Ignatieff, *The Lesser Evil: Political Ethics in an Age of Terror* (Princeton, N.J.: Princeton University Press, 2005).

5. John Yoo quoted in Scott Shane and Charlie Savage, "Bin Laden Raid Revives Debate on the Value of Torture," *New York Times*, May 3, 2011, and Scott Shane, "The Role of Torture Revisited in bin Laden Narrative," *New York Times*, April 30, 2012.

6. Daniel R. Brunsletter and Arturo Jimenez-Bacardi, "Clashing over Drones: The Legal and Normative Gap Between the United States and the Human Rights Community," *International Journal of Human Rights* 19 (2015): 176–198; Sebastian Wuschka, "The Use of Combat Drones in Current Conflicts—A Legal Issue or a Political Problem," *Goettingen Journal of International Law* 3 (2011): 891–905, and "Self-Defence Targetings of Non-State Actors and Permissibility of U.S. Use of Drones in Pakistan," *Journal of Transnational Law and Policy* 19 (Spring 2010): 237–280.

7. Roger Normand and Sarah Zaidi, *Human Rights at the UN: The Political History of Universal Justice* (Bloomington: Indiana University Press, 2008).

8. Tom J. Farer, "The UN and Human Rights: More Than a Whimper, Less Than a Roar," in *United Nations, Divided World: The UN's Roles in International Relations*, ed. Adam Roberts and Benedict Kingsbury, 2nd ed. (New York: Oxford University Press, 1993), 129.

9. Julie A. Mertus, *The United Nations and Human Rights: A Guide for a New Era*, 2nd ed. (London: Routledge, 2009); Martin J. Rochester, *Between Peril and Promise: The Politics of International Law* (Washington, D.C.: CQ Press, 2006); and Michael Byers, ed., *The Role of Law in International Politics: Essays in International Relations and International Law* (Oxford: Oxford University Press, 2000).

10. Michael G. Schechter, *United Nations Global Conferences* (London: Routledge, 2005), 128–134.

11. Joanne R. Bauer and Daniel A. Bell, eds., *The East Asian Challenge for Human Rights* (Cambridge: Cambridge University Press, 1999).

12. Greg Dinsmore, "Debate: When Less Is Really Less—What's Wrong with Minimalist Approaches to Human Rights," *Journal of Political Philosophy* 15, no. 4 (2007): 473–483.

13. Jack Donnelly, *Universal Human Rights in Theory and Practice*, 2nd ed. (Ithaca, N.Y.: Cornell University Press, 2003), 7–21.

14. Michael Ignatieff, *Human Rights as Politics and Idolatry* (Princeton, N.J.: Princeton University Press, 2001).

15. Stephen James, *Universal Human Rights: Origins and Development* (New York: LFB Scholarly Publishing, 2007); and David P. Forsythe, ed., *Encyclopedia of Human Rights*, 3rd ed. (New York: Oxford University Press, 2009).

16. Bertrand G. Ramcharan, *Contemporary Human Rights Ideas* (London: Routledge, 2008).

17. Micheline R. Ishay, T*he History of Human Rights: From Ancient Times to the Globalization Era* (Berkeley: University of California Press, 2004).

18. John F. Hutchinson, "Rethinking the Origins of the Red Cross," *Bulletin of Historical Medicine* 63 (1989): 557–578, and *Champions of Charity: War and the Rise of the Red Cross* (Boulder, Colo.: Westview, 1996).

19. Jan Herman Burgers, "The Road to San Francisco: The Revival of the Human Rights Idea in the Twentieth Century," *Human Rights Quarterly* 14, no. 2 (1992): 447–478.

20. David P. Forsythe, *The Humanitarians: The International Committee of the Red Cross* (Cambridge: Cambridge University Press, 2005).

21. François Bugnion, Le Comité International de la Croix-Rouge et la protection des victimes de la guerre (Geneva: ICRC, 1994); and Edwin M. Smith, "The Law of War and Humanitarian War: A Turbulent Vista," *Global Governance* 9, no. 1 (2003): 115–134.

22. David P. Forsythe and Barbara Ann J. Rieffer, *The International Committee of the Red Cross: A Neutral Humanitarian Actor*, 2nd ed. (London: Routledge, 2016).

23. Nicholas J. Wheeler, *Saving Strangers: Humanitarian Intervention in International Society* (Oxford: Oxford University Press, 2000).

24. Gary J. Bass, *Freedom's Battle: The Origins of Humanitarian Intervention* (New York: Knopf, 2008).

25. Paul Gordon Lauren, *Power and Prejudice: The Politics and Diplomacy of Racial Discrimination* (Boulder, Colo.: Westview, 1988), 76–101; Burgers, "Road to San Francisco," 449.

26. Ernst Haas, *Human Rights and International Action* (Stanford, Calif.: Stanford University Press, 1970); Hector G. Bartolomei de la Cruz et al., *The International Labor*

Organization: The International Standards System and Basic Human Rights (Boulder, Colo.: Westview, 1996); Steve Hughes, *The International Labour Organization* (London: Routledge, 2009).

27. Farer, "UN and Human Rights," 97.

28. Jack Donnelly, "International Human Rights: A Regime Analysis," *International Organization* 40, no. 3 (1985): 599–642.

29. Timothy Snyder, *Bloodlands: Europe Between Stalin and Hitler* (New York: Basic Books, 2010).

30. See Burgers, "Road to San Francisco." Compare Samuel Moyn, *The Last Utopia: Human Rights in History* (Cambridge, Mass.: Harvard University Press, 2012).

31. Cathal J. Nolan, *Principled Diplomacy: Security and Rights in U.S. Foreign Policy* (Westport, Conn.: Greenwood, 1993), 181–202.

32. Burgers, "Road to San Francisco," 475.

33. David P. Forsythe, "Human Rights and Peace," in *Encyclopedia of Human Rights*, 3rd. ed. (New York: Oxford University Press, 2009), 187–196.

34. Nolan, *Principled Diplomacy.*

35. Daniel C. Thomas, *The Helsinki Effect: International Norms, Human Rights, and the Demise of Communism* (Princeton, N.J.: Princeton University Press, 2001); and William Korey, *The Promises We Keep: Human Rights, the Helsinki Process, and American Foreign Policy* (New York: St. Martin's Press, 1993).

36. Robert W. Tucker and David C. Hendrickson, *The Imperial Temptation: The New World Order and America's Purpose* (New York: Council on Foreign Relations Press, 1992), 86.

37. Bruce Russett, "Politics and Alternative Security: Toward a More Democratic, Therefore More Peaceful, World," in *Alternative Security: Living Without Nuclear Deterrence*, ed. Burns Weston (Boulder, Colo.: Westview, 1990), 107–136.

38. Samuel P. Huntington, *The Third Wave: Democratization in the Late Twentieth Century* (Norman: University of Oklahoma Press, 1991).

39. Bruce M. Russett and John R. Oneal, *Triangulating Peace: Democracy, Interdependence, and International Organizations* (New York: W. W. Norton, 2001).

40. David P. Forsythe, "Democracy, War, and Covert Action," *Journal of Peace Research* 29, no. 4 (1992): 385–396.

41. David N. Gibbs, *The Political Economy of Third World Intervention: Mines, Money, and U.S. Policy in the Congo Crisis* (Chicago: University of Chicago Press, 1991).

42. David P. Forsythe, *Human Rights and Peace: International and National Dimensions* (Lincoln: University of Nebraska Press, 1993).

43. Steven C. Poe and C. Neal Tate, "Repression of Human Rights to Personal Integrity in the 1980s: A Global Analysis," *American Political Science Review* 88, no. 4 (1994): 853–872.

44. Johannes Morsink, *The Universal Declaration of Human Rights: Origins, Drafting and Intent* (Philadelphia: University of Pennsylvania Press, 1999); and Mary Ann Glendon, *A World Made New: Eleanor Roosevelt and the Universal Declaration of Human Rights* (New York: Random House, 2001).

45. William F. Felice, *The Global New Deal: Economic and Social Human Rights in World Politics* (Lanham, Md.: Rowman & Littlefield, 2003); and A. Belden Fields, *Rethinking Human Rights for the New Millennium* (New York: Palgrave, 2003).

46. UNDP, *Human Development Report 2000* (New York: Oxford University Press, 2000).

47. John F. Murphy, *The United States and the Rule of Law in International Affairs* (Cambridge: Cambridge University Press, 2004).

48. Human Rights Watch, "Civil Society Denounces Adoption of Flawed ASEAN Human Rights Declaration," accessed October 1, 2014, http://www.hrw.org/news/2012/11/19/civil-society-denounces-adoption-flawed-asean-human-rights-declaration.

49. Philip Alston and Ryan Goodman, *International Human Rights. The Successor to International Human Rights in Context: Law, Politics and Morals* (Oxford, Oxford University Press: 2013), 1025.

50. Mike Pflantz, "African Union Leaders Give Themselves Immunity from War Crimes Prosecution," *Telegraph*, July 2, 2014, accessed September 13, 2014, http://www.telegraph.co.uk/news/worldnews/africaandindianocean/10940047/African-leaders-vote-to-give-themselves-immunity-from-war-crimes-prosecutions.

51. The ICRC and the government of Switzerland signed a headquarters agreement protecting its premises and personnel from review or intrusion by Swiss authorities, as if the ICRC were an intergovernmental organization. The ICRC seems neither fully public nor fully private, legally speaking; rather it is sui generis (or in a category by itself). See Forsythe, *The Humanitarians*.

CHAPTER 7

Applying Human Rights Standards: The Roles of the First and Second UN

THE APPLICATION OF INTERNATIONAL human rights and humanitarian norms varies according to the part of the UN system we are talking about. At the first UN, through their governmental authorities, states make the key decisions. Almost always, state policy on human rights and humanitarian affairs is filtered through the prism of national interest. States rarely criticize or condemn their friends and allies publicly. They rarely pursue decisive policies to protect the rights of foreigners especially if costly in terms of blood and treasure. States almost always consider to some extent their "sovereignty costs"—namely, the extent to which international human rights and humanitarian norms constrain national independence and tradition. At the first UN, concerns about human rights and humanitarian affairs are thus almost always politicized in the sense of being affected by concerns about national self-interest (subjectively defined, of course). For example, in 2015 Russia vetoed a Security Council resolution calling attention to the massacre of Bosnian Muslim men and boys at Srebrenica in 1995 by its ally Serbia; the United States repeatedly has vetoed various council resolutions critical of the treatment of Palestinians by Israel, which has a special relationship to many Americans; China often has vetoed Security Council resolutions pertaining to its neighbor North Korea, as Beijing fears a mass migration from instability there; and in the Human Rights Council in 2015 the United States did not support an effort to investigate alleged Saudi war crimes in the fighting in Yemen because that might prove embarrassing to one of its main allies in the Middle East. Such developments provoked the French human rights activist Bernard Kouchner, founder of Doctors Without Borders (Médecins sans Frontières) and former foreign minister of France, to lament that even democratic states, such as France, could not formulate a consistent human rights policy because of the requirement to defend national interests.[1]

In contrast, a variety of UN organs, offices, and agencies try to see that states apply the norms of internationally recognized human rights and humanitarian affairs as intended—that is, with a view to the advancement of human dignity.[2] The overall UN processes of helping to apply international human rights standards are exceedingly broad and complex. The structure of the main organizational components underpinning that process is illustrated in Figure 7.1.

This chapter's focus is on the activities and operations of the first UN of member states and the second UN of international secretariats on behalf of human rights and humanitarianism. As will be further explored in the next chapter, the third UN is also deeply engaged in trying to improve human rights and humanitarian endeavors both at the level of policy and behavior. For the time being, readers should keep in mind that such nongovernmental organizations (NGOs) as Amnesty International and Human Rights Watch feed information to UN monitoring mechanisms that supervise human rights treaties. NGOs such as Save the Children and Oxfam work side by side in the field with UN agencies to implement rights to adequate nutrition and health. The officially private International Red Cross and Red Crescent Movement (ICRC) coordinates with various UN organs and agencies regarding humanitarian law and the codified humanitarian protection and assistance that is supposed to occur in armed conflict. For example, in 2015 the UN secretary-general and the ICRC's president issued a joint statement urging all fighting parties to pay more attention to human rights and humanitarian law applicable in armed conflicts and to better protect those fleeing such conflicts.

HUMAN RIGHTS AND THE FIRST UN

The Security Council

The Security Council has the authority to declare a situation a threat to or a breach of the peace, which enables it to play an important role in promoting and protecting human rights and humanitarian law. It can invoke Chapter VII of the Charter and reach a decision binding on all states. On several occasions the Security Council has linked human rights violations to a threat to or breach of the peace, or it has otherwise reached a legally binding decision declaring that member states must adopt various necessary steps to correct a human rights problem. In 1992 a Security Council presidential statement, reflecting agreement of the states in that body, indicated that threats to international peace and security could have many sources, including human rights violations and humanitarian crises.

Space does not permit a case-by-case examination of how the UN Security Council has linked security concerns to human rights and humanitarian disasters. Suffice it to say that positive developments generally have been accompanied by defects and disappointments. On the one hand, we can note that most modern

FIGURE 7.1 UN HUMAN RIGHTS ORGANIZATIONAL STRUCTURE

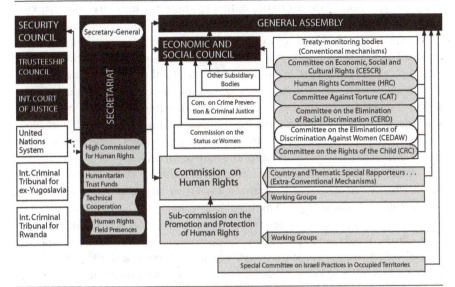

UN Human Rights Organizational Structure. Source: United Nations High Commissioner for Human Rights. (The Human Rights Council now replaces the Commission on Human Rights.)

forms of UN field operations now contain a human rights or humanitarian dimension. Indeed, one of the main purposes of deployment of some UN military forces is precisely to protect civilians from being targeted or persecuted by combatants. On the other hand, a blizzard of ambitious resolutions by the council in New York has not always been matched by vigorous action in the midst of violent conflict. For example, the Security Council declared certain safe areas in the Balkan Wars of the early 1990s so as to safeguard civilians but then did not follow through to authorize and deploy adequate military force to defend them.

Given that the concept of "humanitarian intervention" remains controversial, with weaker states fearing its misuse by stronger states, the Security Council has tended to rely rather on the concept of threat to or breach of the peace. This has sometimes led to legal gymnastics. The deployment of military forces to Somalia in the early 1990s was said to be necessary for international peace and security, but this was surely a strained interpretation. The main problems were internal starvation and stealing from relief efforts. In Iraq (also in the early 1990s), the council took action on the basis of refugee flight from horrific human rights violations by the Saddam Hussein regime but was reluctant to address the original violations per se as compared to the international subject of flight to neighboring Turkey. The specifics of resolutions linking security to human rights reflect political calculations about what wording will pass in that chamber. Thus, council resolutions about Rhodesia back in the 1970s, before it became Zimbabwe, were vague about the exact reason for invoking Chapter VII and imposing mandatory economic sanctions. Was it discrimination by the white minority? Internal violence? Transborder flight?

The end of the Cold War led to a renaissance in international criminal justice, and the UN Security Council was at its origins. In 1993 and 1994 the council used its Chapter VII authority to create two ad hoc criminal courts to try natural persons charged with war crimes, crimes against humanity, and/or genocide in the former Yugoslavia after 1991 and in Rwanda during 1994. This set in motion developments leading to a permanent International Criminal Court (ICC) in 2000. Hence, there was a renewed effort to hold persons, not states, legally accountable for certain violations of human rights and humanitarian law.

Council efforts to use judicial enforcement of rights on a case-by-case basis led to the effort to create a standing criminal court. A large diplomatic conference during 1998 in Rome succeeded in this objective, but at the cost of defection from the project by a number of states, including three of its five permanent members (P5): China, Russia, and the United States. Washington wanted the council to control which cases reached the court, which of course would allow the United States and its allies to escape judicial action. When this proved unacceptable to the majority of states, the United States and others refused to ratify the Rome statute creating the ICC.

For a time, the U.S. opposition to the ICC was clear; however, from 2005 on this opposition has not meant that Washington would stand in the way of using the ICC to pressure those seen as responsible for atrocities. The Security Council has referred the situations in Sudan and Libya to the ICC as well, which has in turn issued important arrest warrants for certain top officials. The Security Council, with significant U.S. political and financial assistance, has also enabled the hybrid courts associated with Sierra Leone, Cambodia, East Timor, and Lebanon. Whether this proliferation of international courts, cases, and prosecutions is the result of states "learning" about the utility of international criminal law, in which individuals are said to be responsible for atrocities, is debatable. Sometimes the recourse to criminal law through the United Nations occurs because member states do not want to engage in more costly—if potentially decisive—actions.

The International Tribunal for the former Yugoslavia (ICTY) and International Tribunal for Rwanda (ICTR) have prosecuted a number of high-level political and military officials. And in a narrow sense these two ad hoc UN courts have been successful not only in convicting and incarcerating a number of criminal defendants but also in engaging in a major rewriting of modern international criminal law.[3] Whether these courts have had a broader ameliorative impact on national and regional politics is still uncertain. The Special Court for Sierra Leone convicted Charles Taylor, the former president of Liberia, and sentenced him to fifty years in prison for his role in supporting rebel atrocities. In the same year the ICC saw its first conviction and sentencing of Thomas Lubanga, for his recruitment of child soldiers in the Democratic Republic of the Congo. Because of these and other cases, various dictators and warlords—at least those in small and weak states—cannot be assured that their evil deeds will go unpunished.

But in some circles of opinion, dissatisfaction is evident with the selective application of the law.[4] The criminal courts established thus far have dealt almost always with situations in powerless countries. Take, for example, an ICC process in Kenya, involving important public figures including the sitting president Uruhu Kenyatta. The ICC managed to issue indictments related to the aftermath of violence following the disputed 2007 presidential elections; however, the prosecutor was forced to adjourn the case against Kenyatta in 2014, citing a lack of cooperation by the government and the unwillingness of key witnesses to testify. Moreover, most international trials have been exceedingly slow and costly, leading to complaints about expenses and the coddling of heinous defendants, despite the complexity of the cases.[5] There are also complaints about the way certain ICC prosecutions have been managed. Still further, there is the central question of whether pursuit of criminal justice at least sometimes impedes a diplomatic solution to a problem. After all, if one wants al-Assad to step down in Syria, would threat of prosecution not be an impediment to that objective?[6]

The Security Council has a long way to go to achieve a balanced and systematic record concerning the protection of human rights, especially under Chapter VII. Many more persons died in Rwanda during 1994 or in Syria in 2012 than died in Kosovo in 1999. Yet the council, pushed by Western states, showed far more interest in the human rights violations in the western Balkans than in Africa or the Middle East, even if it failed formally to approve a decision in the Kosovo case. Double standards stemmed partly from the media coverage of Western-based reporting, partly from the interests of Western governments. Racism may also have been involved. China and Russia, which have less than stellar human rights records themselves, have sometimes protected notorious violators of human rights from Security Council scrutiny. In January 2007, a council resolution sponsored by the United States and the United Kingdom, condemning human rights violations by Myanmar (formerly Burma) and declaring the situation a threat to international peace and security, was blocked by China and Russia, which admitted that human rights violations existed but asserted there was no threat to international peace and security. After Myanmar's bloody crackdown on demonstrators in September 2007, China blocked a council resolution calling for sanctions.[7] The same two countries similarly have exercised double vetoes on three occasions to block council attempts to apply pressure on Syria, despite clear atrocities by forces loyal to the government (see next section). These countries did not block council resolutions referring the Sudanese and Libyan situations to the ICC; however, they did veto a resolution to refer the Syrian conflict to the ICC.[8] In an issue far closer to Moscow, in mid-2015 the Russians vetoed a council resolution designed to create an international tribunal to prosecute and punish those responsible for shooting down a Malaysian civilian airliner over eastern Ukraine in July 2014, killing almost three hundred people on board. This veto was not surprising, given the widespread belief that either Russian military personnel or Russian-supported rebels operating in the area had been responsible for the action, a judgment later substantiated by a Dutch-inspired international panel.

The General Assembly

Beyond setting standards, the General Assembly indirectly protects human rights in two ways. It passes resolutions to condemn or otherwise draw attention to violations of human rights. In 2012, after China and Russia double vetoed a Security Council Chapter VII resolution on the violence in Syria, the General Assembly passed a resolution strongly condemning widespread and systematic human rights violations by Syrian authorities. The vote (with only 12 of 193 countries voting against) was a remarkably clear rebuke of Syrian intransigence as supported by Russia, China, Iran, and a few others. More generally, about one third of the General Assembly's resolutions each year deal with human rights, which keeps one of its main standing committees—the Third Committee—quite busy dealing with social, humanitarian, and cultural affairs. Many of these resolutions are adopted by consensus and constitute a rough barometer of which rights policies are judged most acceptable or egregious. When a resolution targets a specific country or violation, evaluating the resolution's effect over time is difficult. The assembly's repeated condemnations of apartheid in South Africa may have had some impact on changing attitudes among South Africans. At the same time, words divorced from coercive power cannot have much effect in the short term. In trying to account for change in South Africa, violence against apartheid, formal economic sanctions, and the shrinking of investments by the international business community all played a role.

A General Assembly resolution on human rights can also backfire and work against the protection of those rights. General Augusto Pinochet in Chile used critical assembly resolutions to rally nationalistic support for his rule despite the gross violations of basic rights that he was overseeing.[9] The assembly's 1975 declaration that Zionism was a form of racism not only antagonized Israel but also alienated some of Israel's supporters. The resolution did nothing for the practice of rights in either Israel proper or the occupied territories that Israel controlled militarily, and the resolution was repealed in 1991.

The General Assembly has created a segment of the UN Secretariat to deal with Palestinian rights and a committee to oversee Israeli practices pertaining to human rights in the territories militarily occupied since 1967. The assembly also voted to hold the World Conference on Human Rights during June 1993 in Vienna—a follow-up from the one twenty-five years earlier in Tehran. Sometimes the assembly takes a half step to help with rights. It created the Fund for Victims of Torture, but it refused to make the fund part of the regular UN budget. The fund relies on voluntary donations. This and other compensatory funds for the victims of human rights violations have usually been poorly supported.

When decisions are not made by consensus, human rights policies reflect the majority controlling the General Assembly. From 1945 until about 1955, the

Western majority was not very sensitive to issues of racial discrimination and tended to focus instead on such issues as forced labor under communism. In the period that followed, the assembly tended to emphasize issues of national self-determination and an end to racial discrimination, reflecting the desires of the developing countries, which had become a different "automatic majority" with decolonization. After the end of the Cold War, an intensified North-South conflict dominated human rights proceedings in the assembly. In the late 1980s and 1990s, developing countries successfully reaffirmed the principle of state sovereignty in the face of the industrialized countries' expressed desire to emphasize a right of humanitarian assistance that would supersede state sovereignty. Now, in the second decade of the twenty-first century, little has changed.

While the members of the International Commission on Intervention and State Sovereignty (ICISS) could assert "no more Rwandas," many states from the Global South stressed the primacy of state sovereignty. While more stable states from the North, such as Sweden, emphasize international obligations to interfere to protect the interests of the victims of violence or deprivation, many developing countries still see the discourse of human rights as menacing. For some of them, for instance, responsibility to protect (R2P) may be seen as a Trojan horse for Western imperialism.[10] In short, no consensus in the assembly exists as to the proper limits of state sovereignty or when the UN is justified in approving action without state consent in the name of human rights.

In other manifestations, the General Assembly is also characterized by fragmented views that shift from issue to issue. On the question of human rights in Iraq during the 1990s, for example, a number of Islamic states thought that the Security Council had gone too far in restricting Iraqi sovereignty. Yet on the question of human rights for Muslims in Bosnia, many Islamic states in the assembly wanted the Security Council to go further in challenging the policies of an orthodox Serbia toward Bosnia. Thus, Western states do not have a monopoly on double standards for human rights.

Although developing countries control the majority of votes in the General Assembly and despite the rise of the likes of India, China, and Brazil, the West has predominant economic and military power. This situation provides the recipe for some accommodation between the North and Global South, especially since the number of developing countries with more democratic governments prone to compromise rather than to confrontation has grown substantially. Still, developing states are much more likely to seek to advance human rights through dialogue and standard setting rather than through public criticism or punitive sanctions.[11]

Commission on Human Rights (1946–2006)

If, when dealing with human rights, the broad and complex UN system is thought of as a wheel, the Commission on Human Rights (CHR) was the hub from its establishment in 1946 until its abolition in 2006.[12] This commission was eventually made up of fifty-three states elected by the Economic and Social Council

(ECOSOC), and its history reflects in microcosm the legal and diplomatic revolution on human rights. Despite Western domination of the UN during its early years, the commission was content to promote rights by setting standards rather than by trying to protect them, even indirectly, through various forms of diplomatic pressure. When private complaints about rights violations came to the UN, the CHR buried them in an elaborate process leading nowhere, one of the most complicated trash baskets ever devised. The early commission, in the words of one careful observer, displayed a "fierce commitment to inoffensiveness."[13]

A North-South compromise, however, opened up new possibilities between 1967 and 1970. The commission began to deal with specific states and began to examine private complaints more seriously. Developing states wanted to focus on Israel and South Africa, but developed states broadened the commission's mandate so that such states as Greece under military rule (1967–1974) and Haiti under the Duvalier dynasty (1957–1986) also became targets of scrutiny. Member states of the commission agreed that private petitions could lead, after screening, to quiet diplomacy and even the publication of a "blacklist" of states with a pattern of gross violations of human rights. These private petitions, however, were treated in a confidential process that minimized the negative publicity that could be directed at an offending government. Ironically, a state could minimize public scrutiny of its rights record by responding somewhat to private petitions in the confidential process.[14]

The Commission on Human Rights struggled to find ways of working meaningfully. It created "thematic procedures" to deal with certain violations. That is, it created either working groups of states or independent experts, called rapporteurs, to examine such issues as forced disappearances, arbitrary detention, summary execution, torture, religious discrimination, mercenaries, and deprived or suffering children.[15] The subject of human rights affects crucial questions of governmental power, and thus this intergovernmental commission was highly politicized. Various double standards and inconsistencies are well documented. The United States at times focused on rights violations in Cuba out of proportion to events there, especially compared to more serious rights violations in such U.S. allies as Guatemala and El Salvador.[16] During the Cold War, the Soviet Union was openly opportunistic in the commission, using human rights as a weapon against U.S. allies, such as Augusto Pinochet's Chile, but remained silent about major violations of human rights in communist states. Again, human rights language was put at the service of ideological and strategic calculations.

In 2002 Libya was nominated by the African caucus for president of the commission. Given Libya's poor record on many civil and political rights, the African caucus obviously placed more emphasis on equitable geographical representation and friendly relations than on performance in these human rights matters. Since, according to UN tradition, it was "Africa's turn" to hold the presidency of the commission, Libya was duly elected over the protests of the United States and other Western governments—although in a precedent, in 2011 it was thrown off the Human Rights Council, the successor to the Commission on Human Rights.

Adding fuel to the fire, other prominently repressive governments, such as Cuba and Saudi Arabia, were also elected to the commission by their regional caucuses. The commission was never made up of "a club of the clean" who acted consistently on principle and without regard to strategic calculation, but it had often become a mechanism to protect abusers and to promote sovereignty rather than human rights. These developments gave the UN a bad name in the field of human rights.

The double standards by states operated side by side with the more consistently principled work of human rights NGOs that participated in commission proceedings. NGOs played a more significant role in Geneva in the CHR than they played on other issues or in UN institutions elsewhere. NGOs focused on the commission and increased their numbers and influence.[17] By the 1990s large numbers of NGOs were active in all phases of the commission's proceedings.[18] The reports from these groups at least brought some diplomatic pressure to bear on the problems addressed, although decisive and short-term improvement in the practice of rights was rare to nonexistent.

The obvious shortcomings of the Commission on Human Rights figured prominently in the 2004 report from the High-level Panel on Threats, Challenges and Change (HLP). Viewed from Washington as well as many other capitals, the performance of the UN's human rights machinery was scandalous. The primary evidence for the travesty was the commission's fifty-three elected members, who in 2005 included Sudan while it was pursuing genocide in Darfur, and Zimbabwe while it was bulldozing the houses of seven hundred thousand opposition supporters and rounding up journalists and other critics. That China and Cuba played prominent roles and that Libya was a former chair of the commission added to the litany of embarrassments. The HLP recognized the "eroding credibility and professionalism" and that "states have sought membership of the Commission not to strengthen human rights but to protect themselves against criticism or to criticize others."[19]

However, the HLP's proposed solution was counterintuitive: universal membership instead of "only" one quarter of the members. Advancing serious attention to human rights is not served by having matters discussed by a committee of the whole, at that time 192 state delegations. This idea deservedly found its way to the trash heap of diplomatic history. The secretary-general, in his only serious dissent from the HLP's recommendations, went out on a limb and proposed that member states "replace the Commission on Human Rights with a smaller standing Human Rights Council."[20] By the 2005 World Summit, the word *discredited* was used to describe the CHR, and member states agreed to replace it.

Any obituary should also include the CHR's accomplishments. Although it was politicized and prone to double standards and hypocrisy, the commission did target states that were egregious violators of human rights.[21] Commission activities may have had only a limited role in improving human rights conditions in target countries, but they served to socialize and educate all states on the importance of human rights over time. The commission also amassed an impressive record of originating and developing human rights instruments.[22] The CHR held its final session in Geneva in March 2006 and was abolished in June 2006. At that session, then high commissioner of human rights Louise Arbour noted, "It would, however, be a distortion of fact, and a gross disservice to this institution, if we failed on this occasion to celebrate the achievements of the Commission even as we, in full knowledge of its flaws, welcome the arrival of its successor." She listed those accomplishments as setting standards, establishing the system of special procedures, considering the situations in specific countries, creating global forums, and nurturing a unique relationship with civil society.[23]

Human Rights Council (2006–Present)

At the 2005 World Summit, the assembled heads of state and government resolved to create a Human Rights Council (HRC) as a subsidiary of the General Assembly.[24] The General Assembly was assigned the responsibility for creating it (as Charter Article 22 so provides) and deciding its "mandate, modalities, functions, size, composition, membership, working methods, and procedures."[25] Bitter disputes quickly emerged over the shape of the new council, but the General Assembly reached an agreement. Jan Eliasson, the assembly's president and later the UN deputy secretary-general, managed to push for a vote on the HRC with three-year terms with the assent of a simple majority of the General Assembly. Some were disgruntled because the numbers in the new council had decreased only to forty-seven—hardly a big decrease from fifty-three and perhaps still too large to be businesslike.

Membership is subject only to a simple majority vote instead of the more stringent two-thirds requirement that the secretary-general had proposed and the United States desired. However, membership in the council entails special scrutiny designed to discourage the candidacy of the worst human rights offenders. As part of the overall reform effort, all member states undergo a staggered peer review process called the Universal Periodic Review (UPR) conducted by the HRC to assess how states are meeting their obligations under international human rights law. States sitting on the council are subject to the UPR during their first term, forcing such abusers as Libya and Zimbabwe to think twice about running for the HRC. The council also would meet for ten weeks at least three times a year, which was a step in the right direction; in fact, the HRC has been in almost continual session since 2006. Still, the United States voted against the creation of the HRC and decided at first not to stand for election. Instead, it opted for permanent observer status.

Unfortunately, the first election to the HRC yielded such human rights "stalwarts" as Algeria, China, Pakistan, Saudi Arabia, and Cuba, confirming U.S. fears that the council was more like "a caterpillar with lipstick on" than a "butterfly."[26] John Bolton's picturesque imagery ignored the fact that UN larvae require nourishment by important states to grow. Many viewed the U.S. choice not to stand for election not as a protest but a tactic to avoid embarrassment because it might not have had enough votes to be elected. After all, the Bush administration was flagrantly violating international human rights with regard to detainees in its war on terrorism.

A general view of participants during the thirtieth regular session of the Human Rights Council in Geneva, Switzerland. October 1, 2015. (UN PHOTO 647275/JEAN-MARC FERRÉ)

The Human Rights Council's record is, as expected, mixed.[27] In terms of promoting and protecting human rights in specific states, the council spent its first year investigating Israel, which was the only state drawing a critical council resolution. Meanwhile, Sudan, China, Myanmar, and Zimbabwe were not criticized. By the council's second year, Israel had been criticized fifteen times and Myanmar only once (after its junta's bloody crackdown on monks and demonstrators). The HRC's biased and unbalanced focus on Israel drew a rare rebuke from Secretary-General Ban Ki-moon, who stated that he was "worried by its disproportionate focus on violations by Israel." The council, he said, "has clearly not justified all the hopes that so many of us placed on it."[28]

After the election of Barack Obama, the United States ran for the HRC and was elected in 2009. The U.S. approach has been to attempt to reform the HRC from within. This participation was generally positive until Washington distanced itself from the council-sponsored Goldstone Report, which accused Israel and Palestinian authorities of war crimes in Gaza and called for the perpetrators to be brought to justice.[29] Moreover, the United States underwent the UPR in 2010, when its domestic and international human rights record was explored. The U.S. death penalty and its voter identification laws were called into question, and Washington still has not ratified the UN Convention on the Elimination of All Forms of Discrimination against Women (CEDAW), the UN Convention on the Rights of the Child, and the Covenant on Economic, Social, and Cultural Rights. U.S. domestic politics and decisions not to adhere to important human rights treaties are not popular in Geneva, the HRC's home. The United States also rejects the authority of the HRC and its special rapporteur on extrajudicial, summary, and arbitrary executions, who has concerns about Washington's war on terror and its use of drones to target terror suspects.[30]

In a number of ways the Human Rights Council has evolved to be more equitable than many expected, given that its membership is still made up of states and is not that dissimilar from its predecessor commission.[31] A promising development is the use of fact-finding commissions and independent commissions of inquiry made up of independent experts rather than state representatives, and the continued use of special rapporteurs and working groups. Discussed in more detail in the next chapter, these commissions, individuals, and groups provide the nexus between the second and third UN. While not technically employees of the UN, these civil society actors bring objective, expert knowledge to bear on complex situations, helping states and UN officials promote and protect human rights. In many respects, the HRC resembles its predecessor: sometimes politicized and almost always ineffective in the short term at tangibly improving human rights conditions in some of the worst-offending states. But the glass is perhaps half full when considering the council's standard-setting activities, which can help educate and socialize states over the long term. And it has certainly been dynamic in shining the diplomatic spotlight on problem areas in several states, even if specific advances in protection of rights still prove elusive.

HUMAN RIGHTS AND THE SECOND UN

The various moving parts of the second UN encourage, prod, push, and sometimes embarrass states to take active steps to protect and promote rights as properly understood. Fundamentally, most UN diplomacy for human rights involves informal education or socialization in that the second UN seeks to "teach" new attitudes that advance human dignity. Changing attitudes may take quite some time, as with slavery and decolonization.[32] As part of this long-term socialization process, the second UN is extensively engaged in promoting human rights and encouraging states to adopt international human rights standards.

The Office of the Secretary-General

Before Kofi Annan took office in 1997, UN secretaries-general did not publicly display a major commitment to human rights.[33] Perhaps they had seen their primary role as producing progress on peace and security. This emphasis was understood to mean that they could not speak out on specific human rights violations. Had Javier Pérez de Cuéllar, for example, made protection of individual human rights his primary concern, his office probably would have been unacceptable as mediator between Iran and Iraq, or between the Salvadoran armed forces and the Farabundo Marti National Liberation Front (FMLN), or in the Afghan situation after the Soviet invasion.

Virtually all secretaries-general have engaged in good offices or quiet mediation for the advancement of human rights.[34] But only Annan systematically, though cautiously, threw the full weight of his office behind human rights protection. Secretary-General Ban Ki-moon spoke out on Darfur, Côte d'Ivoire, Libya, and Syria; however, his nonconfrontational personality and style meant that he used the UN's bully pulpit to a far lesser degree than his immediate predecessor.

Whether one speaks of Dag Hammarskjöld or Kurt Waldheim, however, the point on human rights remains the same. Hammarskjöld was personally not much interested in human rights at the United Nations, and Waldheim was even less dynamic. Much the same could be said for U Thant, who was not as personally committed to individual rights as he was to the collective right of peoples to self-determination. As human rights became more institutionalized in UN proceedings, however, secretaries-general took a higher profile on rights. Pérez de Cuéllar is instructive in this regard. A cautious Peruvian diplomat, he entered office showing great deference to states, especially Latin ones. One of his first acts was to not renew the contract of his most senior human rights official, Theo van Boven, who had irritated the Argentine junta, then in the process of murdering at least nine thousand Argentines. By the end of his term, Pérez de Cuéllar had projected the UN, by his own authority, into the affairs of both El Salvador and Nicaragua, including deep involvement on human rights. In Nicaragua during his tenure, the UN came to oversee a regional peace accord, to supervise national elections for the first time in a sovereign state, and to collect weapons from a disbanding rebel force. He also oversaw human rights observers in Haiti in 1991, the first time UN election verification had taken place in a country not wracked at the time by civil war.

When human rights were linked to peace, Pérez de Cuéllar and his office came to be bold and innovative. And the two issues were indeed inseparable in such places as El Salvador, Nicaragua, Namibia, Angola, Cambodia, Bosnia, East Timor, and Kosovo. The Office of the Secretary-General took initiatives and then obtained the backing of both the General Assembly and the Security Council. Increasingly, the secretary-general was drawn into rights questions that had previously been considered the domestic affairs of states or seen as in opposition to U.S. desires.

Boutros Boutros-Ghali followed in his predecessors' footsteps. Upon becoming secretary-general in 1992, he seemed uninterested in human rights, even appointing an old friend without a human rights record as head of the UN Centre for Human Rights in Geneva. But within the year, Boutros-Ghali was as deeply involved in human rights issues as Pérez de Cuéllar had been. In El Salvador, for example, Boutros-Ghali was active in supporting President Alfredo Cristiani as he tried to purge the army of most of those who had committed gross violations of internationally recognized human rights. Boutros-Ghali was outspoken in promoting democratic or participatory values as part of the quest for economic development. This stand may not have been completely desired by some developing countries, but his speeches and reports in support of democratic development were backed by many donor countries. In the early 1990s the major donor countries pushed for more grassroots participation in the search for sustainable development, whether through bilateral programs, the World Bank, or agencies of the UN. The secretary-general's position fit nicely within this paradigm shift in favor of the human right to participation in public affairs.

Moreover, Boutros-Ghali appointed the Swedish diplomat who had mediated the Iran-Iraq War, Jan Eliasson, to a new position as emergency relief coordinator (ERC) responsible for pulling together the various parts of the UN system to provide humanitarian assistance. This post evolved toward being a type of general troubleshooter for humanitarian affairs, which were difficult to insulate from wider human rights issues.

Below the highest levels of the Office of the Secretary-General, from the earliest days parts of the secretariat have often actively tried to improve behavior under human rights norms.[35] Van Boven, who had annoyed the Argentine junta before his "nonrenewal" by Pérez de Cuéllar, was the clearest example, but other UN officials also were active, frequently behind the scenes. Nevertheless, the secretary-general sets the tone on human rights for the entire secretariat, and van Boven's fate showed that these officials could do only so much without the support of the secretary-general.[36]

The UN's seventh secretary-general, Kofi Annan was a more activist leader, including in his priority concerns the encouragement and advocacy of human rights, the rule of law, and the universal values of equality, tolerance, and human dignity as articulated in the UN Charter. One of his most eloquent statements in this regard was the 1998 address to the United Nations Educational, Scientific and Cultural Organization (UNESCO) ceremony marking the fiftieth anniversary of the Universal Declaration of Human Rights. In part he said:

> Our belief in the centrality of human rights to the work and life of the United Nations stems from a simple proposition: that States which respect human rights respect the rules of international society. States which respect human rights are more likely to seek cooperation and not confrontation, tolerance and not violence, moderation and not might, peace and not war. States which treat their own people with fundamental respect are more likely to treat their neighbors with the same respect. From this proposition, it is clear that human rights—in practice, as in principle—can have no walls and no boundaries.[37]

One of Annan's pet projects was to try to galvanize the for-profit sector into a greater interest in human rights, in partnership with the UN. Recognizing the economic power of transnational corporations (TNCs), he tried to get them to take a broad approach to their role in the world, one that reflected more social responsibility. In 1999 he launched the idea of a Global Compact at the World Economic Forum in Davos, Switzerland, which projected certain universal principles relevant to business practices in the areas of human rights and the environment. The four main UN agencies that participated in this venture were the Office of the High Commissioner for Human Rights (OHCHR), the International

Labour Organization (ILO), the UN Development Programme (UNDP), and the UN Environment Programme (UNEP). Hoping to reduce especially what some called economic exploitation of labor (and damage to the environment), Annan worked hard to create this partnership, which had great implications for many human rights, even if much of the discourse was about social responsibility. The secretary-general's efforts reflect the growing realization that states are not the only entities that can have an impact on human rights and dignity.

Human rights are on the agenda of the eighth secretary-general, Ban Ki-moon, but appear to rank below other less controversial priorities, such as global climate change. He got off to a rough start when he declined to oppose or criticize the execution of Saddam Hussein in 2006 despite the UN's long-standing condemnation of the death penalty as a violation of human rights. Moreover, he stated that "the issue of capital punishment is for each and every member state to decide."[38] He later clarified his remarks by acknowledging the growing trend among states to abolish the death penalty; however, he is not as powerful a voice for human rights as Annan. In spite of his low-key, nonconfrontational approach, Ban has publicly denounced human rights violations in Myanmar, Sudan, Kenya, Côte d'Ivoire, Libya, and Syria and on occasion appointed special envoys. Arguably, Ban's leadership in Côte d'Ivoire built the necessary consensus and provided international coordination for the UN mission.

Human rights will undoubtedly be high on the agenda for the ninth secretary-general who will take office on January 1, 2017.

The Office of the High Commission for Human Rights (OHCHR)

Debate about the need for a UN high commissioner for human rights started in the 1940s. The 1993 UN Vienna conference on human rights recommended that the General Assembly create such a post. After a heavy lobbying campaign by a variety of actors—including many NGOs, the Carter Center, and the U.S. government—the General Assembly finally created the post that autumn. The office had a vague mandate with weak authority. Secretary-General Boutros-Ghali appointed as the first occupant José Ayala-Lasso of Ecuador, who had held several national diplomatic posts, including foreign minister under a repressive military government. He began his activities in 1994.

The first UN high commissioner for human rights practiced quiet diplomacy out of the limelight rather than being a visible public advocate. This approach helped alleviate some of the developing countries' fears that the post would be used exclusively to emphasize civil and political rights favored by Western states, with developing countries serving as "primary targets." The first high commissioner met with any number of developing countries with questionable human rights policies; during these visits, those policies presumably were discussed. Among other activities, Ayala-Lasso tried to interject more attention to economic and social rights into the work of the UN regional commissions for economic development. This emphasis was continued by his successor.

Beyond an annual report on international human rights at the UN, probably the most important work of the first high commissioner was to establish human rights field missions inside countries either as part of, or as separate from, UN peacekeeping operations. The first of these missions was established in Rwanda, where the human rights field staff broke new ground in legal and diplomatic theory but achieved little in practical terms during its early deployment. Ayala-Lasso then tried to turn Rwanda into a precedent by creating field missions elsewhere, the first of which were in Abkhazia, Georgia, Colombia, and Zaire.

By the end of the decade and with High Commissioner for Human Rights Mary Robinson's enthusiastic backing, a UN field presence for human rights had expanded to include Cambodia, the Central African Republic, the Democratic Republic of the Congo, El Salvador, Gaza, Guatemala, Indonesia, Liberia, Malawi, Mongolia, Sierra Leone, South Africa, southern Africa, and Southeast Europe. Once more, in the name of universal human rights, the UN was acting on matters that had once been considered fully part of domestic affairs. In addition to debates about human rights in New York and Geneva, the second high commissioner was trying to make a difference "on the ground."[39]

The establishment of this post after the Vienna conference in 1993 created some confusion about the overall management and coordination of UN human rights work. Sometimes the high commissioner, the Office of the Secretary-General, and the UN Commission on Human Rights did not seem to be reading the same sheet of music; nor was it always clear who, if anyone, was the conductor. The division of labor has since largely been worked out. In 1997 the Centre for Human Rights was merged with OHCHR, but the Office of the High Commissioner remains chronically short of staff and funds. Robinson ran afoul of the United States, and in 2002 she stepped down under pressure. Just as Washington had seen to it that Boutros-Ghali did not continue as secretary-general, so, too, it made clear that Robinson's high-profile discussion of human rights violations in such places as China and Israeli-occupied territories did not coincide with U.S. policies. In China, for instance, the United States had adopted a bipartisan policy of engagement with authoritarian Beijing, in which human rights was relegated to quiet diplomacy, not public pressure. Regarding Israel, the United States had long declined to take up seriously Israel's repeated violations of the Fourth Geneva Convention of 1949 regulating occupied territory, as affirmed by various UN agencies as well as the ICRC. Because Robinson was more committed to raising awareness about human rights and violations than to quiet diplomacy, she became an irritant not only to those states with serious human rights violations but also to the United States, which had close relations with some of these same states. Robinson also openly criticized U.S. policy regarding interrogation and other treatment of "enemy combatants" after 9/11. The final straw for Washington was the perceived way that Robinson ran the World Conference against Racism, Racial Discrimination, Xenophobia, and Related Intolerance in Durban, South Africa, in September 2001, which featured attacks on Israel and Zionism. She also championed socioeconomic rights, which the United States rejected.

Secretary-General Annan, whose diplomatic skills were normally commensurate with the demands of his position, then nominated, and the General Assembly approved, Brazil's Sergio Vieira de Mello as high commissioner. He had considerable UN experience in humanitarian and refugee matters—in UNHCR as emergency relief coordinator, and head of UN operations in Kosovo and East Timor—and he was known as a much more polished diplomat than Robinson. Some private human rights groups thought he might be too polished, in an effort to get along with the governments that violate human rights. His good relations with the George W. Bush administration made him the U.S. choice to be the secretary-general's representative in postcombat Iraq. Tragically, he and twenty-one other colleagues were killed during a suicide bombing of UN headquarters in August 2003. After Vieira de Mello's death, Bertrand Ramcharan of Guyana became acting high commissioner.

In July 2004, Louise Arbour assumed the key human rights post, having been a judge on Canada's Supreme Court and chief prosecutor for the international criminal tribunals for the former Yugoslavia and Rwanda. Arbour had a judicial temperament and for a while took a lower-key approach. But over time, she spoke out more. And like her predecessors, she wound up in public conflict with Washington, especially when she took exception to some U.S. policies pertaining to the detention and interrogation of suspected terrorists. Arbour's statements caused her to be publicly rebuked by U.S. permanent representative John Bolton.[40]

In 2008 Secretary-General Ban Ki-moon selected a distinguished South African female jurist, Navanethem (Navi) Pillay, to succeed Arbour. Pillay was a strong voice for human rights but not without generating controversy. The UN's troubled relationship with Rwanda was made worse in 2010, when a report issued by her office on the violence in Congo labeled actions by the Rwandan government as "possible genocide." In 2011 Sri Lanka expressed outrage over her call for an independent investigation into alleged atrocities and war crimes by the government in defeating the Tamil Tigers. Pillay, who is of Tamil descent, was vilified as a bullying, racist "Tamil Tigress."[41] She managed to annoy many governments by highlighting the violence and human rights violations experienced by lesbian, gay, bisexual, and transgender (LGBT) people. She called on governments to protect the rights of LGBT people and to repeal discriminatory laws.[42] More recently she was a vocal critic of the Syrian government's crackdown on antigovernment demonstrators. She called for a UN intervention to protect civilians and condemned the violence there before a special session of the General Assembly.[43]

Pillay's term officially ended in 2012; however, it was extended for another two years, making her the longest-serving high commissioner for human rights. Her successor, Prince Zeid Ra'ad Al-Hussein, came to the post with a long Jordanian diplomatic record and a reputation as a human rights advocate. Since taking office in 2014, Al-Hussein has had to contend with the humanitarian catastrophe in Syria and Iraq and sex abuse scandals involving peacekeepers in the Central African Republic.

States like to be associated with the notion of human rights as a matter of principle, but they often take exception when UN officials criticize their own policies

UN high commissioner for human rights Zeid Ra'ad Al-Hussein addresses the thirtieth session of the Human Rights Council in Geneva. September 21, 2015. (UN PHOTO 643134/JEAN-MARC FERRÉ)]

or those of their allies. The UN high commissioner for human rights, like the secretary-general, has found it difficult to be a public advocate for human rights and to satisfy the human rights NGO community, which often demands clear and decisive action, while maintaining the support of member states. Both the secretary-general and the high commissioner have impossible jobs and must walk a diplomatic high wire. They must galvanize member states and mobilize them to act, without alienating them. The high commissioner for human rights, in particular, knows that different conceptions and priorities surround the implementation of human rights.

The high commissioner is now supported by a staff of over one thousand in this crucial office in the second UN. The duties and responsibilities of the OHCHR are extensive, including implementing a rights-based approach within the UN as well as helping states meet their international human rights obligations. It does the latter by setting standards and building national capacity. It advises state officials on incorporating international human rights standards in domestic law and institutions and encourages the creation of national ombudsmen offices to help mediate allegations of human rights abuses. The OHCHR also maintains a network of field missions and regional offices and has staff based with peacekeeping missions. It supports the Human Rights Council and the work of independent commissions and special rapporteurs. OHCHR regional offices ensure liaisons with regional intergovernmental agencies (IGOs), such as the African Union, to enhance regional human rights capacities. The OHCHR also plays an important educative role. It routinely produces training manuals, fact sheets, and reports that help move disparate actors toward a global consensus. In crisis situations, it is ready to deploy human rights advisers and rapid-response personnel to gather facts, document abuses, and take testimony.

UN High Commissioner for Refugees

The Office of the UN High Commissioner for Refugees (UNHCR) warrants special mention, given the sheer numbers of people falling under the UNHCR's formal and informal mandates.[44] In the past ten years, the number of persons of concern to the UNHCR has ranged between 15 and 25 million; however, in 2015 the UNHCR estimated the number of persons assisted by it to be some 40 million—out of the record-breaking 60 million forcibly displaced persons worldwide.[45] The UNHCR was created by the General Assembly in 1950 and functions largely under the 1951 Refugee Convention and its 1967 protocol, providing protection and assistance to refugees and people in refugee-like situations. Originally the UNHCR mandate centered on de jure refugees, or "convention refugees," defined by the 1951 convention/1967 protocol as those who have crossed an international border because of a well-founded fear of persecution. Over time, the UNHCR's mandate has expanded to include those who are in refugee-like situations, which means the General Assembly has authorized the UNHCR to deal, at least sometimes, with persons displaced within a state—internally displaced persons (IDPs), in official parlance—and with those fleeing war or a breakdown in public order.

States themselves make the final determination of who is a convention refugee and therefore entitled to temporary asylum from persecution. The exact role of the UNHCR in protection can vary according to national law, but in general one of its primary roles is to help states determine who should not be returned to a situation of possible persecution. The agency calls this "legal" or "diplomatic" protection, and it can involve interviewing those who claim to be refugees, advising executive branches of government, and helping legislators draft new norms. The UNHCR also often submits legal papers in court cases.

Particularly when faced with a large influx of unwanted persons, states may show a racial, ideological, religious, ethnic, or other bias in their procedures to determine who is recognized as a legal refugee and entitled not to be returned to a dangerous situation. At times the UNHCR will publicly protest what a government is doing. For example, even though the United States is the largest contributor to the agency's voluntary budget, in 1992 the UNHCR officially protested the forced return of Haitians without a proper hearing about their refugee status. During the 2015 record-setting influx of refugees from Syria, Libya, Afghanistan, and Iraq into Europe, several states in Eastern Europe openly expressed unease with the largely Muslim backgrounds of refugees, either because of the fear of importing future terrorists or because of national bias. Catholic Poland indicated it wanted only limited numbers of Christian refugees.

The agency also is involved in assistance. Rather than being an operating agency itself, the UNHCR normally supervises material and medical assistance to refugees, broadly defined, by subcontracting with NGOs to provide for the delivery of necessary goods and services to both refugees and internally displaced persons. In 2015 the agency had operations in 123 countries with a staff of over 9,300. About 425 NGOs were implementing partners—a reminder that the members of the third UN are essential additions to decisions by the first UN and to operational efforts by the second UN.

In the 1990s the UNHCR became deeply enmeshed in the Balkans, devoting about a third of its total resources there. In 1994 the agency was responsible for coordinating relief to some 2 million persons who had fled Rwanda. The growing emphasis on assistance has led some observers to criticize the diminishing role of its traditional legal protection in the organization's priorities. A basis for this criticism is that many institutions can provide aid but only the UNHCR can protect refugees. The growing numbers of IDPs are also of concern to the UNHCR, as they experience refugee-like situations but have been unwilling or unable to flee their war-torn countries.[46] When IDPs were first counted in 1982, there were only 1 million, at which time there were about 10.5 million refugees.[47] IDPs have since become twice as numerous as refugees, numbering almost 40 million in 2015.

The rapid evolution of measures on behalf of IDPs in the 1990s and the embrace of their plight by IGOs and NGOs demonstrate the increasing weight of human rights in state decision making. Efforts accelerated as individuals and private institutions pushed governments and intergovernmental organizations to find new ways to deal with the growing problem of internal displacement. Roberta Cohen recalls that "as early as 1991, NGOs began calling for the consolidation into a single document of the different international standards that apply to IDPs."[48] Francis M. Deng, a former Sudanese diplomat, was designated as the first representative of the secretary-general on internally displaced persons. The development of a comprehensive global approach for effective assistance and protection of IDPs was independently formulated and financed. He and colleagues formulated "sovereignty as responsibility." Between his appointment in 1992 and his replacement by Swiss jurist and professor at the University of Berne Walter Kälin in 2004, Deng's efforts put the issue of IDPs squarely on the international agenda, including the development of "soft law," embodied in the *Guiding Principles of Internal Displacement*. In 2010 Chaloka Beyani, a Zambian lawyer teaching at the London School of Economics and NGO activist, assumed the position. Still, IDPs have no institutional home in the UN system.[49]

Whether for IDPs or refugees, the UNHCR has always found it difficult to negotiate what it calls "durable solutions." The preferred option is repatriation, but this usually entails fundamental political change in the country of origin, something the UNHCR obviously cannot produce. The UNHCR does not deal with Palestinian refugees; they are serviced by the UN Relief and Works Agency (UNRWA).[50] But the fundamental problems remain the same. In the Middle East, at least two generations of refugees have been born in camps; durable solutions have proven elusive.

The UNHCR and UNRWA share other frustrations. Both depend on host-state cooperation for security and other policies in refugee camps. For Rwandan refugees in the Democratic Republic of the Congo (formerly Zaire), as for Palestinian refugees in Lebanon or Syria, the host state decides what groups are allowed to have arms or engage in political activity. In both examples, refugees have been active, respectively, in preparing to launch cross-border armed attacks in Rwanda or Israel. UN refugee agencies are caught in these types of political struggles without either the legal authority or the power to make a difference.[51] Because of such considerations in Zaire and Tanzania in the mid-1990s, some NGOs, or at least some of their national sections, such as Doctors Without Borders, refused to service refugee needs, believing the NGO was contributing to a resumption of violence. The UNHCR decided to stay, as it did not want to abandon civilians who really were being held hostage by armed militias. In the view of the UNHCR, the Security Council has the responsibility to provide proper security in refugee camps.

Another durable solution entails resettlement. This option is made difficult because of the large numbers of people involved in many migrations. Permanent resettlement for most refugees was out of the question as far as host states were concerned. For example, almost five million persons, or a third of the population, left Afghanistan during the fighting there in the 1980s. Iran and Pakistan hosted many of these persons. Resettlement was not a serious option, given the sheer numbers and the lack of economic infrastructure of the two host states. And most refugees do not want to settle in a strange land if there is any hope of a sufficient change to make their home country safe.

Restricting numbers is relatively easy when a country is one of second asylum, or resettlement. Such a state, even one that is a party to the 1951 Refugee Convention, is not obligated to accept any refugees for resettlement if they first went to another country. When dealing with refugees from Vietnam who are in Hong Kong, for example, the United States can select whomever it wishes for entry into the United States. Only a country of first asylum is legally obligated not to return those with a well-founded fear of persecution. Economic migrants can be returned legally, but for genuine refugees under the UN convention of 1951, no ceiling exists on the number entitled to temporary safe haven in the form of asylum.

The 1951 Refugee Convention was drafted with an eye to coping with small numbers fleeing European communism. By contrast, one sees large numbers fleeing not only targeted persecution but also general violence and repression—which is often accompanied by a lack of economic opportunity. In these situations, states of first asylum almost always feel overwhelmed and want to control numbers. This reality was true of Asian states faced with Vietnam's boat people in the 1970s; the United States facing waves of fleeing Cubans and Haitians somewhat later; and Europeans facing large numbers of Syrians, Afghans, Iraqis, Libyans, and others at present. In the most recent case, every European country has a resurgent right wing of nativists who oppose accepting more foreigners. National leaders, such as Angel Merkel in Germany, who have sought to be welcoming have seen their poll numbers decline. The UNHCR is caught in the middle of these complex developments, advocating for the rights and needs of those in flight but lacking the authority to implement its preferences.

In 1981 the UNHCR was awarded the Nobel Peace Prize; however, it still has faced criticism. One high commissioner, Jean-Pierre Hocké of Switzerland, resigned in the midst of controversy over his spending habits and other policies, such as autocratic management. In 1990 Sadako Ogata of Japan became the first woman to head the agency, which regained some of its previous high ground. But by the end of the 1990s, questions continued about what had become a sizable bureaucracy. Ogata was replaced after two five-year terms by a former Dutch prime minister, Ruud Lubbers. Responding to the desires of the Western states that funded his budget, he instituted a series of cost-cutting measures but then resigned in early 2005 amid allegations of sexual harassment.[52] António Guterres, a former Portuguese prime minister, replaced him and focused on voluntary repatriation initiatives and the refugee/IDP situation stemming from the wars in Sudan. Subsequently, he has been challenged by the increased migration from North Africa and the Middle East to a Europe that feels overwhelmed. Part of the UNHCR's role is to get states to accept migrants of uncertain legal status on humanitarian grounds, regardless of which state was the "country of first asylum" or whether the individual or group is entitled to formal legal protection.

Refugees and those in refugee-like situations usually are fleeing human rights violations. Hence, the root causes of these human flows must be addressed if the preferred durable solution, repatriation, is to be achieved. This requires political commitment by member states, which are increasingly recognizing that they cannot ignore the nexus between security, human rights, extreme poverty, and environmental degradation. It also requires a comprehensive and coordinated approach.

In 2015 the intertwined problems of refugees and IDPs were undeniable in the situation in Syria. The internationalized internal armed conflict there had uprooted about half of the prewar population in the form of 4 million refugees and perhaps 8 million IDPs—in addition to over 250,000 deaths. The IDPs were especially hard to reach as the violence went largely unchecked, with irregular militias and shifting battle zones without clear safe areas. Neighboring Lebanon, Jordan, and Turkey were severely affected by those fleeing persecution and violence, as was regional stability. Outside parties, particularly in the West, were mostly reluctant to accept large numbers of foreigners in the context of slow economic growth and rising anti-immigrant feelings. The major Western donors to the UNHCR voluntary budget provided a certain amount of financial support for refugee assistance "over there." Admission and resettlement were another matter. Once again the UNHCR was left to manage intractable problems whose resolution depended on state political will to deal with the root causes of dislocation. Western attention to Syria tended to eclipse media coverage of other dire situations confronting the UNHCR, as in South Sudan. All of these challenges awaited the recently appointed head of UNHCR, Filippo Grandi of Italy, who assumed office in 2016, replacing Guterres.

The Office for the Coordination of Humanitarian Affairs

Human rights are at particular risk during war, public emergencies, and natural disasters (sometimes combined with corruption or incompetence). Various UN organizations exist either to prepare for these disasters or to respond to them.[53] In 1992 the Department of Humanitarian Affairs (DHA) incorporated the UN Disaster Relief Office (UNDRO); it was created to coordinate international humanitarian relief. In January 1998, as part of the secretary-general's reform initiative, the department was restructured and renamed the Office for the Coordination of Humanitarian Affairs (OCHA). OCHA is headed by an undersecretary-general who serves as emergency relief coordinator (ERC) responsible for coordinating disaster assistance both within and outside the UN system. The UNHCR and the United Nations Children's Fund (UNICEF) usually play active, and sometimes lead, roles in coordinating international relief. The World Food Programme (WFP) is usually involved in logistics. And the UN Development Programme (UNDP), which is supposed to coordinate all UN activities within a country, is also involved. The ERC has been mandated the responsibility of overseeing the rapid deployment of staff during crisis situations and ensuring that appropriate coordination mechanisms are set up.

Moreover, a galaxy of private relief organizations is also active. The International Federation of Red Cross and Red Crescent Societies, which loosely coordinates over 185 national units, sees natural-disaster work as one of its primary reasons for being. Hundreds of other private agencies, such as Oxfam, Caritas, and Save the Children, try to respond to natural disasters with emergency assistance.

The budgets of humanitarian organizations registered a fivefold increase from about $800 million in 1989 to some $4.4 billion in 1999, with an additional quadrupling to $16.7 billion in 2009. After peaking at just over $20 billion in 2010, the figures drifted downward to $19.4 billion in 2011 and $17.9 billion in 2012, but then increased dramatically to $22 billion in 2013, the last year for which solid data are available. Preliminary indications suggest a further increase in 2014 to $24 billion.[54] While the number of UN organizations has not grown, their budgets have (accounting for about two-thirds of total Development Assistance Committee [DAC] humanitarian disbursements).

The major problem with humanitarian assistance is that no one is really in charge. "Coordination" is oft-used to describe a loosely knit network of IGOs and NGOs as well as state agencies active in humanitarian relief. Every agency is in favor of coordination in principle, but few wish to be coordinated in practice. UN organizations have been protective of their decentralized independence. Private agencies have resisted coming under the full control of public authorities. As such, agencies compete among themselves for a slice of the action and for credit for whatever accomplishments can be achieved. The result is often confusion and duplication of services.

The ERC chairs an Inter-Agency Standing Committee (IASC), which includes major UN and non-UN humanitarian actors. This body strives to facilitate interagency analysis and decision making in response to humanitarian emergencies. Also, in his role as a UN undersecretary-general, the head of OCHA serves as convener of the Executive Committee for Humanitarian Affairs (ECHA), a cabinet-level forum for coordinating humanitarian policies within the UN. The relevance of OCHA was demonstrated in the aftermath of the 2004 Southeast Asian tsunami, which killed approximately 275,000 people and left tens of millions homeless and without basic services, such as food, water, housing, and medical care. The undersecretary-general at the time, Jan Egeland, prodded many donor countries, which eventually contributed billions of dollars in the largest relief operation in history. OCHA shifted into high gear again to respond to the 2005 earthquake in the Kashmir region, which left approximately thirty thousand people dead and millions homeless.

After the devastating January 2010 earthquake in Haiti, OCHA led the humanitarian charge. Over two hundred thousand Haitians died, and millions were injured and left homeless. In one of the largest humanitarian efforts ever, OCHA "coordinated" the emergency responses of hundreds governments and aid groups with a devastated (and largely corrupt) Haitian government. After the initial emergency needs were met, OCHA worked to maintain international support for reconstruction efforts. More recently, it has led the response to the cholera epidemic through treatment and large-scale vaccination. While Haiti still has a long way to go, the operational support and advocacy of OCHA brought some order to a large, complicated, and decentralized response to an unexpected emergency situation. Nevertheless, reports abounded claiming inefficiencies and imperial attitudes by various NGOs, such as the American Red Cross, and five years after the Haitian natural disaster the country remained in its all too common disorganized and impoverished condition.

The Second UN and Humanitarian Assistance in Armed Conflict

Humanitarian assistance in armed conflict is exceptionally problematic. The disorganization of the UN system regarding assistance again comes into play as no institutionalized UN agency exists to take the system's lead in armed conflicts. The secretary-general or General Assembly may ask an agency on an ad hoc basis to take the lead; for example, that was the case for the UNHCR in the western Balkans during 1992–1995. More recently the UN has experimented with "cluster" leaders: the UNHCR taking the lead for forcibly displaced persons, for example. The undersecretary-general for humanitarian affairs still must negotiate operational details from a welter of options. The situation is even more complicated in internal armed conflict in which one or more fighting parties do not represent a widely recognized state and most of the fighting occurs primarily in the territory of one state.[55] The laws of war (which sometimes are called humanitarian law, the law of armed conflict, or the law for human rights in war) do not create a clear obligation to cooperate with the purveyors of humanitarian assistance. Moreover, states and other fighting parties frequently disagree on whether an internal armed conflict exists as compared to a rebellion or insurrection falling under national rather than international law. The number of interstate wars has declined since 1945, but the number of violent situations seen by some as "internal wars" has risen, accompanied by great civilian loss of life and other suffering.

Neither the second UN nor the third UN (humanitarian NGOs, including the ICRC) can claim consistent success in delivering humanitarian assistance in what are sometimes called "complex emergencies." Given governments' opposition to admitting that they face an internal armed conflict, some have hoped that humanitarian progress could be made by referring to such situations by this euphemism. The logistics of delivery involve foreign militaries, local and national officials, private companies, and NGOs, all of which can cause bottlenecks that must be overcome through diplomacy.[56] The second UN is perhaps best situated for this task, but officials also need the political support of the first UN. Moreover, permitting such assistance has limited meaning to parties using starvation as a weapon and who are engaged in intentional ethnic cleansing, genocide, widespread rape, and deliberate attacks on civilians and aid personnel. Child soldiers and ragtag local militias make the inculcation of humanitarian values difficult.[57] Given the difficulties encountered by both the UN and the ICRC in obtaining the consent of fighting parties in internal wars and public emergencies, some NGOs, such as Doctors Without Borders, began cross-border operations without consent, a practice that is now widespread.

As a practical matter, trying to proceed without the consent of the warring parties can lead—and has led—to lethal attacks on international and local relief staff. The number of attacks has skyrocketed in recent years along with the size of humanitarian disbursements.[58] Since 1990, more journalists and aid workers have died than military peacekeepers. For aid agencies, this kind of insecurity represents a very acute challenge. In the Syrian conflict, some forty-five staff from the Syrian Arab Red Crescent were killed during 2011–2015. Jan Egeland noted in his memoirs that "The age of innocence has gone. . . . I had expected to spend all my energies in the UN on the security and survival of disaster and conflict victims, not the security and survival of our own UN staff."[59] The *Economist* also opined, "It was not until the American-led wars in Afghanistan and Iraq that the UN and other aid agencies began to be deliberately hunted down."[60]

Until recently, the two most essential humanitarian principles (neutrality and impartiality) had been relatively uncontroversial, along with the key operating procedure of seeking consent from belligerents.[61] These principles, too, became casualties as "these Maginot line principles defending humanitarianism from politics crumbled during the 1990s."[62] A host of factors have challenged the classic posture: the complete disregard for international humanitarian law by war criminals and even by child soldiers; the direct targeting of civilians and relief personnel; the use of foreign aid to fuel conflicts and war economies; and the protracted nature of many so-called emergencies.[63]

In many ways, international humanitarian law seems to have been formulated to deal with a different world, one populated by governments and regular armies whose reciprocal interests were often served by respecting the laws of war.[64] In writing of old-fashioned humanitarianism, David Rieff has gone so far as to suggest "the death of a good idea."[65] At the end of the day, he returned to the view that traditional, neutral, limited humanitarianism was the right course of action after earlier having been a proponent of blowing the whistle on atrocities.[66] In fact, over time, Doctors Without Borders has found it difficult to operate in the field and also at the same time bear witness about atrocities. The organization has inconsistently edged closer to the Red Cross tradition of discretion in order to avoid the media spotlight and provide goods and services to victims of political violence.

In spite of these problems—and "identity crisis"[67] is not too strong a term to describe the individual and collective soul-searching by "aid workers"—the preceding pages should have made clear that humanitarian values and expenditures on emergency relief have expanded substantially.[68] The substantial bottom lines have led such harsh critics as Mark Duffield to question whether humanitarian assistance has not become a necessity for maintaining Western hegemony.[69] And at a minimum, the marketplace determines an environment of scarce resources that in turn creates a competitive dynamic for status, power, and authority among competitive UN agencies and NGOs whose staffs and budgets depend on expanding resources.[70] As Michael Barnett and Thomas Weiss noted, humanitarians are no longer necessarily on the side of the angels.[71]

Because of insecurity and the nature of contemporary humanitarian crises, the militaries of member states have moved into the humanitarian space formerly occupied almost exclusively by UN organizations and NGOs. Coupled with the increased use of private contractors by militaries, the distinction between a neutral and impartial humanitarian aid organization and an agent of a state becomes difficult to discern.[72] The raid that killed Osama bin Laden in Pakistan resulted from intelligence gathered by a Pakistani physician working for the CIA. Under the guise of a vaccination program the doctor also was collecting DNA to determine whether bin Laden or his relatives were in the area. That physician, who has since been arrested, interrogated, and convicted of treason by Pakistani authorities, claimed that he had been introduced to the CIA by Save the Children, the largest international aid agency in Pakistan.[73] This has led the government of Pakistan to clamp down on NGO operations and restrict their access to those most in need. In 2015 the Pakistan government ordered Save the Children to leave, but it later rescinded that order after intense Western diplomatic pressure.

Normative developments and political reality are rarely in sync. The idea of an international responsibility to protect reflects a steady and clear normative growth since the early 1990s, whereas the operational capacity and political will to address the root causes of human rights violations and displacement have been on a roller coaster. While the international community of states stood by in Darfur, it intervened militarily in Côte d'Ivoire and Libya. While it failed to deal decisively with South Sudan, it did better in Mali and the Central African Republic—ironically because of France's willingness to put its troops on the ground in certain former colonies.[74] Even as Russia increased its military presence, in 2015 hesitation characterized most government reactions to Syria, while aid organizations of both the second and third UN were trying desperately to create a humanitarian space to treat the victims of the conflict and protect the most fundamental of human rights: the right to life.

HUMAN RIGHTS AND NATIONAL INTEREST

The meaning of "national interest" is not fixed, especially not for human rights.[75] Like "state sovereignty," it is a social construct. Humans derive ideas about national interest in a process of change over time. Whether human rights should be, or can be, linked to national interests is a matter of debate. How they are linked—as with the securitization of human rights and humanitarian aid—also matters. At times states of the first UN have pursued human rights at the United Nations as a weapon in power struggles. The objective has been to delegitimize a certain government; the means has been to emphasize human rights violations. We are witnesses to this as Muslim states and others target Israel in the Human Rights Council.

Some states have adopted a broad definition of their own self-interests. Like Canada or Sweden, for instance, they seek not just territorial integrity, political independence, and other goals directly related to the narrow and expedient interests of the state. They also define their interests in terms of an international society in which human dignity is advanced by serious attention to human rights. Just as governments have defined their domestic interests beyond physical security and economic welfare, so have they used their foreign policies to advance human rights and humanitarian goals.

In contrast, sovereignty is often used as a defense against UN action on human rights by different states on different issues at different times. The principle is especially favored as a defense mechanism by the authorities of weaker and younger developing countries that fear losing status and influence at the hands of more powerful states. Older and more powerful states also do not hesitate to trot out the tired slogans of sacrosanct state sovereignty when some UN agency or regional organization criticizes their actions. The United States chastises others for politicizing the Human Rights Council even while it resists UN rapporteurs and agencies trying to implement UN standards on the U.S. policies toward torture and the treatment of prisoners or terrorists, and the death penalty.

The member states of the first UN have nevertheless found the necessary consensus to muster over time the political will to create UNHCR, the OHCHR, and the ICC. The second UN has done much to bridge the many political divides and help member states address human rights and humanitarian issues in spite of mixed motives and geostrategic rivalries. By playing an imperfect, synthesizing role, the second UN often moves disparate groups forward by setting standards and monitoring progress toward human rights. Its humanitarian relief operations have improved the lives and dignity of millions of people.

The second UN has adopted modest reforms that have advanced its operational efficiency; however, most member states simply will not empower UN organizations with significant independence or decision-making authority. Often, it seems member states want to do something and then ask the second UN to act without approving the necessary resources or displaying sufficient political will. As such, the record of the first and second UN in advancing human rights and humanitarian principles is uneven at best.

NOTES

1. Steven Erlanger, "French Foreign Minister Voices Doubt on Human Rights Push," *New York Times,* December 1, 2008, A8.

2. Julie A. Mertus, *The United Nations and Human Rights: A Guide for a New Era,* 2nd ed. (London: Routledge, 2009); Philip Alston, ed., *The United Nations and Human Rights: A Critical Appraisal,* 2nd ed. (Oxford: Clarendon, 2002); and David P. Forsythe, *Human Rights in International Relations,* 3rd ed. (Cambridge: Cambridge University Press, 2012).

3. Martin J. Burke and Thomas G. Weiss, "The Security Council and Ad Hoc Tribunals: Law and Politics, Peace and Justice," in *Security Council Resolutions and Global Legal Regimes,* ed. Trudy Fraser and Vesselin Popovksi (London: Routledge, 2014), 241–265.

4. Darryl Robinson, "Inescapable Dyads: Why the International Criminal Court Cannot Win," *Leiden Journal of International Law* 28 (2015): 323–347.

5. Stuart Ford, "Complexity and Efficiency at International Criminal Courts," *Emory International Law Review* 29 (2014): 1–69.

6. Eric A. Posner, *The Perils of Global Legalism* (Chicago: University of Chicago Press, 2009), 205–206.

7. David Lague, "China Braces for Prospect of Change," *New York Times,* September 27, 2007.

8. *Harvard Law Review,* "International Law—The Responsibility to Protect—Draft Security Council Resolution Referring Syrian Conflict to the International Criminal Court Vetoed," 128 (2015): 1055–1062.

9. David P. Forsythe, *Human Rights and World Politics,* 2nd ed. (Lincoln: University of Nebraska Press, 1989), chap. 3.

10. For a contrary view, see Rama Mani and Thomas G. Weiss, eds., *The Responsibility to Protect: Cultural Perspectives from the Global South* (London: Routledge, 2011).

11. David Petrasek, "New Powers, New Approaches? Human Rights Diplomacy in the 21st Century," *Journal of International Human Rights* 19 (2013): 6–15.

12. Howard Tolley Jr., *The UN Commission on Human Rights* (Boulder, Colo.: Westview, 1987), was the last in-depth scholarly overview of the commission. For a general picture, see Roger Normand and Sarah Zaidi, *Human Rights at the UN: The Political History of Universal Justice* (Bloomington: Indiana University Press, 2008); and James H. Lebovic and Eric Voeten, "The Politics of Shame," *International Studies Quarterly* 50, no. 4 (2006): 861–888.

13. Tom J. Farer, "The UN and Human Rights: More Than a Whimper, Less Than a Roar," in *Human Rights and the World Community: Issues and Action*, ed. Richard Pierre Claude and Burns H. Weston, 2nd ed. (Philadelphia: University of Pennsylvania Press, 1992).

14. For a different interpretation of the history of international human rights, see Samuel Moyn, *The Last Utopia: Human Rights in History* (Cambridge, Mass.: Harvard University Press, 2012). Also see Stephen Hopgood, *The Endtimes of Human Rights* (Ithaca, N.Y.: Cornell University Press, 2013).

15. Paulo Sérgio Pinheiro, "Musings of a UN Special Rapporteur on Human Rights," *Global Governance* 9, no. 1 (2003): 1–13.

16. Morris B. Abram, "Human Rights and the United Nations: Past as Prologue," *Harvard Human Rights Law Journal* 4 (1991): 69–83.

17. Tolley Jr., *Commission on Human Rights*, 179.

18. Joe W. Pitts III and David Weissbrodt, "Major Developments at the UN Commission on Human Rights in 1992," *Human Rights Quarterly* 15, no. 1 (1993): 122–196.

19. *A More Secure World: Our Shared Responsibility—Report of the High-level Panel on Threats, Challenges, and Change* (New York: United Nations, 2004), paras. 283 and 285.

20. Kofi Annan, *In Larger Freedom: Towards Development, Security and Human Rights for All*, UN document A/59/2005, March 21, 2005, para. 183.

21. Lebovic and Voeten, "The Politics of Shame."

22. See Thomas Buergenthal, "The Evolving International Human Rights System," *American Journal of International Law* 100 (October 2006): 791.

23. Louise Arbour, "Statement by High Commissioner for Human Rights to Last Meeting of Commission on Human Rights," March 27, 2006, 3–6. See further David P. Forsythe, with Baekkwan Park, "Turbulent Transition," in *The United Nations: Past, Present, and Future—Proceedings of the 2007 Francis Marion University UN Symposium*, ed. Scott Kaufman and Alissa Warters (New York: Nova Science, 2009).

24. Bertrand G. Ramcharan, *The UN Human Rights Council* (New York: Routledge, 2011).

25. General Assembly, *2005 World Summit Outcome*, UN resolution A/60/1, September 24, 2005, paras.157 and 160.

26. "A Caterpillar in Lipstick," *Economist*, March 2, 2016.

27. Eduard Jordaan, "South African and Abusive Human Rights Regimes at the UN Human Rights Council," *Global Governance* 20 (2014): 233–254.; Rosa Freedman, "The United Nations Human Rights Council: More of the Same," *Wisconsin International Law Journal* 31 (2013): 208–251; Nico Schrijver, "The UN Human Rights Council: 'A Society of the Committed' or Just Old Wine in New Bottles?" *Leiden Journal of International Law* 20, no. 4 (2007): 809–823; and Yvonne Terlingen, "The Human Rights Council: A New Era in UN Human Rights Work?" *Ethics & International Affairs* 21, no. 2 (2007): 167–178.

28. Quoted in Warren Hoge, "Dismay Over New U.N. Human Rights Council," *New York Times*, March 11, 2007.

29. Kenneth Roth, "Empty Promises," *Foreign Affairs* 89, no. 1 (2010): 10–16. See also Tom Farer, Dinah PoKempner, Ed Morgan, Richard Falk, and Nigel S. Rodley, "The Goldstone Report on the Gaza Conflict: An Agora." *Global Governance* 16, no. 2 (2010): 139–207.

30. Philip Alston, Jason Morgan-Foster, and William Abresch, "The Competence of the UN Human Rights Council and Its Special Procedures in Armed Conflicts: Extrajudicial Executions in the 'War on Terror,'" *European Journal of International Law* 19 (2008): 183–209.

31. Bertrand G. Ramcharan, *The Law, Policy, and Politics of the UN Human Rights Council* (Leiden, Netherlands: Martinus Nijhoff, 2015); Edward McMahan and Marta Ascherio, "A Step Ahead of Promoting Human Rights? The Universal Periodic Review and UN Human Rights Council, *Global Governance* 18 (2012): 231–248.

32. Michael J. Barnett, *Empire of Humanity: A History of Humanitarianism* (Ithaca, N.Y.: Cornell University Press, 2011); Neta C. Crawford, *Argument and Change in World Politics: Ethics, Decolonization, and Humanitarian Intervention* (Cambridge: Cambridge University Press, 2002); and Paul Gordon Lauren, *Power and Prejudice: The Politics and Diplomacy of Racial Discrimination*, 2nd ed. (Boulder, Colo.: Westview, 1996).

33. David P. Forsythe, "The UN Secretary-General and Human Rights," in *The Challenging Role of the UN Secretary-General: Making "The Most Impossible Job in the World" Possible*, ed. Benjamin Rivlin and Leon Gordenker (Westport, Conn.: Greenwood Press, 1993), 211–232. See also Kent J. Kille, ed., *The UN Secretary-General and Moral Authority: Ethics and Religion in International Leadership* (Washington, D.C.: Georgetown University Press, 2008).

34. Bertrand G. Ramcharan, *Preventive Diplomacy at the UN* (Bloomington: Indiana University Press, 2008).

35. John P. Humphrey, *Human Rights and the United Nations: A Great Adventure* (New York: Transaction Books, 1984).

36. A joke circulating about the various recent heads of the UN Centre for Human Rights involved these characters: van Boven was supposedly the most active and committed; his successor, Kurt Herndl, having seen what happened to van Boven, supposedly kept a low profile; his successor, Jan Martenson, was supposedly preoccupied with a public image for himself and his office; his successor, Antoine Blanca, was supposedly an old crony of the secretary-general who had no interest in human rights. So, the joke went like this: van Boven (in fact) wrote the book *People Matter*; then Herndl supposedly wrote *States Matter*; Martenson, *I Matter*; and Blanca, *It Doesn't Matter*.

37. Press Release SG/SM/6825 HR/4391, December 8, 1998.

38. Julia Preston, "New U.N. Chief Invites Controversy by Declining to Oppose Hussein Execution," *New York Times*, January 3, 2007.

39. Bertrand G. Ramcharan, ed., *Human Rights Protection in the Field* (Leiden, Netherlands: Martinus Nijhoff, 2006).

40. David P. Forsythe, "U.S. Policy Toward Enemy Detainees," *Human Rights Quarterly* 28, no. 2 (2006): 465–491. And Forsythe, *The Politics of Prisoner Abuse: The United States and Enemy Prisoners After 9/11* (Cambridge: Cambridge University Press, 2011).

41. "A Tigress and Her Tormentors," *Economist* (October 8, 2011), 74.

42. "Gay People Around the World Face Bias, Abuse and Violence," *New York Times*, December 16, 2011; and Navi Pillay, "Ending Violence and Criminal Sanctions Based on Sexual Orientation and Gender Identity: Statement by the High Commissioner," September 17, 2010, http://www.ohchr.org/EN/NewsEvents/Pages/DisplayNews.aspx?NewsID =10717&LangID=E.

43. Rick Gladstone and Neil MacFarquhar, "U.N. Official Rebukes Syria Over Violence," *New York Times*, February 14, 2012.

44. Gil Loescher, *The UNHCR and World Politics: A Perilous Path* (Oxford: Oxford University Press, 2001); Arthur C. Helton, *The Price of Indifference: Refugees and Humanitarian Action in the New Century* (Oxford: Oxford University Press, 2002); and Niclaus Steiner, Mark Gibney, and Gil Loescher, eds., *Problems of Protection: The UNHCR, Refugees, and*

Human Rights (New York: Routledge, 2003); and Alexander Betts, Gil Loescher, and James Milner, *The United Nations High Commissioner for Refugees (UNHCR): The Politics and Practice of Refugee Protection*, 2nd ed. (London: Routledge, 2011).

45. "Figures at a Glance," accessed November 5, 2015, http://www.unhcr.org/pages /49c3646c11.html.

46. Thomas G. Weiss, "Internal Exiles: What Next for Internally Displaced Persons?" *Third World Quarterly* 24, no. 3 (2003): 429–447; and Kathleen Newland, with Erin Patrick and Monette Zard, *No Refuge: The Challenge of Internal Displacements* (New York: UNOCHA, 2003).

47. The changing numbers of "persons of concern" to the UNHCR can be followed by checking the different editions of *The Refugee Survey Quarterly*, published by the UNHCR, or by going to http://www.unhcr.org. For complete statistics on IDPs, see http://www.idp project.org, maintained by the Norwegian Refugee Council.

48. Michael Ignatieff, "Human Rights: The Midlife Crisis," *New York Review of Books* 46, no. 9 (1999): 58.

49. Roberta Cohen, "Lessons from the Guiding Principles on Internal Displacement," *Forced Migration Review* 45 (2014): 12–14. Thomas G. Weiss and David A. Korn, *Internal Displacement: Conceptualization and Its Consequences* (London: Routledge, 2006).

50. Benjamin N. Schiff, *Refugees unto the Third Generation: UN Aid to Palestinians* (Syracuse, N.Y.: Syracuse University Press, 1995).

51. Fiona Terry, *Condemned to Repeat? The Paradox of Humanitarian Action* (Ithaca, N.Y.: Cornell University Press, 2002).

52. UNHCR local staff in East Africa were accused of exchanging services for sexual favors, a controversy that did not enhance the agency's reputation. Loescher found in his 2001 study that parts of the UNHCR headquarters could be insensitive to refugee needs.

53. Thomas G. Weiss and Cindy Collins, *Humanitarian Challenges and Intervention*, 2nd ed. (Boulder, Colo.: Westview, 2000); and Jonathan Moore, *The UN and Complex Emergencies* (Geneva: UN Research Institute for Social Development, 1996).

54. http://www.huffingtonpost.com/2015/06/12/red-cross-haiti-spending_n_7571258 .html.

55. Peter J. Hoffman and Thomas G. Weiss, *Sword & Salve: Confronting New Wars and Humanitarian Crises* (Lanham, Md.: Rowman & Littlefield, 2006).

56. Jan Egeland, "Humanitarian Diplomacy," in *The Oxford Handbook of Modern Diplomacy*, ed. Andrew F. Cooper, Jorge Heine, and Ramesh Thakur (Oxford: Oxford University Press 2013), 356–357.

57. Simon Chesterman, ed., *Civilians in War* (Boulder, Colo.: Lynne Rienner, 2001); P. W. Singer, *Children at War* (New York: Pantheon, 2005).

58. Jan Egeland, Adele Harmer, and Abby Stoddard, *To Stay and Deliver: Good Practice for Humanitarians in Complex Security Environments* (New York: OCHA, 2011).

59. Jan Egeland, *A Billion Lives: An Eyewitness Report from the Frontlines of Humanity* (New York: Simon & Schuster, 2008), 8.

60. "More Dangerous to Work Than Ever," *Economist*, November 20, 2004, 49.

61. Thomas G. Weiss, "Principles, Politics, and Humanitarian Action," *Ethics & International Affairs* 13 (1999): 1–22, as well as "Responses" by Cornelio Sommaruga, Joelle Tanguy, Fiona Terry, and David Rieff, 23–42.

62. Michael Barnett, "Humanitarianism Transformed," *Perspectives on Politics* 3, no. 4 (2005): 724.

63. Michael Maren, *The Road to Hell: The Ravaging Effects of Foreign Aid and International Charity* (New York: Free Press, 1997); Alex de Waal, *Famine Crimes: Politics and the Disaster Relief Industry in Africa* (Oxford: James Currey, 1997); John Borton, "The State of the International Humanitarian System," Overseas Development Institute Briefing Paper no. 1 (March 1998); Myron Wiener, "The Clash of Norms: Dilemmas in Refugee Policies," *Journal of Refugee Studies* 11, no. 4 (1998): 1–21; Mark Duffield, "NGO Relief in War Zones: Toward an Analysis of the New Aid Paradigm," in *Beyond UN Subcontracting: Task-Sharing with Regional Security Arrangements and Service-Providing NGOs*, ed. Thomas G. Weiss (London: Macmillan, 1998), 139–159; Joanna Macrae and Anthony Zwi, eds., *War and Hunger: Rethinking International Responses to Complex Emergencies* (London: Zed Books, 1994); and David Keen, *The Economic Functions of Violence in Civil Wars*, Adelphi Paper 320 (Oxford: Oxford University Press, 1998).

64. Adam Roberts, "Implementation of the Laws of War in Late 20th Century Conflicts," Parts 1, 2, *Security Dialogue* 29, nos. 2 and 3 (1998): 137–150 and 265–280; and a special issue on "Humanitarian Debate: Law, Policy, Action," *International Review of the Red Cross* 81, no. 833 (1999).

65. David Rieff, "The Death of a Good Idea," *Newsweek*, May 10, 1999, 65.

66. David Rieff, *A Bed for the Night: Humanitarianism in Crisis* (New York: Simon & Schuster, 2002).

67. David Rieff, "Humanitarianism in Crisis," *Foreign Affairs* 81, no. 6 (2002): 111–121.

68. David P. Forsythe, "*Humanitarianism in Question: Politics, Power, Ethics* (Review)," *Human Rights Quarterly* 31, no. 1 (2009): 269–277.

69. Mark Duffield, *Global Governance and the New Wars: The Merging of Development and Security* (London: Zed Books, 2001). See also Philip White, "Complex Political Emergencies—Grasping Contexts, Seizing Opportunities," *Disasters* 24, no. 4 (2000): 288–290, and Des Gasper, "'Drawing a Line'—Ethical and Political Strategies in Complex Emergency Assistance," *European Journal of Development Research* 11, no. 2 (1999): 87–114.

70. Andrew Cooley and James Ron, "The NGO Scramble: Organizational Insecurity and the Political Economy of Transnational Action," *International Security* 27, no. 1 (2002): 5–39.

71. Michael Barnett and Thomas G. Weiss, eds., *Humanitarianism in Question: Politics, Power, Ethics* (Ithaca, N.Y.: Cornell University Press, 2008); and Michael Barnett and Thomas G. Weiss, *Humanitarianism Contested: Where Angels Fear to Tread* (London: Routledge, 2011).

72. Roisin Shannon, "Playing with Principles in an Era of Securitized Aid: Negotiating Humanitarian Space in Post-9/11 Afghanistan," *Progress in Developing Studies* 9, no. 1 (2009): 15–36.

73. Declan Walsh, "Fallout of Bin Laden Raid: Aid Groups in Pakistan Are Suspect," *New York Times*, May 2, 2012.

74. Thomas G. Weiss and Martin Welz, "The UN and the African Union in Mali and Beyond: A Shotgun Wedding?" *International Affairs* 90, no. 4 (2014): 889–905.

75. David P. Forsythe, ed., *Human Rights and Comparative Foreign Policy* (Tokyo: United Nations University Press, 2000).

CHAPTER 8

The Third UN in Human Rights and Humanitarian Affairs: The Role of Independent Experts and NGOs

EXPERTS AND NONGOVERNMENTAL ORGANIZATIONS (NGOs) make numerous contributions to promoting and protecting human rights and humanitarian principles at the UN. Arguably, experts provide independence, a view that is not filtered through state interests, and intellectual depth. Experts also help the politicized intergovernmental bodies at the first UN transcend entrenched biases and offer recommendations that can inform policy. Specialized NGOs advocate on behalf of human rights and humanitarian principles, and pressure public officials from member states and the second UN on policy directions.[1] They are subcontractors who deliver humanitarian goods and services, and monitor detention facilities. Independent experts and NGOs collectively form a "talent bank" from which state and UN officials can draw upon as needed. In short, they can be important catalysts for change.[2]

The growing importance of the third UN does not mean that UN intergovernmental bodies and entities are declining in significance. Rather, the third UN complements and challenges the existing pathways of human rights and humanitarian diplomacy. State representatives and UN officials retain a great deal of influence over the third UN because decisions to appoint special rapporteurs, working groups, and commissions of inquiry are the result of complicated political processes that involve extensive behind-the-scenes negotiations. Furthermore, member states can always ignore recommendations, and state and UN officials can certainly impede NGOs during the humanitarian "scramble." UN-appointed experts often must proceed with state consent, and their investigations can be thwarted by uncooperative governments. States must be willing to provide NGO personnel with transit and work visas, as well as physical protection. Still, the third UN can add considerable value to international efforts to advance human rights and humanitarian principles.

EXPERTS AND THE HUMAN RIGHTS COUNCIL

In 2015 forty-one thematic and fourteen country mandates involved UN-appointed human rights experts. Thematic mandates focus on human rights challenges that cut across national boundaries. Recent examples of thematic mandates include human rights and transnational corporations, the enjoyment of human rights of people with albinism, and arbitrary detention. Country mandates focus on the human rights situations in specific member states, for instance the Democratic People's Republic of Korea, Eritrea, and Cambodia.

Special Procedures: Special Rapporteurs, Independent Experts, and Working Groups

The Human Rights Council (HRC) has continued the precedent of using "special procedures" initially set by the Commission on Human Rights (CHR) to help member states and UN agencies address country-specific and thematic issues. Special procedures involve tapping human rights experts to investigate situations and make recommendations regarding courses of action or steps for improvement. Experts working individually are referred to as special rapporteurs or independent experts, while "working groups" involve five members (one from each of the UN's main regional groups). These experts serve in their own personal capacity and technically are not UN employees. To ensure their independence and autonomy, they are only compensated for their expenses and have fewer constraints than the typical UN official. Their work is supported by the Office of the High Commissioner for Human Rights (OHCHR).

The work of these experts usually involves country visits (with state consent). They investigate complaints and situations by meeting with victims and local NGOs. They also consult with governmental officials. If human rights concerns and abuses are verified, rapporteurs usually act first by communicating with the government(s) and making recommendations regarding corrective measures.[3] Rapporteurs and independent experts generally take a quiet approach when dealing with government officials, at least until their report is published, because governments can be more responsive when they are not publicly embarrassed. At the same time, these experts know that much of what they do will be seeds falling on barren ground.[4] Still, the reports and recommendations are important inputs to the OHCHR when deciding to send country teams or deploy field missions. They also affect HRC decisions to renew mandates.

The educative function of special procedures is often overlooked. Through their activities (albeit constrained), these experts bring together the very different perspectives of state officials, NGOs, and victims in complicated human rights

Urmila Bhoola, special rapporteur on contemporary forms of slavery, including its causes and consequences, addresses the thirtieth regular session of the Human Rights Council. June 23, 2015, Geneva, Switzerland. (UN PHOTO 642412/JEAN-MARC FERRÉ)

situations. They employ their expert views on the current status of human rights (which is always changing) and offer a roadmap for the parties to move forward. They also socialize representatives of states, UN organizations, and NGOs regarding current norms, standards, and expected behavior. This socialization function also extends to the publics of member states. Rapporteurs cultivate relationships with the media and can engage in "megaphone diplomacy" to raise public awareness and provide expert views in the overall public debate. [5] At the end of the day, if the activities under "special procedures" lead to some positive developments 40 percent of the time, as one exhaustive study found, that is a development not to be taken lightly.[6]

Independent Commissions of Inquiry

The HRC also appoints commissions of inquiry on an ad hoc basis to investigate situations involving possible gross violations of human rights or major violations of international humanitarian law. In 2015, the UN had four ongoing operational commissions of inquiry concerning human rights in Eritrea, the Democratic People's Republic of Korea (DPRK), Syria, and Gaza. A fact-finding investigation was ongoing on Sri Lanka, but that was being conducted by OHCHR personnel. Another concerning Gaza was under the aegis of the Office of the Secretary-General. Commissions of inquiry and fact-finding missions are similar to special procedures in that they gather evidence and collect testimony. They also assess responsibility and issue reports that may be given to the Security Council and the General Assembly as well as the HRC.

As with rapporteurs, the normative and operational contributions of independent commissions of inquiry are often dismissed because the first UN frequently ignores reports or fails to act and hold those identified accountable for their actions. Yet commissions may play an important socializing role and serve as a catalyst for moving the first and second UN forward. Arguably, the HRC's appointment of independent commissions of nongovernmental personnel at least delays, for a time, the politicization of an issue and allows for a compilation of evidence not tainted by preexisting biases. For example, the Independent Commission on Human Rights in the DPRK made important contributions to institutionalizing the responsibility to protect (R2P) in UN operations. Their report prompted the UN human rights machinery to engage reclusive North Korea and encouraged the Security Council to consider the rights situation in light of its obligations under R2P.[7] While little can be done directly, especially because of North Korea's nuclear weapons, the commission's report does pressure the regime to improve conditions and documents the human rights conditions experienced by the citizens of North Korea.

One should not underestimate the potential for controversy in third UN human rights activities. The report of the UN Fact-Finding Mission on the Gaza Conflict was established in 2009 and is an illustrative example. Also known as the Goldstone Report (named after the head of the mission, the former South African judge Richard Goldstone), the report detailed evidence of war crimes and crimes against humanity during the military conflict between Israel and Hamas in the Gaza Strip in late 2008 and early 2009. The mission found that both Israel and Hamas had committed war crimes and possibly crimes against humanity. The central and most provocative finding was the report's conclusion that rather than acting in narrow self-defense against rocket attacks, Israel's plan was to target the people of Gaza as a whole, which is a violation of several norms in international humanitarian law.[8] The reaction of the Israeli government, which did not cooperate with the mission, was swift. It rejected the commission's findings, claiming the commission had an anti-Israeli bias. Israel said it had a responsibility to protect its citizens and soldiers from terrorist attacks and that it had acted properly.

The United States objected to the commission's methodology and pointed to the disproportionate attention paid to Israel by the HRC.[9] At the same time, Washington seemed to accept the basic recommendation that Israel conduct its own internal investigation. The report may have little meaning in the face of geopolitical realities (such as Israeli suspicion of anything from the UN, or the virtually automatic U.S. endorsement of any Israeli position); however, it is important in terms of the "legitimacy wars" that may shift opinion over time.[10] Since the report was issued, several developments have occurred. Israel has conducted a major internal review as well as investigations of individual allegations of misconduct. The result was additional information and evidence that has been verified by a UN committee of independent experts that was convened to follow up on the report. Goldstone (under intense personal pressure from various pro-Israeli circles of opinion) publicly reconsidered the report's central conclusion that Israel was targeting civilians as a matter of policy in an extraordinary op-ed piece in the *Washington Post*;[11] however, the other members of the commission of inquiry did not change their views. They argued that no new, compelling evidence had come to light.[12] The Israeli military has adopted a new code of ethics and the Israeli judiciary is considering evidence of war crimes—although in the past Israeli internal investigations of possible war crimes have not led to serious charges or sanctions.

In a later continuation of armed conflict in Gaza in 2014, more or less the same scenario played out at the UN. The Human Rights Council appointed a commission of inquiry to look into violations of international law. Israel objected to the neutrality of the appointed chair and refused to cooperate with the commission. The secretary-general appointed a second commission of inquiry; apart from the HRC, Israel launched its own internal investigation. At issue was Hamas's use of civilian structures to camouflage attacks aimed at Israeli civilians and Israeli attacks of an indiscriminant and disproportionate nature on Palestinian civilian targets (including several UN refugee centers). Whatever the outcome of the various investigations, few observers think that the United States would allow the Security Council to sanction Israel for any violations of humanitarian law, especially since Hamas hardly had pristine hands. Rockets fired in the general direction of Israeli civilian population centers were incompatible with international humanitarian law's core injunction that belligerents distinguish between active combatants and civilians.

To what extent commissions of inquiry and fact-finding missions are meaningful or effect changes in official policies is debatable. What is clear is that member states and the UN machinery react to these reports and use them in subsequent actions. At the same time, while independent experts may compile the facts of a situation rather than governmental representatives, they report to intergovernmental bodies where the usual political biases come into play. It should also be kept in mind that the reports of the HRC fact-finding commissions can become evidence at the International Criminal Court (ICC) or other courts. In 2014, over strong Israeli and U.S. objections, Palestine was granted nonmember state observer status at the UN General Assembly and subsequently joined the ICC. The Palestinian Authority no doubt will seek to introduce the findings of the HRC investigation critical of Israel's policies in Gaza into that court's proceedings.

SUPPLEMENTAL HUMAN RIGHTS AND TREATY MONITORING BODIES

Supplemental human rights and treaty monitoring bodies, made up of individual experts rather than governmental representatives, advance respect for human rights in several ways.[13] Some committees are permitted to consider individuals' petitions and complaints. This is an important legal innovation that permits individuals to seek redress for human rights violations. All the treaty monitoring bodies are authorized to receive and review reports by state parties regarding the domestic implementation of human rights law. The bodies can pose questions, which creates an important dialogue between state officials and civil society actors. Also, the treaty monitoring bodies issue "general comments" that interpret treaty provisions and suggest ways that state parties can improve human rights protection. The process, while lacking the authority to mandate immediate corrections of violations, helps legitimize and institutionalize international human rights law.[14]

Human Rights Committee

Not to be confused with the Human Rights Commission, which existed through mid-2006, the UN Human Rights Committee was created under the International Covenant on Civil and Political Rights (ICCPR). It is composed of individual experts elected by parties to that treaty, and functions only in relation to monitoring the implementation of the civil and political rights codified in the ICCPR. It reports to the General Assembly but is not part of the "regular" UN bureaucracy.

Since the late 1970s, the Human Rights Committee has processed state reports about implementing the civil-political covenant and handled individual petitions when state parties have allowed their citizens that procedural right. Despite the Cold War, European communist states became parties to the covenant, and the committee managed to question many states objectively about their record on civil and political rights. Many states are lax about reporting, and about fifty have adhered to the covenant but not consented to the right of individual petition. The United States is among this group, having ratified the covenant with significant and controversial reservations in 1992. The committee has seemed most influential when dealing with states committed to human rights but that perhaps need some prodding to conform to all international obligations.

Committee on Economic, Social, and Cultural Rights (CESCR)

The International Covenant on Economic, Social, and Cultural Rights first authorized the Economic and Social Council (ECOSOC) to supervise the application of the treaty. State parties are obligated to submit a report periodically on state action to implement the covenant. This provision allows some members of ECOSOC to comment on state behavior under the treaty, even if the state making the comments is not a party to the treaty. The United States falls into this category.

In 1979 ECOSOC created the Committee of Governmental Experts to process these state reports. The committee was unable to encourage serious attention to treaty obligations,[15] and in 1985 ECOSOC replaced it with the Committee of Individual Experts. Since it first met in 1987, this committee has proved more dynamic than its predecessor. Initially taking a cooperative or positive approach toward reporting states, it tried to get states to establish national guidelines for minimum standards of food, shelter, health care, and the other rights found in the socioeconomic covenant. Rather than attempt to create a global standard, it prodded states to think seriously about what the covenant meant in their jurisdictions. The focus was on "the extent to which the most disadvantaged individuals in any given society are enjoying a basic minimum level of subsistence rights."[16] Alone among the UN's monitoring mechanisms, the Committee of Individual Experts accepts written submissions from NGOs and intergovernmental organizations (IGOs). But most human rights NGOs have traditionally not been active regarding these socioeconomic rights.[17] The most visible advocacy groups, such as Amnesty International and Human Rights Watch, concentrate primarily on civil and political rights. Most NGOs working for adequate food, clothing, shelter, and health care conduct humanitarian or development programs rather than human rights campaigns. Thus, NGOs, such as Oxfam, have been oriented more toward practical results in a country based on humanitarian concerns and less toward lobbying for socioeconomic rights through the Committee of Individual Experts. However, change is under way as a human rights approach to development is gaining ground with both UN development agencies and private organizations.

Despite praise for its independence, effective procedures, and constructive recommendations, several problems have plagued the committee. It has functioned in a political vacuum, since few powerful actors have wanted to devote diplomatic efforts to helping implement socioeconomic rights internationally. It considers only a few state reports each year because reports are late and are delayed at the request of states. This UN effort to monitor and improve state behavior pertaining to socioeconomic rights is a long-term project.

Other Supervising Committees

Four other human rights treaties create supervising committees of individual experts that function in similar ways: the Committee on the Elimination of Racial Discrimination (CERD), the Committee on the Elimination of Discrimination against Women (CEDAW), the Committee against Torture (CAT), and the Committee on the Rights of the Child (CRC). They have generated some influence on states that are parties to the treaties but not enough to merit detailed study here. The CERD and its parent treaty against racial discrimination, for example, help outline the gap between normative theory and behavioral reality and thus serve as a template for similar procedures. More than 130 states are parties to this human rights treaty, and much rhetoric has been expended within the UN system about the evils of racial discrimination. Every four years state parties are required to submit comprehensive reports regarding compliance with treaty provisions, with briefer updating reports due every two years. Such reports serve as the primary input into the committee's work. Yet many states routinely fail to comply, thus making it difficult for the committee to fulfill its mandate. Only a few states permit their citizens to bring a private petition to CERD claiming violation of the treaty, as specified under the treaty's Article 14. These kinds of problems are common to the overall monitoring of human rights treaties. State reports are filed late and are not always serious. Private petitions do not often lead to clear protection of rights within a reasonable time. The media do not often cover proceedings or outcomes. Consequently, various proposals to improve the fractured UN system of monitoring human rights treaties have had little impact. Proposals to merge the supervising committees have not led to significant change, although the committees do now meet to try to coordinate their efforts.[18]

NONGOVERNMENTAL ORGANIZATIONS

Member states may be the principal building blocks in the foundation of the United Nations, but NGOs have been especially active and influential in human rights and humanitarian matters.[19] Precision is difficult when gauging the influence generated by NGOs on human rights. In a speech at the United Nations just after the adoption of the Universal Declaration in December 1948, Eleanor Roosevelt aptly predicted that "a curious grapevine" of private action would spread the ideas contained in the declaration far and wide.[20] That image in fact captures the reality, because human rights have a momentum and life of their own in a sprawling and tangled sort of way.

The most general analytical problem, then, is that the impact of NGOs becomes intertwined with governmental and other influences, often making it impossible to say where NGO influence leaves off and governmental influence begins. If Amnesty International lobbies for new standards and monitoring mechanisms concerning torture, and if states in the General Assembly approve these ideas in treaty form, it is difficult to pinpoint what has occurred because of whose efforts.[21] What appears clear is that international relations, as it relates to human rights, is shifting away from a system in which states are the only important actors, to a more complex order in which NGOs and other civil society actors sometimes play important roles as well.

Transnational networks of state and nonstate actors were crucial to two developments of potential significance for human rights—namely the ICC and the treaty banning antipersonnel land mines. Further, NGOs have been active on a wide range of human rights issues at the United Nations. They probably have generated influence for the promotion and protection of human rights. Their cumulative impact has been such that various states have opposed UN consultative status for some of the more assertive NGOs. In 1991 Cuba and some Arab states temporarily prevented Human Rights Watch from obtaining consultative status via the Economic and Social Council. NGOs want that status because they gain the right to circulate documents and speak in UN meetings. During the Cold War several human rights NGOs were excluded from consultative status by communist and developing governments, a practice that continues only somewhat attenuated. At the 1993 Vienna World Conference on Human Rights, the tensions between governments and human rights NGOs were evident. Some governments feared the influence that might be generated by NGOs, perhaps by releasing damaging information to the world press. At the earlier 1968 UN International Conference on Human Rights in Tehran, NGOs had participated in the intergovernmental sessions. In Vienna in 1993, governments denied NGO participation in the official meetings but agreed to a separate, parallel NGO conference. This formula was followed at the 1995 Beijing Fourth UN World Conference on Women and at the 2002 World Conference against Racism, Racial Discrimination, Xenophobia, and Related Intolerance in Durban, South Africa. In 1995 Freedom House, like Human Rights Watch (also based in New York), was temporarily denied consultative status by a coalition of states, including democracies such as India and the Philippines, that disliked the rating system used by Freedom House. Had NGOs generated no influence, governments would not try so hard to keep them out of UN proceedings.

States that cannot completely suppress human rights NGOs often try in other ways to limit their influence. Toward the end of 2007 the government of Vladimir Putin tried to obstruct the activities of a number of Western-based NGOs active on human rights in Russia. He adopted a variety of policies that reduced individual freedom, and his crackdown on human rights NGOs, both domestic and international, was part of that orientation. Had human rights NGOs generated no influence in Russia on behalf of the UN's International Bill of Human Rights, it is unlikely that Putin, as president or as prime minister, would have devoted so much effort to harassing them. He also blocked effective election monitoring by the Organization on Security and Cooperation in Europe (OSCE) in 2008 and regained notoriety after regaining the presidency and then prosecuting Pussy Riot—a feminist punk rock group that harshly criticized him.

In 2012 Egypt raided the offices of several human rights NGOs and shut down those of Freedom House and the National Democratic Institute. Officials of these NGOs were arrested, and many were prevented temporarily from leaving the country in spite of the supposed opening of the Arab Spring's largest country. At the same time, the Universal Periodic Review of the Human Rights Council created substantial space for NGOs, especially local and national ones, to externalize their concerns about Egypt's human rights situation. [22]

The influence of NGOs in human rights and humanitarian affairs stems, in part, from their ability to bring growing resources to bear. As we saw earlier and as Ian Smillie and Larry Minear have noted, "humanitarianism has become a big business."[23] To be sure the "humanitarian marketplace" unleashes an "NGO scramble,"[24] as various organizations compete for publicity and fund-raising in some cases.

The International Committee of the Red Cross

In armed conflicts and public emergencies stemming from human-made disasters, the politics of providing emergency relief to civilians is usually more complicated than in natural disasters, and the task of effectively protecting war victims may be impossible, depending on the security situation and the stance of a government or political authorities. By law and by tradition, the International Committee of the Red Cross (ICRC) coordinates international relief in international wars on behalf of the International Red Cross and Red Crescent Movement. The 1949 Geneva Conventions for victims of war, and the supplemental 1977 Protocol I, give the ICRC a preferred position for this task, especially since protecting powers (neutral states appointed by the fighting parties for humanitarian tasks) are rarely named anymore. The Security Council has affirmed the right of civilians to international assistance in such wars, and belligerents have a general legal duty to cooperate with neutral relief efforts. Protocol I from 1977 states clearly that starvation of civilians is not legally permitted in warfare and that belligerents are not legally permitted to attack objects vital to the survival of the civilian population.

The ICRC is a private agency whose sources of funds are summarized in Table 8.1. The agency is specifically recognized in public international law and by the General Assembly, which has accorded the ICRC observer status along with the Federation of Red Cross and Red Crescent Societies. For large-scale relief the assembly prefers that UN organizations, along with NGOs, be the primary operational agents of humanitarian assistance and that the ICRC adopt a monitoring role.[25] Nonetheless, the ICRC continues with its own relief program stressing the norms of independence, neutrality, and impartiality. In Somalia in the early 1990s, the ICRC remained to play a central role in relief, even after the Security Council authorized the use of force to deliver that relief. In other violent situations, as on the Indian subcontinent in 1971, the ICRC worked closely with the UN system in monitoring the delivery of food and other socioeconomic relief to East Pakistan/Bangladesh. More recently in Syria, the ICRC worked closely with the Syrian Arab Red Crescent to try to bring assistance to civilians caught in harm's way. In such situations accomplishments were accompanied by heavy restrictions from the authorities. Over forty staff members of the Syrian Red Crescent, for instance, had lost their lives by 2015.

What is now called the Red Cross and Red Crescent Movement is either disorganized or decentralized; the ICRC does not fully control national Red Cross or Red Crescent units and certainly not their international federation. Long-standing suggestions concerning how to improve the broad international response to civilian needs in violent situations remain just suggestions.[26]

Other NGO Roles

In addition to urging member states and UN staff to do more to promote and protect human rights, NGOs also perform other important functions. A major aspect of advocacy centers on information-related activities. NGOs document human rights violations and engage in fact-finding.[27] They produce educational materials and give expert testimony for national and international bodies. Large numbers of NGOs had consultative status and participated in meetings of the Commission on Human Rights, which is also now true of the Human Rights Council. They

TABLE 8.1 TOP FINANCIAL CONTRIBUTORS TO THE
INTERNATIONAL COMMITTEE OF THE RED CROSS, 2013

Governments
United States
United Kingdom
Switzerland
European Commission
Sweden
Norway
Germany
Netherlands
Canada
Australia
Japan

Source: Annual Report 2014, pp. 578–579, https://www.icrc.org/en/document/ICRC-annual-report-2014

submit private complaints about patterns of gross violations of human rights to the UN system. Their information is officially used in most of the monitoring of such agencies of the UN system as the Human Rights Committee; Committee on Economic, Social, and Cultural Rights; Committee on the Elimination of Racial Discrimination; Committee on the Elimination of Discrimination against Women; Committee against Torture; Committee on the Rights of the Child; and others. Some NGOs have played influential roles behind the scenes in the adoption of General Assembly resolutions concerning human rights.

Just as private human rights groups have had an impact on national policies, so have they influenced UN proceedings. A formal UN vote or document, reflecting the policy of a majority of governments, may have started or been advanced by one or more NGOs. For instance, NGOs advanced the UN Declaration on Minorities and the Declaration on Indigenous Peoples, although states voted for it. Approximately one thousand NGOs attended the 1993 World Conference on Human Rights, conducting their own proceedings and engaging in the specific criticisms that state delegations at the conference had agreed to avoid. Just as private groups have teamed with the U.S. Congress to improve human rights reporting by the Department of State,[28] NGOs have teamed with interested governments to improve rights activity through the United Nations. Just as a group of secular and faith-based private groups pressured Congress to do more about the violation of religious freedom in the world, so these and other groups constantly pressure states at the UN to take action for human rights. If human rights NGOs had been absent at the UN, it is unlikely that the world organization's record would be as good as it is. That record is disappointing in the view of these same NGOs, but some positive steps have been taken.[29]

Analyses of intergovernmental bodies, UN organizations, independent commissions, and NGOs often lose sight of the individuals who also make a difference. John P. Humphrey of Canada, the first UN director-general of human rights, undoubtedly influenced the content of the Universal Declaration of Human Rights. Other secretariat personnel have advanced ideas or proposals that eventually were accepted by governments voting in UN bodies. Executive heads of such UN organizations as UNICEF, the WHO, the UNHCR, the ILO, and UN Women have clearly taken action on their own for children's health care, the right to adequate health care in general, refugee rights, labor rights, and the rights of women. All this is apart from the human rights activity of the Office of the Secretary-General itself.

Most of the monitoring entities created by treaty have been staffed by individuals acting in their personal capacity. Most have been truly independent from their governments as well as serious about and dedicated to human rights. U.S. ambassador to the UN Samantha Power argues that the tireless effort of one private person, Raphael Lemkin, led to the creation of the genocide convention.[30] She also credits the individual efforts of U.S. senator William Proxmire for helping get the United States to accept that treaty. Similarly, Canadian foreign minister Lloyd Axworthy helped lead the coalition of states and NGOs to adopt the Ottawa Treaty that banned antipersonnel land mines.

Analytically, one can focus on the overall UN system and analyze "the UN," or on state foreign policy at the UN, or on subnational actors, such as NGOs and working groups, or on individuals as individuals. The level of analysis can affect the conclusions that one draws about which actor exercises significant influence.[31] The proliferation of actors complicates the examination and assessment of politics at the UN but also brings additional perspectives to defining, understanding, and advancing human rights. The NGOs and independent experts of the third UN are very much a part of the changing landscape of contemporary human rights protection.

NOTES

1. Beth A. Simmons, *Mobilizing for Human Rights: International Law in Domestic Politics* (Cambridge: Cambridge University Press, 2009); and Thomas Risse, Stephen C. Ropp, and Kathryn Sikkink, eds., *The Power of Human Rights: International Norms and Domestic Change* (Cambridge: Cambridge University Press, 1999).

2. Ted Piccone, *Catalysts for Change: How the UN's Independent Experts Promote Human Rights* (Washington, D.C.: Brookings Institution, 2012).

3. Rosa Freedman, *The United Nations Human Rights Council: A Critique and Early Assessment* (New York: Routledge, 2013), 111. See also Bertrand G. Ramcharan, *The Human Rights Council* (London: Routledge, 2011).

4. Paulo Sergio Pinheiro, "Being a Special Rapporteur: A Delicate Balancing Act," *International Journal of Human Rights* 15 (2011): 169.

5. Ibid., 168.

6. Ted Piccone, *Catalysts for Change: How the UN's Independent Experts Promote Human Rights* (Washington, D.C.: Brookings Institution, 2012).

7. Alex Bellamy, "A Chronic Protection Problem: The DPRK and the Responsibility to Protect," *International Affairs* 91, no. 2 (2015): 225–244.

8. "Human Rights in Palestine and Other Occupied Territory: Report of the UN Fact-Finding Mission on the Gaza Conflict," A/HRC/12/48, September 25, 2009, http://www2.ohchr.org/english/bodies/hrcouncil/docs/12session/A-HRC-12-48.pdf, para. 1883.

9. Michael Posner, "U.S. Response to the Report of the United Nations Fact-Finding Mission on the Gaza Conflict," September 2009, http://www.state.gov/documents/organization/153510.pdf.

10. Richard Falk, "The Goldstone Report: Ordinary Text, Extraordinary Event," *Global Governance* 16 (2010): 173–190, 173.

11. Richard Goldstone, "Reconsidering the Goldstone Report on Israel and War Crimes," *Washington Post* (April 1, 2011), http://www.washingtonpost.com/opinions/reconsidering-the-goldstone-report-on-israel-and-war-crimes/2011/04/01/AFg111JC_story.html.

12. See Tom Farer, Dinah PoKempner, Ed Morgan, Richard Falk, and Nigel S. Rodley, "The Goldstone Report on the Gaza Conflict: An Agora." *Global Governance* 16, no. 2 (2010): 139–207; and Adam Horowitz, Lizzy Ratner, and Philip Weiss, eds., *The Goldstone Report: The Legacy of the Landmark Investigation of the Gaza Conflict* (New York: Nation Books, 2011).

13. Michael O'Flaherty, "The United Nations Human Rights Treaty Bodies." In *Human Rights Diplomacy: Contemporary Perspectives,* ed. Michael O'Flaherty Zdzisław Kędzia, Amrei Müller, and George Ulrich (Leiden, the Netherlands: Martinus Nijhoff Publishers, 2011), 157.

14. Helen Keller and Geir Ulfstein, eds. *UN Human Rights Treaty Bodies: Law and Legitimacy* (Cambridge: Cambridge University Press, forthcoming 2015),

15. David Harris, "Commentary by the Rapporteur on the Consideration of States Parties' Reports and International Cooperation," paper presented at the Implementation of the International Covenant on Economic, Social and Cultural Rights Symposium, *Human Rights Quarterly* 9, no. 1 (1997): 149.

16. Philip Alston and Bruno Simma, "First Session of the UN Committee on Economic, Social and Cultural Rights," *American Journal of International Law* 81, no. 3 (1987): 750.

17. Scott Leckie, "An Overview and Appraisal," *Human Rights Quarterly* 13, no. 3 (September 1991): 566–567.

18. Philip Alston and James Crawford, eds., *The Future of UN Human Rights Treaty Monitoring* (Cambridge: Cambridge University Press, 2000), and Anne Bayefsky, *The UN Human Rights Treaty System: Universality at the Crossroads* (Ardsley, N.Y.: Transnational Publishers, 2001).

19. Melissa Labonte, *Human Rights and Humanitarian Norms, Strategic Framing, and Intervention* (London: Routledge, 2013); Linda Polman, *The Crisis Caravan: What's Wrong with Humanitarian Aid?* (New York: Henry Holt, 2010); and Rachel M. McCleary, *Global Compassion: Private Voluntary Organizations and U.S. Foreign Policy since 1939* (Oxford: Oxford University Press, 2009).

20. Quoted by William Korey, *NGOs and the Universal Declaration of Human Rights: "A Curious Grapevine"* (New York: St. Martin's Press, 1998), 9. See also Bertrand G. Ramcharan, *Contemporary Human Rights Ideas* (London: Routledge, 2008).

21. Peter R. Baehr, "The General Assembly: Negotiating the Convention on Torture," in *The United Nations in the World Political Economy,* ed. David P. Forsythe (London: Macmillan, 1989), 36–53; and Steven Hopgood, *Keepers of the Flame: Understanding Amnesty International* (Ithaca, N.Y.: Cornell University Press, 2006).

22. Laura Landolt, "Externalizing Human Rights: From Commission to Council, the Universal Periodic Review and Egypt," *Human Rights Review* 14, no. 2 (2013): 107–129.

23. Ian Smillie and Larry Minear, *The Charity of Nations: Humanitarian Action in a Calculating World* (Bloomfield, Conn.: Kumarian, 2004), 8.

24. Andrew Cooley and James Ron, "The NGO Scramble: Organizational Insecurity and the Political Economy of Transnational Action," *International Security* 27, no. 1 (2002): 5–39.

25. David P. Forsythe, "Choices More Ethical Than Legal: The International Committee of the Red Cross and Human Rights," *Ethics & International Affairs* 7 (1993): 131–152.

26. Thomas G. Weiss and Larry Minear, eds., *Humanitarianism Across Borders: Sustaining Civilians in Times of War* (Boulder, Colo.: Lynne Rienner, 1993).

27. Tina Rosenberg, "The Body Counter: Meet Patrick Ball, a Statistician Who's Spent His Life Lifting the Fog of War," *Foreign Policy* (March/April 2012).

28. David P. Forsythe, *Human Rights and U.S. Foreign Policy: Congress Reconsidered* (Gainesville: University Press of Florida, 1988).

29. Rodney Bruce Hall and Thomas J. Biersteker, eds., *The Emergence of Private Authority in Global Governance* (Cambridge: Cambridge University Press, 2002).

30. Samantha Power, *"A Problem from Hell": America and the Age of Genocide* (New York: Basic Books, 2002).

31. See further Kenneth Waltz, *Man, the State, and War: A Theoretical Analysis* (New York: Columbia University Press, 1954, 1959, 2001).

CHAPTER 9

Theories of Change

THE DYNAMICS OF ACTIVITY on human rights at the UN represent an important evolution of world politics. Representatives of states, the UN bureaucracy, and nongovernmental organizations (NGOs) have come together to advance the cause of human dignity in multifaceted ways. Can we theorize why this activity has been what it has been? And can we project what directions this activity will take in the future?

Two related views are relevant. The first focuses on the notion of knowledge. Ernst Haas argues that if private communities of knowledge come to an agreement on human rights, this agreement eventually will produce a policy consensus in the public sector.[1] When this public consensus emerges, the United Nations and other intergovernmental organizations (IGOs) become empowered to take action for human rights, which could mean complete and not just partial change at the world organization. For example, if most human rights groups could prove that civil and political rights were necessary for economic growth or that socioeconomic rights were necessary for stable democracy, such private understandings would eventually affect public policy through the UN and would lead to dramatic change.

The second and related view emphasizes learning. George Modelski returns to the ideas of Immanuel Kant to suggest that those who speak for states are in the process of learning a commitment to human rights, especially to the civil and political rights making up democracy.[2] In this view, historical evolution shows expanded learning of the benefits of democracy—whether in terms of human dignity or in terms of international peace. This chapter explores the dimensions of change at the UN related to human rights and applies these notions of knowledge and learning to the International Criminal Court (ICC), the value of democracy, and the importance of development to human dignity.

THEORETICAL CONSIDERATIONS

If Haas's view is correct about the state of knowledge in epistemic communities, several generalizations emerge. First, if all or most private groups active on human rights agreed on particulars, this consensus of knowledge should eventually inform public policy in such a way that the United Nations would be mandated by governments to take more authoritative and effective action for human rights. We may see a paradigm shift. Even the World Bank, which long sought to avoid the "political" matter of human rights, now says that economic growth should be pursued with attention to "good governance." The World Bank and its supporters have concluded— at least for now—that at least some authoritarian models of economic growth do not work very well. In fact, good governance—rule of law, transparency, market-oriented policies—has essentially been defined as the opposite of what authoritarian Third World and Soviet bloc countries did in the 1960s, 1970s, and 1980s. Clearly, these approaches have substantial and positive human rights dimensions.

However, knowledge about human rights is not so much scientific knowledge as moral judgment. Achieving widespread agreement on morality is more difficult than on empirically supported science. Even within one country with a dominant culture, private groups differ over such human rights issues as abortion, the death penalty, health care, and adequate nutrition. Getting private groups to agree that children are better off if vaccinated is relatively easy, as most societies do not disagree with vaccination programs that have proved beneficial. (Taliban executions of health personnel working to eliminate polio nonetheless indicate that members of many societies fear various vaccination programs on the basis of religion or concern about negative health considerations.) Getting private circles of opinion to agree that internationally recognized human rights should be applied in all cultures and situations is far more difficult as the knowledge is hardly scientific. Not all medical experts agree that health care should be treated as a human right. Not all medical personnel agree that abortion should be legal. They may agree on the technical process of how to perform an abortion, for that is based on science. But they disagree on whether abortion should be legal, for that is based on moral judgment. Moral judgment is greatly affected by varieties of opinion because moral argument cannot be easily proved or disproved.

Not everyone will necessarily be better off if rights are applied. If repressive governments respect civil and political rights, many if not most of them will lose power. This may usher in a period of disorder and economic decline. The former Soviet Union is a clear example and may help explain why Russia has often backed authoritarian rule. The disorder in Libya, Syria, Mali, and the Central African Republic are more contemporary examples. In repressive China, many persons have been advancing economically, since state-driven macroeconomic growth (stimulated by an expanding private sector) has averaged around 10 percent annually for over two decades. Many do not believe that rights, especially political rights, would do anything but interrupt this beneficial process in China. Spectacular economic growth has been achieved in Singapore since the 1970s, but without full civil and political rights. Important religious circles in Islamic nations believe freedom of religion and gender equality would hurt their societies.

Even actors that generally seek to protect rights do not insist on the application of rights in every situation. Many Western private groups do not press the issue of the practice of human rights in Saudi Arabia, a stable ally in the Middle East. They also deferred judgment about a military coup in Algeria that prevented the election of a fundamentalist Islamic party. Some of these groups believe on moral grounds that Western access to oil or blocking fundamentalist Islam justifies repressive governments. Elections in such places as Sri Lanka and Iraq have led to illiberal governments that discriminate against minorities and commit other rights violations. A commitment to human rights, such as democratic political participation, is therefore less a matter of scientific proof of inherent progress and more a matter of moral and political choice in context.

Beyond the essential distinction between scientific knowledge and moral judgment in private networks, the public policy consensus across governments at the UN concerning human rights is incomplete, to say the least. The formal consensus is broad, but the real consensus is thin and weak. In other words, human rights treaties are widely accepted in law and widely violated in practice.[3]

Inconsistency is to be expected. The Security Council may authorize humanitarian intervention in Somalia, but at roughly the same time it will fail to sponsor decisive action in similar situations in Liberia or Sudan, Rwanda, or Burundi. The council may set the stage for the use of force in Iraq, at least partially in the name of persecuted civilians, but it will be lethargic about similarly appalling conditions in the Democratic Republic of the Congo. Learning of "correct" policies thus has been more formal than substantive. As long as actual consensus remains weak, human rights activity will not lead to systematic and authoritative protection by the United Nations, broadly defined.

THE INTERNATIONAL CRIMINAL COURT: KNOWLEDGE AND LEARNING

The issue of the UN and international courts provides a good application of the Haas theory of change, linked to knowledge, and the Modelski theory of change, linked to learning.[4] Under the Modelski theory the question is raised whether states, acting through the world organization, have shown a propensity to learn that international relations can be governed by a humane rule of law. Are states learning that they will be more secure, and their citizens better off, if there is a permanent international criminal court? To use semantics from Haas, have private groups used their knowledge to push states into agreement on the demonstrable truth that just as all national societies have institutionalized procedures for criminal cases, so, too, should international relations?

The creation and operation of the International Criminal Court, while technically not a UN body, illustrates that learning varies. After a decade of efforts by NGOs and like-minded public officials, a global network of five hundred civil society actors, called Coalition for the International Criminal Court, generated the shared norms and political pressure necessary to prod states to begin serious negotiations on a permanent international court.[5] In addition to prodding by the General Assembly and certain subsidiary bodies, such as the International Law Commission, 160 member states met in Rome during June and July 1998 to finalize a treaty on international criminal justice.

Against difficult odds, the United Nations Conference of Plenipotentiaries on the Establishment of an International Criminal Court resulted in the Rome Statute, which entered into force four years later upon ratification by sixty states (July 1, 2002). By early 2003, the first set of judges (who sit in their individual capacity rather than as state representatives) had been elected and took up their positions in The Hague. Canada's Philippe Kirsch was the court's first president, and Argentina's Luis Moreno Ocampo was its first chief prosecutor. He has since been replaced by the current chief prosecutor Fatou Bensouda of Gambia. The UN had thus helped establish a permanent international criminal court to try individuals for certain egregious human rights violations, the first such court in history,[6] although the wartime UN War Crimes Commission had begun the process.[7] The ICC's jurisdiction is complementary to states in that, unlike the two ad hoc criminal tribunals for the former Yugoslavia and Rwanda, states retain the primary responsibility to respond to allegations of mass-atrocity crimes. Through the independent prosecutor, who, like the judges, is elected by states that have accepted the Rome Statute, the court becomes active only if a state is unwilling or unable to investigate such allegations and, if warranted, prosecute. By 2015 over one hundred states, including most NATO members, had accepted the Rome Statute and hence the ICC's jurisdiction and authority, which was encouraging for the protection of fundamental human rights. Yet important states such as the United States, Israel, Russia, China, India, and others still reject the court's jurisdiction.

The United States led an active opposition up until 2005 by concluding agreements with states in which they agreed not to turn over each other's citizens to the court. In 2002 the United States delayed extending deployments of UN blue helmets until the Security Council granted it a one-year renewable exemption from the court's jurisdiction. Also in 2002, the U.S. Congress passed legislation, subsequently signed into law by President George W. Bush and informally dubbed "The Hague Invasion Act," which among other sections authorized the United States to use force to liberate any American citizen detained in relation to the ICC. In many ways 2002 represented the last major effort by the United States to kill the ICC. By 2005 Washington decided to utilize the court when dealing with others, as in Sudan, and the Obama administration continued that policy—without, however, seeking U.S. Senate consent to the Rome Statute. The United States claimed that it feared politically motivated and false charges against its citizens by other states, a rogue prosecutor who would engage in the same behavior, and legal exposure to its citizens that was unacceptable, given the extensive security operations taken in the name of the UN or NATO. Furthermore, the Rome Statute was vague about the crime of "aggression," and so signing onto the court potentially could limit U.S. use of military force without UN authorization. Washington's opposition to the court could also be more ideological than pragmatic. Given that, for example, the prosecutor could not proceed with charges against a U.S. citizen unless such proceedings had been approved by a special panel of judges of the court, it seems that Washington was more interested in defending a more absolute conception of state sovereignty and national independence on doctrinaire grounds than in resisting potential and unwarranted dangers to its citizens.[8]

Theoretically, the ICC still could come into play when and if the United States were to select targets and weapons that might contradict international humanitarian law and thus constitute war crimes or crimes against humanity. The latter concept pertains to a systematic attack on civilians, whether in peace or war. Such charges about illegal U.S. policies arose in regard to military strikes on a TV station and the Chinese embassy in Belgrade in 1999, and the use of cluster bombs in civilian areas in Afghanistan in 2001. The International Tribunal for the former Yugoslavia (ICTY) prosecutor undertook a preliminary investigation about certain U.S. military operations in or over Serbia but declined to pursue the matter further. Decisions pertaining to bombing targets and other tactical matters were never independently investigated either by the U.S. Congress or federal courts. It was precisely in such situations that the ICC might become operational and threatening with regard to U.S. citizens, if the state in which events occurred was a party to the court's statute. Either the state where the alleged crime took place or the state of the defendant would have to be a party to the Rome Statute for the ICC to have jurisdiction. When the United States engaged in armed conflict in Iraq in 2003, neither U.S. nor Iraqi citizens were subject to the court's jurisdiction since neither state had exercised the necessary consent. But British policymakers and military personnel were. Thus, theoretically a state, such as France, could file a complaint in the ICC about systematic policy in Iraq against a British national but not against an American or an Iraqi. As events played out, the United Kingdom itself investigated a number of war crimes allegations against its troops in Iraq. The ICC thus was not involved.

The court is a historical milestone in the evolution of efforts to improve the protection of important human rights. The ICC can be "pulled off the shelf" if states do not exercise their responsibility to seriously follow up on allegations of certain mass-atrocity crimes. Future events will determine whether it will actually play an active and important deterrent or enforcement role in international relations. While the ICC is accepted by the likes of Britain, France, Italy, and Canada, it continues to be viewed with reservation by the United States and other important states, such as Russia and China.[9] Indeed, two scholars of realist orientation warned that the ICC was an example of "international idealism run amok."[10] Yet the Bush administration utilized the ICC for Darfur in 2005, and the Obama administration for Libya in 2011.

Powerful states are not the only ones with complicated relationships with the ICC. By 2007 the governments of Uganda, the Democratic Republic of the Congo, and the Central African Republic had authorized the ICC to conduct investigations in their states regarding possible genocide, crimes against humanity, or war crimes. In reality, these governments were using the court to try to go after troublesome figures in their countries. For example, Uganda wanted help in suppressing Joseph Kony and his rebel movement, the Lord's Resistance Army, but at the same time, the Museveni government did not want any ICC investigations into its own human rights violations, which included tolerance for murderous attacks on gay people. In 2005 the Security Council instructed the prosecutor to inquire into bringing charges against certain individuals in Sudan because of policies in the Darfur region that might constitute one or more of the crimes covered by the ICC's statute. In 2008 Moreno Ocampo sought an arrest warrant for Sudanese president Omar Hassan al-Bashir, along with two of his colleagues in the government, and in March 2009 an arrest warrant was issued. Thus, the court was increasingly busy, despite tepid support or opposition by a number of important states.

Although 20 African countries were among the founders of the ICC and 34 of the court's 122 state parties today are African, a communiqué from the African Union in 2008 asking the Security Council to suspend the court's proceedings against al-Bashir (see Chapter 4) suggests that, at least in that situation, a number of African states prioritized diplomatic relations rather than judicial proceedings. In 2012, however, Mali refused to allow al-Bashir to enter that country to attend an African Union (AU) meeting, which was moved to a different location. This showed that an ICC arrest warrant could at least complicate politics as usual. China, on the other hand, allowed al-Bashir into that country for two state visits, even though China had declined to veto the council resolution referring the Sudanese situation to the ICC. In 2015 al-Bashir was attending an AU summit in South Africa when the Southern Africa Litigation Center filed suit in South African courts, asking that al-Bashir be arrested by the South African authorities and transferred to The Hague. The South African Supreme Court initially ruled that al-Bashir not be allowed to leave while it considered the merits of the case. The South African government claimed that al-Bashir had diplomatic immunity and allowed him to leave the summit, which struck another blow to the political viability of the ICC.

The African Union and many African states appear to no longer be as sympathetic to the ICC as they were at the outset.[11] In 2011 the African Union was not supportive of referring the Libyan situation to the ICC, once again giving the official reason of preferring diplomatic approaches to the conflict between the Gaddafi regime and its opponents. Furthermore, a number of African governments expressed some concern when the ICC became deeply involved in Kenya's politics, investigating a number of high politicians for playing a role in ethnic violence. The ICC prosecutor was forced to withdraw or dismiss charges against Kenyan officials in 2014 because of a lack of cooperation by the government and evaporating evidence. In the words of Chief Prosecutor Bensouda, her pursuit of the case had been "undermined by a relentless campaign that has targeted individuals who are perceived to be prosecution witnesses, with threats or offers of bribes, to dissuade them from testifying or persuade witnesses to recant their prior testimony."[12] All of the ICC's current cases have arisen out of Africa, which leads to charges of bias, even though many cases were self-referrals. The Security Council may have referred situations to the ICC, but its member states have not seen fit to enforce arrest warrants or punish governments who do not fulfill their obligations to arrest and transfer indicted suspects.

Member states appear to be just muddling through on this issue. Incomplete agreement has led to the piling up of actions at the UN without any clear and firm overall position on authoritative and effective criminal courts. Learning—to the extent that it occurred—is clearly not universal. Some member states, especially those that contemplate use of their militaries in armed conflict, are reluctant to create a judicial organ to which they might, as a last step under the principle of complementarity, have to turn over their citizens—for example, for charges of violations of the laws of war. Neither George W. Bush nor Barack Obama nor the U.S. Congress has fully supported the ICC. The United States has not learned the advantages of having a permanent mechanism for international criminal prosecution, even though it originally proposed such a mechanism after World War II and has called upon the court to render judgments about Sudan and Libya; nor is it clear that knowledge compels movement in this direction.

Emotive or romantic nationalism may trump expert knowledge about the benefits of international criminal justice. So may tough-minded realism. In general, state learning pertaining to international criminal law showed differences and inconsistencies. States approved ad hoc criminal courts now and then, but at the end of 2015 only just over one hundred countries were parties to the Rome Statute of the International Criminal Court. Optimists were buoyed by the extent of state support, while pessimists pointed out that almost half of the UN members were not sure they wanted to be under the jurisdiction of a UN standing criminal court. State actors might feel the need to show a response to mass atrocities by creating ad hoc courts, but some of the same states might still eschew the costs of a decisive involvement that would curtail the atrocities and punish those responsible. States might agree in theory that individual punishment for atrocities is a good idea, but in particular situations they might like the freedom to negotiate and strike deals for impunity with war criminals. Peace and justice can be sought through both diplomacy and criminal proceedings.

LEARNING AND DEMOCRACY

The relation between knowledge, learning, and UN human rights activity can be summarized by acknowledging the difficulty in achieving a broad consensus about human rights among private networks because the issue deals more with morality than with science. Without NGO and expert agreement about human rights specifics, the consensus among governments on human rights and public policy will remain incomplete. The situation is one of varied learning and incomplete change. The UN acts more for human rights now than before, but it still falls short of being fully systematic and institutionalized as well as authoritative and effective.

For example, it is illustrative to examine the question of whether states are learning, on the basis of cumulative knowledge, a commitment to liberal democracy (meaning popularly elected governments that are rights-protective). The UN certainly now advocates democratic development. Some evidence seems encouraging. Immanuel Kant suggested that over time liberal democracies would become more numerous. A wave of democratization from about the mid-1970s to the early 1990s seemed to verify that Kantian view. Francis Fukuyama argued in the early 1990s that right-thinking persons had to necessarily conclude that liberal democracy was the best way to respect individuals and limit governmental power. Thus, the development of the norms of liberal democracy represented the "end of history," at least in political theory, and a liberal democrat became the last "political man."[13]

If it holds, a historical trend toward liberal democracy would suggest a growing acceptance not only of civil and political rights but of economic and social ones as well. Almost all democracies, except the United States, endorse the latter as well as the former. Thus most liberal democracies are also social democracies that recognize a human right to basic health care and other socioeconomic public goods as provided by the state.[14] The core economy remains capitalist, but an extensive welfare state leads to the label of social democracy. Within the empirical democratic trend, however, there are illiberal democracies that are genuinely supported by majority opinion but do not protect basic rights. Serbia under Slobodan Milošević and Croatia under Franjo Tudjman were clear examples. No more than about one third of UN member states have truly stable or consolidated liberal democracies. Moreover, earlier waves of democracy suffered setbacks, which could happen again. Many states with elected governments still have strong militaries not fully controlled by elected leaders. And the results of elections in some former Soviet republics, as in other parts of the world, might even suggest nostalgia for authoritarian government, which seems to have evolved to mimic democracy and civil society. The new authoritarianism has the trappings of democracy (elections and a few civil society institutions) but with government control,[15] including censoring the media. The government determines who has access to higher education and lucrative business dealings, and the legal system is not independent and can be highly politicized. All of this bodes ill for actualizing UN human rights norms domestically.

Clearly there are parts of the world where political elites articulate a counter narrative to the UN's international bill of rights, which includes norms supportive of liberal and social democracy. Indeed, Stephen Hopgood has argued that we are now in "the endtimes of human rights" because there is more pushback than ever from non-Western countries that are more and more powerful on the world's economic and political stages.[16] Chinese leaders associate liberal democracy with the West and a Western imperialism that divided and exploited China in the past. Furthermore, Chinese leaders are aware that the Russian effort under Mikhail Gorbachev to liberalize the Soviet Union led to the disappearance of that state from the world scene. By 2014–2015 the Chinese leadership was clearly asserting that internationally recognized human rights, and especially genuine democracy, were threats to stability in China.[17] Vladimir Putin's Russia is characterized by growing authoritarianism, suppression of dissent, and the harassment or even murder of advocates for genuine democracy. It is increasingly clear that Moscow sees itself as a noble alternative to Western decadence and that internationally recognized human rights run counter to its dominant view, which pushes authoritarian nationalism blessed by the Russian Orthodox Church.[18] Likewise in the Middle East, Egypt's new dictator, Abdel Fattah al-Sisi, sees attention to internationally backed human rights as troublesome meddling in a country destined by culture to be ruled by various modern pharaohs. Almost seven decades after the General Assembly adopted the Universal Declaration, UN-defined human rights are still rejected by several important states. A dominant local narrative blocked learning that favored the UN's version of human rights.

Despite the rejection of human rights by various key states, the advantages of liberal democratic government have received increased recognition in general and over time. Respect for civil and political rights has grown, albeit in a zigzag or dialectal rather than a linear progression. This learning had been enhanced, at least temporarily, by the various failures of authoritarian communism in Europe and similar models among developing countries. But in many countries ruled by newly democratic governments, major obstacles to the consolidation—meaning stabilization and maturation—of democracy remain. To state the obvious, elections do not a democracy make, and long-term commitments are necessary to consolidate fledgling states.[19] Perhaps most important, economic growth was slow or nonexistent, and the benefits of the economic system were widely perceived as inequitable. New democratic governments, confronted with particularly daunting economic problems, continue to struggle to create the socioeconomic context that would sustain a new and fragile democracy. Particularly in Latin America, but elsewhere as well, democracy has been created but not necessarily consolidated. Indeed, as Thomas Carothers argues, "Of the nearly 100 countries considered as 'transitional' in recent years, only a relatively small number—probably fewer than 20—are clearly en route to becoming successful, well-functioning democracies or at least have made some democratic progress and still enjoy a positive dynamic of democratization."[20] In a number of countries, something of a hybrid regime—combining democratic practices with enduring authoritarian institutions—has emerged and often appears quite stable.[21] Were civil and political rights being learned systematically, or was democratic learning frequently followed by a re-learning of the supposed advantages of authoritarianism?

HUMAN RIGHTS AND DEVELOPMENT

Despite resolutions from the General Assembly and Commission on Human Rights about socioeconomic rights and a claimed right of development, the early history of the United Nations witnessed few concrete efforts to translate this diplomatic rhetoric into policy. For much of the UN's history, government policymakers and decision makers made little effort to devise programs that promoted economic growth in developing countries while integrating internationally recognized human rights. As a former head of the UN Centre for Human Rights documented, rhetoric about human rights and planning for economic growth were kept in separate compartments at the UN.[22] The World Bank (the Bank), UN Development Programme (UNDP), UNICEF, the WHO, the WFP, and other UN organizations went about their traditional business without much regard for the language of international human rights.

This situation began to change in the late 1980s and early 1990s. Important opinion leaders in developed countries became dissatisfied with the record of attempts to achieve economic growth through authoritarian governments. The record in Africa was especially poor. Political changes, particularly in Latin America but to a lesser extent elsewhere, gave rise to more democratic governments in developing countries. Seeking macro-national economic growth without attention to human rights could lead to the marginalization of sectors of society. Even the World Bank, which had long claimed that human rights factors were "political" and therefore not within the Bank's mandate, began to reconsider its stance—albeit under the confusing concept of "good governance." This could and sometimes did entail attention to civil and political rights, even though competing interpretations abounded. Although the Bank still sought to avoid taking a stand about democracy at the national level, it did endorse participatory development. Within the concept of social assessment, it made judgments about the extent of popular participation in development projects.[23]

As part of this broad shift by various actors toward incorporating human rights considerations into "development," the UNDP created indices trying to measure "human freedom" and "human development" in a socioeconomic context, as illustrated in Table 9.1. The effort began in 1990 under the guidance of the late Pakistani economist Mahbubul Haq,[24] and the annual *Human Development Report* provoked a storm of controversy. Some judged that the UNDP may have exceeded the responsibilities of an international civil service because it touched on human rights and domestic jurisdiction. Developing countries had long been sensitive to secretariat officials' passing judgment about how states measured up to international standards. But to its credit, the UNDP stood its ground and even devoted an entire issue to human rights in the *Human Development Report 2000: Human Rights and Human Development*. The UNDP abandoned its freedom index, but like the World Bank, the agency talked more about participatory development. It endorsed an active role for citizens' groups in development projects. This approach entailed defense of civil rights such as freedom of speech and freedom of association.

The UNDP continues to experiment with related indices, including the Inequality-Adjusted Human Development Index (which takes into account the average achievements of a country related to health, education, and income as well as how well those achievements are distributed among the population) and the Gender Inequality Index (which measures gender inequalities related to reproductive health, empowerment, and economic status). Development experts note that gender

TABLE 9.1 HUMAN DEVELOPMENT INDEX, 2013

Top Ten	Bottom Ten
Norway	Mozambique
Australia	Guinea
Switzerland	Burundi
Netherlands	Burkina Faso
United States	Eritrea
Germany	Sierra Leone
New Zealand	Chad
Canada	Central African Republic
Singapore	Democratic Republic of the Congo
Denmark	Niger

Source: Based on information from the UN Development Programme found in the 2014 Human Development Report available at http://hdr.undp.org/en/content/table-1-human-development -index-and-its-components.

discrimination remains a principal obstacle to human development; the Gender Inequality Index therefore measures women's access to health care, education, seats in parliaments, and participation in the labor force. The UNDP seeks to reconceptualize development beyond simple economic indicators to include the many dimensions of human dignity and well-being. As is demonstrated in Part 3, the three UNs strive for sustainable human development, not only as a means of maintaining international peace and security, but so as to improve the quality of life for the world's more than 7 billion inhabitants.

A WEB OF NORMS RESULTING IN CHANGE?

Most situations in which human rights are respected are produced by national conditions, with only secondary influence from international factors.[25] This axiom contains considerable truth but can be overstated. The relaxation of the Soviet grip on Eastern Europe in the late 1980s was the key factor in unleashing local human rights forces. By 1996 more IGO, NGO, and state policies operated in support of international human rights in that region than ever before. In some cases, as in Haiti in 1994, international factors were decisive, at least in the short run, as the United States engineered the departure of a long-standing dictator. The international normative context for human rights had definitely changed for the better, at least temporarily after the Cold War.

A theory of transnational change and human rights is relevant to our discussion here. According to *The Power of Human Rights*, a transnational advocacy network made up of both private and public actors can sometimes bring about progressive change with regard to rights of personal integrity.[26] A merger of international and national actors can, over time, institutionalize human rights norms pertaining to summary execution, torture, and mistreatment and other fundamental civil rights referred to collectively as rights of personal integrity. Hence in this view domestic private groups, acting in tandem with foreign actors of various sorts, can bring effective pressure for rights-protective change on repressive governments. In this theory, UN norms and UN actors play important roles, allowing for considerable variation in which actors in the transnational coalition exert the most influence on behalf of human rights: NGOs, domestic private groups, officials of international organizations, officials of states. The sum total of the efforts of these various and shifting actors accounts for progressive change. While the rise of "the rest" (especially the emerging countries of the Global South) may call into question some of these advances and slow the pace of change, they do not necessarily signal "the endtimes of human rights."

This theory about the importance of human rights norms and discourse over time is linked to transnational pressure, which eventually binds states in their own stated commitments to human rights. If true, the theory can incorporate incidental knowledge about human rights and help explain change. At the world organization, disagreements about human rights protection abound. We are dealing with moral and political more than scientific knowledge, and states in particular have "learned" a variety of things from experience. Given the legal starting point of sovereignty, the international community of states has come a long way in generating respect for the idea of human rights. If we compare international action on human rights at the League of Nations and at the United Nations, the latter changes seem revolutionary. But all three UNs—states, staff, and relevant nonstate actors—still have a long way to go before achieving the systematic observance of human rights as called for in the Charter "without distinction as to race or nationality, sex, language or religion."[27]

NOTES

1. Ernst B. Haas, *When Knowledge Is Power: Three Models of Change in International Organizations* (Berkeley: University of California Press, 1990).

2. George Modelski, "Is World Politics Evolutionary Learning?" *International Organization* 44 (Winter 1990): 1–24.

3. See further Emilie Hafner-Burton, *Making Rights a Reality* (Princeton, N.J.: Princeton University Press, 2012).

4. Steven R. Ratner and Jason S. Abrams, *Accountability for Human Rights Atrocities in International Law: Beyond the Nuremberg Legacy* (Oxford: Clarendon, 1997); Aryeh Neier, *War Crimes: Brutality, Genocide, Terror, and the Struggle for Justice* (New York: Times Books, 1998); and Sarah B. Sewall and Carl Kaysen, eds., *The United States and the International Criminal Court: National Security and International Law* (Lanham, Md.: Rowman & Littlefield, 2000).

5. Helen Durham, "The Role of Civil Society in Creating the International Criminal Court Statute: Ten Years On and Looking Back," *International Humanitarian Legal Studies* 3 (2012): 8, 3–42.

6. Richard J. Goldstone and Adam Smith, *International Judicial Institutions: The Architecture of International Justice at Home and Abroad* (London: Routledge, 2008); Gary

Jonathan Bass, *Stay the Hand of Vengeance: The Politics of War Crimes Tribunals* (Princeton, N.J.: Princeton University Press, 2000); Steven R. Ratner and James L. Bischoff, eds., *International War Crimes Trials: Making a Difference* (Austin: University of Texas Law School, 2004); and Eric Stover and Harvey M. Weinstein, eds., *My Neighbor, My Enemy: Justice and Community in the Aftermath of Mass Atrocity* (New York: Cambridge University Press, 2004).

7. William Schabas, Carsten Stahn, Dan Plesch, Shanti Sattler, and Joseph Powderly, eds., *The United Nations War Crimes Commission: The Origins of International Criminal Justice*, special double issue of *Criminal Law Forum* 25, nos. 1 and 2 (2014).

8. In general, the United States pledges abstract support for international law but consistently seeks to chart a unilateralist path unencumbered by legal obligation to international courts and other authoritative international organizations. See Shirley Scott, *International Law, US Power: The US Search for Legal Security.* (Cambridge: Cambridge University Press, 2012).

9. David P. Forsythe, "The United States and International Criminal Justice," *Human Rights Quarterly* 24, no. 4 (2002): 974–991.

10. John Goldsmith and Stephen D. Krasner, "The Limits of Idealism," *Daedalus* 132, no. 1 (2003): 47–63.

11. Yvonne M. Dutton, *Committing to the Court: Rules, Politics, and the International Criminal Court* (London: Routledge, 2013).

12. "Kenya: International Court Seeks Two Suspected of Bribing Witnesses," *New York Times*, September 11, 2011.

13. Francis Fukuyama, *The End of History and the Last Man* (New York: Free Press, 1992).

14. Amartya Sen, *Development as Freedom* (New York: Knopf, 1999); and Cass R. Sunstein, *The Second Bill of Rights: FDR's Unfinished Revolution and Why We Need It More Than Ever* (New York: Basic Books, 2004).

15. Freedom House, "Freedom in the World 2014," accessed October 11, 2014, http://freedomhouse.org/report/freedom-world/freedom-world2014?gclid=CJqhmPubpcE CFQMT7Aod1CoA8Q#.VDl1Yo10yYN.

16. Stephen Hopgood, *The Endtimes of Human Rights* (Ithaca, N.Y.: Cornell University Press, 2013).

17. Malcolm Moore, "China's Human Rights Situation 'Worst in Decades,'" *The Telegraph*, March 2, 2014, http://www.telegraph.co.uk/news/worldnews/asia/china/10670520 /Chinas-human-rights-situation-worst-in-decades.html.

18. Mark Galeotti and Andrew S. Bowen, "Putin's Empire of the Mind," *Foreign Policy*, April 21, 2014, http://foreignpolicy.com/2014/04/21/putins-empire-of-the-mind.

19. Paul Collier, *Wars, Guns, and Votes: Democracy in Dangerous Places* (New York: HarperCollins, 2009); and Roland Paris, *At War's End: Building Peace After Civil Conflict* (Cambridge: Cambridge University Press, 2004).

20. Thomas Carothers, "The End of the Transition Paradigm," *Journal of Democracy* 13, no. 1 (2002): 9.

21. Terry Lynn Karl, "The Hybrid Regimes of Central America," *Journal of Democracy* 6, no. 3 (1995): 73–86; David Collier and Steven Levitsky, "Democracy with Adjectives: Conceptual Innovation in Comparative Research," *World Politics* 49, no. 3 (1997): 434–435; and Larry Diamond, "Thinking About Hybrid Regimes," *Journal of Democracy* 13, no. 2 (2002): 21–35.

22. Theo van Boven, "Human Rights and Development: The UN Experience," in *Human Rights and Development*, ed. David P. Forsythe (London: Macmillan, 1989), 121–135.

23. Internal World Bank documents increasingly dealt with human rights. See, for example, C. Mark Blackden, "Human Rights, Governance, and Development: Issues, Avenues, and Tasks," October 10, 1991, 17 plus attachments. For an overview, see David P. Forsythe, "Human Rights, Development, and the United Nations," *Human Rights Quarterly* 19, no. 2 (1997): 334–349.

24. Khadija Haq and Richard Ponzio, eds., *Pioneering the Human Development Revolution: An Intellectual Biography of Mahbubul Haq* (Delhi: Oxford University Press, 2008).

25. Jack Donnelly, "Human Rights in the New World Order: Implications for Europe," in *Human Rights in the New Europe*, ed. David P. Forsythe (Lincoln: University of Nebraska Press, 1994), 7–35.

26. Thomas Risse, Stephen C. Ropp, and Kathryn Sikkink, eds., *The Power of Human Rights: International Norms and Domestic Change* (Cambridge: Cambridge University Press, 1999).

27. David P. Forsythe, *Human Rights in International Relations* (Cambridge: Cambridge University Press, 2000), chapter 3.

PART THREE

SUSTAINABLE HUMAN DEVELOPMENT

CHAPTER 10

Theories of Development
at the United Nations

POVERTY PLAGUES A SUBSTANTIAL portion of humankind. Over a billion people are going hungry today, and half the population in the Global South is undernourished. Nearly 3 billion people struggle to survive on less than $2 a day, not to mention the nearly 1 billion who have less than $1.25. Dire as these statistics are, the situation is improving. In its quest to mitigate the human condition, the UN has made poverty eradication one of its highest priorities.

Development is central to alleviating poverty and is inextricably linked to peace and security and the actualization of human rights. It is also linked both positively and negatively to international economic processes and structures and global environmental conditions. How the UN came to pursue sustainable human development through concerted efforts by the first, second, and third UN is another important dimension of its story.

Development has long dominated much of the discourse and practice throughout the UN system, in part because the very concept may be interpreted differently by different people or groups. To some it may mean economic growth defined in macroeconomic terms, such as increases in gross domestic product (GDP), import-export figures, or levels of industrialization. To others, development includes human and social elements, such as the ability of individuals and communities to meet their basic needs through their own initiative. It may also mean sustainability, in that economic growth and the ability of humans to meet their basic needs should not deplete natural resources to the extent that those resources become unavailable for future generations or in other ways impede future generations from satisfying their basic human needs and values.

In consequence of these multiple views, the international community of states is ever challenged to successfully arrive at strategies for pursuing agreed-upon notions of development. The UN role in promoting economic and social development has evolved to include forging compromises, setting agendas, creating norms, and building relative consensus among diverse constituencies. After all, none of these conceptions or definitions of development is mutually exclusive. For example, a certain amount of prosperity is inherent to economic development in macroeconomic terms and necessary for individuals to achieve housing, food, health care, and a basic education. At the same time, healthy and educated individuals are necessary to achieve macroeconomic growth.

These complex, evolving, and controversial definitions of development and, therefore, the different approaches to it, are not necessarily shared by all parts of the UN. Some member states of the first UN may champion neoliberal economic development policies ("free" markets and limited government regulation) as a way to generate growth and the efficient use of resources. Others may support state-led growth, or economic and environmental regulation to protect against the excesses of unbridled capitalism. Agencies within the second UN attempt to bridge the differences among member states and provide them with quality information that hopefully will shape their domestic and international policies. The private actors of the third UN are also part of the mix, usually as actors on the ground trying to build capacity and alleviate extreme poverty or advocating for policy changes at home and in the headquarters of the various agencies of the UN system.

We begin by reviewing the historical evolution of the UN's development work in the context of changing theories of development. As Kenneth Dadzie suggests, the world organization has gone through roughly four phases in dealing with the issue of development,[1] which reflect the evolution of economic thought since World War II. The transition from one phase to another represents an intellectual shift as regards the causes of underdevelopment and the appropriate policies for combating poverty and allowing individuals to fulfill their potential.

PHASE ONE: NATIONAL STATE CAPITALISM (1945–1962)

At the first UN, early approaches to development were characterized by the ideological divide between the United States and the Soviet Union, between capitalism and communism. Since the member states of the West were in a more dominant position at the UN, development focused on liberal reconstruction and development policies after World War II.[2] The concept of development, as it has come to be embraced in UN discourse and practice over the past seven decades, entered quickly through the back door in the form of national economic development, which was endorsed by the UN through decentralized economic liberalism.

This position was informed by the economist John Maynard Keynes. In this view states would pursue a large, private, for-profit sector based on extensive property rights, while the national government would manage the economy at the macro level. This approach recognized the dangers of unregulated capitalism, which gave rise to inequality, exploitation of labor, and harsh living conditions under industrialized capitalism, not to mention the indignities suffered during the Great Depression. At the same time it recognized the benefits generated by markets and capitalism. It also realized that the immediate postwar world economy was in shambles and that a certain amount of multilateral management was needed to restore stability. The Keynesian synthesis sought to harness markets to the development interests of states while acknowledging the state's role in promoting economic growth and full employment, with social protections. This synthesis reflected the initial dominance of Western capitalist states in the world organization and the weakness of communist states in voting and other UN arrangements along with their poor economic records. Most of the Global South still existed as colonies that were subject to the choices made by powerful governments in the West, and especially their respective colonial capitals. The communist countries of the Eastern bloc as well as China were largely frozen out of the discourse.

Development at the second UN was generally thought of primarily in national economic terms, and the emphasis was on lending through the World Bank and other types of foreign assistance, through either state bilateral policies or the UN Expanded Programme of Technical Assistance (EPTA). The goal was to create national infrastructures that would provide the basis for economic growth led by the private, for-profit sector. Although the EPTA was symbolically important for establishing a role for the UN in the development area, its expenditures were nominal. Beginning with an initial operating fund of $20 million in 1951, the program grew only moderately over the next decade. The United States reduced its contribution from 60 percent downward over the years, and other rich countries failed to take up the slack.[3]

At the UN during this time, the global economic situation was seen and portrayed as neutral or benign, although prone to periodic instability. If "proper" national decisions were taken, national macroeconomic growth would eventually occur over time. The role of international organizations centered on international infrastructure, such as agreements on monetary exchange rates, communications, transport, and the like. States were obligated by the UN Charter to cooperate internationally on development matters and to report to the United Nations. But the principal UN organs, including the Economic and Social Council (ECOSOC), were not seen as having a major operational role in advancing development. ECOSOC and the General Assembly were viewed as legitimating and coordinating mechanisms. In part, this approach reflected the wariness of the Western capitalist states in affording too great a role to first UN bodies with broad membership and majority voting.

From the very outset of the UN, the important member states preferred the World Bank (the Bank) and the International Monetary Fund (IMF).[4] The Bank and IMF were created prior to the United Nations proper at a conference in Bretton Woods, New Hampshire, in 1944 by the members of the U.S.-led United Nations alliance.[5] Hence, they are often referred to as the "Bretton Woods institutions." These agencies, although officially or technically part of the UN system from 1945, by design make their decisions entirely independently from ECOSOC and the General Assembly, with proportional voting as determined by funding

Forty-four United Nations and associated nations meeting in Bretton Woods, New Hampshire, to discuss monetary stabilization as an aid to postwar trade. The United Nations Monetary and Financial Conference was held in July 1944. (UN PHOTO 97323)

provided mostly by the assembly's member states (the World Bank also raises money in capital markets). The differences in resources give the reader an idea of first UN preferences. While in recent years the rest of the UN system (UN regular budget plus peacekeeping) spent some $12 to $15 billion annually, the World Bank Group in 2015 managed a loan portfolio totaling nearly $223 billion.

This arrangement has given the United States and other wealthy states not only control over decisions taken in the name of the Bank and the IMF but also significant influence in selecting the executive heads of these two agencies. The president of the Bank has always been American, and the managing director of the IMF has always been European—a practice that continued with the election of Christine Lagarde from France as the IMF's managing director in 2011 and American Jim Yong Kim to the Bank's presidency in 2012. True, European and U.S. governments do not necessarily see eye to eye on many development approaches, with the United States having more of a libertarian streak. For example, the two often disagree on the extent of government ownership of economic enterprises and regulations. The United States is less Keynesian than most states in Europe; however, all developed Western countries believe in the core virtues of markets, entrepreneurship, and private property. This was and is true even in Scandinavian states that also believe in extensive economic regulation, with much emphasis on social and community objectives in addition to personal freedoms.

Among many decisions at the Bank, the major donor countries agreed in 1960 to create the International Development Association (IDA), the so-called soft-loan window for developing countries. In large part this was a response to an early 1950s initiative by developing countries, which had used their growing numbers to vote into being the Special United Nations Fund for Economic Development (SUNFED) to augment technical assistance activities of the second UN with long-term low-interest loans aimed at building infrastructure. The word *special* was added after officials recognized that without it the acronym was UNFED (which actually would have been more accurate, since Western donors never put re-sources into it and were committed to the Bretton Woods institutions). The move to create such a fund was opposed by major donors. Washington first objected on grounds that the American people could not support such a capital fund while underwriting a war in Korea. Besides, the United States had just pumped over $13 billion—approximately $110 billion in current dollars—into sixteen European countries under the Marshall Plan. But even after 1953 and the end of the Korean War, the United States continued its opposition. In the last analysis, SUNFED was stillborn for lack of resources. Developing countries demonstrated that their increasing numbers at the UN could be translated into General Assembly and ECOSOC resolutions, but such initiatives amounted to little without financial resources.

Almost from the beginning, regional development bodies were created to en-courage economic growth and different regional approaches: the economic com-missions for Europe (ECE in 1947); for Asia and the Far East (ECAFE in 1947, which later became ESCAP for "Asia and the Pacific"); for Latin America (ECLA, created in 1948, which later became ECLAC to include the Caribbean); for Africa (ECA in 1958); and for Western Asia (ESCWA, in 1973).[6] Some of these came to be quite important in the evolution of ideas and norms, as was true of ECLA in the Western Hemisphere. Some of these commissions never achieved their promise, and the one in Europe was eclipsed by other regional economic arrangements, such as the European Economic Community (EC), which evolved into the Eu-ropean Union (EU). These regional commissions were created within ECOSOC, which had been mandated the responsibility of coordinating the social and eco-nomic work of the UN itself and the specialized agencies.

Coordination was vexing, however, as specialized agencies were set up as au-tonomous organizations, and many preceded the founding of the UN proper. The International Labour Organization (ILO), for example, had been carried over from the League of Nations. Others, such as the World Meteorological Or-ganization (WMO), the International Telecommunications Union (ITU), and the Universal Postal Union (UPU), were even older. But then a host of new agen-cies, such as the World Health Organization (WHO), the Food and Agriculture Organization (FAO), the UN Educational, Scientific and Cultural Organization (UNESCO), as well as the Bretton Woods institutions, were also created as part of the postwar UN system. While de jure part of that system, the Bretton Woods in-stitutions are de facto autonomous. Each of these and other agencies had its own chartering legal instrument, assessed dues system for funding, executive head, and separate headquarters building.

States could join or withdraw from certain institutions independently of their membership in the United Nations itself. At one point the United States withdrew from both the ILO and UNESCO to protest certain policies—and for ideological reasons, in the case of UNESCO.[7] Such withdrawal did not affect its membership in the UN or U.S. voting in the Security Council and General Assembly. Although ECOSOC was nominally to be the coordinator of all UN economic and social organizations, the legal and financial arrangements of the specialized agencies ensured their independence. They report to the General Assembly through ECOSOC, but these two of the UN's six principal organs do not really control the specialized agencies.[8] So, from the beginning, the way that the UN was set up ensured a shotgun approach to development. The primary idea (promoting national economic liberalism with minimal international involvement beyond basic infrastructure) was to be accomplished collectively through the work of a constellation of agencies, funds, and programs.

Moreover, numerous UN specialized agencies indicated a "theory within a theory." Beyond the UN's central idea of encouraging states to make the "right" decisions to achieve economic growth, the theory of functionalism supposedly explained how to achieve international peace. Functionalism, as developed by David Mitrany, purported to lead to world peace not by a frontal assault on aggression and other "political" questions but by sidestepping these issues and concentrating on the separate elements of development.[9] A functional approach to development—concentrating on labor issues, children's issues, science, education, culture, agriculture, and so on—would not only advance economic and social development but also build strong operational networks so that states would learn cooperation in these functional areas. This functional cooperation would eventually spillover into other areas, even political ones, thereby allowing international agreement on sovereignty, aggression, self-defense, intervention, and the other subjects entailed in international peace and security.

So, in this early UN approach to development, the Keynesian theory of economic growth, through state-regulated capitalism and international economic liberalism, gave guidance on economic and social matters. And the theory of functionalism purportedly explained how international state capitalism could contribute to peace; and it made possible a totally decentralized UN development system whose components often function separately rather than as a team, as we see later in this volume.[10] However, actual attempts to apply the theory of functionalism, and its variant, neofunctionalism, to development, particularly in Europe, led to reconsideration of functionalism as a path to peace.[11] First, development proved to be as political and contentious as any other issue. Building infrastructure through specialized agencies involved both governmental decisions and controversy. Second, "spillback" as well as "spillover" could occur. The controversies over monetary policy and other technical issues led to such intergovernmental conflict that further advances of an economic nature could be halted or even set back for a time—a phenomenon that was again evident during the 2014–2015 Eurozone crisis. Third, political issues beyond the immediate development process intruded on policymaking. In Western Europe, Cold War considerations spawned by power struggles between the NATO and Warsaw Pact countries affected decisions about building Europe. Policy decisions about what would become the European Union were not well explained by a functionalist theory that posited regional technical issues as dominant. Global great-power struggles proved as important, or more important, than functionalist theory applied regionally.

The early UN approach to poverty and economic development in many countries was to reiterate for the globe the standard recipe of economic liberalism understood as national state-capitalism informed by the Keynesian compromise discussed earlier. The need for some international institutions did not detract from the central propositions of capitalist theory, namely that the role of public agencies was mainly to provide the infrastructure for private entrepreneurship and manage the economy using regulation and macroeconomic policies.

PHASE TWO: INTERNATIONAL
AFFIRMATIVE ACTION (1962–1981)

By 1961 the first UN had expanded to 104 member states, more than double the original 51 members. The increase in membership mostly was due to the decolonization process. One consequence was that the new majority of UN members, most of whom were confronted with an unequal global economic playing field, preferred more transnational public regulation of private economic activity. This regulation was intended to benefit the poorer countries by redressing global imbalances and leveling the playing field. Even the World Bank, which did not completely share the new orientation to development found in the General Assembly and ECOSOC, began to rethink the causes of underdevelopment and poverty. The automatic nature of development through traditional capitalist recipes and national economic liberalism was questioned.

The institutional turning point was the beginning of the preparations for the UN Conference on Trade and Development (UNCTAD).[12] Beginning in the mid-1960s, UN development activity focused on persistent income inequalities between the rich North and the poor South, between developed and developing countries, between industrialized and Third World countries. The 1960s were also designated the first UN Development Decade. The origins of this reorientation lay primarily in the thinking of Raúl Prebisch and his colleagues in ECLA, who argued that the international capitalist system was stacked against poorer countries. Their economic worldview, which is often perceived to have been based in Marxist critiques of capitalism, focused on the structural dependence created and reinforced by the unequal playing field between grossly unequal participants in the capitalist world system. Thus, whereas the Bretton Woods agencies were based on the view that economics and economic development could be largely separated from politics, the postcolonial states saw their economic condition as the product of the colonial policies of the past and the power politics of the present, which created an uneven economic playing field.

The charters of the Bank and IMF specify that they are to be nonpolitical, but the new developing countries saw them as inherently political. On the basis of their experience mainly in the Western Hemisphere, Prebisch and his colleagues saw the countries of the "periphery" trapped in relationships of dependency with regard to the "core"—namely, the wealthy developed countries at the center of world trade and finance. Since, for example, the price of finished goods exported by the rich continued to rise, while the price of most raw materials exported by the poor fluctuated greatly and tended to decline over time, the global terms of trade were inimical to the interests of most countries in the Global South. Those societies caught in conditions of dependency could not accumulate capital and grow without external infusions of capital from the North. This view supposedly explained the growing gap between the rich and poor countries. It also was diplomatically supported by the Soviet Union and communist bloc states which, certainly in the 1950s and 1960s, sought to undermine capitalism as an economic mode of production.

In the view of critics of global capitalism, the General Agreement on Tariffs and Trade (GATT) governed an inherently discriminatory trading system that helped make the rich richer and the poor poorer. The GATT was geared toward liberalizing trade in manufactured goods (exports from the core) but did little to liberalize trade in primary products and agricultural products (exports from the periphery). Developing states were placed at a structural disadvantage, as their exports were discriminated against while at the same time they were forced to abide by liberal trade rules for manufactured goods. This led to deteriorating terms of trade, poverty, and debt—in a word, dependency.

The many variants of "dependency theory"[13] proved attractive, not only to Latin Americans, but also to the growing number of newly independent and former colonial territories that attributed underdevelopment to the legacy of colonialism and the structure of the capitalist system. In 1964 the General Assembly created UNCTAD as a permanent voice of the Third World within the UN system. With Prebisch as its first secretary-general, it advocated a restructuring of global economic relations to the advantage of the poorer countries. The views UNCTAD championed were largely synonymous with the views of the Group of 77 (G77, the UN caucus of developing countries, which over time has grown to some 130 members but maintains its original label because of its historic significance).[14]

During a series of conferences in the mid-1970s, the G77 formulated its agenda for restructuring the global political economy.[15] The main thrust came during the Sixth Special Session of the General Assembly in late spring 1974, at which the Declaration and Programme of Action on the Establishment of a New International Economic Order (NIEO) was adopted, but with significant reservations by many Western countries and the United States in particular. The demands of the declaration were wide-ranging but can be classified into four broad themes:

economic sovereignty, trade, aid, and participation.[16] These issues were raised time and again in various ways and in various settings during the remainder of the decade. The North-South battle lines quickly became unambiguously drawn. A number of "global ad hoc conferences"[17] focusing on specific issues, such as population and food, and the more broad-based Conference on International Economic Cooperation, which met in December 1975 and June 1977 under the auspices of the French government, provided additional forums for expanding at the global level what some called "dialogue" between North and South but would more accurately be labeled "invective." Neither side seemed willing to listen, and neither seemed to hear or wished to hear what the other was saying.

The General Assembly majority presented a demand for a New International Economic Order intended to modify the fabric of economic relations between the Global North and South. The NIEO was supposed to be made up of a series of treaties that would greatly regulate transnational economics and redistribute power and wealth. Specific measures on trade, investment, transnational corporations, and official development assistance were informed by the notion that wealth and resources should be authoritatively redistributed rather than allowing the "invisible hand" of the market to determine that distribution. Markets were seen by most governments in the Global South as inherently biased toward and too easily manipulated by the wealthy and the powerful.

The short-lived fate of the NIEO was sealed by changes in the political and economic environment. The majority of states at the UN might call special sessions of the General Assembly and have the votes to create revolutionary new schemes on paper to alter the distribution of economic power. But even with the newly found (and temporary) power of the Organization of Petroleum Exporting Countries (OPEC) as a result of the 1973–1974 oil crisis, the Global South was unable to persuade the North of the wisdom of such economic restructuring. In the wake of the 1973 war in the Middle East between Israel and principally Egypt, OPEC was able to implement an oil embargo for a time (to several countries) and a more general slowdown in oil deliveries (to the rest of the oil-importing countries). But in the last analysis OPEC was not able to force the United States and other Western countries to alter their support for Israel, and OPEC was not able to maintain its unity. More generally, OPEC was unable for long to use oil as a weapon in the larger struggle to compel rich countries to radically transform international economics so as to close the gap between developed and developing countries. On balance, the impact of OPEC's actions was more profound in the Global South, which depended heavily on petroleum to fuel its agricultural and industrial development, than the Global North. The major international oil companies took advantage of the situation to greatly enhance their wealth, and the United States and the rest of the West maintained the power to resist demands for a New International Economic Order and adapted their economies to the increased price of oil.

The second UN increased technical assistance to the poorer countries through the UN Development Programme (UNDP), created in 1965.[18] The UNDP reflected a merger of the earlier EPTA and the stillborn SUNFED. Still, the UNDP and

TABLE 10.1 UN DEVELOPMENT MILESTONES
WITH A STRONG ECOLOGICAL FLAVOR, 1948–1982

1948	International Union for the Conservation of Nature and National Resources (IUCN)[a]
1964	International Biological Program[a]
1968	Intergovernmental Conference on Biosphere[a]
1970	Scientific Committee on Problems of the Environment (SCOPE)/ International Council of Scientific Unions (ICSU)[a]
1972	UN Conference on the Human Environment (UNCHE) Environmental Forum
	Limits to Growth published by the Club of Rome
	UN Environment Programme (UNEP)[a]
1973	Convention for the Prevention of Pollution by Ships (MARPOL)
1974–1981	UN Conference on the Law of the Sea
1976	UN Conference on Human Settlements (HABITAT)
1979	World Climate Conference
	Convention on Long-Range Transboundary Air Pollution
1980	Committee of International Development Institutions on the Environment (CIDIE)[a]
	World Conservation Strategy (IUCN/UNEP)
	Convention on Conservation of the Arctic Living Resources
1982	Convention on the Law of the Seas

[a] Denotes the establishment of the body or commencement of the activity.

other agencies refused to yield their independence. The so-called Jackson Report of 1969, named after its primary drafter, Sir Robert Jackson, called for more centralization of development efforts in the UN system but fell mostly on deaf ears.[19] Funding for the new UNDP was an important factor for improved development in many countries, but its resources remained decidedly meager. The UNDP is funded entirely through voluntary contributions and the top contributors are the United States, Japan, and Norway. With roughly $5 billion, its focus is on technical assistance and pre-investment studies, because donor countries prefer the World Bank and the IMF as the principal vehicles for multilateral development finance.

In a significant change and recognizing the importance of sustainable development, during Phase Two the UN increased its activities on behalf of the environment, as indicated in Table 10.1. In 1972 the UN sponsored a global ad hoc United Nations Conference on the Human Environment (UNCHE) in Stockholm, which led to the United Nations Environment Programme (UNEP).[20] This was largely a new initiative from certain developed countries, mostly European and led by Sweden, concerned that the pursuit of economic growth was causing fundamental harm to the environment. This "green movement"—the color came later—was not always welcomed by poorer countries. Many saw a focus on the environment as interfering with their development. As such, the environmental movement was often viewed in the Global South as a form of neocolonialism, because industrialized countries had grown rich without giving much consideration to environmental destruction, whereas developing countries were supposed to face a different cost structure in pursuing growth while protecting the environment. Thus, some developing countries did not see environmental protection as an inherent part of development but rather as an impediment to a development defined in strictly economic terms.

Leaders of the G77, especially China and India, did not lead on development-related issues, unless by "leadership" one means leading the opposition. These states saw environmental damage as being caused primarily by the capitalist development of just seven countries (G7), and now these same countries were trying to pass the cost of their development on to the South.[21] They believed that the G7 caused most of the damage and therefore should pay for environmental protection. These and other developing countries could be brought on board only for certain green treaties, such as the 1987 Montreal Protocol (designed to protect the ozone layer), with the carrots of compensatory financing for making costly changes.[22]

Meanwhile, the IMF and the World Bank were stymied by the lack of rapid economic progress according to prevailing doctrines in many parts of the Global South. The Bank continued to emphasize export-led development, meaning precisely the emphasis on participation in the world economy that Prebisch and UNCTAD thought so detrimental to the developing countries under the rules of the game established by GATT. So, the World Bank, in particular, was not on the same page as UNCTAD and the UN's other development organizations. A number of Asian states, dubbed at the time the "East Asian Tigers," began to make rapid economic gains through, among other policies, emphasis on investment and trade. Singapore, for example, in a period of about twenty years, surpassed Britain, its former colonial master, in per capita income. But these tigers, such as South Korea, also continued various forms of "statism," similar to how agriculture was treated in the rich countries, by protecting key national industries from full global competition. Such states as Japan had already proved successful at export-led economic growth through an industrial policy that amounted to state subsidies for, and other benefits to, selected national industries. There was extensive trade, but it was not free trade in the sense of pure economic competition. Clearly East Asia was not Latin America. A certain type of authoritarian development worked well in such places as China, Singapore, Malaysia, South Korea, and Taiwan. In the latter two cases, authoritarian development gradually became more democratic.

The East Asian Tigers notwithstanding, the Bank and the IMF continued to press for policy changes in developing countries in light of the low rates of economic growth in Africa and some other parts of the Global South. Increasingly the World Bank was concerned about how noneconomic factors like corruption and cronyism could affect rates of economic growth. According to its charter, as noted, the Bank was a nonpolitical organization, but it came to adopt the policy that it should take into account factors that might not be strictly economic but that did affect economic growth.

Especially after Robert McNamara, former U.S. secretary of defense and head of the Ford Motor Company, became its president in 1967, the Bank began to target poverty within developing countries. McNamara was committed to dramatically increasing the resources available for fighting poverty. Between 1969 and 1973, the Bank provided twice the amount of assistance as in the preceding five years. The Bank's poorest members were given special consideration, and the Bank began to make loans with a view to changing things at the grass roots. Under McNamara's leadership, development became more than just economic growth. Agriculture, population planning, water supply, pollution control, nutrition, and other problems took center stage on the agenda. By June 1972, lending for agriculture became the single leading sector of the Bank's lending. In his thirteen-year tenure as president, McNamara increased World Bank Group lending twelvefold, from $1 billion to $12 billion. Whether his leadership was a mea culpa for his role in the Vietnam War is still debated.

The World Bank still undertook projects designed to promote macroeconomic growth. Some of these projects, such as funding for large hydroelectric dams, proved enormously controversial, given the displacement of people and destruction of the environment that often occurred. But increasingly the Bank focused on pockets of poverty rather than just macroeconomic growth. The Bank pursued its own version of international affirmative action, but not by focusing on terms of trade and other issues championed by UNCTAD. The Bank made loans at very low interest rates to the poorest of the poor. It made loans and even grants to, for example, poor families in South Asia so that their children could attend schools rather than work as child laborers. Thus, much of the UN system along with the World Bank rethought the prevailing wisdom about economic development—even if they did not necessarily adopt precisely the same revisions. The UN's emphasis was on the overall international economic structure, while the Bank focused more on domestic policies. The Bank's changing views were sometimes seen as progressive, because of the broader focus on social if not political factors, but it was still criticized for a top-down approach and for not consulting enough with the persons affected by its policies.

PHASE THREE: RETURN TO NEOLIBERALISM (1981–1989)

Mainstream economic thinking evolved with the elections of Margaret Thatcher in the United Kingdom and Ronald Reagan in the United States. They were adherents of the writings of Friedrich von Hayek, an Austrian economist who stressed individual freedom and relatively unregulated markets as the path to economic prosperity. An intellectual rival to Keynes, Hayek stressed government regulation and management of the economy as causes of economic stagnation and high inflation. The Keynesian compromise that dominated much of the post–World War II era was replaced with a return to a relatively more laissez-faire, free-market capitalist approach first articulated by Adam Smith, the father of capitalism. Given the power of London and Washington in the world and in the UN system, they also led the charge for a return to classical economic thinking within the world organization. During the 1980s, the United States insisted that the IMF and the World Bank implement structural adjustment programs, conditioning loans on the willingness of developing states to prune back public spending and other public involvement in economic matters. Structural adjustment became code for implementing market reforms and economic liberalization in developing countries seeking multilateral development assistance. During a financial crisis, the IMF made emergency loans contingent on reforms.

The fall of the Berlin Wall in 1989 and the end of the Cold War showed that communism as practiced by the Soviet Union and its allies was bankrupt. The United States and other Western governments had mostly resisted but on occasion been obliged to accommodate Third World economic demands during the Cold War; but after its end there was no viable alternative to Western views on global capitalism—and no political reason for the West to compromise. Thus, a new packaging of an old vision took place, what World Bank economist John Williamson called the "Washington consensus."[23] The IMF and the World Bank are based in Washington—hence, the "Washington consensus," and the consensus represented their policy advice informed by neoliberal principles. It stressed that the private sector and freer markets, not government, would pave the way to more satisfactory development. The new orthodoxy in international economics represented a return to minimal regulation and maximum private entrepreneurship. Governments needed to practice fiscal discipline and tax reform. This time around, the IMF, the World Bank, and the development agencies of the UN system, at least for a while, were mostly in agreement.

The Global South was in a weakened position both economically and politically. Not only had it already demonstrated its inability to force acceptance of the idea of an NIEO, but suddenly the Soviet Union disintegrated as an ideological partner. The G77 fragmented as an effective political force. So, the return of neoliberal economics was complete. After a long silence and toward the end of the period, some UN organizations began to criticize the impact of economic liberalization—the most notable being the United Nations Children's Emergency Fund (UNICEF)'s concern with the impact on children and the Economic Commission for Africa (ECA)'s with the devastating impact on Africa.[24]

Over the first three UN Development Decades—the 1960s, 1970s, and 1980s—development thus had taken on various meanings as the global political context shifted. In these years, development was defined largely in terms of national economic growth as measured in aggregate and per capita income. It also meant seeking national self-reliance for Third World countries. Slowly the added, and somewhat different, value of satisfying people's basic needs while protecting the environment came into mainstream thinking in the 1970s. This definition gradually yielded ground to the incorporation of popular participation and local self-reliance in the satisfaction of basic needs. In this way, development discourse has come to embrace simultaneously three widely shared global values: peace, human security (including human rights), and sustainable human development. And the importance of the private sector became, once again in the 1980s, an essential component of development thinking.

UNICEF holds a press conference as the General Assembly adopts the United Nations Convention on the Rights of the Child. From left to right are James Grant (executive director of UNICEF), Jan Mårtenson (undersecretary-general for human rights and director, United Nations, Geneva), and Audrey Hepburn (goodwill ambassador of UNICEF). November 20, 1989, United Nations, New York. (UN PHOTO 275920/JOHN ISAAC)

PHASE FOUR: SUSTAINABLE DEVELOPMENT AND GLOBALIZATION (1989–PRESENT)

While important member states at the first UN largely pursued neoliberal economic development through the IMF and World Bank (and the World Trade Organization [WTO] after its creation in 1995), the second and third UN were calling attention to a growing problem.[25] Building on the 1972 Stockholm conference mentioned above, the need to simultaneously foster economic development and ensure the availability of resources for future generations, or "sustainable development," was framed by a commission headed by then Norwegian prime minister Gro Harlem Brundtland, who later headed WHO.[26] The dialectical interchange between those stressing the role of markets and free trade versus those emphasizing public regulation and assistance for both social and economic reasons has yet to yield a complete synthesis. These tensions have continued, as the second UN sought to shift its attention to the idea of sustainable development. In 1992 the UN Conference on Environment and Development (UNCED), better known as the Rio Conference or the Earth Summit, was held and produced Agenda 21, a nonbinding, complicated action plan for how member states, UN agencies, and nongovernmental agencies (NGOs) should pursue sustainable development. It also yielded two binding framework treaties on biodiversity and climate change, which would require state parties to pursue negotiations to finalize important details at a future point.

The Earth Summit also yielded a new UN coordinating body, the Commission on Sustainable Development (CSD), whose mandate incorporated ecological concerns and sustainability. Created as a functional commission under the ECOSOC, this first UN intergovernmental body was comprised of fifty-three member states, elected by the ECOSOC on a regional basis. It was responsible for monitoring and reviewing progress on implementing Agenda 21 at the international, regional, and national levels. While designed to be the cornerstone for focusing member states on sustainable development, the CSD was weak in legal authority. Hence, it had a difficult time moving states along the same path. But its name had symbolic importance and was able to keep sustainable development on the international agenda of many member states. At the 2012 United Nations Conference on Sustainable Development (called "Rio+20" because this follow-up meeting took place two decades after the first session in Rio de Janeiro, which had occurred two decades after Stockholm), member states voted to replace the CSD with the High-level Political Forum on Sustainable Development, which held its first session in 2015.

In 1994 Secretary-General Boutros Boutros-Ghali followed up on the Earth Summit when he presented the General Assembly with *An Agenda for Development*.[27] Declaring development to be a fundamental human right, which built on a General Assembly resolution on the same point, he presented a framework that highlighted the interdependence of peace, economy, civil society, democracy, social justice, and environment as indispensable components of the development process. In this regard, he pointed to the special position, role, and responsibility of the United Nations in promoting development in all its aspects but with specific regard to setting priorities and facilitating cooperation and coordination.

The administrations of George H. W. Bush (elected in 1988) and then Bill Clinton (elected in 1992) were less ideological, in terms of devotion to free-market orthodoxy, than the preceding Reagan administration. They also demonstrated a greater commitment to multilateral approaches to complex global problems—in fact, President Bush had served as the U.S. ambassador to the United Nations. The demise of communism and the increase in pragmatism by the Global South also contributed. Still, the tension between regulation, at either the state or the international level, and market-oriented approaches plagued international efforts to promote sustainable development. The same debate occurred within countries. For example, strategies for protecting the environment while achieving economic development could involve market-based solutions. Markets use resources more efficiently and generate the kind of wealth and technologies that in theory could allow societies to concentrate more on environmental protection. From the neoliberal perspective, markets are the solution to environmental problems. From a Keynesian perspective, both government regulations and markets should be brought to bear on environmental problems. From a more engaged "pro-green" environmentalist perspective, unregulated capitalism is the cause of environmental degradation, and the economy should be properly regulated to protect against environmental damage. These competing worldviews about the causes of and the solutions to international problems complicate international negotiations and make compromise difficult.

Neoliberalism was (and still is) alive and well among powerful member states of the first UN. The tension between those who favor a more laissez-faire capitalism and those who see public regulation, especially for environmental sustainability, as a global public good explains the discontinuities in the pursuit of sustainable development. This situation is exacerbated by the lack of coordination between the World Bank, IMF, and WTO, on the one hand, and UN agencies representing sustainable development, ecological, and human rights concerns, on the other. In 1995 GATT was transformed into the World Trade Organization, whose rules endorse free trade and minimal social regulation, whether that regulation is to protect the environment, human rights, or any other concern. So single-minded was the WTO's focus on strictly economic matters that U.S. national legislation to protect endangered sea turtles from certain fishing nets was struck down by a WTO dispute settlement panel as an inappropriate restraint on free trade.[28] The WTO seemed to undermine the multilateral progress made at the Earth Summit; unlike the World Bank and IMF that are at least on paper part of the UN system, the WTO is neither de jure nor de facto part of that system.

Given the number of persons—in industrialized as well as developing countries—left behind by the forces of globalization, the unalloyed advantages of the freer markets and technology-led specialization championed by the WTO have been less than obvious. As this is an important topic in contemporary UN debates, it is worth a lengthy aside because a veritable cottage industry has developed for scholarship on "globalization."[29] Globalization as a concept is useful for understanding contemporary world affairs. However, it has no widely accepted definition. At its core, globalization refers to the movement of goods, services, ideas, and people across national borders in an ever-shrinking world. In this sense it is related to internationalization, interconnectedness, and interdependence.[30] At the beginning of the twenty-first century, global transactions in foreign exchange markets had already reached a level nearly eighty times larger than world trade. The growth in foreign direct investment and portfolio capital flows in developing countries has also outpaced international trade. The expansion of global markets and production and other aspects of the worldwide diffusion of capitalism, however, is only one dimension of the social transformations involved in globalization.[31] The expansion of markets, for example, challenges the state and institutions and has led to the rise of new social and political movements.[32]

Globalization is profoundly changing the face of world politics and the nature of human social interaction and existence, and thus it should also change the face of multilateralism.[33] The nature, structure, geographical pattern, and magnitude of world trade and investment, for example, are in transformation. As the 2008 financial crisis in the United States made clear, globalization also means that serious economic problems in the world's largest economy cause serious economic problems in many other parts of the world. Similarly, the 2012 sovereign debt crisis in Europe threatened to throw the entire world economy into recession, just as the 2015 slowdown in China was unsettling for Asian economies in particular.

Economic liberalization has fostered the diffusion of multinational production networks, capital mobility, and new technologies, which has tended in many cases to place downward pressures on wages and working conditions and otherwise make labor in developing societies increasingly susceptible to global forces. The development of financial markets and institutions, along with the tremendous growth in foreign direct investment, short-term portfolio investment, and other transnational capital flows in developing regions, has dramatically transformed those regions' political and economic climate.

The concept of globalization provides a context within which to frame and understand issues and challenges of global governance and assess the work of international institutions in fulfilling their mandates in promoting human security and sustainable human development. These changes have had an especially hard impact on poorer developing countries in terms of growth, poverty, and income inequality.

The central challenge facing the United Nations is to find ways to use the opportunities inherent in globalization to help people everywhere better cope with its undesirable side effects. Opportunities are related to increased access to information and communications technology, greater public exposure to and awareness of their interdependence and vulnerabilities, and "real-time" social exchanges.

Globalization signaled new wealth and freedom for some, but to others the process seemed uninvited and cruel. This particular tide did not lift all boats. It brought a cornucopia of benefits to many in developed countries, but its wake brought inequality unprecedented in human history.[34] Given such rules, decisions, and emphases within the WTO, its policies received broad and intense negative reactions. The "battle of Seattle" was a highly visible reminder of this reaction, as violent street demonstrations and civil disobedience accompanied the WTO meeting in that city in late 1999. Other kinds of civil disobedience have come to be a feature of WTO, IMF, and Group of 8 (G8, the G7 with Russia, which was suspended in 2014 after Russia's invasion of the Crimea) meetings. The WTO, an important multilateral agency, has approached development in an exceedingly narrow way, as if trade and development are purely economic processes in which human rights and ecology and culture do not matter. For example, it says nothing about labor rights.

The creation of the WTO certainly did not mean that UNEP or UNCTAD went out of business, any more than the emphasis on free trade meant that the ILO went out of business. But the continuing prevalence of the Washington consensus left unresolved the relationship between trade and other strictly economic processes and matters like ecology and labor rights that had increasingly been considered part of a broader and legitimate conception of development. To date, no formal link has been established between the WTO, the ILO, and UNEP with human rights agencies, and other environmental organizations. It is as if the thinking within the WTO had reverted to the 1940s and the view that development is an economic and nonpolitical matter. The division in worldviews explains

The Economic and Social Council meets in a special high-level meeting with the Bretton Woods institutions, the World Trade Organization (WTO), and the United Nations Conference on Trade and Development (UNCTAD). April 18, 2005, United Nations, New York. (UN PHOTO 71219/ESKINDER DEBEBE)

why the WTO has been unable to hold a successful round of trade negotiations and why many states wanting a freer trading system have pursued policies bilaterally, or more recently regionally, for example by negotiating the controversial Trans-Pacific Partnership (TPP). One of the major reasons it was controversial was that its draft terms once again raised the possibility that human rights and ecological measures might be struck down as restraints on trade by arbitration panels stacked in favor of private enterprise.

Some progress was made at the World Bank, as protecting the environment was increasingly seen as a legitimate part of its approach to investing in development. In 1991 the Bank launched a $1 billion pilot program, the Global Environmental Facility (GEF), to support sustainable development initiatives. The GEF later combined Bank funding with UNEP and UNDP programming. Thus, the Bank's operations were much more intertwined with parts of the UN system, even if key decision making remained fragmented. After the 1992 Earth Summit, the GEF was moved out of the World Bank and restructured to serve as the financial mechanism for several environmental treaties to help defray the costs of implementing sustainable development policies. The creation of the GEF was a clear recognition of the relationship between development and the environment, and represents incremental progress toward achieving sustainable economic growth.

Another sign of progress was seen at forums related to the financing of development. In 2002, at the first International Conference on Financing for Development in Monterrey, Mexico, both the North and South agreed that governments of developing countries had an obligation to reform themselves to promote transparency and the rule of law and to end corruption (in addition to market liberalization reforms), while those in developed countries had an obligation to provide meaningful assistance for that improved process of development. The numerical measure of "meaningful" meant the governments of the Global North would commit 0.7 percent of their GDP to overseas development assistance (ODA). Termed the "Monterrey consensus," this approach attempted to reconcile the need for political and structural/market reforms and the need to authoritatively redistribute some wealth of the rich North to the impoverished South. This shift in thinking shows that even when more purely economic considerations dominate the agenda, a compromise can be reached, at least on guiding principles. These same emphases remained in July 2015 at the third Financing for Development Conference in Addis Ababa.

In addition to creating and building awareness around focusing on poverty and sustainable development, the second UN also began to focus more attention on the role of women and gender in development in the 1990s.[35] Building on the work of feminist economists, such UN agencies as UNDP, UNICEF, and the United Nations Development Fund for Women (UNIFEM; now part of UN Women after its creation in 2010) began to research how men and women are positioned differently in the world economy and in poverty. Under particular scrutiny were the structural adjustment programs affecting women in countries experiencing economic crises. Through an examination of how the policies of governments and multilateral institutions affect the everyday lives of women, strategies could be developed to avoid any ill effects or unintended consequences. Even at the organizations preferred by the first UN, the World Bank and the IMF have conducted their own research and have modified their policies such that structural adjustment loans can now be used, in part, for the alleviation of poverty and not just for market reforms. Furthermore, the World Bank now considers gender equality as fundamental to economic development. While the inclusion of women and gender issues on the development agenda has obvious benefits, it also complicates multilateral diplomacy in that the respective conceptions regarding the status of women and their rights are markedly different among countries, with many Middle Eastern and Asian countries having views that clash with those in much of the rest of the world.[36]

The intensive series of international conferences in the 1990s led to a reasonably coherent framework of development goals, objectives, and policies.[37] That framework formed the foundation for the Millennium Declaration and was couched in the language of shared fundamental values: freedom, equality, solidarity, tolerance, respect for nature, and shared responsibility. For those who read it even casually, Secretary-General Annan's Millennium Report was reminiscent of President Franklin D. Roosevelt's "Four Freedoms" speech.[38] The UN's foundations in liberal capitalist ideology appear not only to be still firmly in place but greatly strengthened by the absence of any potential significant challengers. Like Roosevelt's New Deal, the new international agreement contained elements of social democracy, although these ideas are not necessarily reflected in the policies of the World Bank, IMF, and WTO.

At the 2000 UN Millennium Summit member states adopted the Millennium Development Goals (MDG) as an action plan to alleviate poverty and lay the foundation for sustainable development. The MDG project (discussed in detail in Chapter 12) set out eight goals with eighteen measurable and time-bound targets to assess progress. The goals were eventually succeeded by the Sustainable Development Goals in 2015; however, the MDGs paid particular attention to the importance of broad private sector partnerships and technology in achieving improvements in gender equality, education, health (with special emphasis on combating HIV/AIDS, malaria, and other infectious diseases), and environmental sustainability. The first UN had essentially endorsed the idea of human security—which includes the elimination of poverty and the promotion of sustainable development—as the world organization's highest priority. In doing so, member states recognized the link between the UN's work in economic and social domains and its mandate for international peace and security, which emphasizes the promotion of social and economic development and the protection of human rights as indirect approaches to peace. Economic equity, the pursuit of economic growth, and the satisfaction of basic human needs could do more than just improve the material quality of life. They could arguably reduce the likelihood of violent conflict. The causes of violence between and within states could be decreased by reducing gross social and economic inequalities and deprivations. In the oft-cited *An Agenda for Peace*, Boutros Boutros-Ghali highlighted this link and identified economic despair, social injustice, and political oppression among the "deepest causes of conflict."[39]

The conventional wisdom within the second UN has more or less come to embrace the proposition, as formulated by the UNDP, that "the concept of security must change—from an exclusive stress on national security to a much greater stress on people's security, from security through armaments to security through human development, from territorial security to food, employment, and environmental security."[40]

Creating the foundation for sustainable human security entails empowering individuals, groups, and communities to become engaged constructively and effectively in satisfying their own needs, values, and interests, thereby providing them with a genuine sense of control over their futures. This was given an additional boost with a report from an eminent group of persons, headed by former UN high commissioner for refugees Sadako Ogata and Nobel laureate in economics Amartya Sen, which focuses on "shielding people from acute threats and empowering them to take charge of their own lives."[41] Sen was certainly interested in traditional notions of development, but along with that focus he was also interested in various "unfreedoms," such as lack of education and health care.

The George W. Bush administration, not known for its fondness for the UN or multilateralism, followed the Millennium Summit with an announcement of a new bilateral Millennium Challenge Account (MCA) of foreign assistance to the poorest countries. Recipient countries would have to meet certain criteria dealing with both economic effectiveness and good governance. The MCA would not be a multilateral arrangement but would be administered by an independent corporation—the Millennium Challenge Corporation—of the United States. Congressional appropriations for the MCA, however, have consistently fallen short by about half of the administration's budgetary requests, which average roughly $1 billion a year. Given the restrictive nature of funding criteria, very few of the world's poorest countries are able to qualify for this assistance. Budget deficits and pressing problems both at home and abroad have led many observers to question the future of the MCA, especially given that foreign assistance had for a long time not been very popular in Washington. Nevertheless, President Obama continued to devote significant resources to the MCA, requesting nearly $1.5 billion in 2015.

The Bush administration also initiated the President's Emergency Plan for AIDS Relief (PEPFAR) in 2003, which committed $15 billion over five years to combat HIV/AIDS. Nearly all of the funds were tied to bilateral aid programs in fifteen countries, and of the $1 billion available for multilateral assistance, a substantial portion was restricted to abstinence education. It is estimated that PEPFAR provided antiretroviral therapy to over 2 million people, and helped train thousands of health-care personnel in areas where the AIDS problem is particularly acute. The program was renewed by Congress in 2008 and increased to $48 billion over the following two years. The Obama administration shifted some resources from PEPFAR to the Global Fund for AIDS, Tuberculosis, and Malaria, but most of U.S. AIDS funding goes to PEPFAR. While these bilateral programs are large and generous, they may have the effect of weakening rather than complementing global efforts.

At the 2005 World Summit, over 150 heads of state and government met in New York to review progress toward achieving the MDGs and to endeavor to agree on reforms to enhance the capacity and effectiveness of the world organization. The UN diplomats negotiating the final summit outcome agreement in August 2005 were initially stunned when the U.S. permanent representative to the UN, John Bolton, suddenly proposed removing all references to the MDGs by name and substituting only broad support for development objectives in general. There was a predictable uproar from all three UNs at the move. Within days, Bolton reversed course and allowed specific references to the MDGs—given their worldwide profile and acceptance—to go back into the final agreement, albeit with language that permitted Washington to maintain a distinction between what states had agreed on in 2000 and the specifics attached afterward by the UN Secretariat. This partial change of heart is credited to the intercession of Secretary of State Condoleezza Rice and Undersecretary Nicholas Burns. President Bush's address to the summit on September 14, 2005, included this unexpectedly categorical statement: "We are committed to the Millennium Development Goals."[42] Beyond restoring the goals by name, the United States also backed away from other proposed deletions on such subjects as the Kyoto agreement on climate change, which was only slightly fuzzed in the final document to indicate there was not universal agreement.[43] We will see, however, that state fidelity to the MDGs was anything but certain.

We know that where development falls short, turmoil often follows. The links among poverty, underdevelopment, and violent conflict are hard to ignore, even if the causal link is empirically hard to prove. The poverty and human rights abuses in Afghanistan undoubtedly allowed Al Qaeda to flourish there. That terrorist organization and its leader, Osama bin Laden, also initially found refuge in Sudan, and Al Qaeda and its offshoots have found havens in such places as Yemen and Somalia. Islamic extremism and virulent nationalism have some roots in economic deprivation and the problems of persistent poverty, even if some leaders are wealthy, as bin Laden was.[44] Leaders from the upper classes often mobilize followers who are frustrated by poverty and unemployment. According to Thomas Friedman, it is often the "stand around guys" from the unemployed ranks who turn out to be suicide bombers and other terrorists. As Amartya Sen stated, "Even though definitive empirical work on the causal linkages between political turmoil and economic deprivations may be rare, the basic presumption that the two phenomena have firm causal links is widespread. . . . Of course, avoidance of war and eradication of destitution are both important ends, and it is quite plausible that each feeds the other."[45] Discourse and practice among developed and developing countries in the UN continue to reflect the importance of this development-conflict nexus.

With this overview of changing development thinking in mind, we now turn to the UN and international cooperation for development at more specific and operational levels. We look at the record of the first and second UN in advancing development and assess their value added. We examine the role of the UN in the creation and advancement of norms and the extent to which development efforts respect a right of participation by the stakeholders. We also explore how all three UNs have pursued sustainable development in the real world of national interests, humanitarian crises, and environmental degradation.

NOTES

1. Kenneth Dadzie, "The UN and the Problem of Economic Development," in *United Nations, Divided World: The UN's Roles in International Relations*, ed. Adam Roberts and Benedict Kingsbury, 2nd ed. (Oxford: Clarendon, 1995), 297–326.

2. The word *liberal* means many things to many people. Here it is used in the strictly economic sense of an emphasis on private enterprise, private markets, and minimal government intervention and regulation.

3. Olav Stokke, *International Development Assistance: The UN Contribution* (Bloomington: Indiana University Press, 2007).

4. Devesh Kapur, John P. Lewis, and Richard Webb, *The World Bank: Its First Half Century*, 2 vols. (Washington, D.C.: Brookings Institution, 1997). The previous history was written by Edward S. Mason and Robert E. Asher, *The World Bank Since Bretton Woods: The Origins, Policies, Operations, and Impact of the International Bank for Reconstruction and Development and the Other Members of the World Bank Group* (Washington, D.C.: Brookings Institution, 1973). For the IMF, see, for example, Margaret G. de Vries, *The International Monetary Fund, 1945–1965: The Twenty Years of International Monetary*

Cooperation (Washington, D.C.: IMF, 1969), *The International Monetary Fund, 1966–1971: The System Under Stress* (Washington, D.C.: IMF, 1976), and *The International Monetary Fund, 1972–1978: Cooperation on Trial* (Washington, D.C.: IMF, 1985); and James Boughton, *Silent Revolution: The International Monetary Fund, 1979–1989* (Washington, D.C.: IMF, 2001). See also Norman K. Humphreys, ed., *Historical Dictionary of the IMF* (Washington, D.C.: IMF, 2000); Ngaire Woods, *The Globalizers: The IMF, the World Bank, and Their Borrowers* (Ithaca, N.Y.: Cornell University Press, 2006); Ariel Buira, ed., *Reforming the Governance of the IMF and World Bank* (London: Anthem, 2005); and Nancy Birdsall and John Williamson, *Delivering on Debt Relief: From IMF Gold to a New Aid Architecture* (Washington, D.C.: Institute of International Economics, 2002).

5. James Raymond Vreeland, *The International Monetary Fund: Politics of Conditional Lending* (London: Routledge, 2007); and Katherine Marshall, *The World Bank: From Reconstruction to Development to Equity* (London: Routledge, 2008).

6. Yves Berthelot, ed., *Unity and Diversity in Development Ideas: Perspectives from the UN Regional Commissions* (Bloomington: Indiana University Press, 2004).

7. Roger A. Coate, *Unilateralism, Ideology, and U.S. Foreign Policy: The United States in and out of UNESCO* (Boulder, Colo.: Lynne Rienner, 1988); and J. P. Singh, *UNESCO* (London: Routledge, 2011).

8. See Erskine Childers with Brian Urquhart, *Renewing the United Nations System* (Uppsala, Sweden: Dag Hammarskjöld Foundation, 1994).

9. David Mitrany, *A Working Peace System* (Chicago: Quadrangle Books, 1966), and *The Progress of International Government* (New Haven, Conn.: Yale University Press, 1933). Later, a "neofunctionalist" school formed around such ideas linked to European integration, including Ernst B. Haas, *Beyond the Nation State* (Stanford, Calif.: Stanford University Press, 1964).

10. See Thomas G. Weiss, *What's Wrong with the UN and How to Fix It*, 3rd ed. (Cambridge: Polity, 2016), chaps. 3 and 7.

11. Robert O. Keohane and Stanley Hoffmann, eds., *The New European Community: Decisionmaking and Institutional Change* (Boulder, Colo.: Westview Press, 1991).

12. Ian Taylor, *UN Conference on Trade and Development* (London: Routledge, 2007); John Toye and Richard Toye, *The UN and Global Political Economy: Trade, Finance, and Development* (Bloomington: Indiana University Press, 2004); and Thomas G. Weiss, *Multilateral Development Diplomacy in UNCTAD, 1964–84* (London: Macmillan, 1986).

13. André Gunder Frank, *Development and Underdevelopment in Latin America* (New York: Monthly Review Press, 1967); and Fernando Henrique Cardoso, *Dependency and Development in Latin America* (Berkeley: University of California Press, 1979).

14. See www.g77.org.

15. Michael G. Schechter, ed., *United Nations-Sponsored World Conferences: Focus on Impact and Follow-Up* (Tokyo: UN University Press, 2001); and Michael G. Schechter, *United Nations Global Conferences* (London: Routledge, 2005).

16. Robert S. Jordan, "Why an NIEO? The View from the Third World," in *The Emerging International Economic Order: Dynamic Processes, Constraints and Opportunities*, ed. Harold K. Jacobson and Dusam Aidjanski (Beverly Hills, Calif.: Sage, 1982), 59–80.

17. Thomas G. Weiss and Robert S. Jordan, *The World Food Conference and Global Problem Solving* (New York: Praeger, 1976).

18. Digambar Bhouraskar, *United Nations Development Aid: A History of UNDP* (New Dehli: Academic Foundation, 2013); Stephen Browne, *The United Nations Development Programme and System* (London: Routledge, 2011).

19. *A Study of the Capacity of the United Nations Development System* (Geneva: UN, 1969), document DP/5.

20. Elizabeth R. DeSombre, *Global Environmental Institutions* (London: Routledge, 2006).

21. Hugo Dobson, *The Group of 7/8* (New York: Routledge, 2006).

22. Richard Benedick, *Ozone Diplomacy: New Directions in Safeguarding the Planet*, 2nd ed. (Cambridge, Mass.: Harvard University Press, 1998).

23. John Williamson, ed., *Latin America Adjustment: How Much Has Happened?* (Washington, D.C.: Institute for International Economics, 1990); and John Williamson, "The Washington Consensus Revisited," in *Economic and Social Development in the 21st Century*, ed. Louis Emmerij (Baltimore: Johns Hopkins University Press, 1997), 48–61.

24. Giovanni A. Cornia, Richard Jolly, and Frances Stewart, eds., *Adjustment with a Human Face: Country Case Studies* (Oxford: Oxford University Press, 1992).

25. See Nico Schrijver, *Sovereignty over Natural Resources: Balancing Rights and Duties* (Cambridge: Cambridge University Press, 1997); and *Development Without Destruction: The UN and Global Resource Management* (Bloomington: Indiana University Press, 2010).

26. World Commission on Environment and Development, *Our Common Future* (Oxford: Clarendon, 1987). For a discussion, see Tappio Kanninen, *Crisis of Global Sustainability* (London: Routledge, 2013).

27. Boutros Boutros-Ghali, *An Agenda for Development, 1995: With Related UN Documents* (New York: United Nations, 1995).

28. Bernard M. Hoekman and Petros C. Mavroidis, *The World Trade Organization: Law, Economics, and Politics*, 2nd ed. (London: Routledge, 2015); and Rorden Wilkinson, *What's Wrong with the World Trade Organization and How to Fix It* (Cambridge: Polity, 2014).

29. David Held and Anthony McGrew, eds., *Governing Globalization: Power, Authority and Global Governance* (Cambridge: Polity, 2002); James H. Mittelman, *Whither Globalization? The Vortex of Knowledge and Ideology* (London: Routledge, 2004); Volker Rittberger, ed., *Global Governance and the United Nations System* (Tokyo: United Nations University Press, 2002); Paul Kennedy, Dirk Messner, and Franz Nuscheler, *Global Trends and Global Governance* (London: Pluto, 2002); Andrew F. Cooper, John English, and Ramesh Thakur, eds., *Enhancing Global Governance: Towards a New Diplomacy* (Tokyo: UN University Press, 2002); Anthony Giddens, *Runaway World: How Globalization Is Reshaping Our Lives* (New York: Routledge, 2000); John H. Dunning, ed., *Making Globalization Good: The Moral Challenge of Global Capitalism* (Oxford: Oxford University Press, 2003); Rodney Bruce Hall and Thomas J. Biersteker, eds., *The Emergence of Private Authority in Global Governance* (Cambridge: Cambridge University Press, 2002); Tagi Sagafinejad with John Dunning, *The UN and Transnational Corporations: From Code of Conduct to Global Compact* (Bloomington: Indiana University Press, 2008); Georg Sørensen, *A Liberal World Order in Crisis: Choosing Between Imposition and Restraint* (Ithaca, N.Y.: Cornell University Press, 2011); and James A. Caporaso and Mary Anne Madeira, *Globalization, Institutions, and Governance* (London: Sage, 2012).

30. David P. Forsythe, Patrice C. McMahon, and Andrew Wedeman, eds., *American Foreign Policy in a Globalized World* (New York: Routledge, 2006).

31. Dic Lo, *Alternatives to Neoliberal Globalization: Studies in the Political Economy of Institutions and Late Development* (New York: Palgrave Macmillan, 2012); Jon Carlson, *Myths, State Expansion, and the Birth of Globalizations: A Comparative Perspective* (New York: Palgrave Macmillan, 2012); and Natalie Goldstein, *Globalization and Free Trade* (New York: Facts on File, 2012).

32. Ngaire Woods, ed., *The Political Economy of Globalization* (New York: St. Martin's Press, 2000).

33. David Singh Grewal, *Network Power: The Social Dynamics of Globalization* (New Haven, Conn.: Yale University Press, 2008).

34. Anthony Giddens, *Runaway World: How Globalization Is Reshaping Our Lives* (New York: Routledge, 2000); David Held, Anthony McGrew, David Goldblatt, and Jonathan Perraton, *Global Transformations: Politics, Economics, and Culture* (Stanford, Calif.: Stanford University Press, 1999); Joseph E. Stiglitz, *Globalization and Its Discontents* (New York: W. W. Norton, 2002); and James H. Mittelman, *Globalization: Critical Reflections* (Boulder, Colo.: Lynne Rienner, 1996), *The Globalization Syndrome: Transformation and Resistance* (Princeton, N.J.: Princeton University Press, 2000), and *Whither Globalization? The Vortex of Knowledge and Ideology* (London: Routledge, 2004).

35. Devaki Jain, *Women, Development, and the UN: A Sixty-Year Quest for Equality and Justice* (Bloomington: Indiana University Press, 2005); Lourdes Benería, *Gender, Development and Globalization: Economics As If All People Mattered* (New York: Routledge, 2003); Hilkka Pietila, *Engendering the Global Agenda: The Story of Women and the United Nations* (New York: UN Non-Governmental Liaison Service, 2002); Suzanne Bergeron, *Fragments of Development: Nation, Gender, and the Space of Modernity* (Ann Arbor: University of Michigan Press, 2006); and Jael Silliman and Ynestra King, *Dangerous Intersections: Feminist Perspectives on Population, Environment and Development* (Cambridge, Mass.: South End, 1999).

36. Ellen Chesler and Terry McGovern, *Women and Girls Rising: Progress and Resistance Around the World* (London: Routledge, 2016). See also UN Women, *Transforming Economies, Realizing Rights* (New York: UN Women, 2015).

37. Michael Schechter, *United Nations Global Conferences* (London: Routledge, 2005).

38. Kofi A. Annan, *We the Peoples: The United Nations in the 21st Century* (New York: United Nations, 2000).

39. Boutros Boutros-Ghali, *An Agenda for Peace: Preventive Diplomacy, Peacemaking, and Peace-Keeping* (New York: United Nations, 1992), para. 15.

40. UNDP, *Human Development Report 1993* (New York: Oxford University Press, 1993), 5.

41. Commission on Human Security, *Human Security Now* (New York: Commission on Human Security, 2003), iv.

42. "Statement of H. E. George W. Bush, President of the United States of America, 2005 World Summit, High Level Plenary Meeting, September 14, 2005," www.un.org/webcast/summit2005/statements/usa050914.pdf.

43. Thomas G. Weiss and Barbara Crossette, "United Nations: Post-Summit Outlook," in *Great Decisions 2006*, ed. Karen M. Rohan (New York: Foreign Policy Association, 2006), 9–20.

44. Steve Coll, *Ghost Wars: The Secret History of the CIA, Afghanistan, and bin Laden, from the Soviet Invasion to September 10, 2001* (New York: Penguin, 2004).

45. Amartya Sen, "Global Inequality and Persistent Conflicts," paper presented at the Nobel Awards Conference 2002, reprinted in Commission on Human Security, *Human Security Now*, 132.

CHAPTER 11

Sustainable Development as Process: UN Organizations and Norms

T HE WORK OF THE United Nations in the development arena was born decentralized and remains the same today—indeed, many argue that it has become even more compartmentalized and expansive because of the seemingly ever-growing number of agencies, funds, and programs.[1] Development began largely as an implicit and secondary goal but has since become one of the world organization's primary activities. Over the decades, scores of development-related agencies, funds, programs, commissions, and committees have continued to spring up, thereby creating an ever more complex institutional web (see Appendix A).

Unpacking the complex structure of UN development reveals two main clusters of somewhat autonomous activity. The first cluster centers on the United Nations proper. Here, the first and second UN operate more or less in tandem. While important to the development process as a whole, especially in terms of norm creation, the operational efficacy of this cluster is challenged because important member states pursue multilateral development policies outside the UN proper in institutions that are more or less guided by neoliberal economic thought. Thus, and as we saw in the previous chapter, the second cluster focuses on the International Monetary Fund (IMF) and the World Bank (the Bank), which often go their own way although they are de jure are parts of the UN system, and the activities of the World Trade Organization (WTO).[2] As with the other substantive issue areas governed by the UN, the third UN of nongovernmental agencies (NGOs) and independent experts complements the development process through data collecting, monitoring, and advocacy.

Beyond the specific contributions by individual organizations, the UN system's collective contribution to development in the longer term is more notable for

nurturing agreement on ideas and principles about sustainable human development than for its operational impact with assistance projects on the ground. Ideas
are a powerful explanation for human progress, and the UN's contribution is not
an exception. Secretary-General Boutros Boutros-Ghali wrote that "the United
Nations is the mechanism in place and is best prepared to facilitate the work of
achieving a new development rationale."[3]

THE UN PROPER

The UN system—even for seasoned observers—is a bewildering alphabet soup
of acronymic semiautonomous programs, funds, committees, commissions, and
agencies, mostly strikingly in the development arena. A 2012 survey, like the ones
before and after it, demonstrated that respondents worldwide favored fewer moving parts and acronyms; still the system remains complex.[4] Some observers use
the term "UN family" instead of "system"; the former has the advantage of easy
association with the adjective "dysfunctional" to describe the kinds of routine
battles and quarrels that occur.[5] Few would dispute that the UN has failed to perform at the level expected of the world organization and is "punching below its
weight."[6] Or as one analyst bluntly summarized: "There is no point in mincing
words: the UN is a structural monstrosity."[7] The following discussion is an effort
to simplify activities encompassing some thirty development-related bodies (or
as many as seventy, depending on how one is counting), each with distinct governance, funding, and staffing arrangements and with different, though not necessarily distinct, mandates. [8]

The First UN and Sustainable Development

At the core of the UN system is the General Assembly, one of the six principal
organs, whose agenda grows longer from year to year.[9] Its influence, however, may
be the inverse. Most development issues are dealt with in the assembly's Second
Committee (Economic and Financial), which is made up of representatives of all
member states (in UN parlance, "a committee of the whole"). The General Assembly, for example, voted in 1983 to create what came to be called the Brundtland Commission—a part of the third UN—which was an important milestone in
changing ideas about development by fusing the seemingly clashing perspectives
about economic growth versus environmental protection. Some of the assembly's
most important work in the development field has taken place in special sessions
or in global ad hoc conferences convened to consider specific issues or topics, such
as women, population, development financing, and HIV/AIDS. Normally the assembly deals with substantive ideas, or the big picture, rather than the details of
management, administration, and coordination.

The General Assembly elects fifty-four of its member states to the Economic
and Social Council (ECOSOC), which, under Article 55 of the Charter, is another

Secretary-General Kofi Annan (second from left) delivers his statement to the high-level segment of the fourteenth session of the Commission on Sustainable Development, at UN Headquarters in New York. José Antonio Ocampo, undersecretary-general for economic and social affairs, is on the left. May 10, 2006. (UN PHOTO 118008/ESKINDER DEBEBE)

principal organ mandated with the responsibility for promoting and coordinating UN development activities. The ECOSOC attempts to coordinate social and development activities through ten functional commissions and five regional commissions that are overseen by member states. The central functional commission related to development is the new High-level Political Forum on Sustainable Development (HLPF), which replaced the Commission of Sustainable Development (CSD). Growing out of the Earth Summit in Rio de Janeiro in 1992, the CSD was, at least early on, a promising vehicle for first UN cooperation and second and third UN coordination. The CSD was given dual responsibilities for overseeing the implementation of the provisions of Agenda 21, the policy blueprint for the environment, and coordinating the sustainable development activities of the various organizations within the UN system.[10] Although the CSD was assigned the role of being the primary mechanism within the UN system for coordinating sustainable development, its relationship to other intergovernmental entities, especially the autonomous agencies, was ill-defined.

The CSD also had a mandate to strengthen and integrate the role of major societal groups and civic actors as effective participants in sustainable development decision making at all levels. The text of Agenda 21 specifically addressed the roles of ten major groups, all members of the third UN: NGOs, indigenous peoples, local governments, workers, businesses, scientific communities, farmers, women, children, and youth. Exactly how this mandate for mainstreaming was to be institutionalized in practice, however, was left undefined. Only 18 NGOs were represented at the first CSD meeting, although ECOSOC had authorized the CSD to consider including all 1,400 NGOs represented at the Earth Summit. As recognized in both Agenda 21 and the Rio Declaration, fulfilling this mandate effectively is the fundamental cornerstone for successfully implementing sustainable development programs and practices. The mandate was a challenge for the CSD as well as for the UN system and multilateral organizations more generally. Establishing an effective relationship between the sovereignty-based world of states and intergovernmental organizations and the global civil society within which that interstate order exists was an elusive quest.[11]

While the CSD did serve as a focal point for reviewing and assessing progress toward fulfilling Agenda 21 goals and objectives, its overall efficacy is an open question.[12] The fifteenth session of the CSD in May 2007 proved contentious, as delegates were unable to reach an agreement for implementing commitments, including target dates for increased energy efficiency and reduced air pollution. This session ended with no final outcome agreement; the compromise document was ultimately rejected by the European Union.[13] To complicate matters, CSD members elected Zimbabwe—a development, human rights, and environmental disaster—to chair the commission for 2008. Viewed in a pessimistic light, Zimbabwe's election illustrates the hollow and hypocritical nature of the CSD. But, as the *Economist* rather cheekily noted, this odd choice might not necessarily be a bad thing. After all, "few things are more dull than a worthy cause run by a do-gooding country. It is a fair bet that if, say, Sweden or Canada were chairing the commission no one outside the aid industry would hear a squeak about its doings over the next year. Zimbabwe's stewardship, by contrast, will attract much scrutiny."[14]

The CSD survived Zimbabwe as chair but not the 2012 UN Conference on Sustainable Development (the UNCSD, or Rio+20) where member states voted to replace the CSD with the HLPF. The HLPF is mandated to provide political leadership for sustainable development and steward progress toward the newly adopted Sustainable Development Goals (SDGs) that replaced the MDGs after 2015. As with its predecessor, the HLPF is scheduled to meet annually under the auspices of the ECOSOC; however, the process is supposedly improved because it will convene the heads of state and government every four years as well. Whether this moves the first UN more cohesively toward sustainable development remains to be seen.

Through the General Assembly and the ECOSOC, the member states of the first UN comprise the governing bodies of many of the second UN's development-related programs and funds. This includes such bodies as the UN Development Programme (UNDP), Children's Fund (UNICEF), (Conference on Trade and Development (UNCTAD), Population Fund (UNFPA), and Environment Programme (UNEP), as well as the World Food Programme (WFP). The mandates and work programs of these various agencies overlap, which has made the job of coordination daunting. In many respects, the UN system reflects that functional specialization and the powerlessness of ECOSOC.[15] It also represents how institutionalized agencies can take on a life of their own, even outside the preferences of major donor states. The ECOSOC continuously encounters the challenges of coordination and in reality is something of a mailbox between the General Assembly and the second UN of the socioeconomic agencies involved in development.

The Second UN and Sustainable Development

The General Assembly, ECOSOC, and other UN governing bodies are composed of states but rely on the UN's administrative branch—the secretariat—for staffing and support. Most of the activities of the ECOSOC are serviced by the UN Department for Economic and Social Affairs (DESA). DESA provides substantive support to ECOSOC and UN member states in a variety of areas by collecting data, formulating development policies, and monitoring the implementation of international agreements. DESA has been on the front lines in assessing the impact of the global financial crisis on development, poverty reduction, and climate change.

Boutros Boutros-Ghali focused attention on the role of the United Nations in promoting development in his 1994 *An Agenda for Development*. Yet the second UN was inadequate for the task. In January 1997, when Kofi Annan assumed the post of secretary-general, he was the first person to hold the office who had spent virtually his entire professional career, nearly three decades, working his way up through the ranks and being exposed to the best and the worst of the world organization. He committed himself and the UN to a reform process.[16] This subject was also important for the United States, which, as the largest donor to both the regular and the voluntary UN budgets, had long been pressing for administrative and structural reform.

At the heart of Annan's reform program was the reorientation and reorganization of the UN's administration and management. More change has actually taken place than is customarily appreciated, although the remaining organizational chart and decentralization undoubtedly would drive a management consultant to reconsider his or her profession. In his effort to bring unity of purpose to the diverse activities of the UN and provide clear lines of responsibility, in 1997 Annan created—for the first time in the UN's half century—a cabinet structure. This Senior Management Group (SMG) is made up of the various undersecretaries-general, the heads of UN funds and programs, and the deputy secretary-general. This last post was created in 1998 to oversee the reform process and coordinate development activities (although more in theory than reality because the deputy most often is used as a substitute for the secretary-general). Similarly, four thematic executive committees (Peace and Security, Humanitarian Affairs, Economic and Social Affairs, and the UN Development Group) were created and charged with overseeing the coordination of policy development, management, and decision making. The conveners of each of these committees sit on the SMG.

Two of these executive committees are of particular importance for development. The Economic and Social Affairs Executive Committee (EC-ESA) is convened by the undersecretary-general for economic and social affairs and comprises representatives from eighteen UN bodies. Like all the other executive committees, the EC-ESA serves as a consultative body for facilitating decision making, policy development and coordination, and better management.

The United Nations Development Group Executive Committee is convened by the administrator of UNDP and includes the UNFPA, UNICEF, and WFP. This body serves as the secretariat for the United Nations Development Group (UNDG) to provide better coordination among the numerous UN funds, programs, and other bodies that have proliferated over the years in the development area. The UNDG consists of twenty-eight member agencies plus five observers. In addition to its own operational activities, the UNDP administers several special-purpose funds and programs, including the UN Capital Development Fund (UNCDF). And in cooperation with the World Bank and UNEP, the UNDP serves as an implementing agency for Global Environment Facility (GEF), which provides concessional funding and grants for certain environmentally sound development projects.

UN development activities have benefited from enhanced coordination via the Office of the Secretary-General and UNDP. Given that states vote to create all sorts of UN development institutions, it falls to these two parts of the UN system to bring as much order as possible to a multifaceted process that has no real carrots or sticks to induce cooperation. States get the kind of UN for which they vote and otherwise support financially. Unfortunately, all too often, member states vote for or against a particular UN organization or one of its activities as a diplomatic concession to some domestic group or as part of a compromise with other states. The public display of affection or disgruntlement may or may not have a concrete follow-on in the form of necessary diplomatic and financial backing. As such, the UN record for success in promoting sustainable development is mixed at best. We will briefly explore the main development bodies of the second UN in the following sections.

UNDP. Although many UN development bodies were created by member states and given unrealistic mandates and limited resources, they have made important contributions to setting and advancing development goals. The UN Development Programme is perhaps the most influential development agency at the second UN. In 2015 it was operating in more than 170 countries and territories. Its most senior official in developing countries, the UNDP resident representative, also acts as the resident coordinator for the UN system. As the primary unit devoted to capacity building for social and economic development, the program was created in 1965 to take the lead in providing technical assistance.[17] In this regard, it works with other UN units in a wide variety of thematic contexts. It works in the security realm to support elections, demobilization and reconciliation initiatives, and human rights. In the humanitarian field, the agency provides support for disaster prevention, mitigation, and preparedness; the reintegration into society of refugees, former combatants, and internally displaced persons; and the implementation of postdisaster national plans for reintegration, reconstruction, and recovery.

The UNDP activities involve advocacy, advice, pilot projects, and partnerships. Its current priorities are sustainable development, democratic governance and peacebuilding, and climate and disaster resilience. The advisory function focuses on building capacity in a variety of areas, including legal, political, and regulatory frameworks as well as infrastructure for basic social and economic development. Given the agency's limited budget, it concentrates on actions that can serve as catalysts for mainstreaming particular policy agendas as opposed to taking on expensive, large-scale projects. Technical assistance and preinvestment studies have been in its portfolio since it began operations in 1966.

The UNDP's partnership function is wide-ranging, focusing on integrating diverse elements of society and the private sector into development. The agency sees promoting sustainable development as requiring new forms of cooperation and involving complex interventions from a wide variety of actors: governments at all levels, NGOs, private business enterprises, and local community groups. The focus is on empowering people and creating the conditions necessary for "people-centered" development. The guiding philosophy is that "people should guide both the state and the market, which need to work in tandem, with people sufficiently empowered to exert a more effective influence over both."[18] Basically, the UNDP's underlying theme has been getting the product to the poor and empowering them with the capacity for good governance. Priority is placed on democratization and empowerment through participation. This means, among other things, that the UNDP has "mainstreamed" human rights considerations into its development work.

Of course, empowerment, like most development activities, requires resources, especially financial resources and a commitment from the central as well as local authorities within states. In this regard, the UNDP, working with other UN organizations, has undertaken initiatives to provide financial services to the poor at the local level. Its Special Unit for Microfinance is devoted to supporting the creation of start-up microfinancial institutions in rural areas to provide not only loans but also savings products. In the context of the shrinking financial resources for multilateral development assistance over the past two decades, the UNDP adds value to the overall development process. It is both a coordinator of UN development-related activities and a development agency in its own right, although the latter role can create problems for the former in terms of competition with other UN organizations for limited funds.[19]

The UNDP's core operating budget and the size of its headquarters staff have been cut, but it remains prominent in promoting sustainable human development through its fieldwork and by building cooperative relationships. Former UNDP administrator Mark Malloch Brown once opined, "When I took office the agenda was clear: Reform of UNDP. . . . The message was close to reform or die."[20] By the time he left the agency to become chief of staff for the secretary-general and then the deputy secretary-general, the UNDP was at the forefront of the MDG process. But as Malloch Brown has acknowledged, "in the final analysis, we cannot judge our reform by its impact on UNDP alone, but rather on how we help strengthen the critical role of the United Nations system as a whole in all aspects of development cooperation."[21]

Malloch Brown also claimed that the UNDP annual *Human Development Report* gives the agency a "special voice and pulpit and authority to develop alternative ideas," a view also favored by his immediate successor, Kemal Derviş, and by the current administrator, Helen Clark.[22] The now broadly shared conception of sustainable human development was the central component in the UNDP's *Human Development Reports*.[23] Started in 1990 by a prominent Pakistani economist, Mahbubul Haq, and then carried on by Richard Jolly of the United Kingdom and others, the annual reports analyzed international cooperation for development in a broad, multifaceted way. The annual report sometimes stressed human rights, sometimes women, sometimes ecology. It ranked countries not just by GDP per capita but by a more complex formula attempting to measure quality of life. Wealth and prosperity loomed large, of course, but so did education and medical care. Various indices sought to measure discrimination against women not only legally and politically but also in terms of basic health and education. In its approach to development, the UNDP dovetailed and embraced the Overseas Development Council (ODC), a private group based in the United States that had pioneered in creating the Physical Quality of Life Index, which sought to measure the quality of life in all countries according to wealth, medical care, and education. More recently, the UNDP and other organizations, including the World Bank, are making increasing use of the Gini coefficient, which measures income inequality within countries. This adds legitimacy to this important statistical measure that gauges the distribution of wealth within societies and says more about equitable human development of a society than GDP. How the UN and other important organizations measure development is important, especially when assessing how the UN can improve human dignity.

The first few issues of the *Human Development Report* were controversial for several reasons. First, a United Nations agency "rated" countries according to debated criteria; states on the bottom disliked the publicity, while states not quite at the top, including the United States, grumbled. Second, many governments resented the fact that poorer neighbors got higher ratings because they were better at making decisions about priorities, having devoted more of their limited resources to education and health instead of spending them on other items. Third, sometimes the methodology the UNDP used to establish its comparative ratings was, in fact, open to serious criticism, as in the 2000 volume stressing human rights. Accurate statistics are difficult to come by in many countries. Moreover, given the subjectivity involved in choosing measures of human development, debates raged about what to include in the Human Development Index as well as how the variables were weighted.

Still, what was once a counterdiscourse to the neoliberal notions of development defined as increases in GDP, trade flows, and industrial capacity is now a mainstream concept with widespread global agreement.[24] If the UNDP is supposed to assist in the creation of successful market democracies, then democracy and human rights are as important as efficient markets. Of course, the human rights–based approach to development, especially with its emphasis on civil and political rights, does create resistance from states sensitive to outside intrusions into their political affairs.[25] Most analyses of the linkages between human rights and development focus on economic and social rights and economic growth. The UNDP focus on democratic governance and peacebuilding is fraught with controversy as disagreements abound on how to best pursue peace and democracy.

UNCTAD. The UN Conference on Trade and Development began in 1964 as a debating forum and think tank for developing countries and their advocates. The G77 sought a counterforum to the General Agreement on Tariffs and Trade, which was perceived to ignore their trade interest and create terms of trade favorable to the advanced industrialized countries. For most of its existence, it largely served that function. The conference itself meets in formal session every four years, but the Trade and Development Board (TDB) meets annually, and the secretariat in Geneva operates continuously. UNCTAD served as the focal point for formulating and articulating the ideas that framed the failed attempt to establish a New International Economic Order. However, the end of the Cold War brought with it hard times. After the creation of the WTO in 1995, UNCTAD adopted a more conciliatory tone by seeking finally to end impediments to trade in agricultural products.[26] UNCTAD remains an important forum in that it continues to articulate the unintended consequences of trade liberalization on development in the Global South. It highlights alternative theories that may be more suitable for impoverished states as they pursue development in a globalized world.[27] UNCTAD is also instrumental in exposing how certain trade rules are biased against developing states, especially those related to agricultural subsidies in the Global North.

UNCTAD was part of Secretary-General Kofi Annan's initiative of forging innovative partnerships with other international organizations, local governments, NGOs, the private sector, and civil society. UNCTAD's role has taken on a wide variety of forms and complexions. In 1999, for example, UNCTAD, along with UNDP and Habitat (the UN Center for Human Settlements), initiated a global partnership—World Alliance of Cities Against Poverty (WACAP)—with civil society, the private sector, and local governments to carry out the goals of the 1995 World Summit for Social Development in Copenhagen. This alliance quickly became formalized and has grown substantially. It seeks to strengthen networks among cities around the world. During the Third UN Conference on Least Developed Countries in Brussels in 2001, for instance, WACAP organized a parallel Mayors Meeting, bringing together representatives from 216 cities around the world. The primary purpose of this conference was action. A "city-to-city solidarity market" was held in which requests for assistance were matched with offers. On the spot, twelve formal agreements of cooperation were concluded between cities in Belgium and cities in Africa, Asia, and Latin America. The requests of 120 other cities from developing regions were tendered and are currently either under consideration or being related to cities throughout the world through the numerous global, regional, national, and city networks that also participated in the meeting.[28]

UNCTAD seeks opportunities for regional and local trading arrangements to negotiate better rules and terms of trade for poor and impoverished countries. It does have to dodge periodic efforts to abolish it as part of the overall UN reform process. Some argue that UNCTAD duplicates the work of the WTO. However, it remains a central voice for the perspectives of the Global South regarding trade-related development and provides an alternative to the free-trade discourse of the WTO.

UNICEF. The UN Children's Fund is better known by its acronym UNICEF, and its work ranges from child and maternal health care and basic education to water and sanitation.[29] UNICEF has special initiatives dealing with HIV/AIDS, participation and rights of adolescent girls, tobacco-free youth, adolescent health and development, and hygiene and nutrition. It also initiates specific appeals to meet challenging crises. Most recently it has focused on reaching and helping children in humanitarian emergencies caused by disease (Ebola) and violent conflict (in Gaza, Iraq, Syria, South Sudan, and the Central African Republic).

UNICEF focuses a great deal on women and mothers as well as on children. Underdevelopment is gendered in that females bear the brunt of poverty. They are often denied adequate education and health care and are victims of various forms of discrimination. Women are excluded from key decision-making positions and their lower political and social status means they and their children are disadvantaged. As such, UNICEF also focuses on girls' education in the context of the "education of every child," because education is the path to empowerment.[30]

More than most UN organizations reviewed here, UNICEF participates across the range of UN activities. It began as a temporary emergency relief organization in Europe after World War II. After it became a permanent part of the UN in 1951, that task was supplemented by a development portfolio, which in many years accounts for about two thirds of UNICEF's annual budget. It now sees itself as a human rights agency, seeking to "mainstream" human rights considerations into its operations, tying itself increasingly to the Convention on the Rights of the Child.[31] The assumption is that using the discourse on children's rights will garner more support for its operations, thereby increasing its effectiveness.[32] UNICEF also educates the first UN and the third UN about the humanitarian action needed on behalf of children. For example, in 2011, UNICEF focused on concrete steps and strategies for building resilience among communities as they face catastrophic emergencies such as earthquakes and violent conflict.[33] Teaching children and the community the skills to pick up the pieces and move forward with their lives is a necessary first step in rebuilding and healing society.

UNESCO. The United Nations Educational, Scientific and Cultural Organization (UNESCO) grew out of the wartime deliberations in London by the Council of

Allied Ministers of Education[34] because, as its constitution notes, "it is in the minds of men [and women] that the defences of peace must be constructed." It began in the 1960s with a wide variety of environmental concerns that cut across its main areas of competence, including science, education, and culture, which are keys to development, broadly defined. In 1965 a ten-year program, the International Hydrological Decade, was launched to promote the study of hydrological resources, including water pollution. This early environmental focus was strengthened with the hosting of the Biosphere Conference, the 1970 Helsinki Interdisciplinary Symposium on Man's Role in Changing His Environment, and the 1972 Convention Concerning the Protection of the World Cultural and Natural Heritage.

UNESCO has been responsible for creating a number of affiliated bodies, such as the International Oceanographic Commission (IOC). This particular body has been important in promoting international marine scientific research with special emphasis on pollution prevention. Since the late 1980s, the UNESCO secretariat in Paris has emphasized coordination of the environmentally related activities and programs within its various divisions. It was actively involved in follow-up activities to the 1992 Rio Conference and the implementation of a variety of related agreements. In recent years, UNESCO's main contributions to the UN system's environmental work have focused on environmental education and its environment-related scientific programs. UNESCO has not been without controversies, however.[35] It lost U.S. and U.K. support in the mid-1980s over allegations of undo politicization and poor performance, and then again from the U.S. in 2011 after the member states of the organization voted to admit Palestine as a member state.

WMO. In addition to UNESCO, most other organizations within the UN system have operational mandates linked to eco-development. The environmental relationships of some of these bodies are more obvious and more direct than others. Most, if not all, of the work of the World Meteorological Organization (WMO), for instance, focuses on eco-development. Its broad, heavily scientific mandate includes atmospheric pollution, meteorological aspects of water pollution, climate change, the effects of pollution on climate change and vegetation, and the relationship between climate, weather, and agricultural practices. Along with the IOC and International Council for Science (ICSU), the WMO cosponsors the World Climate Research Programme (WCRP). This joint initiative examines the dynamic aspects of the earth's climate system and stands as a counterpart to the International Geosphere-Biosphere Programme (IGBP), which studies biological and chemical aspects of global change.

WHO. The work of the World Health Organization (WHO), at its Geneva headquarters and in the field, focuses broadly on the relationship between human beings and their environment with regard to health.[36] This institution is concerned with controlling environmental pollution, as well as all other environmental factors that affect health. The agency undertakes pollution surveys and initiates programs for improving methods for measuring pollution and for designing programs for pollution abatement and control. Just as UNICEF has taken more of a human rights approach to its concern for children around the world, so WHO has been trying to get states to view adequate health and health care as a human right.[37] WHO has undertaken a major effort to reduce the use of tobacco in its various forms and has come close to facilitating in many countries a ban similar to those in effect in Europe and many U.S. states. Here again we see part of the UN system collecting and disseminating scientific information and then trying to advance ideas based on that knowledge—in this case to improve health.

WHO has led the international community's frontline response to emerging deadly diseases such as SARS (severe acute respiratory syndrome), a rare but deadly respiratory disease. SARS was a powerful reminder of how globalization has enabled disease to spread easily. SARS was the first new major communicable disease to emerge in the twenty-first century, with the first case identified in February 2003 in Hanoi, Vietnam. The disease is suspected to have originated in China, except it was identified as an atypical respiratory disease. WHO was quick to act and in mid-March 2003 issued a global alert about mysterious cases of a severe atypical pneumonia with unknown etiology (cause or origin). Two days later, Canadian health authorities reported two deaths from a similar phenomenon. The following day, WHO elevated its alert, as cases were being reported in Singapore and elsewhere. Within weeks the situation worsened in Hong Kong, and mainland China and WHO took the unprecedented step of issuing travel advisories for Beijing, Hong Kong, Guangdong Province, Shanxi Province, and Toronto (the site of a North American outbreak).

The global response to SARS illustrates how effective international cooperation can be in response to a crisis and how important international organizations and their leadership can be. In this case, WHO, under the leadership of Gro Harlem Brundtland, did not hesitate to confront both a great power (China) and a traditional organizational supporter (Canada). The level of cooperation was unprecedented. The potentially rapid spread of the deadly disease (lethal in an estimated 8–10 percent of cases) was successfully checked.[38]

WHO is leading the world's response to the continuing threat of avian influenza, A/(H5N1), which, if it mutates so that it can be passed from human to human, threatens to be a worldwide pandemic that could kill tens of millions of people, because about half of those infected to date have died. The 2007 outbreak of the disease was largely contained, with two thirds of all human cases in one country, Indonesia. WHO was instrumental in tracking and isolating the deadly virus and educating governments. Similarly, WHO has taken the lead in addressing swine flu, H1N1, declaring a pandemic in June 2009. While the initial outbreak proved to be relatively mild to those infected, WHO and governments are coordinating national and international responses should the H1N1 virus become more lethal.

The response of WHO to the 2014–2015 Ebola outbreak in West Africa, however, was widely criticized during and after the crisis.[39] In January 2015, the executive board (a thirty-four-member state governing body, elected by the state members of the WHO assembly) requested an expert review of WHO's Ebola response. At issue was the perceived failure of the organization to take a leadership role, especially after it was empowered by the 2005 International Health Regulations to declare a situation a public health emergency of international concern and recommend health measures to member states. Responding to international public health emergencies has emerged as one of WHO's principal functions, yet it was slow to recognize the threat of Ebola. The expert panel found that WHO had limited operational capacity and relied too much on "good diplomacy to address the crisis."[40] The leadership of Dr. Margaret Chan was also criticized for failing to take courageous steps to push affected African governments. It seems that the WHO headquarters deferred too much to its regional officials, which in some cases have been staffed by political rather than medical appointees. Beyond the Ebola crisis, WHO has also been criticized for not using an international human rights framework to help it implement the International Health Regulations.[41]

FAO. The Food and Agricultural Organization (FAO) focuses on issues related to eco-development from its headquarters in Rome and in its operational projects worldwide.[42] They include sustainable water management through water harvesting, agriculture investment, and addressing radioactive contamination, contamination of food by pesticides, and marine pollution related to fisheries. The agency works to establish criteria for water quality management, soil and water resource management, pesticide control, fisheries management, and general control of pollution. Several important environmental conventions fall under FAO auspices, including the International Convention for the Conservation of Atlantic Tunas, the FAO International Code of Conduct on the Distribution and Use of Pesticides, and the Code of Conduct for Responsible Fisheries.

Marine pollution is important to the work of the International Maritime Organization (IMO), established in 1948 as the Intergovernmental Maritime Consultative Organization. At the heart of this agency's work in London are concerns about legal liability and the rights of parties to seek redress from pollution by ships and equipment operating in marine areas, as well as how to prevent such pollution. Over the years, the agency has promoted more than two dozen international conventions and protocols, ranging from the International Convention for the Prevention of Pollution at Sea by Oil in 1959 to the International Convention on Oil Pollution Preparedness Response and Cooperation in 1990. In fulfilling its environment-related mandate, the IMO has maintained close working relations with UNEP, FAO, ILO, the United Nations Commission on International Trade Law, UNCTAD, and WHO, as well as the International Union for the Conservation of Nature and National Resources (IUCN, also known as the World Conservation Union), the International Chamber of Shipping, and various other nongovernmental organizations.

IUCN. One of the most important international environmental organizations is the hybrid International Union for the Conservation of Nature and National

Resources (IUCN). It comprises states, governmental agencies, and international and national NGOs. Although possessing only a small secretariat, it conducts a remarkably wide range of activities through numerous standing commissions and committees. The IUCN helped forge the conceptual link between development and environment. With the World Wide Fund for Nature and UNEP, and in association with FAO and UNESCO, the IUCN launched the World Conservation Strategy in 1980. As a precursor to sustainable development, this initiative set forth principles promoting the sustainable use of the earth's living resources.

MEMBERS OF THE UN FAMILY?

For most of the UN's existence, the Washington-based international financial institutions functioned autonomously of the UN proper. In many depictions of the so-called UN system, including the one in Appendix A, dotted lines connect to the World Bank and International Monetary Fund, which suggest their independence from the UN and the UN secretary-general. The Geneva-based WTO is vaguely designated a "related" UN organization but does not even have a dotted line. In terms of resources, however, these organizations are the primary vehicles through which member states of the first UN have chosen to pursue development, usually defined as increases in GDP, import-export figures, and levels of industrialization. Hence, the bulk of their financing for development is geared toward promoting macroeconomic growth, albeit with the assumption that such market-oriented growth can enhance the ability of individuals to meet their basic human needs and promote the efficient use of resources, thereby protecting the environment. In this section, the development strategies of the World Bank, IMF, and WTO are reviewed in terms of how they contribute to the UN's sustainable development model.

The World Bank

The Bank group comprises the International Bank for Reconstruction and Development (IBRD) and four associated agencies or affiliates: International Finance Corporation (IFC), International Development Association (IDA), Multilateral Investment Guarantee Agency (MIGA), and International Centre for Settlement of Investment Disputes (ICSID).[43] The IBRD functions much like a traditional bank. Its funding comes from states as well as financing raised on open capital markets. The first affiliate, the IFC, was created in 1956 to encourage private investment in developing countries. Its principal strategy centers on providing seed money for business ventures and domestic infrastructure, which can then attract domestic investment and foreign direct investment by multinational corporations. The IFC also created its own International Securities Group (ISG) to advise developing states on creating a domestic stock market and helping local businesses to issue stock and list their stock on the major exchanges. The IBRD and the IFC are clearly wedded to economic development in a neoliberal sense, but they also consider environmental impacts of proposed projects and assist states in preparing loan requests with an eye toward sustainable development.

In 1960 the IDA was created to help alleviate poverty by providing soft loans to the poorest of the poor. "Soft" loans, with extremely low interest rates and unusually long repayment periods, actually amount to overseas development assistance (ODA). In 1988 the MIGA was created to help war-torn and/or extremely impoverished states, not by making loans or investments, but by insuring private investors against loss. Through this insurance program, private investment in high-risk states can be encouraged. Finally, the ICSID was created by treaty in 1965. It serves as an impartial forum for resolving international investment disputes among its 143 members. These latter affiliates demonstrate that the World Bank is aware of the special situation of extremely poor and postconflict societies; nevertheless, it still prefers to devote a significant portion of its resources to encourage market-based, private solutions.

The World Bank experienced a crisis of leadership in the first decade of the twenty-first century. President Paul Wolfowitz, a former Pentagon neoconservative supported by the Bush administration, left office in 2007 under a cloud of allegations relating to his companion's employment at the World Bank. Since anticorruption is a cornerstone of World Bank lending, this made its work more difficult under the next president, Robert Zoellick, the former U.S. trade representative to the WTO. A special commission, headed by Paul Volcker, the former head of the U.S. Federal Reserve, recommended that the World Bank work on improving its relations with developing countries and examine its own corruption before pushing its anticorruption agenda.[44] Thus, the multilateral institution that receives and distributes the lion's share of multilateral development assistance was put on the defensive.

Although Zoellick began his tenure under the gray cloud of his predecessor, governments were more than willing to move ahead quickly and put the divisiveness and bitterness of the Wolfowitz years behind them. Under Zoellick, the World Bank improved its relations with many members of the Global South through a number of measures. It defended the eligibility of middle-income states, such as India and China, for development loans. It also provided assistance to developing countries experiencing food shortages because of the global spike in commodity prices in 2007–2008, recognizing that land was being diverted for crops that could be used for biofuels (which were competitive because of increasing oil prices) rather than for food. The World Bank began stressing development programs that would help states achieve a measure of domestic food security, even if it was cheaper and more efficient to import food in the long run.

In 2012 President Barack Obama nominated Jim Yong Kim, the former president of Dartmouth College, to become the World Bank president, which continued the tradition of Washington's selecting the organization's head. His nomination involved a series of firsts.[45] It was the first time that other countries put up nominees, challenging the sixty-six-year-old tradition of U.S. control of the top spot. The financial crisis called into question American leadership on economic issues at a time when many developing countries were more vocally questioning why the president of the World Bank had to necessarily be an American. China, for instance, holds the largest foreign exchange reserves, about three times more than Japan, in second place, and seven of the top ten holders are from developing countries.[46] Should not the most qualified person, regardless of nationality, be selected? It was also the first time that someone outside of finance and government was nominated. Kim's expertise is in health, and prior to his time in academia, he worked to combat HIV and tuberculosis in extremely impoverished areas. Although an American citizen, Kim was born in Korea, which gave the U.S. choice a more global flavor. His credentials as a physician, rather than as a banker or political leader, mean he is more reform-minded and willing to provide more focus to World Bank lending. Such health issues as malaria, HIV/AIDS, and tuberculosis remain obstacles to sustainable development.

The IMF

The International Monetary Fund was created to handle the UN system of national accounts and help attenuate currency fluctuations and balance-of-payments problems in the international monetary system based on fixed exchange rates (which in part explains its de facto independence from the UN).[47] Over time, and with the collapse of the fixed-exchange-rate system in the 1970s, the IMF reinvented itself as the "lender of last resort." This means that the IMF's role in development has been that of a crisis troubleshooter, providing financial assistance to otherwise uncreditworthy states. Such states usually experience an economic crisis that also involves a run on their currency, greatly reducing its value. During these kinds of crises, the IMF works with states and the World Bank to put together loan packages designed to stabilize currency values and stave off economic catastrophe. The loan packages come with strings attached: namely, conditions designed to fundamentally change the underlying situations that, in theory, gave rise to the crisis in the first place. These structural adjustment loans require states to implement market reforms, privatize government-owned industries, and reduce government deficits through austerity.

The IMF and its structural adjustment programs (SAPs) have numerous detractors on both sides of the political spectrum. On the left, critics claim that structural adjustment loans increase poverty and the costs of restructuring the economy are borne by the poor, especially women. Some maintain that Bank and IMF SAPs reinforce authoritarian governments, in that only repressive governments can carry out the unpopular cost-cutting programs. For instance, Naomi Klein argues in *The Shock Doctrine: The Rise of Disaster Capitalism* (the book's subtitle says it all) that much structural reform has nothing to do with the origins of economic problems but instead attempts to advance the ideology of the market.[48] On the right, the IMF is seen as interventionist, bailing out states and private investors/creditors/banks making high-risk and, ultimately, poor choices.

Bailouts like the one that the United States implemented at home in 2008–2009 could have the effect of rewarding bad behavior, and the same type of reasoning applies internationally. At the same time, governments cannot sit idly by while an economy crashes or the financial system implodes. Most governments and international financial institutions (IFIs) tend to be pragmatic rather than dogmatic in selecting economic policy tools.

The IMF remains the only mechanism to coordinate multilateral responses to monetary crises. In an interesting twist of fortune, both the IMF and, to a lesser extent, the World Bank are facing identity crises. According to former IMF managing director Dominique Strauss-Kahn, "What might be at stake today is the very existence of the I.M.F. as a major institution providing financial stability to the world, a global public good. . . . In sum, the two main issues are relevance and legitimacy."[49] With globalization and massive financial transfers occurring daily, the IMF can no longer handle a financial crisis like that in Asia in the late 1990s or Argentina at the start of the twenty-first century, let alone the ongoing one. States assisted in the 1990s have, for the most part, only partially repaid loans. However, relations between those states have soured given the heavy-handed approach of the IMF's structural adjustment programs.

The IMF and the World Bank are significantly challenged by the ongoing global financial crisis. In November 2008, European leaders sought to hold a major conference seen by many as Bretton Woods II, whereby the IMF and World Bank would be reformed to address the financial challenges of the twenty-first century. The Bush administration resisted any initiative that would lead to a global financial management scheme but did call a meeting of the G20 in Washington because the smaller G8 did not include either the largest potential creditors or sources of possible growth.

By 2011 Europe was in a full-fledged, sovereign-debt crisis. It began in Greece but soon spread to Portugal, Ireland, Spain, and Italy; the borrowing costs for these governments rose beyond their ability to pay and continue to service debt. Greece needed a bailout almost immediately, and contagion concerns forced Europe into a multilateral response. Financial crises have happened in the past but never to an advanced industrialized country integrated into one of the world's most important currencies and largest regional economies. The EU (led by Germany and France), the IMF, and the United States were forced into immediate and short-term action. This involved emergency loans (in exchange for austerity) and building up a firewall both in Europe and at the IMF. This meant having sufficient resources in place to stave off any future speculative runs on the euro. The size of the crisis also meant that the G20 would have to be involved, especially with the BRICS (Brazil, Russia, India, China, and South Africa) contributing additional resources to the IMF. The significance of the G20 during the economic and financial meltdown was an indication that the "rest" (or at least the largest and most important economic powers in the Global South) were essential to the West.[50]

Complicating the euro crisis, the IMFs then managing director Strauss-Kahn was accused of sexually assaulting a maid at a hotel in New York, creating a global scandal. Prior to his service at the IMF, he had served as France's minister of economy, finance, and industry and oversaw the launch of the euro; he was widely expected to be a strong candidate for the presidency in 2012. His abrupt resignation and departure created a critical vacuum, which was filled by Christine Lagarde, the first woman to head the IMF. Her appointment generated controversy, as developing countries again questioned why the leadership of the IMF should be determined by Europe. Meanwhile, Europeans worried that Lagarde was too schooled in the American version of international finance, which earned her the moniker of "l'Américaine."[51]

In a repetition of the long-standing debate on the virtues of stimulus versus austerity in a crisis (albeit with a reversal of roles), Germany and northern European states, bolstered by the European Central Bank, insisted on austerity and adjustment. The U.S. Federal Reserve made dollars more available to European banks, temporarily keeping them solvent. The IMF, which oversaw half a billion dollars in emergency loans, warned against too much austerity. In its 2012 *World Economic Outlook*, the IMF warned that austerity should not come at the expense of growth, as the resulting social instability threatened the overall economy.[52] In July 2015, the IMF argued, in contrast to the European Central Bank and European creditor countries, that Greece's debt was unsustainable.[53] The irony of the IMF's calling for a human face on structural adjustment when applied to Europe cannot be lost on many in the Global South.

The WTO

Trade and development are linked: trade brings the goods, services, and technology necessary for economic growth and increased standards of living. Moreover, trade promotes the efficient use of resources contributing to sustainability. The development success stories are those of trade-related, export-led growth. In 1995 the World Trade Organization was created as the last order of business of the Uruguay Round of the General Agreement on Tariffs and Trade (GATT) to help states overcome several problematic trade issues. While the GATT had been quite successful at reducing tariffs, duties, and quotas on manufactured goods, it could not deal with emerging new protectionist measures (known as nontariff barriers, or NTBs) and had little success in liberalizing the agricultural and services sectors of the world economy. Also important to many trading states was the Agreement on Trade-Related Aspects of Intellectual Property Rights (TRIPS) and rules regarding trade-related investment measures (TRIMS). The WTO was created to help member states overcome their differences on these issues through consensus-based rule making and the Dispute Settlement Body (DSB), a mechanism through which disputes can be authoritatively decided by neutral trade experts and trade rules enforced. While the DSB determines what trade practices are in accord with WTO rules (or not), it is states that decide whether to impose sanctions—such as, ironically, higher tariffs—against those whose policies have been held to violate the rules. As of this writing, the Doha Round that began with the WTO's establishment in 1995 is not completed, as many countries of the North and South are negotiating bilateral and regional agreements.[54] Clearly there are problems with the WTO.[55]

The differences among member states on trade issues are real and sometimes intractable because free trade may bring many benefits that are distributed unevenly between and within societies. Free trade also brings many problems: local businesses and industries can be threatened, and workers can be displaced. This makes it difficult for states in the Global South, and to a lesser extent the North, to ensure the basic human needs of their people and stable sustainable economic growth. Hence, reaching consensus on trade rules has proven difficult and contentious.

Coordination among all of these different development mechanisms in the UN family is not all it could be. Kofi Annan's "Quiet Revolution" sought to redress this situation and bring the UN, the international financial institutions, and the WTO into closer working relations.[56] The subject is essential and goes beyond budgets and finances, because a greater integration of these organizations is necessary for policy coherence as well. The World Bank, especially in regard to a narrow and rather technical approach to economic growth, leaves out many important human aspects of the development process.[57] At the same time, the UN system manifests a broader coherent development rationale through the MDGs, and now the SDGs, but has precious few resources to test its more theoretical propositions. The IMF may use structural adjustment programs to reform a state's economy, but UNICEF knows how to put a human face on such conditionality.[58] A reasonably coherent and pragmatic framework to fight poverty and promote human development and the wherewithal and expertise to pursue that agenda exist among a host of decentralized international organizations that are all supposedly part of the UN development system.

NORM CREATION AND COHERENCE: A PARTIAL HISTORY OF IDEAS

The United Nations, broadly defined, plays two basic kinds of roles in world politics: ideational and operational.[59] Creating norms and building relative consensus around those norms is essential for moving disparate states, organizations, and peoples (with different values and preferences) in the same general direction. The international community did not just arrive at a shared understanding of "development" as meaning sustainable human development.[60] That understanding was forged through diplomacy and compromise. The process is difficult, inconsistent, and often ineffective. At the same time, that process defined problems (poverty, inequality, resource depletion, pollution, climate change) and their causes, and created strategies for addressing those problems.

From Stockholm to Rio de Janeiro

As an example of the ideational process, we take the example of the rise of an ecological perspective. The process of norm creation began in 1971 in Stockholm with the United Nations Conference on the Human Environment (UNCHE). During the preparations for this conference, experts in Founex, Switzerland, led by then UNCHE secretary-general Maurice Strong, probed the concept of eco-development, thereby integrating development and the environment. The Club of Rome and others had also put forward similar notions, although these largely intellectual exercises did not carry the same force or impact as the Founex report.[61] Under Strong's leadership, the participants were able to bridge some important political divides, in particular the clash of priorities between developing countries in pursuit of economic growth and developed countries concerned about conservation of natural resources. The clash was captured by India's prime minister, Indira Gandhi, who opened the Stockholm conference by arguing that in developing countries "poverty is the greatest polluter."[62] By arguing that long-term development was necessary to combat the poverty that contributed to pollution but that such growth also depended on dealing with shorter-term environmental problems, Strong was able to bridge the North-South divide. He also suggested that the governments of industrialized countries help defray the costs of environmental protection that developing countries would be forced to bear. The concept of "additionality," meaning to increase resources so as to apply them to a new problem rather than to subtract them from another use, helped overcome skepticism in the South over global economic inequities.[63]

Two decades later, the issues were revisited. Previously, in 1987, the Brundtland Commission, created by the General Assembly in 1983 to intellectually bridge the divide between economic growth and environmental protection, had reframed the debate as "sustainable development." This in turn fed into the preparations for and activities surrounding the 1992 UN Conference on Environment and Development (UNCED), also known as the Earth Summit, held in Rio de Janeiro. The Earth Summit far exceeded almost all normal conceptions of a conference, as did the extensive documentation.[64] The Rio process was massive. In addition to the intergovernmental conference, which incorporated a summit meeting of heads of state or government during its final days, the Rio gathering included a series of related events, unparalleled in scope and sponsored by civic-based entities that together were referred to as the Global Forum. These parallel activities of the emerging third UN drew tens of thousands of participants and an estimated two hundred thousand onlookers. A record number of national governmental delegations attended the Earth Summit, and some fourteen hundred NGOs with approximately eighteen thousand participants were at the parallel Global Forum.

The "road to Rio" was arduous.[65] Participants were engaged in the preparatory process almost continuously for three years. Maurice Strong, who after twenty years was selected to serve again as secretary-general of the conference secretariat, repeated what he had said about UNCHE, namely that in many important respects "the process was the policy."[66] The process of building consensus was regarded by many participants as being just as important an outcome of UNCED as any set of declarations, treaties, or other specific products. However, that process was not always an easy one, and the end products were not satisfactory to a majority of the participants. After three years of laborious and often tedious negotiations (for example, the specification of timetables), qualitative and quantitative targets and acceptable limits still eluded negotiators as they rushed to finalize agreement on the conventions, statements of principles, and plan of action.

The North-South tensions so evident in many other aspects of UN diplomacy, not surprisingly, also appeared in the sustainability debate, and they continue today. Southern governments were then and today remain skeptical about the North's push to impose ecological imperatives on the global development agenda. From their perspective, ozone depletion, hazardous waste pollution, and global climate change were products of industrialization and overconsumption in the North, but suddenly the new priority to protect the environment was to come at the expense of development in the Global South. Cooperation from developing countries was conditioned on the willingness of developed countries to pay the bill for at least part of their past environmental sins. If the North wanted the active partnership of the South in redressing these problems, northern donor governments would need to make available additional financial and technical resources.

These North-South tensions were brought into particularly sharp focus during the debate over deforestation. Southern negotiators were led by the Brazilians, Indians, and Malaysians—in an echo of what we heard earlier when sovereignty was under siege in the security and human rights arenas—and forcefully resisted any incursion into the principle of sovereignty over natural resources. Similarly, tensions prevailed in drafting the Rio Declaration, which was to guide governments and nongovernmental actors in implementing the many provisions of Agenda 21. With its unmistakable flavor of compromise between negotiators from industrialized countries and those from developing ones, this declaration integrated many of the most important elements of the development and environment perspectives of both sides. Even as the right to exploit resources within a state's geographical boundaries was reaffirmed, the responsibility of states to exercise control over environmentally damaging activities within their boundaries also was proclaimed. In addition, among the twenty-seven principles embodied in the declaration was one stating that the cost of pollution should be borne at the source and should be reflected in product cost at all stages of production.

Two legally binding international conventions—on biodiversity and on climate change—were incorporated as part of the larger Rio process. The Convention on Biodiversity requires signatories to pursue economic development in such a way as to preserve existing species and ecosystems. The Convention on Climate Change embodies a general set of principles and obligations aimed at reducing greenhouse gases. Largely as a result of the intransigent position of the first Bush

administration during the negotiation process, formal intergovernmental negotiations over the creation of these two legal conventions proved to be difficult
to finalize. The final documents emerging from the Earth Summit represented
"framework conventions." Although these conventions designated general principles and obligations, specific timetables and targets were left unspecified and
subject to future negotiations over protocols—that is, additional treaties.

Agenda 21 comprised more than six hundred pages and covered a large array
of issues. Although most of this text was agreed to before UNCED, a number of
contentious items were carried to the Earth Summit itself. In keeping with the
general tenor of debates, problems included issues related to biodiversity, biotech-
nology, and deforestation, and institutional and procedural issues involving financing, technology transfer, and institutional arrangements for carrying out the
elements of the action agenda.

A number of these issues proved to be intractable and remained unresolved
at the close of UNCED. Foremost among them was how to generate the financial
resources needed to implement the program of action and associated activities.
Estimates varied; the calculations made by the UNCED secretariat put the price
tag at well over $100 billion per year for the first decade alone. These figures re-
flected the massive scope of the components inherent in the marriage between
development and environment as they had come together within the Rio process.

Linked to the issue of financing was governance. At the core was the following
question: Who decides when and how such resources are to be spent? As the negotiations during the Rio process clearly revealed, some minimal basic agreement
about governance is a prerequisite for agreement over financing. Again, North-
South tensions fueled the debate. The northern negotiators, led by Washington,
pressed to have all such financing channeled through the World Bank group. In
that setting, the locus of control would be well established, with the G8 possessing
effective veto power. Also, the World Bank and the IMF tended to approach environmental protection through markets. The Global Environment Facility was in
place and might be expanded to encompass a broader mandate.

This proposed solution was not acceptable to most southern participants, who
preferred what they called a "more democratic" arrangement. These governments
proposed the creation of a new green fund, which would operate on more egali-
tarian voting principles. Most major northern donors found this proposal wholly
unacceptable. For them to commit significant levels of funding, some guarantee
of control was required. A compromise was achieved to enhance the South's participation while retaining elements of control for donor states. Interim financing
for Agenda 21 implementation would be provided under the aegis of the World
Bank group. The GEF would be expanded and its rules altered to provide for decision making by consensus among equally represented groupings of donors and
recipients. The governance issue has, at least temporarily, been put to rest. But the
matter of securing the requisite financial resources remains problematic, with
only a very small fraction of the necessary funds actually being delivered.

Beyond Rio

In the years immediately following the Earth Summit, two overriding challenges arose. The first was how to generate and sustain effective cooperation. This problem had both horizontal and vertical dimensions. Effective cooperation would be required horizontally across different autonomous organizational domains, legal jurisdictions, and sectors of society as well as vertically across different levels of social aggregation, from individuals in their roles in groups and communities to representative governance in international forums.

The second challenge was how to reorient UN discourse and practice to overcome the constraints inherent in the organization's legal foundations in state sovereignty. The UN's involvement in eco-development rejoins our earlier treatment of its activities in international peace and security and human rights matters. They all highlight the limits of working with a system circumscribed by the concept of sovereignty. The foundations of the UN Charter, especially Article 2 (7), prohibit the UN from intervening in the domestic jurisdiction of states. Additionally, the institutional structures and practices of multilateral diplomacy constrain attempts to incorporate nonstate and market actors into a full partnership in global policy processes.

These challenges seem forbidding, but as the heads of government at Rio pointed out, the costs of not rising to the challenge could be perilous. As they warned in the preamble of Agenda 21, "humanity stands at a defining moment in history. We are confronted with a perpetuation of disparities between and within nations, a worsening of poverty, hunger, ill health and illiteracy, and the continuing deterioration of the ecosystems on which we depend for our well-being." The Agenda 21 text argues that only by creating global partnerships and involving all sectors of world society can the world's peoples expect "the fulfillment of basic needs, improved living standards for all, better-protected and better-managed ecosystems and a safer, more prosperous future." Creating the necessary global partnerships on an unprecedented scale will, in turn, require meeting the twin challenges of cooperating effectively and moving beyond the confines of sovereignty. Before exploring the nature and scope of those challenges, however, we need a better understanding of the dynamic interplay of the forces and tensions that have given shape to the contemporary discourse and practice of sustainable development.

The debate over sustainable development places people-centered development at the core of the UN's work, even if the World Bank, the IMF, and the WTO are generally thought to contribute less to this concept than they should.[67] This was also the case with respect to issues such as population, human settlements, health, food, and women. This evolving emphasis on people-centered development was given enhanced visibility through the reports of a series of special high-level, independent global commissions comprising eminent persons. These began with the Pearson Commission in 1969 but shifted away from an almost exclusive focus on governments and economic development toward engaging other actors in the work of the world organization. We have discussed the three most prominent recent ones—on global governance (1995), intervention and state sovereignty (2001), and human security (2003)—as essential contributions to the normative climate, and in each of them the third UN played an essential role.[68]

The role sustainable development played in traversing the turf and ideological divide that otherwise separates actors in the global arena provides insight about the future of the UN's development work. In the Rio process and beyond, sustainability has served as an important bridge in institutional bargaining. The associated political processes have been characterized by bargaining among autonomous and self-interested participants striving for consensus. Operating under a veil of uncertainty about the likely effects of their alternative choices, participants engage in transnational alliance formation and politics that link issues. Many may be associated with specific communities of knowledge, but the political process is a pluralistic one in which groups of participants perceive and act on differing perceptions of problems, values, interests, and stakes.

Despite numerous difficulties, the general ideas articulated at Rio in 1992 on behalf of sustainable development increasingly took hold. In the mid-1990s the UNDP/UNFPA Executive Board decision 94/14 adopted "sustainable human development" as a new mission for technical assistance. Like other development concepts before it, sustainable human development was viewed as a prerequisite for creating and maintaining a secure and peaceful world order. The barrage of political discourse over development in the 1990s led most member states to expect the UN to play a meaningful role in realizing such a goal.

The decade of the 1990s witnessed an almost continuous negotiating process. Member states were constantly involved in, preparing for, or actually attending a major international socioeconomic gathering. And this was especially the case when planning follow-up sessions at five-, ten-, and most recently twenty-year intervals. The 2012 United Nations Conference on Sustainable Development (UNCSD) sought a joint endeavor to recommit to sustainable development by focusing on economic development, social development, and environmental protection. This Rio+20 conference identified the priority areas of decent jobs, energy, sustainable cities, food security, sustainable agriculture, water, oceans, and disaster readiness. In a slight shift, Rio+20 applied the norms of environmental protection developed at Rio in 1992 to these priority areas.

Was the gathering in Brazil yet another anticlimax? For those still reading a hard copy of the Sunday *New York Times*, a small article appeared on page 8, "Progress on the Sidelines as Rio Conference Ends," in contrast to June 1992, when several feature articles appeared over several days, many starting on the front page. Among the summaries cited about the 2012 summit's 283-paragraph agreement were those from CARE and Greenpeace: "nothing more than a political charade" and "a failure of epic proportions."[69]

The presence of more than a hundred heads of state amid fifty thousand participants led to no new intergovernmental agreement—unlike the 1992 conference,

From left: Secretary-General Ban Ki-moon; Dilma Rousseff, president of Brazil; and Muhammad Shaaban, undersecretary-general for General Assembly affairs and conference management. All are pictured at the podium during the plenary session of the UN Rio+20 Conference on Sustainable Development, in Rio de Janeiro, Brazil. June 20, 2012. (UN PHOTO 518067/MARIA ELISA FRANCO)

which produced two landmark policies in the form of conventions on climate change and biodiversity and a set of objectives in Agenda 21. Although many judge that these treaties have failed to live up to their promises and publicity, nonetheless these policies indicated a willingness among governments at the beginning of the 1990s to move ahead that had evaporated two decades later. Europe and the United States were distracted by the ongoing financial crisis that started in 2008, and the emerging powers of the South were unwilling to move toward compromise and enforceable commitments on climate change. It is worth recalling that views initially were largely negative toward the outcomes in 1992, but the conference ended up shaping many national policies and actions over the following two decades. In retrospect then, perhaps Rio+20 will resemble Rio 1992 and will have a more positive impact than appears at present.

The UN's goal-setting agenda—the three-year process that resulted in the formulation of the Sustainable Development Goals—did grow directly from the Rio+20 conference. In addition, after earlier disappointments in a host of gatherings, in particular in Copenhagen in 2009, conversations to address climate change continued among all three UNs in Paris in December 2015. The outcome was a landmark agreement by which states from both the North and the Global South agreed to take concrete, verifiable steps to reduce greenhouse gas emissions. The accord, whose details are discussed in the next chapter, does not get the world to where scientists say it needs to be; however, it was an important diplomatic success that moved states, businesses, and NGOs forward in a shared direction. After treading water for many

Secretary-General Ban Ki-moon poses for a group photo with world leaders attending the UN Climate Change Conference (COP21) in Paris, France. November 30, 2015. (UN PHOTO 654969/RICK BAJORNAS)

years (following the collapse in Copenhagen in 2009), finally the international political sentiment has begun to respond to climate change in a way that seems commensurate with the nature of the threat.

THE UN'S SUSTAINABLE HUMAN DEVELOPMENT MODEL

Sustainable human development is part of an overall human security framework that has been in the making since the early 1990s, although many would say that the combination of security, human rights, and sustainable development in separate streams has constituted the history of the international organization.[70] Making human beings secure, the approach argues, means more than protecting them from armed violence and alleviating suffering. If international organizations are to contribute meaningfully to the promotion of human security, security needs to be defined in much broader terms. Protecting civilians in war zones or from thuggish repression or grinding poverty is, of course, a fundamental objective and is far from guaranteed, as viewers of the evening news or readers of daily newspapers are all too aware.

Doing these simultaneously, as human security proposes, is logical but hardly easy. The *Human Development Report 1994* was a precursor to one a decade later from the Commission on Human Security in that both agreed this concept "must stress the security of people, not only of nations."[71] Thus, the way that citizens and their governments, and also scholars and international officials, think about security would be altered: people and their needs would trump such calculations as bombs and bullets, and considerations like access to food would be as important as military budgets. Thus sustainable human development can be viewed as a process of improving and sustaining human security.

Sustainable development, like human security, is a qualitative condition that entails individual and collective perceptions of threats to physical and psychological well-being from all agents and forces that could degrade lives, values, and property.[72] At a minimum, people may be considered secure if they are protected from the threat of the physical destruction of their lives or property as a result of assault from others. At the opposite extreme, maximum human security can be imagined in a totally threat-free environment, where human beings are protected against all threats to their lives, values, and property. Various qualities of human security can be imagined depending on the relative ordering of the priorities that people place on the satisfaction of various needs, values, and interests.

Human security bridges the traditional divisions of the silo-like agendas established by different international organizations, in which questions of war and peace have been largely insulated from economic and social ones. According to this alternative conceptualization, peace as the absence of direct massive violence is only one attribute of a secure environment, and international organizational action is one means of establishing this so-called negative peace. Further, the notion of human security focuses the attention of international organizations directly on individuals and their circumstances, thereby constituting a subtle challenge to state sovereignty. Making people psychologically secure may, under some circumstances, be the antithesis of making the governments of states and their territorial boundaries physically secure, especially when states themselves are the perpetrators of many individual insecurities. Pressing international organizations into the service of individually focused human security could therefore constitute an incremental step toward circumventing or marginalizing states and legitimizing supranational governance.

Most important, conceptualizing the mission of multilateral organizations as one of comprehensively promoting human security rather than separately promoting economic and social development, sustainable development, military security, human rights, and a variety of other goals frees the policy imagination to contemplate more holistically the nature and variety of threats to individual environments. Although critics rightly point out that such a blanket concept can lead to fuzzy thinking with little intellectual traction,[73] human security can free the policy imagination to consider how such threats may be removed and to formulate policy prescriptions for how international organizations might contribute to removing them.[74] Because the sources of human insecurity vary from region to region, so, too, will the definition of human security and the priorities for international organizations. It may be that in many, if not most, cases the organizations of the UN development system are not very appropriate, efficient, or effective mechanisms for transferring material development assistance. They appear to be relatively better suited to promoting and enhancing human security via policies, programs, and activities that focus on nonmaterial resource transfers and exchanges, including training and the exchange of ideas and information. But such a shift of institutional focus requires rethinking the nature and meaning of sustainable human development.

The foundations for sustainable human development require individuals, groups, and communities to take charge of their own destinies. They thereby themselves become engaged significantly in the satisfaction of their own needs, values, and interests. In short, they control their own futures according to the classic UNDP *Human Development Report*: "Human development is development of the people for the people by the people. . . . Development for the people means ensuring that the economic growth they generate is distributed widely and fairly. . . . Development by the people [means] giving everyone a chance to participate."[75] Yet the concept of popular participation has proven to be woolly and the debate about its meaning unfocused. In the World Bank, for example, popular participation has at various times and in various contexts been articulated as and associated with the "empowerment" of NGOs and the enhancement of their involvement in making Bank policy; increased Bank accountability and control of the Bank's programs, projects, and activities by "domestic" actors; and the active engagement in project planning of previously excluded individuals and groups with an emphasis on the importance of local knowledge and the satisfaction of local needs.

These aspects of participation are important, but this discourse has so far done little to change the essential course of the World Bank's policy and enhance its role in promoting some aspects of human security or to construct new models of development focusing on the satisfaction of basic human needs and values. Development models and institutional policies that fail to take adequate account of human needs may actually work to erode human security and inhibit sustainable human development.

The next chapter examines this new global development agenda in the context of the Millennium Development Goals (2000–2015) and the Sustainable Development Goals (2016–2030). Most world leaders acknowledge that "security" in the twenty-first century includes "human security" and that the UN's development agenda is a necessary component. Nevertheless, finding sufficient political will and operational capacity to move fast enough to confront and manage the ill effects of HIV/AIDS, extreme poverty, and climate change clearly remains a challenge.

NOTES

1. See the series of public opinion surveys by the Future UN Development System Project at http://www.futureun.org/en/Publications-Surveys/Article?newsid=34&teaserId=2. See also Stephen Browne, *The United Nations Development Programme and System* (London: Routledge, 2011); and Thomas G. Weiss, *What's Wrong with the UN and How to Fix It*, 3rd ed. (Cambridge: Polity, 2016).

2. The WTO is not formally part of the UN system but is considered a UN-related organization. See Bernard M. Hoekman and Petros C. Mavroidis, *The World Trade Organization: Law, Economics, and Politics* (London: Routledge, 2007); and Rorden Wilkinson, *The WTO: Crisis and the Governance of Global Trade* (London: Routledge, 2006).

3. Boutros Boutros-Ghali, "A New Departure on Development," *Foreign Policy* 98 (1995): 47. This is the working assumption behind the United Nations Intellectual History Project, which is producing fourteen volumes and an oral history around this theme. For details, see http://www.unhistory.org.

4. Stephen Browne and Thomas G. Weiss, *Making Change Happen: Enhancing the UN's Contributions to Development* (New York: WFUNA, 2012). See also http://www.futureUN.org.

5. Mourad Ahmia, ed., *The Group of 77 at the United Nations: Environment and Sustainable Development* (Oxford: Oxford University Press, 2012).

6. Bruce Jenks and Bruce D. Jones, *Punching Below Its Weight: The UN Development System at a Crossroads* (New York: Center for International Cooperation, 2012).

7. Jussi M. Hanhimäki, *The United Nations: A Very Short Introduction* (Oxford: Oxford University Press, 2008), 1. See also Stephen Browne and Thomas G. Weiss, "Is the UN Development System Becoming Irrelevant?" Development Dialogue paper no. 4 (December 2013), Dag Hammarskjöld Foundation.

8. Alisa Clarke, "Organizational Culture, System Evolution, and the United Nations of the 21st Century," *Journal of International Organizations Studies* 4, no. 1 (2013): 127–133.

9. Nassir Abdulaziz Al-Nasser, *A Year at the Helm of the United Nations General Assembly* (New York: New York University Press, 2014); M. J. Peterson, *The UN General Assembly* (London: Routledge, 2006).

10. For an overview of the CSD and other institutions, see Elizabeth R. DeSombre, *Global Environmental Institutions* (London: Routledge, 2006).

11. Helmut Anheier, Marlies Glasius, and Mark Kaldor, *Global Civil Society 2001* (Oxford: Oxford University Press, 2001); Peter Willetts, *Non-Governmental Organizations in World Politics: The Construction of Global Governance* (New York: Routledge, 2011); and Merritt Polk, ed. *Co-Producing Knowledge for Sustainable Cities: Joining Forces for Change* (New York: Routledge, 2015).

12. Stine Madland Kaasa, "The UN Commission On Sustainable Development: Which Mechanisms Explain Its Accomplishments?" *Global Environmental Politics* 7 (2007): 107–129.

13. Elsa Tsioumani, "CSD-15 Concludes with No Final Outcome Adopted," *Environmental Policy and Law* 37 (2007): 288–289.

14. "Hot Seats," *Economist*, May 19, 2007, 19.

15. Thomas G. Weiss, "ECOSOC Is Dead, Long Live ECOSOC," *Friedrich Ebert Stiftung Perspectives* 2010, and "ECOSOC and the MDGs: What Can Be Done?" in *Beyond the Millennium Development Goals: Global Development Goals Post-2015*, ed. David Hulme and Rorden Wilkinson (London: Routledge, 2012).

16. Kofi A. Annan, *Renewing the United Nations: A Programme for Reform* (New York: UN, 1997).

17. Crain N. Murphy, *United Nations Development Programme: A Better Way?* (Cambridge: Cambridge University Press, 2006).

18. UNDP, *Human Development Report 1993* (New York: Oxford University Press, 1993).

19. Stephen Browne, *United Nations Development Programme and System* (London: Routledge, 2011).

20. Mark Malloch Brown, "Opening Statement at the UNDP/UNFPA Executive Board," New York, June 10, 2003, 1.

21. Ibid., 11.

22. UNDP, Annual Report of the Administrator, June 19, 2003. The *Journal of Human Development: Alternative Economics in Action* has been published three times a year since 2000.

23. Craig Murphy, *The United Nations Development Programme: A Better Way?* (Cambridge: Cambridge University Press, 2006); and Khadija Haq and Richard Ponzio, eds., *Pioneering the Human Development Revolution: An Intellectual Biography of Mahbubul Haq* (Delhi: Oxford University Press, 2008).

24. See Richard Ponzio and Arunabha Ghosh, *Human Development and Global Institutions: Evolution, Impact, Reform* (London: Routledge, 2016); Desmond McNeill, "Human Development: The Power of the Idea," *Journal of Human Development* 8 (March 2007): 5–23; and Desmond McNeill and Asunción Lera St. Clair, *Global Poverty: Ethics and Human Rights: The Role of Multilateral Organisations* (London: Routledge, 2009).

25. Joel E. Oestreich, "The United Nations and the Rights-Based Approach to Development in India," *Global Governance* 20 (2014): 77–94.

26. Ian Taylor, *UN Conference on Trade and Development* (London: Routledge, 2007); and John Toye and Richard Toye, *The UN and Global Political Economy: Trade, Finance, and Development* (Bloomington: Indiana University Press, 2004).

27. John Toye, "Assessing the G-77: 50 Years After UNCTAD and 40 Years After the NIEO," *Third World Quarterly* 35 (2014): 1759–1774 and Charles Gore, "Which Growth Theory Is Good for the Poor?" *European Journal of Development Research* 19 (March 2007): 30–48.

28. UNCTAD-UNDP-HABITAT, Press Release, May 16, 2001.

29. Yves Beigbeder, *New Challenges for UNICEF: Children, Women, and Human Rights* (New York: Palgrave, 2001); and Richard Jolly, *UNICEF* (London: Routledge, 2013).

30. You Danzen, Lucia Hug, and David Anthony, "UNICEF Report Generation 2030 Africa Calls Upon Investing in and Empowering Girls and Young Women," *Reproductive Health* 12 (2015): 1–4.

31. Laura Lundy, Ursula Kilkelly, and Bronagh Byrne, "Incorporation of the United Nations Convention on the Rights of the Child in Law: A Comparative Review," *International Journal of Children's Rights* 21 (2013): 442–463.

32. Joel Oestreich, *Power and Principle* (Washington, D.C.: Georgetown University Press, 2007).

33. UNICEF, *Humanitarian Action for Children 2011* (New York: UNICEF, 2011), http://www.unicef.org/publications/files/HAC2011_EN_030911.pdf.

34. Miriam Intrator, "Educators Across Borders, The Conference of Allied Ministers of Education, 1942–45," in *Wartime Origins and the Future United Nations*, ed. Dan Plesch and Thomas G. Weiss (London: Routledge, 2015), 56–75.

35. J. P. Singh, *United Nations Educational, Social and Cultural Organization (UNESCO)* (London: Routledge, 2011).

36. Gian Luca Burci and Claude-Henri Vignes, *World Health Organization* (The Hague: Kluwer Law International, 2004); Kelley Lee, *The World Health Organisation (WHO)* (London: Routledge, 2009); and Sophie Harman, *Global Health Governance* (Abingdon, U.K.: Routledge, 2011); Nitsan Chorev, *The World Health Organization Between North and South* (Ithaca, N.Y.: Cornell University Press, 2014).

37. Alicia Ely Yamin and Ole Frith Norheim, "Taking Equality Seriously: Applying Human Rights Frameworks to Priority Setting," *Human Rights Quarterly* 36 (2014): 296–324.

38. WHO, Press Release, May 22, 2003.

39. Laurie Garrett, "Ebola's Lessons: How the WHO Mishandled the Crisis," *Foreign Affairs* 94, no. 5 (2015).

40. "Report of Ebola Interim Assessment Panel," July 2015, http://www.who.int/csr /resources/publications/ebola/ebola-panel-report/en.

41. Andraz Zidar, "WHO International Health Regulations and Human Rights: From Allusions to Inclusion," *International Journal of Human Rights* 19 (2015): 505–526.

42. D. John Shaw, *Global Food and Agricultural Organizations* (London: Routledge, 2008).

43. Edward S. Mason and Robert E. Asher, *The World Bank Since Bretton Woods: The Origins, Policies, Operations, and Impact of the International Bank for Reconstruction and Development and the Other Members of the World Bank Group* (Washington, D.C.: Brookings Institution, 1973); Devesh Kapur, John P. Lewis, and Richard Webb, *The World Bank: Its First Half Century*, vol. 1, *History* (Washington, D.C.: Brookings Institution, 1997); Morten Bøås and Desmond McNeill, *Global Institutions and Development: Framing the World?* (London: Routledge, 2004); and Katherine Marshall, *The World Bank: From Reconstruction to Development to Equity* (London: Routledge, 2008).

44. Paul Volcker et al., *The Independent Panel Review of the World Bank Group Department of Institutional Integrity*, September 13, 2007, available at http://siteresources.world bank.org/NEWS/Resources/Volcker_Report_Sept._12,_for_website_FINAL.pdf

45. Howard Schneider, "Jim Yong Kim Named World Bank President," *Washington Post*, April 16, 2012.

46. http://www.investopedia.com/articles/investing/033115/10-countries-biggest-forex -reserves.asp.

47. Margaret G. de Vries, *The International Monetary Fund, 1945–1965: The Twenty Years of International Monetary Cooperation* (Washington, D.C.: IMF, 1969), *The International Monetary Fund, 1966–1971: The System Under Stress* (Washington, D.C.: IMF, 1976), and *The International Monetary Fund, 1972–1978: Cooperation on Trial* (Washington, D.C.: IMF, 1985); Norman K. Humphreys, ed., *Historical Dictionary of the IMF* (Washington, D.C.: IMF, 2000); and James Vreeland, *The International Monetary Fund: Politics of Conditional Lending* (New York: Routledge, 2006).

48. Naomi Klein, *The Shock Doctrine: The Rise of Disaster Capitalism* (London: Macmillan, 2007).

49. Steven Weisman, "I.M.F. Faces a Question of Identity," *New York Times*, September 28, 2007.

50. Andrew F. Cooper and Ramesh Thakur, *The Group of Twenty (G20)* (London: Routledge, 2013).

51. Liz Alderman, "Mme Lagarde Goes to Washington," *New York Times*, September 24, 2011.

52. See IMF, *World Economic Outlook*, April 2012, http://www.imf.org/external/pubs/ft /weo/2012/01/pdf/text.pdf.

53. "Greece: An Update of IMF Staff's Preliminary Public Debt Sustainability Analysis, IMF Country Report No. 15/186, July 14, 2015, available at https://www.imf.org/external /pubs/ft/scr/2015/cr15186.pdf.

54. Rorden Wilkinson and James Scott, eds., *Trade, Poverty, Development: Getting Beyond the WTO's Doha Deadlock* (London: Routledge, 2013).

55. Rorden Wilkinson, *What's Wrong with the WTO and How to Fix It* (Cambridge: Polity, 2015).

56. Kofi Annan, "The Quiet Revolution," *Global Governance* 4, no. 2 (1998): 123–138.

57. Jonathan R. Pincus and Jeffrey A. Winters, eds., *Reinventing the World Bank* (Ithaca, N.Y.: Cornell University Press, 2002). As for the IMF, see Devesh Kapur, "The IMF: A Cure or a Curse?" *Foreign Policy* 111 (Summer 1998): 114–131; and Graham Bird and Joseph P. Joyce, "Remodeling the Multilateral Financial Institutions," *Global Governance* 7, no. 1 (2001): 75–94.

58. UNICEF report, "Structural Adjustment with a Human Face" (Oxford: UNICEF /Oxford University Press, 1987).

59. Stephen Brown and Thomas G. Weiss, "The Future UN Development Agenda: Contrasting Visions and Contrasting Operations," *Third World Quarterly* 35, 7 (2014): 1326–1340.

60. David Hulme, *Global Poverty: How Global Governance Is Failing the Poor* (London: Routledge, 2010); and Jennifer Clapp and Rorden Wilkinson, eds., *Global Governance, Poverty, and Inequality* (London: Routledge, 2010).

61. UNEP, "Development and Environment: The Founex Report—In Defense of the Earth," *The Basic Texts on Environment*, UNEP Executive Series 1, Nairobi, 1981.

62. Quoted by Maurice Strong, "Policy Lessons Learned in a Thirty Years' Perspective," in *Stockholm Thirty Years On: Proceedings from an International Conference 17–18 June 2002* (Stockholm: Ministry of the Environment, 2002), 18.

63. W. Bradnee Chambers and Jessica F. Green, eds., *Reforming International Environmental Governance: From Institutional Limits to Innovative Reforms* (Tokyo: UN University Press, 2005); Pamela S. Chasek, David L. Downie, and Janet Welsh Brown, *Global Environmental Politics*, 4th ed. (Boulder: Colo.: Westview, 2005); and Pamela S. Chasek, *Earth Negotiations: Analyzing Thirty Years of Environmental Diplomacy* (Tokyo: UN University Press, 2001).

64. Shanna Halpren, *The United Nations Conference on Environment and Development: Process and Documentation* (Providence, R.I.: Academic Council on the United Nations System, 1992).

65. Michael McCoy and Patrick McCully, *The Road from Rio: An NGO Guide to Environment and Development* (Amsterdam: International Books, 1993). For a more general discussion, see Kerstin Martens, *NGOs and the United Nations: Institutionalization, Professionalization and Adaptation* (New York: Palgrave Macmillan, 2005). See also the three reports in 2001, 2002, and 2003 by Helmut Anheier, Marlies Glasius, and Mary Kaldor, eds., *Global Civil Society* (Oxford: Oxford University Press, 2001, 2002, and 2003).

66. Maurice Strong, *Where on Earth Are We Going?* (New York: W. W. Norton, 2001).

67. Richard Jolly, Louis Emmerij, and Thomas G. Weiss, *The Power of UN Ideas: Lessons from the First Sixty Years* (New York: United Nations Intellectual History Project, 2005), and *UN Ideas That Changed the World* (Bloomington: Indiana University Press, 2009).

68. Commission on International Development, *Partners in Development* (New York: Praeger, 1969); *Our Global Neighborhood: The Report of the Commission on Global Governance* (Oxford: Oxford University Press, 1995); *The Responsibility to Protect: Report of the International Commission on Intervention and State Sovereignty* (Ottawa: International Development Research Centre, 2001); and Commission on Human Security, *Human Security Now* (New York: Commission on Human Security, 2003). This was also a view expressed in oral histories from some of the main participants in Thomas G. Weiss, Tatiana

Carayannis, Louis Emmerij, and Richard Jolly, *UN Voices: The Challenge of Development and Social Justice* (Bloomington: Indiana University Press, 2005), part three; for the complete transcripts, see the CD-ROM *The Complete Oral History Transcripts from "UN Voices"* (New York: United Nations Intellectual History Project, 2006).

69. Simon Romero and John M. Broder, "Progress on the Sidelines as Rio Conference Ends," *New York Times*, June 24, 2012.

70. Fen Hampson and Christopher Penny, "Human Security," in *The Oxford Handbook on the United Nations*, ed. Thomas G. Weiss and Sam Daws (Oxford: Oxford University Press, 2007), 539–557; Susan Pick de Weiss and Jenna Sirkin, *Breaking the Poverty Cycle: The Human Basis for Sustainable Development* (Oxford: Oxford University Press, 2010).

71. UNDP, *Human Development Report 1993*, 2.

72. Sheldon Leader and David Ong, eds., *Global Project Finance, Human Rights and Sustainable Development* (Cambridge: Cambridge University Press, 2011).

73. S. Neil MacFarlane and Yuen Foong Khong, *The UN and Human Security: A Critical History* (Bloomington: Indiana University Press, 2005); and Roland Paris, "Peacebuilding and the Limits of International Liberalism," *International Security* 22 (Fall 1997): 54–89.

74. Fen Osler Hampson et al., *Madness in the Multitude: Human Security and World Disorder* (Toronto: Oxford University Press, 2001).

75. UNDP, *Human Development Report 1993*, 2.

CHAPTER 12

The UN and Development in a Globalizing World

THE GLOBALIZING WORLD OF the late twentieth and early twenty-first centuries presents a plethora of economic, social, and political challenges and opportunities. The forces and processes at play are not really new but are ever more apparent in today's shrinking world. While the globalizing world economy yields many benefits, especially to some in wealthier countries and perhaps the upper classes of all countries, it also has brought in its wake unprecedented inequality. Secretary-General Kofi Annan reflected on this problem in *"We the Peoples": The Role of the United Nations in the 21st Century*: "The benefits of globalization are plain to see: faster economic growth, higher living standards, accelerated innovation and diffusion of technology and management skills, new economic opportunities for individuals and countries alike." Yet these benefits are distributed very unequally and inequitably. They are "highly concentrated among a relatively small number of countries and are spread unevenly within them."[1] The globalized world economic-political order has a malevolent side, giving rise to different, often criminal, kinds of violence and threats to human security.[2]

The impact of globalizing forces varies dramatically from region to region and case to case. As underscored in an earlier report by Annan, the "actual experience of globalization, to a great degree, varied with the level of development at which a country experienced it."[3] In some cases, where national economies were well positioned in terms of capacity and economic orientation, rapid economic growth has ensued. Elsewhere the result has been much less positive, contributing to increased poverty, inequality, marginalization, and human insecurity. In some places, globalization may actually undermine many of the development efforts by UN agencies.

The 2000 Millennium Declaration identified several development challenges that were translated into eight concrete Millennium Development Goals (MDGs). It also identified globalization as a key issue confronting the international community of states. UN member states accordingly pledged to act "to ensure that globalization becomes a positive force for all the world's people."[4] This chapter details the fifteen-year international effort to achieve the MDGs in an increasingly global world, and assesses the status of world politics as the UN embarks on a strategy to actualize the successor to MDGs, the Sustainable Development Goals (SDGs). The MDG and SDG strategies reflect the loose partnership between governments, UN agencies, civil society actors, and local communities striving to advance sustainable human development and human security.

THE MDG STRATEGY

International gatherings over the past two decades have resulted in a largely consensual strategy for assessing progress toward dealing with the negative impacts of globalization and eradicating extreme poverty. At the same time, these gatherings reflected a tension between states favoring a more authoritative, regulative state-driven approach to promoting development and those seeking to harness market forces to this end. This tension has resulted in an ambiguous compromise whereby both strategies are pursued, albeit with asymmetrical resources. The consensual strategy was organized at the turn of the millennium around eight main objectives—the MDGs—and eighteen related targets to be achieved by 2015. (See Table 12.1)

Seven of the eight main goals focused on substantive objectives. The eighth MDG dealt with creating the capacity to achieve the other seven. Cumulatively, the MDGs were envisioned to be both mutually reinforcing and intertwined. Eradicating extreme poverty, for example, would most likely drastically reduce infant mortality, improve maternal health, and better ensure environmental sustainability. Similarly, achieving universal primary education, promoting gender equality, empowering women, and combating HIV/AIDS, malaria, and other diseases would undoubtedly contribute to the eradication of poverty.

A UN system-wide strategy was designed for mobilizing support and monitoring progress toward achieving the MDGs. The strategy had four main components: the Millennium Project, the Millennium Campaign, Millennium Reports, and country-level monitoring and operational country-level activities. The Millennium Project sought to mobilize scholars from around the world and focus their collective wisdom and research efforts on achieving the MDGs. The purpose of this initiative was to help member states and UN agencies develop implementation strategies for reaching MDG targets. It also endeavored to identify priorities and financing mechanisms. At its inception, the project was directed by Columbia University's Jeffrey Sachs, who served as special adviser to the secretary-general. Ten expert task forces were set up to carry out the necessary research and report their findings to the secretary-general and the UN Development Programme (UNDP) administrator. Each task force focused on a specific set of MDG targets. Part of the process was the *Human Development Report 2003*, which focused on the MDGs.[5] Also, the campaign sought to promote and reinforce cooperation

TABLE 12.1 MILLENNIUM DEVELOPMENT GOALS AND TARGETS

Goal 1: Eradicate extreme poverty and hunger

Target 1   Halve, between 1990 and 2015, the proportion of people whose income is less than $1 a day

Target 2   Halve, between 1990 and 2015, the proportion of people who suffer from hunger

Goal 2: Achieve universal primary education

Target 3   Ensure that, by 2015, children everywhere, boys and girls alike, will be able to complete a full course of primary schooling

Goal 3: Promote gender equality and empower women

Target 4   Eliminate gender disparity in primary and secondary education, preferably by 2005, and to all levels of education no later than 2015

Goal 4: Reduce child mortality

Target 5   Reduce by two-thirds, between 1990 and 2015, the under-five mortality rate

Goal 5: Improve maternal health

Target 6   Reduce by three-quarters, between 1990 and 2015, the maternal mortality ratio

Goal 6: Combat HIV/AIDS, malaria, and other diseases

Target 7   Have halted by 2015 and begun to reverse the spread of HIV/AIDS

Target 8   Have halted by 2015 and begun to reverse the incidence of malaria and other major diseases

Goal 7: Ensure environmental sustainability

Target 9   Integrate the principles of sustainable development into country policies and programs and reverse the loss of environmental resources

Target 10   Halve, by 2015, the proportion of people without sustainable access to safe drinking water

Target 11   By 2020, achieve significant improvement in the lives of at least 100 million slum dwellers

Goal 8: Develop a global partnership for development

Target 12   Develop further an open, rule-based, predictable, nondiscriminatory trading and financial system (includes a commitment to good governance, development, and poverty reduction—both nationally and internationally)

Target 13   Address the special needs of the least developed countries (includes tariff- and quota-free access for LDC exports; enhanced program of debt relief for Heavily Indebted Poor Countries (HIPC) and cancellation of official bilateral debt; and more generous ODA for countries committed to poverty reduction)

Target 14   Address the special needs of landlocked countries and small island developing states (through the Program of Action for the Sustainable Development of Small Island Developing States and the outcome of the twenty-second special session of the General Assembly)

Target 15   Deal comprehensively with the debt problems of developing countries through national and international measures in order to make debt sustainable in the long term

Target 16   In cooperation with developing countries, develop and implement strategies for decent and productive work for youth

Target 17   In cooperation with pharmaceutical companies, provide access to affordable, essential drugs in developing countries

Target 18   In cooperation with the private sector, make available the benefits of new technologies, especially information and communications

Source: http://www.unmillenniumproject.org/goals/gti.htm.

among UN agencies, the International Monetary Fund (IMF) and the World Bank (the Bank), and the World Trade Organization (WTO).

The final summary report by Sachs's team, *Investing in Development*, was published in March 2005 as background for the World Summit. It noted that the development aid system was still not MDG-based and lacked a coherent approach to poverty. The ten accompanying reports provided statistical backup in some depth for the argument. Although some low-level coordination has taken place, the IMF, the Bank, and the regional development banks still are not well linked to UN agencies for local projects.[6] In 2006, MDG Support replaced the Millennium Project and worked with countries to develop and implement their national development strategies.

The Millennium Campaign was designed to mobilize support for the MDGs. This entailed coaching member states to comply with the commitments already made and convincing them that greater consistency across trade, finance, education, health, development, and other ministries was crucial to MDG success. At least one positive outcome of the campaign at the 2005 World Summit was to garner U.S. support for the MDGs, and it helped recommit and refocus the UN at the MDG Summit in 2010.

The Millennium Reports constituted the third pillar of the strategy. The reports were individual country report cards. Country-level monitoring entailed collecting and analyzing data on progress toward achieving individual MDGs. UN teams assisted countries in designing and implementing policies necessary for successful progress. While not all countries submitted reports, the vast majority did, and the reports indicated significant progress toward meeting the MDGs in 2015.[7]

The UN's Non-Governmental Liaison Service (NGLS) reported, "The Millennium Development Goals, over a relatively short period of time, have gained tremendous currency, primarily in development circles but increasingly in related trade and finance circles. Many actors are now counting on the goals . . . to galvanize disparate and sometimes competing development agendas and are imagining how they might become a powerful political tool to hold governments and international institutions accountable."[8] The MDGs provided a widely used framework for examining the development work of the UN system.

The financial crisis of 2008 and the continuing economic slowdown caused instability in the world economy. Recession in many parts of Europe and little or no growth elsewhere in the advanced industrialized economies impacted the willingness of donor states to commit the resources necessary to meet the MDGs. In spite of initial concerns that the crisis would threaten progress toward the MDGs,[9] the effect was uneven: developing countries (such as in Latin America) that were more integrated into the world economy were suffering more than states in sub-Saharan Africa.[10] The UN Department for Economic and Social Affairs (DESA) remained concerned that high unemployment, especially among young people and women, coupled with austerity and the threat of a double-dip recession, will lead to setbacks in reducing poverty.[11] In spite of the economic challenges, the UN continued to implement the MDG strategy, adjusting and adapting along the way.[12]

Miguel d'Escoto Brockmann, president of the sixty-third session of the General Assembly, joined by Secretary-General Ban Ki-moon, addresses a high-level event of world leaders, private-sector representatives, and civil society partners to discuss specific ways to energize collaboration to achieve the Millennium Development Goals. (UN PHOTO 196894/MARCO CASTRO)

IMPLEMENTING THE MDGS

Unpacking the MDGs helps assess the progress and shortcomings in achieving sustainable human development. All three UNs contributed to the MDG process in an often uneasy partnership. As the UN's *Millennium Development Goals Report 2015* (*MDGR 2015*) indicates, tremendous advances in poverty reduction have been made but inequalities persist and progress is uneven.[13] The *MDGR 2015* is the final "report card" of the MDG effort and lays the foundation for the SDGs, which will frame the UN development agenda until 2030.

Poverty and Hunger

Poverty eradication lay at the core of the MDGs and the UN's sustainable development efforts. The world organization measures extreme poverty by determining the number of people living on less than $1.25 a day (previously the level was $1.00 a day). Given this measure, *The Millennium Development Goals Report 2012* (*MDGR 2012*) indicated that poverty rates have declined in all regions since 1990. The absolute number of extremely poor in the developing world fell from over 2 billion in 1990 to under 1.4 billion in 2008, and the proportion of people living in extreme poverty fell from 47 percent in 1990 to 24 percent in 2008.[14] As reflected in the *MDGR 2011*, "despite significant setbacks for the 2008–2009 economic downturn, exacerbated by the food and energy crisis, the world is still on track to reach the poverty-reduction target."[15]

Although extreme poverty worldwide is in decline, the benefits of growth measured by overall statistics disguise the uneven distribution of benefits. China made impressive progress and, along with India, was statistically responsible for progress measured globally because the two account for a third of the world's population (and for an even higher percentage of the MDG developing countries being measured). China is distinctive in having made tremendous strides during the 1990s in reducing the number of extremely poor. This Chinese success correlated highly with its unprecedented economic growth during the same time period, which has accelerated in the twenty-first century. A number of other East Asian and Pacific countries made impressive gains, too, cutting by half the number of extremely poor in the region as a whole.[16] The international community met the first MDG target globally in 2015; however, sub-Saharan Africa and South Asia remain a concern. The vast majority of those living in extreme poverty reside in these two regions.

Hunger and malnutrition are highly correlated with poverty. The specific target was to halve the proportion of people who suffer from hunger between 1990 and 2015. This target was narrowly missed, according to the *MDGR 2015*. In 1997, the number of chronically hungry people stood at 791 million, which represented a dramatic reduction from 1970, when the figure was 959 million. Yet, in the late 1990s, a strong reversal occurred, and by 2002 the number had risen to 852 million. In 2002, the MDG hunger target was being met in only 3 percent of the countries, and only 46 percent were on track. Of the remaining 51 percent, about half (24 percent of the total) were lagging far behind. On a somewhat more positive note, child hunger has declined in most regions.

Education

The education target (MDG 2) was to ensure that by 2015 "children everywhere, boys and girls alike, will be able to complete a full course of primary education." The *MDGR 2015* indicated mixed results toward achieving MDG 2. The enrollment rate in developing countries globally was 91 percent in 2015, up from 83 percent in 2000.[17] Illiteracy remained a major problem, with more than one hundred million people between the ages of fifteen and twenty-four unable to read or write. To spearhead the drive for universal literacy, the General Assembly declared 2003–2012 "The UN Literacy Decade." This UN system-wide effort, coordinated by UNESCO, focused on extending literacy to all who were not currently literate, children and adults alike. Thus, the poorest and marginalized population segments were key targets for the campaign, which was conducted under the banner of "Literacy for All: Voice for All, Learning for All." Creating sustainable, local "literacy environments" was a primary objective of the initiative.[18] By at least one measure, the worldwide literacy rate of youths between fifteen and twenty-four increased from 83 to 90 percent, with South Asia and North Africa leading the way.[19]

Various UN agencies attempted to bolster the global effort to achieve MDG 2. For example, there was a UN system-wide initiative, the United Nations Girls' Education Initiative, assisted governments in eliminating gender disparities in education. The International Labour Organization (ILO) placed special focus on promoting free and universally accessible education. Member states were called on to enforce compulsory schooling up to a minimum age for employment. The Food and Agriculture Organization (FAO) and the UN Educational, Scientific and Cultural Organization (UNESCO) spearheaded a partnership—Education for Rural People—with other international agencies, governments, and civil society, to reduce rural-urban disparities and improve the quality of rural education. UNESCO, the UN Children's Emergency Fund (UNICEF), the World Health Organization (WHO), the World Bank, and Education International launched a program called Focusing Resources on Effective School Health. UN organizations, individually and collectively, could do only so much, however. Real and sustainable progress depends on commitments and follow-through at the national and international levels by a host of partners.

One of the keys to increasing school enrollment has been abolishing school fees, which has been especially critical in Africa. In one year alone, between 2004 and 2005, public school enrollment in Ghana's most deprived districts increased from 4.2 to 5.4 million. In Kenya the change was even more dramatic: from 2003 to 2004 primary school enrollment vaulted from 1.3 million to just over 6 million. Other African countries, including Burundi, Democratic Republic of the Congo, Ethiopia, Malawi, Mozambique, Tanzania, and Uganda, experienced significant, albeit much less dramatic, results. Considerable progress was also made in Benin, Bhutan, Burkina Faso, Mali, and Niger, where enrollment ratios increased by 25 percent, with the abolition of school fees being the main driving force.[20]

Gender Equality

Efforts to ameliorate gender disparities were perhaps the most important global antipoverty effort of the MDGs, one that arguably has improved the lives, dignity, and security of millions, if not billions, of people. Poor women are the most marginalized of social groups who do not benefit from globalization. MDG 3 focused on gender inequality and empowering women. Globalization can clearly be a powerful force for development,[21] but women are often victims of structural violence, in that they are systematically excluded from the resources necessary to develop their human potential.[22] While promoting gender equality is an important objective in itself, enhancing the status of women in society is also important for a variety of reasons. Reducing gender differences in education may lead to other positive effects, such as increased creation of sustainable livelihoods and increases in productivity, improved maternal health, reduced fertility rates, and higher primary school retention. As UNDP administrator Mark Malloch Brown argued, "Empowering women is not just one of the goals; it plays a critical role in the achievement of the other seven as well." He continued, "Women are the poorest of the poor: disproportionately, women lack access to land, water, and sources of energy; women lack access to education and other social services; and too often women are absent from decision-making, not only at the national, regional, or local level, but even within their own families."[23]

The main target specified for this goal was to eliminate gender disparity in primary and secondary education, preferably by 2005, and in all levels of education no later than 2015. By 2005 a large number of countries were on track. In East and Southeast Asia, Latin America, the Caribbean, and the Council of International Schools (CIS), basic parity had been attained, and despite problems, much progress had been made in South Asia. However, substantial disparities persisted in sub-Saharan Africa, North Africa, the Middle East, and West Asia. In 2005, 113 countries had failed to achieve parity in primary and secondary education, and at the then-current rates only 18 of these were on track to achieve the target by 2015. The situation with regard to secondary education was bleaker. Only about one third of the developing countries had attained parity in secondary education. The *MDGR 2012* announced that parity had been achieved in primary education in the developing world as a whole.[24] Of the 131 developing countries reporting data by sex, 71 had achieved gender parity. Again, however, sub-Saharan Africa and Western Asia lagged behind and the *MDGR 2015* indicated that these regions were struggling to gain ground.

A May 2003 UNIFEM report, *Progress of the World's Women 2002: Gender Equality and the Millennium Development Goals*, disclosed that "although women have progressed relatively slowly in the last two years in the areas of education, literacy and employment, there have been encouraging signs of improvement in women's legislative representation." The report pointed out that this MDG indicator was the only gender inequality indicator not linked to poverty and disparities between rich and poor countries: "The United States, France and Japan, where women's share of parliamentary seats is 12, 11.8, and 10 percent respectively, lag behind thirteen developing countries in sub-Saharan Africa, which is experiencing the greatest regional poverty in the world. In South Africa and Mozambique, women's share of seats is 30 percent, while Rwanda and Uganda have 25.7 and 24.7 percent respectively."[25] As the *MDGR 2007* noted, the existence of a government-required quota system makes all the difference. In a quota system, women's inclusion in politics is authoritatively mandated by setting aside seats in legislatures and positions in government specifically for women. In 2003, for example, Rwanda adopted a new constitution that mandates a minimum of 30 percent of parliamentary seats go to women. As a result, Rwanda now has the largest proportion of women in parliament in the world. The *MDGR 2015* summarized that efforts to politically empower women resulted in the doubling of women in parliament, but still only one in five members are women.[26]

Underlying the UN's work in this area for the past two and a half decades has been the Convention on the Elimination of All Forms of Discrimination against Women. The convention binds acceding states to several important obligations.

State parties agree to incorporate the principles of equality of men and women in their legal system, abolish all discriminatory laws, and adopt appropriate ones prohibiting discrimination against women; establish tribunals and other public institutions to ensure the effective protection of women against discrimination; and ensure elimination of all acts of discrimination against women by persons, organizations, or enterprises.[27] Although the United States is a signatory, it has never ratified the convention. Some 170 other countries have ratified it.

Founded and merged with the United Nations Development Fund for Women (UNIFEM, formed in 1976) in 2010—UN Women builds on the earlier organization's work and plays a key advocacy role in promoting women's rights and the implementation of the convention against the discrimination of women. UN Women is committed to eliminating discrimination against women and girls and to empower women so they can achieve equality as "partners and beneficiaries of development, human rights, humanitarian action and peace and security."[28] The MDGs and the follow-up SDGs are a central focus area for UN Women, which places the goals at the center of its operations and programs, and monitors and analyzes system-wide progress. It works with other agencies and bodies to identify gender gaps and plays the role of advocate.

Transnational Public Health

Three MDGs dealt with various health-related topics: reducing child mortality; improving maternal health; and combating HIV/AIDS, malaria, and other diseases. In addition, one of the targets for the eighth MDG called for a global partnership with pharmaceutical companies to provide access to affordable, essential drugs in developing countries. All of these health-related goals were mutually reinforcing and were highly associated with the overall goal of poverty reduction. Disease and poor health provide a drag on economic growth and development. HIV/AIDS is particularly acute in this regard and threatens to undermine the development efforts of the entire sub-Saharan African region.

The issue of the role of child mortality in development is complex, and reducing infant and child mortality is problematic because of the lack of adequate medical treatment and immunization, unsafe drinking water, poor sanitation, civil strife, endemic disease, and malnutrition. Approximately 70 percent of child deaths are associated with some combination of disease and/or malnutrition, with pneumonia being the leading cause of death. "Rapid improvements before 1990 gave hope that mortality rates of children under five could be cut by two-thirds in the following 25 years. But progress slowed almost everywhere in the 1990s, and in parts of Africa infant mortality rates increased."[29] More children die from disease and malnutrition than the total number of adults who die from the three great endemic killer diseases: HIV/AIDS, malaria, and tuberculosis. Still, strides have been made. The global under-five mortality has declined by more than half.[30] Unfortunately, the highest levels remain in sub-Saharan Africa and the international community fell far short of the target of reducing the mortality rate by two thirds.

Malnutrition is a leading cause of child death, and poor, rural areas have a disproportionate number of deaths regardless of geographic location. Malaria and other diseases are also leading causes. According to a 2008 UN MDG fact sheet,[31] the "Nothing but Nets" campaign to provide insecticide-treated bed nets in malaria-prone countries has made a real difference. In Kenya, for example, there was a 44 percent reduction in child deaths among those sleeping under insecticide-treated nets compared with children who were not. Measles is another child killer, which strikes some 30 to 40 million children each year and kills nearly half a million. The Global Measles Initiative to vaccinate children, launched in 2001, represents another success story: measles mortality declined by 68 percent between 2000 and 2006. In sub-Saharan Africa the results were even more dramatic, with a 91 percent reduction in child measles deaths. Bangladesh's measles eradication program gained world attention in 2006, when 33.5 million children were vaccinated in twenty days. By 2015, it was calculated that measles vaccinations had prevented 15.6 million deaths between 2000 and 2013.[32]

MDG 5 centered on improving maternal health care. The target for this goal was to reduce by three quarters, between 1990 and 2015, the maternal mortality ratio. Maternal health problems are the leading cause of death of women of reproductive age: every minute, a woman dies of complications of pregnancy or childbirth. Nearly all maternal-related deaths occur in developing countries, and most are preventable. Inadequate delivery services and prenatal and postnatal care as well as unsafe abortions account for a large number of such deaths. For every woman who dies during childbirth, twenty more sustain debilitating pregnancy-related injuries. In the context of high-income countries the answer seems simple: adequate prenatal and postnatal maternal health care, family planning, skilled birth attendants, clean birthing facilities with adequate and safe blood supplies, and prevention of unsafe abortions. Unfortunately, in poor countries such luxuries often simply are not available, especially to the poor. Progress toward achieving the MDG target for maternal health was mixed and very disappointing in parts of Asia and nearly all of sub-Saharan Africa. Sub-Saharan Africa and Southern Asia account for 85 percent of maternal deaths worldwide.[33]

Several reports have indicated that maternal deaths have declined sharply. In 2010, the *Lancet* issued a report contradicting the perception that little or no progress was being made.[34] The study, funded by the Bill and Melinda Gates Foundation using different data and methods from those used by the UN, found a 1 to 3 percent annual decline in maternal mortality rates since 1980. While some countries such as Zimbabwe, showed an increase, many countries showed substantial progress toward MDG 5. The study also found that more than 50 percent of the maternal deaths in 2008 occurred in six countries (India, Nigeria, Pakistan, Afghanistan, Ethiopia, and the Congo). The reasons for the overall improvement were lower pregnancy rates, higher income and education for women, and the increasing availability of skilled attendants.[35] The rising rates in eastern and southern Africa were the result of HIV infection and the lack of access to antiretroviral drugs. The findings were initially viewed with skepticism, but the UN confirmed the findings with its own report, *Trends in Maternal Mortality 1990–2010*, issued in May 2012.

Adequately measuring and assessing maternal mortality is difficult for a variety of reasons. Most countries do not have good vital registration systems, and underreporting is acute in situations where a skilled health attendant is absent. The proportion of births attended by skilled health personnel is used as an important indicator because of the high correlation between maternal mortality and the absence of skilled personnel. The *MDGR 2015* indicated that globally, births attended by skilled personnel rose from 59 to 71 percent between 1990 and 2014.[36] Still, within countries, great gaps existed as the rich are far more likely than the poor to have access to a skilled attendant. The target of reducing maternal mortality by three quarters was not met.

The United Nations Population Fund (UNFPA) initiated a Campaign to End Fistula in 2006. Obstetric fistula afflicts many women in developing countries and is highly correlated with maternal death. Obstetric fistula is a complication of pregnancy in high-risk areas whereby the excretory organs attach to the reproductive organs, poisoning the woman. Even if death does not result, the woman often faces incontinence and an inability to control bowel movements. The campaign operates in forty countries in sub-Saharan Africa, South Asia, and the Arab states; in late 2008, significant progress was reported in twenty-five of those countries. Several NGOs are also working to combat the problem, most notably the Worldwide Fistula Fund (WFF), which operates primarily in Niger and received attention in 2012 for its success saving women and improving the quality of their lives.[37]

Maternal mortality is also linked to HIV/AIDS, malaria, and other endemic diseases. This connection is one of the reasons that combating these diseases was made MDG 6. HIV/AIDS is currently the most devastating health pandemic of our time—or, for that matter, any time in history—and challenges international cooperation.[38] HIV/AIDS has become the fourth largest cause of death in the world. The MDG target related to AIDS was to have halted and begun to reverse the spread of HIV/AIDS by 2015. Yet this task was daunting, especially in Africa and other low-income countries, and the goal was not met.

The situation in Africa clearly illustrates how the implications of AIDS for development go far beyond economic factors. One of the most significant impacts has been on educational systems. In the most highly infected countries, "HIV/ AIDS kills teachers faster than they can be trained, makes orphans of students, and threatens to derail efforts . . . to get all boys and girls into primary school by 2015." Moreover, AIDS has resulted in a widening gender gap. In addition to being more susceptible to infection than boys, girls are more prone to dropping out of school to care for sick family members.[39]

The effort to combat HIV infection illustrates the partnership between the three UNs. The Sachs Millennium Project report and the HLP report on threats, challenges, and change both stressed the need to commit the resources required to deal effectively and quickly with AIDS. Nearly all the AIDS-related recommendations in these reports found their way into the secretary-general's 2008 report to the General Assembly on Progress Made in the Implementation of the Declaration of Commitment on HIV/AIDS. One of the secretary-general's key recommendations focused on the need to mobilize the financial resources required to fund a comprehensive response to the pandemic. He argued that an estimated $18 billion above what was currently pledged would be required to fund worldwide HIV/AIDS efforts over three years, including treatment, care, and prevention.

Funding for anti–HIV/AIDS programs globally has grown tremendously. The amounts raised, however, represent less than half of what is estimated to be necessary annually to make headway in the fight against the disease. Largely as a result of increased funding from the Global Fund to Fight AIDS, Tuberculosis and Malaria (Global Fund) and the U.S. program, the President's Emergency Plan for AIDS Relief (PEPFAR), there was a significant increase in access to antiretroviral therapy. The Global Fund is a health financing organization that brings together governments, civil society, and the private sector, and PEPFAR is the largest bilateral program providing antiretroviral drugs and financing for AIDS prevention. UNAIDS, a small UN agency, coordinates international efforts and provides technical assistance. The *MDGR 2015* showed that the target of universal access to HIV/AIDS treatment was missed. At the same time access to antiretroviral therapy (ART) has increased at a remarkable pace. "By June 2014, 13.6 million people living with HIV were receiving ART globally. Of those, 12.1 million were living in developing regions, a massive increase from just 375,000 in 2013. In 2013 alone the number of people receiving ART rose by 1.9 million in the developing regions. This is 20 percent more than in 2012 and the largest annual increase ever."[40] Despite the increase, most people living with HIV in developing regions (some 31.5 million people) do not have access to ART. Such access will require sustained effort post-2015.

The second target for MDG 6 was to have halted by 2015 and begun to reverse the incidence of malaria and other major diseases. Malaria is the most prevalent tropical disease in the world, with between 200 and 500 million cases a year, resulting in nearly 1 million deaths. Although malaria is found in 109 countries, approximately 90 percent of the cases are located in sub-Saharan Africa, with other pockets of prevalence in tropical climates. The death rate from malaria in sub-Saharan Africa is truly staggering. About 90 percent of those deaths are children under the age of five.[41] The UN has pursued a variety of prophylactic measures,[42] the most promising of which is the use of insecticide-treated bed nets. The global target was met but regionally, sub-Saharan Africa still struggles with prevention and treatment.[43]

One third of the world's population—over 2 billion people—is infected with tuberculosis (TB). Luckily, most such individuals, especially in more affluent countries, will never develop active TB. The developing world is home to about 90 percent of all active cases. In terms of impact, TB is the single most devastating disease among adults in the developing world, and sub-Saharan Africa and South Asia are the most affected regions. TB and HIV/AIDS are highly associated diseases. In sub-Saharan Africa, three quarters of those infected with HIV/

AIDS develop active TB. Despite a slow rate of decline, the UN predicts all regions should meet the goal of halting the spread and reducing the incidence of TB.[44]

One of the success stories in international health has been the battle against polio. Only a few small pockets of the disease persist. Of all remaining cases, 99 percent are located in three countries—India, Nigeria, and Pakistan—with most of the remaining 1 percent located in just four additional countries. WHO, UNICEF, the U.S. Centers for Disease Control and Prevention (CDC), and Rotary International announced the new Global Polio Eradication Initiative in 2003. This program focuses its efforts in these seven most affected countries and in six others where there exists significant risk of reinfection.[45] In spite of progress, new cases were reported in 2012, prompting Secretary-General Ban Ki-moon to make a public appeal for more funding, as the Global Polio Eradication Initiative has only half of the $2 billion necessary for vaccines and staff.

Ensuring Environmental Sustainability

The MDG 7 of ensuring environmental sustainability centered on integrating the principles of sustainable development in development efforts and reversing the loss of environmental resources. The list of environmental problems plaguing the world's poor is daunting, including access to safe water and sanitation, modern energy supplies, deforestation, and desertification. Climate change has emerged as a major environmental problem facing the international community. As articulated by the Intergovernmental Panel on Climate Change (IPCC), climate change is primarily caused by the burning of fossil fuels, which contributes to the buildup of greenhouse gases, such as carbon dioxide and methane, in the atmosphere. Climate change is also exacerbated by other environmental problems, such as deforestation and desertification.

In 1989, the UN held a conference in the Netherlands to map out a strategy for tackling climate change. The three-part strategy that emerged centered on first getting all states to commit to stabilizing and reducing carbon dioxide emissions by a fixed date. Second, only the advanced industrialized states should have binding targets and they should pay for new environmentally friendly technologies to be used by developing countries to help them reduce their emissions without compromising their economic development. The third part was to conduct more research to reach a scientific consensus as to the causes and effects of climate change. This strategy served as the basis for the 1992 Earth Summit in Rio de Janeiro, which resulted in the 1992 Framework Convention on Climate Change and the follow-up treaty, the 1997 Kyoto Protocol.

The Kyoto Protocol was innovative in many respects. First, it set binding reductions on greenhouse-gas emissions on developed states whereby the European Union, the United States, and Japan agreed to reduce their emissions by 8 , 7, and 6 percent respectively below 1990 levels. To encourage efficiency and growth, Kyoto also included transferable emissions permits that would allow states to buy and sell the right to pollute. This works by assigning each country a certain amount of emitting rights, determined by their contribution to world gross domestic product (GDP) and other considerations, and placing a cap on overall global emissions. For example, China, which is experiencing tremendous economic development (and emitting more greenhouse gases as a result), should not have to sacrifice economic growth because it has exceeded its emissions limit. Rather, China could buy the pollution rights of a sub-Saharan African country, which probably emits very little. Under this kind of "cap and trade" arrangement, China can continue its economic development without externalizing the costs, and the sub-Saharan country earns money that can be used to achieve its own development goals. The main drawback of the Kyoto Protocol resulted from a negotiating concession, namely that developing countries only had "voluntary" reduction targets. Despite the drawbacks, the Clinton administration agreed to the protocol but did not submit it to the U.S. Senate, as the prospects for passage were slim. In 2001, the Bush administration rejected the protocol.

With the world's largest greenhouse-gas emitter on the sidelines, the international community struggled along with a series of conferences in Marrakech (2001) and Montreal (2005). The United States participated in these conferences but only as a nonbinding member. In November 2006 a framework for UN collaboration in assisting countries to develop the capacity to respond effectively to climate change—the Nairobi Framework—grew out of a climate change conference in that city. In 2007 the theme of the annual opening of the General Assembly was climate change. Bolstered by the Academy Award–winning film by former U.S. vice president Al Gore, *An Inconvenient Truth*, and the awarding of the Nobel Peace Prize to Gore and the IPCC, global warming and climate change moved front and center on the international agenda. Once contested, climate change is now almost universally regarded as a central problem facing humanity. Prior to leaving office, George W. Bush also recognized the seriousness of global warming, though he sought to approach it in his own way, as evidenced by his decision to skip the 2007 UN meetings on the subject in New York and instead hold his own conference at the same time.[46]

Multilateral efforts on addressing climate change were boosted somewhat in 2007, when Kevin Ruud was elected as Australia's prime minister and agreed to sign on to Kyoto. He also fully participated in the 2007 Bali Conference, which produced a "road map" for producing a binding treaty in Copenhagen in 2009 and replacing Kyoto in 2012. However, these efforts and the election of Barack Obama did not amount to any substantive immediate progress in the UN-based negotiations. Ruud was forced out of office, and Obama did not stress environmental action during his first administration; subsequent gatherings from 2010 to 2012 in Cancún and Durban as well as Rio were disappointments. The 195 Parties to the Convention met again in Lima in December 2014 in an attempt to jump-start the process. A month prior, President Obama and President Xi Jinpeng of China announced a joint declaration on carbon emissions, so there was some optimism. Yet negotiations in Lima were intense and problematic. Two of the major stumbling blocks revolved around developing a consensus over a transparent way to measure and report emissions and providing assistance to poorer countries to do so.

The *MDGR 2015* noted that emissions have increased by 50 percent since 1990 and the rise of greenhouse gases is unabated globally.[47] Unchecked, these emissions will have a catastrophic impact on the planet. Rising temperatures, melting ice caps, and weather extremes threaten coastal and urban areas, islands, and biodiversity. The continued increase in greenhouse gases may make large areas of the planet uninhabitable. Thus, combating climate change remains a critical challenge, especially for the first UN. A fledgling step occurred in Paris in December 2015, where member states for the first time forged an agreement among 195 countries. This time, U.S. President Obama moved the United States into a leadership role on the issue. On August 31, 2015, he challenged: "This year, in Paris, has to be the year that the world finally reaches an agreement to protect the one planet that we've got while we still can."[48]

The 2015 Paris conference, known as COP21 (or the 21st Conference of the Parties for the UN Framework Convention on Climate Change) took a different tack from the top-down approach of past negotiations. Rather than setting a universal target, all states were challenged to set their own national reduction targets and come to the conference with their best plans. From there, negotiators would broker a deal to improve transparency and secure funding—issues that stymied discussions in Lima. The COP21 outcome, while insufficient for reversing climate change or even keeping the temperature increases below the thresholds established by most scientists, is noteworthy for several reasons. First, while the initial national targets were not enough to meet the long-term goal of keeping global warming below 2 degrees Celsius (3.6 degrees Fahrenheit), the parties agreed to review their national targets every few years. Second, wealthy states agreed to continue to offer financial support to help poorer countries to adapt, and on a voluntary basis, emerging economies would also contribute resources. Third, the agreement has transparent rules for documenting and reporting progress, while building in flexibility for developing states. Fourth, the agreement recognizes loss and damage from climate change, although such recognition does not specify liability and compensation. Fifth, while there is no legal requirement dictating how or how much countries should reduce emissions, there are legally binding provisions to ratchet up the stringency of their approaches over time, reconvene every five years beginning in 2020 with tighter plans, and meet every five years beginning in 2023 to report on progress using a common accounting system. The name-and-shame system will hopefully encourage countries to enact necessary measures so as not to appear as laggards before their peers.

The agreement has problems. It is not a legally binding treaty (as the United States is unlikely to get any such treaty ratified). Moreover, the long-term goal of keeping warming below 2 degrees Celsius is not enough to stave off ill effects. There are also no penalties if countries miss their targets—there is an obligation to formulate voluntary plans, but no penalties for failing to comply. Private sector actors, such as Bill Gates, argue that new clean technologies are needed and the fossil-fuel industry remains an obstacle. Gates announced that he and other philanthropists had created a multibillion-dollar clean-energy fund at the start of the Paris talks, but the details of the necessary public-private partnership to make this initiative effective remain sketchy. So, in many respects, COP21 represents a glass half full. The agreement has many firsts; however, its implementation and adaptation over time will determine the degree to which it is successful.

Although climate change looms large and receives the lion's share of environmental attention, of much greater immediate concern for an overwhelming number of people are the scarcity of fresh water and a lack of sanitation. By 2010 the MDG target of halving the proportion of the world's population without sustainable access to safe drinking water had been met—five years ahead of schedule—but the challenge is that over 750 million people still have no access to safe drinking water. Worldwide more than 2.8 billion people, or about 40 percent of the world's population, are experiencing either physical or economic water shortages.[49]

WHO estimates that half the world's hospital beds are occupied by patients suffering from water-related diseases, and nearly 2 million people die from diarrhea and other water-borne diseases each year.[50] In many places entire communities are exposed to considerable health hazards as a result of inadequate sanitation facilities. Although sanitation has improved in most developing regions, almost half the people in those regions still lack access to improved sanitation facilities. The final report card shows that the target of providing sanitation was missed, and 946 million people still use open defecation, which brings people into direct contact with human waste.[51]

A GLOBAL PARTNERSHIP FOR DEVELOPMENT

The focus of MDG 8 was to build a global partnership for sustainable human development. In essence, it addressed the steps that the international community needed to take to attain the other seven goals. This goal specified seven targets: developing an open, rule-based, predictable, and nondiscriminatory trading and financial system; addressing the special needs of least developed countries, including better access to developed country markets, increased aid, enhanced debt relief, and cancellation of official bilateral debt; addressing the needs of landlocked countries and small island states; increasing development assistance; dealing effectively and comprehensively with debt sustainability problems; developing and implementing strategies for youth employment; providing access to affordable essential drugs; and making certain that the benefits of new technologies are available to all. To meet these targets, UN agencies and the Bretton Woods institutions (the World Bank and the IMF) have created new partnerships and become directly involved with diverse elements of society, including nongovernmental organizations (NGOs), the private business sector, and many other types of civil society organizations.

Business in General

Secretary-General Annan and the core staff of the UNDP sought to build an array of partnerships with business primarily through the Global Compact because development, especially for poorer developing countries, cannot occur through governmental or intergovernmental means alone, even when augmented by assistance from the multitude of nongovernmental development assistance organizations. Neither can it occur through unbridled market forces. Creating local, national, and international enabling environments is essential, and a broad-based partnership involving all relevant "stakeholders" is required.

Of course, this may be deemed inappropriate or unacceptable for some—often of quite diverse and even opposing ideological perspectives—who see various types of stakeholders as being unacceptable or illegitimate partners.[52] Nonetheless, the Global Compact has been steadily expanding since it got under way following the Millennium Summit. By 2015, over seven thousand corporate partners had joined the agreement.[53] One of its underlying principles is that UN organizations should "undertake a deeper examination of issues related to corporate governance" in the context of developing countries' specific legal, social, and cultural environments "to develop and implement international accounting, reporting and auditing standards." While encouraging information sharing about potential investment opportunities, the UN development framework cautions that "international institutions involved in supporting FDI [foreign direct investment] flows should evaluate the development impact of investment flows in recipient countries, including social development concerns."[54] Similarly, by joining the Global Compact, businesses recognized that they had a responsibility for helping to meet the MDGs.[55] Corporations have effectively become part of an extended "international community."

At the same time, corporations, especially those with headquarters or subdivisions in the United States, were pleased with the Kiobel decision by the U.S. Supreme Court. This judgment made it almost impossible for victims of human rights violations to hold corporations liable for complicity in human rights violations abroad. Thus, when victims and their NGO sponsors sought to utilize U.S. courts to hold businesses responsible for cooperating with repressive governments abroad, the Supreme Court's majority ruled that this type of petition would unwisely undermine international stability and respect for foreign sovereignty—which could open up retaliation against American interests under foreign court rulings. Kiobel pertained to actions by Royal Dutch Shell in Nigeria in a case with major ecological overtones, but other cases dealt with questionable foreign corporate behavior in apartheid South Africa, Argentina during the junta, and so on. The George W. Bush administration had lobbied for this kind of ruling, as had various business associations, by submitting "friend of the court" papers. Thus, the idea that the UN Global Compact showed the willingness of transnational corporations to shoulder increased social responsibility was accompanied by a significant caveat.[56] The Kiobel decision and following judgments showed that conservative justices, business interests, and their governmental backers favored business as usual over social responsibility. The Global Compact is perhaps too weak to adequately address human rights concerns and may even help gloss over poor corporate behavior.

Trade and Finance

Enhancing an "open, rule-based, predictable, nondiscriminatory trading and financial system" involves a commitment to good governance, development, and poverty reduction—both nationally and internationally. However, one of the major problems confronting the UN system almost since its inception has been that the management of trade and finance has seldom, if ever, functioned as the broad and coherent system that may appear on paper. The UN proper is but one of a group of institutions, and most of the important decisions are made by the WTO and the Bretton Woods institutions. The 2008 recession put considerable strain on international efforts to liberalize trade. The *MDGR 2011* stated that while most protectionist measures were avoided, significant challenges remained ahead, as countries responded to little or no growth or fell back into recession.[57] As world trade recovered from the crisis, many developing countries have rebounded well. The *MDGR 2015*, however, noted that in 2013 and 2014, the amount of goods from developing countries admitted duty-free dipped, suggesting a slight backslide toward increased protectionism.[58]

The latest set of trade talks at the WTO is the most complex ever. This so-called Doha Development Agenda round of talks, launched in 2001 in Doha, Qatar, has taken up many of the items that were left unsettled by the Uruguay Round, which lasted from 1986 to 1994, such as agricultural subsidies; special, less stringent adherence to trade rules for poor countries; and access to vital medicines and treatments. Although originally scheduled for completion in January 2005, Doha negotiations have dragged on and are still incomplete as of this writing.[59] The main stumbling block for negotiations centers on a split between North and South regarding trade priorities. Developed countries want greater liberalization of financial and other services as well as an agreement involving trade-related investment measures (TRIMS). Developing countries, on the other hand, clearly linked agreement in those areas to the reduction of agricultural subsidies in the developed countries, especially Europe, whose position has proven intractable. For example, subsidies to farmers in Organization for Economic Co-operation and Development (OECD) countries in 2003 totaled more than $349 billion. As David Lynch reminds us, "This is nearly $1 billion per day and is approximately the same amount as the combined annual GDP of all Sub-Saharan Africa."[60]

In 2004, the World Bank proposed a "trade for aid" initiative to help incorporate trade into development and poverty reduction. At the 2005 WTO Ministry Meeting in Hong Kong, this initiative was adopted and was officially placed on the WTO agenda in 2007. However, the timing raised questions among many developing states. According to then WTO director-general Pascal Lamy, "aid for trade" is designed to "break the shackles that have been holding back the trade potential of many poor countries, such as substandard infrastructure, lack of modern technology and inadequate financing."[61] Yet developing countries see this as the WTO waving carrots in front of them to get them to make trade conces- sions on services and TRIMS without corresponding concessions related to re- ducing agricultural subsidies in the advanced industrialized countries.[62] A brief glimmer of hope emerged in June 2007, when trade talks resumed and the G4— Brazil, the European Union, India, and the United States—attempted to hammer out closure on critical issues, but again talks broke down, and agreement failed. Since 2009, with the global financial crisis triggering doubt and protectionist pol- icies, the Doha negotiations have been limping along. As such, states have been pursuing alternative free trade agreements, such as the multilateral Trans-Pacific Partnership and the Transatlantic Trade and Investment Partnership, as well as assorted bilateral trade deals. The secretive nature of negotiations raises human rights and transparency questions. A group of UN independent human rights experts publicly expressed concern that these trade agreements had the poten- tial to threaten the right to life, food, water and sanitation, health, housing, and education.[63] These members of the third UN have spoken out on behalf of inter- nationally recognized human rights and, indirectly, in support of the MDGs. The likelihood of concluding such treaties is in doubt because, during periods of slow economic growth and stagnant wages, domestic publics have little appetite for trade agreements that threaten national industries and jobs. Nevertheless, gov- ernments continue to seek freer trade that will benefit exports and businesses.

Development Assistance

Making sustainable human development a reality requires resources, especially financial resources. At the summit-level UN-sponsored Conference on Financ- ing for Development in Monterrey, Mexico, in March 2002, donor countries ex- pressed an increased rhetorical commitment to fighting poverty.[64] The Monterrey gathering for the first time brought together stakeholders representing govern- ments, business, civil society, and international institutions to formally exchange views. The Monterrey Consensus recognized the need to increase official develop- ment significantly in order to meet the MDGs.[65] At the same time, the Monterrey Consensus recognized the deleterious effects of corruption on economic growth and the development process because individuals and groups use public agencies and resources for financial gain.

After the Monterrey Consensus, overseas development assistance (ODA) reached a new high in 2005 of $106.8 billion. In 2006, a downturn set in, and ODA declined by 5.1 percent, and 2007 continued this pattern with an 8.4 percent drop. Although the G8 had committed in 2005 to double aid to Africa by 2010, ODA to the region (excluding debt relief to Nigeria) increased only 2 percent between 2005 and 2006. Only five donor countries—Denmark, Luxembourg, the Netherlands, Norway, and Sweden—have reached the 0.7 percent of their gross national income

(GNI) target.[66] By 2015 the picture had not changed dramatically, but the United Kingdom had joined those countries that had attained the target. With the advent of new funds, the overall amount of ODA provided by the twenty-eight OECD/ DAC donors has grown in real terms from $80 billion in 2000 to almost $130 billion in 2010. Since 2010, there has been a more modest increase to $135 billion in 2014, reflecting the economic crisis that affected most of the rich world.[67]

The United States falls at the bottom of the OECD Development Assistance Committee (DAC) list and devotes a mere 0.16 percent of its GNI to development assistance. It is, however, the largest donor by volume. The European Union collectively provided 55 percent of all ODA, though the continued stagnation in Europe coupled with the Greek debt/euro crisis has meant Europe has not been as generous. The *MDGR 2015* indicated that ODA from DAC countries represented 0.29 percent of GNI, falling short of the 0.7 target.[68]

Two interesting occurrences have been the creation of the Asian Infrastructure and Investment Bank (AIIB) and the New Development Bank (NDB) in 2015. The AIIB is a China-led multilateral development bank that seeks to provide loans and other financing for infrastructure throughout Asia. The United States has opposed the AIIB because it would challenge the primacy of the World Bank and the regional Asian Development Bank (led by Japan). It has also expressed concern that the AIIB would apply looser standards on the environment, transparency, and governance.[69] The United Kingdom, Germany, Italy, and France have joined as founding members, although China provided the bulk of the financing and retains veto power over AIIB decisions. The NDB is a BRICS (Brazil, Russia, India, China, and South Africa) institution that provides loans and emergency funding. How these banks challenge or complement existing development banks remains to be seen. How they relate to the UN proper is also unclear, although their creation is welcomed by some parts of the UN system.[70] The BRICS members do not appear to be enthusiastic about adapting their positions within the UN proper to exercise greater influence.[71]

Debt Relief

More concrete action can be found in the area of debt relief.[72] A vexing issue for many developing countries is making their debt burden sustainable. In 1996 the World Bank and IMF launched a plan to provide debt relief for the world's poorest, most heavily indebted countries. Under this Heavily Indebted Poor Countries Initiative (HIPC), creditors collectively move to provide exceptional assistance aimed at bringing the debtor country into a position of debt sustainability. By 2005, debt-reduction programs had been approved for twenty-eight of the forty-one eligible countries. The total collective debt reduction as of that date was $33 billion, with the possibility of a cumulative total of $61 billion, should the remaining thirteen countries reach their decision points for receiving relief. About half comes from bilateral lenders and the remainder from international financial institutions (IFIs).[73]

At the July 2005 G8 meeting, heads of government proposed a new Multilateral Debt Relief Initiative to supplement HIPC. Under this plan, three IFIs—the IMF, World Bank (specifically the International Development Association), and African Development Bank—would be allowed to provide 100 percent debt relief for countries completing the HIPC process.[74] According to the *MDGR 2007*, "By April 2007, 22 of the 40 HIPC countries had fulfilled all conditions and had been granted debt relief; eight had completed the first stage of the process and received debt relief on a provisional basis."[75] For the eligible countries, 90 percent of their external debt will be canceled. So, important progress has been made, but there is a lot more work to do. Ten HIPC countries are still eligible but need help with the process, while eleven others remain ineligible because of violent conflict and corruption. Indicating the significance of this problem, more than fifty countries spend more on debt servicing than on public health. The global economic and financial crisis and the resulting sharp drop in exports from developing countries in 2009 interrupted progress toward reducing their debt-service ratios.[76] But in 2015, the downward trend of developing countries' debt-service ratios resumed.[77]

Access to Affordable, Essential Drugs

Key to dealing with endemic diseases, such as HIV/AIDS, malaria, and TB, is to provide affordable access to medicines and treatments. Access to affordable drugs for all diseases on a sustainable basis is not available to over one third of the developing world's population. The *MDGR 2015* acknowledges that global and regional data are lacking; however, estimates are that on average, generic medicines were available in 58 percent of public health facilities and 67 percent of private facilities.[78] Solving this problem is challenging because any solution is bundled with a variety of economic, political, legal, and moral issues. Access to medicines to treat those afflicted with HIV/AIDS has sparked a heated debate between developing and the most developed countries. Over 90 percent of the persons currently living with HIV/AIDS live in the developing world. Yet nearly all the drugs that have been developed to treat the disease and its symptoms are produced and controlled under license by pharmaceutical companies in the developed world.

At the center of the controversy over the access issue in recent years has been the Agreement on Trade-Related Aspects of Intellectual Property Rights (TRIPS). Negotiated in the context of WTO, TRIPS represented an attempt to strike a balance between protecting the property rights of the inventor and providing access to the consumer. Article 7 of TRIPS recognizes that the protection of intellectual property contributes to the promotion of technological innovation and to the transfer and dissemination of technology, to the mutual advantage of users and producers of technological knowledge. At the same time, TRIPS attempts to balance the social and human needs of poor countries. TRIPS emerged from a genuine negotiating process in which the need for balance was very much at the fore.[79]

The TRIPS agreement has three main aspects. First, the agreement sets minimum standards of protection and obligations for each member country. Second, it specifies general principles that must be followed in all intellectual property rights enforcement procedures. Finally, all disputes under it are subject to WTO dispute settlement procedures. In the context of international health, TRIPS has meant trying to find a balance between the interests of pharmaceutical companies and their home states, and non–technologically advanced countries that desire greater access to drugs that are essential for public health reasons. Under Article 31 of the TRIPS agreement, members are allowed to exercise "compulsory licensing" without the authorization of the rights holder under certain conditions, such as public health necessities. However, the nature of this right is ambiguous and subject to dispute. Moreover, many developing countries do not have adequate manufacturing capabilities in pharmaceuticals to enable them even to make effective use of compulsory licensing.

At the WTO Ministerial Conference in Doha in November 2001, this issue came to a head; and while the Doha Round has not been completed as of this writing, the issue of drug availability has moved ahead. Developing-country governments, seeking greater access to drugs for treating HIV/AIDS, tuberculosis, and other endemic diseases, were able to get member states to agree to a compromise. In adopting the Doha Declaration on the TRIPS Agreement and Public Health, the member states affirmed that "the TRIPS Agreement does not and should not prevent members from taking measures to protect public health. Accordingly, while reiterating our commitment to the TRIPS Agreement, we affirm that the Agreement can and should be interpreted and implemented in a manner supportive of WTO members' right to protect public health and, in particular, to promote access to medicines for all."[80]

The declaration specified that the least developed countries would be given until January 2016 before being required to implement or enforce the TRIPS agreement with regard to pharmaceutical products. The declaration, however, still left unresolved the issue of how to deal with those countries that do not have sufficient manufacturing capabilities in pharmaceuticals to enable them even to make effective use of compulsory licensing. In July 2007 Rwanda became the first country to announce that, because of the lack of local production capacity, it would import cheaper generic drugs made elsewhere under compulsory licensing.

This issue remains contested, with the WTO Council on TRIPS attempting to forge a compromise between the United States and other technologically advanced countries as well as less technologically advanced member states that are demanding more flexible patent rules during public health emergencies. The shortage in Europe and the United States of a patented drug that treats the symptoms of avian flu in humans prompted many in the advanced industrialized countries to rethink the primacy of intellectual property rights in the face of a health epidemic.

Information and Communication Technology

Globalization is fueled, in large part, by the continuing revolution of information and communication technologies (ICTs). The challenge centers on making the benefits of ICTs available to all, especially given the inequalities inherent in the present information order—the so-called digital divide. According to the *MDGR 2015*, just over 97 percent of the world's inhabitants were covered by a mobile cellular signal, but more than 450 million people living in rural areas lived out of reach of a mobile signal.[81] Moreover, two thirds of the world's population still does not have access to the Internet, compared to 18 percent in developed countries. And due to the continuing gender disparity, women and girls have far less access than do their male counterparts.[82]

With regard to promoting human development, ICT has a larger context. As suggested in the final report of the UNDP's Digital Opportunity Initiative, "used in the right way and for the right purposes, ICT can have a dramatic impact on achieving specific social and economic development goals as well as play a key role in broader national development strategies."[83] In the highly globalized information age, development cannot occur without such social and economic networks. The UN system has in many ways been energized by the possibilities that ICT presents for promoting human development; however, many prickly political problems plague the path to creating a common global vision of the norms and principles underlying the information society.[84]

FROM THE MDGS TO THE SDGS

The formal consensus about the MDGs, as evidenced by the 2005 World Summit, was not universal. But a generally shared orientation, underpinned by shared meanings and shared values, appeared to be present.[85] Disagreements centered on strategy and commitments. Governments in Zimbabwe or Saudi Arabia may have voted for the MDGs in New York, but their policies and decisions at home reflect anything but a deep commitment to doing what is necessary to enhance human security. Governments in Washington and Paris may also have voted for the MDGs, but whether they are prepared to increase their development assistance and make meaningful trade concessions to developing countries is not always evident. The European Union continues to protect European agricultural producers to the detriment of poor countries attempting to sell their exports in Europe.

Progress toward achieving the MDGs was mixed, especially when global numbers are disaggregated, but as indicated some progress was registered. Indeed for a few months, the declaration enjoyed the familiar fate of many UN outcome statements—nothing happened except for rubber-stamping by the General Assembly. Then, in early 2001, the UN led by UNDP decided to formally identify and label what became the seven MDGs, which were extracted from the declaration, and to initiate a process of regular country monitoring. It was another year before a full set of targets and indicators was drawn up (subsequently expanded) and an eighth goal added at the urging of the G77 and international civil society. Only the UN Secretariat and the funds and programs were involved in this process, and the MDGs only gradually came to be acknowledged as the basis for UN system-wide operations. The specialized agencies were initially not engaged and some took several years before incorporating the MDGs into their programming.

In measuring the successes or failures of the MDG strategy, several questions are often asked. Are people on the whole better off than they were before the MDGs? If so, can we be sure that the MDGs intervention caused the improvement? Most of the statistical successes are the result of China's tremendous economic growth in the last fifteen years. Sub-Saharan Africa and South Asia, on the other hand, missed most of the targets. Yet, missing targets does not mean that lives were not improved, only that goals were not met. Another set of questions center on the performance of the three UNs in implementing the MDG strategy. Was the MDG strategy an efficient use of scarce resources? Operationally, did the three UNs cooperate and perform reasonably well? Many member states only half-heartedly embraced the MDGs and did not deliver on promises. UN development agencies, while great at generating ideas, did not perform particularly well, given their level of expertise and numbers of skilled personnel. The atomized structure of the second UN and lack of systemic coherence make it a marginal partner in the sustainable human development process.[86] NGOs continued to duplicate efforts and important nonprofits such as the Global Fund were plagued by scandal and mismanagement. Despite the mixed record, the UN moves forward as a collection of imperfect human institutions that lack real consensus.

The successes and failures in meeting the MDGs and associated targets have led to new goals, new thinking, and new strategies. In May 2012 Secretary-General Ban announced that Indonesian president Susilo Bambang Yudhoyono, Liberian president Ellen Johnson Sirleaf, and British prime minister David Cameron would lead a high-level panel to advise the international community on the post-2015 way forward. That panel embraced the 2012 UN Conference on Sustainable Development (Rio+20)'s recommendations that framed the Sustainable Development Goals (SDGs).[87] After a series of meetings in London, Monrovia, and Bali, and deep consultations with UN, NGO, and corporate officials, the high-level panel sought to build on the MDGs and lessons learned to create the post-2015 development agenda. The experience with the MDGs showed that strategies need to ensure that no one is left behind; sustainable development must be at the core; economies should be transformed for jobs and inclusive growth; public institutions should be effective, open, inclusive, and accountable; and there needs to be a broad-based global partnership between national governments, local authorities, international institutions, business, academia, scientists, foundations, philanthropists, and NGOs. The post-2015 SDGs need to be SMART: specific, measurable, attainable, relevant, and time bound.[88]

The UN General Assembly established an intergovernmental working group charged with bringing all the relevant stakeholders to the table, all of whom were invited to submit proposals for the SDGs. The SDGs (Appendix E) reflect the high-level panel's desire to keep the eradication of extreme poverty at the heart of development strategies. In what has been termed a "free-for-all" in setting goals and targets,[89] the UN working group produced a set of seventeen goals, with assorted targets that were approved at the 2015 UN General Assembly Meeting—the seventieth anniversary of the founding of the UN. Climate change and a permanent, predictable financing scheme for the SDGs topped the agenda. Of course, there is debate over whether these new goals are realistic, desirable, or measurable. Some stress the importance of eliminating extreme inequality on both economic and ethical grounds.[90] Others stress that current methods of achieving goals, such as trade, are insufficient given the near collapse of the Doha Round.[91] Whether member states can find the estimated $3 trillion a year to effect these goals is also in question.

Compared with the declarations of 2000 and 2005, the SDGs agreed to at the September 2015 General Assembly Summit are more comprehensive in one important respect but much less so in another. Because they grew out of the Rio+20 environment summit in 2012, they are infused with concepts of natural resource and energy sustainability. In fact, the SDGs can be characterized as the MDGs+, the main addition being the amplification of environmental concerns. But the outcome statement confines to a single goal (out of seventeen) perfunctory references to some of the more critical aspects of development that we identified above, such as good governance, rule of law, and democratic accountability (and almost nothing at all on security concerns and human rights). The principles of democratic accountability are not even being applied to the monitoring of SDG progress, which is to be firmly in government hands.

Unlike the MDGs, the SDGs were the product of a protracted, two-year-long process of consultations and intergovernmental negotiations, signed off on by the General Assembly's 193 member states. To that extent, they enjoy the wide legitimacy that comes from universal backing.

While unquestionably the UN has a critical role to play in matters of environmental management, in several other areas covered by the SDGs, experience has shown that the UN is being increasingly eclipsed operationally. At a Future United Nations Development System (FUNDS) briefing in 2014, the former World Bank director-general of evaluation went so far as to state, based on the results of recent surveys of the UN's effectiveness, that "the organization has lost the aid effectiveness race. . . . its key role is in security operations, humanitarian assistance, and global norm building. In these realms, the UN is peerless."[92] It is as if the member states engaged in the SDG discussions have a death wish for the UN, asking it to do more in areas where it enjoys the least comparative advantage.

In the aftermath of the summit, the SDG indicators will be further honed, and countries will be encouraged to draw up their own achievement road maps, although the number of (particularly environmental) targets is so numerous that no country will be able to adopt them all. Yet, despite the length of this putative UN agenda, it is substantially incomplete. Climate change and trade negotiations are highly relevant, but even without the SDGs, there are already established forums for negotiating new agreements. Several of the huge global development challenges that the UN will be called upon to address are not even mentioned— massive forced displacement and voluntary migration, capital flight from the developing countries, corruption, cyber-security, postconflict reconstruction, religious intolerance, international terrorism, and the list goes on. It is more than likely that the important development work of the UN will be found between the lines of the 2015 outcome statement and in arenas unmentioned in the SDGs.

EXPLAINING CHANGE

Change is rarely progressively linear. Occasionally, change is shocking and dramatic, the result of a crisis. But usually it is incremental and setbacks often occur. Beginning in the early 1970s around the time of the Stockholm conference, the concept of eco-development came onto the global agenda. In attempting to lay the foundations of a global plan of action for dealing with environmental issues, Maurice Strong and other UN officials quickly came to perceive the inseparability of development from those issues. This orientation evolved over later decades as the environmental science community, development assistance practitioners and scholars, international financiers, government officials, and many others came to see their own work to be achievable only in the context of a more holistic eco-development worldview. But not everyone was or is in agreement. The convergence of development and environment into sustainable development and the subsequent convergence of sustainable development, human development, and human security into sustainable human development is a widely shared view, but debates on strategy and policy will continue to persist. The global public policy agenda may grow from agreement over eco-development in private communities of knowledge and institutional learning is possible. The normative convergence is a product of a process in which many state officials have recognized (or "learned") the inherent inseparability of the two issues.

Proponents of the consensual-knowledge approach point to the growth and involvement, at least of civic actors in the North, in sustainable development politics at the global, intergovernmental level. They also point to the evolution of the role of NGOs since Stockholm, to the activities of NGOs in the Rio and subsequent conference processes, and to the influence of knowledge communities on issues such as protection of the ozone layer as evidence that this approach is valid.[93] The *MDGR 2015* stated that ozone-depleting substances have virtually been eliminated.[94] Perhaps the same approach can be applied to halt climate change.

The nature of the evolution of NGO involvement in the sustainable human development arena however, is not always positive. Thousands of opinion communities are concerned with sustainable development. Sometimes the diversity and often outright antagonisms among these communities have created their own challenges—consider the windows broken and stores looted in such cities as Seattle, Genoa, Montreal, Evian, and Hong Kong, all sites of G8 or WTO summits.[95] Yet this is not to suggest the absence of a convergence of interests over sustainability issues. Indeed, the concept has come to dominate much of the debate over both development and environment.

Although growing consensus can be observed within specific areas of environmental concern, it has yet to be translated into a coherent global scientific consensus about sustainable development. Moreover, a large gulf still separates basic and applied scientists over many eco-development issues. Still, the idea of sustainable development has served as a common denominator, helping to bridge the turf and ideological divides that otherwise separate the international financial institutions from other members of the UN family.[96]

With respect to learning, of crucial importance is the acceleration of both knowledge and worldwide awareness since the 1987 establishment of the Intergovernmental Panel on Climate Change (IPCC) by the World Meteorological Organization (WMO), with UNEP's support. The importance of epistemic communities is a key subject for contemporary international relations, and the IPCC is a powerful illustration of how under UN auspices some two thousand world-class volunteer scientists from several disciplines translated scientific findings into language comprehensible by policymakers. In a comprehensive, objective, open, and transparent fashion, the scientific, technical, and socioeconomic information relevant to understanding the risk of human-induced climate change, its potential impacts, and options for adaptation and mitigation were all made clear. The 2007 Nobel Peace Prize recognized the UN's comparative advantage because this network put to rest the dispute, other than in the minds of ideologues, over the human role in global climate. We have witnessed the emergence of a true scientific consensus: it has become virtually impossible to ignore not simply record temperatures, storms, and other indicators, but also record agreement among knowledgeable experts (90 percent of them) that climate change is a looming threat that requires urgent action to reverse or at least to slow human-induced damage.[97]

In global debates, delegates from the North usually define sustainability rather narrowly as environmental protection and resource conservation. Southerners normally define the concept with specific reference to meeting basic human needs and reducing poverty, with a focus on people, on promoting economic growth that produces employment and encourages the wider participation of people in economic processes.[98] Economists have their own definition. They say sustainable development is "an economic process in which the quantity and quality of our stocks of natural resources (like forests) and the integrity of biogeochemical cycles (like climate) are sustained and passed on to the future generations unimpaired."[99] The feedback from seemingly endless conferences and the ever-evolving closer relationship among previously discordant agencies—especially the Bretton Woods institutions and other members of the UN system—may have well served to create a genuine learning environment.

Given limited resources and the lack of real sustained leadership on the part of its more powerful members, the UN broadly defined nonetheless has done some remarkable things. The world organization has improved the lives of hundreds of millions of people and launched a host of ideas that have changed the world.[100] The world is far better off with the United Nations than without it. But the world body could do so much more in what Ken Conca has called "an unfinished foundation."[101] The second UN cannot change the priorities of member states so that states put the UN at the center of global governance. The second UN can suggest priorities, seek commitments, coordinate action, and attempt to bridge divides through norm creation. But ultimately the governments of the first UN must choose to work through, and with, the second to manage pressing global problems such as disease, extreme poverty, and environmental degradation. States invest scarce resources into priorities they value, and clearly they continue to value military hardware, subsidies to domestic farmers and industries, and welfare for their own people. Core resources provided to the second UN in general, and to pursue the MDGs and now SDGs in particular, show that the second UN is not a priority for most donor governments. Until the priorities of member states change, the role of the United Nations—first, second, and third—in promoting sustainable human development will be, at best, modest.

NOTES

1. Kofi A. Annan, "We the Peoples": The Role of the United Nations in the 21st Century (New York: United Nations, 2000), 9–10.

2. Jorge Heine and Ramesh Thakur, eds., The Dark Side of Globalization (New York: United Nations University Press, 2011); and Laura Westra, Globalization, Violence, and World Governance (Boston: Brill, 2011).

3. UN document A.AC.253/25, March 22, 2000.

4. UN document A/RES/55/2, September 18, 2000.

5. UNDP, Human Development Report 2003 (New York: Oxford University Press, 2003).

6. Millennium Development Project, Investing in Development: A Practical Plan to Achieve the Millennium Development Goals (New York: UNDP, 2005).

7. World Bank, Global Monitoring Report 2012: Food Prices, Nutrition, and Millennium Development Goals (Washington, D.C.: World Bank, 2012), http://www.worldbank.org/mdgs.

8. NGLS Roundup, "MDGs: Moving Forward on the Millennium Development Goals," November 2002.

9. Joshua Kurlantzich, "An Empty Poor Box at the United Nations," Newsweek, August 16, 2010, 7; Joses M. Kirigia, Benjamin M. Nganda, Chris N. Mwikisa, and Bernardino Cardoso, "The Effects of Global Financial Crisis on Funding for Health Development in Nineteen Countries of the WHO African Region," International Health and Human Rights 11, no. 1 (2011): 1–10.

10. Frances Stewart, "The Impact of the Global Economic Crises on the Poor: Comparing the 1980s and 2000s," Journal of Human Development and Capabilities 13, no. 1 (2012): 83–105.

11. DESA, World Economic Situation and Prospects 2012 (New York: United Nations, 2012), http://www.un.org/en/development/desa//policy/wesp.

12. Stephen Browne and Thomas G. Weiss, eds., Post-2015 UN Development (London: Routledge, 2014); David Hulme and Rorden Wilkinson, eds., Beyond the Millennium Development Goals: Global Development Goals Post-2015 (London: Routledge, 2012); and Sakiko Fukada-Parr, The MDGs, Capabilities, and Human Rights: The Power of Numbers To Shape Agendas (London: Routledge, forthcoming).

13. *The Millennium Development Goals Report 2015* (New York: United Nations, 2015), 3, http://www.un.org/millenniumgoals/2015_MDG_Report/pdf/MDG%202015%20rev %20(July%201).pdf; hereafter *MDGR 2015*.

14. *The Millennium Development Goals Report 2012* (New York: United Nations, 2012), 7, http://www.un.org/millenniumgoals/pdf/MDG%20Report%202012.pdf; hereafter *MDGR 2012*.

15. *The Millennium Development Goals Report 2011* (New York: United Nations, 2011), 4, http://www.un.org/millenniumgoals/11_MDG%20Report_EN.pdf; hereafter *MDGR 2011*.

16. Millennium Project, *Investing in Development*, 13–14. See also "Millennium Indicators Data Base," UN Statistics Division, 2005, http://mdgs.un.org/unsd/mdg/Default. aspx; and Jeffrey Sachs, *The End of Poverty: Economic Possibilities for Our Time* (New York: Penguin Books, 2005).

17. *MDGR 2015*, 24.

18. "Education: Literacy," UNESCO, http://www.unesco.org/new/en/education/themes /education-building-blocks/literacy.

19. *MDGR 2011*, 19; and *MDGR 2012*, 19.

20. *MDGR 2011*, 17.

21. Ian Goldin, *Globalization for Development: Meeting New Challenges* (Oxford: Oxford University Press, 2012).

22. Joia Mukherjee, Donna J. Barray, Hind Satti, Maxi Raymonville, Sarah Marsh, and Mary Kay Smith Fawzi, "Structural Violence: A Barrier to Achieving the Millennium Development Goals for Women," *Journal of Women's Health* 20, no. 4 (2011): 593–597.

23. Mark Malloch Brown, "World's Top Goals Require Women's Empowerment," Message from UN Development Programme, March 8, 2003.

24. *MDGR 2012*, 20.

25. UNIFEM, Press Release, May 1, 2003.

26. *MDGR 2015*, 28.

27. UN, Division for the Advancement of Women, "Convention on the Elimination of All Forms of Discrimination Against Women," http://www.un.org/womenwatch/daw/cedaw.

28. See UN Women's website: http://www.unwomen.org/about-us/about-un-women.

29. World Bank, "Millennium Development Goals Promote Gender Equality," *World Development Indicators 2004* (Washington: International Bank of Reconstruction and Development, 2004).

30. *MDGR 2015*, 32.

31. United Nations, "End Poverty 2014: Millennium Development Goals Fact Sheet," September 25, 2008: 1–2. http://www.un.org/millenniumgoals/2008highlevel/pdf/news room/Goal%204%20FINAL.pdf.

32. *MDGR 2015*, 32.

33. World Bank, "Data: Over 99 Percent of the Maternal Deaths Occur in Developing Countries," May 4, 2012, http://data.worldbank.org/news/over-99-percent-of-maternal -deaths-occur-in-developing-countries.

34. Margaret C. Hogan et al., "Maternal Mortality for 181 Countries, 1980–2008: A Systematic Analysis of the Progress Toward Millennium Development Goal 5," *Lancet* 375, no. 9726 (May 2010): 1609–1623.

35. Denise Grady, "Maternal Deaths Decline Sharply Across the Globe," *New York Times*, April 13, 2010.

36. *MDGR 2015*, 6.

37. See Nicholas Kristof, "Saving the Lives of Moms," *New York Times*, May 12, 2012.

38. See Franklyn Lisk, *Global Institutions and the HIV/AIDS Epidemic* (London: Routledge, 2010); Leon Gordenker, Roger A. Coate, Christer Jönsson, and Peter Söderholm, *International Cooperation in Response to AIDS* (London: Pinter, 1995); and Peter Söderholm, *Global Governance of AIDS: Partnerships with Civil Society* (Lund, Sweden: Lund University Press, 1997).

39. World Bank, Education and HIV/AIDS: A Window of Hope, http://go.worldbank.org /QFZ5LJ5K00.

40. *MDGR 2015*, 46.

41. *MDGR 2011*, 42–23.

42. *MDGR 2007*, 20.

43. *MDGR 2015*, 47.

44. Ibid., 49.

45. UNICEF, Press Release, May 13, 2003.

46. Steven Lee Meyers, "Bush to Skip U.N. Talks on Global Warming," *New York Times*, September 24, 2007.

47. *MDGR 2015*, 53.

48. "Obama Makes Urgent Appeal in Alaska for Climate Change Action," *New York Times*, August 31, 2015.

49. *MDGR 2015*, 55.

50. E. C. Corcoran, C. Nellemann, E. Baker, R. Bos, D. Osborn, and H. Savelli, eds. *Sick Water: The Central Role of Waste Water Management in Sustainable Development.* (New York: UNEP, 2010), 11, http://www.unep.org/pdf/SickWater_screen.pdf.

51. *MDGR 2015*, 58.

52. Ellen Paine, "The Road to the Global Compact: Corporate Power and the Battle Over Global Public Policy at the United Nations," Global Policy Forum, October 2000, http:// www.globalpolicy.org/social-and-economic-policy/social-and-economic-policy-at-the-un /un-and-business/32188.html.

53. Catia Gregoratti, *The UN Global Compact* (London: Routledge, 2013); Oliver F. Williams, *Corporate Social Responsibility* (London: Routledge, 2013); and Christopher May, *Global Corporations in Global Governance* (London: Routledge, 2015).

54. UN document A/AC.257/12.

55. See the UN Global Compact's website, http://www.unglobalcompact.org.

56. For a start on a sizable literature about the U.S. alien tort statute and its use vis-à-vis corporations, among other kinds of defendants, see Center for Justice and Accountability, "*Kiobel v. Shell*: Light Dims on Human Rights Claims in the US," no date, http://cja.org /section.php?id=510.

57. *MDGR 2011*, 60.

58. *MDGR 2015*, 64.

59. Rorden Wilkinson and James Scott, eds., *Trade, Poverty, Development: Getting Beyond the WTO's Doha Deadlock* (London: Routledge, 2012).

60. David Lynch, "Negotiating Between and Across Borders," in *A Global Agenda: Issues Before the 60th General Assembly of the United Nations*, ed. Angela Drakulich (New York: UNA-USA, 2005), 225.

61. "WTO Places Aid for Trade on Its Agenda," *Bangkok Post*, November 16, 2007, B7.

62. Ibid.

63. Office the High Commissioner for Human Rights, "UN Experts Voice Concern over Adverse Impact of Free Trade and Investment Agreements on Human Rights," June 2, 2015, http://www.ohchr.org/EN/NewsEvents/Pages/DisplayNews.aspx?NewsID =16031&LangID=E.

64. David Hulme, *Global Poverty: Global Governance and Poor People in the Post-2015 Era*, 2nd ed. (London: Routledge, 2015); and Jonathan J. Makuwira, *Nongovernmental Development Organizations and the Poverty Reduction Agenda* (London: Routledge, 2014).

65. Barry Herman, "Civil Society and the Financing for Development Initiative at the United Nations," in *Civil Society and Global Finance*, ed. Jan Aart Scholte with Albrecht Schabel (London: Routledge, 2002), 162–177.

66. "Financial Flows to Developing Countries," *World Economic Situation and Prospects 2010,* http://www.un.org/en/development/desa/policy/wesp/wesp_archive/2010chap3.pdf.

67. Organisation for Economic Cooperation and Development, *Multilateral Aid 2015: Better Partnerships for a Post-2015 World* (Paris: OECD, 2015).

68. *MDGR 2015*, 62.

69. Erik Voeten, "Why the US Effort to Curb the Asian Infrastructure Bank Is Doomed to Fail (and Why It Doesn't Matter All That Much)," *Washington Post,* March 19, 2015, http://www.washingtonpost.com/blogs/monkey-cage/wp/2015/03/19/why-the-u-s-effort -to-curb-the-asian-infrastructure-investment-bank-is-doomed-to-fail-and-why-it-doesnt -matter-all-that-much.

70. UNCTAD, *The BRICS Development Bank: A Dream Coming True?"* (Geneva: United Nations, 2014).

71. Silke Weinlich, "Emerging Powers at the UN: Ducking for Cover?" *Third World Quarterly* 35 (2014): 1829–1844. See also Thomas G. Weiss and Adriana Erthal Abdenur, eds., *Emerging Powers and the UN: What Kind of Development Partnership?* (London: Routledge, 2016).

72. Ross P. Buckley, *Debt-for-Development Exchanges: History and New Applications* (Cambridge: Cambridge University Press, 2011).

73. IMF, Fact Sheet: "Debt Relief Under the Heavily Indebted Poor Countries (HIPC) Initiative," December 2005, http://www.imf.org/external/np/exr/facts/hipc.htm.

74. IMF, Fact Sheet: "The Multilateral Debt Relief Initiative (MDRI)," December 2005, http://www.imf.org/external/np/exr/facts/mdri.htm.

75. *MDGR 2007*, 30.

76. *MDGR 2011*, 62.

77. *MDGR 2015*, 62.

78. Ibid., 68.

79. WTO, "Pharmaceutical Patents and the TRIPS Agreement," September 21, 2006, http://www.wto.org/english/tratop_e/trips_e/pharma_ato186_e.htm.

80. WTO, "Doha WTO Ministerial 2001: Ministerial Declaration," November 20, 2001, http://www.wto.org/english/thewto_e/minist_e/min01_e/mindecl_e.htm.

81. *MDGR 2015*, 63.

82. Rekha Pande and Theo van der Weide, *Globalization, Technology Diffusion and Gender Disparity* (Hershey, Pa.: Information Science Reference, 2012).

83. Digital Opportunity Initiative, "Creating a Development Dynamic: Final Report of the Digital Opportunity Initiative," United Nations Development Programme, 2001, http://3nw.com/doi/index.htm#02_executive_summary.

84. Andrew Chadwick, *Internet Politics: States, Citizens, and New Communication Technologies* (New York: Oxford University Press, 2006).

85. David Held, "Toward a New Consensus: Answering the Dangers of Globalization," *Harvard International Review* 27 (Summer 2005): 14–17.

86. Stephen Browne and Thomas G. Weiss, "Is the UN Development System Becoming Irrelevant?" *Development Dialogue Paper* 4 (December 2013): 2, http://www.futureun.org/media/archive1/reports/FUNDS-UNDSBecomingIrrelevant.pdf.

87. The Report of the High-Level Panel of Eminent Persons on the Post-2015 Development Agenda, *A New Global Partnership: Eradicate Poverty and Transform Economies Through Sustainable Development* (New York: United Nations, 2013), http://www.post2015hlp.org/wp-content/uploads/2013/05/UN-Report.pdf.

88. The Report of the High-Level Panel of Eminent Persons on the Post-2015 Development Agenda, *A New Global Partnership: Eradicate Poverty and Transform Economies Through Sustainable Development* (New York: United Nations, 2013), 13, http://www.post2015hlp.org/wp-content/uploads/2013/05/UN-Report.pdf.

89. Eduardo Porter, "At the UN, A Free-For-All on Setting Goals," *New York Times* (May 7, 2014), B1.

90. Jeffery Sachs, *The Age of Sustainable Development* (New York: Columbia University Press, 2015); Michael W. Doyle and Joseph E. Stiglitz, "Eliminating Extreme Inequality: A Sustainable Development Goal, 2015–2030," *Ethics and International Affairs* 28 (2014): 5–13.

91. Bernd G. Janzen and Emily S. Fuller. "Assessing the UN Sustainable Development Goals Through the Lens of International Trade Law," *International Law News* 44 (2015); 22–25.

92. Robert Picciotto, "The UN Has Lost the Aid Effectiveness Race: What Is to Be Done?" *FUNDS Briefing 14*, February 2014, 4, available at www.futureun.org/media/archive1/briefings/FUNDS_Brief14_Feb2014_D5.pdf.

93. Peter Haas, "Banning Chlorofluorocarbons: Epistemic Community Efforts to Protect Stratospheric Ozone," *International Organization* 46, no. 1 (1992): 187–224.

94. *MDGR 2015*, 7, 52.

95. Michael Edwards, *Future Positive: International Cooperation in the 21st Century* (London: Earthscan, 2000), and *NGO Rights and Responsibilities: A New Deal for Global Governance* (London: Foreign Policy Centre, 2000). See also Molly Ruhlman, *Who Participates in Global Governance: States, Bureaucracies, and NGOs in the United Nations* (London: Routledge, 2014); and Peter Willetts, *Non-Governmental Organizations in World Politics* (London: Routledge, 2011).

96. Lynton K. Caldwell, *International Environmental Policy: Emergence and Dimensions*, 2nd ed. (Durham, N.C.: Duke University Press, 1991), 81.

97. Nigel Lawson, *An Appeal to Reason: A Cool Look at Global Warming* (London: Duckworth Overlook, 2008).

98. Alvaro de Soto, "The Global Environment: A Southern Perspective," *International Journal* 15, no. 8 (1992): 679–705; and UNDP, *Human Development Report 1993* (New York: Oxford University Press, 1993).

99. Anil Agarwal, "What Is Sustainable Development?" *Concordare* (Spring 1993): 2.

100. Richard Jolly, Louis Emmerij, and Thomas G. Weiss, *UN Ideas That Changed the World* (Bloomington: Indiana University Press, 2009).

101. Ken Conca, *An Unfinished Foundation: The United Nations and Global Environmental Governance* (Oxford: Oxford University Press, 2015).

CONCLUSION

Learning from Change

In a time when winds of change are blowing very strong, we must rest content with knowing that foresight is always imperfect and that choices must always be made in ignorance of their full consequences. That is the price we pay for being able to make the world over by changing our own behavior, individually and collectively, in response to cherished hopes and shared purposes, framed in words. Our capacity to err is our capacity to learn and thereby achieve partial and imperfect, but real, improvement in the conditions of human life.

—William H. McNeill[1]

The core United Nations organization itself and the broader UN system made up of multiple, autonomous agencies are interdependent. How they will continue to develop in the twenty-first century will be determined by the dynamic interplay of interstate politics and transformations in the global political economy. Given the transnational nature of many problems, member states of the first UN need to transfer more loyalty, power, and authority to the second. But such a radical change is a distant prospect. The goal is not just effective global governance per se but governance that is wise and accountable, with due regard for human rights and human security.[2]

World politics continues to evolve and multilateral organizations can and do influence the course of that evolution. Transnational problems requiring transnational management remain, and in William McNeill's words, it would certainly be nice to know in which direction the winds of change are blowing. Alas, this is not easy. The initial euphoria about the end of the Cold War and optimism about possibilities for democratization on a global scale have given way to a more sober, and perhaps normal, caution. The winds of hyper-nationalism and unilateralism that blew from the George W. Bush administration were followed by the election and reelection of Barack Obama and a friendlier rhetoric, if not always practice, toward multilateralism. And the preferences of the BRICS (Brazil, Russia, India, China, and South Africa), with their growing power and influence, do not necessarily accord with shifting views in Washington.[3]

As a generalization, politics outside the UN are primary, and factors inside the UN are secondary—in theoretical vocabulary, the world organization is a dependent variable. The end of the Cold War, indeed the end of the Soviet Union, primarily explained the renaissance of UN security activities that began in the late 1980s. The Security Council did not end the Cold War. Rather, the end of the Cold War allowed the Security Council to act with renewed consensus, commitment, and vigor.

Once allowed to act, UN personnel and organs may independently influence states and other actors. What was once a secondary factor, dependent on state approval, may come to be a primary factor in the ongoing process to make and implement policy. Once member states decided to create an environmental program, the United Nations Environment Programme (UNEP) came to exert some relatively independent influence—both in cleaning up the Mediterranean Sea and in coordinating scientific evidence about the need to protect the ozone layer. The second UN can help implement the policy choices of the first UN when there is sufficient political will, and the resources to match. In short, it is an important actor in its own right.

MEASURING CHANGE

A first analytical concern centers on what constitutes "change."[4] Kal Holsti's *Taming the Sovereigns* probes the concept of change and ways of measuring it: "These include change as novelty or replacement, change as addition or subtraction, increased complexity, transformation, reversion, and obsolescence."[5] Qualitative change can be defined as difference in kind. Novelty and replacement are types of qualitative change. The presumption is of rupture, or a clear break between what once was and what currently is.[6] To that extent, we are looking for discontinuities, when new forms replace old ones. This is the story of the United Nations, including, for instance, the creation of peacekeeping and its next step of peacebuilding; the introduction of gender and other types of human rights mainstreaming; and the change from protecting the environment to sustainable human development.

UN security operations increased rapidly beginning in 1988 and then declined, only to manifest renewed growth a decade later that continues today. The notion of security has been broadened incrementally, albeit inconsistently, to encompass the idea of human security—a still evolving concept. The demands for global action in the humanitarian affairs and human rights arenas continue to expand. Against the background of clear normative development, discourse certainly has changed, and advances in humanitarian delivery and prevention are evident. Yet the world organization's capacity to respond to violations, even atrocities, has not always kept pace. Budgetary shortfalls hinder effective responses, and the absence of political will is demonstrated by lack of appropriate response to major tragedies in Darfur, the Democratic Republic of the Congo, and Syria. Moreover, challenges to liberal democracy seem to be persisting and even gaining strength, as we see especially in monarchical and fundamentalist political Islamic circles and the tightening of Chinese authoritarianism, as well as Russia's resurgent revanchism and dictatorship. On the human development front, the world is becoming more polarized between rich and poor, with some of the poorest—in sub-Saharan Africa especially—losing absolute as well as relative ground. Yet we have also seen growing formal consensus, in the form of the Millennium Development Goals (MDGs) and Sustainable Development Goals (SDGs), about what should be done to advance sustainable human development. The formal consensus, however, is rather like the formal consensus on the International Bill of Rights: namely, the agreement about norms is not followed by effective implementation.

James Rosenau characterized world politics by "turbulence," in which basic patterns are not clear, making change difficult to measure or grasp.[7] In this view, world politics can be conceptualized as having "macro" and "micro" dimensions, with "macro" covering the world of states and intergovernmental organizations (IGOs) and "micro" covering the world of individuals, local communities, and other elements of civil society. Rosenau's writing envisions a world in which the international and domestic are so intermingled as to be conceptualized as one— or an "intermestic" set of political processes. The micro and macro dimensions are in such turmoil that one can only project alternative scenarios for the future, not specifically describe the likely structure or basic features of world politics. Yet in today's turbulent world order, with the increasingly nonstate character of many threats to global, regional, and local peace, there are mounting pressures to think in terms of human security as opposed to state security. Thus, there is a need to integrate elements and dimensions of civil society into the security sphere where states historically dominated. In the human rights and sustainable development arenas, nongovernmental organizations (NGOs) are already active in analysis, lobbying, and operations. Independent experts lead important UN commissions. Hence, the UN of states and of secretariats would not be the same—in either normative or operational terms—without this third United Nations.

The United Nations is in a perpetual political transition. Old patterns of interaction have broken down or changed significantly, but new patterns may not necessarily have crystallized. Many old norms—such as nonintervention in domestic affairs—are under challenge. Meanwhile new ones—such as the responsibility to protect—have not yet been adequately codified and implemented. Old ways of doing things may prove insufficient for new problems, yet new experiments involve mistakes. States may be dissatisfied with the record of the old United Nations but are slow to provide the political will and resources necessary for a new generation of governance mechanisms to manage global problems.

LEARNING LESSONS?

The lessons of UN history can be helpful in charting the future direction of the world organization while recognizing that history can be misinterpreted and misused as a guide for political choices.[8] Still, one can separate what is known from what is unknown (or presumed). When using historical analogies, precision is required when comparing similarities and differences between the past and the present. Above all, one can clarify current options, guard against presumptions, and avoid stereotypes. In the 1990s the UN Secretariat was fairly criticized for not having a policy-planning group able to draw historical lessons from past use of UN force. Certain state bureaucracies, and many academics, were prepared to evaluate UN peacekeeping against the historical background of what had gone wrong with ONUC in the Belgian Congo from 1960 to 1964, or what had gone right in Central America regarding ONUSAL and ONUCA.

The next time the UN takes enforcement action inside a country, whether to deliver humanitarian relief, disarm belligerents, or protect civilians, it will be only natural to try to draw historical lessons from events in northern Iraq, Somalia, Bosnia, Rwanda, Haiti, Kosovo, East Timor, Libya, and Mali. The lessons from Afghanistan and the 2003 war in Iraq inform UN decisions as it faces the challenges presented by terrorism and the proliferation of weapons of mass destruction (WMDs). These lessons include the usefulness of UN diplomacy and inspections, the necessity of more adequate and accurate intelligence, and the need for multilateral stabilization efforts. The political and financial costs of "going it alone" have affected the United States, which is again using multilateral diplomacy to manage potential crises with Syria, Iran, and North Korea, as it once did during World War II and the birth of the United Nations.[9]

The task of learning is complicated by the pace of change and the culture of the second UN's bureaucracy. As Shashi Tharoor, then UN undersecretary-general in charge of the Department of Public Information, put it, we "too often find ourselves steering a rattling vehicle that is moving at breakneck speed, without an up-to-date roadmap, while trying to fix the engine at the same time."[10] Learning lessons is different from adapting. Adapting is more reactive and less comprehensive and is represented by incremental and often ambiguous institutional change. As two of the foremost analysts of institutional learning, Peter Haas and Ernst Haas, have written, "Organizations characterized by irreconcilable disagreements over desirable world orders or ineptitude may not even be made capable of learning to manage interdependence rather than merely adapting to it."[11] The major players in the first and second UN still have to make a substantial effort to digest the lessons from the recent past in order to formulate a workable strategy for the future.[12] The establishments of lessons-learned units in the Department of Peacekeeping Operations, Department of Political Affairs, and Office for the Coordination of Humanitarian Affairs are steps in the right direction, as are broadened evaluation and research units in many other UN entities and NGOs. There also is evidence of a growing thirst for independent research and knowledge as a basis for organizational learning.[13]

Against the background of historical lessons, three fundamental political tasks are characteristic of policymaking and problem solving: articulating and consolidating interests, making rules, and applying those rules.[14] We conclude this analysis of the United Nations with our evaluation of what has been learned. We chart change at the UN before and after the Cold War, and we suggest what these changes portend for an uncertain future in a shifting geopolitical landscape with emerging powers.

ARTICULATION AND AGGREGATION OF INTERESTS

As a result of decolonization and following the fall of the Berlin Wall, new states have routinely wanted to join the United Nations and other organizations in the system, but none of the old members has wanted to exit. Since 1945 only one state, Indonesia, has withdrawn (soon to rejoin after its quixotic attempt to create a rival organization collapsed). The delegation from South Africa was barred for a time, during part of the apartheid era, from participating in the General Assembly, but the state was still a member of the organization. Even in the doldrums of the 1960s, when the Soviet Union proposed replacing the secretary-general with a troika, or the twenty-first century, when some Washington insiders advocated replacing the UN with a league of democracies, states recognized that they needed the universal world organization to build diplomatic coalitions, make rules, and monitor adherence to and enforce those rules. Simply put, the old adage still applies: if the UN did not exist, it would have to be invented. The United Nations may be in perpetual crisis, but it is very much in demand and needs to be fixed.[15] Even those who displayed an initial proclivity to attack it, such as Ronald Reagan and George W. Bush, wound up utilizing it for many major policy decisions and actions. As a general rule, "the United Nations is successful over the long haul only if it helps to uncover or develop genuinely shared interests."[16] A dominant state or coalition can control policy for a time, but the UN is likely to be more effective if it is used in pursuit of widely shared interests.

After the Cold War as after World War II, the United States was the most important state in the United Nations. It was the only state capable of projecting military power globally and had the world's largest economy. The United States had always been the UN's most important member state, and the UN has never undertaken the use of force, for either peacekeeping or enforcement, without genuine U.S. backing. The UN has occasionally attempted human rights and economic programs in opposition to U.S. policy, but these programs have not achieved much. The rejection of the Special United Nations Fund for Economic Development (SUNFED) and the fate of the New International Economic Order (NIEO) are good examples of the futility of attempting a major program or initiative without U.S. support. However, the survival and even advancement of the International Criminal Court (ICC) and the land mines treaty in the face of U.S. opposition demonstrates the difficulty of generalizations. To be sure, many UN members were not altogether happy with U.S. influence at the UN. The lack of U.S. support for the Convention on the Rights of the Child, the treaty to ban land mines, the Kyoto Protocol to slow global climate change, the diplomacy to restrict the introduction of light arms into conflict zones, and the ICC led to much criticism of U.S. unilateralism.[17] The flow of criticism became a torrent after the United States led an invasion of Iraq in 2003 without Security Council authorization. UN diplomats almost unanimously described the debate surrounding the resolution withdrawn on the eve of the war in Iraq as "a referendum not on the means of disarming Iraq but on the American use of power."[18]

While noting U.S. unilateralism, we can recall issues at the UN for which there was genuine shared interest among UN members. Most states were opposed to the Iraqi aggression against Kuwait in 1991. Most states were appalled at human suffering in Somalia in 1992. Most states have expressed at least diplomatic support for human rights. Most states have recognized the need to promote sustainable development. Most states were opposed to Taliban rule and its support for Al Qaeda.

World politics can be thought of as a multilevel game. On the military level, at least in terms of traditional armed conflict, the United States clearly is predominant. Yet U.S. applied power can be opposed effectively, at least to some extent, by irregular violence such as roadside bombs, hit-and-run attacks, and other measures designed to counter U.S. putative superiority in traditional means of warfare. Even with the presumed primacy of the United States in military affairs, the U.S. quagmires in Iraq after 2003 and Afghanistan after 2001 show that broad cooperation and burden sharing is often the wise course of action in security matters. As Winston Churchill is reported to have said, the only thing worse than going to war with allies is going to war without them.

On the economic level, the cumulative weight of the European Union and Asia (particularly China and India) means that the United States, still with close to a quarter of the world's gross domestic product (GDP), does not dictate with the same authority as in the military arena. Its version of capitalism is no longer attractive and is seen by many as a cause of many of the world's problems. Some widely read authors, such as Kishore Mahbubani and Fareed Zakaria, were already talking about the rise of Asia and the nature of a post-American world even before the 2008–2009 financial crisis.[19] The world's major powers need each other to manage transnational problems.

Beyond the military and economic levels of world politics, the more general diplomatic level reveals many more multilateral elements and the need for compromise. The United States could not block the land mine treaty or the one creating the International Criminal Court. Washington's current short list for UN action includes postconflict reconstruction in Afghanistan, Iraq, and Libya; inspecting energy facilities in Iran; fighting terrorism (sharing information and the fight against money laundering); confronting infectious diseases and pandemics, such as Ebola; pursuing environmental sustainability; monitoring human rights; providing humanitarian aid; rescheduling debt; and fostering trade. As the former head of the National Security Council for George H. W. Bush and president of the Council on Foreign Relations Richard Haass put it, "For all its power, there is virtually nothing the United States can do better without others. The United States needs partners; unilateralism is rarely a viable option."[20] Power also resides in the activities of international organizations.[21]

Barack Obama has enunciated his "belief that the UN is an indispensable—and imperfect—forum."[22] He has also acknowledged that "the global challenges we face demand global institutions that work."[23] The UN's universal membership provides legitimacy and is a unique asset for the United States.[24] Obama and his administration certainly placed more rhetorical emphasis on the UN and multilateralism than his predecessor. At the same time, President Obama authorized many unilateral actions in such places as Pakistan to kill Osama bin Laden and others who were attacking or planning to attack U.S. personnel and allies. For any government, foreign policy is always a mix of unilateralism and multilateralism. The question is one of balance and reasoned choice in context. The Obama administration had to confront growing atrocities in Syria, the disintegration of Libya, and a Security Council with a more assertive Russia and China, both of which are not inclined to acquiesce to the Western powers. This makes it difficult to know which way the winds are blowing, especially in relation to the main issue areas addressed by the three UNs.

Security Issues

In the 1990s the United States led the military charges in the UN campaign to repel Iraqi aggression against Kuwait, to pressure Iraq to comply with various UN resolutions after Desert Storm, to deliver humanitarian relief in Somalia, and to make other UN security operations succeed. In a continuation of past patterns and in light of the U.S.'s veto power and military muscle, no UN security operation was undertaken against the wishes of the United States. Other states were also important in UN security affairs. The British and French deployed relatively large numbers of peacekeeping troops in the Balkans. The French mounted operations in Rwanda and the eastern Congo, as did the British in Sierra Leone, and the Australians led the UN force in East Timor. The Russians kept the lid on violence in Georgia, at least until the summer of 2008, and Nigeria spearheaded two Economic Community of West African States (ECOWAS) missions in West Africa, while Brazil took the lead in Haiti. The European Union took over military responsibilities in Bosnia from NATO, which remained on the ground in Kosovo and Afghanistan. NATO was also central in Libya in 2011 after France, the United Kingdom, and the United States had led in enforcing the no-fly zone. France proved key to curtailing violence and honoring elections in Côte d'Ivoire in 2011, in Mali in 2013, and in the Central African Republic in 2014.

All the permanent members of the Security Council have to at least avoid using their veto for UN decisions about peace and security matters to be made. Apart from permanent Security Council members, numerous states have supported UN peace and security efforts. Japan played a large role in UN Transitional Authority in Cambodia (UNTAC)'s efforts to stabilize and democratize Cambodia. Canada and Norway and some other states have been stalwarts of UN peacekeeping. Costa Rica and other Spanish-speaking states played important roles in supporting mediation by the secretary-general in Central America in the 1980s. For some time, developing countries have provided the vast majority of UN peacekeepers.[25]

The United States wants at least the UN's collective approval, and sometimes the UN's more direct help, in managing international peace and security. The George W. Bush administration took its concerns about Iraq to the Security Council in 2002, but then it attacked Iraq in 2003 without a UN blessing and without a persuasive case for self-defense. Nonetheless, the administration went back to the council for approval of its plans for the occupation and reconstruction of Iraq. The early occupation was directed by the United States, but as difficulties mounted, the Bush team was more amenable to UN involvement. The UN helped in the transfer of authority to an interim Iraqi government in June 2005 and has helped administer elections at several junctures. Despite U.S. unilateral use of force in places such as Grenada (1983), Panama (1989), and Iraq (2003)—along with its almost total exclusion of the UN from the negotiations leading to the Dayton Peace Accord (1995) for the former Yugoslavia—the dominant trend among all states, including Washington, is to involve the UN in managing military security problems. One reason to rely on the UN for the collective management of security issues is that most other regional options offer less prospect of success. Often a "hybrid" is created, as we have seen with the African Union and the UN in the Horn of Africa or the Arab League and the UN in mounting an observer mission in Syria. The Arab League was also important in UN developments concerning Libya in 2012. The African Union and the UN combined efforts in Darfur, although that venture was hardly an unqualified success—as noted previously. At a minimum, the world organization is required to be associated with security efforts to make states and coalitions who are delegated security responsibilities more accountable for actions undertaken in the UN's name. When Nigeria became bogged down in trying to pacify Liberia and Sierra Leone through the use of ECOWAS, this had the effect of increasing, not lessening, demands that the UN become more involved. A slightly different pattern obtained in Côte d'Ivoire in that both a UN force and one from ECOWAS proved inferior to, finally, a French contingent operating as part of the UN operation.

Both great and small powers have sought to confer on the UN an enhanced security role after the Cold War. The articulation and aggregation of interests have varied from issue to issue. And states have not always provided sufficient political and material support to enable UN operations and special representatives to succeed. Nevertheless, most states seem to have learned that major problems are hardly avoided by the pursuit of unilateral action. Apart from direct threats to a state's existence, multilateral security diplomacy has been the option preferred by most states on numerous occasions, including the long-simmering crises in Iran and North Korea and ongoing ones in Syria, South Sudan, the Central African Republic (CAR), and Yemen.

Human Rights Issues

The United States has been less of a dominant or hegemonic leader in human rights than in security and economic affairs.[26] The articulation and aggregation of human rights interests, principally through the Commission on Human Rights (CHR), came about less because of the United States and more because of a series of compromises among a large number of states, mostly Western in their orientation. At the 1993 World Conference on Human Rights, U.S. delegates played the leading role in pushing for reaffirmation of universal human rights. Ironically, UN norms codify economic and social human rights, which Washington rejects in their UN form. At one point the U.S. delegates circulated an informal list of states dragging their diplomatic feet. The United States was initially supportive of the idea of creating a more businesslike Human Rights Council to restore legitimacy to international efforts to protect and promote human rights, but it then voted against its creation, arguing that the council was not sufficiently changed from its predecessor. Still, Washington worked closely with the new body and eventually was elected in 2009. And when it came to the matter of forcefully delivering humanitarian assistance in situations of armed conflict, the UN took the most decisive steps in northern Iraq and Somalia, precisely where the United States displayed the most interest and commitment.

Just as most states sought to involve the UN in the management of security issues, so most states sought to use the world organization to promote human rights through international standards and to give at least some attention to their implementation—mostly by diplomacy, at least until 1993. Particularly after the Cold War, human rights were vigorously articulated by many democratic governments that had succeeded authoritarian ones—whether communist or otherwise. The Czech Republic and Uruguay are just two examples of governments that sought extensive UN action on human rights as a result of their own previous and traumatic experience with the denial of most internationally recognized rights.

Some states—for example, Burma, China, Cuba, Iraq, Sri Lanka, Sudan, Russia, Syria, Venezuela, Vietnam, and Zimbabwe—resisted this dominant trend. The United States, under the George W. Bush administration, invented semantic ways to circumvent the Geneva Conventions and its own constitutional prohibitions to torture prisoners captured in its military operations in Iraq and Afghanistan. Others, such as Saudi Arabia, Algeria, and various states in the Middle East, also opposed UN action on human rights—especially concerning women's reproductive rights and homosexuality—but they found it politically prudent to keep a low profile.

Moral and expedient interests in internationally recognized human rights exist, if one takes governmental statements at face value. States appear to have learned that the advancement of such rights is conducive to human dignity and that such rights have politically desirable consequences—for example, international peace, domestic tranquility, and uninterrupted foreign assistance. States have little choice but to use the United Nations for the articulation and aggregation of global human rights interests. Of course, they also can use regional organizations to develop international human rights norms and programs on a regional basis. In theory universal human rights standards could be developed outside the UN in much the same way that international humanitarian law was developed for human rights in armed conflicts. However, if international society desires widespread, shared understandings of universal human rights, it needs the United Nations.

Sustainable Human Development

The UN has been a—probably *the*—central forum for articulating and aggregating interests regarding sustainable human development and human security. We pointed out how the adoption of the MDGs and their restatement at the World Summit in September 2005 represented a culmination of a long process, one that had taken six decades. The September 2015 World Summit that agreed on the SDGs marked the beginning of the next part of that unfinished journey. The UN network was used mostly by developing countries to define and refine their views of what should be done about poverty and underdevelopment. Some of their demands, such as for SUNFED and the NIEO, did not lead to planetary bargains between North and South, but major compromises have been struck with various UN agencies and personalities playing important roles in facilitating agreements. At the risk of overgeneralization, we would say that over time industrialized countries have come around to the view that UN agencies have important roles to play in bridging the North-South divide and that private markets alone cannot provide all that is necessary to overcome underdevelopment in all its forms. Despite their shortcomings, the SDGs set targets for all countries—not just developing ones. The SDGs are yet another indication of the value of a universal forum in setting the global agenda.

Ecological protection is fundamental to sustainable human development. The 1992 Rio conference, where the lengthy Agenda 21 was hammered out and articulated as a policy guideline for the twenty-first century, and where treaties on biodiversity and rain forests were negotiated, remains part of the road map. Agenda 21 and various conventions and declarations that emerged from Rio are snapshots of an evolving political process rather than static political outcomes. The Commission on Sustainable Development and the United Nations Environment Programme were the result of a compromise among states about what the United Nations could do to interject environmental protection into efforts to produce economic growth. In June 2012 more than one hundred heads of state or government convened in Rio de Janeiro for the United Nations Conference on Sustainable Development, Rio+20. The summit produced a 283-paragraph agreement,

"The Future as We Want It," but from the perspective of many participants and observers, very little had actually been accomplished. The U.S. president failed to attend the summit, and no enforceable commitments resulted for dealing with major environmental challenges. Still, the follow-up process within the first UN managed to articulate the SDGs, and member states adopted them as the development agenda for 2016–2030.

The UN has not exercised a monopoly over efforts to articulate interests related to sustainable development. All developed countries, and many developing ones as well, have individual programs for environmental protection. Regional organizations, particularly the European Union,[27] also have environmental programs that, when added to efforts to ensure economic growth, produce a combined policy framework on sustainable development. But as with security and human rights issues, the UN has been used by various actors to formulate and express a vision of how economic growth can be combined with protection of the environment.

RULE MAKING

Every society requires collective procedures to establish rules that differentiate between permissible and impermissible behavior. The United Nations plays a central role in this essential rule making for international society—largely through the Security Council, General Assembly, and world conferences—but other mechanisms in international society also create rules. Some treaties are made outside the UN system, and regional organizations make rules as well. The murky institution of customary international law, which is greatly affected by the behavior of powerful states, also plays a role. As José Alvarez tells us, "Like the Pope, whose historical influence on states has obviously exceeded the Vatican's military or economic capabilities, IOs' [international organizations'] impact on international law-making actors results from, in substantial part, the moral suasion they exert and not from the law-making powers explicitly."[28] The UN has a major role in rule making for all three of our major issues.

Security Rules

Rules relating to international security are vague. Neither the International Court of Justice nor the Security Council has specified the distinction between a breach of the peace and outright aggression. Moreover, the term "intervention" has never been authoritatively specified, even though a 1974 General Assembly resolution attempted to define aggression. The 1998 Rome Statute for the International Criminal Court recognizes this problem, indicating that no charges can be brought against individuals for aggression until that concept is better specified in international law. Questions remain about whether military reprisals are legal in peacetime and whether force can be used to protect human rights. Questions also remain about the scope of state self-defense of an anticipatory or preventative nature.

The Security Council has used a very broad interpretation of Chapter VII of the UN Charter pertaining to enforcement action in response to threats to and breaches of the peace and acts of aggression. It has determined that peace and security issues may arise from human rights, economic, and ecological situations—and even from HIV/AIDS in Africa—not just from the use of force across borders by states. It has even determined that humanitarian conditions within a state, even those that do not seem to generate external material effects, constitute a threat to international peace and security and merit an enforcement action under Chapter VII. It has decided to authorize such action to restore an elected government overthrown by military force. Along the way, the Security Council has specified that individuals in zones of armed conflict have a right to humanitarian assistance and protection and that to interfere with that right is a war crime for which there can be individual prosecution. The council has also authorized member states to seize the property of a state (Iraq) so as to assist in the implementation of binding sanctions. Under Chapter VII the council has created war-crimes tribunals for the former Yugoslavia and for Rwanda and approved various hybrid courts. International security rules are likely to remain vague because the competing claims of states are rarely authoritatively reviewed by the Security Council or the World Court. Often world politics is about case-by-case decision making and double standards, but the Security Council is a source of international legal precedents.[29] Efforts to clearly delineate the conditions under which force may be authorized stalled at the 2005 World Summit. Nevertheless, the council continues to try to distinguish aggression from self-defense and make use of Chapter VII to organize a legally binding response to threats to and breaches of the peace.

Human Rights Rules

The UN has been codifying rules on internationally recognized human rights since 1948, when the General Assembly adopted the Universal Declaration of Human Rights and also approved the convention on genocide. Since then, there has been sufficient formal or informal consensus (reflecting an aggregation of interests) to produce numerous treaties, declarations, and resolutions.

More particularly, the United Nations has been active in fostering human rights rules since the end of the Cold War. The Security Council has merged human rights and security rules to a great extent, making decisions under Chapter VII pertaining to peace and security that involved such fundamental rights as the one to adequate nutrition (for example, in Somalia) and freedom from repression (for example, in Iraq). Stanley Hoffmann has aptly described "international peace and security" as an "all-purpose parachute."[30] In Haiti, the council voted a binding and comprehensive economic embargo on the country during summer 1993 after military elements deposed an elected civilian president. Moreover, the Commission on Human Rights expanded its rule making even beyond the several dozen treaties and declarations already adopted. The commission took on the complex subjects of the rights of minorities and indigenous peoples. The follow-on Human Rights Council adopted new standards on enforced disappearances and indigenous peoples.

The 1993 Vienna conference witnessed tremendous NGO pressure on all states to continue with UN rule making on human rights. A demand was strong for further attention to rules on women's rights. Even states not genuinely committed to personal rights found it difficult to withstand combined NGO and state pressure in support of expanded UN rule making. The political situation was such that it was easier for these dissenting states to formally accept rules that they did not really support than to stand up and try to oppose them directly. The Vienna process also indicated clearly that established principles of human rights might not be as universally accepted as many UN and human rights observers had previously thought.

The plethora of UN rules on human rights is marked also by remarkable state hypocrisy about those rules. The UN treaty monitoring system is plagued by late and superficial reports, not to mention a lack of adequate funding to ensure their timely review. The systematic election of rights-violating states to the CHR indicated that many states gave preference to traditional bargaining and geographical considerations rather than to serious respect for the rules. This has been slow to change with its successor, the Human Rights Council, even though all members are elected by a majority vote of the General Assembly and are subject to having their human rights performance reviewed. The human rights domain at the UN is characterized by extensive codification and other norm development that reflect a formal statement of interests and/or values, but human rights NGOs properly remain skeptical about state sincerity. This concern remains valid, as the Human Rights Council is now in continual session (instead of meeting only periodically as its predecessor did) but nonetheless seems to many to be little more than old wine in a new bottle.

Rules for Sustainable Development

Many view the Millennium Development Goals as comparable to the Universal Declaration of Human Rights, with specific reference to spelling out an agreed development agenda for member states and the UN development system. These core principles included a focus on poverty and hunger, education, gender equality, children's and maternal welfare, good health and especially the threat of HIV/AIDS, and such general matters as sustainable ecology and broad partnership for development. The MDGs contained measurable targets for human security, although many states had fallen short on some of the targets by the 2015 deadline. Undeterred, the three UNs embarked on the SDGs with the goal of eliminating extreme poverty and inequality in the next fifteen years. Too many pundits dismiss out of hand the role of goal setting, but this has been a singular achievement of the United Nations that has more of an impact on naming and shaming states and thus altering their behavior than is commonly thought. The UN has long-term value as the fount and proponent of ideas and ideals that have spawned numerous global conventions, norms, standards, and principles—here, the UN is "peerless."[31]

UN organizations and international civil servants, along with a phalanx of NGOs, press states to take the MDGs and SDGs seriously. Just as human rights NGOs lobby for attention to the international rules in the domain of human rights and humanitarian affairs, so there will be nonstate actors of various types seeking to follow up the new agenda for development, to help hold states at least modestly accountable for their commitments.

APPLYING RULES

Most striking about the UN system amid changing world politics is the extent to which judgments are made about the behavior of states under UN-sponsored rules, which themselves reflect interests articulated and aggregated through UN channels. The past seven decades reveal important lessons for UN rule application within our three thematic areas.

Applying Security Rules

The Security Council is the locus of supervisory activity concerning state use of force and other security policies. The Security Council cannot be expected to override the permanent members in any serious way. Each still possesses the veto, which guarantees council paralysis when a permanent member's strategic interest is challenged or engaged. This is the result not of poor drafting by the Charter's framers but of a clear recognition of the realities of power. No coalition of states could hope militarily to coerce the United States or Russia into changing its policies; it is doubtful that any coalition could do likewise against Britain, France, or China without enormous disruption to world politics. Avoiding such a major confrontation that could make matters worse was a justification for the UN in the first place. The inability of the Security Council to act after Russia's takeover of the Crimea and support for Russian-speaking rebels in Eastern Ukraine demonstrated in 2014 the same reality as had been evident since 1945, namely the impossibility of a divided council having an impact.

In spring 2003 most of the members of the council were trying to offset U.S. and U.K. military power, then focused on Iraq, with diplomatic and legal arguments. In a sense this was classic balance-of-power politics, with France, Russia, Germany, China, and others trying to restrain the United States (and Britain and Spain) with diplomatic and legal measures. This balancing failed in the short run, in the sense that the United States and a coalition of willing partners were not deterred in their use of force against Iraq. Indeed, given the preponderance of American power, it is difficult to see how such a diplomatic approach could effectively have constituted a real balance. In the long run, obvious postconflict (if that is the word) difficulties in Iraq may make the United States more cautious about unilateralism in the future, or at least help it to better appreciate the limits of military power and the advantages of multilateral diplomacy.

Never before in world history has an intergovernmental body sought to pass judgment on states' security policies to the extent that the Security Council has. In historical perspective, this was a major experiment and the outcome has been mixed. Working closely with the secretary-general, the council could count a number of successes in supervising various policies in such places as South-West Africa/Namibia and Central America in the late 1980s and early 1990s. The result was both independence for Namibia and significant steps toward regional peace and national reconciliation in El Salvador and Nicaragua. From August 1990 the council successfully countered various Iraqi policies that violated international law, primarily because the United States took a strong interest in resisting aggression against Kuwait and in seeing that council follow-up resolutions were enforced. The council was also successful in ameliorating starvation in Somalia in 1992 and early 1993, again because the United States decided, for whatever reason, that the situation was intolerable.

At the same time, the Security Council passed numerous resolutions pertaining to the former Yugoslavia that were not implemented. The state members of the council were diplomatically engaged in supervising the policies of the various parties engaged in armed conflict: Serbians, Croats, Bosnians, Bosnian Serbs, Bosnian Croats, and Bosnian Muslims. Those same council members, however, lacked the will to see that the necessary political and material resources were made available to UN forces and representatives in the field. Multilateral diplomacy was divorced from the threat to use power or the effective use of power, with predictably disappointing results. Serbia's original war aims ended up being the negotiated final solution. Nevertheless, the UN did commendable work in trying circumstances by providing humanitarian relief to many thousands of persons.

From May 1993, the council and its field representatives through the second UN Operation in Somalia (UNOSOM II) tried to accomplish what U.S. forces had been unwilling to do under the Unified Task Force (UNITAF)—namely, to disarm the internal factions that had been threatening civilian life and to protect relief officials. But this task proved difficult, given the inadequate training, coordination, equipment, and overall force levels of UN military contingents. Calling the effort an enforcement operation under Chapter VII did not resolve problems in the field, and the UN had difficulty suppressing factions that had long used force to gain their political objectives.

The situation was similar for the UN Transitional Authority in Cambodia (UNTAC). General elections were supervised in May 1993, but the Security Council found it difficult to fashion a policy that would control the Khmer Rouge while helping competing domestic factions that supported national reconciliation. The delayed reactions to genocide in Rwanda and to the ouster of the elected government in Haiti also tarnished the UN's reputation. But in these and other security situations, state members of the council tended to pass resolutions that they were not committed to implementing unless the costs were deemed to be reasonable and the duration of an operation short.

The United States led NATO to use military force in the former Yugoslavia during 1999 outside the council, because Russia and China were not prepared to support such action against Serbia's persecution of Albanian Kosovars. Russia saw itself as the historical protector of the Serbs, and China was worried about UN approval of strong action against a government's treatment of its own citizens. Over time, an uneasy equilibrium balancing the territorial integrity of states and the right to self-determination has tamped down on violence in the region. Following the Arab Spring, the Security Council was able to find the will to intervene in Libya in 2011 while being unable to muster the necessary consensus to act decisively in the ongoing humanitarian crisis in Syria. This inconsistency is not surprising, but is the result of changing world politics. How states calculate their interests and how much power they think they can apply vary from case to case. Action by the UN is dependent on such calculations. Efforts in Mali have also shown that the second UN is constrained in its capacity to conduct counterterrorism military operations.

Applying Human Rights Rules

Since about 1970 the United Nations, principally via the Commission on Human Rights and since 2006 the Human Rights Council, has been more or less systematically using embarrassment to pressure states violating UN human rights rules to make corrections. But here, as elsewhere, double standards prevail. Before 1970 the UN sporadically supervised rights performance, but only after 1970 did the world organization make this supervision a regular feature of its actions. The realm of domestic jurisdiction has shrunk progressively, and the realm of international supervision has expanded; but again, consistency is not always a characteristic of UN affairs.

Small and weak developing countries were the most likely targets of UN human rights supervision, but no state could be guaranteed immunity from diplomatic pressure. For example, the Expert Committee supervising the UN Covenant on Economic, Social and Cultural Rights took on the Dominican Republic. The UN Committee on Human Rights supervising the UN Covenant on Civil and Political Rights confronted Uruguay. And the Commission on Human Rights broke new diplomatic ground in supervising Guinea-Bissau. More important states, such as China, Iran, Iraq, and Israel, were sometimes targeted for diplomatic supervision. Russia has been the only permanent member of the council officially condemned by the CHR; that occurred because of its heavy-handed policies in the breakaway republic of Chechnya. China has intensely lobbied to avoid censure in that commission and succeeded by the narrowest of votes.

Power greatly affects human rights issues at the United Nations. The United States and Japan were not as likely as Israel to be pressured about racial discrimination. Haiti was more likely to be pressured about the denial of political rights than Myanmar (formerly Burma). China could avoid the issue of suppression of Tibetan rights at the Vienna conference, whereas Israel could not so easily avoid the issue of Palestinian rights to self-determination.

In recent years member states created special tribunals to deal with genocide and other human rights atrocities in particular places, such as Rwanda and Yugoslavia, and then they created the ICC. They also experimented with a hybrid course in Sierra Leone, Cambodia, and Lebanon. There remained, however, considerable disagreement about enforcing some human rights via international criminal proceedings. The ICC has been stymied as member states refuse to arrest indicted suspects and has even been forced to drop cases due to a lack of cooperation. The renaissance of international criminal justice since 1993 is a major development in international relations, and the UN has played a central role, even if the ICC is largely (but not entirely) independent of the United Nations. International criminal justice is not a panacea, but the judicial enforcement of major human rights violations is not the moribund subject it was some decades ago.

Applying Rules on Sustainable Human Development

Judging the UN's record on supervising sustainable human development is a complex task. The MDGs generated general policy statements, and the UN had a mixed record in applying them. The International Labour Organization monitored labor conditions (usually treated as a human rights question); the World Health Organization watched over health conditions (also treated by some as a human rights issue); and UN Educational, Scientific and Cultural Organization (UNESCO) kept an eye on educational issues. But on many core issues of sustainable development, the basic rules, as well as the very meaning of the concept, have only recently met with relative consensus. Deciding what specific data will be used is hardly uncontroversial, and many sustainable development concerns are treated outside the official framework of the United Nations. For example, the Montreal Protocol on the ozone and related agreements have been negotiated outside the UN but with some participation by UNEP. No single national government is able on its own to solve the problem of the thinning ozone layer and states can only secure their long-term interests in a healthy environment through multilateral action. Such situations can lead to the adoption of shared norms and concrete actions by international organizations. The result can create important legal and organizational restrictions on states even if binding national legislation to remedy the problem is lacking in most states.

The UN has never played as definitive and large a role in directly monitoring state economic and ecological policies as it has in supervising security and human rights policies. The new SDG initiative is no different. International supervision in this arena has been performed more authoritatively by the World Bank and the International Monetary Fund, which also have far more resources to encourage compliance with international agreements. Since 1995, the World Trade Organization (WTO) has handled disputes about trading rules and is totally outside the UN. Given the wide range of indicators for MDGs and SDGs, various UN agencies may engage in "naming and shaming" in an effort to prod states into meeting stated targets.

Just how the Security Council, the General Assembly, or some other UN body could impose itself on a fragmented UN system and how such a centralized entity would link to the Washington-based international financial institutions and the WTO is unclear. The proliferation of new China-led and BRICS-led development banks adds new actors with distinct preferences to the mix. As the 2000 Millennium Assembly indicated, sustainable development entails processes and conditions that lie well outside the scope and domain of interstate relations. Sustainable development calls for popular participation in decision-making processes and project implementation. It reaches to the lowest level of social aggregation: local communities, social groups, and individuals. These are elements of sustainable human development and of human security that do not fit well with intergovernmental decision making, UN style, and associated norms about the extent of national state sovereignty and noninterference in domestic affairs. Indeed, in many ways the worldviews underlying interstate relations, on the one hand, and sustainable development, on the other, are distinct. UN specialized agencies were by and large created to facilitate and promote a liberal-economic (that is, laissez-faire) world order. The resulting tensions and turbulence characterize contemporary world politics. Bridging the gap between micro- and macro-phenomena is key to coping with turbulence and promoting human as well as global security.

SOME FINAL THOUGHTS

The primary raison d'être of the United Nations is the promotion and maintenance of international peace and security, whose meaning has evolved considerably since 1945. In this regard, we need to stress the inherent and inextricably linked nature of human security, democratization and human rights, and sustainable human development. The latter is aimed at cumulatively improving and sustaining human security and reducing perceived and actual threats to physical and psychological well-being from all manner of agents and forces that could degrade lives, values, and property. Both sustainable human security and sustainable human development require democracy and the protection of fundamental human rights. In short, enhancing human security is what both development and democracy are about. Nothing could be clearer in the post-9/11 world. But democracy is messy and chaotic, and often leads to illiberal governments more interested in order at the expense of individual freedom.

The United Nations has always been a blend of ideals and reality. Its Charter represents complementary yet contradictory principles. It articulates the idealistic goals of international society, a world of peace and justice with rights and prosperity for all. Its day-to-day operations represent the reality of state foreign policies

Picture of a copy of the "Charter of the United Nations." (UN PHOTO/MARK GARTEN 25148)

mediated by the views of nonstate parties, such as NGOs and international civil servants. The UN thus represents both striving for a better world—more peaceful, with more human dignity and equitable and sustainable prosperity—and the abject failure to fully achieve that world.

The end of the Cold War provided an opportunity for states to cooperate more through the United Nations. The debilitating competition between the United States and the Soviet Union, between NATO and the Warsaw Pact, between capitalist democracies and authoritarian socialist states, disappeared along with the Berlin Wall. States have at least sometimes learned from this post–Cold War opportunity how to cooperate within the security realm (for instance, in the 1991 Gulf War and Somalia), the human rights arena (for instance, in Haiti and El Salvador), and the field of sustainable development (through the MDGs and SDGs).

But interstate cooperation via the United Nations clearly has its limits. States learned conflicting lessons about the wisdom of projecting the UN into armed conflicts in places like the former Yugoslavia or into the human rights situation in such places as China, and how to handle sustainable development in both the North and the Global South. How effective UN efforts will be in helping to reconstitute Afghanistan, Iraq, Somalia, Libya, and Mali is as unknown as the effectiveness of the U.S.-led war on terrorism and regime change. In sum, different states draw different lessons about the desirability of multilateralism via the UN. Yet the organization not only continues but also is asked to take on new problems even as many old ones remain.

Despite all the problems and challenges, perhaps things are not getting worse but better. Perhaps we should discount what John Mearsheimer famously called "the false promise of international institutions"[32] and emphasize what John Ruggie just as famously claimed, that "multilateralism matters."[33] Recent studies have challenged the conventional wisdom that the world is more violent than it used to be.[34] The first decade of the twenty-first century has averaged 55,000 war-related deaths a year, whereas the 1990s averaged approximately 100,000 annual deaths, and the Cold War averaged 180,000 a year between 1950 and 1989.[35] The subtitle for the *Human Security Report 2009–2010* is *The Causes of Peace and the Shrinking Costs of War*, and it puts forward some encouraging data concerning the reduced risks of war. This puzzling reality seemingly results from the demise of colonialism and the Cold War, along with increasing levels of economic interdependence, the number of democracies, and evolving norms.[36] The story of the UN is not always heartwarming, and assessing what might have happened had the UN acted or not is impossible to discern. What is possible to do is to trace how and why the UN was created and how it has adapted in a constantly changing political, economic, and social environment. Most analysts would say that UN norms and operations have had something to do with declining violence over time. We often get depressed by events in Ukraine and Syria and Libya and lose sight of the big picture.

In evaluating the successes and failures attributed to the United Nations, we can take a maximalist or a minimalist position. If we compare the real record of achievement with the lofty goals articulated in the Charter, the world organization's record is bound to be the subject of criticism or even derision. If we recognize that UN actions depend heavily on state foreign policies, which are ever sensitive to calculations about narrowly conceived national interests, and that much of the time the second UN is handed the problems that states have not been able to solve on their own, then criticism is moderated. "SG" is an accepted abbreviation for the UN's head, but it also stands for "scapegoat," a prevalent function in world politics for the secretary-general and the United Nations more generally.

In this respect we may do well to conclude with the central theme with which we began this text. In the words attributed to Secretary-General Dag Hammarskjöld: "The purpose of the UN is not to get us to heaven but to save us from hell." Developments in world politics will determine whether Dag Hammarskjöld's vision of the UN remains relevant in our turbulent twenty-first century.

NOTES

1. "Winds of Change," *Foreign Affairs* 69, no. 4 (1995): 162–172.

2. See Thomas G. Weiss and Rorden Wilkinson, eds., *International Organization and Global Governance* (London: Routledge, 2014).

3. See Jamie Gasgarth, ed., *Rising Powers, Global Governance, and Global Ethics* (London: Routledge, 2015); and Cedric de Coning, Thomas Mandrup, and Liselotte Odgaard, eds., *BRICS and Coexistence: An Alternative Vision of World Order* (London: Routledge, 2014).

4. This discussion draws on Michael Barnett and Thomas G. Weiss, "Humanitarianism: A Brief History of the Present," in *Humanitarianism in Question: Politics, Power, Ethics* (Ithaca, N.Y.: Cornell University Press, 2008), 1–48.

5. Kalevi J. Holsti, *Taming the Sovereigns: Institutional Change in International Politics* (Cambridge: Cambridge University Press, 2004), 12–13.

6. John Campbell, *Institutional Change and Globalization* (Princeton, N.J.: Princeton University Press, 2004), 34.

7. James N. Rosenau, *Turbulence in World Politics: A Theory of Change and Continuity* (Princeton, N.J.: Princeton University Press, 1990). The implications of this view for the United Nations are found in his *The United Nations in a Turbulent World* (Boulder, Colo.: Lynne Rienner, 1992).

8. Ernest R. May, *"Lessons" of the Past: The Use and Misuse of History in American Foreign Policy* (New York: Oxford University Press, 1975); and Richard E. Neustadt and Ernest R. May, *Thinking in Time: The Uses of History for Decision Makers* (New York: Free Press, 1986).

9. Dan Plesch and Thomas G. Weiss, eds., *Wartime Origins and the Future United Nations* (London: Routledge, 2015).

10. Shashi Tharoor, "Foreword," in *Beyond Traditional Peacekeeping*, ed. Donald C. F. Daniel and Bradd C. Hayes (London: Macmillan, 1995), xviii.

11. Peter M. Haas and Ernst B. Haas, "Learning to Learn: Improving International Governance," *Global Governance* 1, no. 3 (1995): 278.

12. Cindy Collins and Thomas G. Weiss, *Review of the Peacekeeping Literature, 1990–1996* (Providence, R.I.: Watson Institute, 1997).

13. See Michael Barnett, "Humanitarianism as a Scholarly Vocation," and Peter J. Hoffman and Thomas G. Weiss, "Humanitarianism and Practitioners: Social Science Matters," in *Humanitarianism in Question: Politics, Power, Ethics*, ed. Michael Barnett and Thomas G. Weiss (Ithaca, N.Y.: Cornell University Press, 2008), chaps. 10 and 11.

14. Harold K. Jacobson, *Networks of Interdependence: International Organizations and the Global Political System* (New York: Knopf, 1979).

15. Thomas G. Weiss, *What's Wrong with the United Nations and How to Fix It*, 3rd ed. (London: Polity, 2016).

16. Robert E. Riggs, *US/UN: Foreign Policy and International Organization* (New York: Appleton-Century-Crofts, 1971), 298.

17. Clyde Prestowitz, *Rogue Nation: American Unilateralism and the Failure of Good Intentions* (New York: Basic Books, 2003); and David M. Malone and Yuen Foong Khong, eds., *Unilateralism and U.S. Foreign Policy: International Perspectives* (Boulder, Colo.: Lynne Rienner, 2003).

18. James Traub, "The Next Resolution," *New York Times Magazine*, April 13, 2003.

19. Kishore Mahbubani, *The New Asian Hemisphere: The Irresistible Shift of Global Power to the East* (New York: PublicAffairs, 2008); and Fareed Zakaria, *The Post-American World* (New York: W. W. Norton, 2008).

20. Richard N. Haass, *The Opportunity: America's Chance to Change the World* (New York: PublicAffairs, 2005), 199. See also David P. Forsythe, Patrice C. McMahon, and Andrew Wedeman, eds., *American Foreign Policy in a Globalized World* (New York: Routledge, 2006).

21. Michael Barnett and Raymond Duvall, eds., *Power in Global Governance* (Cambridge: Cambridge University Press, 2005).

22. Thomas G. Weiss, "Toward a Third Generation of International Institutions: Obama's UN Policy," *Washington Quarterly* 32, no. 3 (2009): 343–364, and "Renewing Washington's Multilateral Leadership," *Global Governance* 18, 3 (2012): 253–266.

23. "The National Security Team," December 1, 2008, http://change.gov/newsroom /entry/the_national_security_team.

24. "Susan Rice's Testimony at Her U.N. Ambassador Hearing, January 15, 2009," http://www.realclearpolitics.com/articles/2009/01/susan_rices_testimony_at_her_u .html. Other quotations are from this testimony as well.

25. Paul D. Williams, *Enhancing U.S. Support for Peace Operations in Africa* (New York: Council on Foreign Relations, 2015).

26. Tony Evans, *U.S. Hegemony and the Project of Universal Human Rights* (New York: St. Martin's Press, 1996); and David P. Forsythe, *Human Rights in International Relations* (Cambridge: Cambridge University Press, 2012).

27. See Henrik Selin and Stacy D. VanDeveer, *The European Union and Environmental Governance* (London: Routledge, 2015).

28. José E. Alvarez, *International Organizations as Law-Makers* (Oxford: Oxford University Press, 2005), 626.

29. Vesselin Popovski and Trudy Fraser, eds., *The Security Council as Global Legislator* (London: Routledge, 2014).

30. Remarks made at a symposium on collective responses to common threats, Oslo, Norway, June 22–23, 1993.

31. Richard Jolly, Louis Emmerij, and Thomas G. Weiss, *UN Ideas That Changed the World* (Bloomington: Indiana University Press, 2009), chap. 5.

32. John Mearsheimer, "The False Promise of International Institutions," *International Security* 19, no. 3 (1994/95): 5–49.

33. John G. Ruggie, ed., *Multilateralism Matters* (New York: Columbia University Press, 1993).

34. Steven Pinker, *The Better Angels of Our Nature: Why Violence Has Declined* (New York: Viking, 2011); and Joshua S. Goldstein, *Winning the War on War: The Decline of Armed Conflict Worldwide* (New York: Dutton, 2011).

35. Joshua S. Goldstein, "Think Again: War," *Foreign Policy* (September/October 2011); and Jon Western and Joshua S. Goldstein, "Humanitarian Intervention Comes of Age," *Foreign Affairs* (November/December 2011).

36. Human Security Report Project, *Human Security Report 2009-2010: The Causes of Peace and the Shrinking Costs of War* (New York: Oxford University Press, 2011).

Appendix A
The United Nations System

UNITED NATIONS

The UNITED NATIONS system

PRINCIPAL ORGANS OF THE UNITED NATIONS

| INTERNATIONAL COURT OF JUSTICE | SECURITY COUNCIL | GENERAL ASSEMBLY | ECONOMIC AND SOCIAL COUNCIL | TRUSTEESHIP COUNCIL | SECRETARIAT |

SECURITY COUNCIL
- Military Staff Committee
- Standing Committee and ad hoc bodies
- International Criminal Tribunal for the Former Yugoslavia
- International Criminal Tribunal for Rwanda
- UN Monitoring, Verification and Inspection Commission (Iraq)
- United Nations Compensation Commission
- Peacekeeping Operations and Missions

GENERAL ASSEMBLY
- Main committees
- Other sessional committees
- Standing committees and ad hoc bodies
- Other subsidiary organs

PROGRAMMES AND FUNDS

UNCTAD United Nations Conference on Trade and Development
- **ITC** International Trade Centre (UNCTAD/WTO)

UNDCP United Nations Drug Control Programme

UNEP United Nations Environment Programme

UNHSP United Nations Human Settlements Programme (UN-Habitat)

UNDP United Nations Development Programme
- **UNIFEM** United Nations Development Fund for Women
- **UNV** United Nations Volunteers

UNFPA United Nations Population Fund

UNHCR Office of the United Nations High Commissioner for Refugees

UNICEF United Nations Children's Fund

WFP World Food Programme

UNRWA** United Nations Relief and Works Agency for Palestine Refugees in the Near East

OTHER UN ENTITIES

OHCHR Office of the United Nations High Commissioner for Human Rights

UNOPS United Nations Office for Project Services

UNU United Nations University

UNSSC United Nations System Staff College

UNAIDS Joint United Nations Programme on HIV/AIDS

RESEARCH AND TRAINING INSTITUTES

INSTRAW International Research and Training Institute for the Advancement of Women

UNICRI United Nations Interregional Crime and Justice Research Institute

UNITAR United Nations Institute for Training and Research

UNRISD United Nations Research Institute for Social Development

UNIDIR** United Nations Institute for Disarmament Research

ECONOMIC AND SOCIAL COUNCIL

FUNCTIONAL COMMISSIONS
- Commission for Social Development
- Human Rights Council
- Commission on Narcotic Drugs
- Commission on Crime Prevention and Criminal Justice
- Commission on Science and Technology for Development
- Commission on Sustainable Development
- Commission on the Status of Women
- Commission on Population and Development
- Statistical Commission

REGIONAL COMMISSIONS
- Economic Commission for Africa (ECA)
- Economic Commission for Europe (ECE)
- Economic Commission for Latin America and the Caribbean (ECLAC)
- Economic and Social Commission for Asia and the Pacific (ESCAP)
- Economic and Social Commission for Western Asia (ESCWA)
- United Nations Forum on Forests
- Sessional and Standing Committees Expert, ad hoc and related bodies

RELATED ORGANIZATIONS

IAEA International Atomic Energy Agency

WTO (trade) World Trade Organization

WTO (tourism) World Tourism Organization

CTBTO Prep.com PrepCom for the Nuclear-Test-Ban-Treaty Organization

OPCW Organization for the Prohibition of Chemical Weapons

SPECIALIZED AGENCIES*

ILO International Labour Organization

FAO Food and Agriculture Organization of the United Nations

UNESCO United Nations Educational, Scientific and Cultural Organization

WHO World Health Organization

WORLD BANK GROUP
- **IBRD** International Bank for Reconstruction and Development
- **IDA** International Development Association
- **IFC** International Finance Corporation
- **MIGA** Multilateral Investment Guarantee Agency
- **ICSID** International Centre for Settlement of Investment Disputes

IMF International Monetary Fund

ICAO International Civil Aviation Organization

IMO International Maritime Organization

ITU International Telecommunication Union

UPU Universal Postal Union

WMO World Meteorological Organization

WIPO World Intellectual Property Organization

IFAD International Fund for Agricultural Development

UNIDO United Nations Industrial Development Organization

SECRETARIAT

OSG Office of the Secretary-General

OIOS Office of Internal Oversight Services

OLA Office of Legal Affairs

DPA Department of Political Affairs

DDA Department for Disarmament Affairs

DPKO Department of Peacekeeping Operations

OCHA Office for the Coordination of Humanitarian Affairs

DESA Department of Economic and Social Affairs

DGACM Department of General Assembly and Conference Management

DPI Department of Public Information

DM Department of Management

OIP Office of the Iraq Programme

UNSECOORD Office of the United Nations Security Coordinator

OHRLLS Office of the High Representative for the Least Developed Countries, Landlocked Developing Countries and Small Island Developing States

ODC Office on Drugs and Crime

UNOG UN Office at Geneva

UNOV UN Office at Vienna

UNON UN Office at Nairobi

*Autonomous organizations working with the United Nations and each other through the coordinating machinery of the Economic and Social Council.
**Report only to the General Assembly.

Published by the United Nations Department of Public Information DPI/2299 - February 2003

Appendix B

Concise List of Internet Sites Relevant to the United Nations

General Information on International Relations with Frequent Attention to the UN

Council on Foreign Relations and *Foreign Affairs* magazine: www.cfr.org
Carnegie Council on Ethics: www.carnegiecouncil.org
Foreign Policy magazine: www.foreignpolicy.com
International Crisis Group: www.intl-crisis-grp.org

General Information on the UN and the UN System

The United Nations homepage*: www.un.org
The United Nations University: www.unu.edu
UN Wire: www.unwire.org
Academic Council on the UN System (ACUNS): www.acuns.org
UN Association of the USA: www.unausa.org
UN Chronicle magazine: www.un.org/Pubs/chronicle

Security Issues

International Security magazine: www.harvard.edarticle 545u/publications/cfm
International Institute for Strategic Studies and Survival magazine: www.iiss.org
Center for Strategic and International Studies: www.csis.org
Women in International Security: www.wiis.org
Security Council Report: www.securitycouncilreport.org

Human Rights and Humanitarian Affairs

International Committee of the Red Cross: www.icrc.org
Amnesty International: www.amnesty.org
Human Rights Watch: www.hrw.org
Coalition for International Justice: www.cij.org
Freedom House: www.freedomhouse.org

Sustainable Human Development

World Bank: www.worldbank.org
Overseas Development Council: www.odc.org
Organisation for Economic Co-operation and Development: www.oecd.org
US Agency for International Development: www.usaid.gov
Center for International Development: www.cid.harvard.edu

---

* All of the websites of the agencies, bodies, programs, and funds of the UN system can be accessed through this site. They are not repeated under substantive headings.

Appendix C
Charter of the United Nations

Preamble

We the Peoples of the United Nations Determined
- to save succeeding generations from the scourge of war, which twice in our lifetime has brought untold sorrow to mankind, and
- to reaffirm faith in fundamental human rights, in the dignity and worth of the human person, in the equal rights of men and women and of nations large and small, and
- to establish conditions under which justice and respect for the obligations arising from treaties and other sources of international law can be maintained, and
- to promote social progress and better standards of life in larger freedom,

And for These Ends
- to practice tolerance and live together in peace with one another as good neighbors, and
- to unite our strength to maintain international peace and security, and
- to ensure by the acceptance of principles and the institution of methods, that armed force shall not be used, save in the common interest, and
- to employ international machinery for the promotion of the economic and social advancement of all peoples,

Have Resolved to Combine Our Efforts to Accomplish These Aims

Accordingly, our respective Governments, through representatives assembled in the city of San Francisco, who have exhibited their full powers found to be in good and due form, have agreed to the present Charter of the United Nations and do hereby establish an international organization to be known as the United Nations.

CHAPTER I: PURPOSES AND PRINCIPLES

Article 1

The Purposes of the United Nations are:
1. To maintain international peace and security, and to that end: to take effective collective measures for the prevention and removal of threats to the peace, and for the suppression of acts of aggression or other breaches of the peace, and to bring about by peaceful means, and in conformity with the principles of justice and international law, adjustment or settlement of international disputes or situations which might lead to a breach of the peace;
2. To develop friendly relations among nations based on respect for the principle of equal rights and self-determination of peoples, and to take other appropriate measures to strengthen universal peace;
3. To achieve international cooperation in solving international problems of an economic, social, cultural, or humanitarian character, and in promoting and encouraging respect for human rights and for fundamental freedoms for all without distinction as to race, sex, language, or religion; and

4. To be a center for harmonizing the actions of nations in the attainment of these common ends.

Article 2

The Organization and its Members, in pursuit of the Purposes stated in Article 1, shall act in accordance with the following Principles.

1. The Organization is based on the principle of the sovereign equality of all its Members.
2. All Members, in order to ensure to all of them the rights and benefits resulting from membership, shall fulfill in good faith the obligations assumed by them in accordance with the present Charter.
3. All Members shall settle their international disputes by peaceful means in such a manner that international peace and security, and justice, are not endangered.
4. All Members shall refrain in their international relations from the threat or use of force against the territorial integrity or political independence of any state, or in any other manner inconsistent with the Purposes of the United Nations.
5. All Members shall give the United Nations every assistance in any action it takes in accordance with the present Charter, and shall refrain from giving assistance to any state against which the United Nations is taking preventive or enforcement action.
6. The Organization shall ensure that states which are not Members of the United Nations act in accordance with these Principles so far as may be necessary for the maintenance of international peace and security.
7. Nothing contained in the present Charter shall authorize the United Nations to intervene in matters which are essentially within the domestic jurisdiction of any state or shall require the Members to submit such matters to settlement under the present Charter; but this principle shall not prejudice the application of enforcement measures under Chapter VII.

CHAPTER II: MEMBERSHIP

Article 3

The original Members of the United Nations shall be the states which, having participated in the United Nations Conference on International Organization at San Francisco, or having previously signed the Declaration by United Nations of January 1, 1942, sign the present Charter and ratify it in accordance with Article 110.

Article 4

1. Membership in the United Nations is open to all other peace-loving states which accept the obligations contained in the present Charter and, in the judgment of the Organization, are able and willing to carry out these obligations.
2. The admission of any such state to membership in the United Nations will be effected by a decision of the General Assembly upon the recommendation of the Security Council.

Article 5

A member of the United Nations against which preventive or enforcement action has been taken by the Security Council may be suspended from the exercise of the rights and privileges of membership by the General Assembly upon the recommendation of the Security Council. The exercise of these rights and privileges may be restored by the Security Council.

Article 6

A Member of the United Nations which has persistently violated the Principles contained in the present Charter may be expelled from the Organization by the General Assembly upon the recommendation of the Security Council.

CHAPTER III: ORGANS

Article 7

1. There are established as the principal organs of the United Nations: a General Assembly, a Security Council, an Economic and Social Council, a Trusteeship Council, an International Court of Justice, and a Secretariat.
2. Such subsidiary organs as may be found necessary may be established in accordance with the present Charter.

Article 8

The United Nations shall place no restrictions on the eligibility of men and women to participate in any capacity and under conditions of equality in its principal and subsidiary organs.

CHAPTER IV: THE GENERAL ASSEMBLY

Composition

Article 9

1. The General Assembly shall consist of all the Members of the United Nations.
2. Each member shall have not more than five representatives in the General Assembly.

Functions and Powers

Article 10

The General Assembly may discuss any questions or any matters within the scope of the present Charter or relating to the powers and functions of any organs provided for in the present Charter, and, except as provided in Article 12, may make recommendations to the Members of the United Nations or to the Security Council or to both on any such questions or matters.

Article 11

1. The General Assembly may consider the general principles of cooperation in the maintenance of international peace and security, including the principles governing disarmament and the regulation of armaments, and may make recommendations with regard to such principles to the Members or to the Security Council or to both.
2. The General Assembly may discuss any questions relating to the maintenance of international peace and security brought before it by any Member of the United Nations, or by the Security Council, or by a state which is not a Member of the United Nations in accordance with Article 35, paragraph 2, and, except as provided in Article 12, may make recommendations with regard to any such questions to the state or states concerned or to the Security Council or to both. Any such question on which action is necessary shall be referred to the Security Council by the General Assembly either before or after discussion.
3. The General Assembly may call the attention of the Security Council to situations which are likely to endanger international peace and security.
4. The powers of the General Assembly set forth in this Article shall not limit the general scope of Article 10.

Article 12

1. While the Security Council is exercising in respect of any dispute or situation the functions assigned to it in the present Charter, the General Assembly shall not make any recommendation with regard to that dispute or situation unless the Security Council so requests.
2. The Secretary-General, with the consent of the Security Council, shall notify the General Assembly at each session of any matters relative to the maintenance of international peace

and security which are being dealt with by the Security Council and shall similarly notify the General Assembly, or the Members of the United Nations if the General Assembly is not in session, immediately the Security Council ceases to deal with such matters.

Article 13

1. The General Assembly shall initiate studies and make recommendations for the purpose of:
   a. promoting international cooperation in the political field and encouraging the progressive development of international law and its codification;
   b. promoting international cooperation in the economic, social, cultural, educational, and health fields, and assisting in the realization of human rights and fundamental freedoms for all without distinction as to race, sex, language, or religion.
2. The further responsibilities, functions, and powers of the General Assembly with respect to matters mentioned in paragraph 1(b) above are set forth in Chapters IX and X.

Article 14

Subject to the provisions of Article 12, the General Assembly may recommend measures for the peaceful adjustment of any situation, regardless of origin, which it deems likely to impair the general welfare or friendly relations among nations, including situations resulting from a violation of the provisions of the present Charter setting forth the Purposes and Principles of the United Nations.

Article 15

1. The General Assembly shall receive and consider annual and special reports from the Security Council; these reports shall include an account of the measures that the Security Council has decided upon or taken to maintain international peace and security.
2. The General Assembly shall receive and consider reports from the other organs of the United Nations.

Article 16

The General Assembly shall perform such functions with respect to the international trusteeship system as are assigned to it under Chapters XII and XIII, including the approval of the trusteeship agreements for areas not designated as strategic.

Article 17

1. The General Assembly shall consider and approve the budget of the Organization.
2. The expenses of the Organization shall be borne by the Members as apportioned by the General Assembly.
3. The General Assembly shall consider and approve any financial and budgetary arrangements with specialized agencies referred to in Article 57 and shall examine the administrative budgets of such specialized agencies with a view to making recommendations to the agencies concerned.

Voting

Article 18

1. Each member of the General Assembly shall have one vote.
2. Decisions of the General Assembly on important questions shall be made by a two-thirds majority of the members present and voting. These questions shall include: recommendations with respect to the maintenance of international peace and security, the election of the non-permanent members of the Security Council, the election of the members of the Economic and Social Council, the election of members of the Trusteeship Council in accordance with paragraph 1(c) of Article 86, the admission of new Members to the United

Nations, the suspension of the rights and privileges of membership, the expulsion of Members, questions relating to the operation of the trusteeship system, and budgetary questions.

3. Decisions on other questions, including the determination of additional categories of questions to be decided by a two-thirds majority, shall be made by a majority of the members present and voting.

Article 19

A Member of the United Nations which is in arrears in the payment of its financial contributions to the Organization shall have no vote in the General Assembly if the amount of its arrears equals or exceeds the amount of the contributions due from it for the preceding two full years. The General Assembly may, nevertheless, permit such a Member to vote if it is satisfied that the failure to pay is due to conditions beyond the control of the Member.

Procedure

Article 20

The General Assembly shall meet in regular annual sessions and in such special sessions as occasion may require. Special sessions shall be convoked by the Secretary-General at the request of the Security Council or of a majority of the Members of the United Nations.

Article 21

The General Assembly shall adopt its own rules of procedure. It shall elect its President for each session.

Article 22

The General Assembly may establish such subsidiary organs as it deems necessary for the performance of its functions.

CHAPTER V: THE SECURITY COUNCIL

Composition

Article 23

1. The Security Council shall consist of fifteen Members of the United Nations. The Republic of China, France, the Union of Soviet Socialist Republics, the United Kingdom of Great Britain and Northern Ireland, and the United States of America shall be permanent members of the Security Council. The General Assembly shall elect ten other Members of the United Nations to be non-permanent members of the Security Council, due regard being specially paid, in the first instance to the contribution of Members of the United Nations to the maintenance of international peace and security and to the other purposes of the Organization, and also to equitable geographical distribution.
2. The non-permanent members of the Security Council shall be elected for a term of two years. In the first election of the non-permanent members after the increase of the membership of the Security Council from eleven to fifteen, two of the four additional members shall be chosen for a term of one year. A retiring member shall not be eligible for immediate re-election.
3. Each member of the Security Council shall have one representative.

Functions and Powers

Article 24

1. In order to ensure prompt and effective action by the United Nations, its Members confer on the Security Council primary responsibility for the maintenance of international peace

and security, and agree that in carrying out its duties under this responsibility the Security Council acts on their behalf.

2. In discharging these duties the Security Council shall act in accordance with the Purposes and Principles of the United Nations. The specific powers granted to the Security Council for the discharge of these duties are laid down in Chapters VI, VII, VIII, and XII.

3. The Security Council shall submit annual and, when necessary, special reports to the General Assembly for its consideration.

Article 25

The Members of the United Nations agree to accept and carry out the decisions of the Security Council in accordance with the present Charter.

Article 26

In order to promote the establishment and maintenance of international peace and security with the least diversion for armaments of the world's human and economic resources, the Security Council shall be responsible for formulating, with the assistance of the Military Staff Committee referred to in Article 47, plans to be submitted to the Members of the United Nations for the establishment of a system for the regulation of armaments.

Voting

Article 27

1. Each member of the Security Council shall have one vote.

2. Decisions of the Security Council on procedural matters shall be made by an affirmative vote of nine members.

3. Decisions of the Security Council on all other matters shall be made by an affirmative vote of nine members including the concurring votes of the permanent members; provided that, in decisions under Chapter VI, and under paragraph 3 of Article 52, a party to a dispute shall abstain from voting.

Procedure

Article 28

1. The Security Council shall be so organized as to be able to function continuously. Each member of the Security Council shall for this purpose be represented at all times at the seat of the Organization.

2. The Security Council shall hold periodic meetings at which each of its members may, if it so desires, be represented by a member of the government or by some other specially designated representative.

3. The Security Council may hold meetings at such places other than the seat of the Organization as in its judgment will best facilitate its work.

Article 29

The Security Council may establish such subsidiary organs as it deems necessary for the performance of its functions.

Article 30

The Security Council shall adopt its own rules of procedure, including the method of selecting its President.

Article 31

Any Member of the United Nations which is not a member of the Security Council may participate, without vote, in the discussion of any question brought before the Security Council whenever the latter considers that the interests of that Member are specially affected.

Article 32

Any Member of the United Nations which is not a member of the Security Council or any state which is not a Member of the United Nations, if it is a party to a dispute under consideration by the Security Council, shall be invited to participate, without vote, in the discussion relating to the dispute. The Security Council shall lay down such conditions as it deems just for the participation of a state which is not a Member of the United Nations.

CHAPTER VI: PACIFIC SETTLEMENT OF DISPUTES

Article 33

1. The parties to any dispute, the continuance of which is likely to endanger the maintenance of international peace and security, shall, first of all, seek a solution by negotiation, enquiry, mediation, conciliation, arbitration, judicial settlement, resort to regional agencies or arrangements, or other peaceful means of their own choice.
2. The Security Council shall, when it deems necessary, call upon the parties to settle their dispute by such means.

Article 34

The Security Council may investigate any dispute, or any situation which might lead to international friction or give rise to a dispute, in order to determine whether the continuance of the dispute or situation is likely to endanger the maintenance of international peace and security.

Article 35

1. Any Member of the United Nations may bring any dispute, or any situation of the nature referred to in Article 34, to the attention of the Security Council or of the General Assembly.
2. A state which is not a Member of the United Nations may bring to the attention of the Security Council or of the General Assembly any dispute to which it is a party if it accepts in advance, for the purposes of the dispute, the obligations of pacific settlement provided in the present Charter.
3. The proceedings of the General Assembly in respect of matters brought to its attention under this Article will be subject to the provisions of Articles 11 and 12.

Article 36

1. The Security Council may, at any stage of a dispute of the nature referred to in Article 33 or of a situation of like nature, recommend appropriate procedures or methods of adjustment.
2. The Security Council should take into consideration any procedures for the settlement of the dispute which have already been adopted by the parties.
3. In making recommendations under this Article the Security Council should also take into consideration that legal disputes should as a general rule be referred by the parties to the International Court of Justice in accordance with the provisions of the Statute of the Court.

Article 37

1. Should the parties to a dispute of the nature referred to in Article 33 fail to settle it by the means indicated in that Article, they shall refer it to the Security Council.
2. If the Security Council deems that the continuance of the dispute is in fact likely to endanger the maintenance of international peace and security, it shall decide whether to take action under Article 36 or to recommend such terms of settlement as it may consider appropriate.

Article 38

Without prejudice to the provisions of Articles 33 to 37, the Security Council may, if all the parties to any dispute so request, make recommendations to the parties with a view to a pacific settlement of the dispute.

CHAPTER VII: ACTION WITH RESPECT TO THREATS TO THE PEACE, BREACHES OF THE PEACE, AND ACTS OF AGGRESSION

Article 39

The Security Council shall determine the existence of any threat to the peace, breach of the peace, or act of aggression and shall make recommendations, or decide what measures shall be taken in accordance with Articles 41 and 42, to maintain or restore international peace and security.

Article 40

In order to prevent an aggravation of the situation, the Security Council may, before making the recommendations or deciding upon the measures provided for in Article 39, call upon the parties concerned to comply with such provisional measures as it deems necessary or desirable. Such provisional measures shall be without prejudice to the rights, claims, or position of the parties concerned. The Security Council shall duly take account of failure to comply with such provisional measures.

Article 41

The Security Council may decide what measures not involving the use of armed force are to be employed to give effect to its decisions, and it may call upon the Members of the United Nations to apply such measures. These may include complete or partial interruption of economic relations and of rail, sea, air, postal, telegraphic, radio, and other means of communication, and the severance of diplomatic relations.

Article 42

Should the Security Council consider that measures provided for in Article 41 would be inadequate or have proved to be inadequate, it may take such action by air, sea, or land forces as may be necessary to maintain or restore international peace and security. Such action may include demonstrations, blockade, and other operations by air, sea, or land forces of Members of the United Nations.

Article 43

1. All Members of the United Nations, in order to contribute to the maintenance of international peace and security, undertake to make available to the Security Council, on its call and in accordance with a special agreement or agreements, armed forces, assistance, and facilities, including rights of passage, necessary for the purpose of maintaining international peace and security.

2. Such agreement or agreements shall govern the numbers and types of forces, their degree of readiness and general location, and the nature of the facilities and assistance to be provided.
3. The agreement or agreements shall be negotiated as soon as possible on the initiative of the Security Council. They shall be concluded between the Security Council and Members or between the Security Council and groups of Members and shall be subject to ratification by the signatory states in accordance with their respective constitutional processes.

Article 44

When the Security Council has decided to use force it shall, before calling upon a Member not represented on it to provide armed forces in fulfillment of the obligations assumed under Article 43, invite that Member, if the Member so desires, to participate in the decisions of the Security Council concerning the employment of contingents of that Member's armed forces.

Article 45

In order to enable the United Nations to take urgent military measures Members shall hold immediately available national air-force contingents for combined international enforcement action. The strength and degree of readiness of these contingents and plans for their combined action shall be determined, within the limits laid down in the special agreement or agreements referred to in Article 43, by the Security Council with the assistance of the Military Staff Committee.

Article 46

Plans for the application of armed force shall be made by the Security Council with the assistance of the Military Staff Committee.

Article 47

1. There shall be established a Military Staff Committee to advise and assist the Security Council on all questions relating to the Security Council's military requirements for the maintenance of international peace and security, the employment and command of forces placed at its disposal, the regulation of armaments, and possible disarmament.
2. The Military Staff Committee shall consist of the Chiefs of Staff of the permanent members of the Security Council or their representatives. Any Member of the United Nations not permanently represented on the Committee shall be invited by the Committee to be associated with it when the efficient discharge of the Committee's responsibilities requires the participation of that Member in its work.
3. The Military Staff Committee shall be responsible under the Security Council for the strategic direction of any armed forces placed at the disposal of the Security Council. Questions relating to the command of such forces shall be worked out subsequently.
4. The Military Staff Committee, with the authorization of the Security Council and after consultation with appropriate regional agencies, may establish regional subcommittees.

Article 48

1. The action required to carry out the decisions of the Security Council for the maintenance of international peace and security shall be taken by all the Members of the United Nations or by some of them, as the Security Council may determine.
2. Such decisions shall be carried out by the Members of the United Nations directly and through their action in the appropriate international agencies of which they are members.

Article 49

The Members of the United Nations shall join in affording mutual assistance in carrying out the measures decided upon by the Security Council.

Article 50

If preventive or enforcement measures against any state are taken by the Security Council, any other state, whether a Member of the United Nations or not, which finds itself confronted with special economic problems arising from the carrying out of those measures shall have the right to consult the Security Council with regard to a solution of those problems.

Article 51

Nothing in the present Charter shall impair the inherent right of individual or collective self-defense if an armed attack occurs against a Member of the United Nations, until the Security Council has taken measures necessary to maintain international peace and security. Measures taken by Members in the exercise of this right of self-defense shall be immediately reported to the Security Council and shall not in any way affect the authority and responsibility of the Security Council under the present Charter to take at any time such action as it deems necessary in order to maintain or restore international peace and security.

CHAPTER VIII: REGIONAL ARRANGEMENTS

Article 52

1. Nothing in the present Charter precludes the existence of regional arrangements or agencies for dealing with such matters relating to the maintenance of international peace and security as are appropriate for regional action, provided that such arrangements or agencies and their activities are consistent with the Purposes and Principles of the United Nations.
2. The Members of the United Nations entering into such arrangements or constituting such agencies shall make every effort to achieve pacific settlement of local disputes through such regional arrangements or by such regional agencies before referring them to the Security Council.
3. The Security Council shall encourage the development of pacific settlement of local disputes through such regional arrangements or by such regional agencies either on the initiative of the states concerned or by reference from the Security Council.
4. This Article in no way impairs the application of Articles 34 and 35.

Article 53

1. The Security Council shall, where appropriate, utilize such regional arrangements or agencies for enforcement action under its authority. But no enforcement action shall be taken under regional arrangements or by regional agencies without the authorization of the Security Council, with the exception of measures against any enemy state, as defined in paragraph 2 of this Article, provided for pursuant to Article 107 or in regional arrangements directed against renewal of aggressive policy on the part of any such state, until such time as the Organization may, on request of the Governments concerned, be charged with the responsibility for preventing further aggression by such a state.
2. The term enemy state as used in paragraph 1 of this Article applies to any state which during the Second World War has been an enemy of any signatory of the present Charter.

Article 54

The Security Council shall at all times be kept fully informed of activities undertaken or in contemplation under regional arrangements or by regional agencies for the maintenance of international peace and security.

CHAPTER IX: INTERNATIONAL ECONOMIC AND SOCIAL COOPERATION

Article 55

With a view to the creation of conditions of stability and well-being which are necessary for peaceful and friendly relations among nations based on respect for the principle of equal rights and self-determination of peoples, the United Nations shall promote:

- a. higher standards of living, full employment, and conditions of economic and social progress and development;
- b. solutions of international economic, social, health, and related problems; and international cultural and educational cooperation; and
- c. universal respect for, and observance of, human rights and fundamental freedoms for all without distinction as to race, sex, language, or religion.

Article 56

All Members pledge themselves to take joint and separate action in cooperation with the Organization for the achievement of the purposes set forth in Article 55.

Article 57

1. The various specialized agencies, established by intergovernmental agreement and having wide international responsibilities, as defined in their basic instruments, in economic, social, cultural, educational, health, and related fields, shall be brought into relationship with the United Nations in accordance with the provisions of Article 63.
2. Such agencies thus brought into relationship with the United Nations are hereinafter referred to as specialized agencies.

Article 58

The Organization shall make recommendations for the coordination of the policies and activities of the specialized agencies.

Article 59

The Organization shall, where appropriate, initiate negotiations among the states concerned for the creation of any new specialized agencies required for the accomplishment of the purposes set forth in Article 55.

Article 60

Responsibility for the discharge of the functions of the Organization set forth in this Chapter shall be vested in the General Assembly and, under the authority of the General Assembly, in the Economic and Social Council, which shall have for this purpose the powers set forth in Chapter X.

CHAPTER X: THE ECONOMIC AND SOCIAL COUNCIL

Composition

Article 61

1. The Economic and Social Council shall consist of fifty-four Members of the United Nations elected by the General Assembly.

2. Subject to the provisions of paragraph 3, eighteen members of the Economic and Social Council shall be elected each year for a term of three years. A retiring member shall be eligible for immediate re-election.
3. At the first election after the increase in the membership of the Economic and Social Council from twenty-seven to fifty-four members, in addition to the members elected in place of the nine members whose term of office expires at the end of that year, twenty-seven additional members shall be elected. Of these twenty-seven additional members, the term of office of nine members so elected shall expire at the end of one year, and of nine other members at the end of two years, in accordance with arrangements made by the General Assembly.
4. Each member of the Economic and Social Council shall have one representative.

Functions and Powers

Article 62

1. The Economic and Social Council may make or initiate studies and reports with respect to international economic, social, cultural, educational, health, and related matters and may make recommendations with respect to any such matters to the General Assembly, to the Members of the United Nations, and to the specialized agencies concerned.
2. It may make recommendations for the purpose of promoting respect for, and observance of, human rights and fundamental freedoms for all.
3. It may prepare draft conventions for submission to the General Assembly, with respect to matters falling within its competence.
4. It may call, in accordance with the rules prescribed by the United Nations, international conferences on matters falling within its competence.

Article 63

1. The Economic and Social Council may enter into agreements with any of the agencies referred to in Article 57, defining the terms on which the agency concerned shall be brought into relationship with the United Nations. Such agreements shall be subject to approval by the General Assembly.
2. It may coordinate the activities of the specialized agencies through consultation with and recommendations to such agencies and through recommendations to the General Assembly and to the Members of the United Nations.

Article 64

1. The Economic and Social Council may take appropriate steps to obtain regular reports from the specialized agencies. It may make arrangements with the Members of the United Nations and with the specialized agencies to obtain reports on the steps taken to give effect to its own recommendations and to recommendations on matters falling within its competence made by the General Assembly.
2. It may communicate its observations on these reports to the General Assembly.

Article 65

The Economic and Social Council may furnish information to the Security Council and shall assist the Security Council upon its request.

Article 66

1. The Economic and Social Council shall perform such functions as fall within its competence in connection with the carrying out of the recommendations of the General Assembly.
2. It may, with the approval of the General Assembly, perform services at the request of Members of the United Nations and at the request of specialized agencies.

3. It shall perform such other functions as are specified elsewhere in the present Charter or as may be assigned to it by the General Assembly.

Voting

Article 67

1. Each member of the Economic and Social Council shall have one vote.
2. Decisions of the Economic and Social Council shall be made by a majority of the members present and voting.

Procedure

Article 68

The Economic and Social Council shall set up commissions in economic and social fields and for the promotion of human rights, and such other commissions as may be required for the performance of its functions.

Article 69

The Economic and Social Council shall invite any Member of the United Nations to participate, without vote, in its deliberations on any matter of particular concern to that Member.

Article 70

The Economic and Social Council may make arrangements for representatives of the specialized agencies to participate, without vote, in its deliberations and in those of the commissions established by it, and for its representatives to participate in the deliberations of the specialized agencies.

Article 71

The Economic and Social Council may make suitable arrangements for consultation with non-governmental organizations which are concerned with matters within its competence. Such arrangements may be made with international organizations and, where appropriate, with national organizations after consultation with the Member of the United Nations concerned.

Article 72

1. The Economic and Social Council shall adopt its own rules of procedure, including the method of selecting its President.
2. The Economic and Social Council shall meet as required in accordance with its rules, which shall include provision for the convening of meetings on the request of a majority of its members.

CHAPTER XI: DECLARATION REGARDING NON-SELF-GOVERNING TERRITORIES

Article 73

Members of the United Nations which have or assume responsibilities for the administration of territories whose peoples have not yet attained a full measure of self-government recognize the principle that the interests of the inhabitants of these territories are paramount, and accept as a sacred trust the obligation to promote to the utmost, within the system of international peace and security established by the present Charter, the well-being of the inhabitants of these territories, and, to this end:

a. to ensure, with due respect for the culture of the peoples concerned, their political, economic, social, and educational advancement, their just treatment, and their protection against abuses;
b. to develop self-government, to take due account of the political aspirations of the peoples, and to assist them in the progressive development of their free political institutions, according to the particular circumstances of each territory and its peoples and their varying stages of advancement;
c. to further international peace and security;
d. to promote constructive measures of development, to encourage research, and to cooperate with one another and, when and where appropriate, with specialized international bodies with a view to the practical achievement of the social, economic, and scientific purposes set forth in this Article; and
e. to transmit regularly to the Secretary-General for information purposes, subject to such limitation as security and constitutional considerations may require, statistical and other information of a technical nature relating to economic, social, and educational conditions in the territories for which they are respectively responsible other than those territories to which Chapters XII and XIII apply.

Article 74

Members of the United Nations also agree that their policy in respect of the territories to which this Chapter applies, no less than in respect of their metropolitan areas, must be based on the general principle of good-neighborliness, due account being taken of the interests and well-being of the rest of the world, in social, economic, and commercial matters.

CHAPTER XII: INTERNATIONAL TRUSTEESHIP SYSTEM

Article 75

The United Nations shall establish under its authority an international trusteeship system for the administration and supervision of such territories as may be placed thereunder by subsequent individual agreements. These territories are hereinafter referred to as trust territories.

Article 76

The basic objectives of the trusteeship system, in accordance with the Purposes of the United Nations laid down in Article 1 of the present Charter, shall be:
a. to further international peace and security;
b. to promote the political, economic, social, and educational advancement of the inhabitants of the trust territories, and their progressive development towards self-government or independence as may be appropriate to the particular circumstances of each territory and its peoples and the freely expressed wishes of the peoples concerned, and as may be provided by the terms of each trusteeship agreement;
c. to encourage respect for human rights and for fundamental freedoms for all without distinction as to race, sex, language, or religion, and to encourage recognition of the interdependence of the peoples of the world; and
d. to ensure equal treatment in social, economic, and commercial matters for all Members of the United Nations and their nationals and also equal treatment for the latter in the administration of justice without prejudice to the attainment of the foregoing objectives and subject to the provisions of Article 80.

Article 77

1. The trusteeship system shall apply to such territories in the following categories as may be placed thereunder by means of trusteeship agreements:
   a. territories now held under mandate;
   b. territories which may be detached from enemy states as a result of the Second World War; and
   c. territories voluntarily placed under the system by states responsible for their administration.
2. It will be a matter for subsequent agreement as to which territories in the foregoing categories will be brought under the trusteeship system and upon what terms.

Article 78

The trusteeship system shall not apply to territories which have become Members of the United Nations, relationship among which shall be based on respect for the principle of sovereign equality.

Article 79

The terms of trusteeship for each territory to be placed under the trusteeship system, including any alteration or amendment, shall be agreed upon by the states directly concerned, including the mandatory power in the case of territories held under mandate by a Member of the United Nations, and shall be approved as provided for in Articles 83 and 85.

Article 80

1. Except as may be agreed upon in individual trusteeship agreements, made under Articles 77, 79, and 81, placing each territory under the trusteeship system, and until such agreements have been concluded, nothing in this Chapter shall be construed in or of itself to alter in any manner the rights whatsoever of any states or any peoples or the terms of existing international instruments to which Members of the United Nations may respectively be parties.
2. Paragraph 1 of this Article shall not be interpreted as giving grounds for delay or postponement of the negotiation and conclusion of agreements for placing mandated and other territories under the trusteeship system as provided for in Article 77.

Article 81

The trusteeship agreement shall in each case include the terms under which the trust territory will be administered and designate the authority which will exercise the administration of the trust territory. Such authority, hereinafter called the administering authority, may be one or more states or the Organization itself.

Article 82

There may be designated, in any trusteeship agreement, a strategic area or areas which may include part or all of the trust territory to which the agreement applies, without prejudice to any special agreement or agreements made under Article 43.

Article 83

1. All functions of the United Nations relating to strategic areas, including the approval of the terms of the trusteeship agreements and of their alteration or amendment, shall be exercised by the Security Council.

2. The basic objectives set forth in Article 76 shall be applicable to the people of each strategic area.
3. The Security Council shall, subject to the provisions of the trusteeship agreements and without prejudice to security considerations, avail itself of the assistance of the Trusteeship Council to perform those functions of the United Nations under the trusteeship system relating to political, economic, social, and educational matters in the strategic areas.

Article 84

It shall be the duty of the administering authority to ensure that the trust territory shall play its part in the maintenance of international peace and security. To this end the administering authority may make use of volunteer forces, facilities, and assistance from the trust territory in carrying out the obligations towards the Security Council undertaken in this regard by the administering authority, as well as for local defense and the maintenance of law and order within the trust territory.

Article 85

1. The functions of the United Nations with regard to trusteeship agreements for all areas not designated as strategic, including the approval of the terms of the trusteeship agreements and of their alteration or amendment, shall be exercised by the General Assembly.
2. The Trusteeship Council, operating under the authority of the General Assembly, shall assist the General Assembly in carrying out these functions.

CHAPTER XIII: THE TRUSTEESHIP COUNCIL

Composition

Article 86

1. The Trusteeship Council shall consist of the following Members of the United Nations:
    a. those Members administering trust territories;
    b. such of those Members mentioned by name in Article 23 as are not administering trust territories; and
    c. as many other Members elected for three-year terms by the General Assembly as may be necessary to ensure that the total number of members of the Trusteeship Council is equally divided between those Members of the United Nations which administer trust territories and those which do not.
2. Each Member of the Trusteeship Council shall designate one specially qualified person to represent it therein.

Functions and Powers

Article 87

The General Assembly and, under its authority, the Trusteeship Council, in carrying out their functions, may:

consider reports submitted by the administering authority;
accept petitions and examine them in consultation with the administering authority;
provide for periodic visits to the respective trust territories at times agreed upon with the administering authority; and
take these and other actions in conformity with the terms of the trusteeship agreements.

Article 88

The Trusteeship Council shall formulate a questionnaire on the political, economic, social, and educational advancement of the inhabitants of each trust territory, and the administering authority for each trust territory within the competence of the General Assembly shall make an annual report to the General Assembly upon the basis of such questionnaire.

Voting

Article 89

1. Each member of the Trusteeship Council shall have one vote.
2. Decisions of the Trusteeship Council shall be made by a majority of the members present and voting.

Procedure

Article 90

1. The Trusteeship Council shall adopt its own rules of procedure, including the method of selecting its President.
2. The Trusteeship Council shall meet as required in accordance with its rules, which shall include provision for the convening of meetings on the request of a majority of its members.

Article 91

The Trusteeship Council shall, when appropriate, avail itself of the assistance of the Economic and Social Council and of the specialized agencies in regard to matters with which they are respectively concerned.

CHAPTER XIV: THE INTERNATIONAL COURT OF JUSTICE

Article 92

The International Court of Justice shall be the principal judicial organ of the United Nations. It shall function in accordance with the annexed Statute which is based upon the Statute of the Permanent Court of International Justice and forms an integral part of the present Charter.

Article 93

1. All Members of the United Nations are ipso facto parties to the Statute of the International Court of Justice.
2. A state which is not a Member of the United Nations may become a party to the Statute of the International Court of Justice on conditions to be determined in each case by the General Assembly upon the recommendation of the Security Council.

Article 94

1. Each Member of the United Nations undertakes to comply with the decision of the International Court of Justice in any case to which it is a party.
2. If any party to a case fails to perform the obligations incumbent upon it under a judgment rendered by the Court, the other party may have recourse to the Security Council, which may, if it deems necessary, make recommendations or decide upon measures to be taken to give effect to the judgment.

Article 95

Nothing in the present Charter shall prevent Members of the United Nations from entrusting the solution of their differences to other tribunals by virtue of agreements already in existence or which may be concluded in the future.

Article 96

1. The General Assembly or the Security Council may request the International Court of Justice to give an advisory opinion on any legal question.
2. Other organs of the United Nations and specialized agencies, which may at any time be so authorized by the General Assembly, may also request advisory opinions of the Court on legal questions arising within the scope of their activities.

CHAPTER XV: THE SECRETARIAT

Article 97

The Secretariat shall comprise a Secretary-General and such staff as the Organization may require. The Secretary-General shall be appointed by the General Assembly upon the recommendation of the Security Council. He shall be the chief administrative officer of the Organization.

Article 98

The Secretary-General shall act in that capacity in all meetings of the General Assembly, of the Security Council, of the Economic and Social Council, and of the Trusteeship Council, and shall perform such other functions as are entrusted to him by these organs. The Secretary-General shall make an annual report to the General Assembly on the work of the Organization.

Article 99

The Secretary-General may bring to the attention of the Security Council any matter which in his opinion may threaten the maintenance of international peace and security.

Article 100

1. In the performance of their duties the Secretary-General and the staff shall not seek or receive instructions from any government or from any other authority external to the Organization. They shall refrain from any action which might reflect on their position as international officials responsible only to the Organization.
2. Each Member of the United Nations undertakes to respect the exclusively international character of the responsibilities of the Secretary-General and the staff and not to seek to influence them in the discharge of their responsibilities.

Article 101

1. The staff shall be appointed by the Secretary-General under regulations established by the General Assembly.
2. Appropriate staffs shall be permanently assigned to the Economic and Social Council, the Trusteeship Council, and, as required, to other organs of the United Nations. These staffs shall form a part of the Secretariat.
3. The paramount consideration in the employment of the staff and in the determination of the conditions of service shall be the necessity of securing the highest standards of efficiency, competence, and integrity. Due regard shall be paid to the importance of recruiting the staff on as wide a geographical basis as possible.

CHAPTER XVI: MISCELLANEOUS PROVISIONS

Article 102

1. Every treaty and every international agreement entered into by any Member of the United Nations after the present Charter comes into force shall as soon as possible be registered with the Secretariat and published by it.
2. No party to any such treaty or international agreement which has not been registered in accordance with the provisions of paragraph I of this Article may invoke that treaty or agreement before any organ of the United Nations.

Article 103

In the event of a conflict between the obligations of the Members of the United Nations under the present Charter and their obligations under any other international agreement, their obligations under the present Charter shall prevail.

Article 104

The Organization shall enjoy in the territory of each of its Members such legal capacity as may be necessary for the exercise of its functions and the fulfillment of its purposes.

Article 105

1. The Organization shall enjoy in the territory of each of its Members such privileges and immunities as are necessary for the fulfillment of its purposes.
2. Representatives of the Members of the United Nations and officials of the Organization shall similarly enjoy such privileges and immunities as are necessary for the independent exercise of their functions in connection with the Organization.
3. The General Assembly may make recommendations with a view to determining the details of the application of paragraphs 1 and 2 of this Article or may propose conventions to the Members of the United Nations for this purpose.

CHAPTER XVII: TRANSITIONAL SECURITY ARRANGEMENTS

Article 106

Pending the coming into force of such special agreements referred to in Article 43 as in the opinion of the Security Council enable it to begin the exercise of its responsibilities under Article 42, the parties to the Four-Nation Declaration, signed at Moscow October 30, 1943, and France, shall, in accordance with the provisions of paragraph 5 of that Declaration, consult with one another and as occasion requires with other Members of the United Nations with a view to such joint action on behalf of the Organization as may be necessary for the purpose of maintaining international peace and security.

Article 107

Nothing in the present Charter shall invalidate or preclude action, in relation to any state which during the Second World War has been an enemy of any signatory to the present Charter, taken or authorized as a result of that war by the Governments having responsibility for such action.

CHAPTER XVIII: AMENDMENTS

Article 108

Amendments to the present Charter shall come into force for all Members of the United Nations when they have been adopted by a vote of two-thirds of the members of the General Assembly and ratified in accordance with their respective constitutional processes by two-thirds of the Members of the United Nations, including all the permanent members of the Security Council.

Article 109

1. A General Conference of the Members of the United Nations for the purpose of reviewing the present Charter may be held at a date and place to be fixed by a two-thirds vote of the members of the General Assembly and by a vote of any seven members of the Security Council. Each Member of the United Nations shall have one vote in the conference.
2. Any alteration of the present Charter recommended by a two-thirds vote of the conference shall take effect when ratified in accordance with their respective constitutional processes by two-thirds of the Members of the United Nations including all the permanent members of the Security Council.
3. If such a conference has not been held before the tenth annual session of the General Assembly following the coming into force of the present Charter, the proposal to call such a conference shall be placed on the agenda of that session of the General Assembly, and the conference shall be held if so decided by a majority vote of the members of the General Assembly and by a vote of any seven members of the Security Council.

CHAPTER XIX: RATIFICATION AND SIGNATURE

Article 110

1. The present Charter shall be ratified by the signatory states in accordance with their respective constitutional processes.
2. The ratifications shall be deposited with the Government of the United States of America, which shall notify all the signatory states of each deposit as well as the Secretary-General of the Organization when he has been appointed.
3. The present Charter shall come into force upon the deposit of ratifications by the Republic of China, France, the Union of Soviet Socialist Republics, the United Kingdom of Great Britain and Northern Ireland, and the United States of America, and by a majority of the other signatory states. A protocol of the ratifications deposited shall thereupon be drawn up by the Government of the United States of America which shall communicate copies thereof to all the signatory states.
4. The states signatory to the present Charter which ratify it after it has come into force will become original Members of the United Nations on the date of the deposit of their respective ratifications.

Article 111

The present Charter, of which the Chinese, French, Russian, English, and Spanish texts are equally authentic, shall remain deposited in the archives of the Government of the United States of America. Duly certified copies thereof shall be transmitted by that Government to the Governments of the other signatory states.

IN FAITH WHEREOF the representatives of the Governments of the United Nations have signed the present Charter.

DONE at the city of San Francisco the twenty-sixth day of June, one thousand nine hundred and forty-five.

Appendix D

United Nations Universal Declaration of Human Rights

Adopted and Proclaimed by General Assembly Resolution 217 A (III) of December 10, 1948

On December 10, 1948, the General Assembly of the United Nations adopted and proclaimed the Universal Declaration of Human Rights the full text of which appears in the following pages. Following this historic act the Assembly called upon all Member countries to publicize the text of the Declaration and "to cause it to be disseminated, displayed, read and expounded principally in schools and other educational institutions, without distinction based on the political status of countries or territories."

Preamble

Whereas recognition of the inherent dignity and of the equal and inalienable rights of all members of the human family is the foundation of freedom, justice and peace in the world,

Whereas disregard and contempt for human rights have resulted in barbarous acts which have outraged the conscience of mankind, and the advent of a world in which human beings shall enjoy freedom of speech and belief and freedom from fear and want has been proclaimed as the highest aspiration of the common people,

Whereas it is essential, if man is not to be compelled to have recourse, as a last resort, to rebellion against tyranny and oppression, that human rights should be protected by the rule of law,

Whereas it is essential to promote the development of friendly relations between nations,

Whereas the peoples of the United Nations have in the Charter reaffirmed their faith in fundamental human rights, in the dignity and worth of the human person and in the equal rights of men and women and have determined to promote social progress and better standards of life in larger freedom,

Whereas Member States have pledged themselves to achieve, in co-operation with the United Nations, the promotion of universal respect for and observance of human rights and fundamental freedoms,

Whereas a common understanding of these rights and freedoms is of the greatest importance for the full realization of this pledge,

Now, Therefore THE GENERAL ASSEMBLY proclaims THIS UNIVERSAL DECLARATION OF HUMAN RIGHTS as a common standard of achievement for all peoples and all nations, to the end that every individual and every organ of society, keeping this Declaration constantly in mind, shall strive by teaching and education to promote respect for these rights and freedoms and by progressive measures, national and international, to secure their universal and effective recognition and observance, both among the peoples of Member States themselves and among the peoples of territories under their jurisdiction.

Article 1

All human beings are born free and equal in dignity and rights. They are endowed with reason and conscience and should act towards one another in a spirit of brotherhood.

Article 2

Everyone is entitled to all the rights and freedoms set forth in this Declaration, without distinction of any kind, such as race, colour, sex, language, religion, political or other opinion, national or social origin, property, birth or other status. Furthermore, no distinction shall be made on the basis of the political, jurisdictional or international status of the country or territory to which a person belongs, whether it be independent, trust, non-self-governing or under any other limitation of sovereignty.

Article 3

Everyone has the right to life, liberty and security of person.

Article 4

No one shall be held in slavery or servitude; slavery and the slave trade shall be prohibited in all their forms.

Article 5

No one shall be subjected to torture or to cruel, inhuman or degrading treatment or punishment.

Article 6

Everyone has the right to recognition everywhere as a person before the law.

Article 7

All are equal before the law and are entitled without any discrimination to equal protection of the law. All are entitled to equal protection against any discrimination in violation of this Declaration and against any incitement to such discrimination.

Article 8

Everyone has the right to an effective remedy by the competent national tribunals for acts violating the fundamental rights granted him by the constitution or by law.

Article 9

No one shall be subjected to arbitrary arrest, detention or exile.

Article 10

Everyone is entitled in full equality to a fair and public hearing by an independent and impartial tribunal, in the determination of his rights and obligations and of any criminal charge against him.

Article 11

1. Everyone charged with a penal offence has the right to be presumed innocent until proved guilty according to law in a public trial at which he has had all the guarantees necessary for his defence.
2. No one shall be held guilty of any penal offence on account of any act or omission which did not constitute a penal offence, under national or international law, at the time when it was committed. Nor shall a heavier penalty be imposed than the one that was applicable at the time the penal offence was committed.

Article 12

No one shall be subjected to arbitrary interference with his privacy, family, home or correspondence, nor to attacks upon his honour and reputation. Everyone has the right to the protection of the law against such interference or attacks.

Article 13

1. Everyone has the right to freedom of movement and residence within the borders of each state.
2. Everyone has the right to leave any country, including his own, and to return to his country.

Article 14

1. Everyone has the right to seek and to enjoy in other countries asylum from persecution.
2. This right may not be invoked in the case of prosecutions genuinely arising from non-political crimes or from acts contrary to the purposes and principles of the United Nations.

Article 15

1. Everyone has the right to a nationality.
2. No one shall be arbitrarily deprived of his nationality nor denied the right to change his nationality.

Article 16

1. Men and women of full age, without any limitation due to race, nationality or religion, have the right to marry and to found a family. They are entitled to equal rights as to marriage, during marriage and at its dissolution.
2. Marriage shall be entered into only with the free and full consent of the intending spouses.
3. The family is the natural and fundamental group unit of society and is entitled to protection by society and the State.

Article 17

1. Everyone has the right to own property alone as well as in association with others.
2. No one shall be arbitrarily deprived of his property.

Article 18

Everyone has the right to freedom of thought, conscience and religion; this right includes freedom to change his religion or belief, and freedom, either alone or in community with others and in public or private, to manifest his religion or belief in teaching, practice, worship and observance.

Article 19

Everyone has the right to freedom of opinion and expression; this right includes freedom to hold opinions without interference and to seek, receive and impart information and ideas through any media and regardless of frontiers.

Article 20

1. Everyone has the right to freedom of peaceful assembly and association.
2. No one may be compelled to belong to an association.

Article 21

1. Everyone has the right to take part in the government of his country, directly or through freely chosen representatives.
2. Everyone has the right of equal access to public service in his country.
3. The will of the people shall be the basis of the authority of government; this will shall be expressed in periodic and genuine elections which shall be by universal and equal suffrage and shall be held by secret vote or by equivalent free voting procedures.

Article 22

Everyone, as a member of society, has the right to social security and is entitled to realization, through national effort and international co-operation and in accordance with the organization and resources of each State, of the economic, social and cultural rights indispensable for his dignity and the free development of his personality.

Article 23

1. Everyone has the right to work, to free choice of employment, to just and favourable conditions of work and to protection against unemployment.
2. Everyone, without any discrimination, has the right to equal pay for equal work.
3. Everyone who works has the right to just and favourable remuneration ensuring for himself and his family an existence worthy of human dignity, and supplemented, if necessary, by other means of social protection.
4. Everyone has the right to form and to join trade unions for the protection of his interests.

Article 24

Everyone has the right to rest and leisure, including reasonable limitation of working hours and periodic holidays with pay.

Article 25

1. Everyone has the right to a standard of living adequate for the health and well-being of himself and of his family, including food, clothing, housing and medical care and necessary social services, and the right to security in the event of unemployment, sickness, disability, widowhood, old age or other lack of livelihood in circumstances beyond his control.
2. Motherhood and childhood are entitled to special care and assistance. All children, whether born in or out of wedlock, shall enjoy the same social protection.

Article 26

1. Everyone has the right to education. Education shall be free, at least in the elementary and fundamental stages. Elementary education shall be compulsory. Technical and professional education shall be made generally available and higher education shall be equally accessible to all on the basis of merit.
2. Education shall be directed to the full development of the human personality and to the strengthening of respect for human rights and fundamental freedoms. It shall promote understanding, tolerance and friendship among all nations, racial or religious groups, and shall further the activities of the United Nations for the maintenance of peace.
3. Parents have a prior right to choose the kind of education that shall be given to their children.

Article 27

1. Everyone has the right freely to participate in the cultural life of the community, to enjoy the arts and to share in scientific advancement and its benefits.
2. Everyone has the right to the protection of the moral and material interests resulting from any scientific, literary or artistic production of which he is the author.

Article 28

Everyone is entitled to a social and international order in which the rights and freedoms set forth in this Declaration can be fully realized.

Article 29

1. Everyone has duties to the community in which alone the free and full development of his personality is possible.
2. In the exercise of his rights and freedoms, everyone shall be subject only to such limitations as are determined by law solely for the purpose of securing due recognition and respect for

the rights and freedoms of others and of meeting the just requirements of morality, public order and the general welfare in a democratic society.

3. These rights and freedoms may in no case be exercised contrary to the purposes and principles of the United Nations.

Article 30

Nothing in this Declaration may be interpreted as implying for any State, group or person any right to engage in any activity or to perform any act aimed at the destruction of any of the rights and freedoms set forth herein.

Appendix E
Sustainable Development Goals

Sustainable Development Goal 1: *No Poverty*

Sustainable Development Targets:
- By 2030, eradicate extreme poverty for all people everywhere, currently measured as people living on less than $1.25 a day
- By 2030, reduce at least by half the proportion of men, women and children of all ages living in poverty in all its dimensions according to national definitions
- Implement nationally appropriate social protection systems and measures for all, including floors, and by 2030 achieve substantial coverage of the poor and the vulnerable
- By 2030, ensure that all men and women, in particular the poor and the vulnerable, have equal rights to economic resources, as well as access to basic services, ownership and control over land and other forms of 13 property, inheritance, natural resources, appropriate new technology and financial services, including microfinance
- By 2030, build the resilience of the poor and those in vulnerable situations and reduce their exposure and vulnerability to climate-related extreme events and other economic, social and environmental shocks and disasters
- Ensure significant mobilization of resources from a variety of sources, including through enhanced development cooperation, in order to provide adequate and predictable means for developing countries, in particular least developed countries, to implement programmes and policies to end poverty in all its dimensions
- Create sound policy frameworks at the national, regional and international levels, based on pro-poor and gender-sensitive development strategies, to support accelerated investment in poverty eradication actions

Sustainable Development Goal 2: *No Hunger*

Sustainable Development Targets:
- By 2030, end hunger and ensure access by all people, in particular the poor and people in vulnerable situations, including infants, to safe, nutritious and sufficient food all year round
- By 2030, end all forms of malnutrition, including achieving, by 2025, the internationally agreed targets on stunting and wasting in children under 5 years of age, and address the nutritional needs of adolescent girls, pregnant and lactating women and older persons
- By 2030, double the agricultural productivity and incomes of small-scale food producers, in particular women, indigenous peoples, family farmers, pastoralists and fishers, including through secure and equal access to land, other productive resources and inputs, knowledge, financial services, markets and opportunities for value addition and non-farm employment
- By 2030, ensure sustainable food production systems and implement resilient agricultural practices that increase productivity and production, that help maintain ecosystems, that strengthen capacity for adaptation to climate change, extreme weather, drought, flooding and other disasters and that progressively improve land and soil quality
- By 2020, maintain the genetic diversity of seeds, cultivated plants and farmed and domesticated animals and their related wild species, including through soundly managed and

diversified seed and plant banks at the national, regional and international levels, and promote access to and fair and equitable sharing of benefits arising from the utilization of genetic resources and associated traditional knowledge, as internationally agreed
- Increase investment, including through enhanced international cooperation, in rural infrastructure, agricultural research and extension services, technology development and plant and livestock gene banks in order to enhance agricultural productive capacity in developing countries, in particular least developed countries
- Correct and prevent trade restrictions and distortions in world agricultural markets, including through the parallel elimination of all forms of agricultural export subsidies and all export measures with equivalent effect, in accordance with the mandate of the Doha Development Round
- Adopt measures to ensure the proper functioning of food commodity markets and their derivatives and facilitate timely access to market information, including on food reserves, in order to help limit extreme food price volatility

Sustainable Development Goal 3: *Good Health and Well-Being*

Sustainable Development Targets:
- By 2030, reduce the global maternal mortality ratio to less than 70 per 100,000 live births
- By 2030, end preventable deaths of newborns and children under 5 years of age, with all countries aiming to reduce neonatal mortality to at least as low as 12 per 1,000 live births and under-5 mortality to at least as low as 25 per 1,000 live births
- By 2030, end the epidemics of AIDS, tuberculosis, malaria and neglected tropical diseases and combat hepatitis, water-borne diseases and other communicable diseases
- By 2030, reduce by one third premature mortality from non-communicable diseases through prevention and treatment and promote mental health and well-being
- Strengthen the prevention and treatment of substance abuse, including narcotic drug abuse and harmful use of alcohol
- By 2020, halve the number of global deaths and injuries from road traffic accidents
- By 2030, ensure universal access to sexual and reproductive health-care services, including for family planning, information and education, and the integration of reproductive health into national strategies and programmes
- Achieve universal health coverage, including financial risk protection, access to quality essential health-care services and access to safe, effective, quality and affordable essential medicines and vaccines for all
- By 2030, substantially reduce the number of deaths and illnesses from hazardous chemicals and air, water and soil pollution and contamination
- Strengthen the implementation of the World Health Organization Framework Convention on Tobacco Control in all countries, as appropriate
- Support the research and development of vaccines and medicines for the communicable and noncommunicable diseases that primarily affect developing countries, provide access to affordable essential medicines and vaccines, in accordance with the Doha Declaration on the TRIPS Agreement and Public Health, which affirms the right of developing countries to use to the full the provisions in the Agreement on Trade Related Aspects of Intellectual Property Rights regarding flexibilities to protect public health, and, in particular, provide access to medicines for all
- Substantially increase health financing and the recruitment, development, training and retention of the health workforce in developing countries, especially in least developed countries and small island developing States
- Strengthen the capacity of all countries, in particular developing countries, for early warning, risk reduction and management of national and global health risks

Sustainable Development Goal 4: *Quality Education*

Sustainable Development Targets:
- By 2030, ensure that all girls and boys complete free, equitable and quality primary and secondary education leading to relevant and Goal-4 effective learning outcomes
- By 2030, ensure that all girls and boys have access to quality early childhood development, care and preprimary education so that they are ready for primary education
- By 2030, ensure equal access for all women and men to affordable and quality technical, vocational and tertiary education, including university
- By 2030, substantially increase the number of youth and adults who have relevant skills, including technical and vocational skills, for employment, decent jobs and entrepreneurship
- By 2030, eliminate gender disparities in education and ensure equal access to all levels of education and vocational training for the vulnerable, including persons with disabilities, indigenous peoples and children in vulnerable situations
- By 2030, ensure that all youth and a substantial proportion of adults, both men and women, achieve literacy and numeracy
- By 2030, ensure that all learners acquire the knowledge and skills needed to promote sustainable development, including, among others, through education for sustainable development and sustainable lifestyles, human rights, gender equality, promotion of a culture of peace and non-violence, global citizenship and appreciation of cultural diversity and of culture's contribution to sustainable development
- Build and upgrade education facilities that are child, disability and gender sensitive and provide safe, nonviolent, inclusive and effective learning environments for all
- By 2020, substantially expand globally the number of scholarships available to developing countries, in particular least developed countries, small island developing States and African countries, for enrolment in higher education, including vocational training and information and communications technology, technical, engineering and scientific programmes, in developed countries and other developing countries
- By 2030, substantially increase the supply of qualified teachers, including through international cooperation for teacher training in developing countries, especially least developed countries and small island developing States

Sustainable Development Goal 5: *Gender Equality*

Sustainable Development Targets:
- End all forms of discrimination against all women and girls everywhere
- Eliminate all forms of violence against all women and girls in the public and private spheres, including trafficking and sexual and other types of exploitation
- Eliminate all harmful practices, such as child, early and forced marriage and female genital mutilation
- Recognize and value unpaid care and domestic work through the provision of public services, infrastructure and social protection policies and the promotion of shared responsibility within the household and the family as nationally appropriate
- Ensure women's full and effective participation and equal opportunities for leadership at all levels of decisionmaking in political, economic and public life
- Ensure universal access to sexual and reproductive health and reproductive rights as agreed in accordance with the Programme of Action of the International Conference on Population and Development and the Beijing Platform for Action and the outcome documents of their review conferences
- Undertake reforms to give women equal rights to economic resources, as well as access to ownership and control over land and other forms of property, financial services, inheritance and natural resources, in accordance with national laws

- Enhance the use of enabling technology, in particular information and communications technology, to promote the empowerment of women
- Adopt and strengthen sound policies and enforceable legislation for the promotion of gender equality and the empowerment of all women and girls at all levels

Sustainable Development Goal 6: *Clean Water and Sanitation*

Sustainable Development Targets:
- By 2030, achieve universal and equitable access to safe and affordable drinking water for all
- By 2030, achieve access to adequate and equitable sanitation and hygiene for all and end open defecation, paying special attention to the needs of women and girls and those in vulnerable situations
- By 2030, improve water quality by reducing pollution, eliminating dumping and minimizing release of hazardous chemicals and materials, halving the proportion of untreated wastewater and substantially increasing recycling and safe reuse globally
- By 2030, substantially increase water-use efficiency across all sectors and ensure sustainable withdrawals and supply of freshwater to address water scarcity and substantially reduce the number of people suffering from water scarcity
- By 2030, implement integrated water resources management at all levels, including through transboundary cooperation as appropriate
- By 2030, protect and restore water-related ecosystems, including mountains, forests, wetlands, rivers, aquifers and lakes
- By 2030, expand international cooperation and capacity-building support to developing countries in water- and sanitation-related activities and programmes, including water harvesting, desalination, water efficiency, wastewater treatment, recycling and reuse technologies

---

* Support and strengthen the participation of local communities in improving water and sanitation management

Sustainable Development Goal 7: *Affordable and Clean Energy*

Sustainable Development Targets:
- By 2030, ensure universal access to affordable, reliable and modern energy services
- By 2030, increase substantially the share of renewable energy in the global energy mix
- By 2030, double the global rate of improvement in energy efficiency
- By 2030, enhance international cooperation to facilitate access to clean energy research and technology, including renewable energy, energy efficiency and advanced and cleaner fossil-fuel technology, and promote investment in energy infrastructure and clean energy technology
- By 2030, expand infrastructure and upgrade technology for supplying modern and sustainable energy services for all in developing countries, in particular least developed countries, small island developing States, and land-locked developing countries, in accordance with their respective programmes of support

Sustainable Development Goal 8: *Decent Work and Economic Growth*

Sustainable Development Targets:
- Sustain per capita economic growth in accordance with national circumstances and, in particular, at least 7 per cent gross domestic product growth per annum in the least developed countries
- Achieve higher levels of economic productivity through diversification, technological upgrading and innovation, including through a focus on high-value added and labour-intensive sectors

- Promote development-oriented policies that support productive activities, decent job creation, entrepreneurship, creativity and innovation, and encourage the formalization and growth of micro-, small- and medium-sized enterprises, including through access to financial services
- Improve progressively, through 2030, global resource efficiency in consumption and production and endeavour to decouple economic growth from environmental degradation, in accordance with the 10-year framework of programmes on sustainable consumption and production, with developed countries taking the lead
- By 2030, achieve full and productive employment and decent work for all women and men, including for young people and persons with disabilities, and equal pay for work of equal value
- By 2020, substantially reduce the proportion of youth not in employment, education or training
- Take immediate and effective measures to eradicate forced labour, end modern slavery and human trafficking and secure the prohibition and elimination of the worst forms of child labour, including recruitment and use of child soldiers, and by 2025 end child labour in all its forms
- Protect labour rights and promote safe and secure working environments for all workers, including migrant workers, in particular women migrants, and those in precarious employment
- By 2030, devise and implement policies to promote sustainable tourism that creates jobs and promotes local culture and products
- Strengthen the capacity of domestic financial institutions to encourage and expand access to banking, insurance and financial services for all
- Increase Aid for Trade support for developing countries, in particular least developed countries, including through the Enhanced Integrated Framework for Trade-Related Technical Assistance to Least Developed Countries
- By 2020, develop and operationalize a global strategy for youth employment and implement the Global Jobs Pact of the International Labour Organization

Sustainable Development Goal 9: *Industry, Innovation, and Infrastructure*

Sustainable Development Targets:
- Develop quality, reliable, sustainable and resilient infrastructure, including regional and transborder infrastructure, to support economic development and human well-being, with a focus on affordable and equitable access for all
- Promote inclusive and sustainable industrialization and, by 2030, significantly raise industry's share of employment and gross domestic product, in line with national circumstances, and double its share in least developed countries
- Increase the access of small-scale industrial and other enterprises, in particular in developing countries, to financial services, including affordable credit, and their integration into value chains and markets
- By 2030, upgrade infrastructure and retrofit industries to make them sustainable, with increased resource-use efficiency and greater adoption of clean and environmentally sound technologies and industrial processes, with all countries taking action in accordance with their respective capabilities
- Enhance scientific research, upgrade the technological capabilities of industrial sectors in all countries, in particular developing countries, including, by 2030, encouraging innovation and substantially increasing the number of research and development workers per 1 million people and public and private research and development spending
- Facilitate sustainable and resilient infrastructure development in developing countries through enhanced financial, technological and technical support to African countries, least developed countries, landlocked developing countries and small island developing States

- Support domestic technology development, research and innovation in developing countries, including by ensuring a conducive policy environment for, inter alia, industrial diversification and value addition to commodities
- Significantly increase access to information and communications technology and strive to provide universal and affordable access to the Internet in least developed countries by 2020

Sustainable Development Goal 10: *Reduced Inequalities*

Sustainable Development Targets:

- By 2030, progressively achieve and sustain income growth of the bottom 40 per cent of the population at a rate higher than the national average
- By 2030, empower and promote the social, economic and political inclusion of all, irrespective of age, sex, disability, race, ethnicity, origin, religion or economic or other status
- Ensure equal opportunity and reduce inequalities of outcome, including by eliminating discriminatory laws, policies and practices and promoting appropriate legislation, policies and action in this regard
- Adopt policies, especially fiscal, wage and social protection policies, and progressively achieve greater equality
- Improve the regulation and monitoring of global financial markets and institutions and strengthen the implementation of such regulations
- Ensure enhanced representation and voice for developing countries in decision-making in global international economic and financial institutions in order to deliver more effective, credible, accountable and legitimate institutions
- Facilitate orderly, safe, regular and responsible migration and mobility of people, including through the implementation of planned and well-managed migration policies
- Implement the principle of special and differential treatment for developing countries, in particular least developed countries, in accordance with World Trade Organization agreements
- Encourage official development assistance and financial flows, including foreign direct investment, to States where the need is greatest, in particular least developed countries, African countries, small island developing States and landlocked developing countries, in accordance with their national plans and programmes
- By 2030, reduce to less than 3 per cent the transaction costs of migrant remittances and eliminate remittance corridors with costs higher than 5 per cent

Sustainable Development Goal 11: *Sustainable Cities and Communities*

Sustainable Development Targets:

- By 2030, ensure access for all to adequate, safe and affordable housing and basic services and upgrade slums
- By 2030, provide access to safe, affordable, accessible and sustainable transport systems for all, improving road safety, notably by expanding public transport, with special attention to the needs of those in vulnerable situations, women, children, persons with disabilities and older persons
- By 2030, enhance inclusive and sustainable urbanization and capacity for participatory, integrated and sustainable human settlement planning and management in all countries
- Strengthen efforts to protect and safeguard the world's cultural and natural heritage
- By 2030, significantly reduce the number of deaths and the number of people affected and substantially decrease the direct economic losses relative to global gross domestic product caused by disasters, including water-related disasters, with a focus on protecting the poor and people in vulnerable situations
- By 2030, reduce the adverse per capita environmental impact of cities, including by paying special attention to air quality and municipal and other waste management

- By 2030, provide universal access to safe, inclusive and accessible, green and public spaces, in particular for women and children, older persons and persons with disabilities
- Support positive economic, social and environmental links between urban, peri-urban and rural areas by strengthening national and regional development planning
- By 2020, substantially increase the number of cities and human settlements adopting and implementing integrated policies and plans towards inclusion, resource efficiency, mitigation and adaptation to climate change, resilience to disasters, and develop and implement, in line with the Sendai Framework for Disaster Risk Reduction 2015–2030, holistic disaster risk management at all levels
- Support least developed countries, including through financial and technical assistance, in building sustainable and resilient buildings utilizing local materials

Sustainable Development Goal 12: *Responsible Consumption and Production*

Sustainable Development Targets:
- Implement the 10-year framework of programmes on sustainable consumption and production, all countries taking action, with developed countries taking the lead, taking into account the development and capabilities of developing countries
- By 2030, achieve the sustainable management and efficient use of natural resources
- By 2030, halve per capita global food waste at the retail and consumer levels and reduce food losses along production and supply chains, including post-harvest losses
- By 2020, achieve the environmentally sound management of chemicals and all wastes throughout their life cycle, in accordance with agreed international frameworks, and significantly reduce their release to air, water and soil in order to minimize their adverse impacts on human health and the environment
- By 2030, substantially reduce waste generation through prevention, reduction, recycling and reuse
- Encourage companies, especially large and transnational companies, to adopt sustainable practices and to integrate sustainability information into their reporting cycle
- Promote public procurement practices that are sustainable, in accordance with national policies and priorities
- By 2030, ensure that people everywhere have the relevant information and awareness for sustainable development and lifestyles in harmony with nature
- Support developing countries to strengthen their scientific and technological capacity to move towards more sustainable patterns of consumption and production
- Develop and implement tools to monitor sustainable development impacts for sustainable tourism that creates jobs and promotes local culture and products
- Rationalize inefficient fossil-fuel subsidies that encourage wasteful consumption by removing market distortions, in accordance with national circumstances, including by restructuring taxation and phasing out those harmful subsidies, where they exist, to reflect their environmental impacts, taking fully into account the specific needs and conditions of developing countries and minimizing the possible adverse impacts on their development in a manner that protects the poor and the affected communities

Sustainable Development Goal 13: *Climate Action*

Sustainable Development Targets:
- Strengthen resilience and adaptive capacity to climate-related hazards and natural disasters in all countries

- Integrate climate change measures into national policies, strategies and planning
- Improve education, awareness-raising and human and institutional capacity on climate change mitigation, adaptation, impact reduction and early warning
- Implement the commitment undertaken by developed-country parties to the United Nations Framework Convention on Climate Change to a goal of mobilizing jointly $100 billion annually by 2020 from all sources to address the needs of developing countries in the context of meaningful mitigation actions and transparency on implementation and fully operationalize the Green Climate Fund through its capitalization as soon as possible
- Promote mechanisms for raising capacity for effective climate change–related planning and management in least developed countries and small island developing States, including focusing on women, youth and local and marginalized communities

---

* Acknowledging that the United Nations Framework Convention on Climate Change is the primary international, intergovernmental forum for negotiating the global response to climate change.

Sustainable Development Goal 14: *Life Below Water*

Sustainable Development Targets:
- By 2025, prevent and significantly reduce marine pollution of all kinds, in particular from land-based activities, including marine debris and nutrient pollution
- By 2020, sustainably manage and protect marine and coastal ecosystems to avoid significant adverse impacts, including by strengthening their resilience, and take action for their restoration in order to achieve healthy and productive oceans
- Minimize and address the impacts of ocean acidification, including through enhanced scientific cooperation at all levels
- By 2020, effectively regulate harvesting and end overfishing, illegal, unreported and unregulated fishing and destructive fishing practices and implement science-based management plans, in order to restore fish stocks in the shortest time feasible, at least to levels that can produce maximum sustainable yield as determined by their biological characteristics
- By 2020, conserve at least 10 per cent of coastal and marine areas, consistent with national and international law and based on the best available scientific information
- By 2020, prohibit certain forms of fisheries subsidies which contribute to overcapacity and overfishing, eliminate subsidies that contribute to illegal, unreported and unregulated fishing and refrain from introducing new such subsidies, recognizing that appropriate and effective special and differential treatment for developing and least developed countries should be an integral part of the World Trade Organization fisheries subsidies negotiation
- By 2030, increase the economic benefits to Small Island developing States and least developed countries from the sustainable use of marine resources, including through sustainable management of fisheries, aquaculture and tourism
- Increase scientific knowledge, develop research capacity and transfer marine technology, taking into account the Intergovernmental Oceanographic Commission Criteria and Guidelines on the Transfer of Marine Technology, in order to improve ocean health and to enhance the contribution of marine biodiversity to the development of developing countries, in particular small island developing States and least developed countries
- Provide access for small-scale artisanal fishers to marine resources and markets
- Enhance the conservation and sustainable use of oceans and their resources by implementing international law as reflected in UNCLOS, which provides the legal framework for the conservation and sustainable use of oceans and their resources, as recalled in paragraph 158 of The Future We Want

Sustainable Development Goal 15: *Life on Land*

Sustainable Development Targets:
- By 2020, ensure the conservation, restoration and sustainable use of terrestrial and inland freshwater ecosystems and their services, in particular forests, wetlands, mountains and drylands, in line with obligations under international agreements
- By 2020, promote the implementation of sustainable management of all types of forests, halt deforestation, restore degraded forests and substantially increase afforestation and reforestation globally
- By 2030, combat desertification, restore degraded land and soil, including land affected by desertification, drought and floods, and strive to achieve a land degradation-neutral world
- By 2030, ensure the conservation of mountain ecosystems, including their biodiversity, in order to enhance their capacity to provide benefits that are essential for sustainable development
- Take urgent and significant action to reduce the degradation of natural habitats, halt the loss of biodiversity and, by 2020, protect and prevent the extinction of threatened species
- Promote fair and equitable sharing of the benefits arising from the utilization of genetic resources and promote appropriate access to such resources, as internationally agreed
- Take urgent action to end poaching and trafficking of protected species of flora and fauna and address both demand and supply of illegal wildlife products
- By 2020, introduce measures to prevent the introduction and significantly reduce the impact of invasive alien species on land and water ecosystems and control or eradicate the priority species
- By 2020, integrate ecosystem and biodiversity values into national and local planning, development processes, poverty reduction strategies and accounts
- Mobilize and significantly increase financial resources from all sources to conserve and sustainably use biodiversity and ecosystems
- Mobilize significant resources from all sources and at all levels to finance sustainable forest management and provide adequate incentives to developing countries to advance such management, including for conservation and reforestation
- Enhance global support for efforts to combat poaching and trafficking of protected species, including by increasing the capacity of local communities to pursue sustainable livelihood opportunities

Sustainable Development Goal 16: *Peace, Justice, and Strong Institutions*

Sustainable Development Targets:
- Significantly reduce all forms of violence and related death rates everywhere
- End abuse, exploitation, trafficking and all forms of violence against and torture of children
- Promote the rule of law at the national and international levels and ensure equal access to justice for all
- By 2030, significantly reduce illicit financial and arms flows, strengthen the recovery and return of stolen assets and combat all forms of organized crime
- Substantially reduce corruption and bribery in all their forms
- Develop effective, accountable and transparent institutions at all levels
- Ensure responsive, inclusive, participatory and representative decision-making at all levels
- Broaden and strengthen the participation of developing countries in the institutions of global governance
- By 2030, provide legal identity for all, including birth registration
- Ensure public access to information and protect fundamental freedoms, in accordance with national legislation and international agreements

- Strengthen relevant national institutions, including through international cooperation, for building capacity at all levels, in particular in developing countries, to prevent violence and combat terrorism and crime
- Promote and enforce non-discriminatory laws and policies for sustainable development

Sustainable Development Goal 17: *Partnerships for the Goals*

Sustainable Development Targets:

Finance

- Strengthen domestic resource mobilization, including through international support to developing countries, to improve domestic capacity for tax and other revenue collection
- Developed countries to implement fully their official development assistance commitments, including the commitment by many developed countries to achieve the target of 0.7 per cent of ODA/GNI to developing countries and 0.15 to 0.20 per cent of ODA/GNI to least developed countries; ODA providers are encouraged to consider setting a target to provide at least 0.20 per cent of ODA/GNI to least developed countries
- Mobilize additional financial resources for developing countries from multiple sources
- Assist developing countries in attaining long-term debt sustainability through coordinated policies aimed at fostering debt financing, debt relief and debt restructuring, as appropriate, and address the external debt of highly indebted poor countries to reduce debt distress
- Adopt and implement investment promotion regimes for least developed countries

Technology

- Enhance North-South, South-South and triangular regional and international cooperation on and access to science, technology and innovation and enhance knowledge sharing on mutually agreed terms, including through improved coordination among existing mechanisms, in particular at the United Nations level, and through a global technology facilitation mechanism
- Promote the development, transfer, dissemination and diffusion of environmentally sound technologies to developing countries on favourable terms, including on concessional and preferential terms, as mutually agreed
- Fully operationalize the technology bank and science, technology and innovation capacity-building mechanism for least developed countries by 2017 and enhance the use of enabling technology, in particular information and communications technology

Capacity building

- Enhance international support for implementing effective and targeted capacity-building in developing countries to support national plans to implement all the sustainable development goals, including through North-South, South-South and triangular cooperation

Trade

- Promote a universal, rules-based, open, non-discriminatory and equitable multilateral trading system under the World Trade Organization, including through the conclusion of negotiations under its Doha Development Agenda
- Significantly increase the exports of developing countries, in particular with a view to doubling the least developed countries' share of global exports by 2020
- Realize timely implementation of duty-free and quota-free market access on a lasting basis for all least developed countries, consistent with World Trade Organization decisions, including by ensuring that preferential rules of origin applicable to imports from least developed countries are transparent and simple, and contribute to facilitating market access

Systemic issues:

Policy and institutional coherence
- Enhance global macroeconomic stability, including through policy coordination and policy coherence
- Enhance policy coherence for sustainable development
- Respect each country's policy space and leadership to establish and implement policies for poverty eradication and sustainable development

Multi-stakeholder partnerships
- Enhance the global partnership for sustainable development, complemented by multi-stakeholder partnerships that mobilize and share knowledge, expertise, technology and financial resources, to support the achievement of the sustainable development goals in all countries, in particular developing countries
- Encourage and promote effective public, public-private and civil society partnerships, building on the experience and resourcing strategies of partnerships

Data, monitoring and accountability
- By 2020, enhance capacity-building support to developing countries, including for least developed countries and small island developing States, to increase significantly the availability of high-quality, timely and reliable data disaggregated by income, gender, age, race, ethnicity, migratory status, disability, geographic location and other characteristics relevant in national contexts
- By 2030, build on existing initiatives to develop measurements of progress on sustainable development that complement gross domestic product, and support statistical capacity-building in developing countries

Sustainable Development Goals—United Nations. (n.d.). Retrieved from http://www.un.org /sustainabledevelopment/sustainable-development-goals/#prettyPhoto

About the Book and Authors

The United Nations celebrated its seventieth anniversary in 2015. Since its inception, the UN has weathered the political polarization of the Cold War, innovated with peacekeeping, managed complex emergencies and humanitarian interventions, rolled back aggression in Iraq, and facilitated the development of international criminal law and war-crimes tribunals. It continues to confront complicated and diverse security challenges in such places as Syria, Iraq, Mali, and the Central African Republic. It promotes and protects international human rights and humanitarian principles, and is building a relatively consensual strategy for combating climate change and achieving sustainable human development.

In this thematic and synthetic text, the authors bring to life the alphabet soup of the United Nations, moving from its historical foundations to its day-to-day expanding role in the governance of global issues. Students at all levels will learn what the UN is, how it operates, and the relationships between the universe of actors and institutions that comprise the UN, from sovereign states to UN officials, and the plethora of nongovernmental and intergovernmental organizations now playing important roles in world politics.

The authors, all of whom have practical as well as academic experience with the UN, show how it has exerted operational and normative influence on issues in three key areas—security, human rights, and sustainable development—even as they make recommendations for improved UN performance in the future. *The United Nations and Changing World Politics* is essential to a comprehensive and contemporary understanding of the world's leading international organization—one that, in the words of Dag Hammarskjöld, may not get us to heaven but could save us from hell.

THOMAS G. WEISS is Presidential Professor at the City University of New York's Graduate Center; he also is Co-Chair, Cultural Heritage at Risk Project, J. Paul Getty Trust, and Eminent Scholar at Kyung Hee University, Seoul. Past Andrew Carnegie Fellow and president of the International Studies Association and recipient of its "2016 Distinguished IO Scholar Award," chair of the Academic Council on the UN System, editor of *Global Governance*, and Research Director of the International Commission on Intervention and State Sovereignty, he has written extensively about international peace and security, humanitarian action, and sustainable development. His latest (2018) single-authored book is *Would the World Be Better Without the UN?*

DAVID P. FORSYTHE is university professor emeritus and professor and Charles J. Mach Distinguished Professor of Political Science at the University of Nebraska–Lincoln. His research interests include international law, organization, and human rights. His research in those areas led to the 2003 Quincy Wright Distinguished Scholar Award given by the Midwest Section of the International Studies Association. He is author or editor of numerous publications, including recently *The Politics of Prisoner Abuse: US Policy and Enemy Prisoners After 9/11; The Humanitarians; Human Rights and Diversity* (with Patrice C. McMahon); *Human Rights in International Relations; Human Rights and Comparative Foreign Policy*; and *The US and Human Rights*. Among other consultancies, he has worked for the International Red Cross and Red Crescent movement and the Office of the United Nations High Commissioner for Refugees.

ROGER A. COATE is Paul D. Coverdell Professor of Public Policy at Georgia College and State University and distinguished professor emeritus of political science at the University of South Carolina and has taught at Arizona State University. He has served as staff consultant to the U.S. secretary of state's Monitoring Panel on UNESCO; a member of the U.S. Delegation to the 31st UNESCO General Conference; adviser to the Bureau of International Organization Affairs, U.S. Department of State; a member of U.S. National Academy of Science's Board of International Scientific Organizations; a member of the UN Secretary-General's Advisory Panel on Housing Rights; and United Nations Fellow at the UN Centre for Human Rights. His books include *Identity Politics in an Age of Globalization*; *United Nations Politics: Responding to a Challenging World*; *International Cooperation in Response to AIDS*; *United States Policy and the Future of the United Nations*; and *Unilateralism, Ideology and United States Foreign Policy: The U.S. In and Out of UNESCO*. He was founding coeditor of the journal *Global Governance: A Review of Multilateralism and International Organization*.

KELLY-KATE PEASE is professor and director of international relations–worldwide at Webster University. She was the founding director of the Institute for Human Rights and Humanitarian Studies, served as the 2012 Manitoba Chair for Global Governance, and has been a visiting professor at Samara State University School of Law in Samara, Russia. She has taught at Webster University's campuses in London, England; Leiden, the Netherlands; and Cha-Am, Thailand. She is author of *International Organizations: Perspectives on Governance in the Twenty-First Century* and *Human Rights and Humanitarian Diplomacy* as well as articles and book chapters centering on human rights, humanitarian intervention, economic rights, moral hazard, and international criminal courts and tribunals.

Index

413